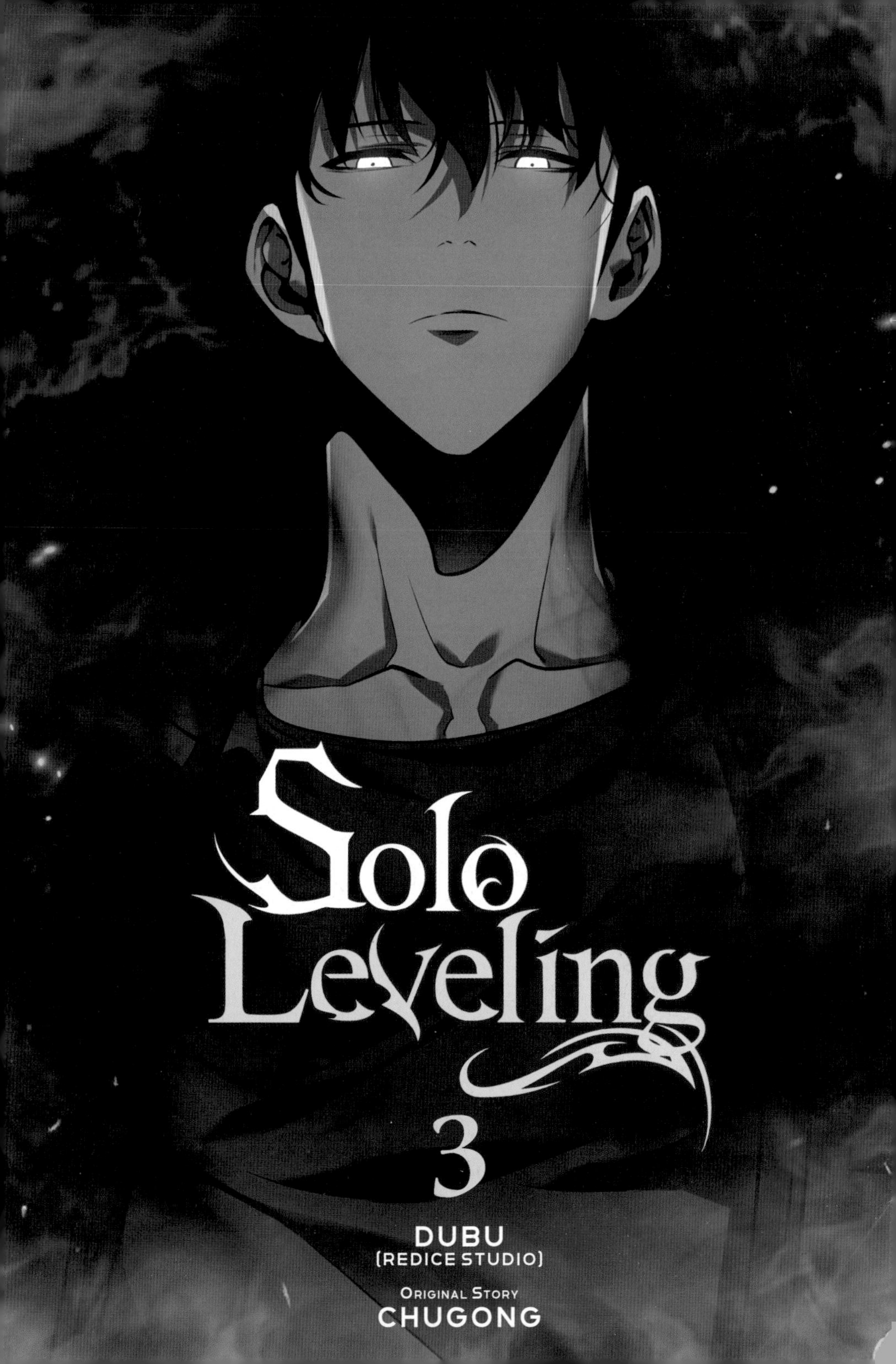
Solo Leveling
3
DUBU
(REDICE STUDIO)
Original Story
CHUGONG

CHARACTERS

Jinwoo Sung

E-rank Hunter

Chiyul Song

C-rank Hunter

Sangshik Kim

D-rank Hunter

Joohee Lee

B-rank Hunter

Taesik Kang

B-rank Hunter

CONTENTS

Solo
Leveling

CHAPTER 6

B-rank
Taesik Kang

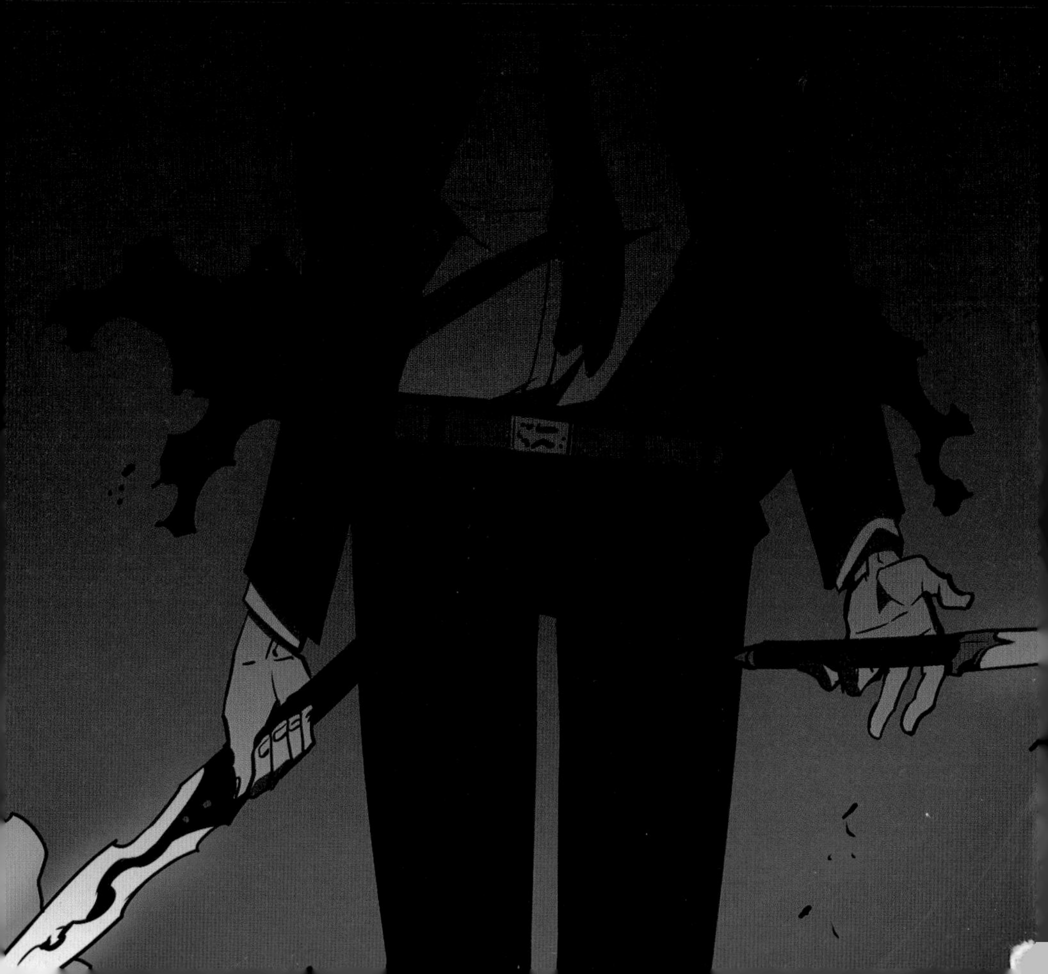

Solo Leveling

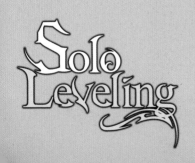

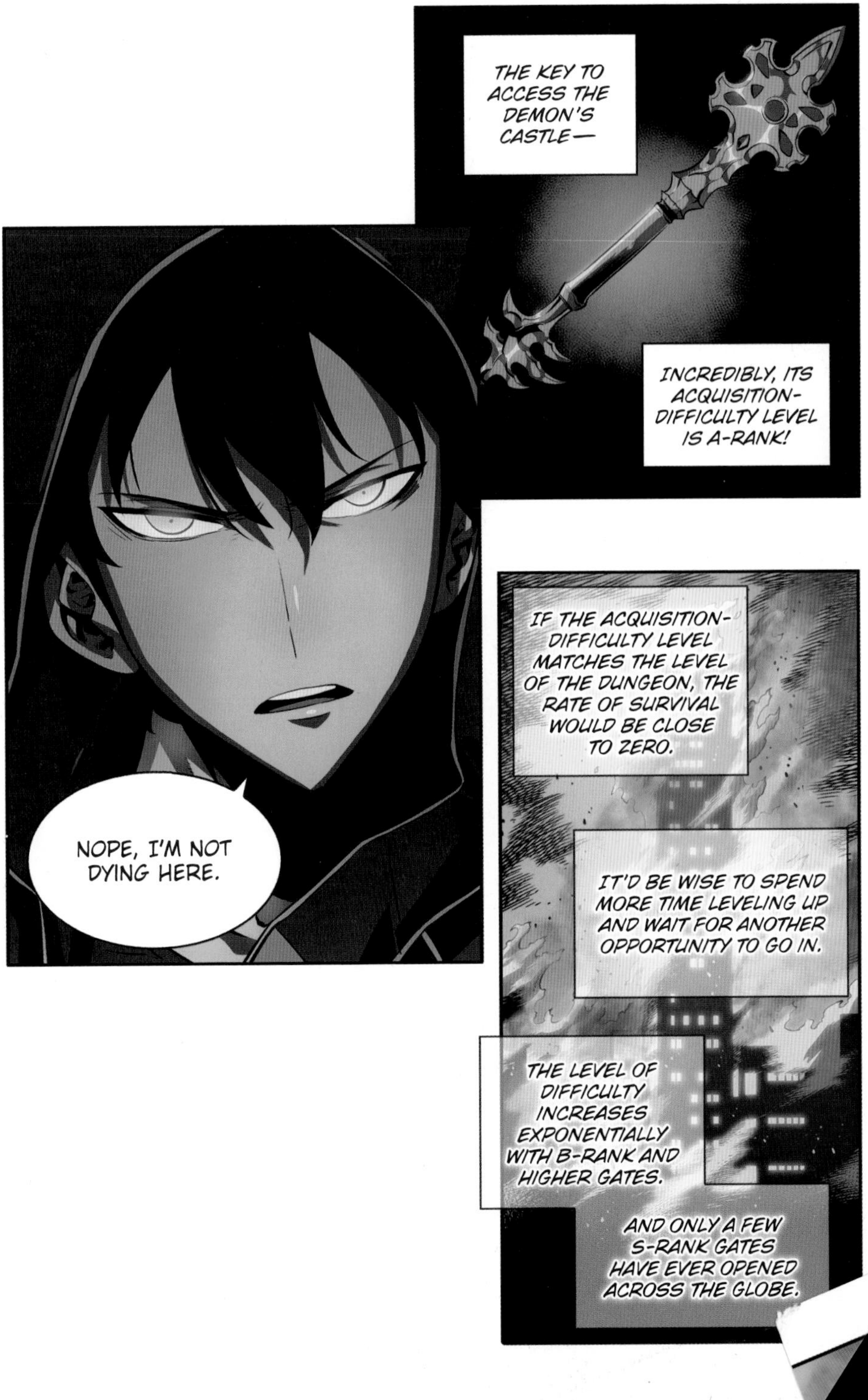
THE KEY TO ACCESS THE DEMON'S CASTLE—
INCREDIBLY, ITS ACQUISITION-DIFFICULTY LEVEL IS A-RANK!
NOPE, I'M NOT DYING HERE.
IF THE ACQUISITION-DIFFICULTY LEVEL MATCHES THE LEVEL OF THE DUNGEON, THE RATE OF SURVIVAL WOULD BE CLOSE TO ZERO.
IT'D BE WISE TO SPEND MORE TIME LEVELING UP AND WAIT FOR ANOTHER OPPORTUNITY TO GO IN.
THE LEVEL OF DIFFICULTY INCREASES EXPONENTIALLY WITH B-RANK AND HIGHER GATES.
AND ONLY A FEW S-RANK GATES HAVE EVER OPENED ACROSS THE GLOBE.

ONE OF THEM OPENED ON JEJU ISLAND.

IT BECAME A NO-MAN'S-LAND FOLLOWING AN S-RANK DUNGEON BREAK.

NO ONE KNOWS IF IT'S POSSIBLE FOR EVEN A TEAM OF S-RANK HUNTERS TO CLEAR AN S-RANK GATE.

SO FAR, NO GOVERNMENT-ORGANIZED TEAM OF HUNTERS HAS BEEN ABLE TO CONTROL AN S-RANK GATE.

GIVEN MY CURRENT LEVEL, I SHOULD NEVER HAVE COME HERE.

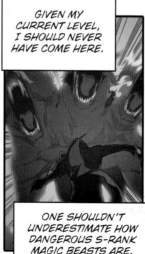

ONE SHOULDN'T UNDERESTIMATE HOW DANGEROUS S-RANK MAGIC BEASTS ARE.

THEY ARE RESISTANT TO THE STRONGEST ATTACKS.

THEY CAN INSTAKILL.

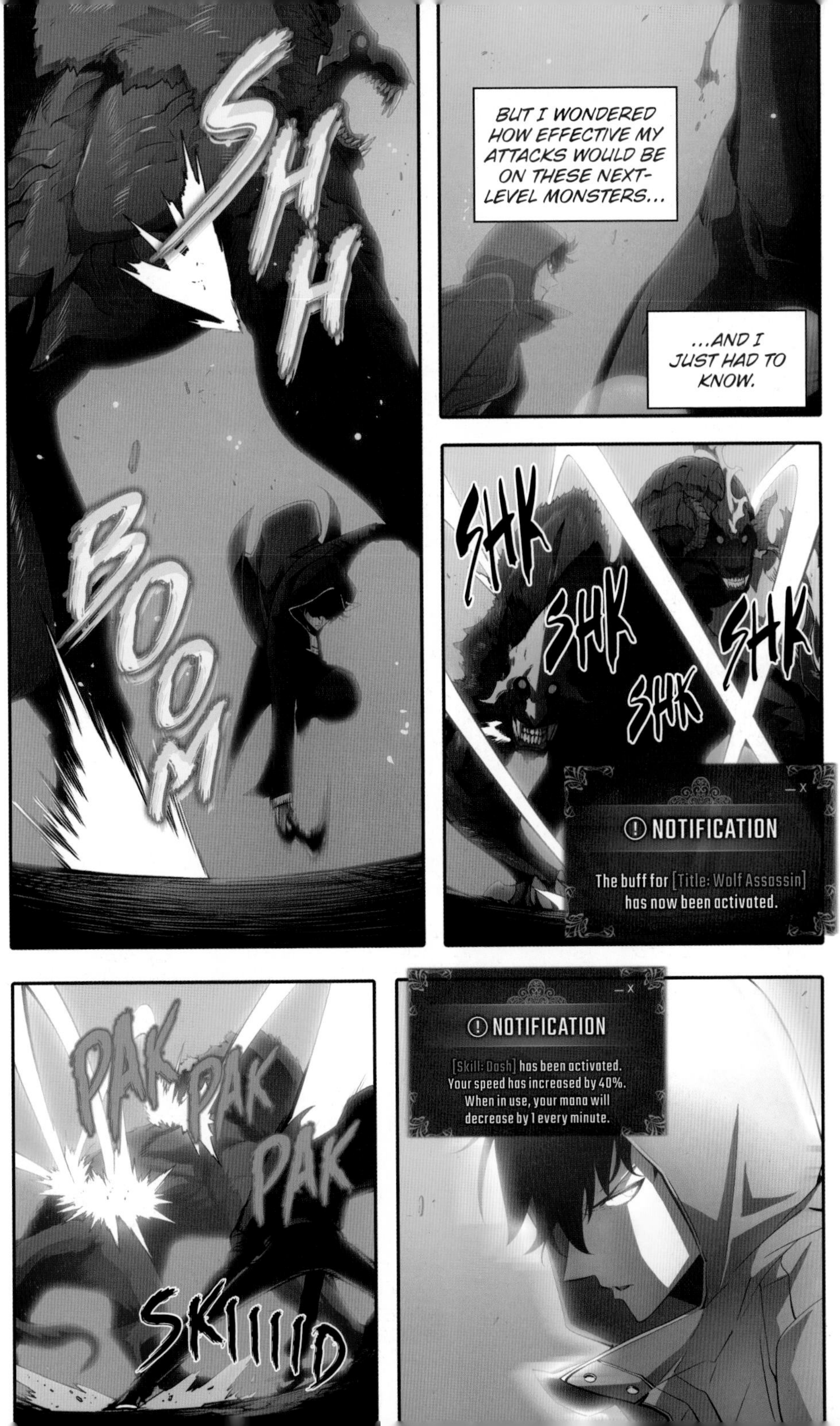
SHHH
BOOM
BUT I WONDERED HOW EFFECTIVE MY ATTACKS WOULD BE ON THESE NEXT-LEVEL MONSTERS...
...AND I JUST HAD TO KNOW.
SHK
SHK
SHK
SHK
NOTIFICATION
The buff for [Title: Wolf Assassin] has now been activated.
PAK PAK PAK
SKIIID
NOTIFICATION
[Skill: Dash] has been activated. Your speed has increased by 40%. When in use, your mana will decrease by 1 every minute.

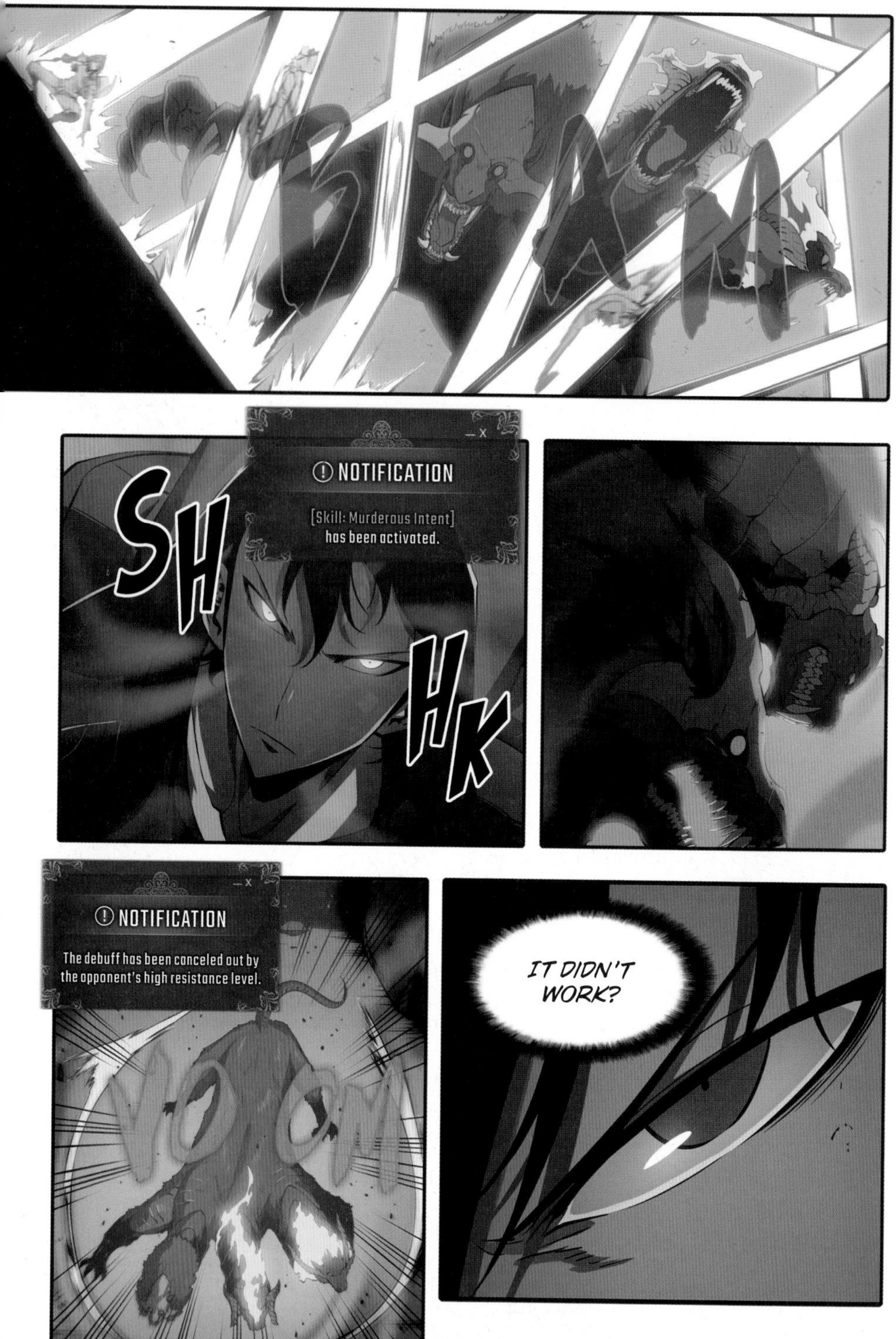
BAM
SHHK
NOTIFICATION
[Skill: Murderous Intent] has been activated.
NOTIFICATION
The debuff has been canceled out by the opponent's high resistance level.
VOOM
IT DIDN'T WORK?

I THOUGHT THAT MONSTER WAS A GOOD MATCH FOR ME...

...BUT MY ATTACKS AREN'T EFFECTIVE.

EVEN WITH THE TITLE BUFF, THEIR LEVEL IS STILL THAT MUCH HIGHER THAN MINE...

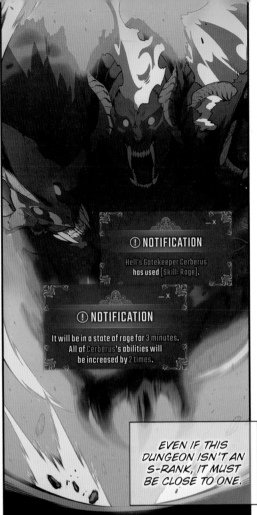

[Title: Wolf Assassin]
A title given to those skilled at hunting wolves. When battling an animal-type monster, all abilities will increase by 40%.

SKRR

! NOTIFICATION

Hell's Gatekeeper Cerberus has used [Skill: Rage].

! NOTIFICATION

It will be in a state of rage for 3 minutes. All of Cerberus's abilities will be increased by 2 times.

EVEN IF THIS DUNGEON ISN'T AN S-RANK, IT MUST BE CLOSE TO ONE.

BAM BAM BAM BAM

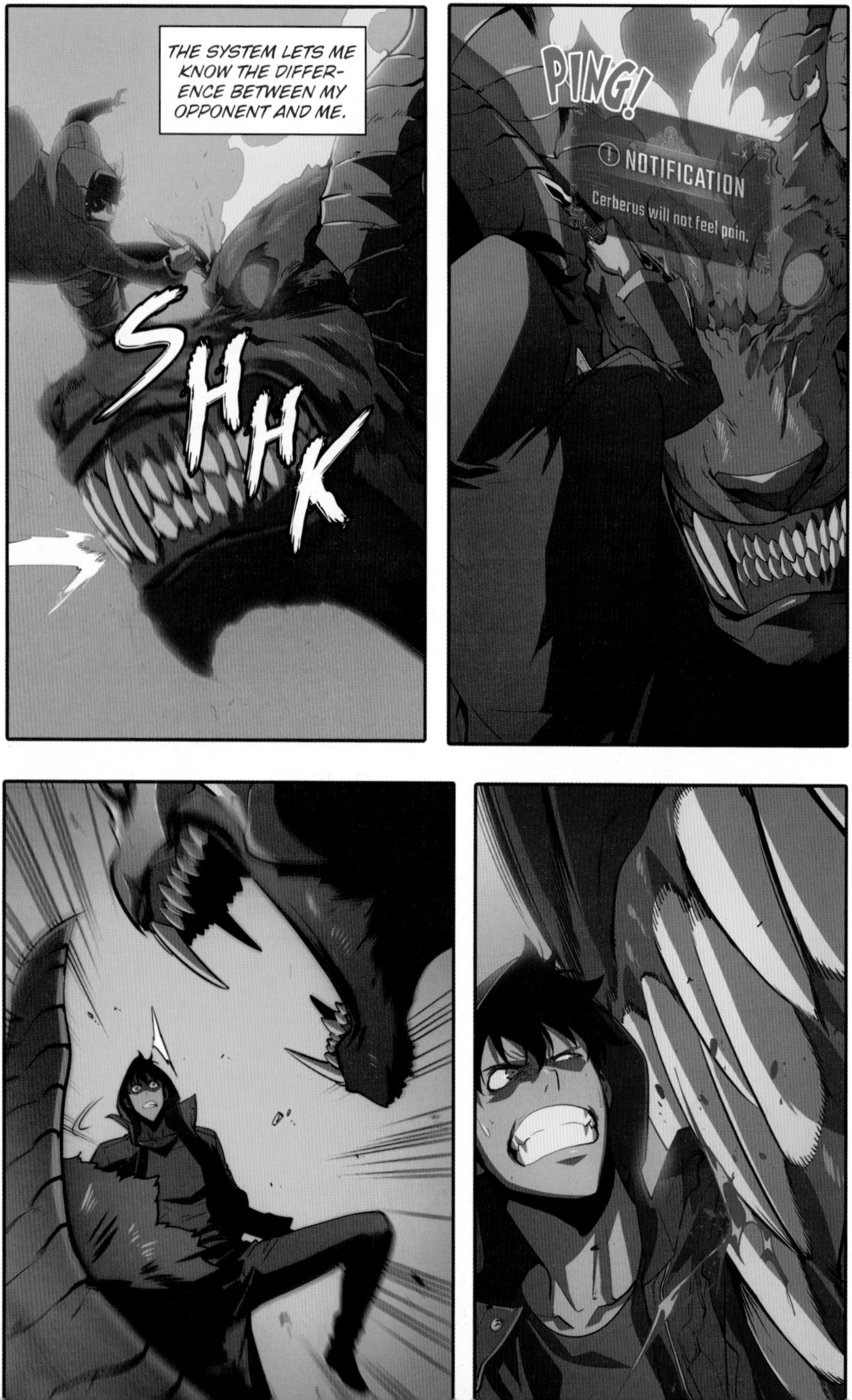
THE SYSTEM LETS ME KNOW THE DIFFERENCE BETWEEN MY OPPONENT AND ME.
SHHK
PING!
NOTIFICATION
Cerberus will not feel pain.

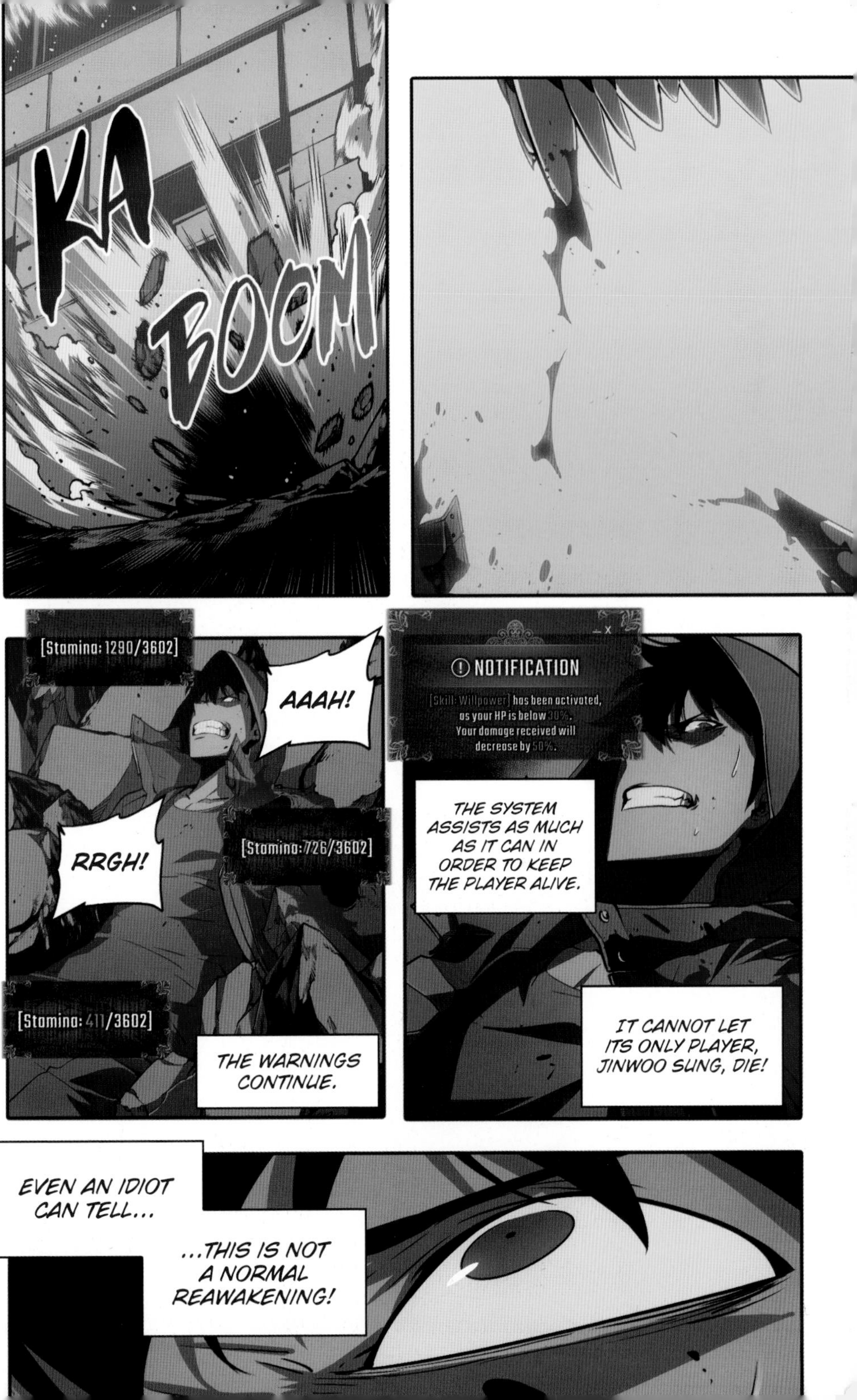
KA BOOM
[Stamina: 1290/3602]
AAAH!
RRGH!
[Stamina: 726/3602]
[Stamina: 411/3602]
THE WARNINGS CONTINUE.
NOTIFICATION
[Skill: Willpower] has been activated, as your HP is below 30%. Your damage received will decrease by 50%.
THE SYSTEM ASSISTS AS MUCH AS IT CAN IN ORDER TO KEEP THE PLAYER ALIVE.
IT CANNOT LET ITS ONLY PLAYER, JINWOO SUNG, DIE!
EVEN AN IDIOT CAN TELL...
...THIS IS NOT A NORMAL REAWAKENING!

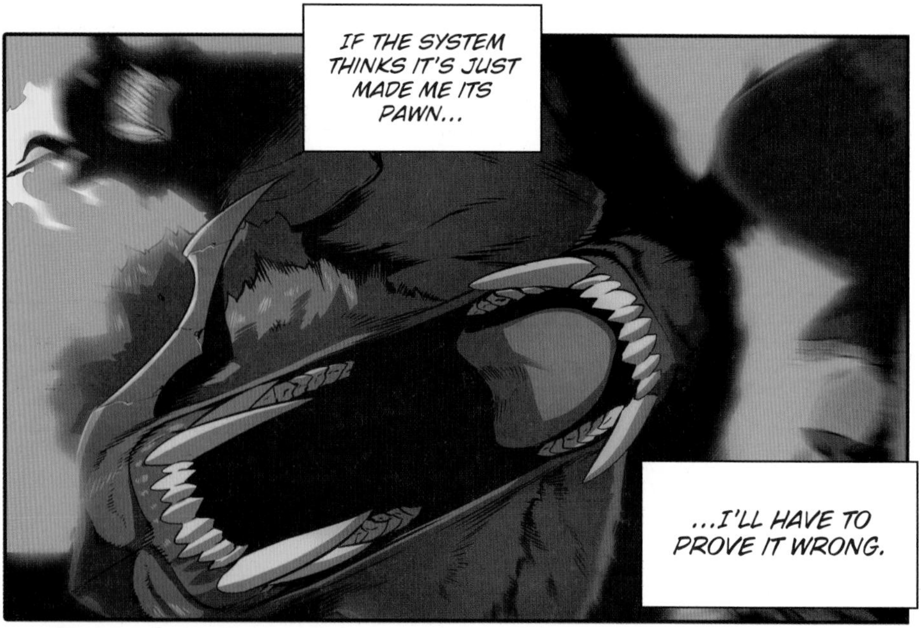
IF THE SYSTEM THINKS IT'S JUST MADE ME ITS PAWN...
...I'LL HAVE TO PROVE IT WRONG.

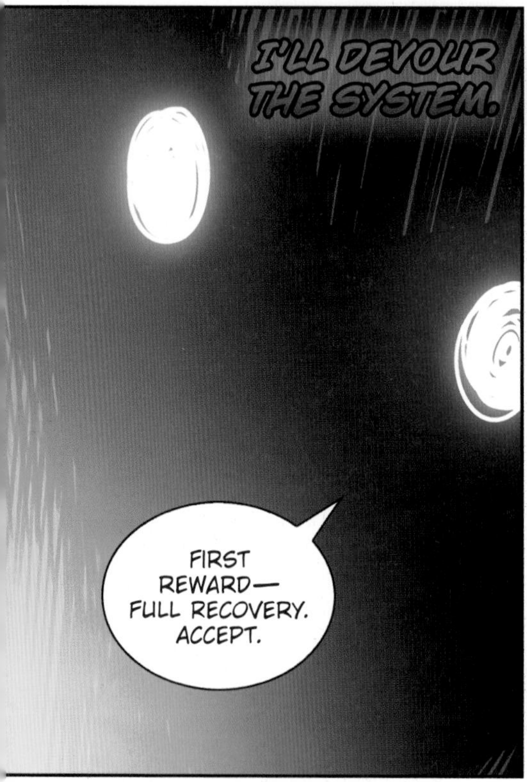
I'LL DEVOUR THE SYSTEM.
FIRST REWARD—FULL RECOVERY. ACCEPT.

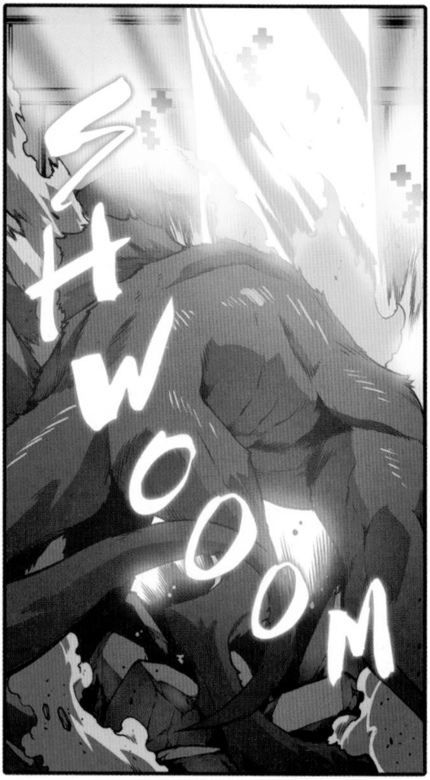
SHWOOOM

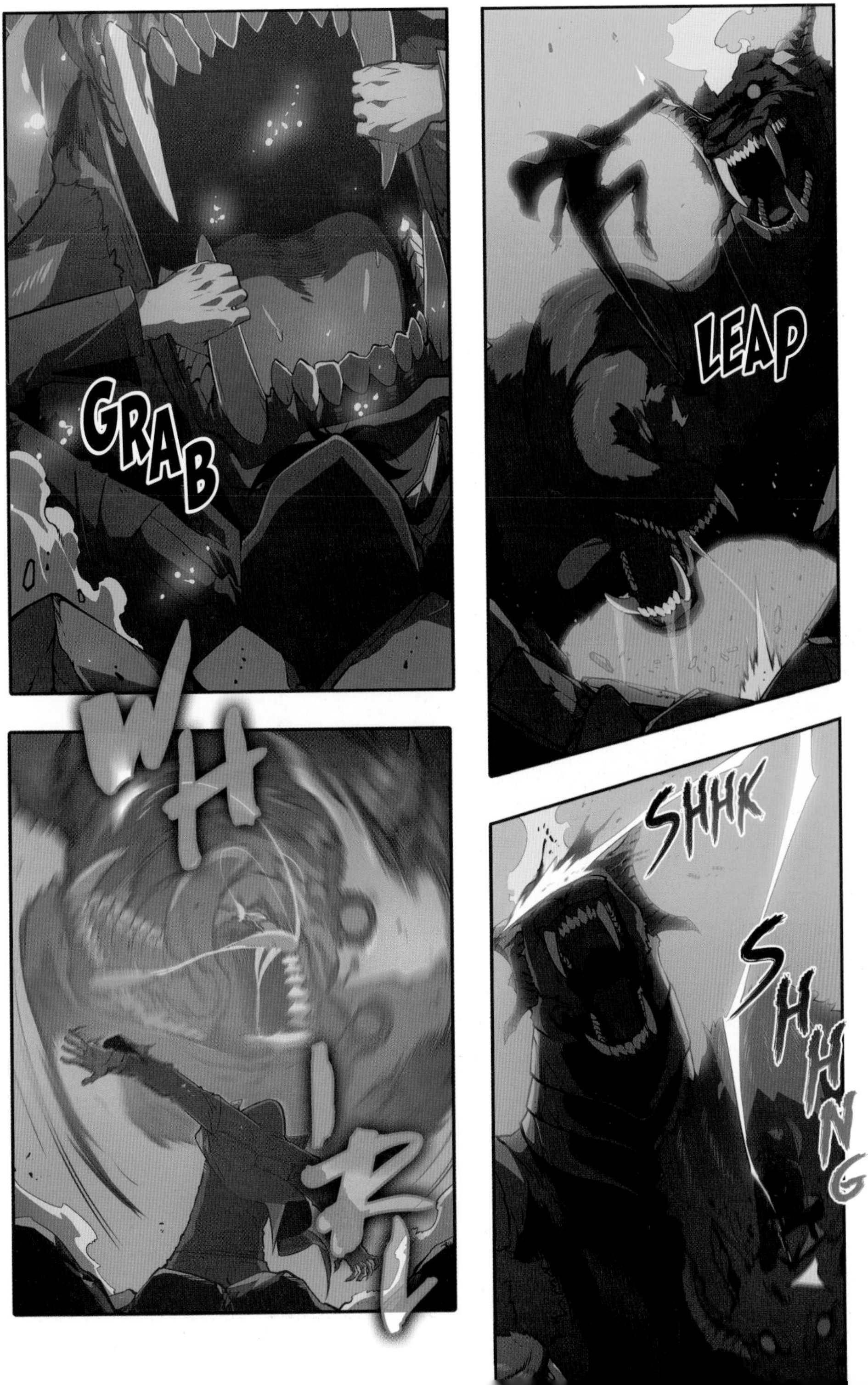
GRAB
LEAP
WHIRL
SHHK
SHHNG

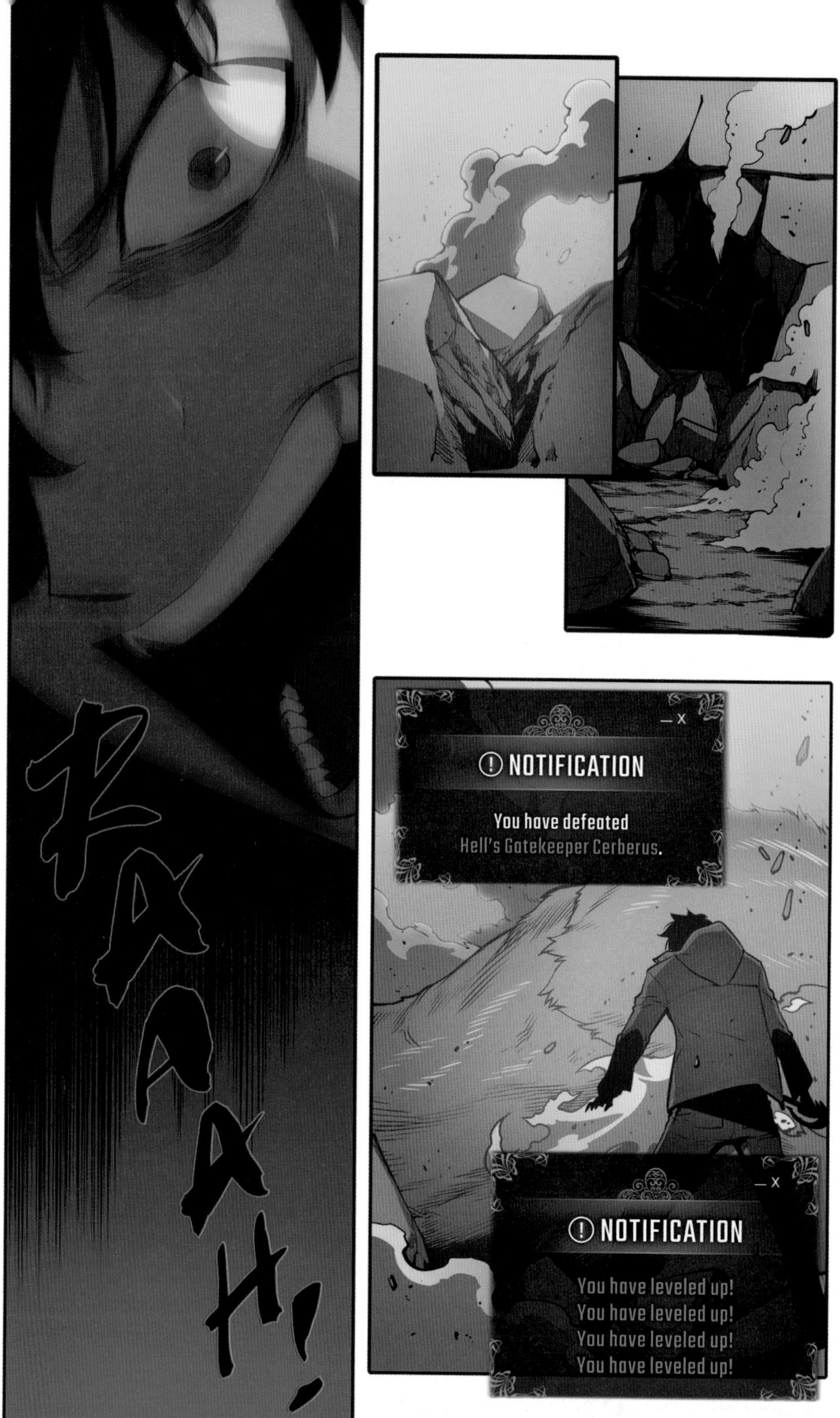
HAAAH!
NOTIFICATION
You have defeated
Hell's Gatekeeper Cerberus.
NOTIFICATION
You have leveled up!
You have leveled up!
You have leveled up!
You have leveled up!

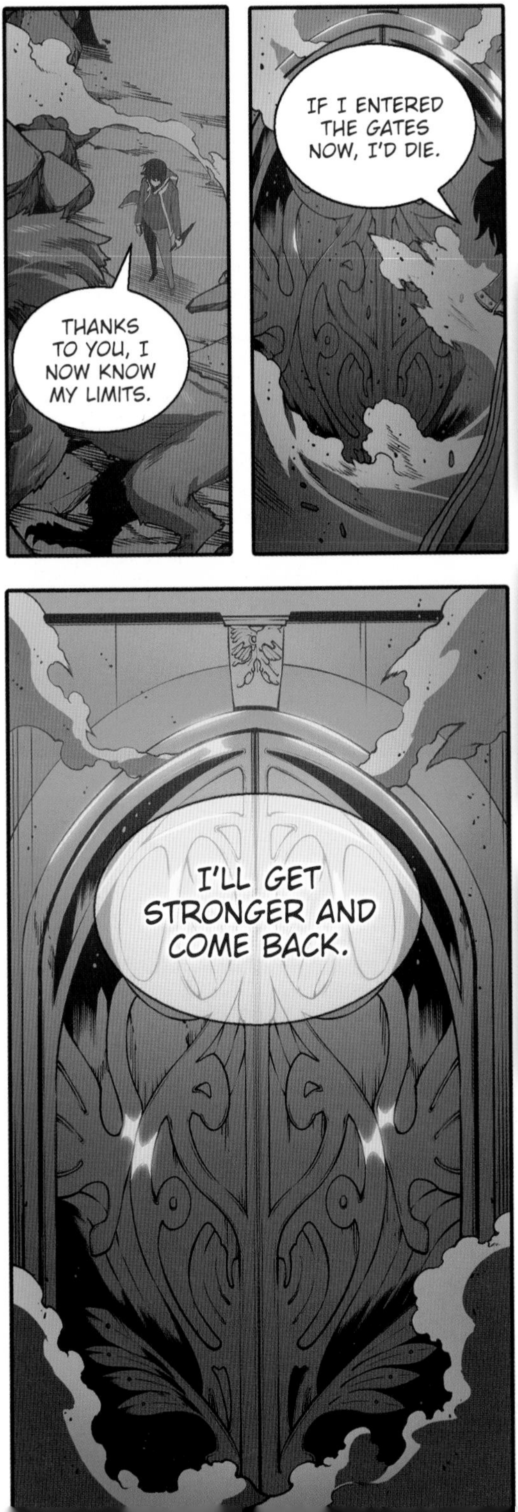
THANKS TO YOU, I NOW KNOW MY LIMITS.
IF I ENTERED THE GATES NOW, I'D DIE.
I'LL GET STRONGER AND COME BACK.

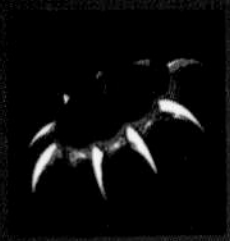

[ITEM: Warden's Collar]
ACQUISITION DIFFICULTY: A
CATEGORY: Collar

AGILITY +20, PERCEPTION +20

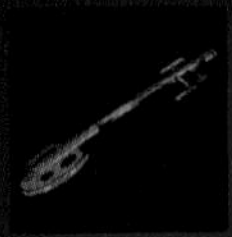

[ITEM: Castle Door Key]
ACQUISITION DIFFICULTY: A
CATEGORY: Key

This key unlocks the door to the Demon's Castle. You can acquire this only when you kill the gatekeeper.

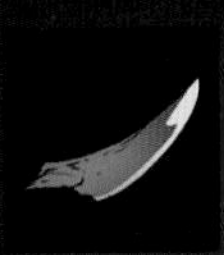

[ITEM: Cerberus's Fang]
ACQUISITION DIFFICULTY: None
CATEGORY: Miscellaneous

You can acquire this fang when you defeat Cerberus.

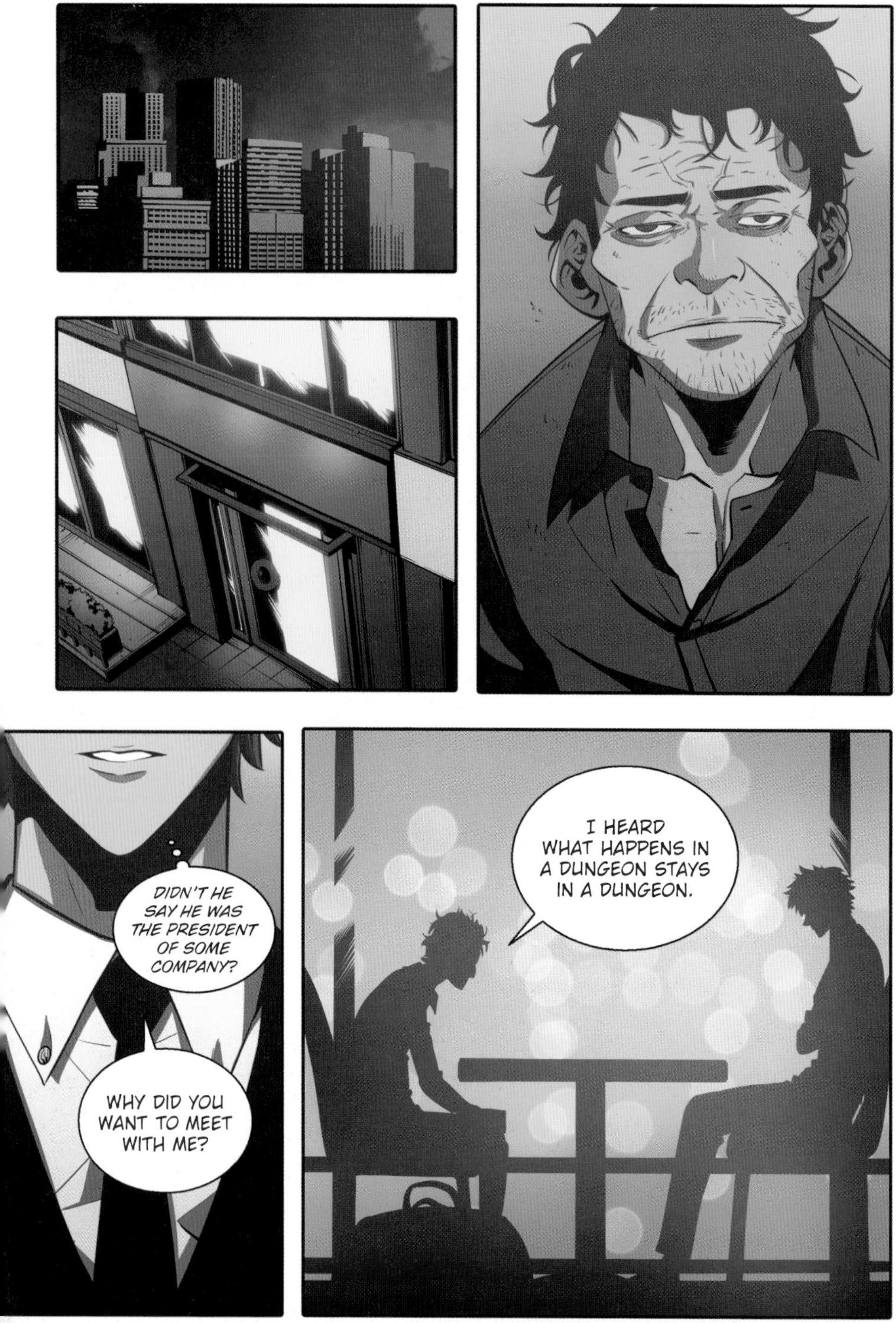
DIDN'T HE SAY HE WAS THE PRESIDENT OF SOME COMPANY?
WHY DID YOU WANT TO MEET WITH ME?
I HEARD WHAT HAPPENS IN A DUNGEON STAYS IN A DUNGEON.

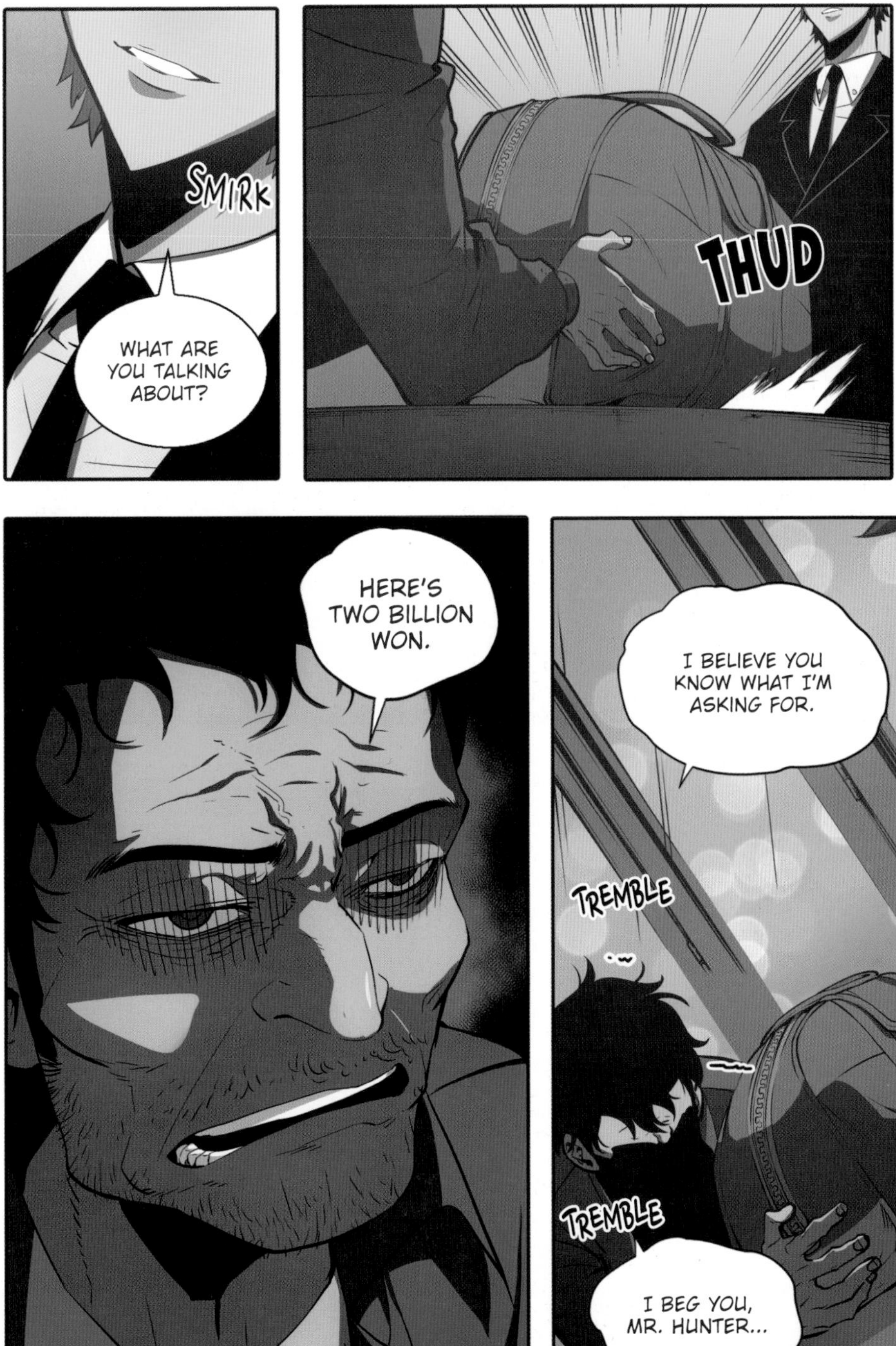
SMIRK
WHAT ARE YOU TALKING ABOUT?
THUD
HERE'S TWO BILLION WON.
I BELIEVE YOU KNOW WHAT I'M ASKING FOR.
TREMBLE
TREMBLE
I BEG YOU, MR. HUNTER...

While exchange rates fluctuate daily, an easy conversion estimate is about 1,000 KRW to 1 USD.

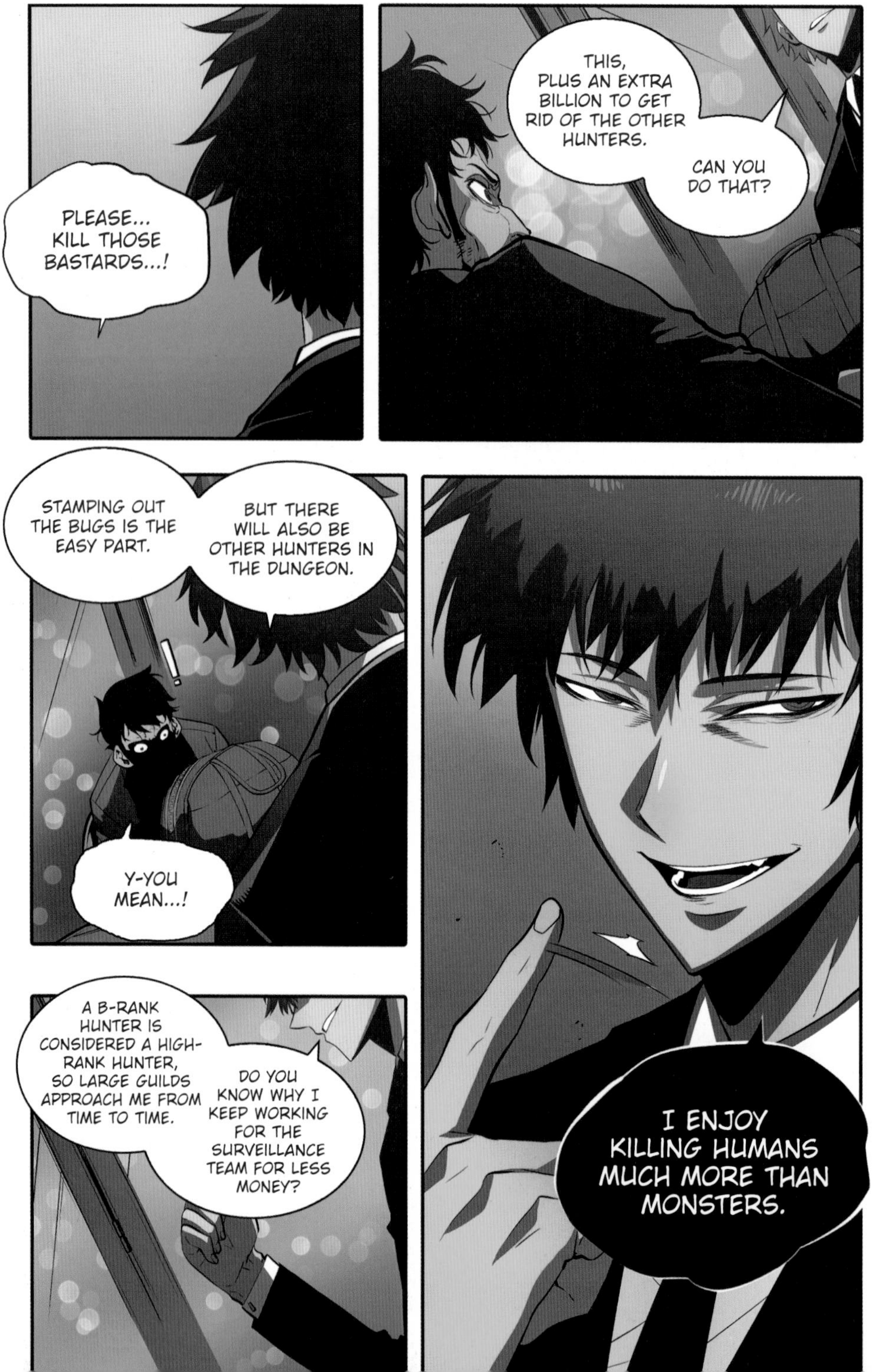
PLEASE... KILL THOSE BASTARDS...!
THIS, PLUS AN EXTRA BILLION TO GET RID OF THE OTHER HUNTERS.
CAN YOU DO THAT?
STAMPING OUT THE BUGS IS THE EASY PART.
BUT THERE WILL ALSO BE OTHER HUNTERS IN THE DUNGEON.
!
Y-YOU MEAN...!
A B-RANK HUNTER IS CONSIDERED A HIGH-RANK HUNTER, SO LARGE GUILDS APPROACH ME FROM TIME TO TIME.
DO YOU KNOW WHY I KEEP WORKING FOR THE SURVEILLANCE TEAM FOR LESS MONEY?
I ENJOY KILLING HUMANS MUCH MORE THAN MONSTERS.

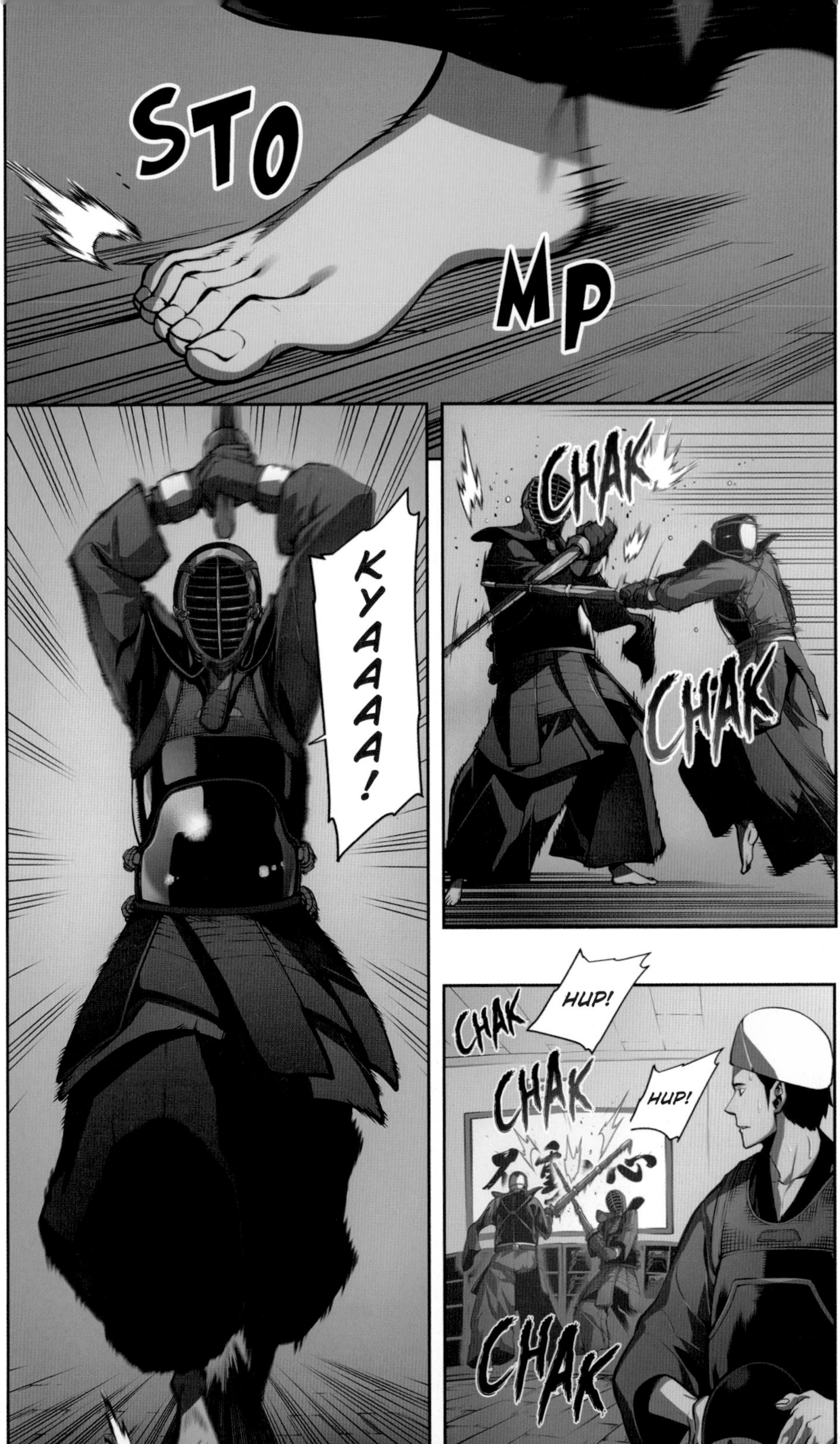

STO
MP
KYAAAAA!
CHAK
CHAK
CHAK
HUP!
CHAK
HUP!
CHAK

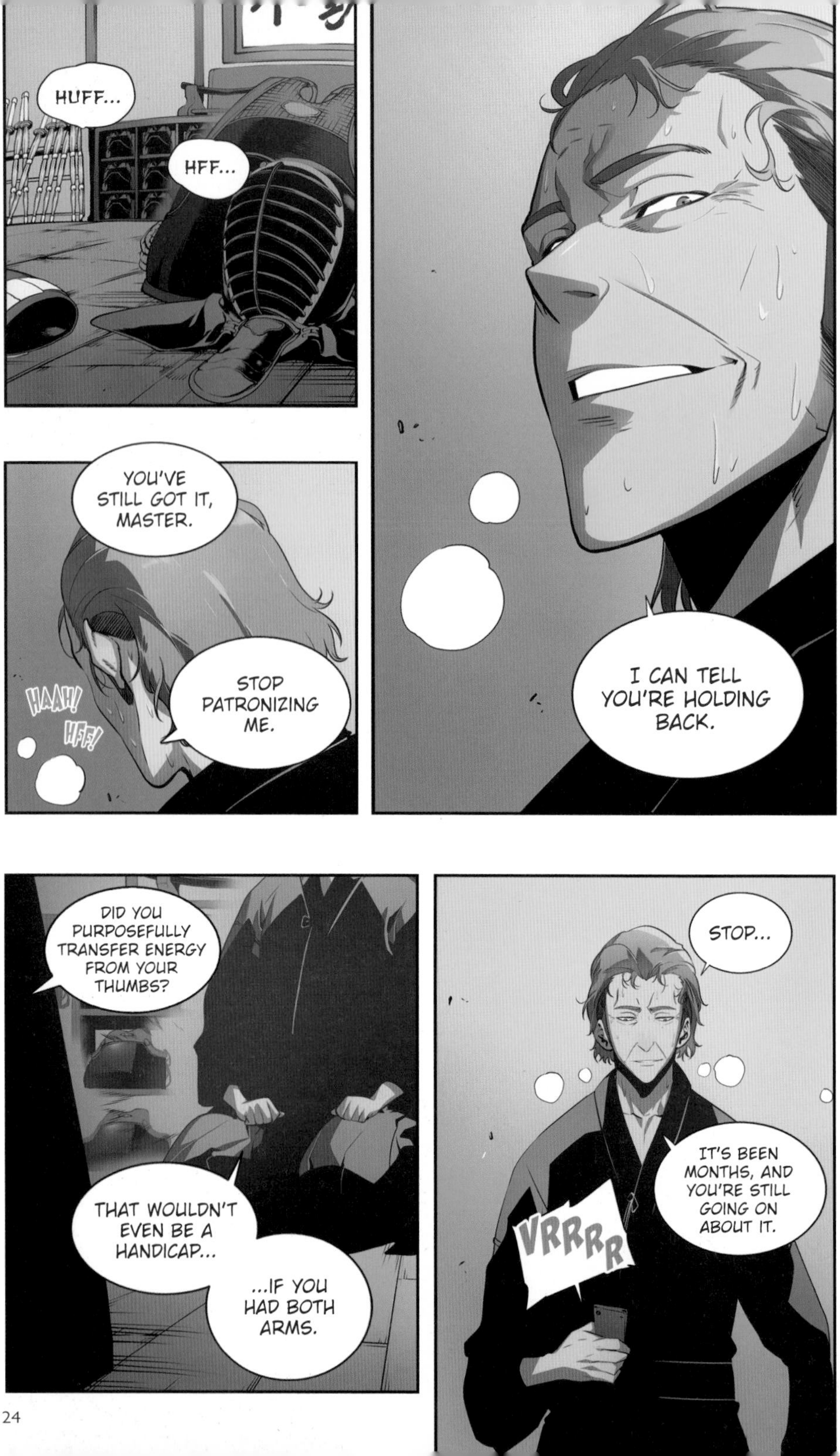
HUFF...
HFF...
YOU'VE STILL GOT IT, MASTER.
STOP PATRONIZING ME.
HAAH!
HFF!
I CAN TELL YOU'RE HOLDING BACK.
DID YOU PURPOSEFULLY TRANSFER ENERGY FROM YOUR THUMBS?
THAT WOULDN'T EVEN BE A HANDICAP...
...IF YOU HAD BOTH ARMS.
STOP...
IT'S BEEN MONTHS, AND YOU'RE STILL GOING ON ABOUT IT.
VRRRR

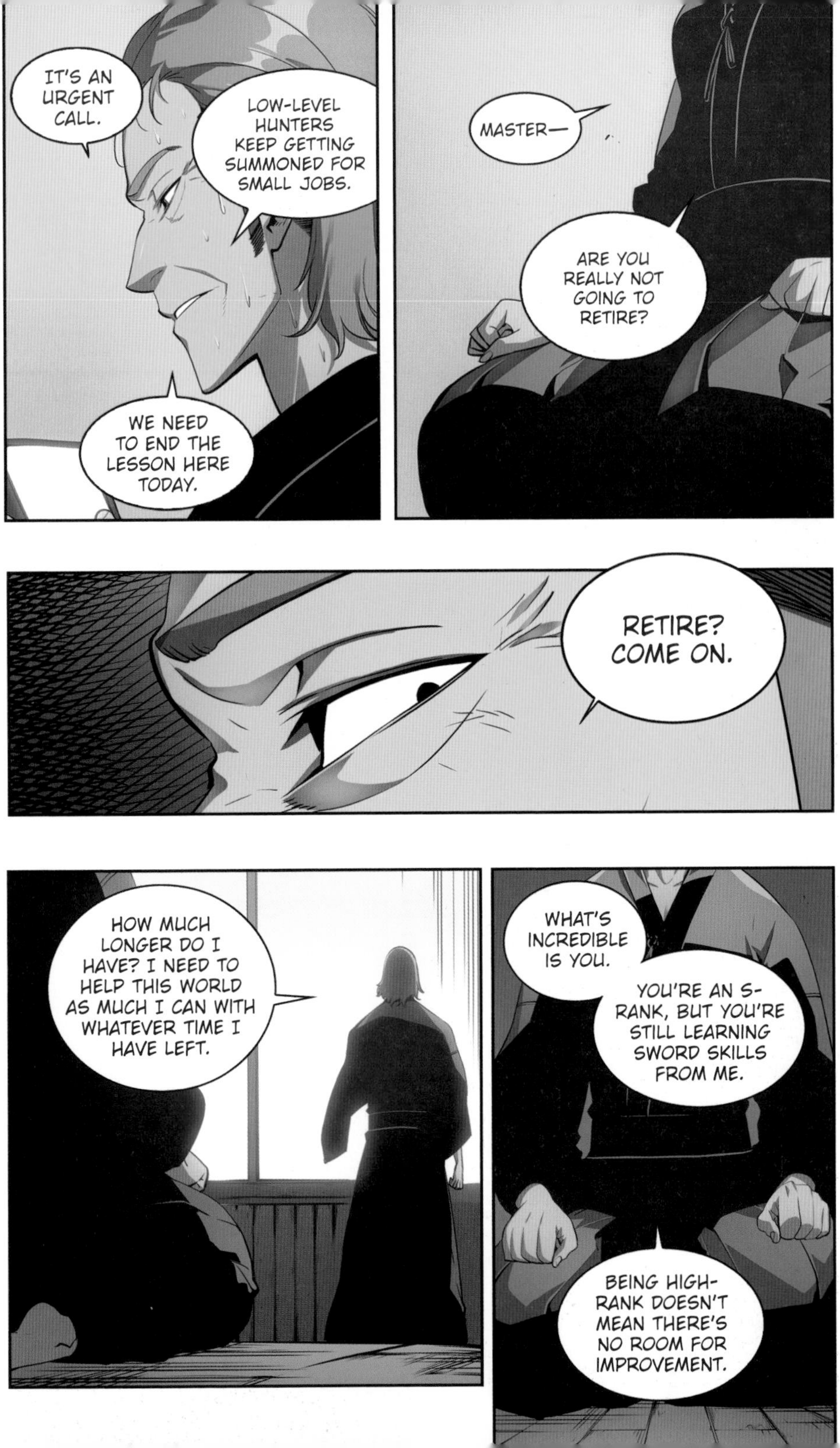
IT'S AN URGENT CALL.
LOW-LEVEL HUNTERS KEEP GETTING SUMMONED FOR SMALL JOBS.
WE NEED TO END THE LESSON HERE TODAY.
MASTER—
ARE YOU REALLY NOT GOING TO RETIRE?
RETIRE? COME ON.
HOW MUCH LONGER DO I HAVE? I NEED TO HELP THIS WORLD AS MUCH I CAN WITH WHATEVER TIME I HAVE LEFT.
WHAT'S INCREDIBLE IS YOU.
YOU'RE AN S-RANK, BUT YOU'RE STILL LEARNING SWORD SKILLS FROM ME.
BEING HIGH-RANK DOESN'T MEAN THERE'S NO ROOM FOR IMPROVEMENT.

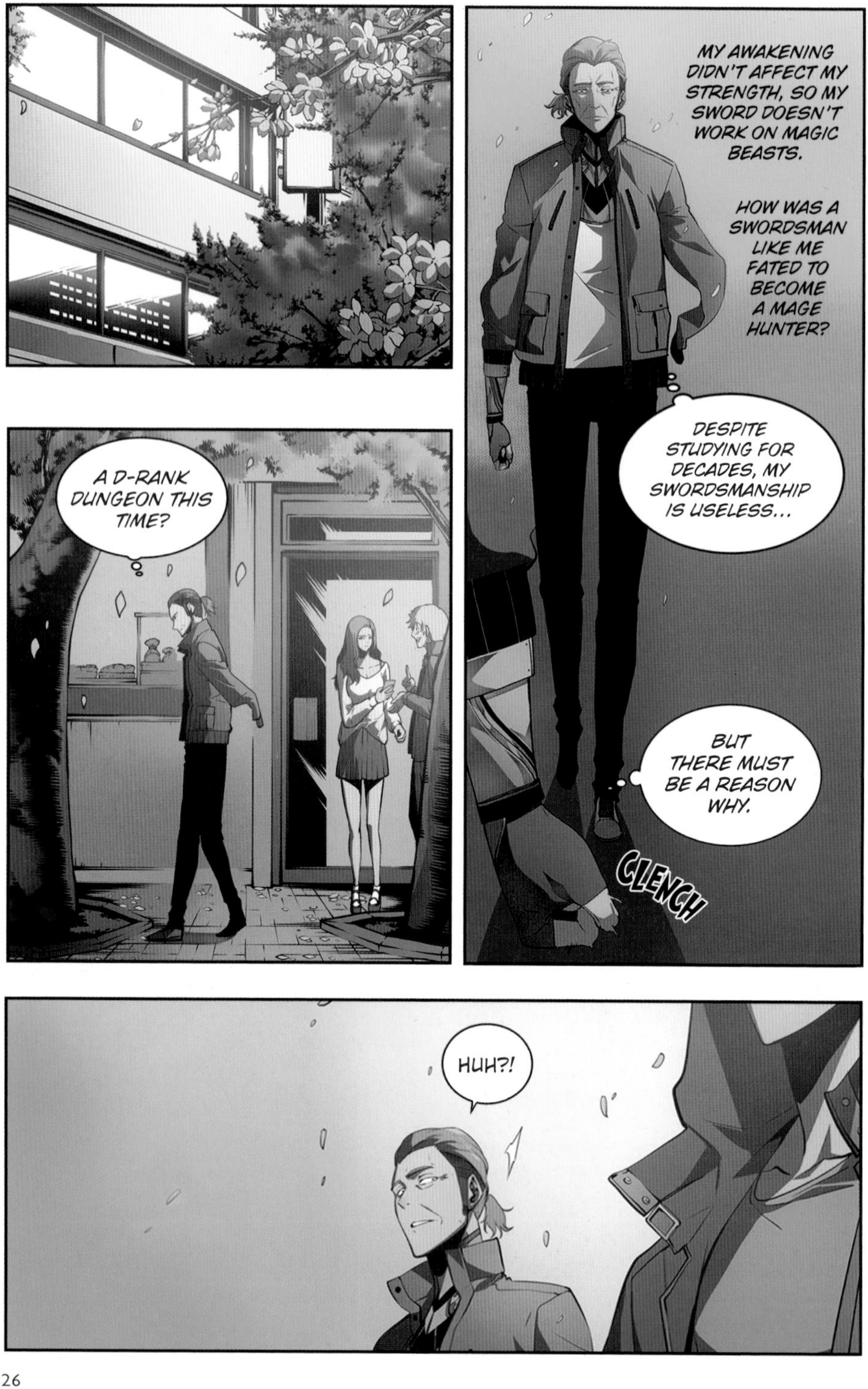
A D-RANK DUNGEON THIS TIME?
MY AWAKENING DIDN'T AFFECT MY STRENGTH, SO MY SWORD DOESN'T WORK ON MAGIC BEASTS.
HOW WAS A SWORDSMAN LIKE ME FATED TO BECOME A MAGE HUNTER?
DESPITE STUDYING FOR DECADES, MY SWORDSMANSHIP IS USELESS...
BUT THERE MUST BE A REASON WHY.
CLENCH
HUH?!

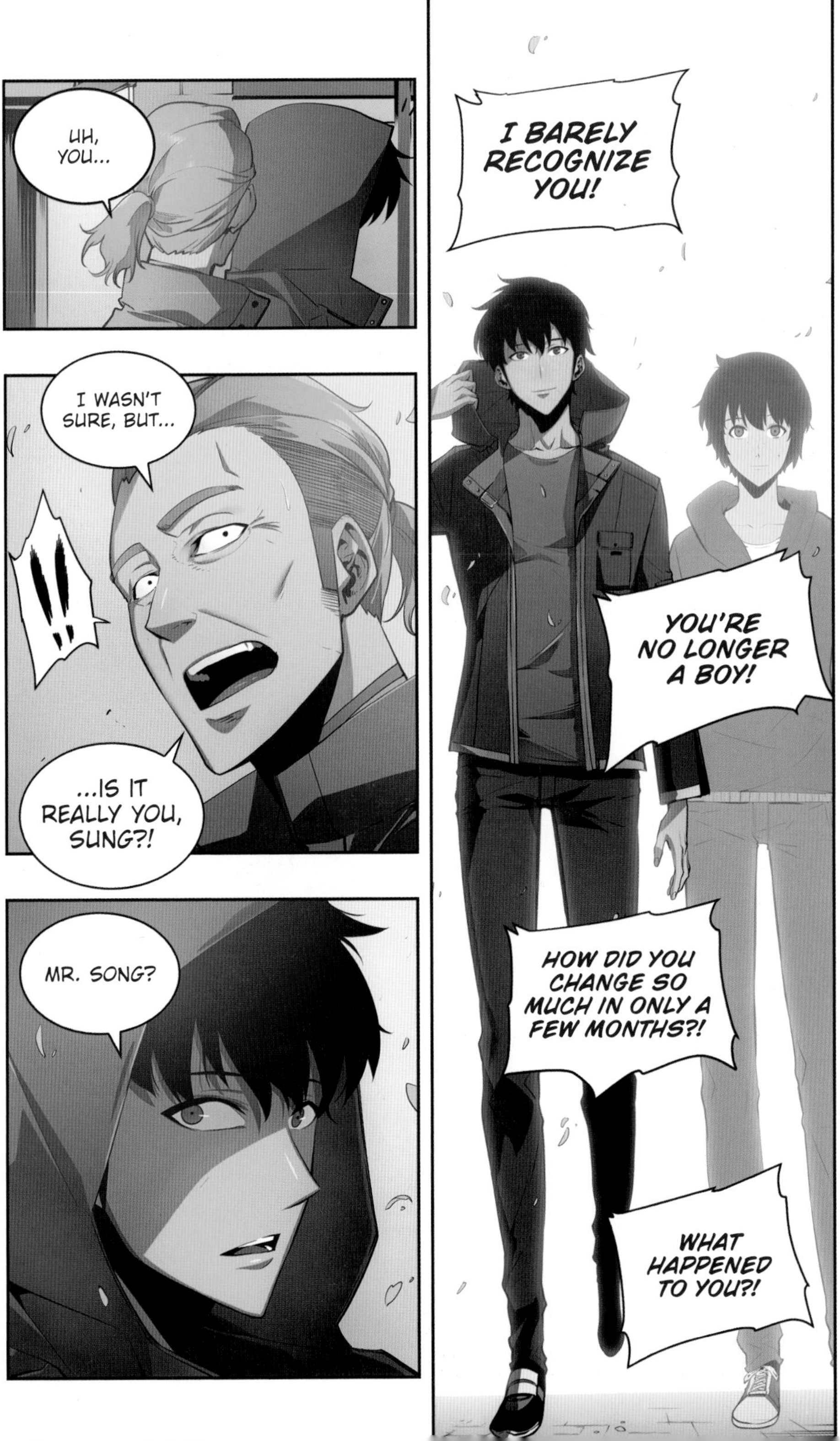
UH, YOU...
I WASN'T SURE, BUT...
!!
...IS IT REALLY YOU, SUNG?!
MR. SONG?
I BARELY RECOGNIZE YOU!
YOU'RE NO LONGER A BOY!
HOW DID YOU CHANGE SO MUCH IN ONLY A FEW MONTHS?!
WHAT HAPPENED TO YOU?!

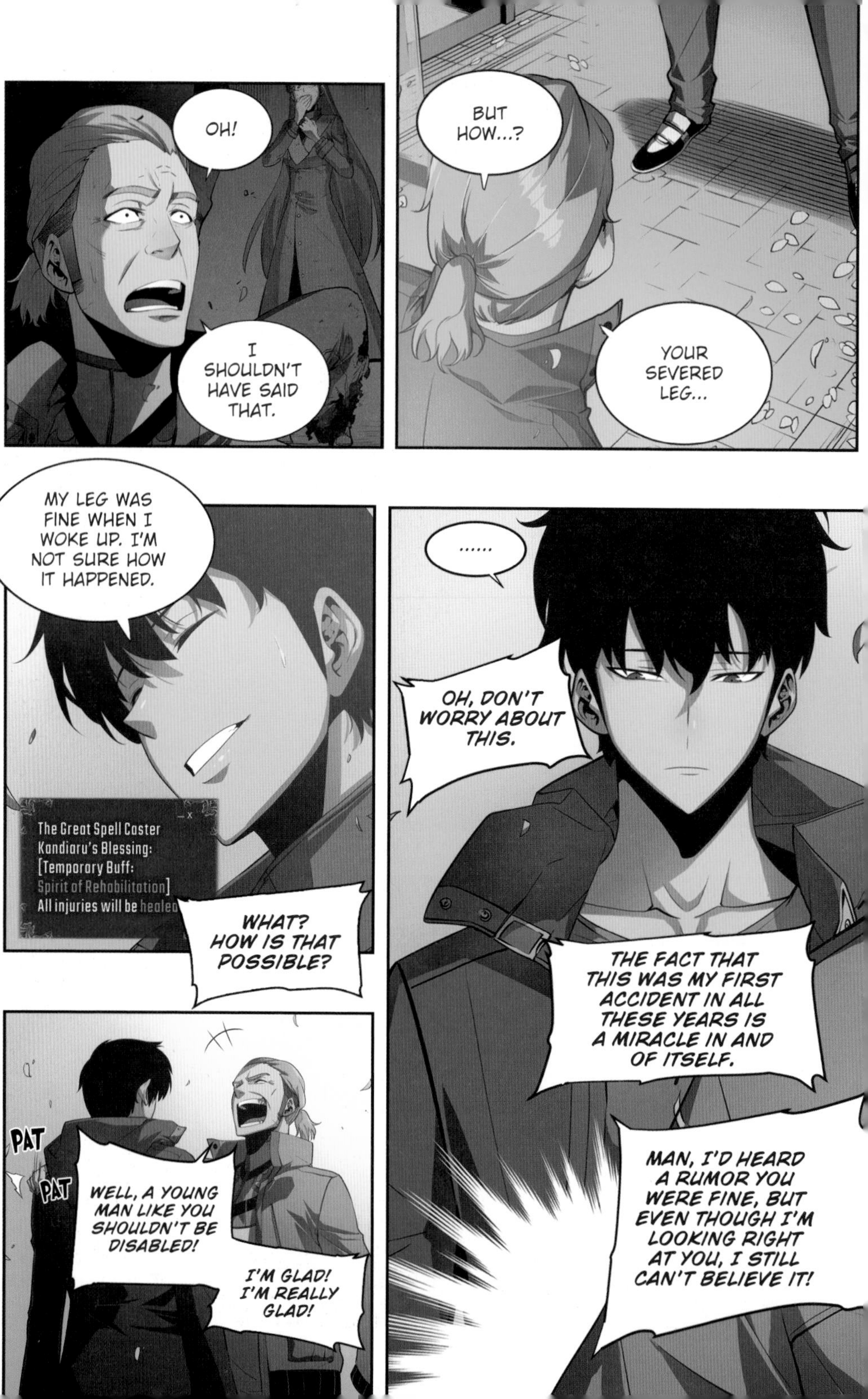
OH!
I SHOULDN'T HAVE SAID THAT.
BUT HOW...?
YOUR SEVERED LEG...
MY LEG WAS FINE WHEN I WOKE UP. I'M NOT SURE HOW IT HAPPENED.
The Great Spell Caster Kandiaru's Blessing: [Temporary Buff: Spirit of Rehabilitation] All injuries will be healed
WHAT? HOW IS THAT POSSIBLE?
PAT
PAT
WELL, A YOUNG MAN LIKE YOU SHOULDN'T BE DISABLED!
I'M GLAD! I'M REALLY GLAD!
......
OH, DON'T WORRY ABOUT THIS.
THE FACT THAT THIS WAS MY FIRST ACCIDENT IN ALL THESE YEARS IS A MIRACLE IN AND OF ITSELF.
MAN, I'D HEARD A RUMOR YOU WERE FINE, BUT EVEN THOUGH I'M LOOKING RIGHT AT YOU, I STILL CAN'T BELIEVE IT!

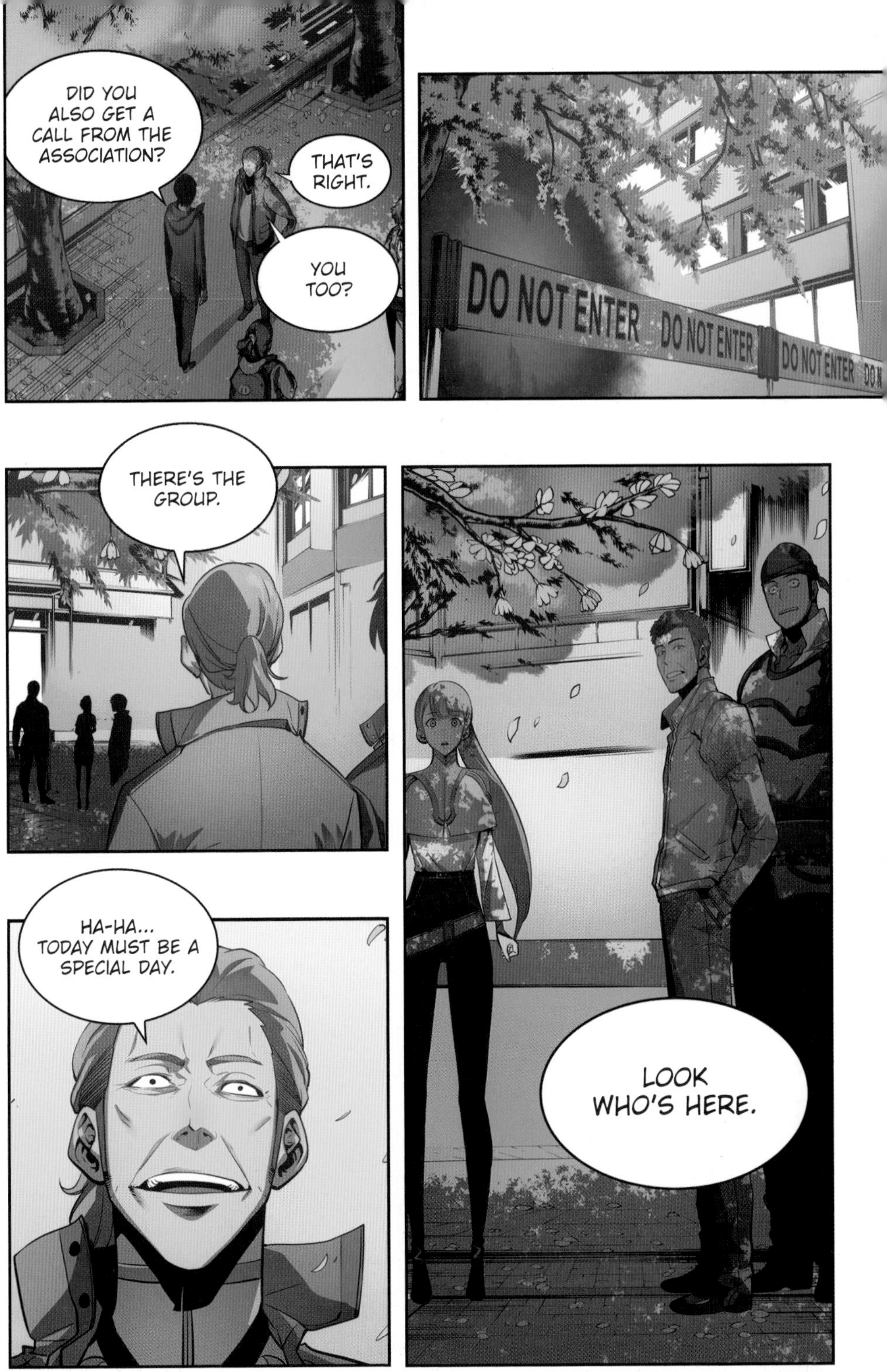
DID YOU ALSO GET A CALL FROM THE ASSOCIATION?
THAT'S RIGHT.
YOU TOO?
DO NOT ENTER
DO NOT ENTER
DO NOT ENTER
THERE'S THE GROUP.
HA-HA... TODAY MUST BE A SPECIAL DAY.
LOOK WHO'S HERE.

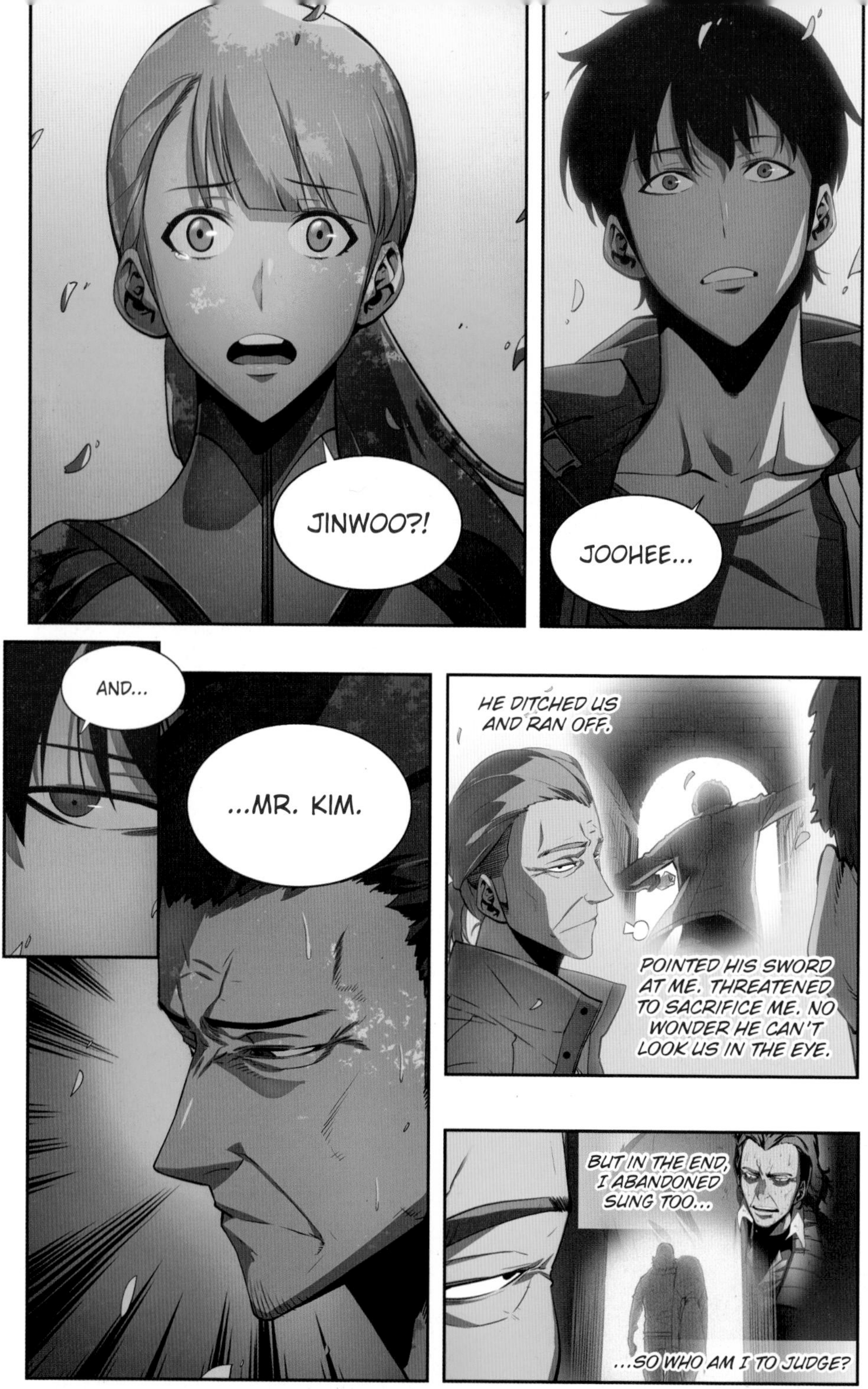
JINWOO?!
JOOHEE...
AND...
...MR. KIM.
HE DITCHED US AND RAN OFF.
POINTED HIS SWORD AT ME. THREATENED TO SACRIFICE ME. NO WONDER HE CAN'T LOOK US IN THE EYE.
BUT IN THE END, I ABANDONED SUNG TOO...
...SO WHO AM I TO JUDGE?

I GUESS I DIDN'T THINK...

UNNH...

MY ARM!

SLRK

THE
MOV

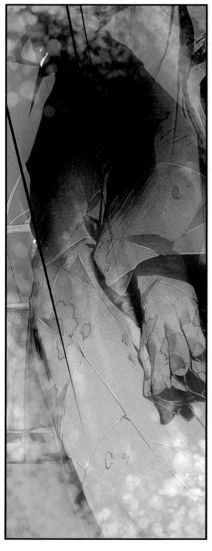

...ANY OF US...

...WOULD GET OUT ALIVE...

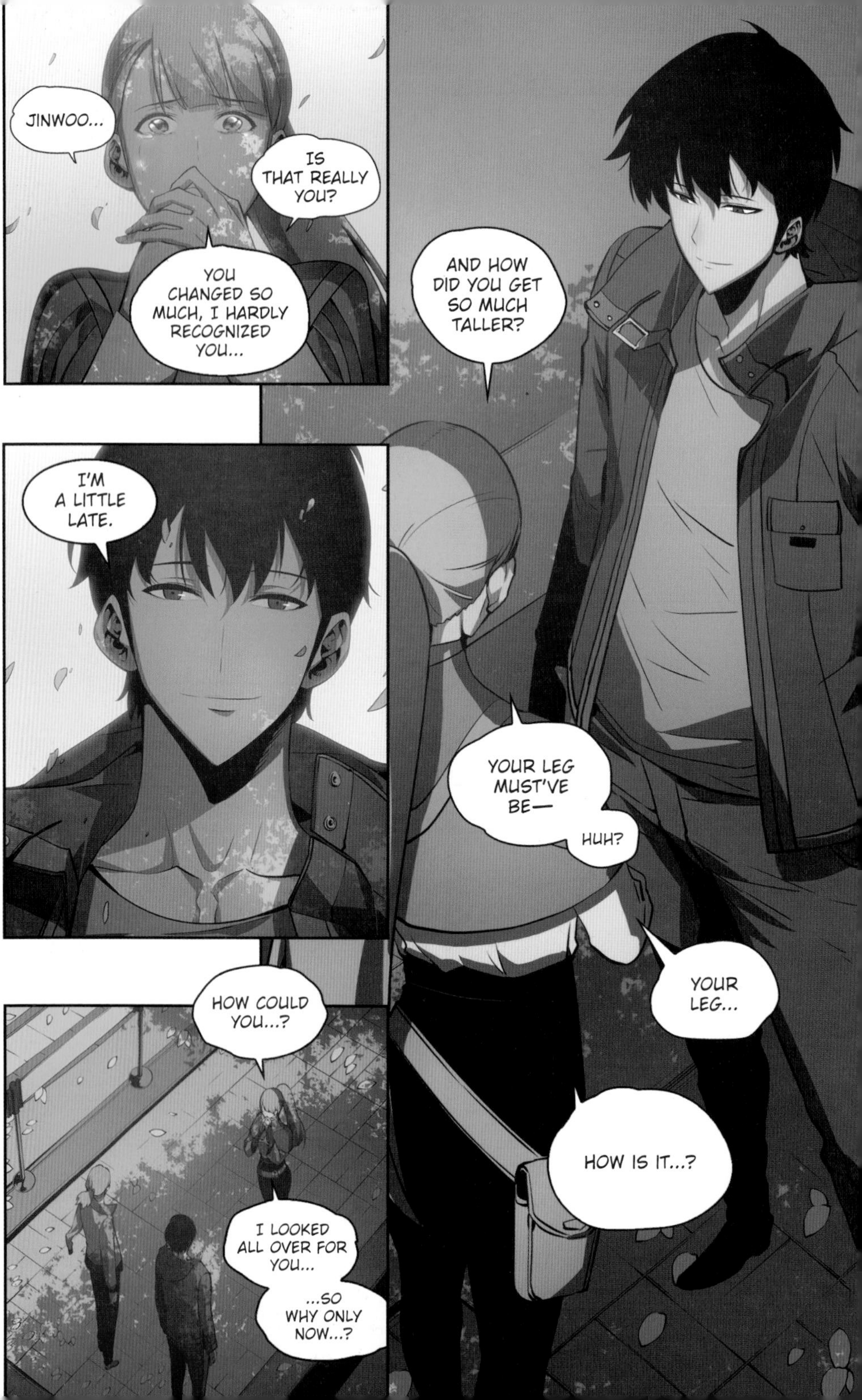
JINWOO...
IS THAT REALLY YOU?
YOU CHANGED SO MUCH, I HARDLY RECOGNIZED YOU...
I'M A LITTLE LATE.
HOW COULD YOU...?
I LOOKED ALL OVER FOR YOU...
...SO WHY ONLY NOW...?
AND HOW DID YOU GET SO MUCH TALLER?
YOUR LEG MUST'VE BE—
HUH?
YOUR LEG...
HOW IS IT...?

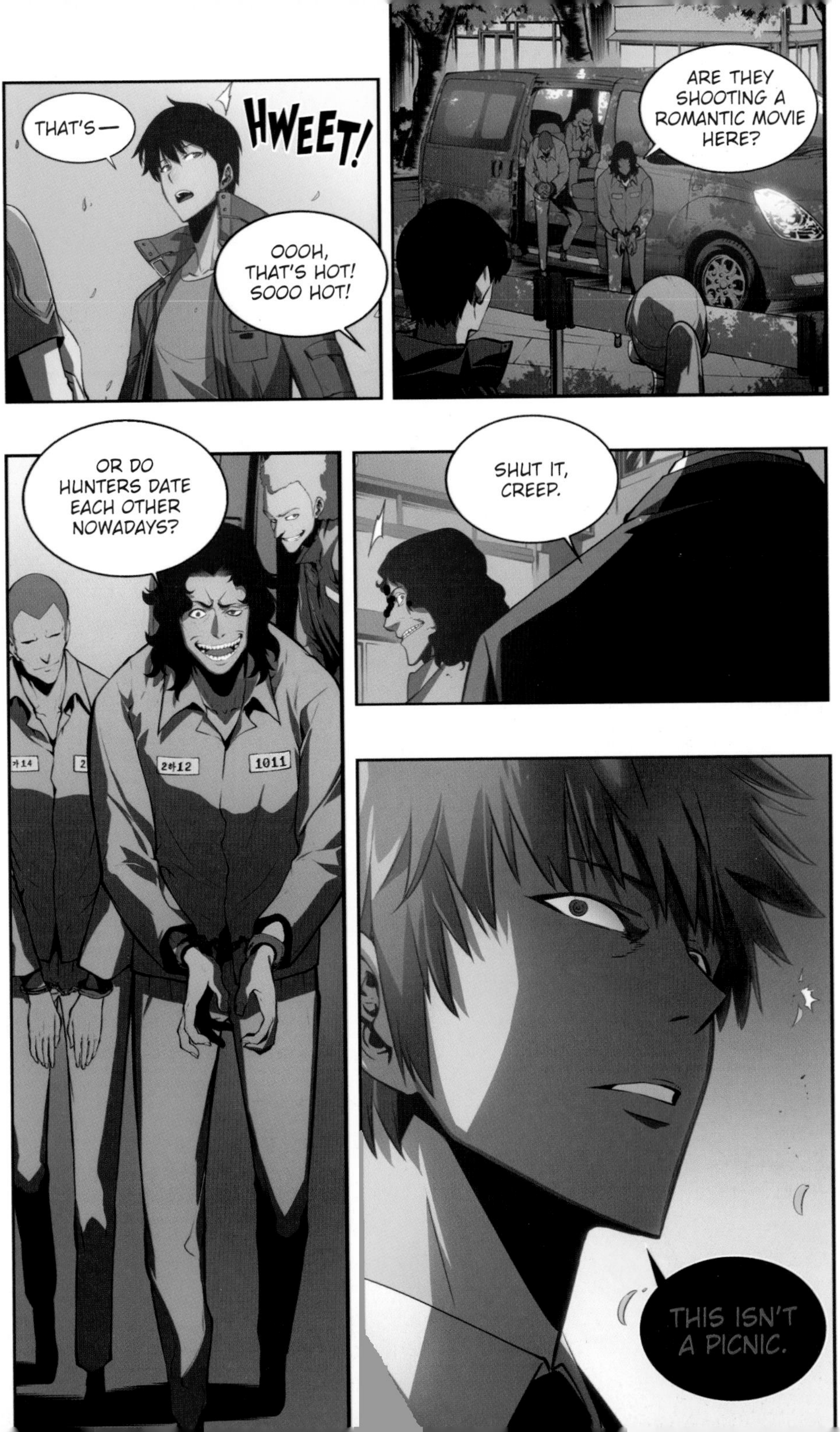
THAT'S—
HWEET!
OOOH, THAT'S HOT! SOOO HOT!
ARE THEY SHOOTING A ROMANTIC MOVIE HERE?
OR DO HUNTERS DATE EACH OTHER NOWADAYS?
2하12
1011
SHUT IT, CREEP.
THIS ISN'T A PICNIC.

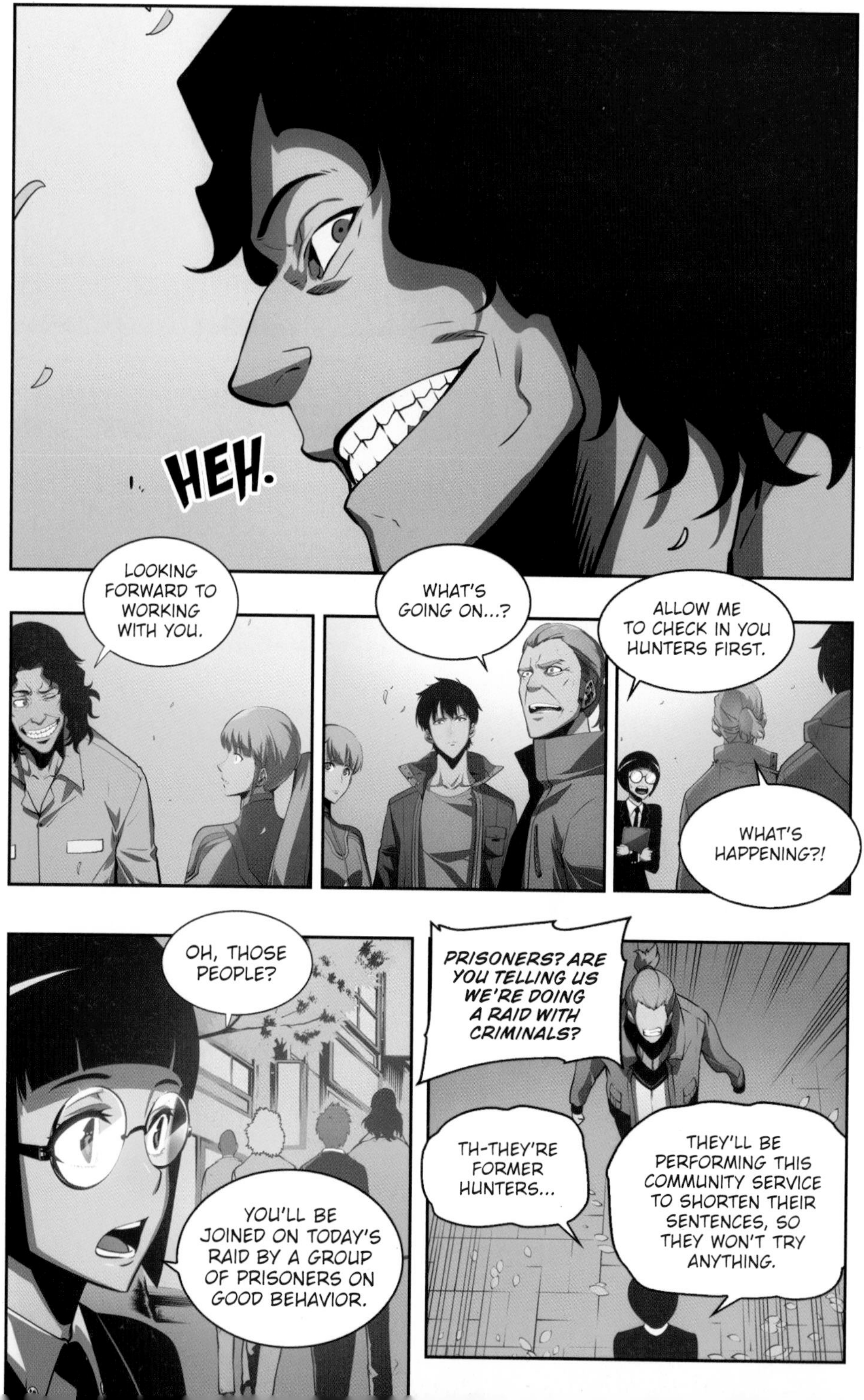
HEH.
LOOKING FORWARD TO WORKING WITH YOU.
WHAT'S GOING ON...?
ALLOW ME TO CHECK IN YOU HUNTERS FIRST.
WHAT'S HAPPENING?!
OH, THOSE PEOPLE?
YOU'LL BE JOINED ON TODAY'S RAID BY A GROUP OF PRISONERS ON GOOD BEHAVIOR.
PRISONERS? ARE YOU TELLING US WE'RE DOING A RAID WITH CRIMINALS?
TH-THEY'RE FORMER HUNTERS...
THEY'LL BE PERFORMING THIS COMMUNITY SERVICE TO SHORTEN THEIR SENTENCES, SO THEY WON'T TRY ANYTHING.

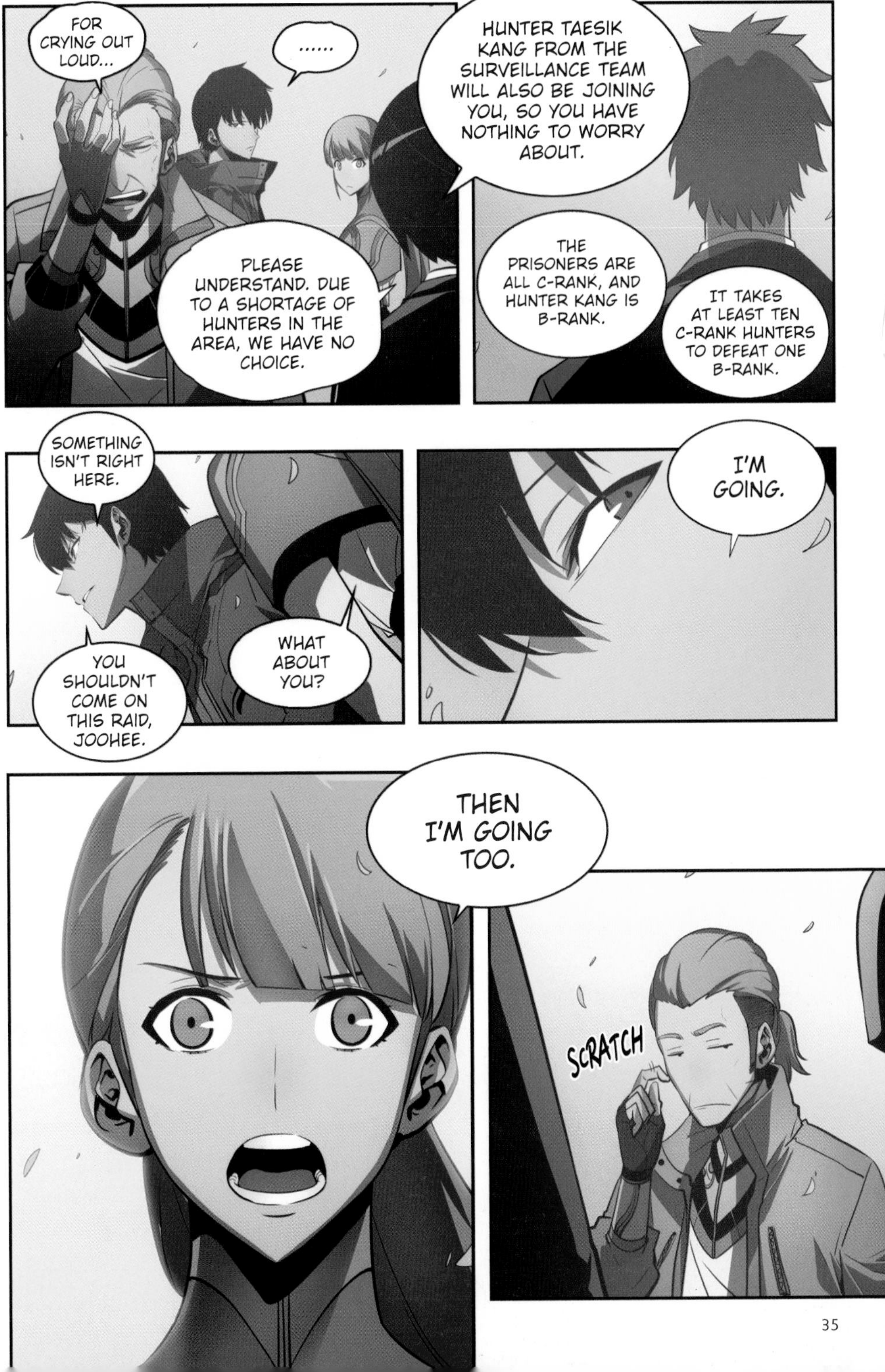
FOR CRYING OUT LOUD...
......
HUNTER TAESIK KANG FROM THE SURVEILLANCE TEAM WILL ALSO BE JOINING YOU, SO YOU HAVE NOTHING TO WORRY ABOUT.
PLEASE UNDERSTAND. DUE TO A SHORTAGE OF HUNTERS IN THE AREA, WE HAVE NO CHOICE.
THE PRISONERS ARE ALL C-RANK, AND HUNTER KANG IS B-RANK.
IT TAKES AT LEAST TEN C-RANK HUNTERS TO DEFEAT ONE B-RANK.
SOMETHING ISN'T RIGHT HERE.
YOU SHOULDN'T COME ON THIS RAID, JOOHEE.
WHAT ABOUT YOU?
I'M GOING.
THEN I'M GOING TOO.
SCRATCH

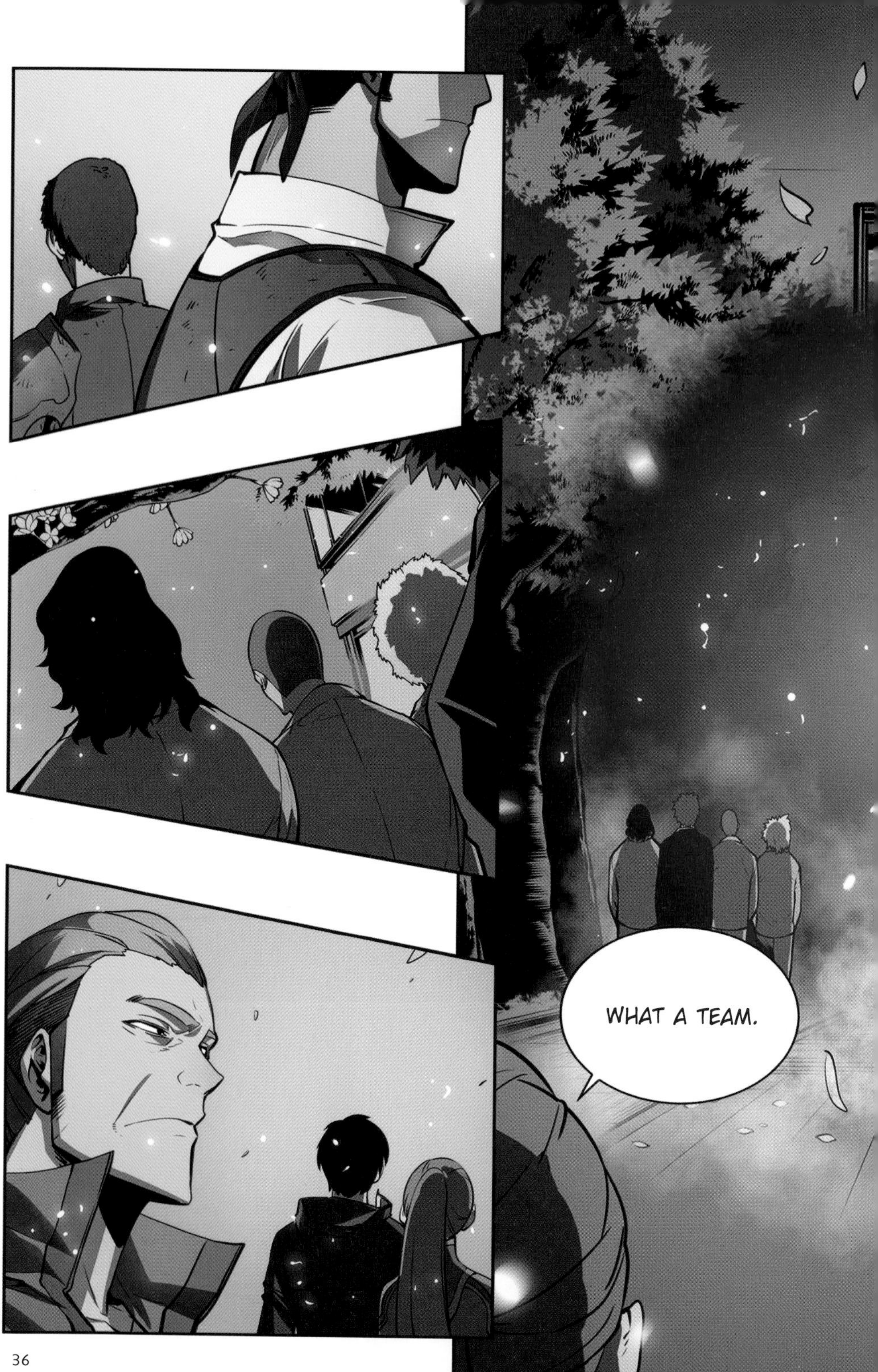
WHAT A TEAM.

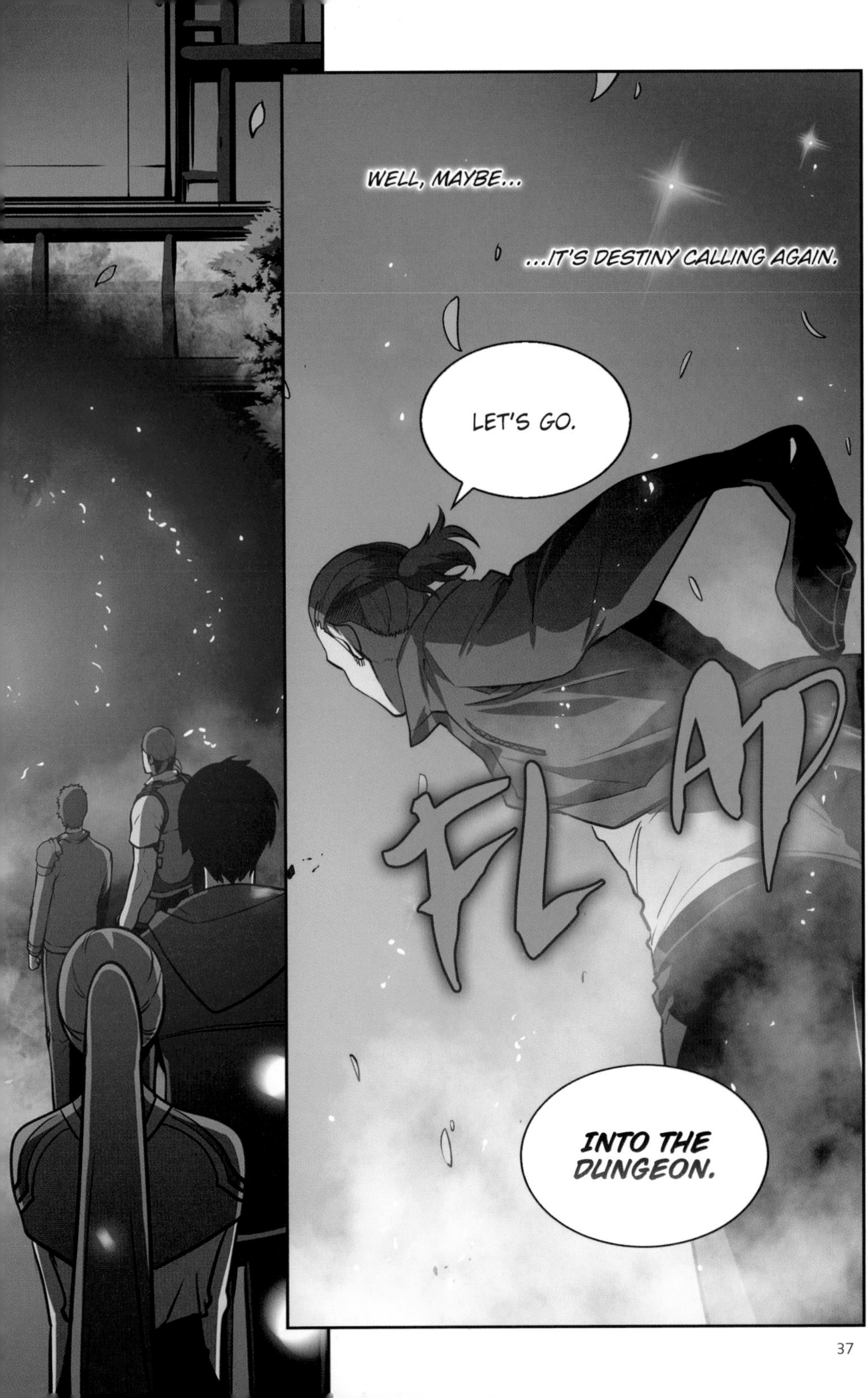
WELL, MAYBE...
...IT'S DESTINY CALLING AGAIN.
LET'S GO.
FLAP
INTO THE DUNGEON.

CLICK

DAMN, THAT WAS SO UNCOMFORTABLE.

KRIK

KRAK

WE'RE NOT SLAVES. HOW CAN THEY DRAG US AROUND LIKE THIS?

I'M TAESIK KANG FROM THE SURVEILLANCE TEAM.

3 가 14

2028

SHUT UP.

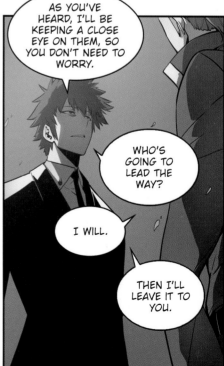

AS YOU'VE HEARD, I'LL BE KEEPING A CLOSE EYE ON THEM, SO YOU DON'T NEED TO WORRY.

WHO'S GOING TO LEAD THE WAY?

I WILL.

THEN I'LL LEAVE IT TO YOU.

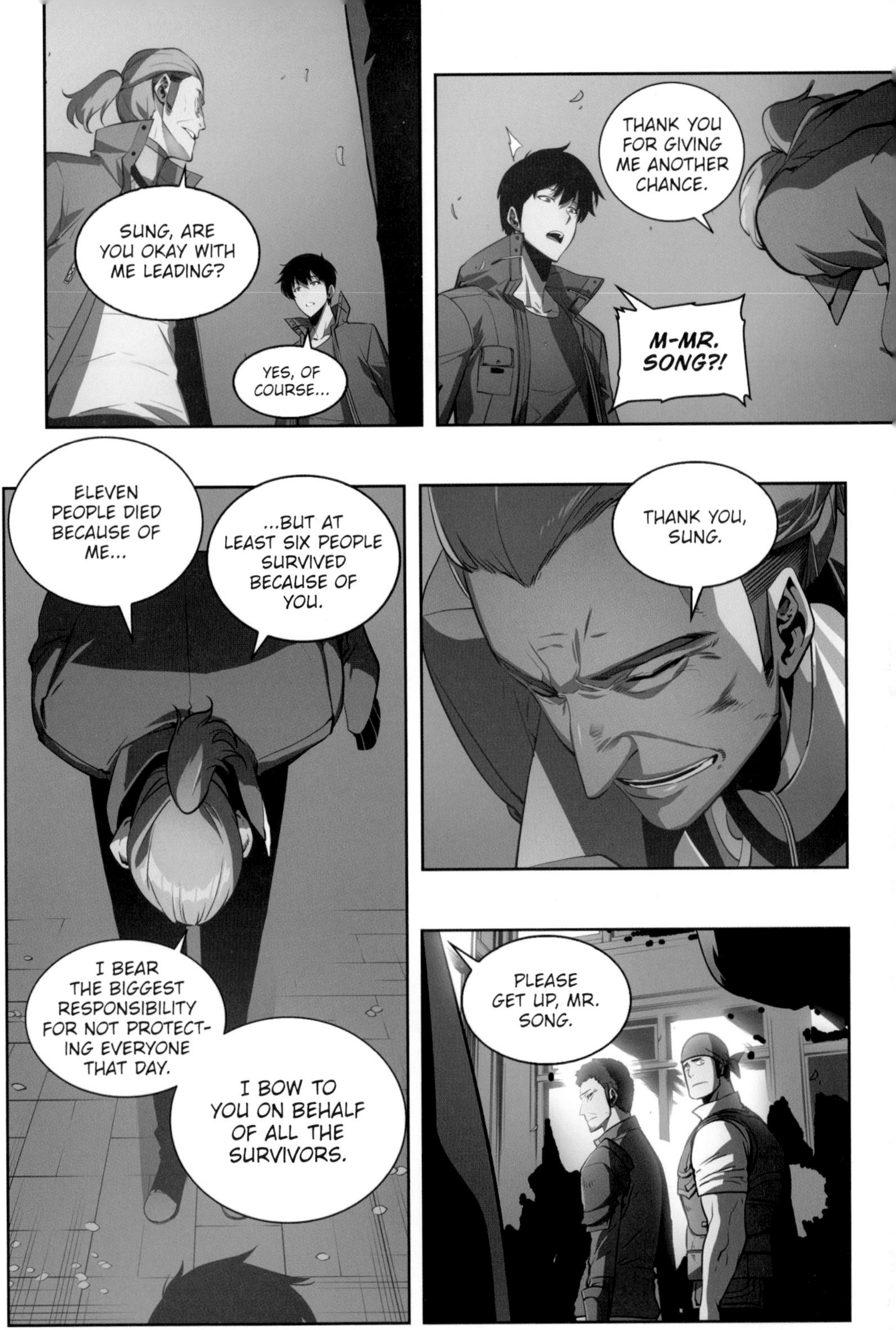
SUNG, ARE YOU OKAY WITH ME LEADING?
YES, OF COURSE...
THANK YOU FOR GIVING ME ANOTHER CHANCE.
M-MR. SONG?!
ELEVEN PEOPLE DIED BECAUSE OF ME...
...BUT AT LEAST SIX PEOPLE SURVIVED BECAUSE OF YOU.
I BEAR THE BIGGEST RESPONSIBILITY FOR NOT PROTECT-ING EVERYONE THAT DAY.
I BOW TO YOU ON BEHALF OF ALL THE SURVIVORS.
THANK YOU, SUNG.
PLEASE GET UP, MR. SONG.

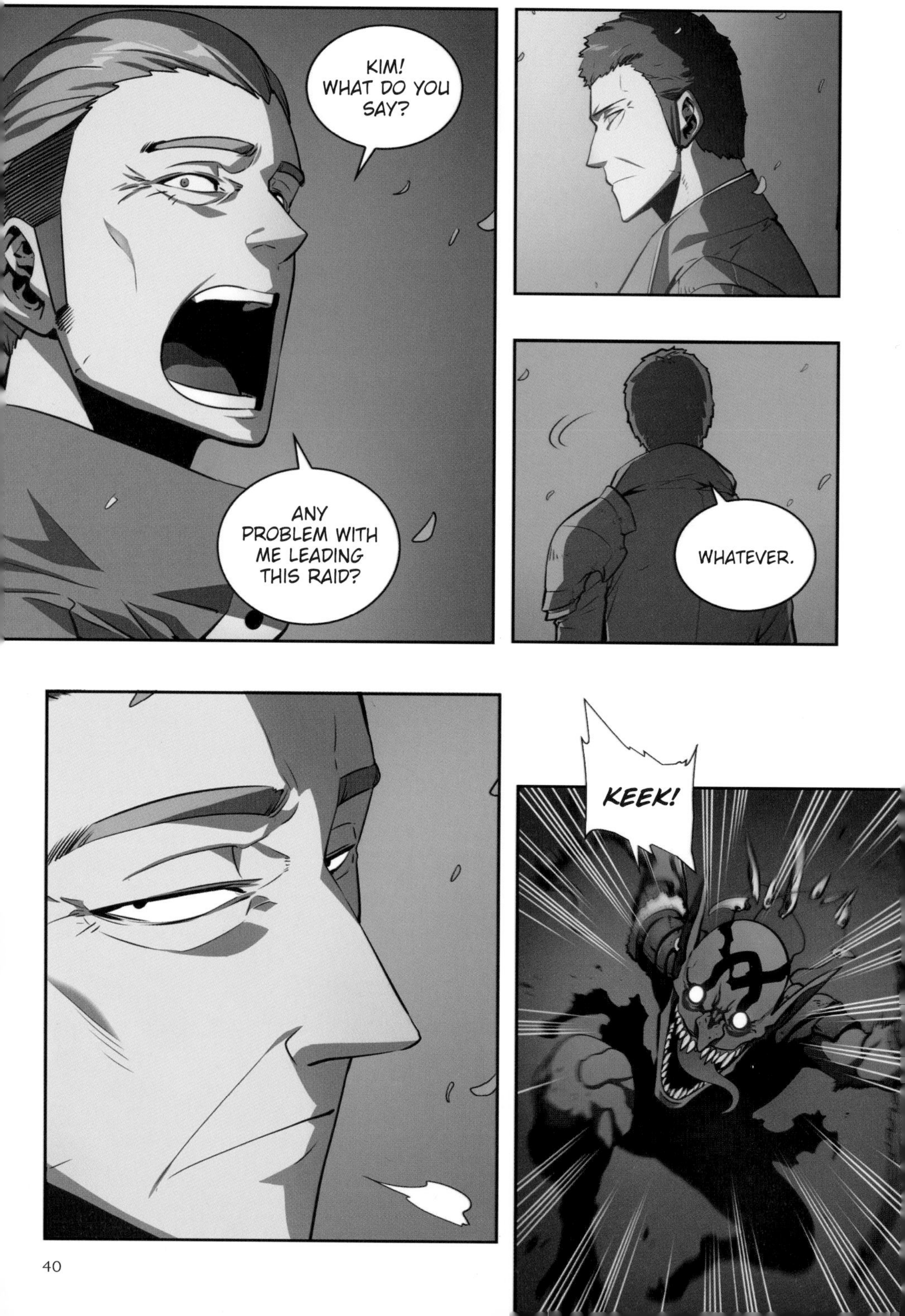
KIM! WHAT DO YOU SAY?
ANY PROBLEM WITH ME LEADING THIS RAID?
WHATEVER.
KEEK!

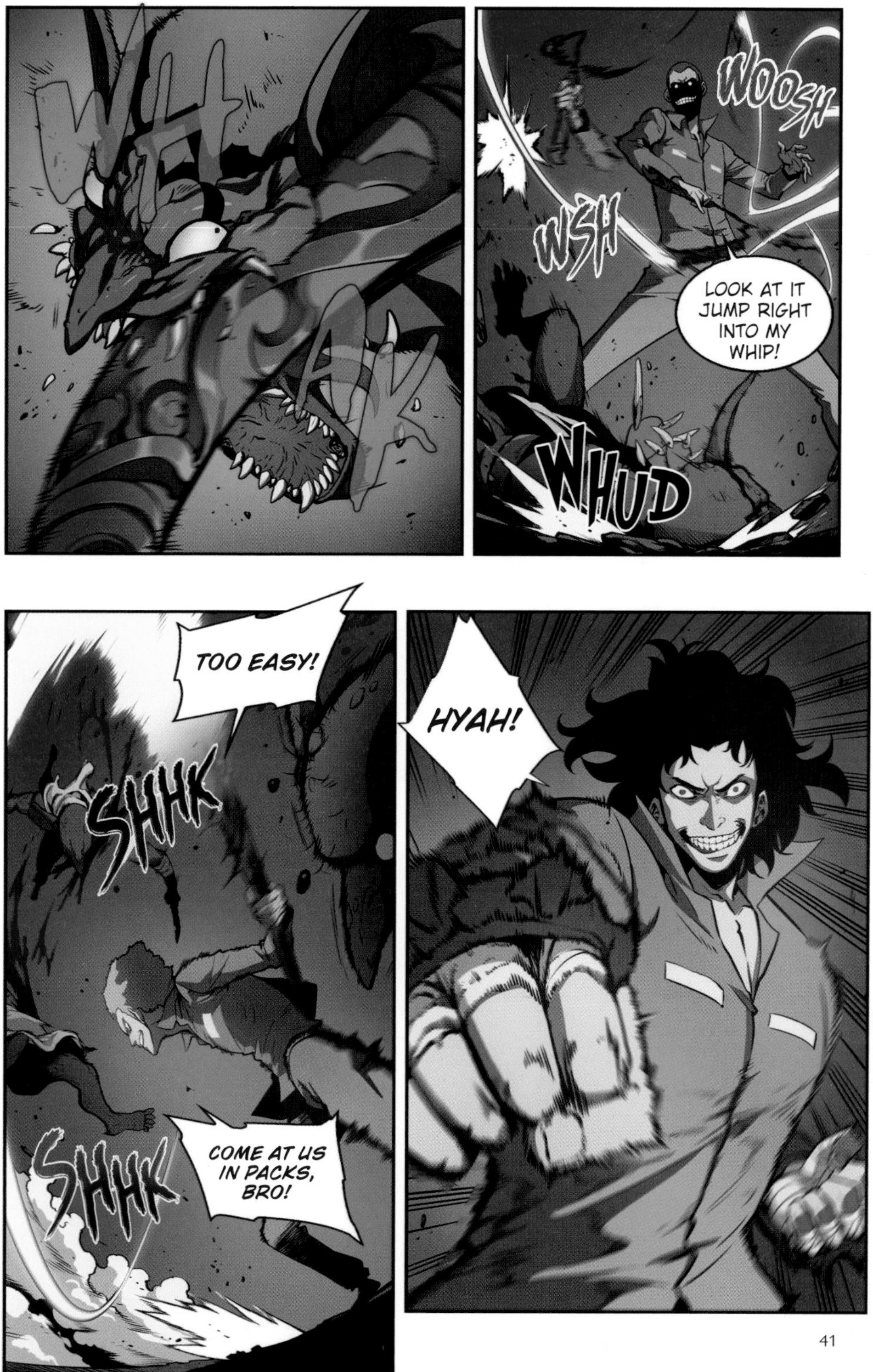
WOOSH
WSH
LOOK AT IT JUMP RIGHT INTO MY WHIP!
WHUD
TOO EASY!
SHHK
SHHK
COME AT US IN PACKS, BRO!
HYAH!

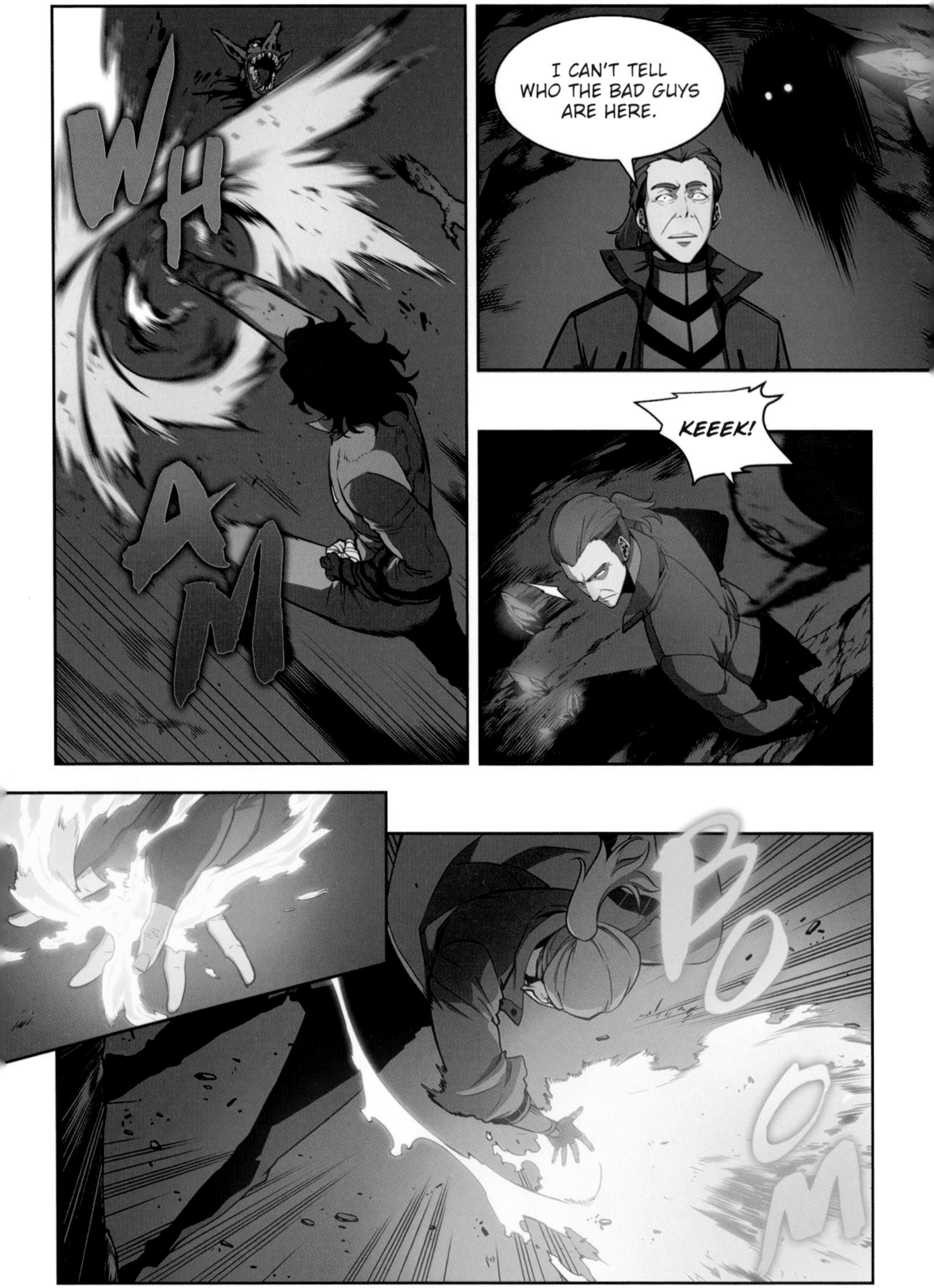
WHAM
I CAN'T TELL WHO THE BAD GUYS ARE HERE.
KEEEK!
BOOOM

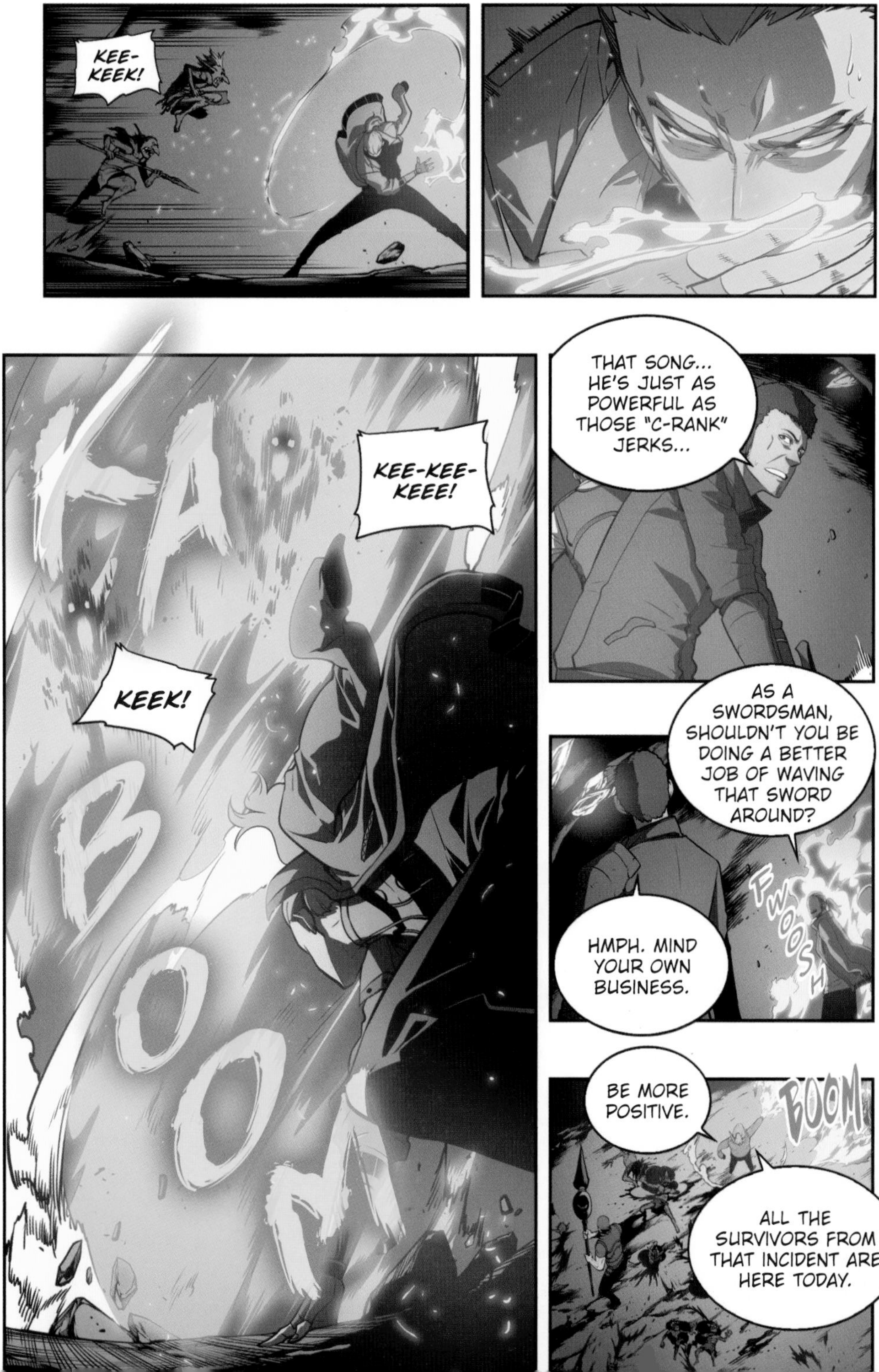
KEE-KEEK!
KEE-KEE-KEEE!
KEEK!
KABOOM
THAT SONG... HE'S JUST AS POWERFUL AS THOSE "C-RANK" JERKS...
AS A SWORDSMAN, SHOULDN'T YOU BE DOING A BETTER JOB OF WAVING THAT SWORD AROUND?
HMPH. MIND YOUR OWN BUSINESS.
FWOOSH
BE MORE POSITIVE.
BOOM
ALL THE SURVIVORS FROM THAT INCIDENT ARE HERE TODAY.

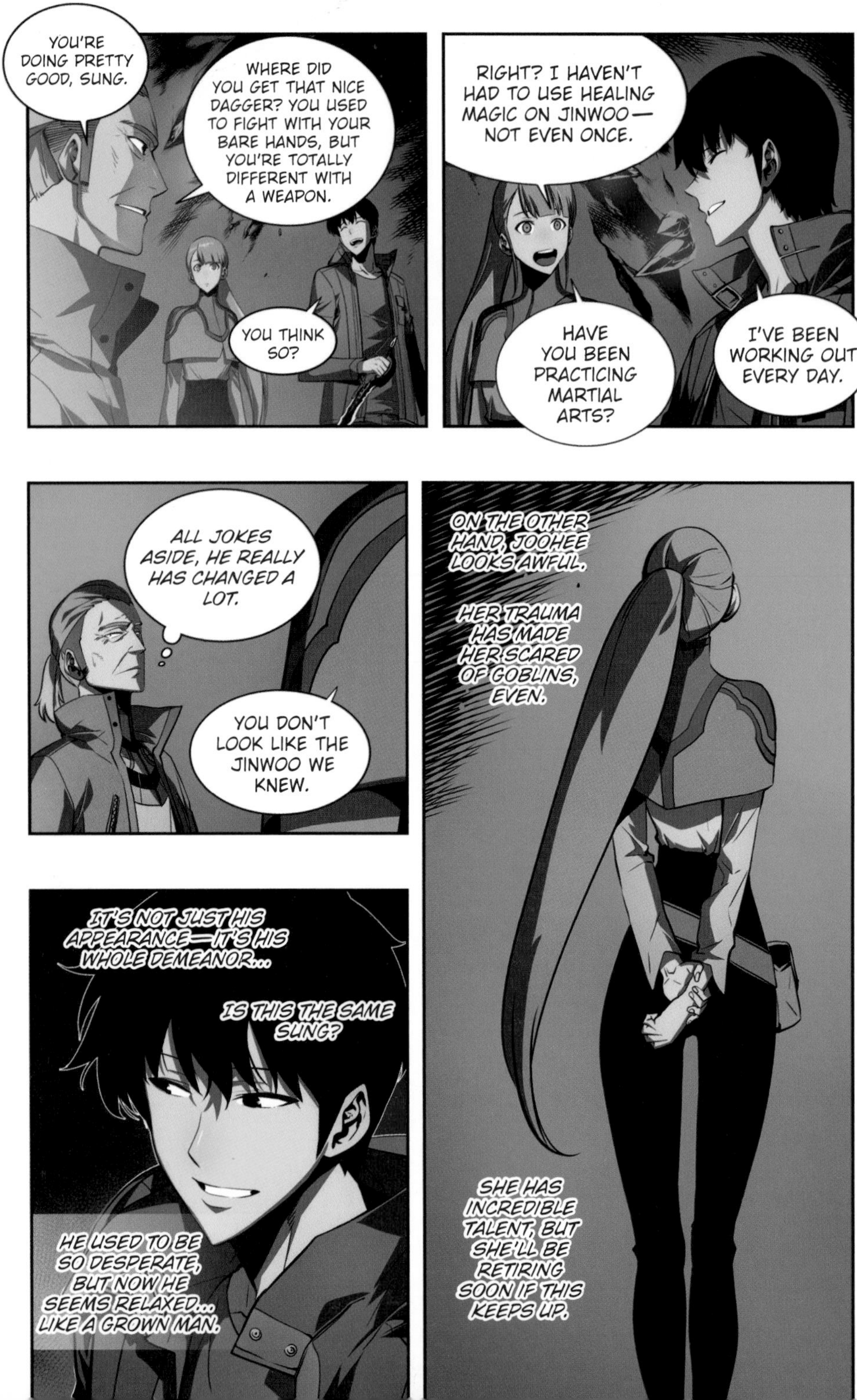
YOU'RE DOING PRETTY GOOD, SUNG.
WHERE DID YOU GET THAT NICE DAGGER? YOU USED TO FIGHT WITH YOUR BARE HANDS, BUT YOU'RE TOTALLY DIFFERENT WITH A WEAPON.
YOU THINK SO?
RIGHT? I HAVEN'T HAD TO USE HEALING MAGIC ON JINWOO— NOT EVEN ONCE.
HAVE YOU BEEN PRACTICING MARTIAL ARTS?
I'VE BEEN WORKING OUT EVERY DAY.
ALL JOKES ASIDE, HE REALLY HAS CHANGED A LOT.
YOU DON'T LOOK LIKE THE JINWOO WE KNEW.
IT'S NOT JUST HIS APPEARANCE—IT'S HIS WHOLE DEMEANOR...
IS THIS THE SAME SUNG?
HE USED TO BE SO DESPERATE, BUT NOW HE SEEMS RELAXED... LIKE A GROWN MAN.
ON THE OTHER HAND, JOOHEE LOOKS AWFUL.
HER TRAUMA HAS MADE HER SCARED OF GOBLINS, EVEN.
SHE HAS INCREDIBLE TALENT, BUT SHE'LL BE RETIRING SOON IF THIS KEEPS UP.

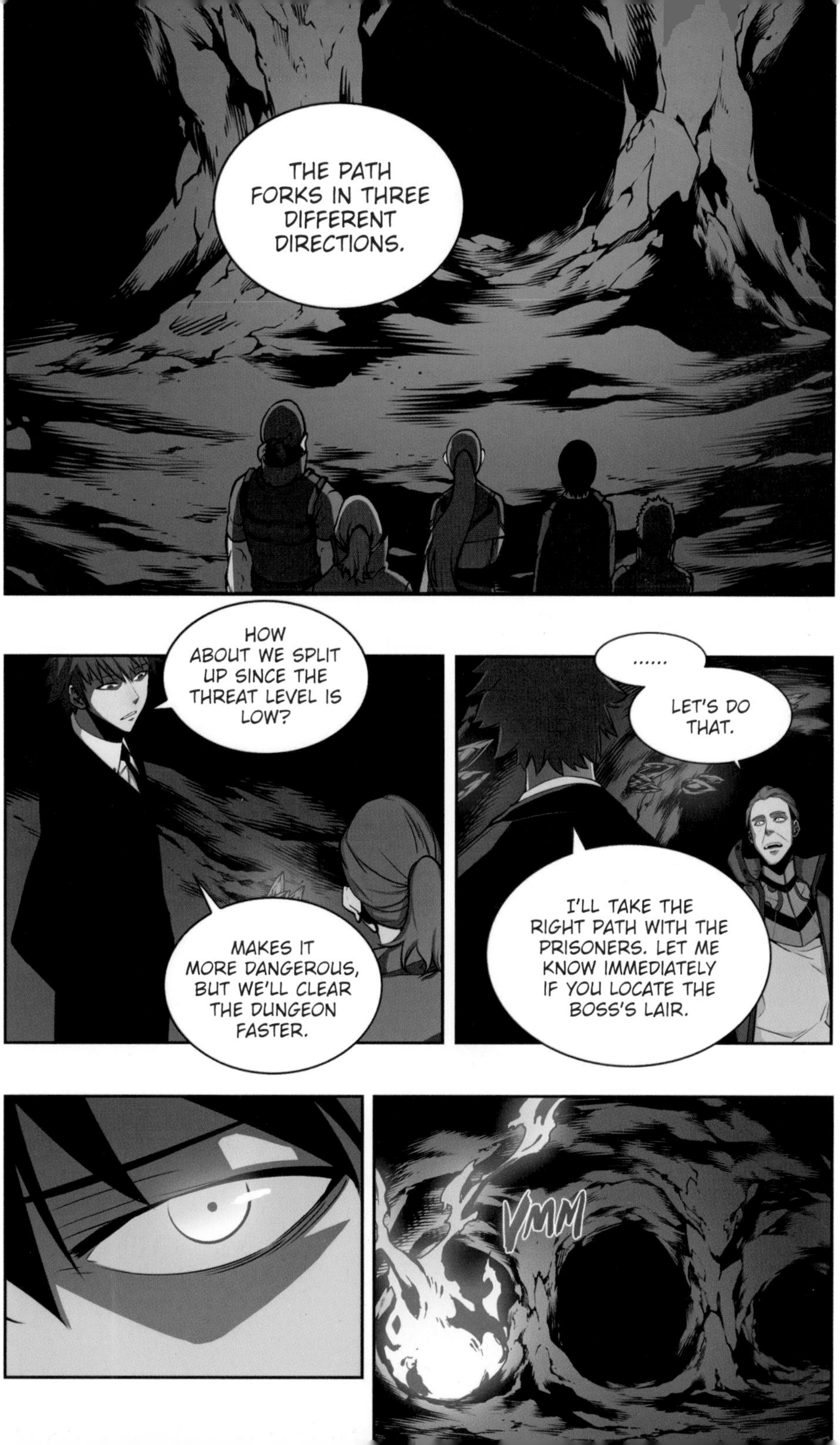
THE PATH FORKS IN THREE DIFFERENT DIRECTIONS.
HOW ABOUT WE SPLIT UP SINCE THE THREAT LEVEL IS LOW?
MAKES IT MORE DANGEROUS, BUT WE'LL CLEAR THE DUNGEON FASTER.
......
LET'S DO THAT.
I'LL TAKE THE RIGHT PATH WITH THE PRISONERS. LET ME KNOW IMMEDIATELY IF YOU LOCATE THE BOSS'S LAIR.
VMM

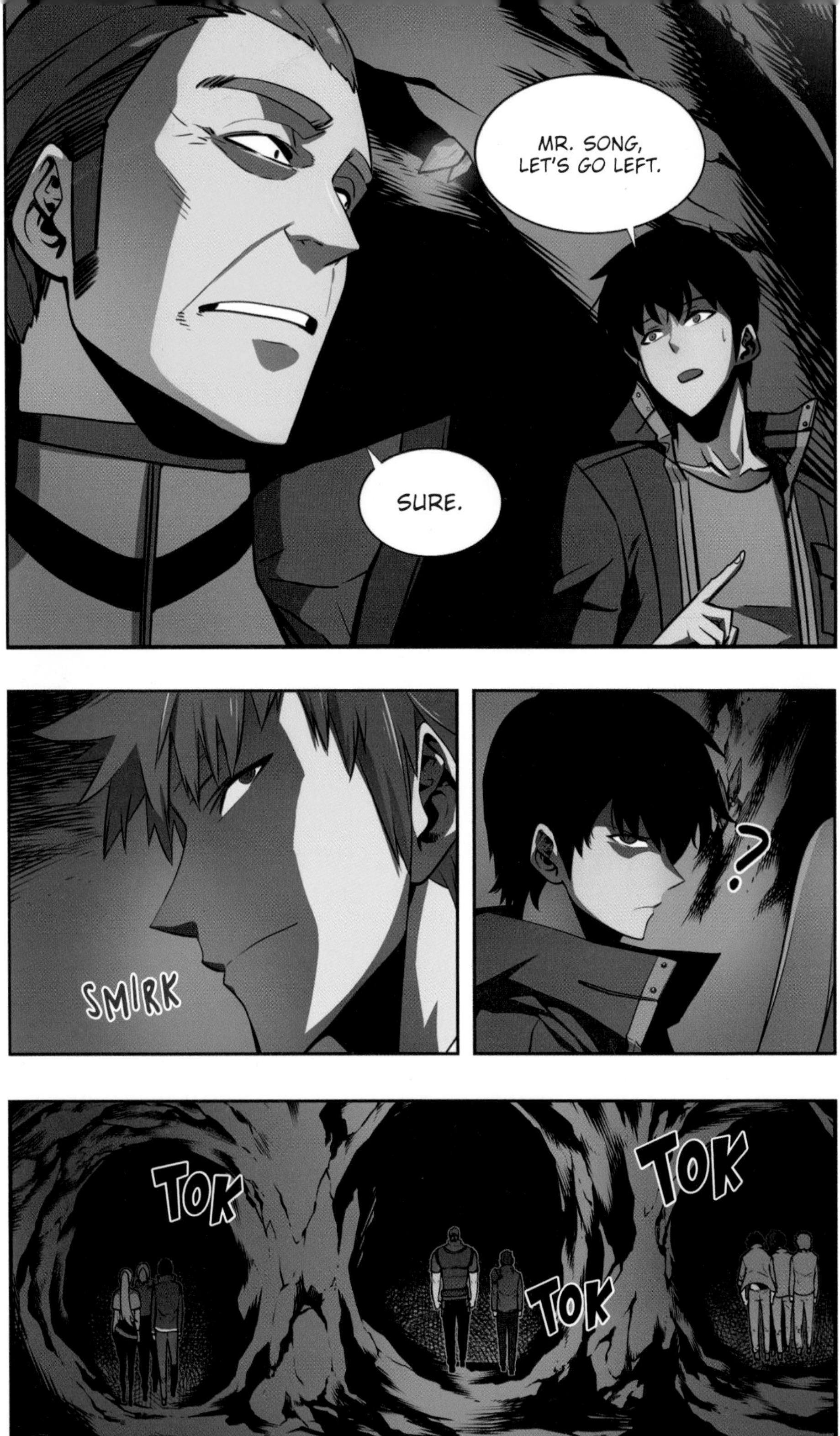
MR. SONG, LET'S GO LEFT.
SURE.
SMIRK
?
TOK
TOK
TOK

THE BOSS IS AT THE END OF THIS PATH.

SINCE I CAN'T GAIN XP WITH GOBLINS, I NEED TO KILL THE BOSS. BUT MORE IMPORTANTLY...

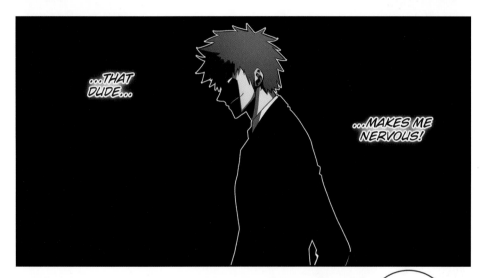

...THAT DUDE...

...MAKES ME NERVOUS!

WHAK

WHAM

ARE YOU DONE?

PIECE OF CAKE.

LAME. SO LAME. GOBLINS ARE NO MATCH FOR US.

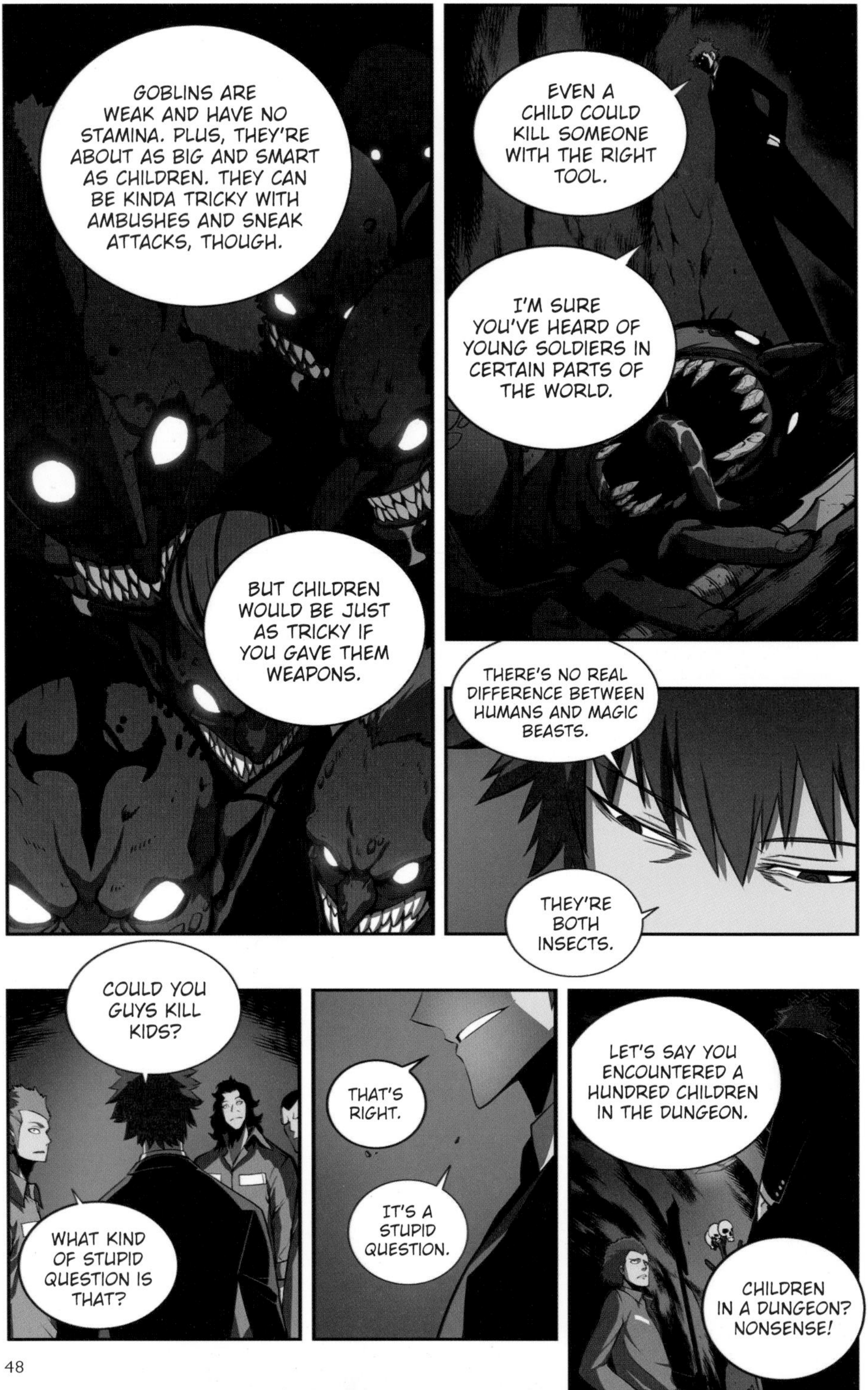
GOBLINS ARE WEAK AND HAVE NO STAMINA. PLUS, THEY'RE ABOUT AS BIG AND SMART AS CHILDREN. THEY CAN BE KINDA TRICKY WITH AMBUSHES AND SNEAK ATTACKS, THOUGH.
BUT CHILDREN WOULD BE JUST AS TRICKY IF YOU GAVE THEM WEAPONS.
EVEN A CHILD COULD KILL SOMEONE WITH THE RIGHT TOOL.
I'M SURE YOU'VE HEARD OF YOUNG SOLDIERS IN CERTAIN PARTS OF THE WORLD.
THERE'S NO REAL DIFFERENCE BETWEEN HUMANS AND MAGIC BEASTS.
THEY'RE BOTH INSECTS.
COULD YOU GUYS KILL KIDS?
WHAT KIND OF STUPID QUESTION IS THAT?
THAT'S RIGHT.
IT'S A STUPID QUESTION.
LET'S SAY YOU ENCOUNTERED A HUNDRED CHILDREN IN THE DUNGEON.
CHILDREN IN A DUNGEON? NONSENSE!

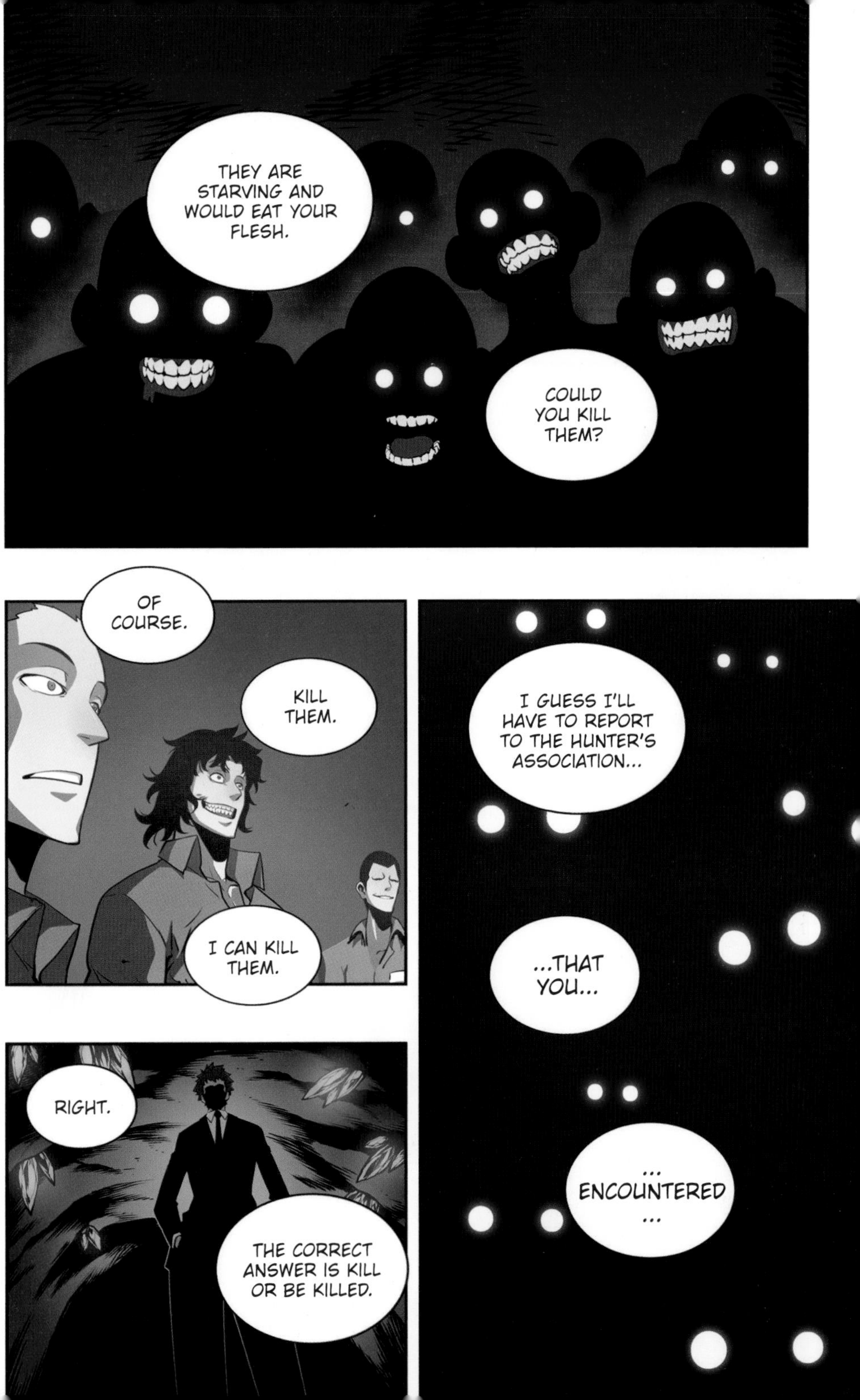
THEY ARE STARVING AND WOULD EAT YOUR FLESH.
COULD YOU KILL THEM?
OF COURSE.
KILL THEM.
I CAN KILL THEM.
RIGHT.
THE CORRECT ANSWER IS KILL OR BE KILLED.
I GUESS I'LL HAVE TO REPORT TO THE HUNTER'S ASSOCIATION...
...THAT YOU...
... ENCOUNTERED ...

...A HUNDRED GOBLINS.

IF GOBLINS ARE THIS EASY, THIS IS DOABLE.

I HOPE THE RAID ENDS WITHOUT ANY INCIDENT.

I DOUBT THERE'LL BE ANY PROBLEMS.

OHH, I FEEL...

HIM BEING HERE...

SHH, HE MIC HEAF H...

WE USED TO SAY IF THE WEAKEST HUNTER WAS HERE...

...THEN THE DUNGEON WAS ALSO WEAK.

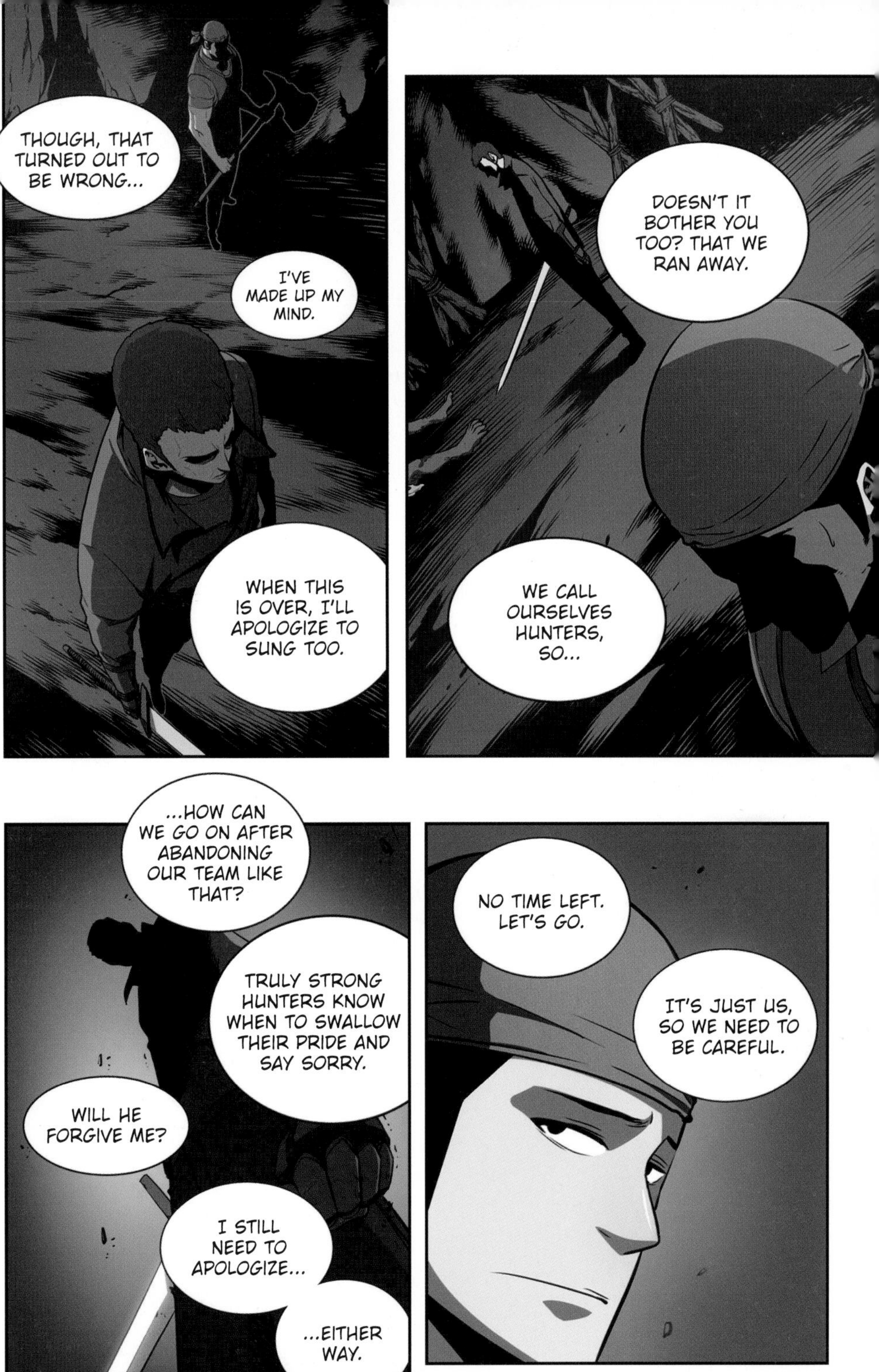
THOUGH, THAT TURNED OUT TO BE WRONG...
I'VE MADE UP MY MIND.
WHEN THIS IS OVER, I'LL APOLOGIZE TO SUNG TOO.
DOESN'T IT BOTHER YOU TOO? THAT WE RAN AWAY.
WE CALL OURSELVES HUNTERS, SO...
...HOW CAN WE GO ON AFTER ABANDONING OUR TEAM LIKE THAT?
TRULY STRONG HUNTERS KNOW WHEN TO SWALLOW THEIR PRIDE AND SAY SORRY.
WILL HE FORGIVE ME?
I STILL NEED TO APOLOGIZE...
...EITHER WAY.
NO TIME LEFT. LET'S GO.
IT'S JUST US, SO WE NEED TO BE CAREFUL.

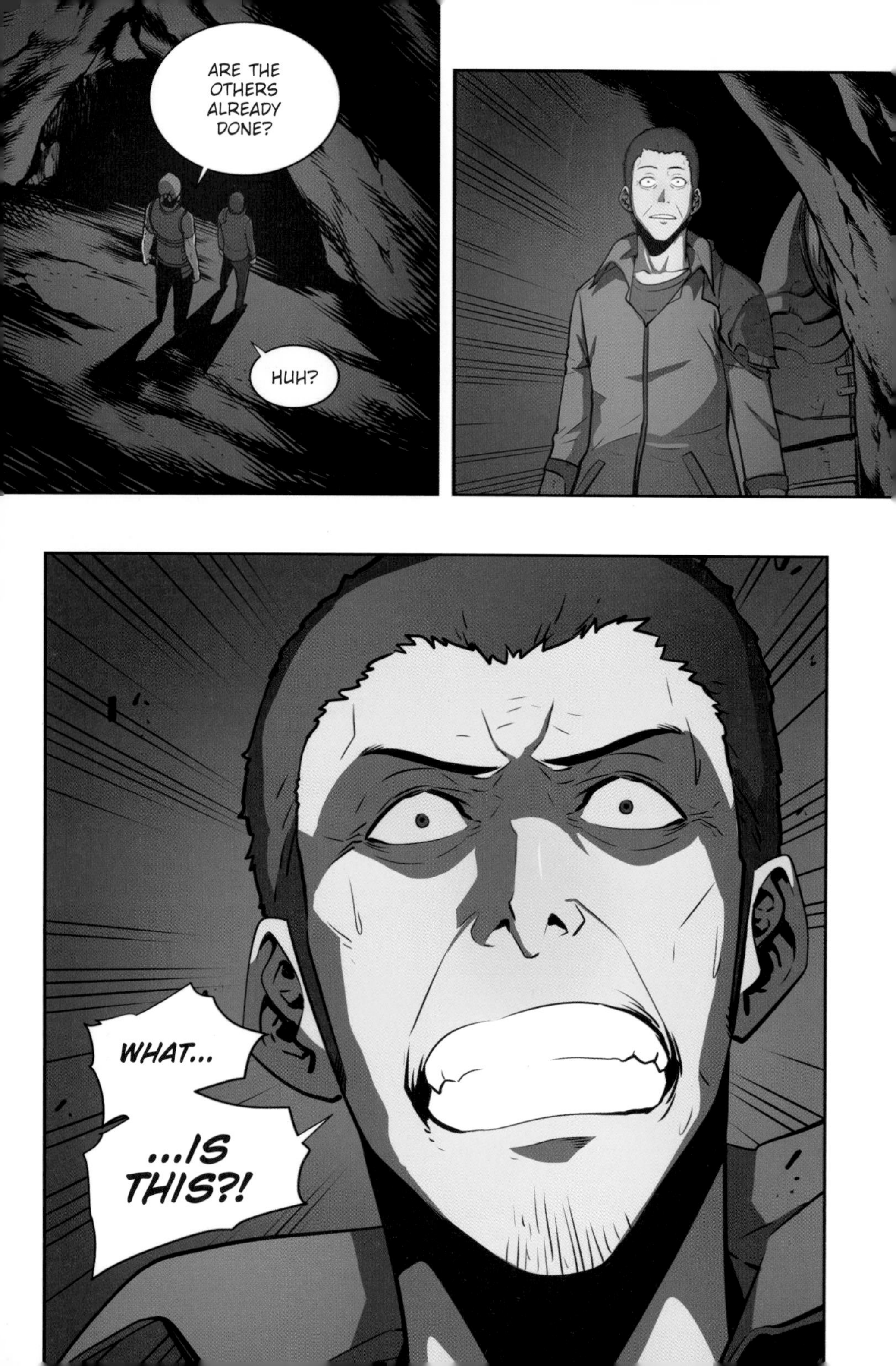
ARE THE OTHERS ALREADY DONE?
HUH?
WHAT...
...IS THIS?!

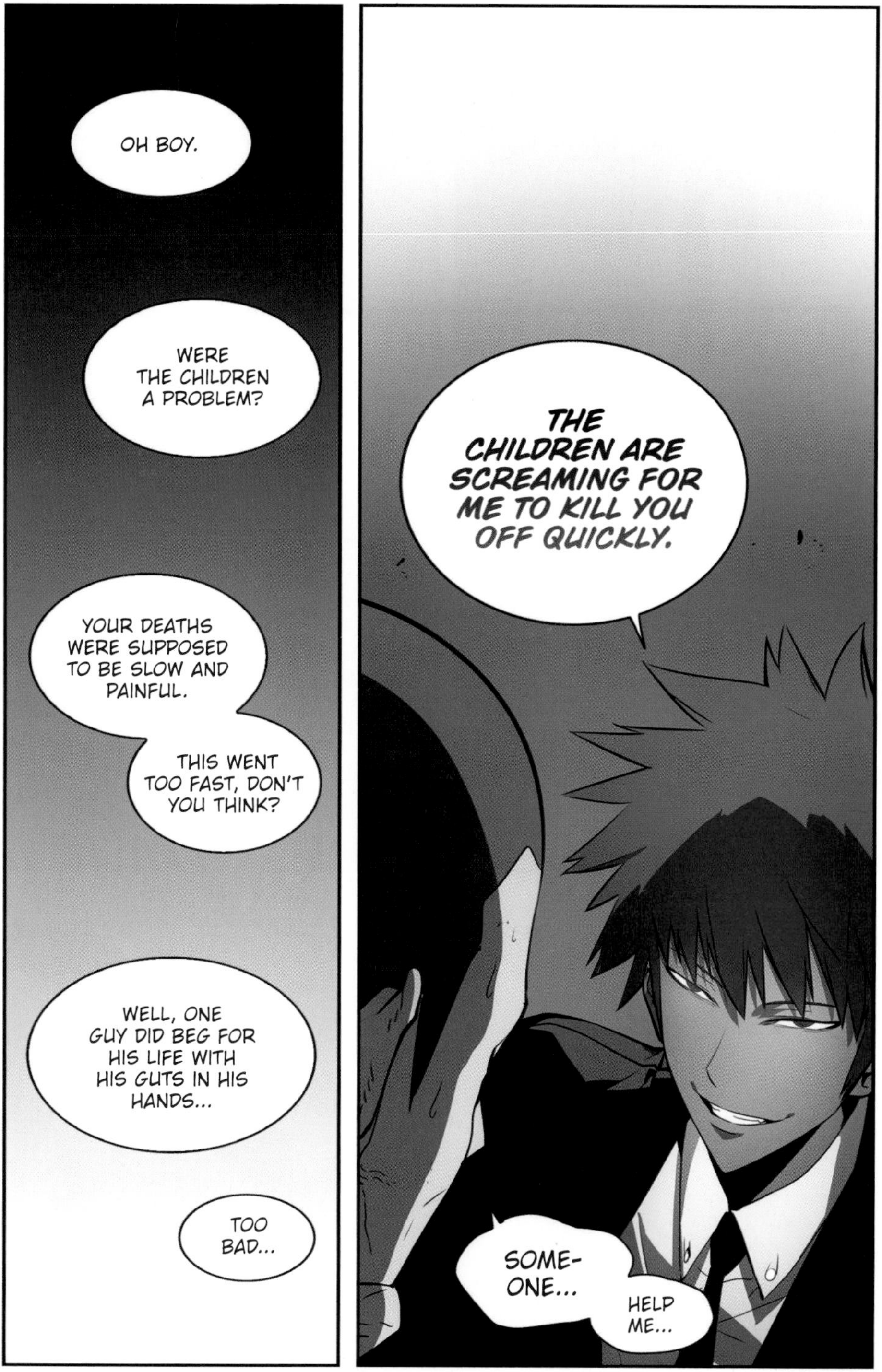
OH BOY.
WERE THE CHILDREN A PROBLEM?
YOUR DEATHS WERE SUPPOSED TO BE SLOW AND PAINFUL.
THIS WENT TOO FAST, DON'T YOU THINK?
WELL, ONE GUY DID BEG FOR HIS LIFE WITH HIS GUTS IN HIS HANDS...
TOO BAD...
THE CHILDREN ARE SCREAMING FOR ME TO KILL YOU OFF QUICKLY.
SOME-ONE...
HELP ME...

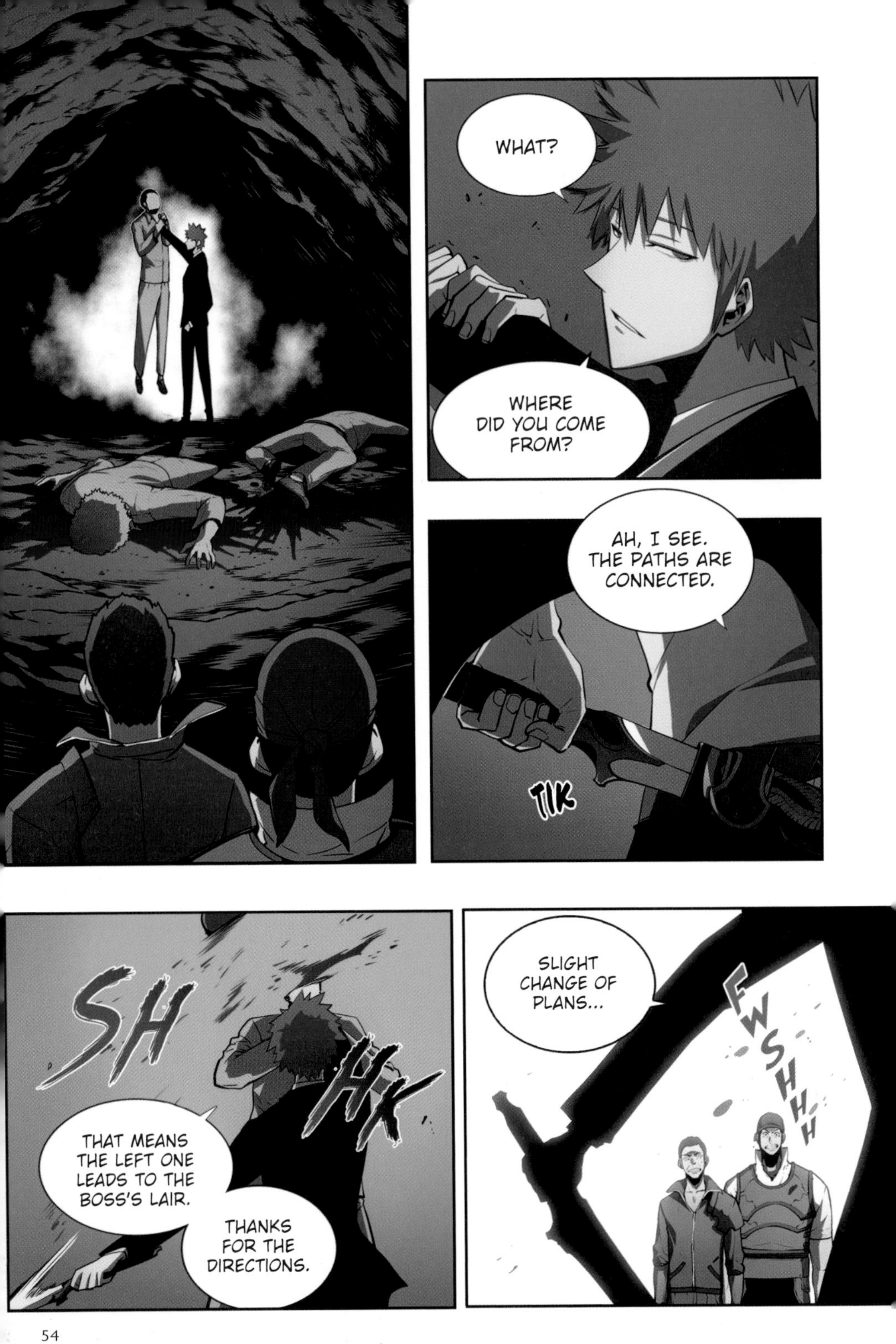
WHAT?
WHERE DID YOU COME FROM?
AH, I SEE. THE PATHS ARE CONNECTED.
TIK
SHHK
THAT MEANS THE LEFT ONE LEADS TO THE BOSS'S LAIR.
THANKS FOR THE DIRECTIONS.
SLIGHT CHANGE OF PLANS...
FWSHHH

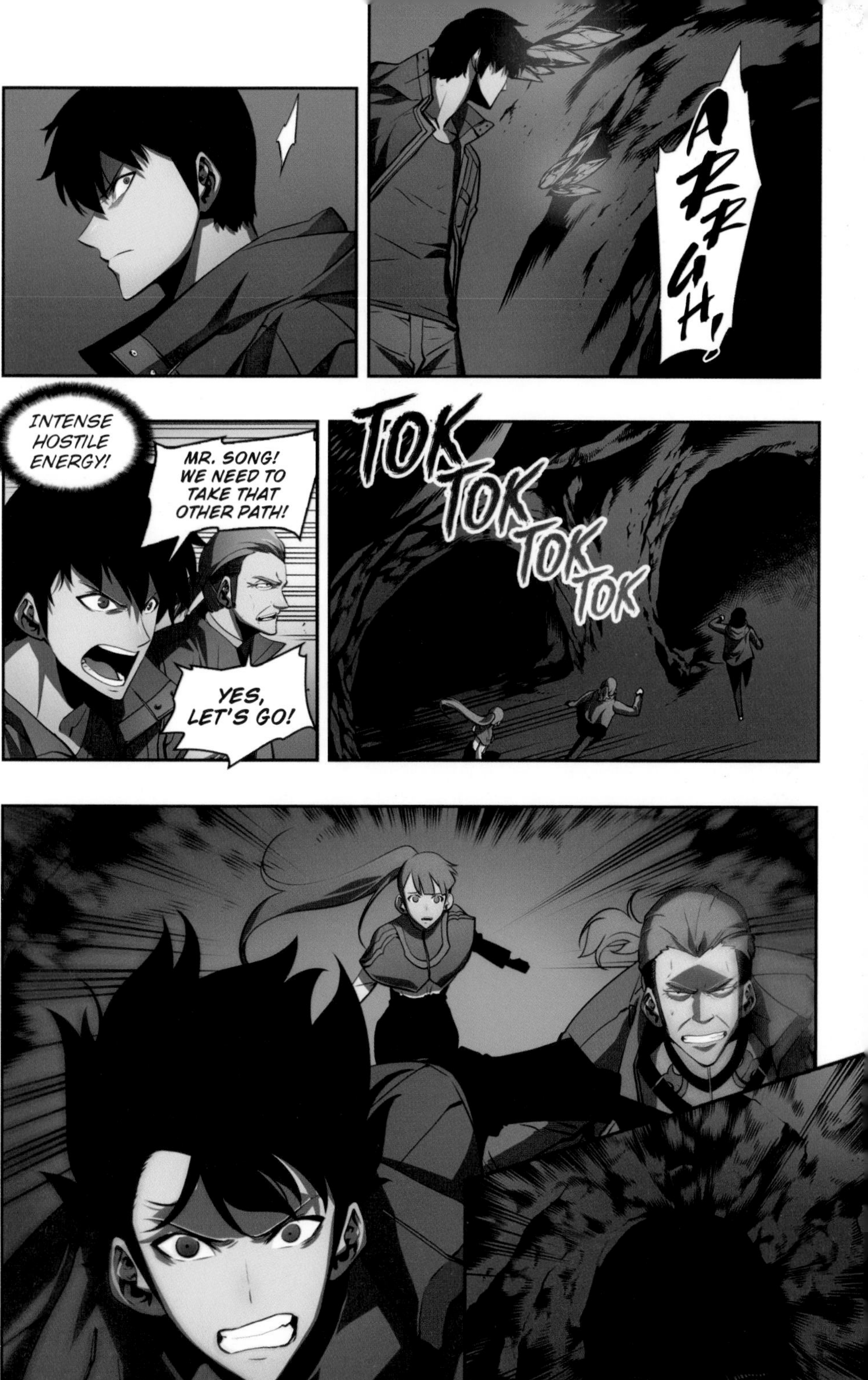
ARRGH!
INTENSE HOSTILE ENERGY!
MR. SONG! WE NEED TO TAKE THAT OTHER PATH!
YES, LET'S GO!
TOK TOK TOK TOK

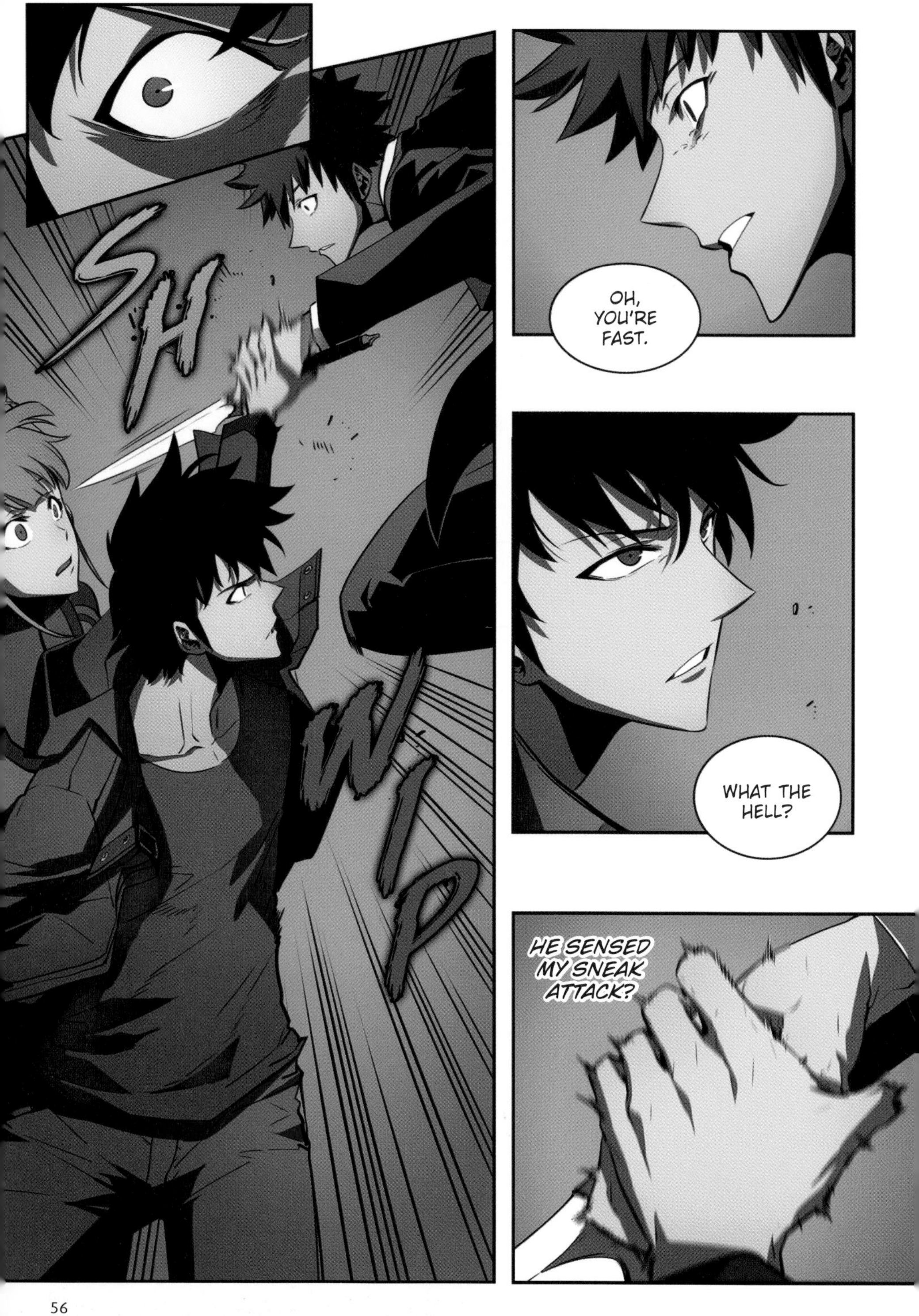
SH
WIP
OH, YOU'RE FAST.
WHAT THE HELL?
HE SENSED MY SNEAK ATTACK?

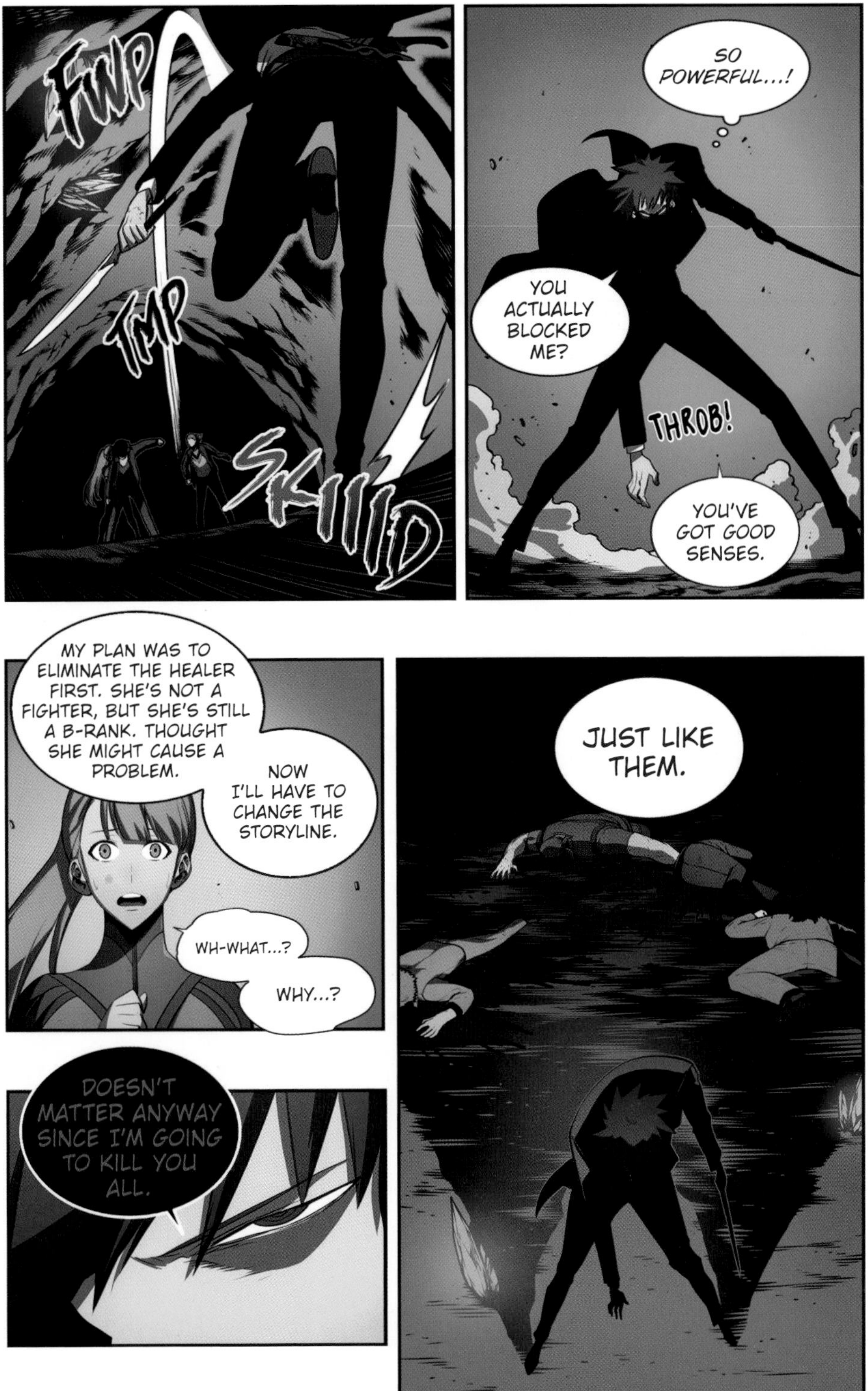
FWP
TMP
SKIIID
SO POWERFUL...!
YOU ACTUALLY BLOCKED ME?
THROB!
YOU'VE GOT GOOD SENSES.
MY PLAN WAS TO ELIMINATE THE HEALER FIRST. SHE'S NOT A FIGHTER, BUT SHE'S STILL A B-RANK. THOUGHT SHE MIGHT CAUSE A PROBLEM.
NOW I'LL HAVE TO CHANGE THE STORYLINE.
WH-WHAT...?
WHY...?
DOESN'T MATTER ANYWAY SINCE I'M GOING TO KILL YOU ALL.
JUST LIKE THEM.

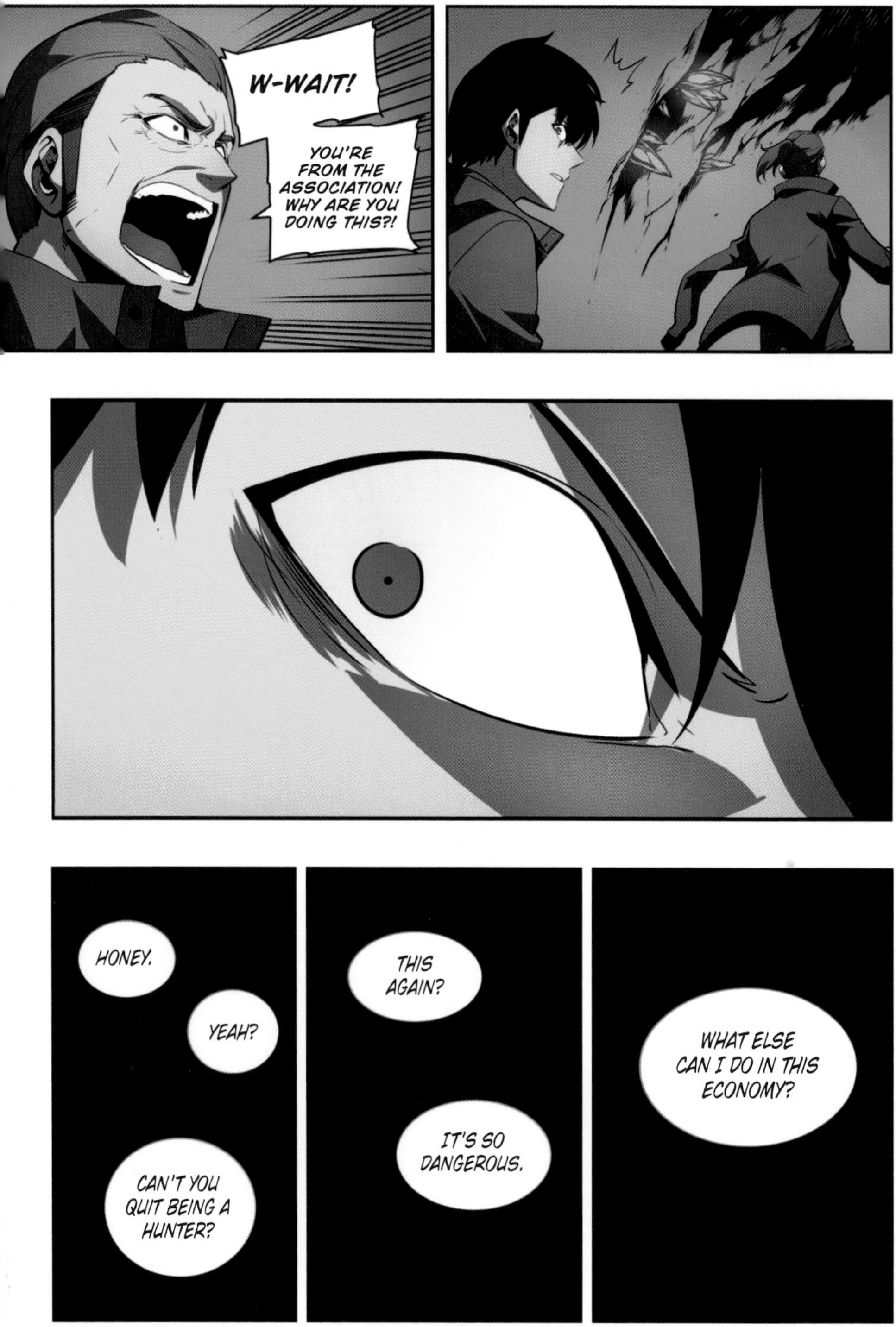
W-WAIT!
YOU'RE FROM THE ASSOCIATION! WHY ARE YOU DOING THIS?!
HONEY.
YEAH?
CAN'T YOU QUIT BEING A HUNTER?
THIS AGAIN?
IT'S SO DANGEROUS.
WHAT ELSE CAN I DO IN THIS ECONOMY?

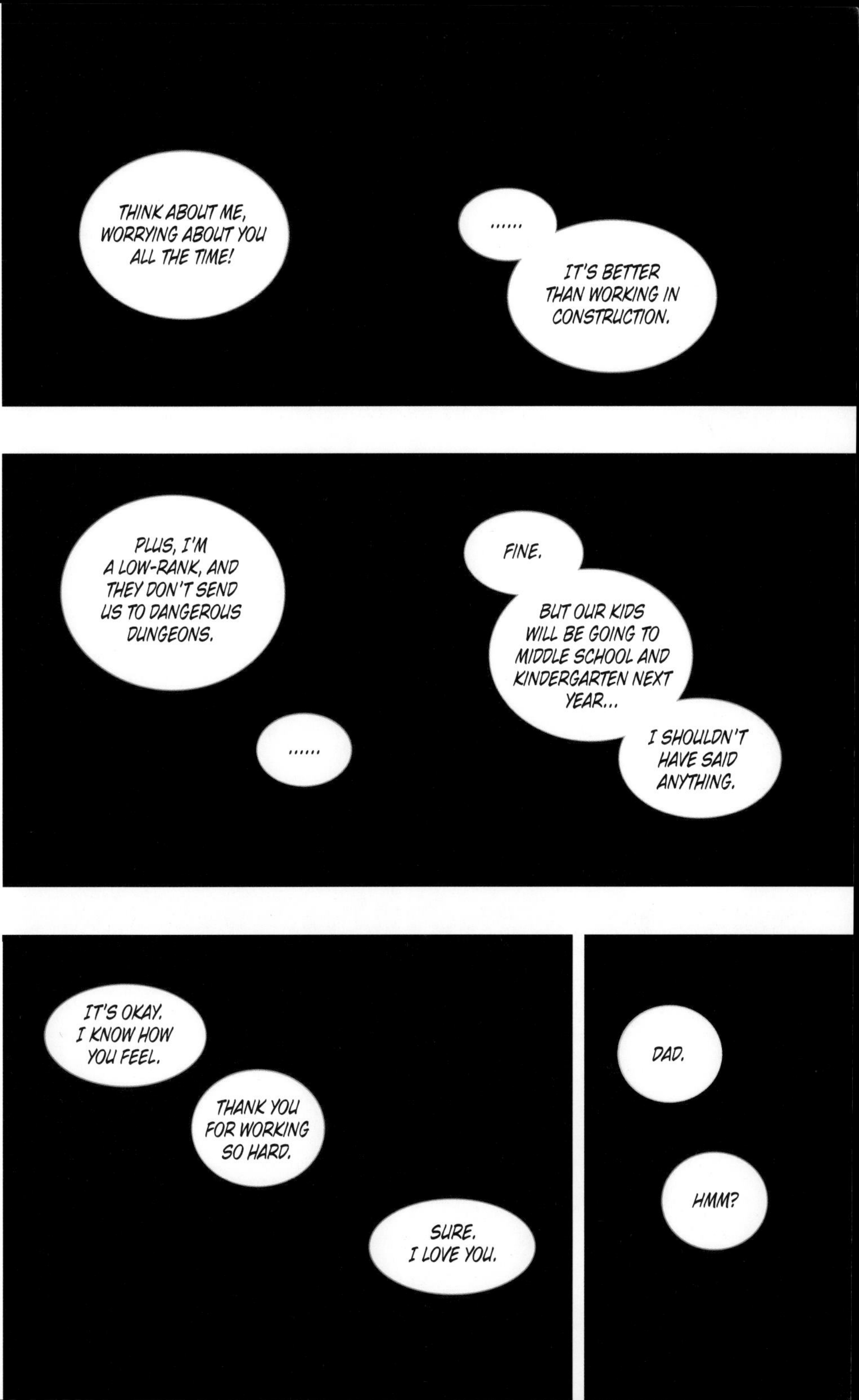
THINK ABOUT ME, WORRYING ABOUT YOU ALL THE TIME!
......
IT'S BETTER THAN WORKING IN CONSTRUCTION.
PLUS, I'M A LOW-RANK, AND THEY DON'T SEND US TO DANGEROUS DUNGEONS.
FINE.
BUT OUR KIDS WILL BE GOING TO MIDDLE SCHOOL AND KINDERGARTEN NEXT YEAR...
......
I SHOULDN'T HAVE SAID ANYTHING.
IT'S OKAY. I KNOW HOW YOU FEEL.
THANK YOU FOR WORKING SO HARD.
SURE. I LOVE YOU.
DAD.
HMM?

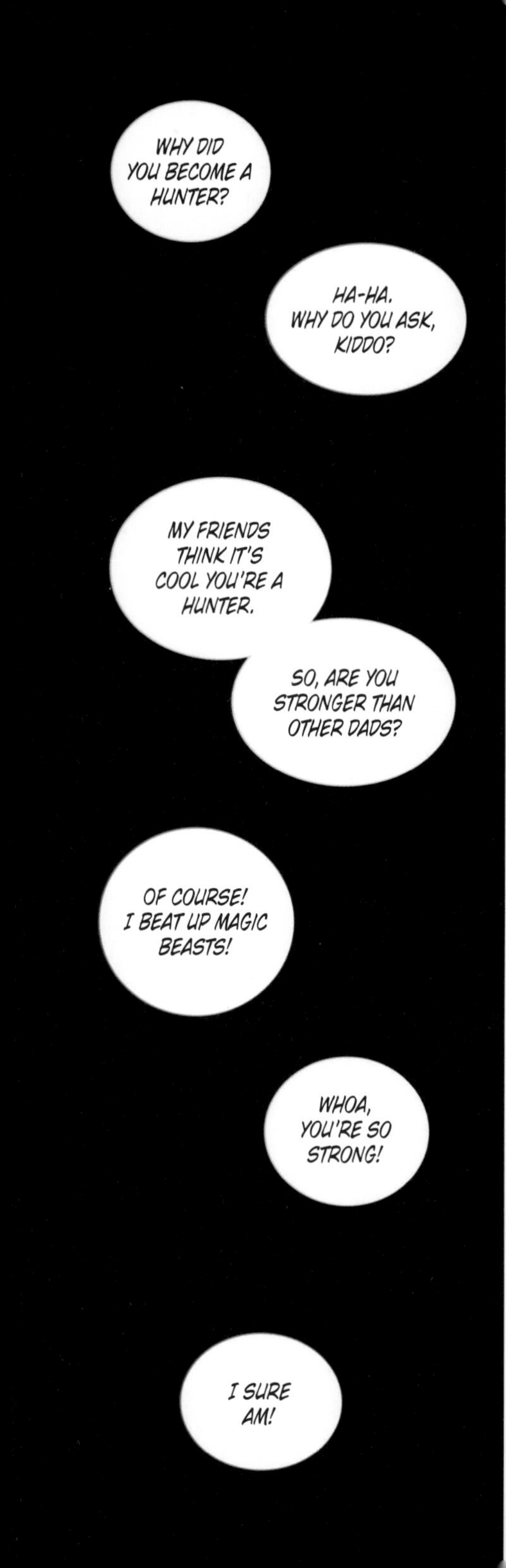
WHY DID YOU BECOME A HUNTER?
HA-HA. WHY DO YOU ASK, KIDDO?
MY FRIENDS THINK IT'S COOL YOU'RE A HUNTER.
SO, ARE YOU STRONGER THAN OTHER DADS?
OF COURSE! I BEAT UP MAGIC BEASTS!
WHOA, YOU'RE SO STRONG!
I SURE AM!
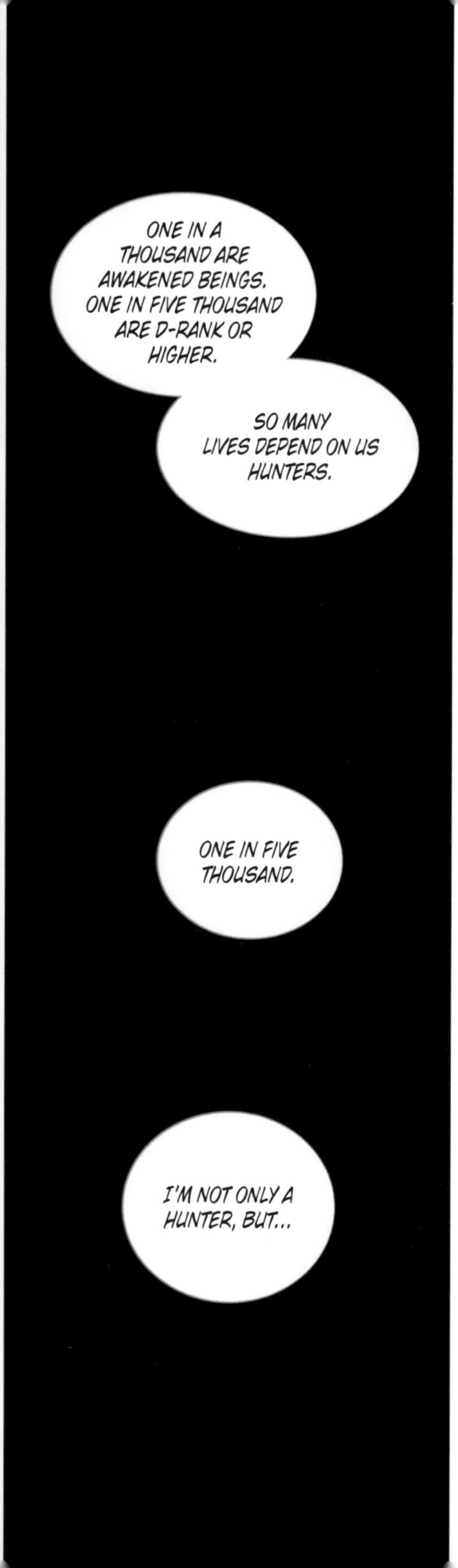
ONE IN A THOUSAND ARE AWAKENED BEINGS. ONE IN FIVE THOUSAND ARE D-RANK OR HIGHER.
SO MANY LIVES DEPEND ON US HUNTERS.
ONE IN FIVE THOUSAND.
I'M NOT ONLY A HUNTER, BUT...

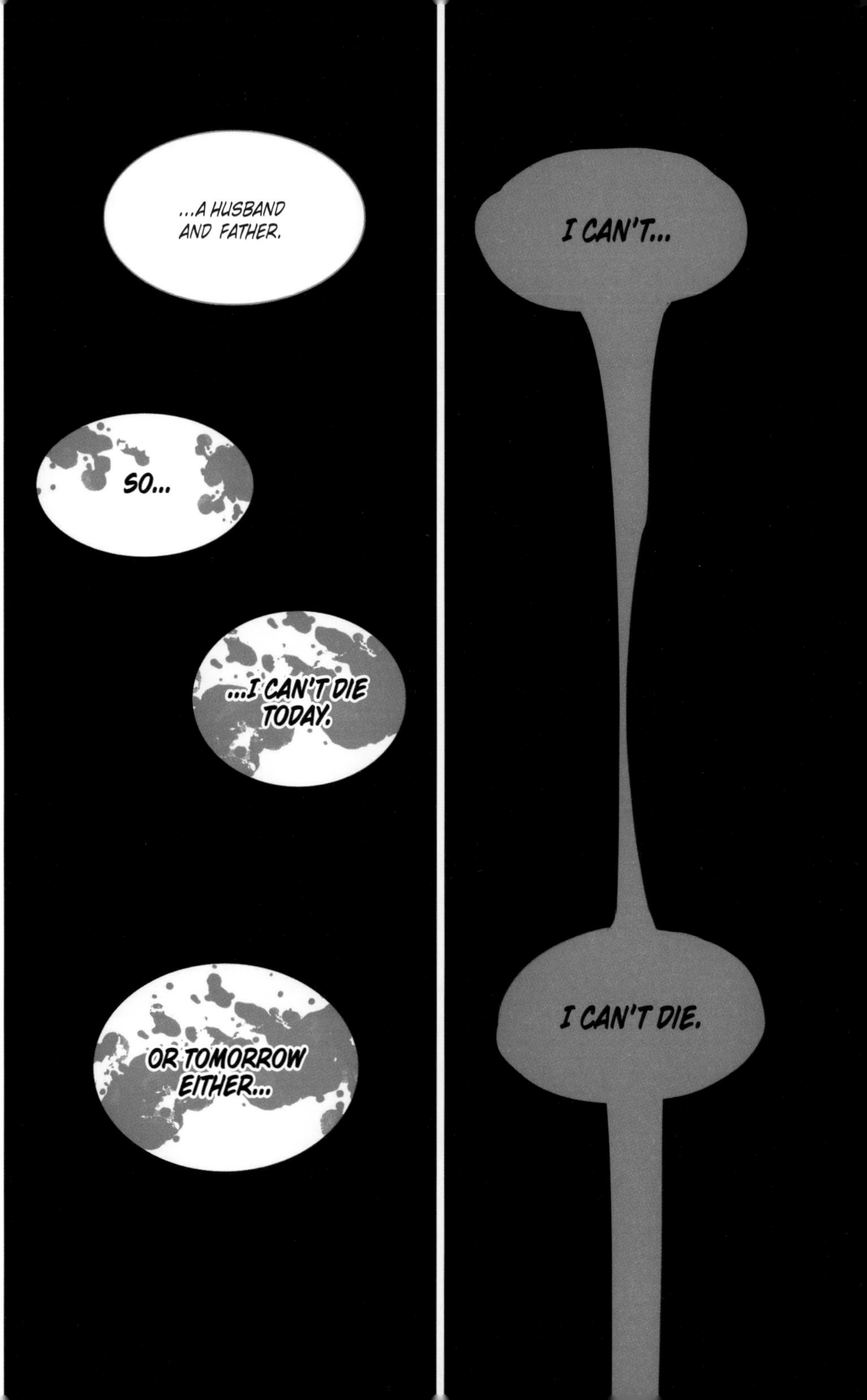
...A HUSBAND AND FATHER.
SO...
...I CAN'T DIE TODAY.
OR TOMORROW EITHER...
I CAN'T...
I CAN'T DIE.

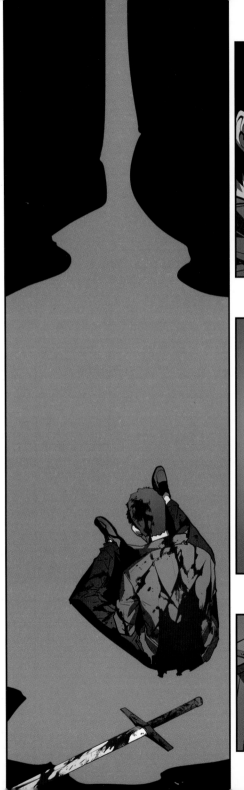

MR. KIM...?

JOOHEE...

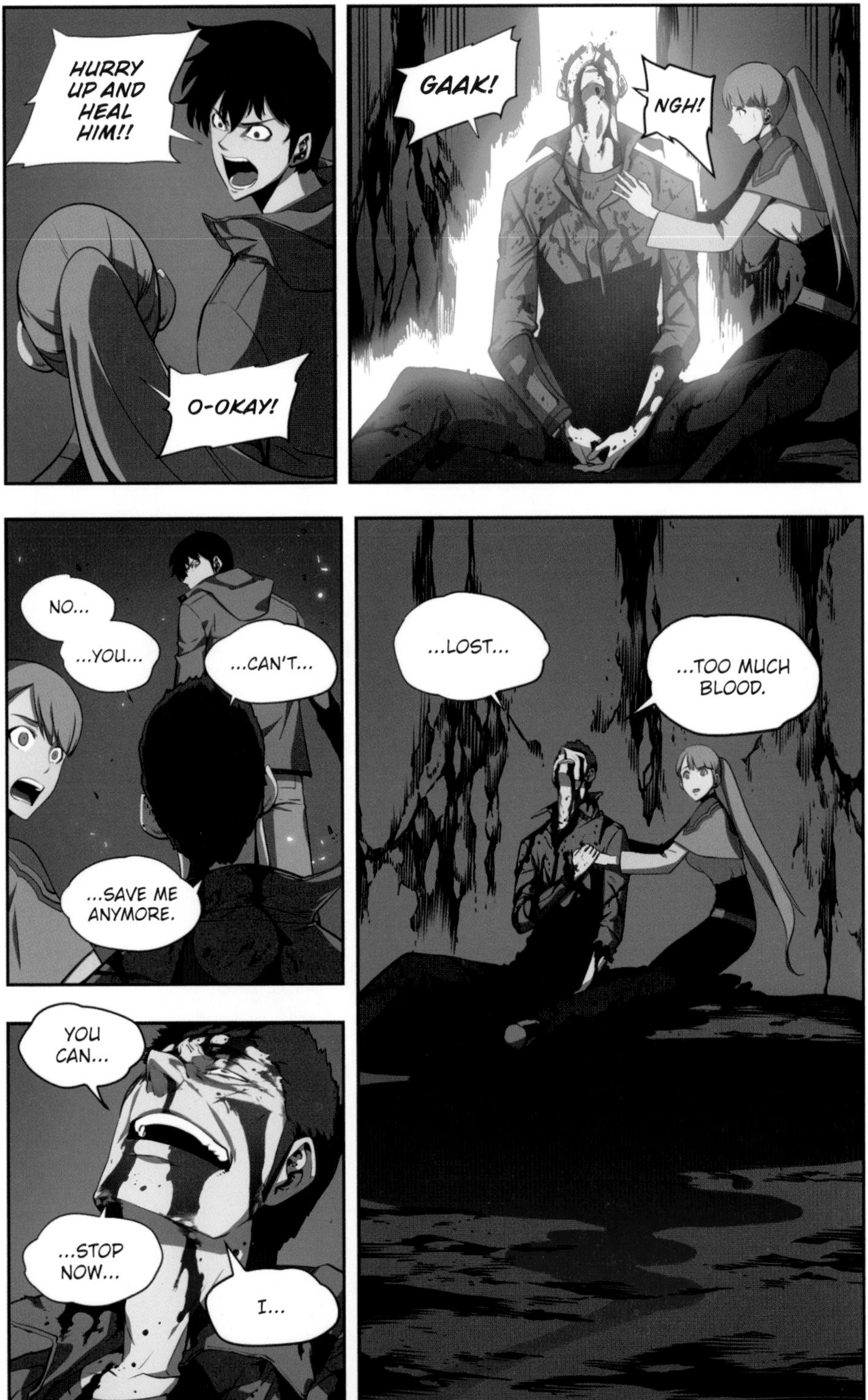
HURRY UP AND HEAL HIM!!
O-OKAY!
GAAK!
NGH!
NO...
...YOU...
...CAN'T...
...SAVE ME ANYMORE.
YOU CAN...
...STOP NOW...
I...
...LOST...
...TOO MUCH BLOOD.

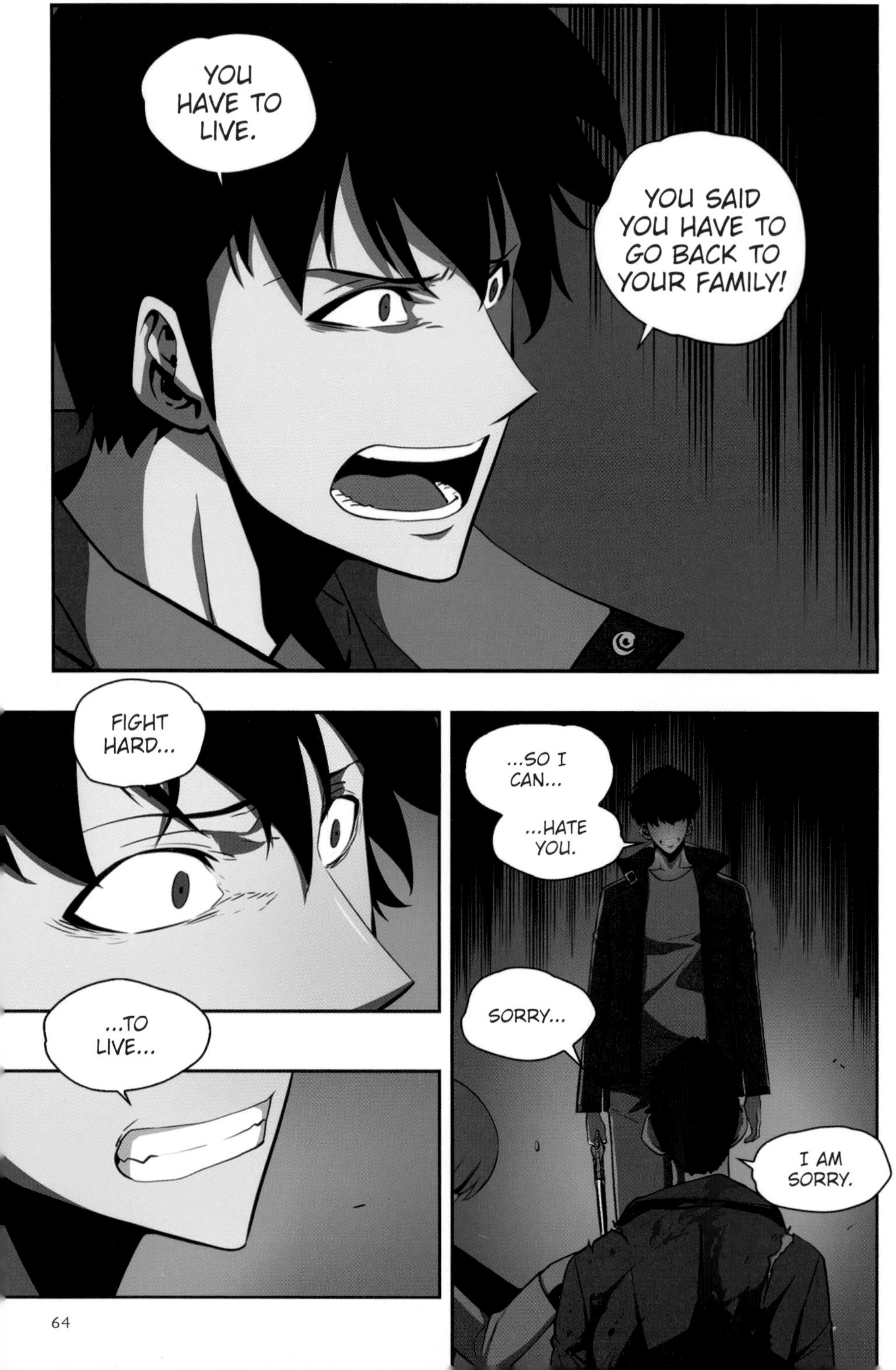
YOU HAVE TO LIVE.
YOU SAID YOU HAVE TO GO BACK TO YOUR FAMILY!
FIGHT HARD...
...TO LIVE...
...SO I CAN...
...HATE YOU.
SORRY...
I AM SORRY.

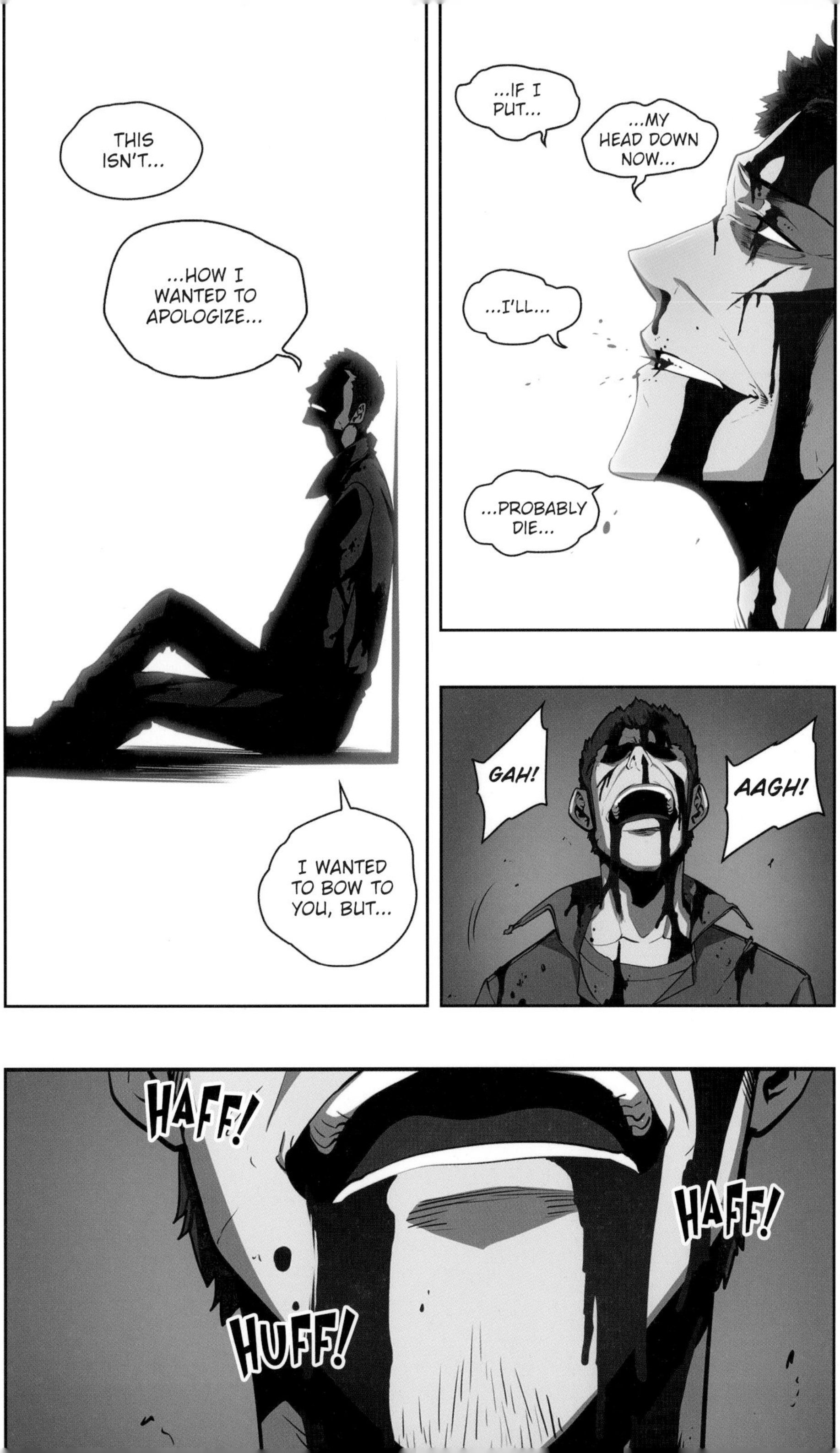
THIS ISN'T...
...HOW I WANTED TO APOLOGIZE...
I WANTED TO BOW TO YOU, BUT...
...IF I PUT...
...MY HEAD DOWN NOW...
...I'LL...
...PROBABLY DIE...
GAH!
AAGH!
HAFF!
HAFF!
HUFF!

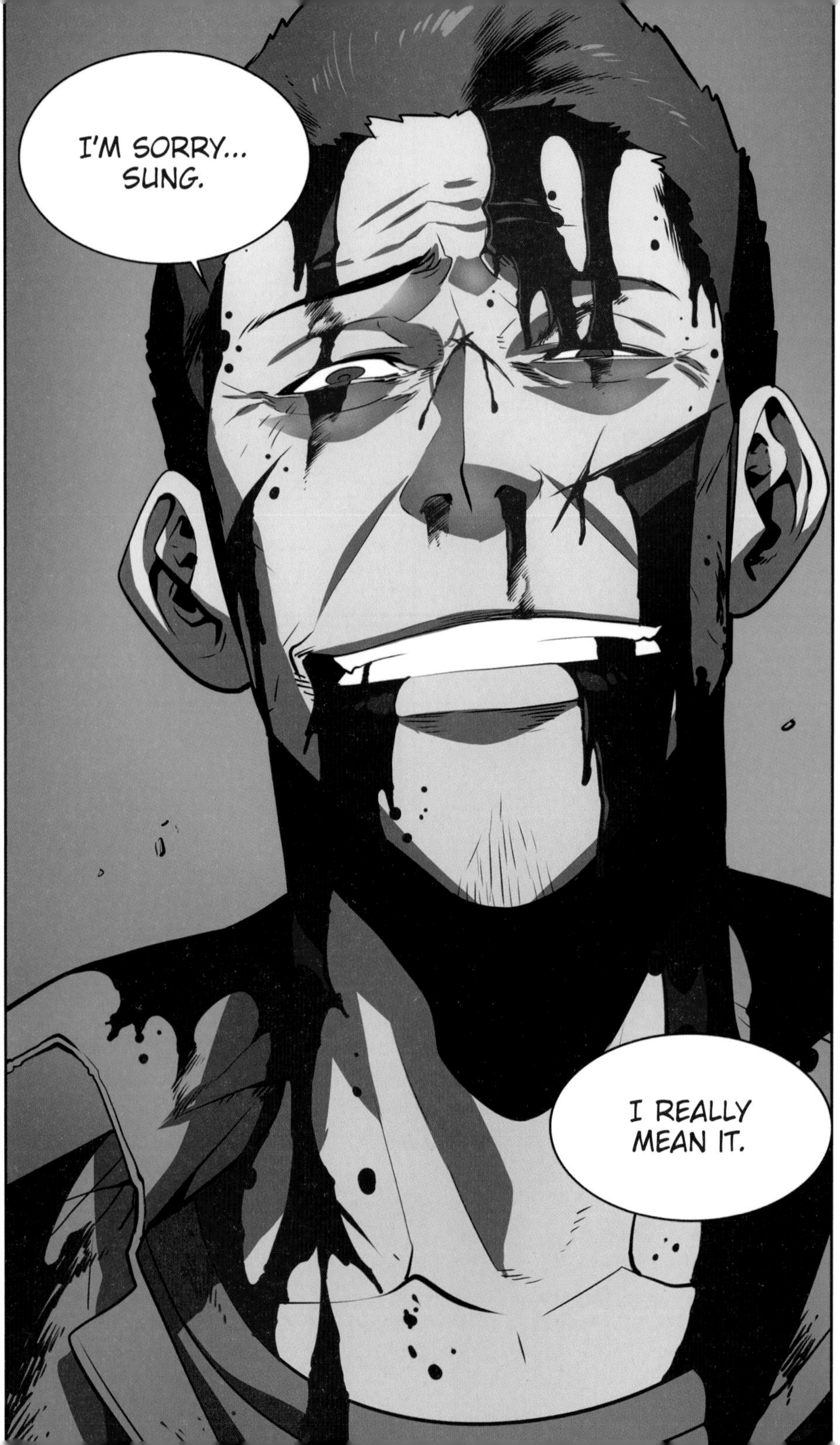
I'M SORRY... SUNG.
I REALLY MEAN IT.

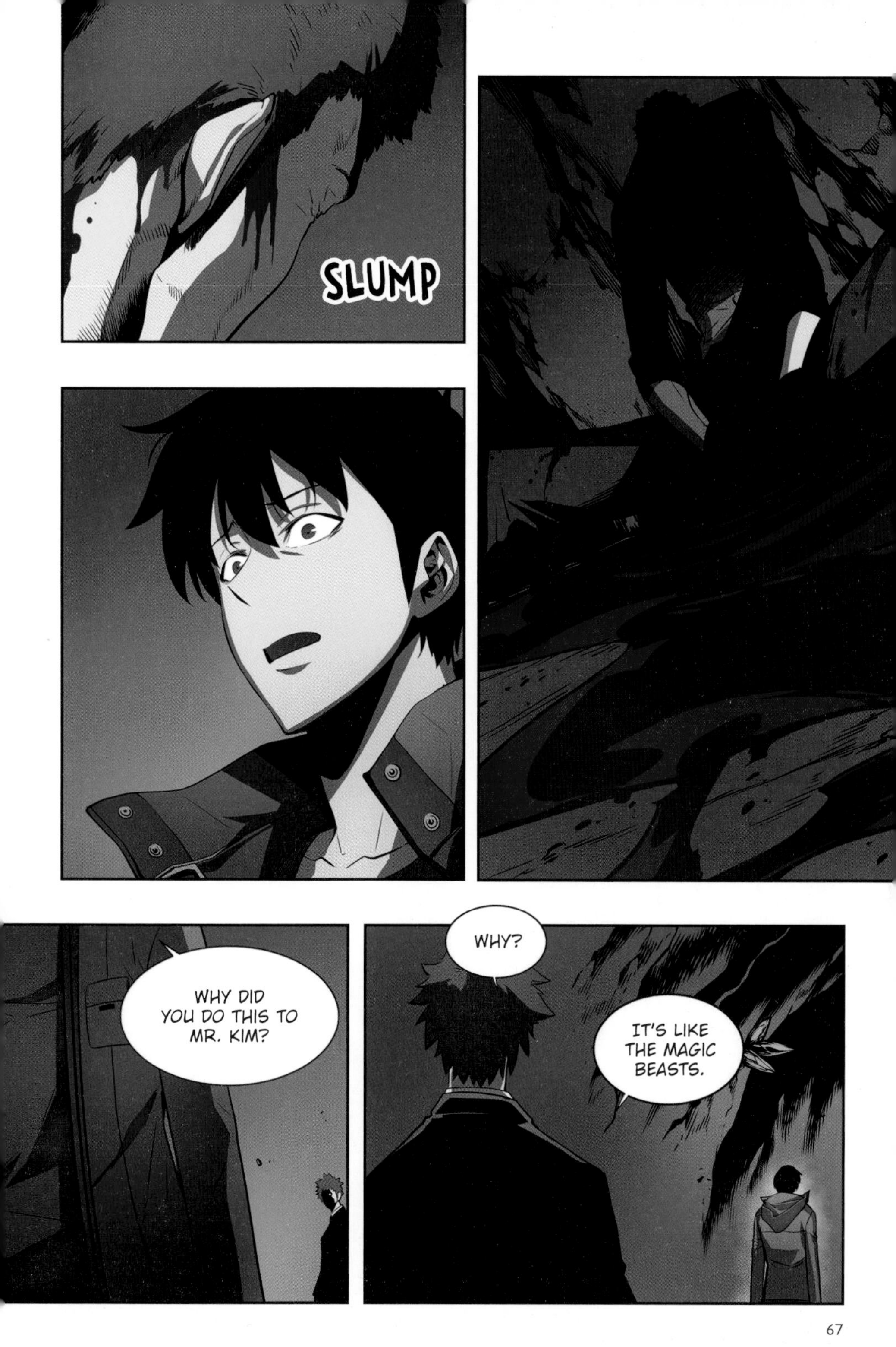
SLUMP
WHY DID YOU DO THIS TO MR. KIM?
WHY?
IT'S LIKE THE MAGIC BEASTS.

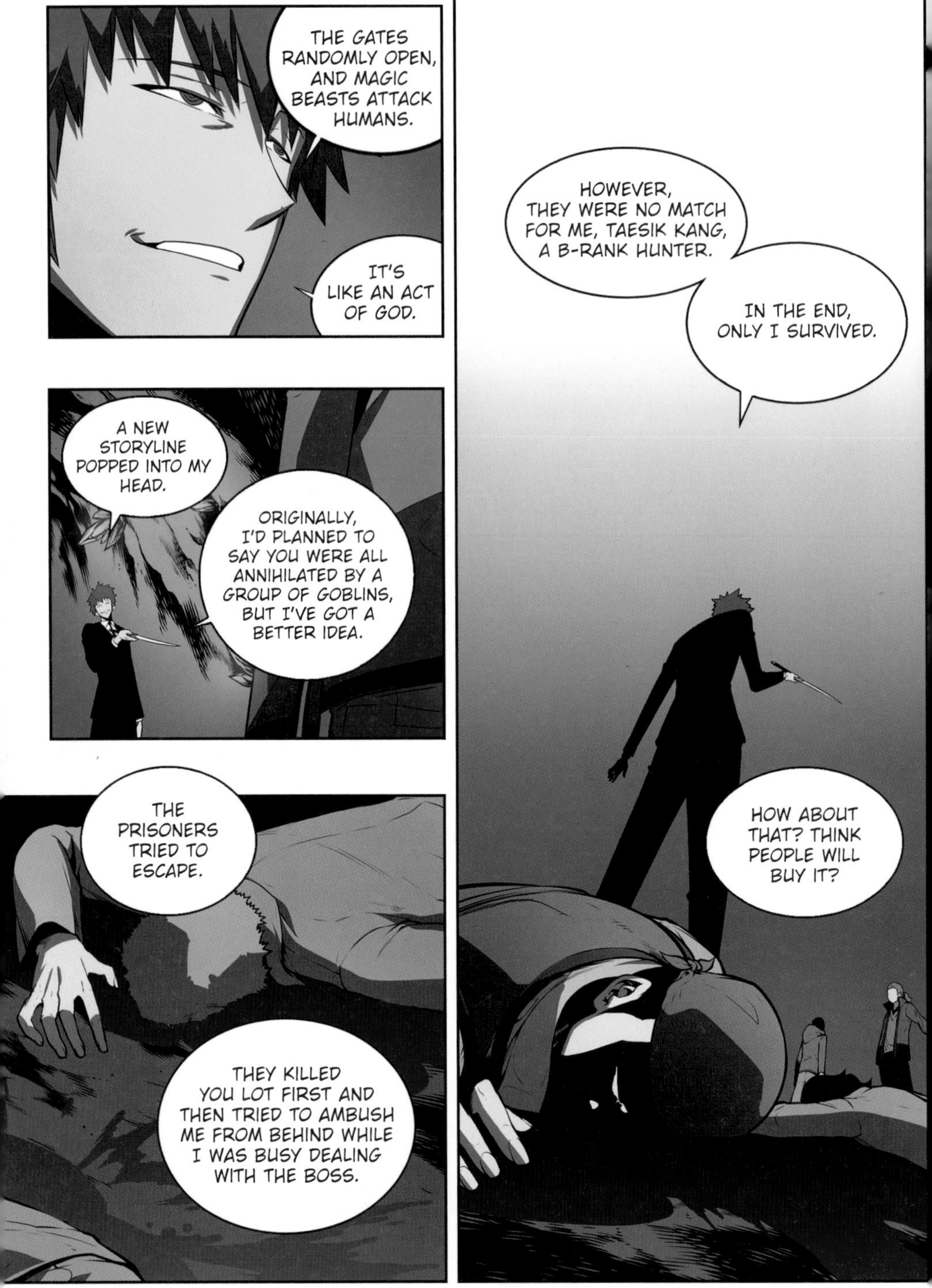
THE GATES RANDOMLY OPEN, AND MAGIC BEASTS ATTACK HUMANS.
IT'S LIKE AN ACT OF GOD.
A NEW STORYLINE POPPED INTO MY HEAD.
ORIGINALLY, I'D PLANNED TO SAY YOU WERE ALL ANNIHILATED BY A GROUP OF GOBLINS, BUT I'VE GOT A BETTER IDEA.
THE PRISONERS TRIED TO ESCAPE.
THEY KILLED YOU LOT FIRST AND THEN TRIED TO AMBUSH ME FROM BEHIND WHILE I WAS BUSY DEALING WITH THE BOSS.
HOWEVER, THEY WERE NO MATCH FOR ME, TAESIK KANG, A B-RANK HUNTER.
IN THE END, ONLY I SURVIVED.
HOW ABOUT THAT? THINK PEOPLE WILL BUY IT?

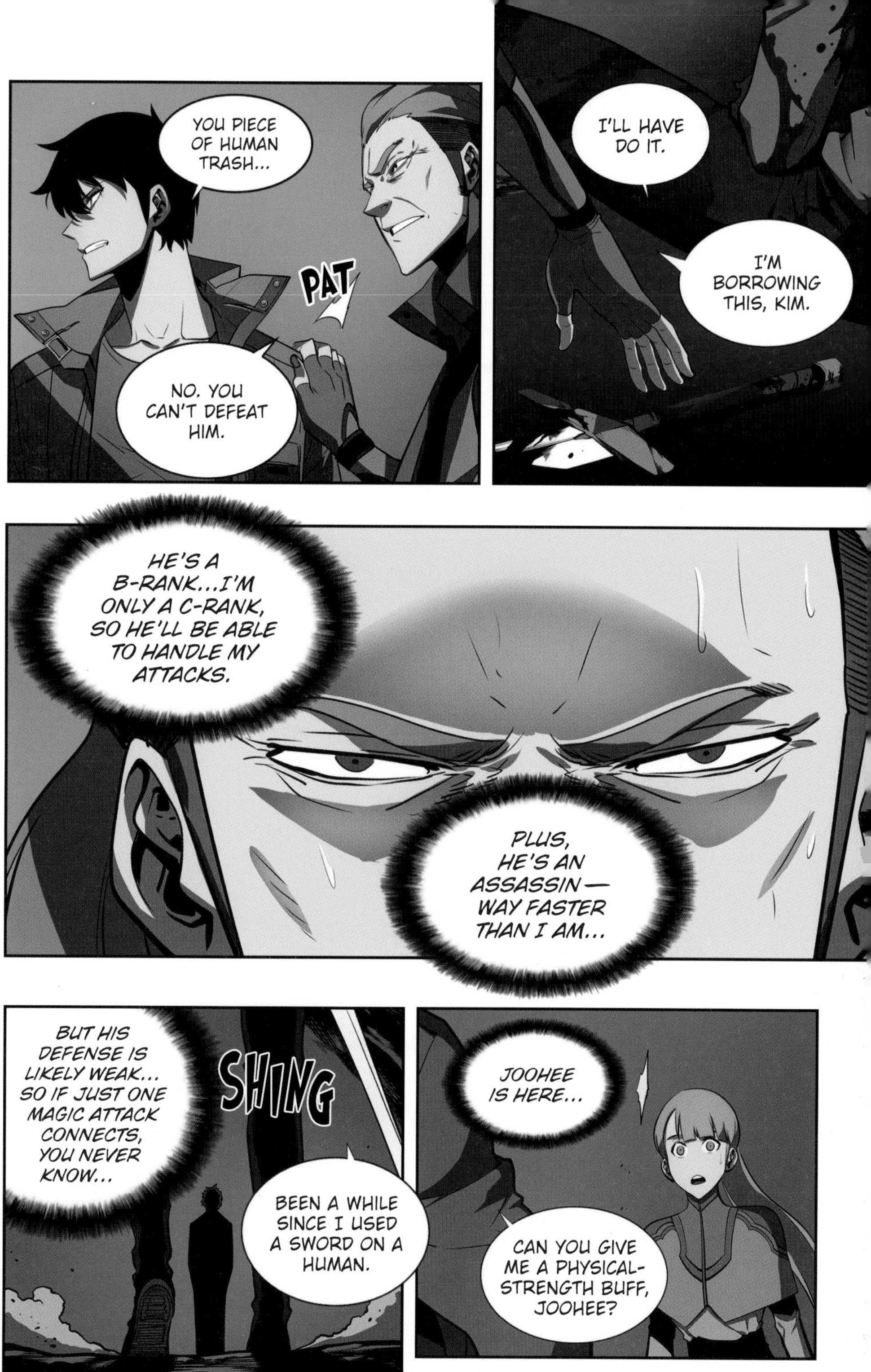
YOU PIECE OF HUMAN TRASH...
PAT
NO. YOU CAN'T DEFEAT HIM.
I'LL HAVE DO IT.
I'M BORROWING THIS, KIM.
HE'S A B-RANK...I'M ONLY A C-RANK, SO HE'LL BE ABLE TO HANDLE MY ATTACKS.
PLUS, HE'S AN ASSASSIN— WAY FASTER THAN I AM...
BUT HIS DEFENSE IS LIKELY WEAK... SO IF JUST ONE MAGIC ATTACK CONNECTS, YOU NEVER KNOW...
SHING
BEEN A WHILE SINCE I USED A SWORD ON A HUMAN.
JOOHEE IS HERE...
CAN YOU GIVE ME A PHYSICAL-STRENGTH BUFF, JOOHEE?

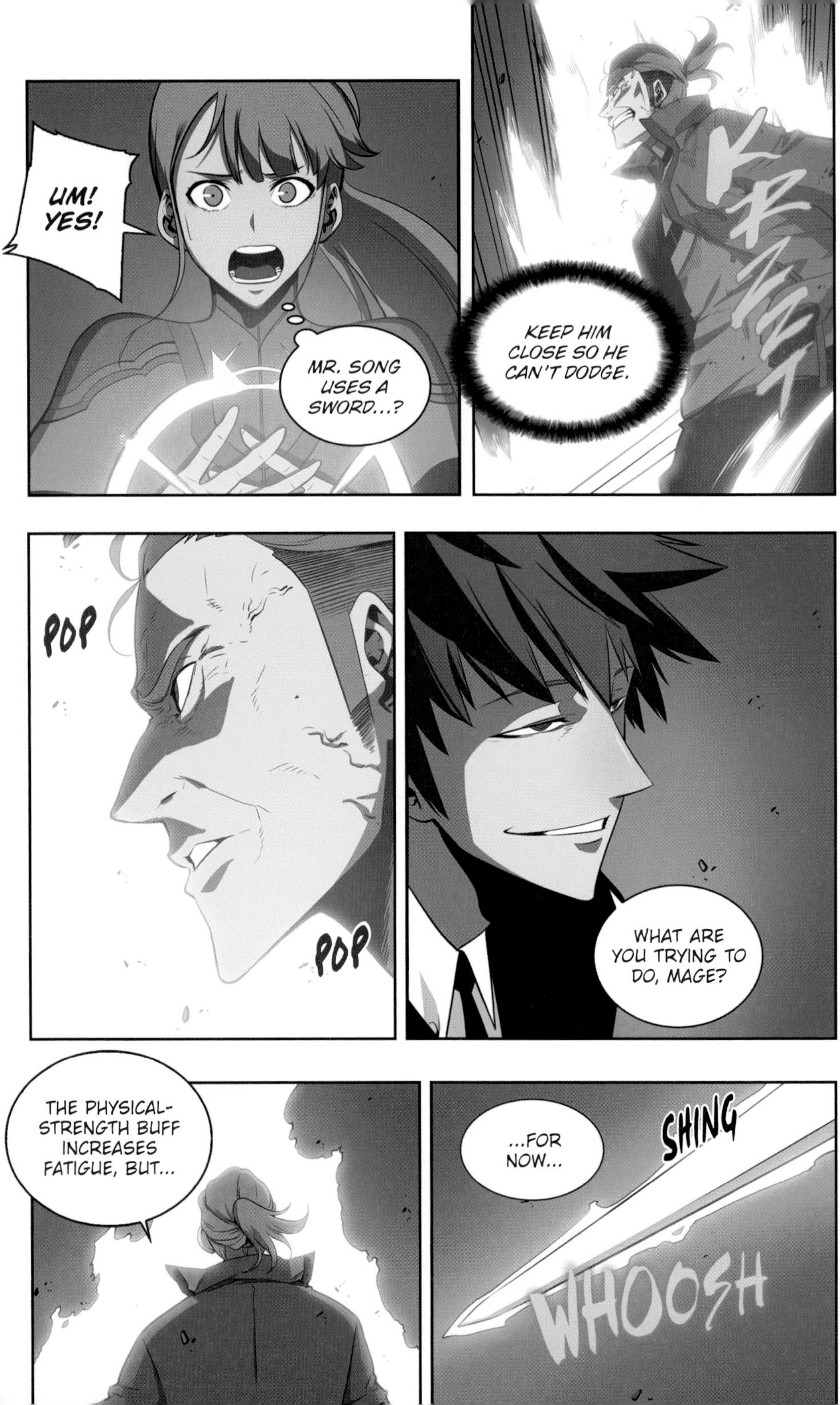
UM! YES!
MR. SONG USES A SWORD...?
KEEP HIM CLOSE SO HE CAN'T DODGE.
POP
POP
WHAT ARE YOU TRYING TO DO, MAGE?
THE PHYSICAL-STRENGTH BUFF INCREASES FATIGUE, BUT...
...FOR NOW...
SHING
WHOOSH

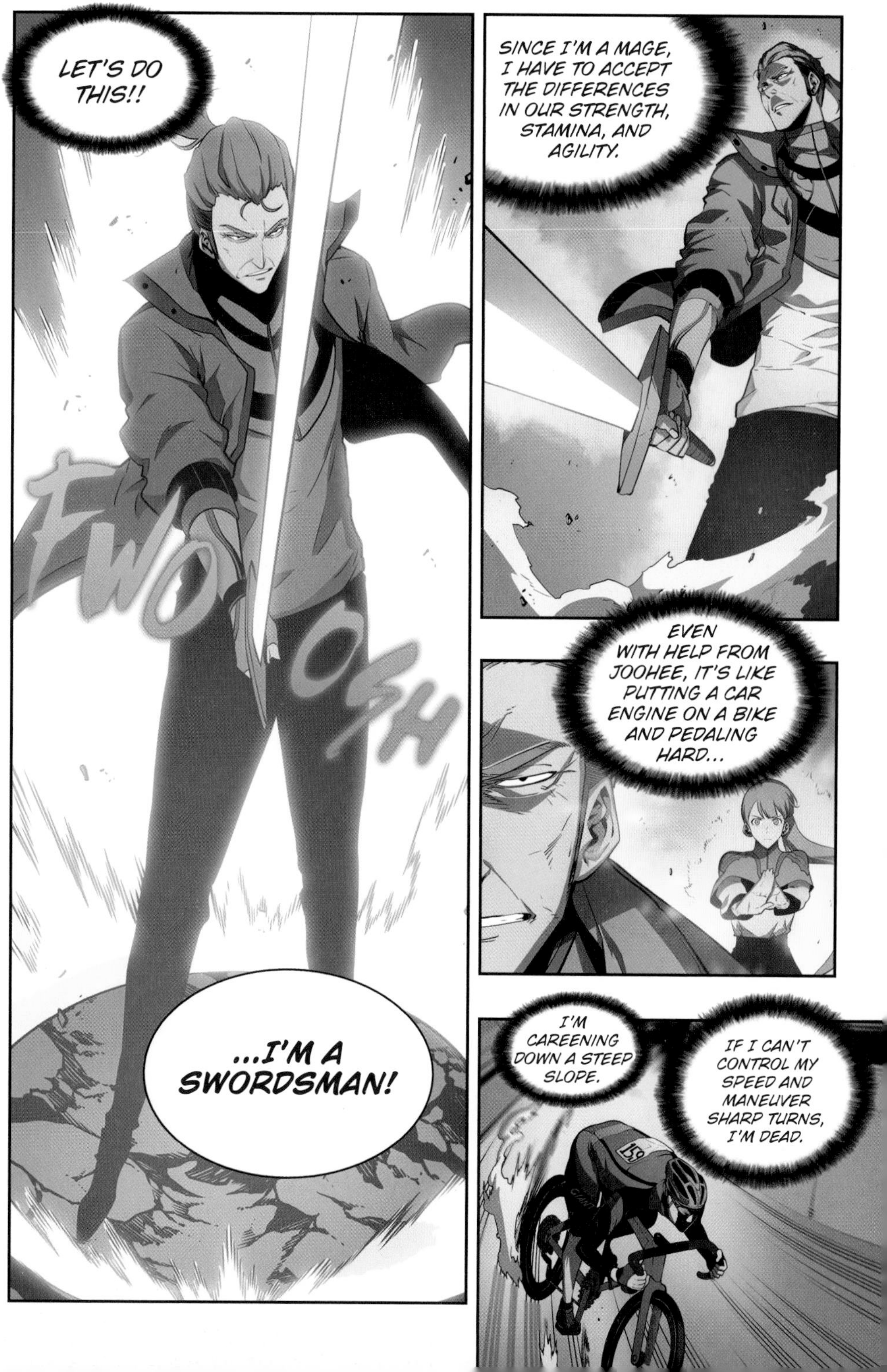
LET'S DO THIS!!
FWOOSH
...I'M A SWORDSMAN!
SINCE I'M A MAGE, I HAVE TO ACCEPT THE DIFFERENCES IN OUR STRENGTH, STAMINA, AND AGILITY.
EVEN WITH HELP FROM JOOHEE, IT'S LIKE PUTTING A CAR ENGINE ON A BIKE AND PEDALING HARD...
I'M CAREENING DOWN A STEEP SLOPE.
IF I CAN'T CONTROL MY SPEED AND MANEUVER SHARP TURNS, I'M DEAD.

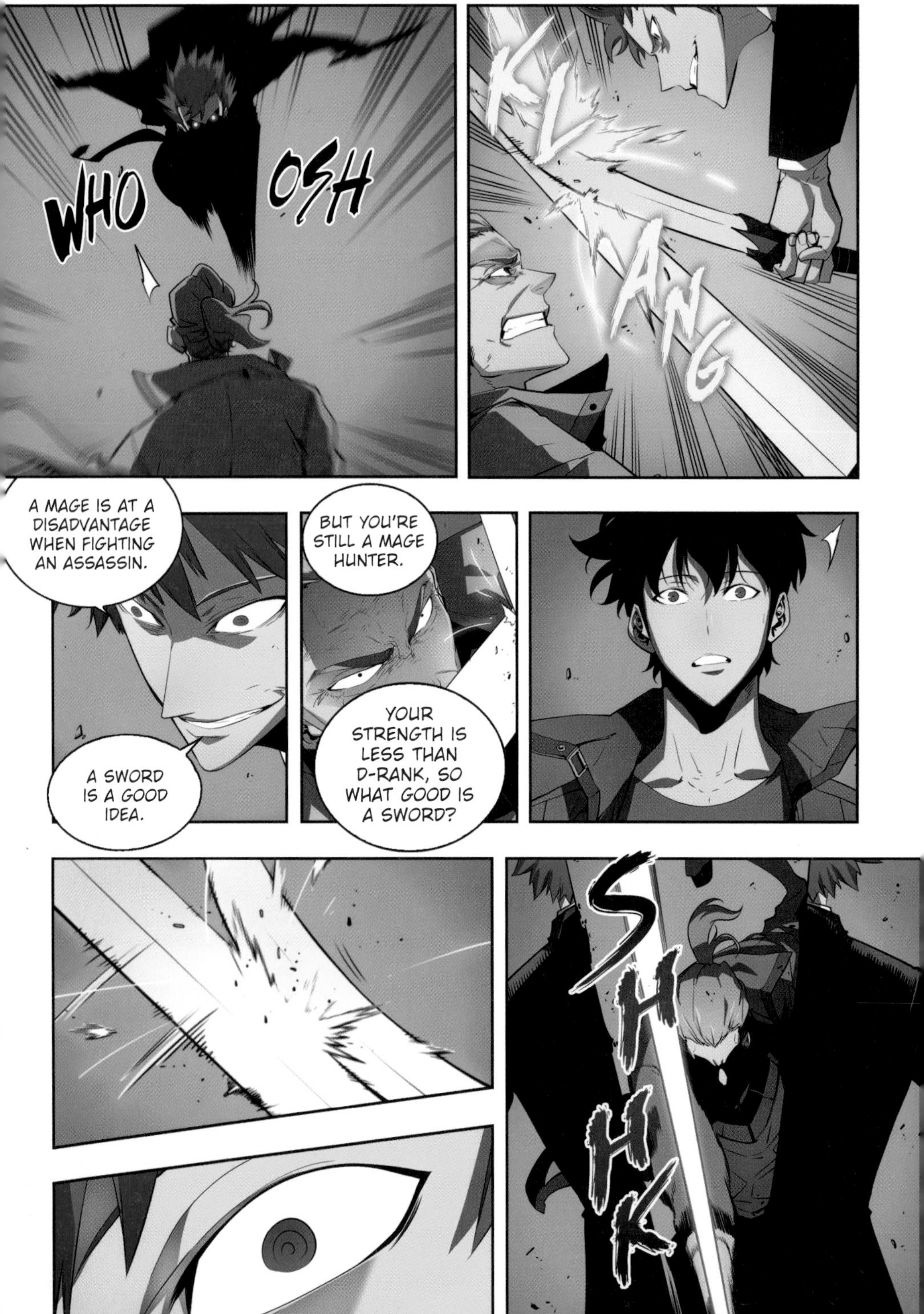
WHOOSH
KLANG
A MAGE IS AT A DISADVANTAGE WHEN FIGHTING AN ASSASSIN.
A SWORD IS A GOOD IDEA.
BUT YOU'RE STILL A MAGE HUNTER.
YOUR STRENGTH IS LESS THAN D-RANK, SO WHAT GOOD IS A SWORD?
SHHK

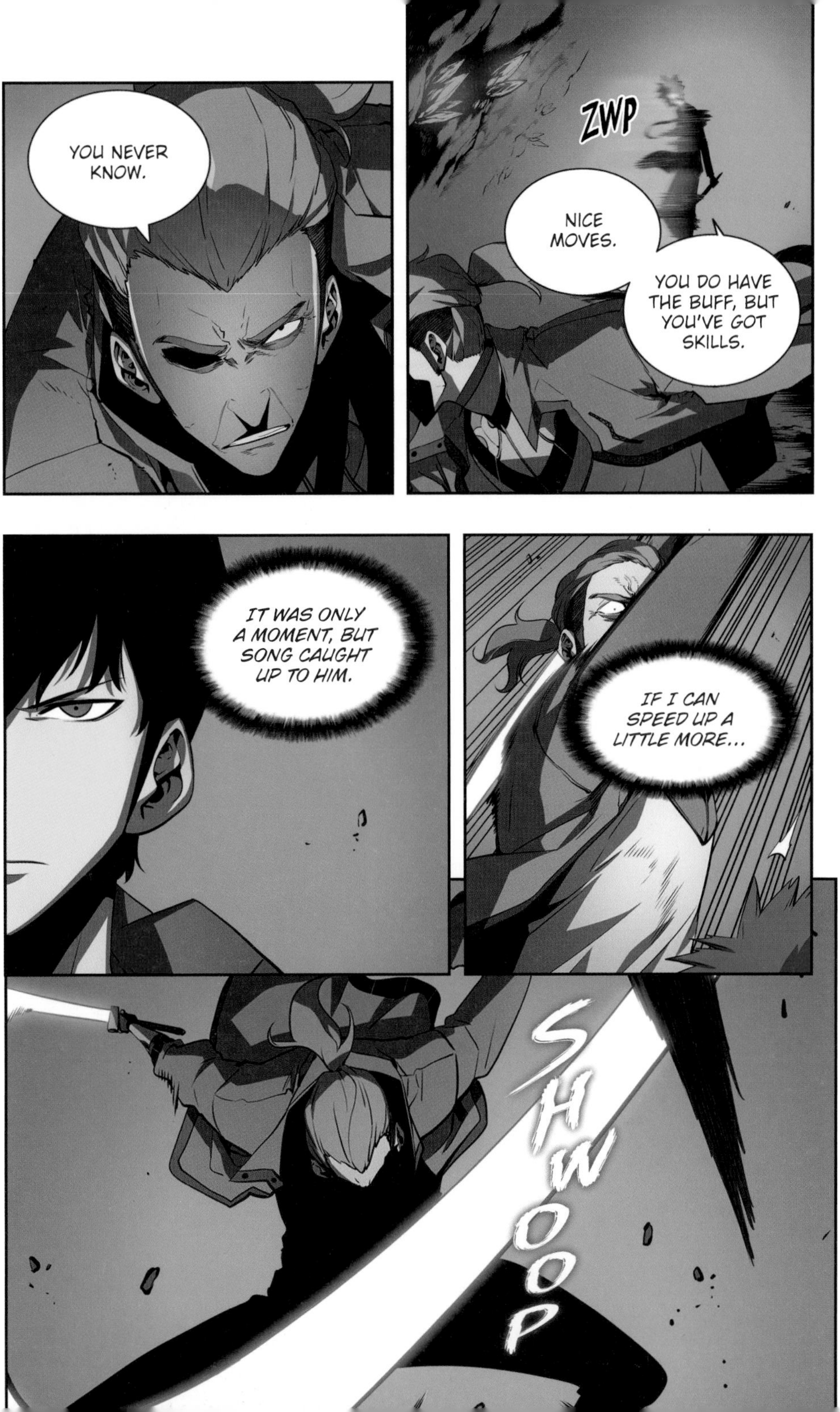
YOU NEVER KNOW.
ZWP
NICE MOVES.
YOU DO HAVE THE BUFF, BUT YOU'VE GOT SKILLS.
IT WAS ONLY A MOMENT, BUT SONG CAUGHT UP TO HIM.
IF I CAN SPEED UP A LITTLE MORE...
SHWOOP

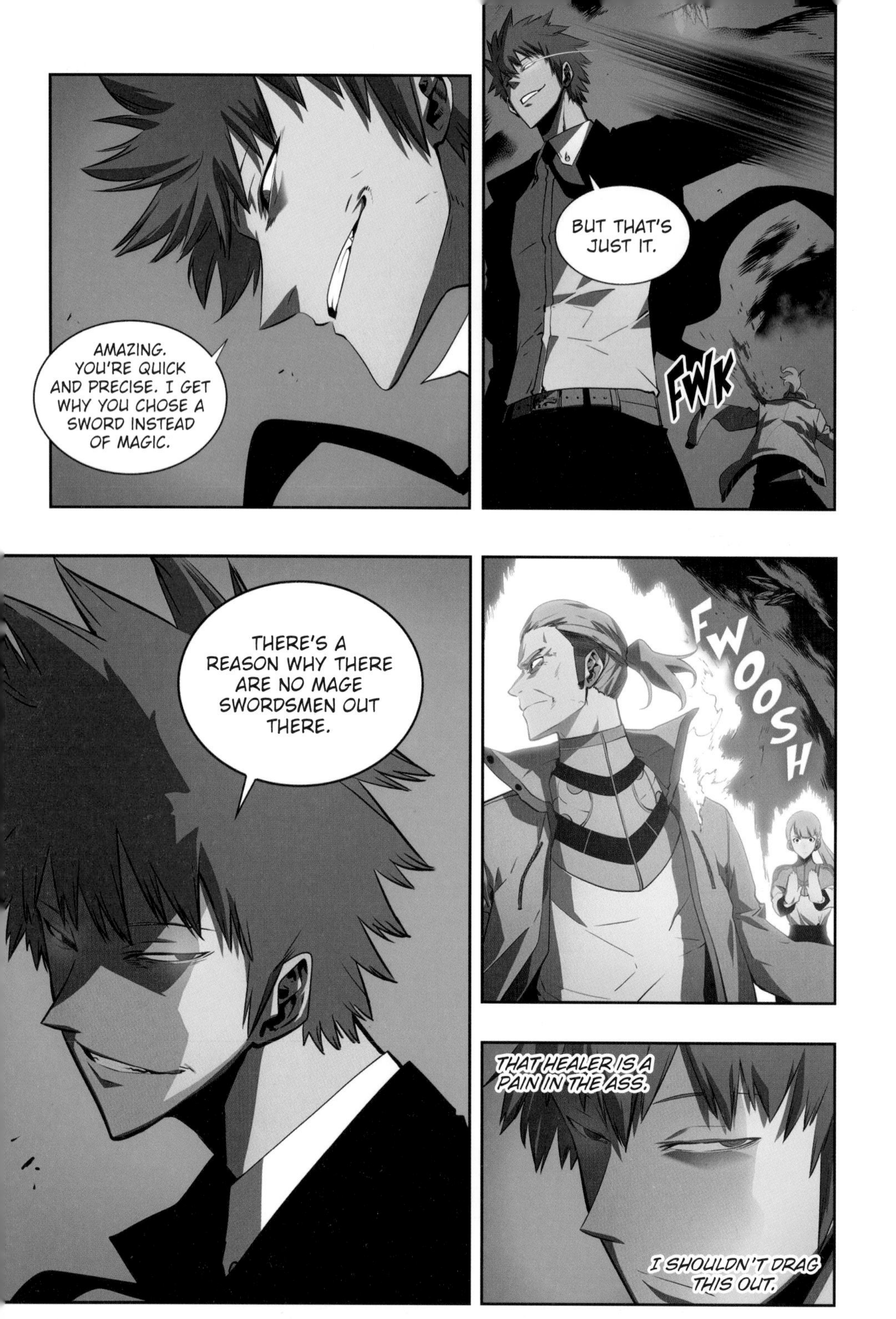
AMAZING. YOU'RE QUICK AND PRECISE. I GET WHY YOU CHOSE A SWORD INSTEAD OF MAGIC.
BUT THAT'S JUST IT.
FWK
THERE'S A REASON WHY THERE ARE NO MAGE SWORDSMEN OUT THERE.
FWOOSH
THAT HEALER IS A PAIN IN THE ASS.
I SHOULDN'T DRAG THIS OUT.

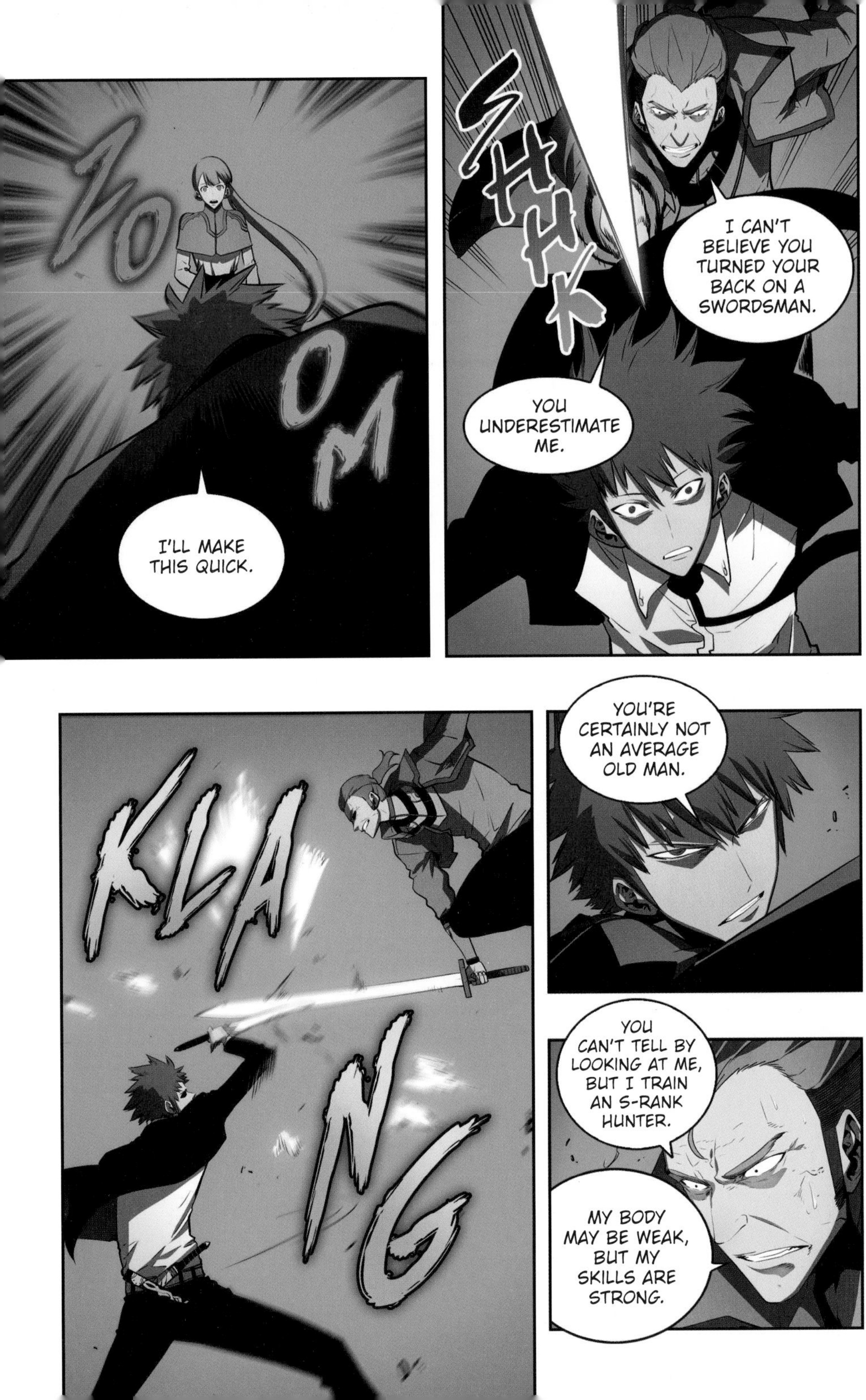
ZOOM
I'LL MAKE THIS QUICK.
SHHK
I CAN'T BELIEVE YOU TURNED YOUR BACK ON A SWORDSMAN.
YOU UNDERESTIMATE ME.
KLANG
YOU'RE CERTAINLY NOT AN AVERAGE OLD MAN.
YOU CAN'T TELL BY LOOKING AT ME, BUT I TRAIN AN S-RANK HUNTER.
MY BODY MAY BE WEAK, BUT MY SKILLS ARE STRONG.

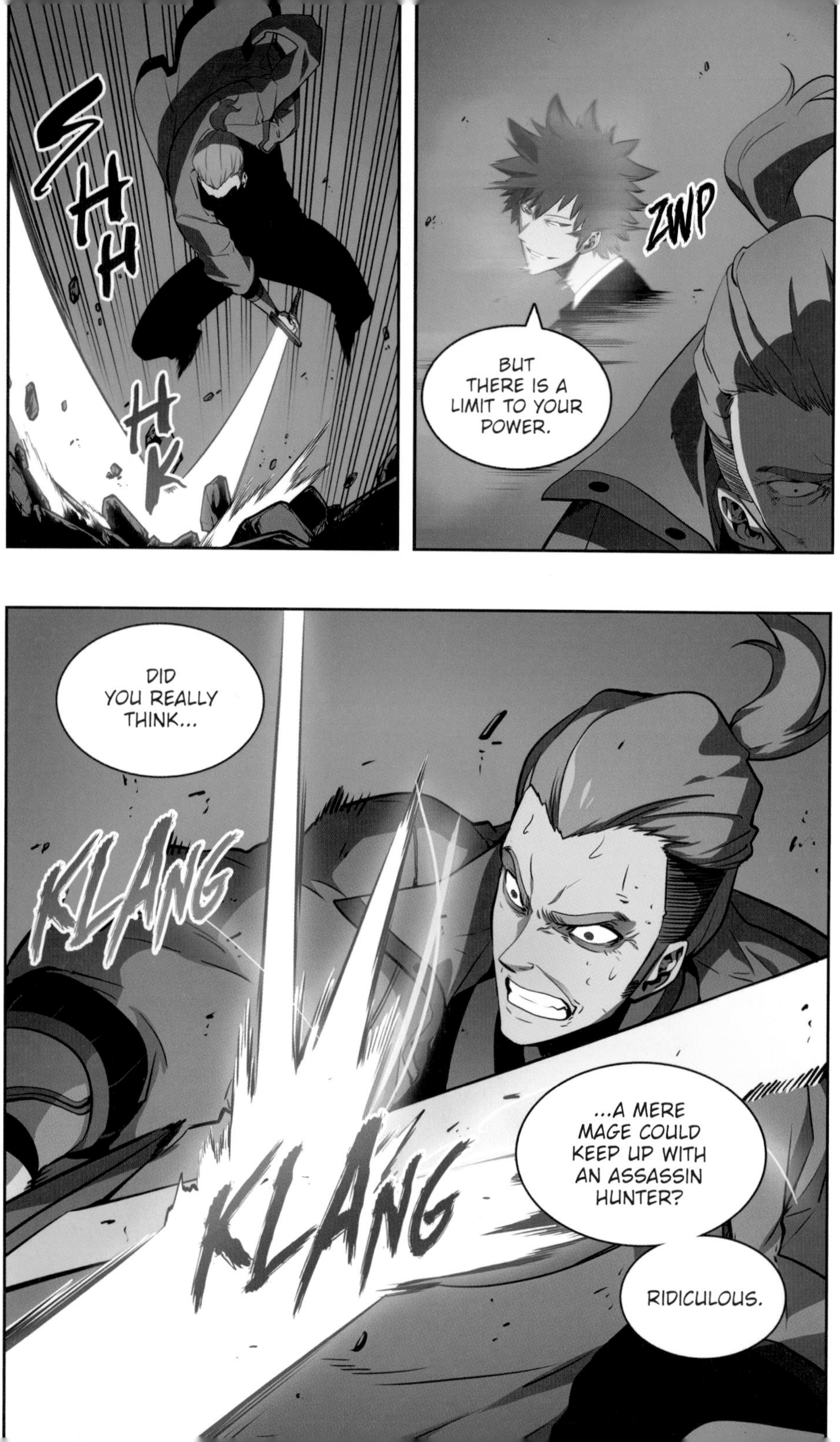
SHHH
HK
ZWP
BUT THERE IS A LIMIT TO YOUR POWER.
DID YOU REALLY THINK...
KLANG
KLANG
...A MERE MAGE COULD KEEP UP WITH AN ASSASSIN HUNTER?
RIDICULOUS.

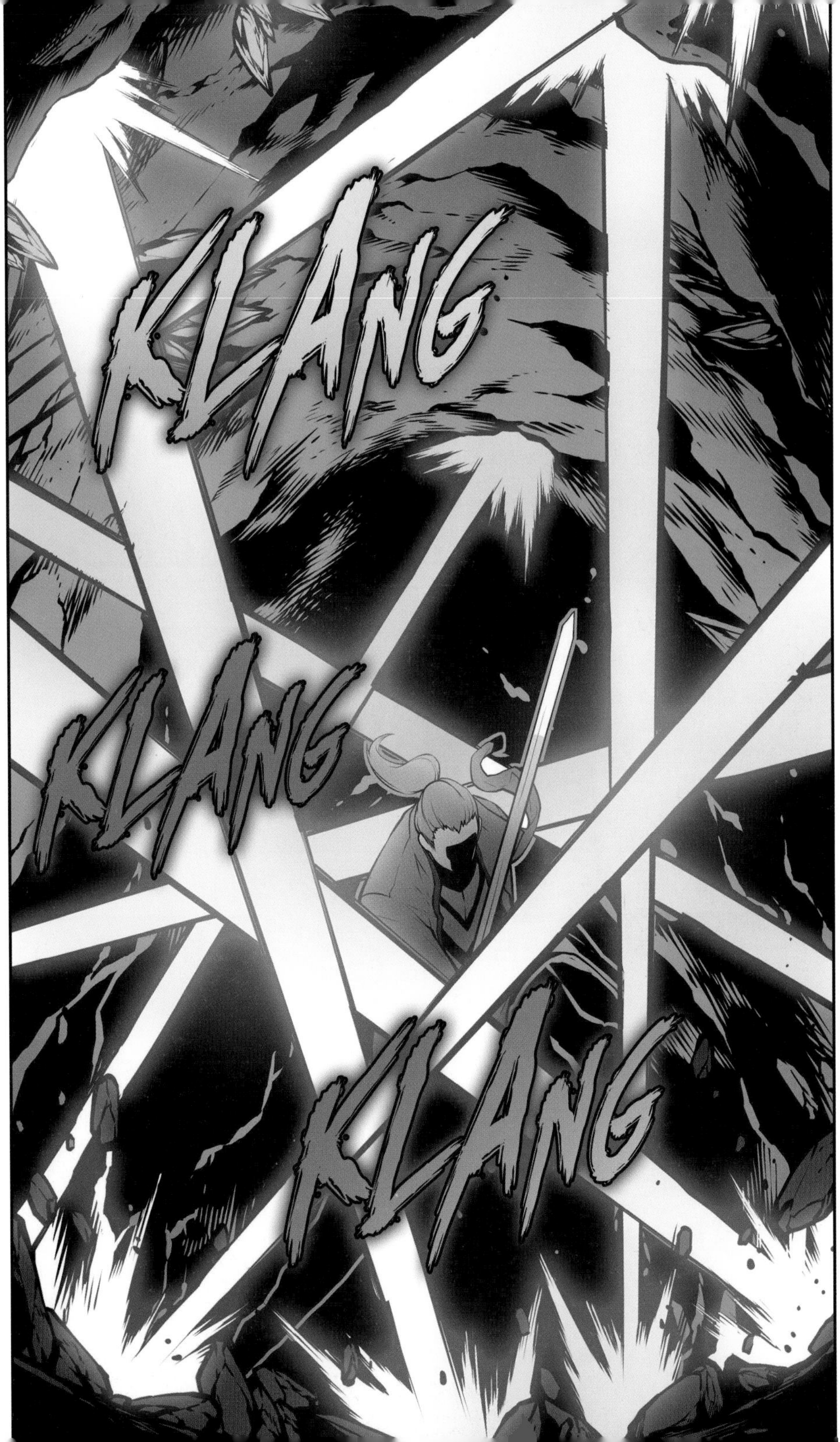
KLANG
KLANG
KLANG

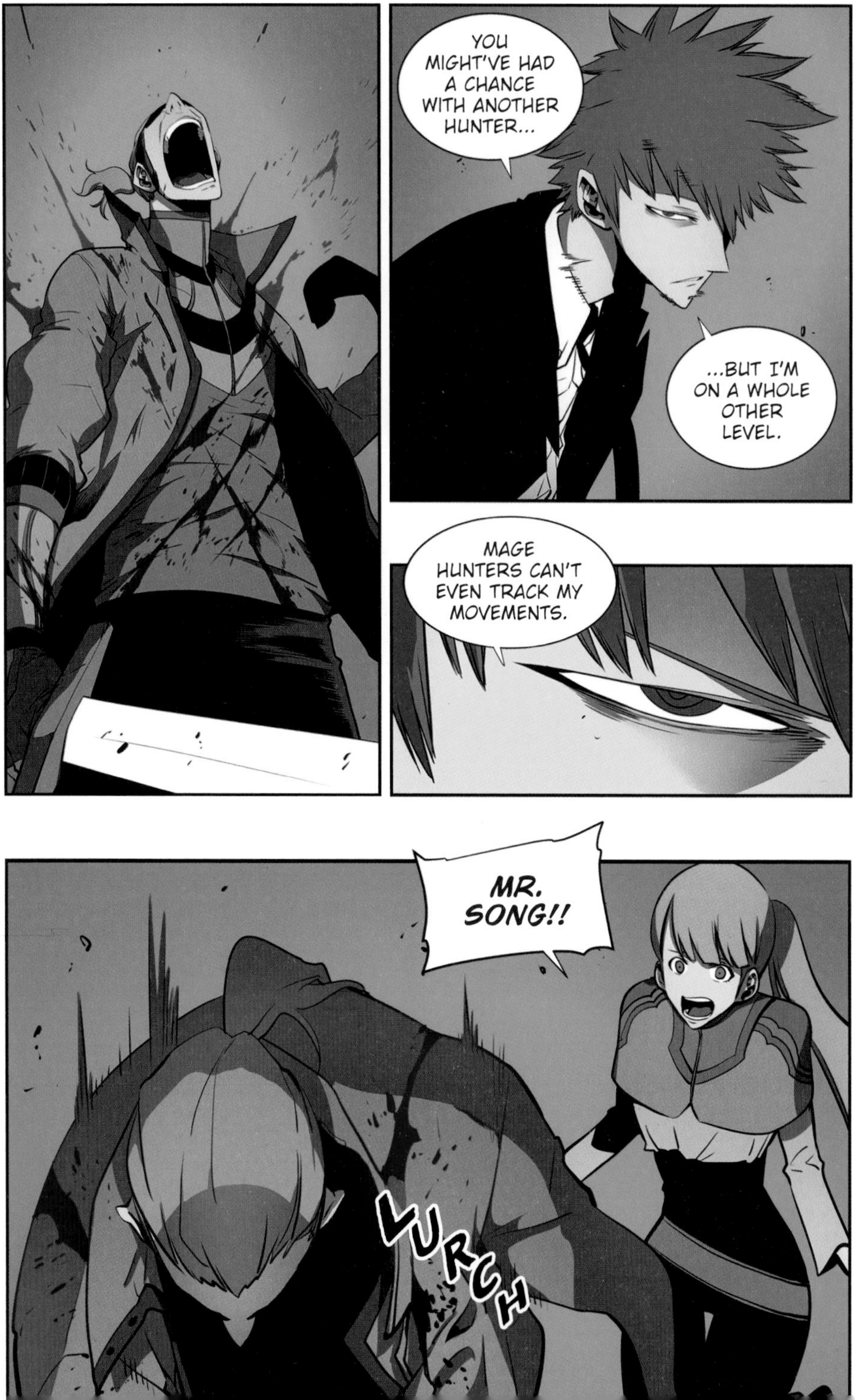
YOU MIGHT'VE HAD A CHANCE WITH ANOTHER HUNTER...
...BUT I'M ON A WHOLE OTHER LEVEL.
MAGE HUNTERS CAN'T EVEN TRACK MY MOVEMENTS.
MR. SONG!!
LURCH

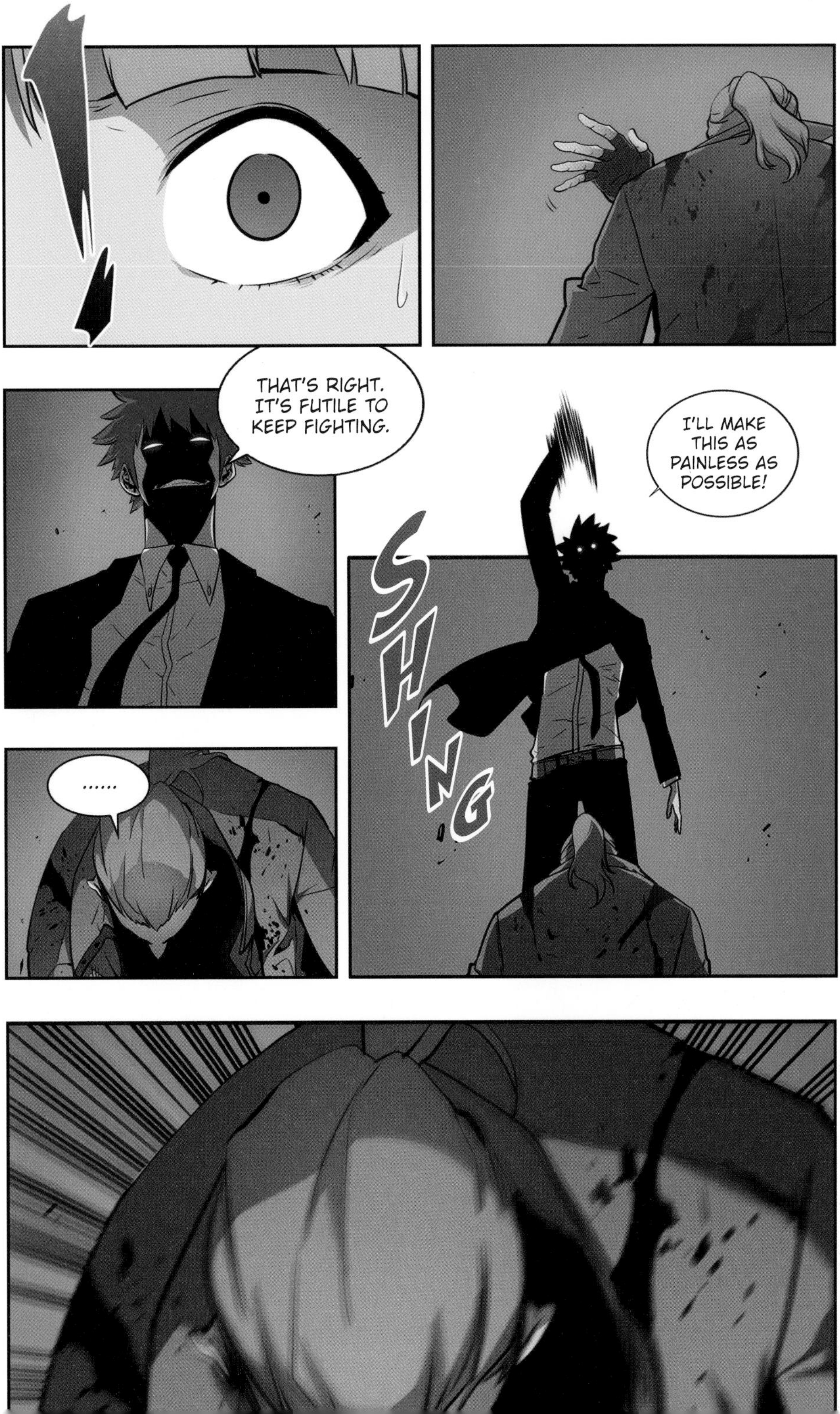
THAT'S RIGHT. IT'S FUTILE TO KEEP FIGHTING.
I'LL MAKE THIS AS PAINLESS AS POSSIBLE!
SHING
......

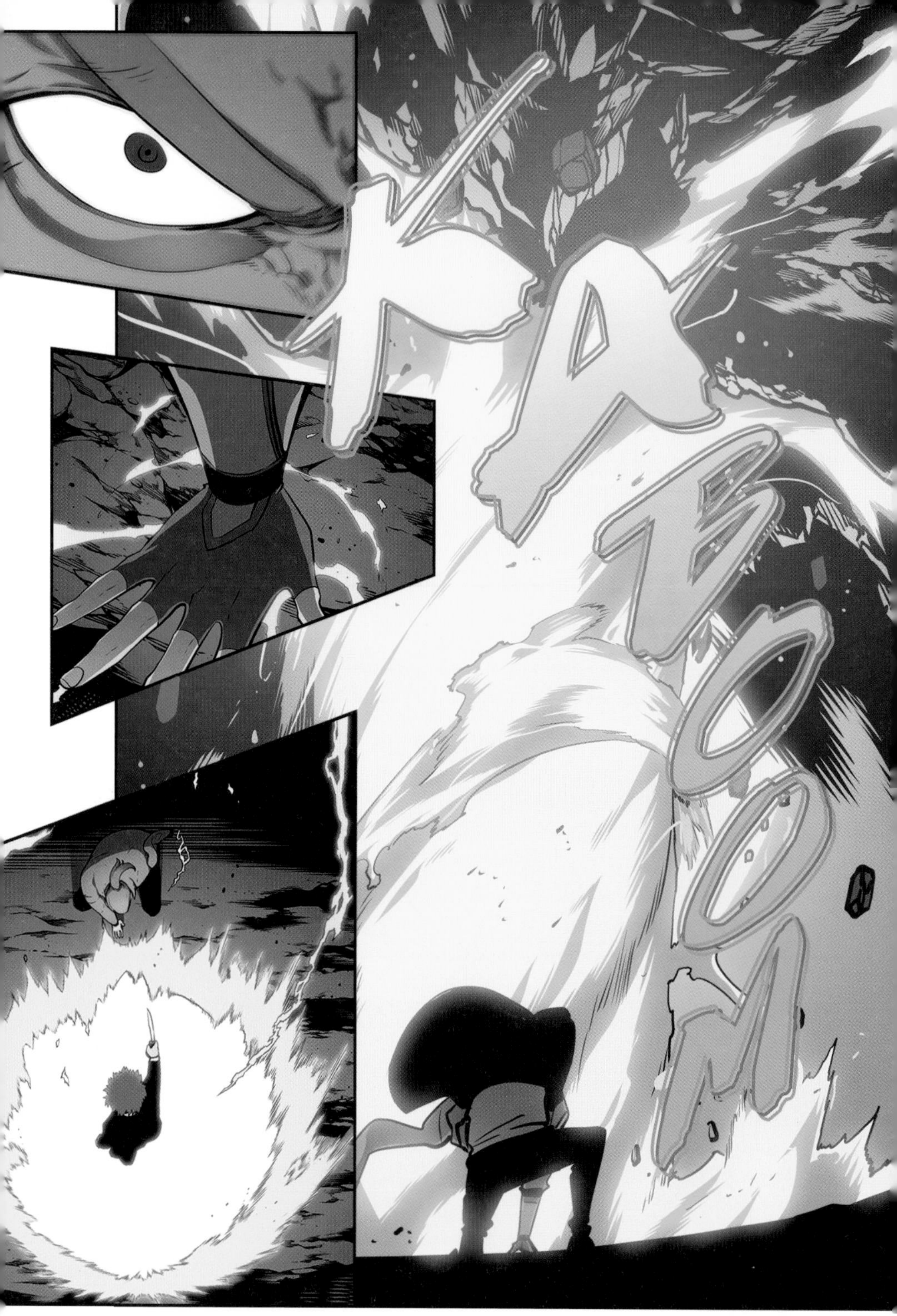
KABOOM

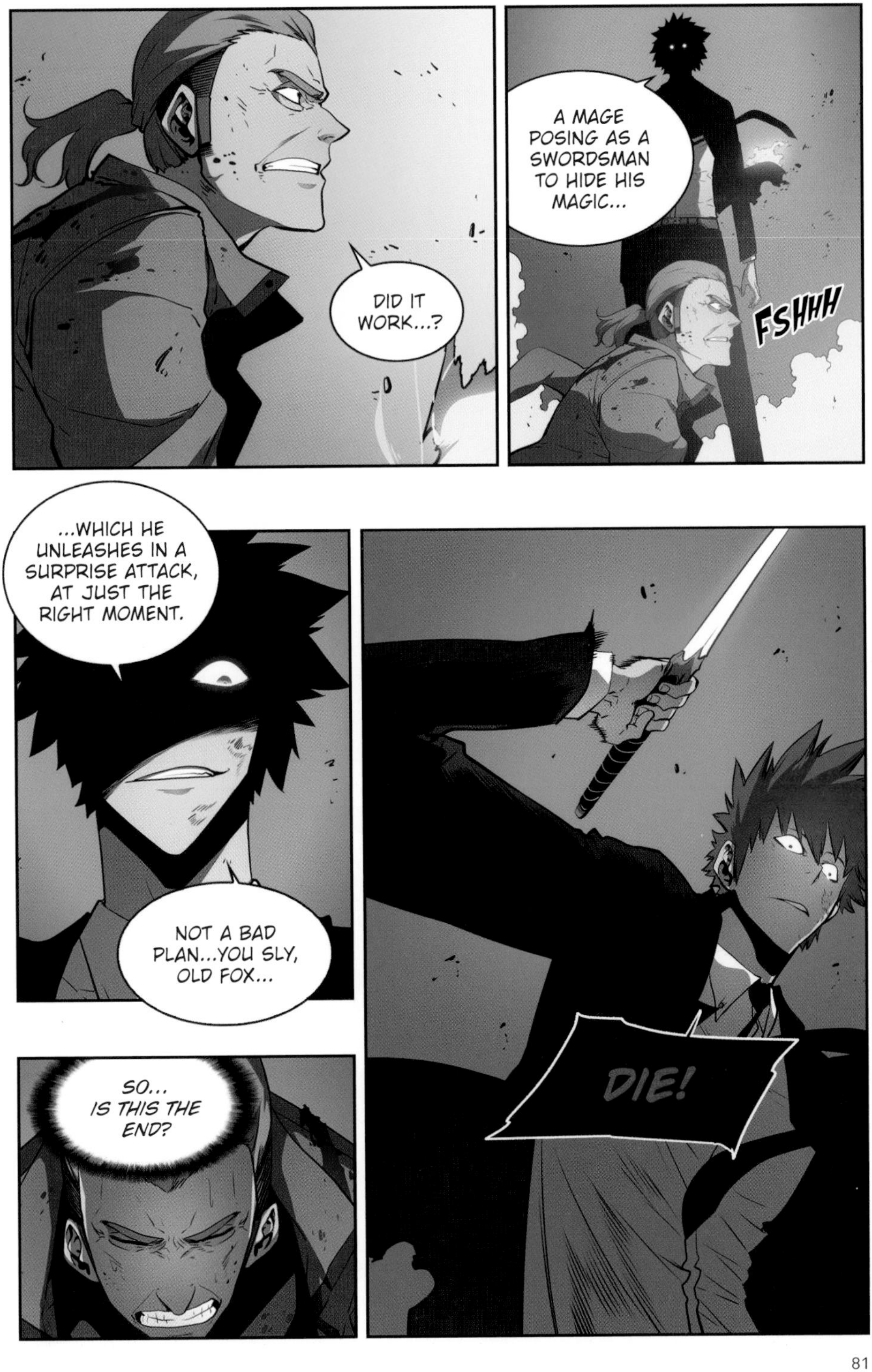
DID IT WORK...?
A MAGE POSING AS A SWORDSMAN TO HIDE HIS MAGIC...
FSHHH
...WHICH HE UNLEASHES IN A SURPRISE ATTACK, AT JUST THE RIGHT MOMENT.
NOT A BAD PLAN...YOU SLY, OLD FOX...
SO... IS THIS THE END?
DIE!

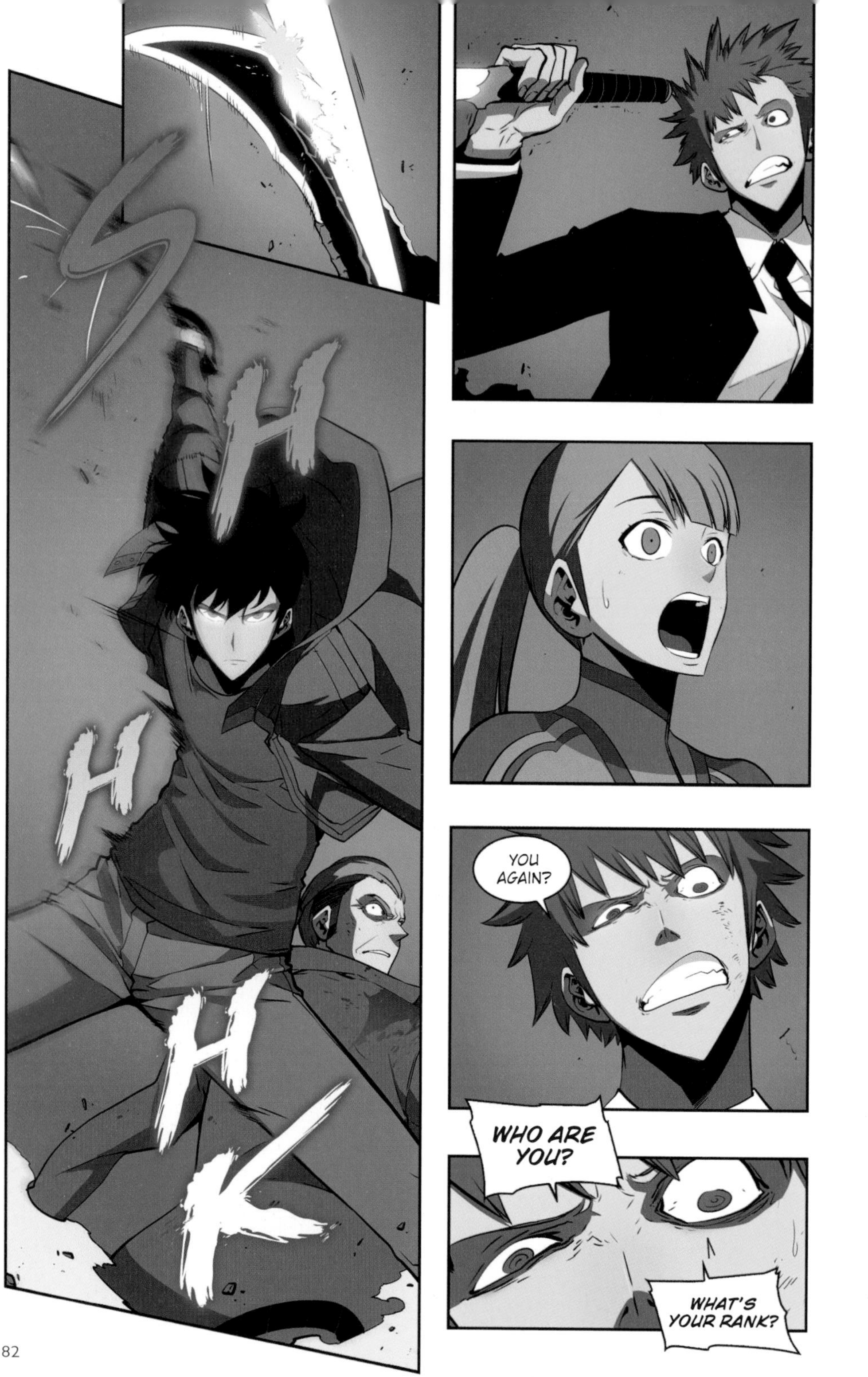
SHHHK
YOU AGAIN?
WHO ARE YOU?
WHAT'S YOUR RANK?

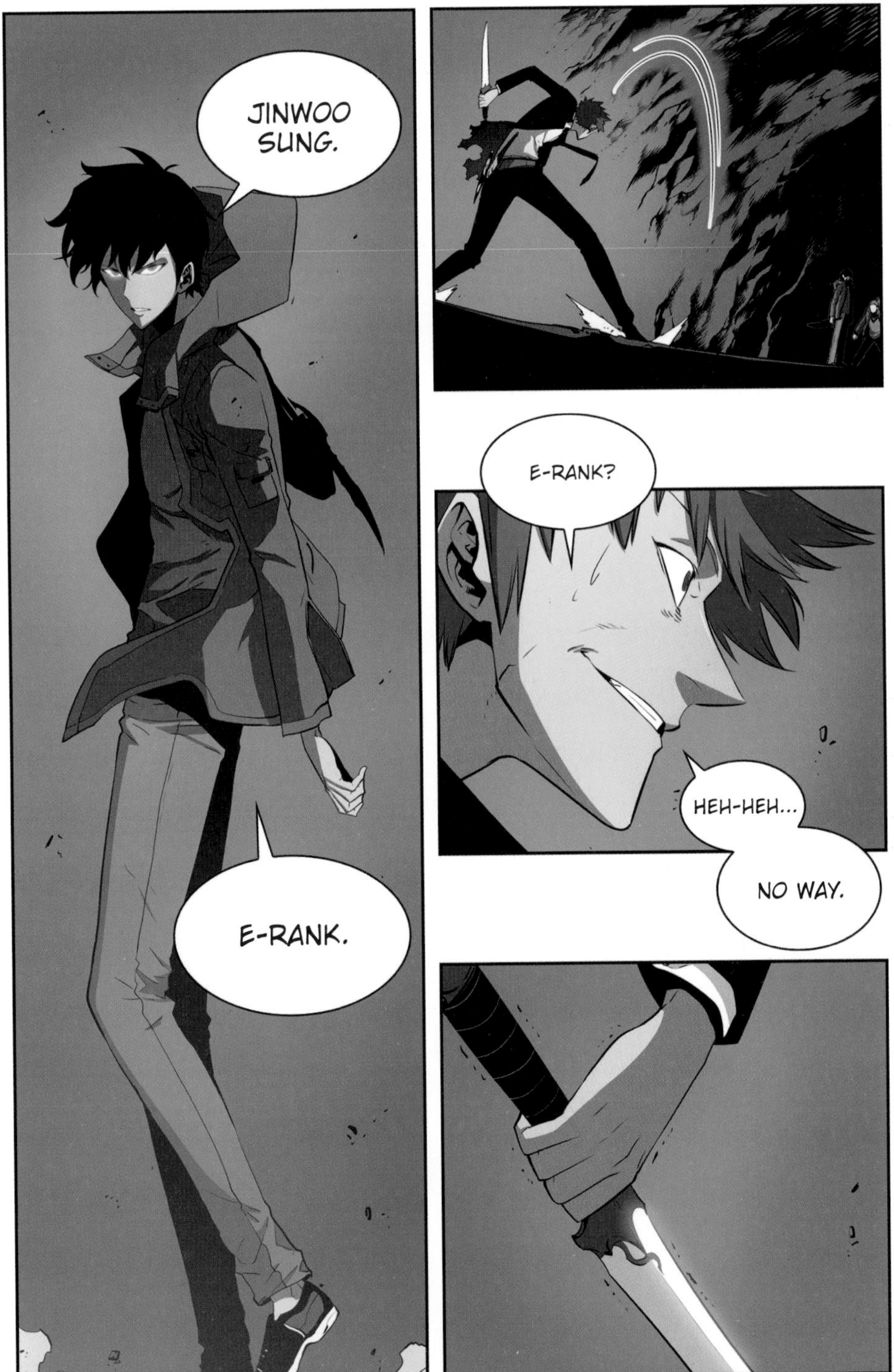
JINWOO SUNG.
E-RANK.
E-RANK?
HEH-HEH...
NO WAY.

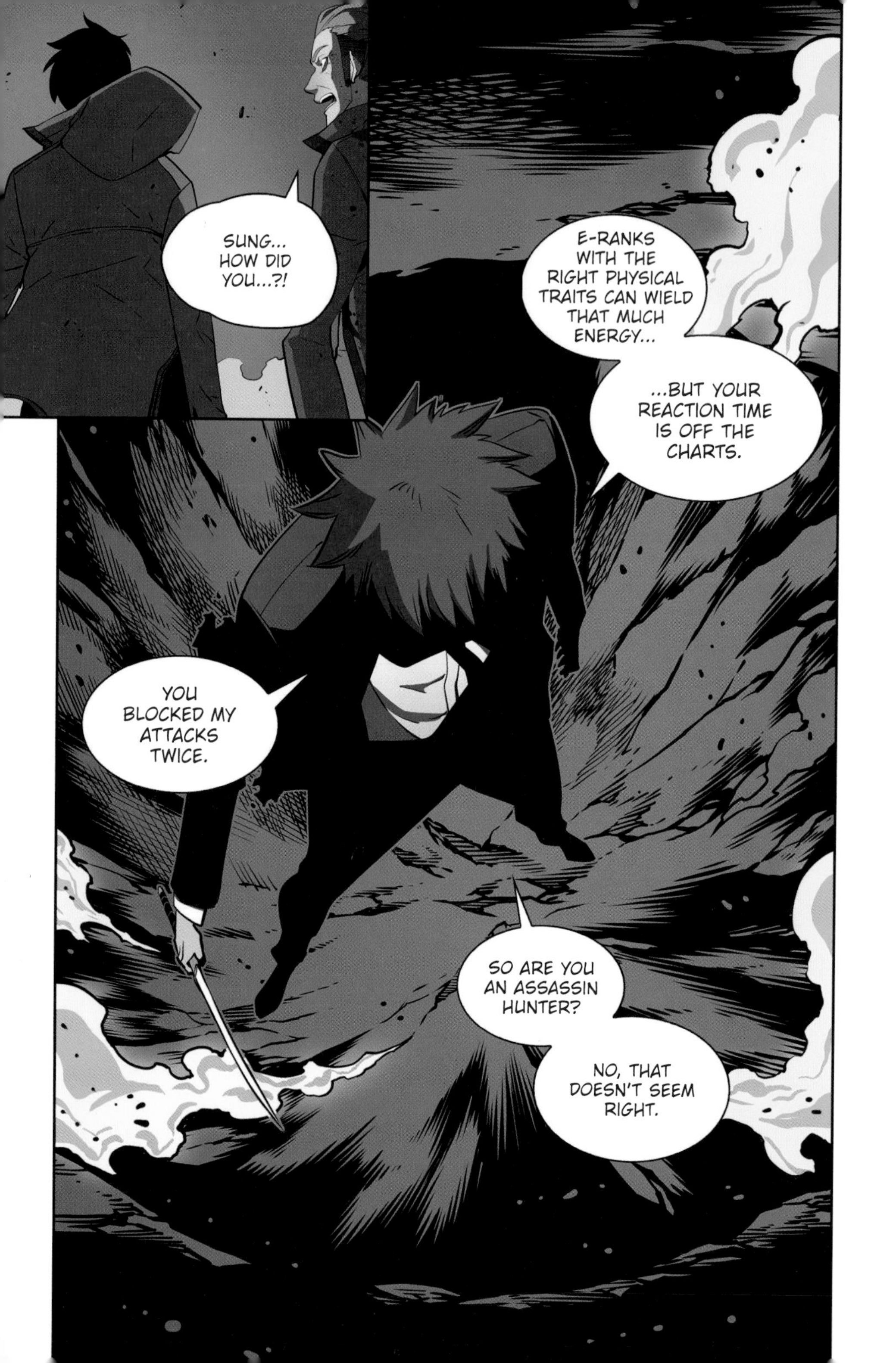
SUNG... HOW DID YOU...?!
E-RANKS WITH THE RIGHT PHYSICAL TRAITS CAN WIELD THAT MUCH ENERGY...
...BUT YOUR REACTION TIME IS OFF THE CHARTS.
YOU BLOCKED MY ATTACKS TWICE.
SO ARE YOU AN ASSASSIN HUNTER?
NO, THAT DOESN'T SEEM RIGHT.

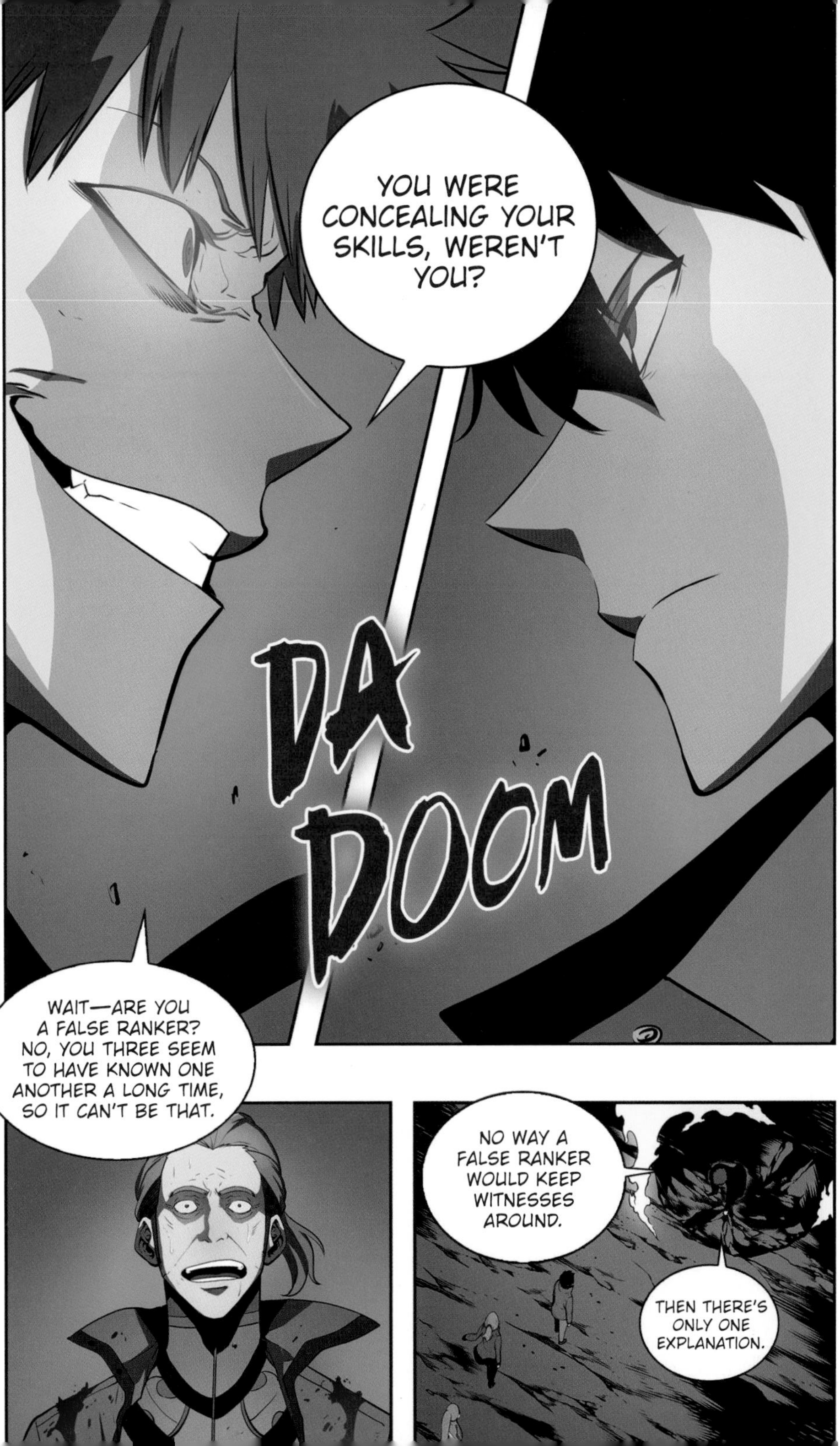
YOU WERE CONCEALING YOUR SKILLS, WEREN'T YOU?
DA DOOM
WAIT—ARE YOU A FALSE RANKER? NO, YOU THREE SEEM TO HAVE KNOWN ONE ANOTHER A LONG TIME, SO IT CAN'T BE THAT.
NO WAY A FALSE RANKER WOULD KEEP WITNESSES AROUND.
THEN THERE'S ONLY ONE EXPLANATION.

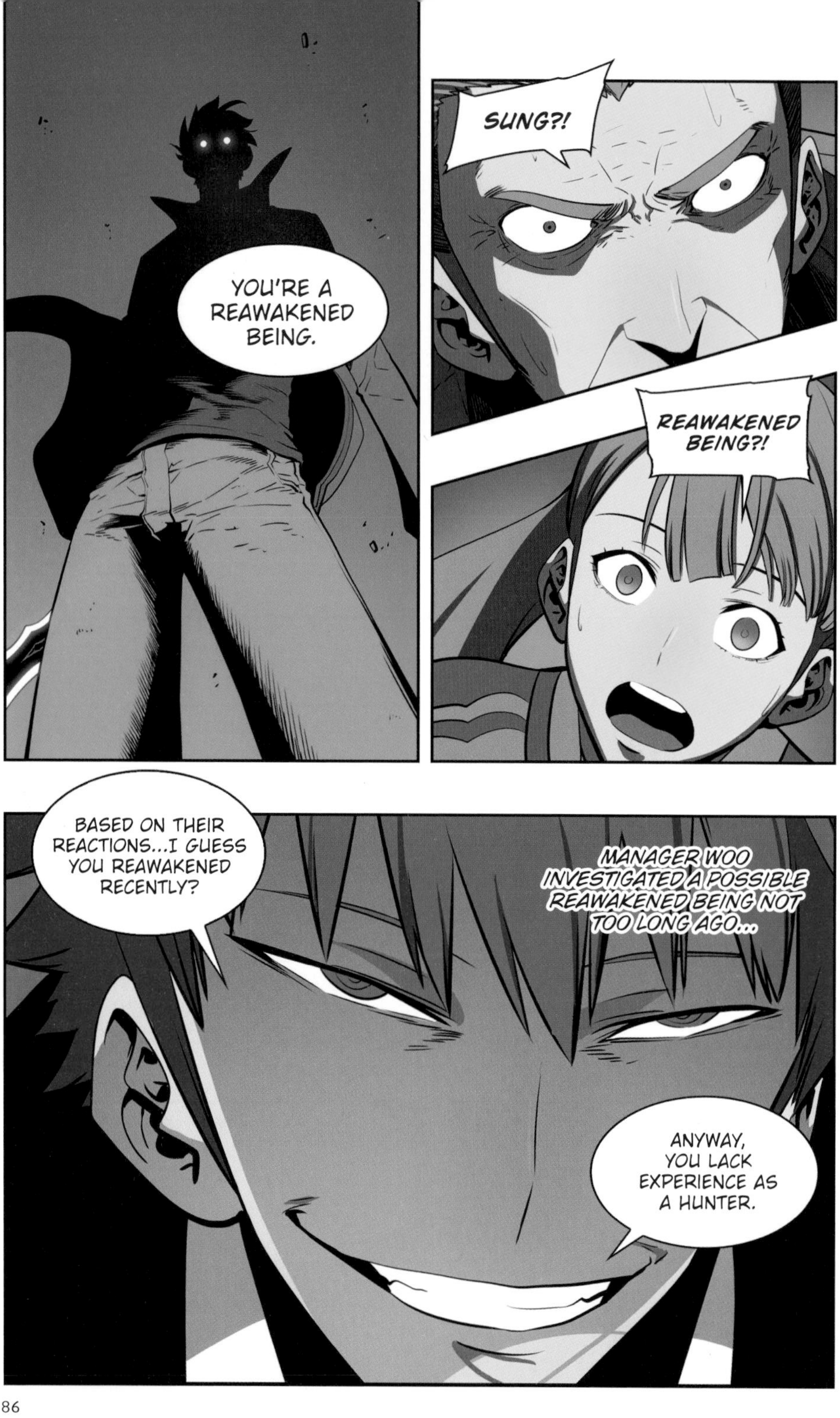
YOU'RE A REAWAKENED BEING.
SUNG?!
REAWAKENED BEING?!
BASED ON THEIR REACTIONS...I GUESS YOU REAWAKENED RECENTLY?
MANAGER WOO INVESTIGATED A POSSIBLE REAWAKENED BEING NOT TOO LONG AGO...
ANYWAY, YOU LACK EXPERIENCE AS A HUNTER.

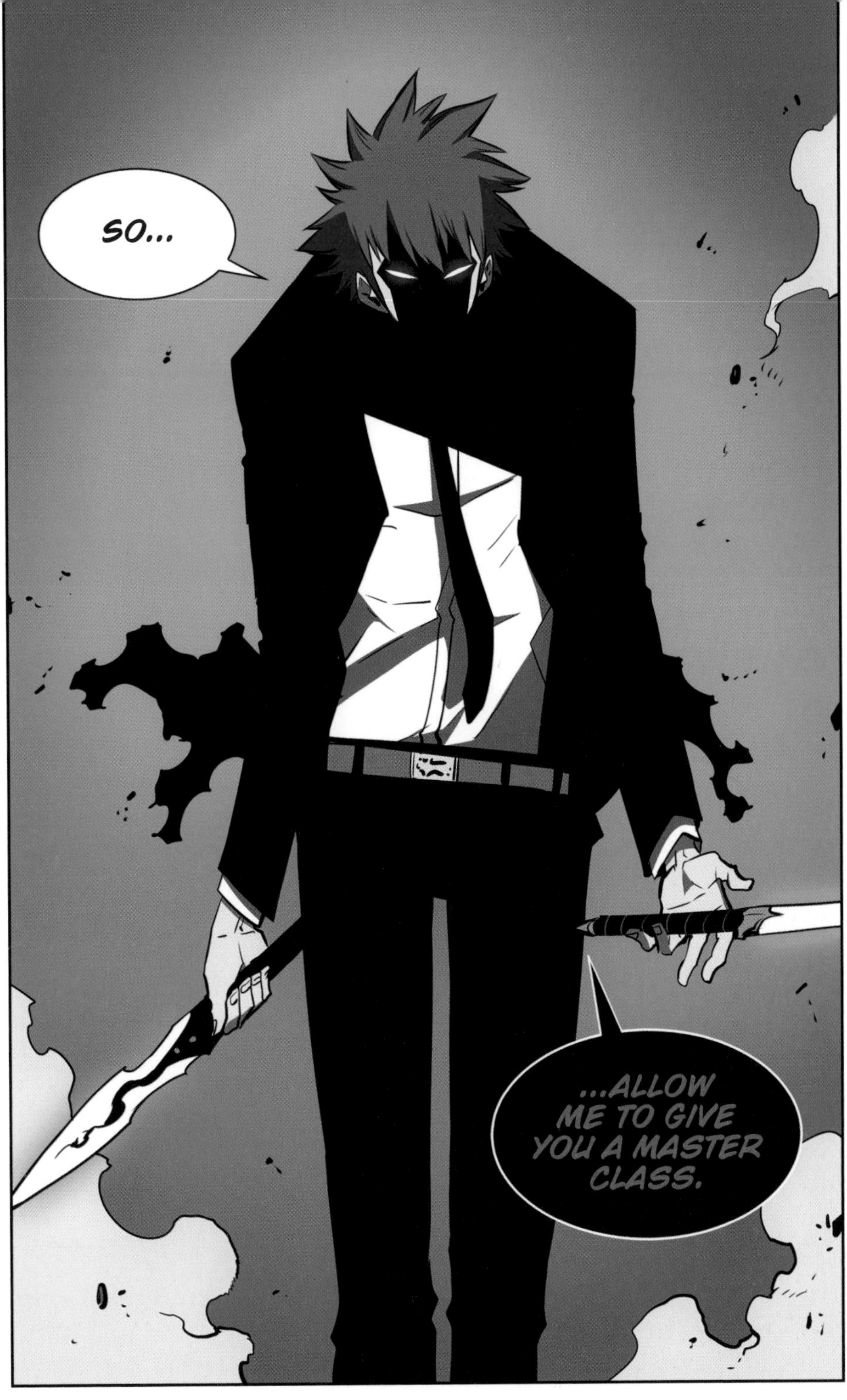
SO...
...ALLOW ME TO GIVE YOU A MASTER CLASS.

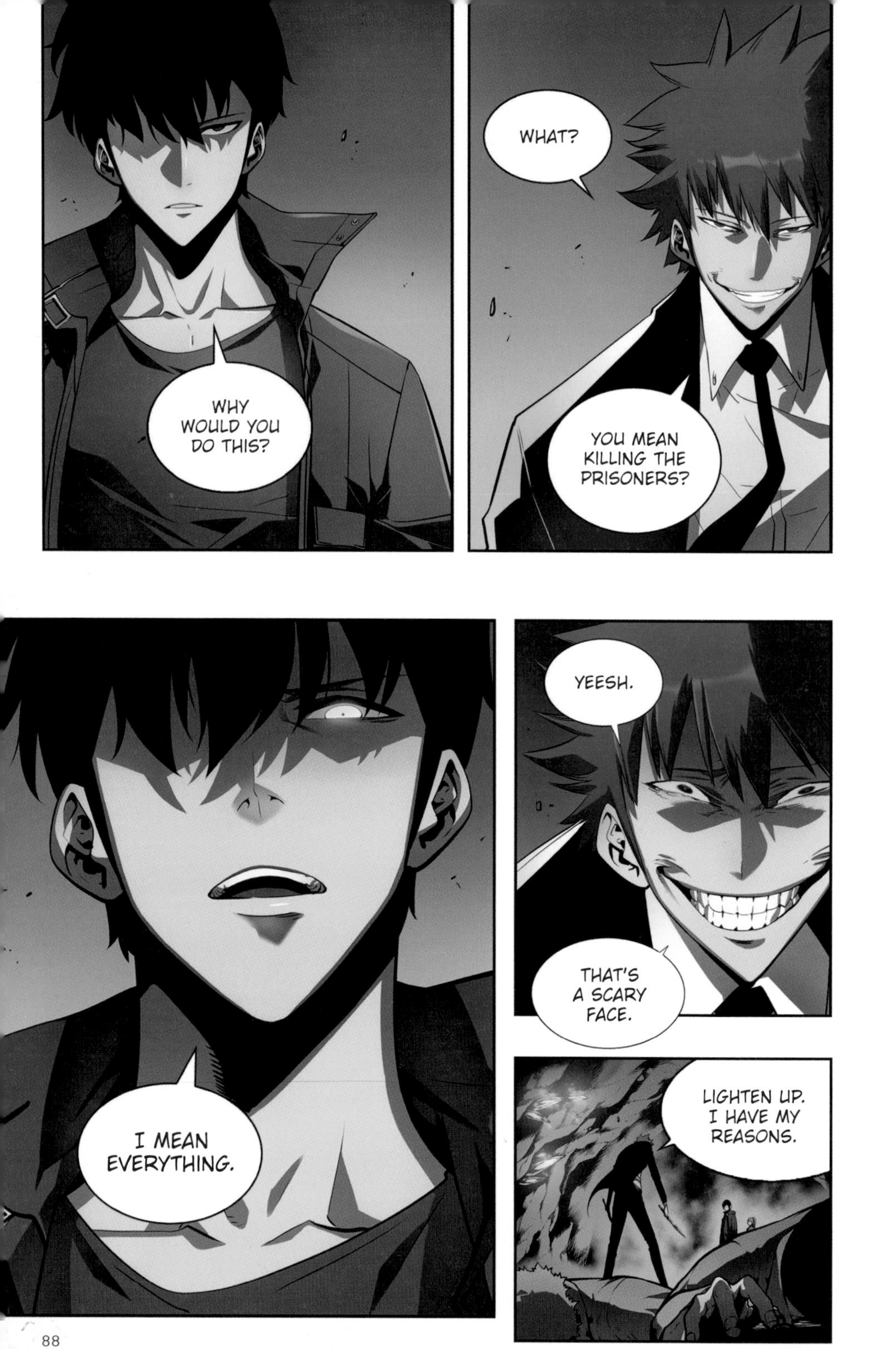
WHY WOULD YOU DO THIS?
WHAT?
YOU MEAN KILLING THE PRISONERS?
I MEAN EVERYTHING.
YEESH.
THAT'S A SCARY FACE.
LIGHTEN UP. I HAVE MY REASONS.

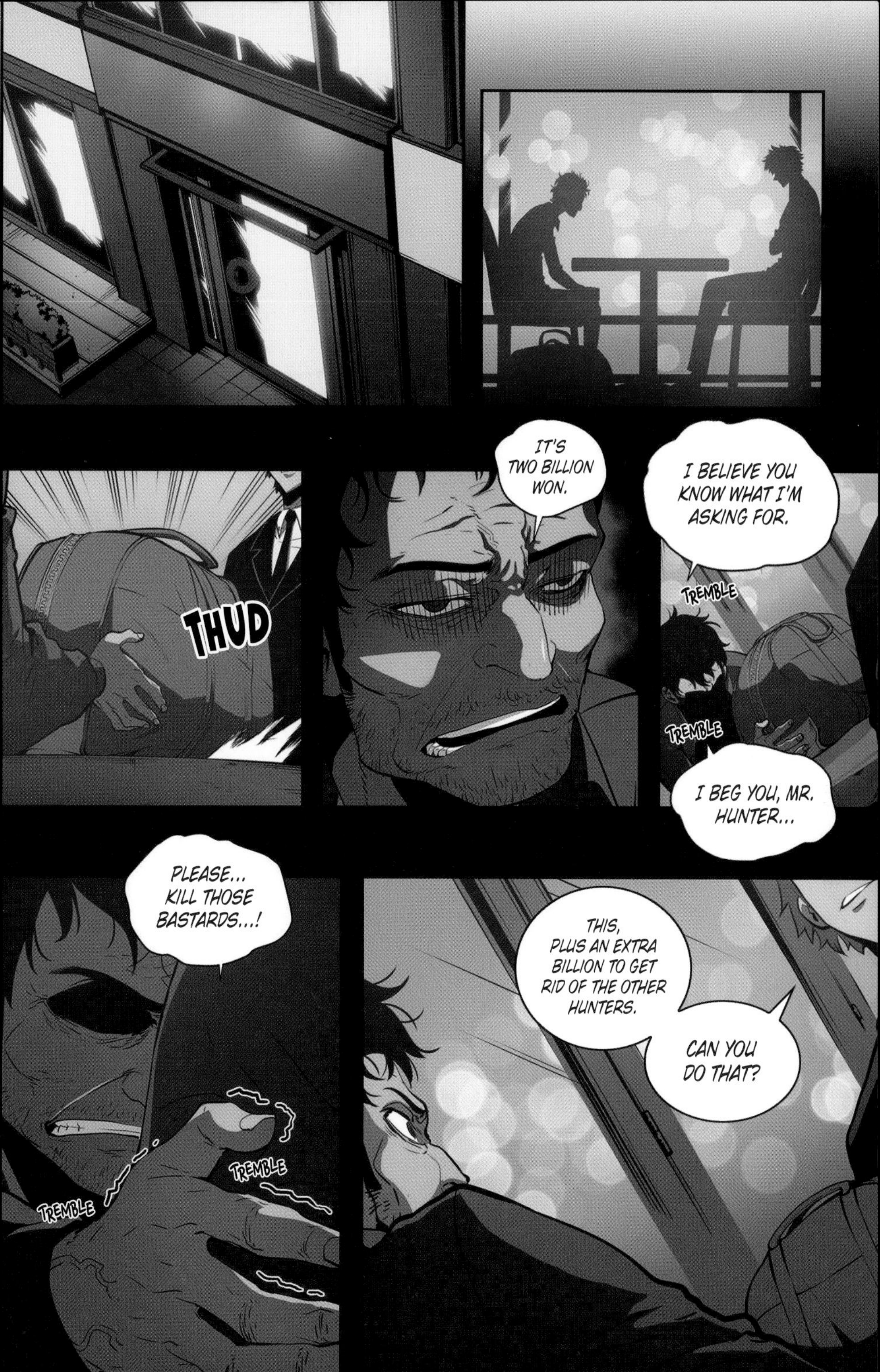
THUD
IT'S TWO BILLION WON.
I BELIEVE YOU KNOW WHAT I'M ASKING FOR.
TREMBLE
TREMBLE
I BEG YOU, MR. HUNTER...
PLEASE... KILL THOSE BASTARDS...!
TREMBLE
TREMBLE
THIS, PLUS AN EXTRA BILLION TO GET RID OF THE OTHER HUNTERS.
CAN YOU DO THAT?

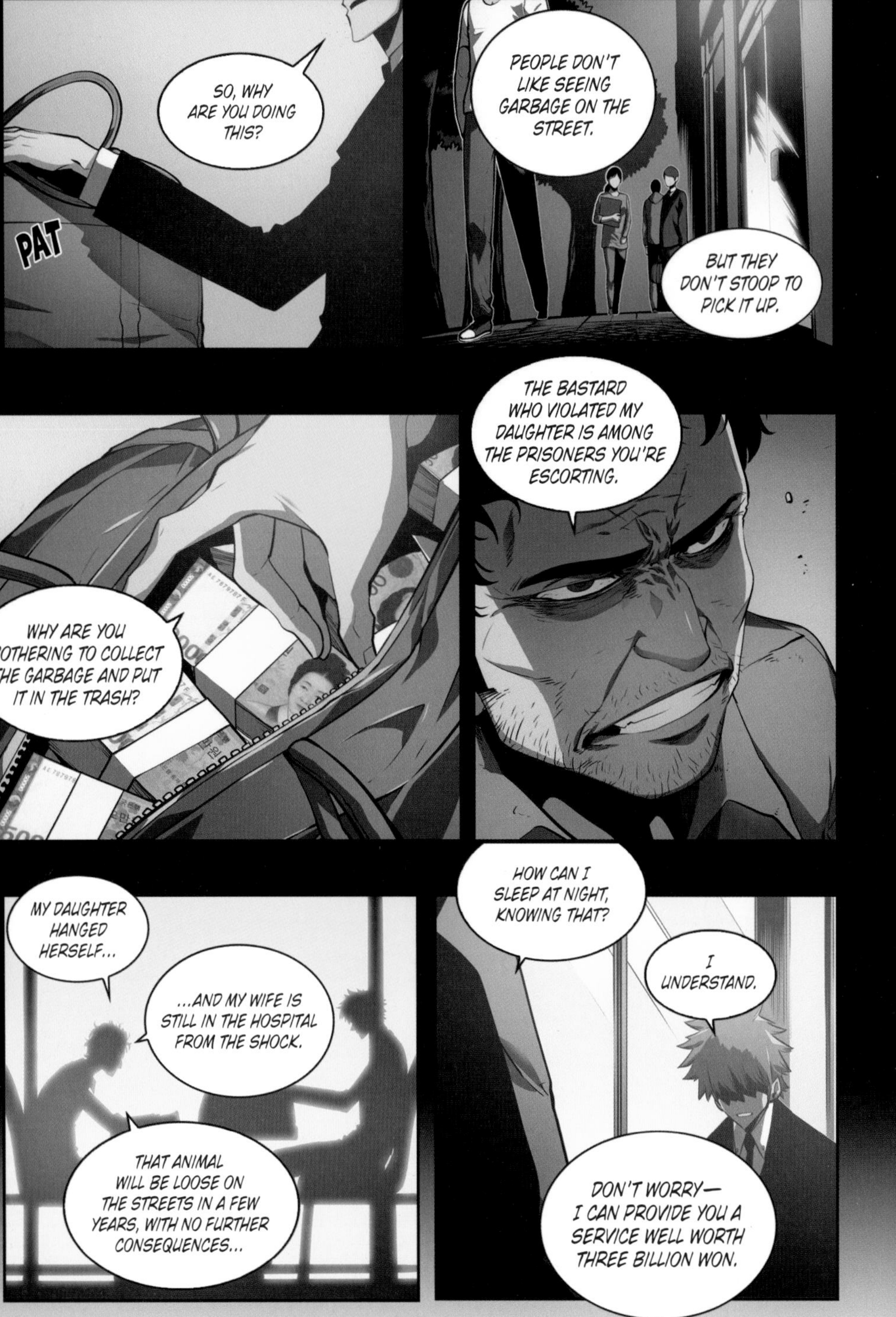
SO, WHY ARE YOU DOING THIS?
PAT
PEOPLE DON'T LIKE SEEING GARBAGE ON THE STREET.
BUT THEY DON'T STOOP TO PICK IT UP.
WHY ARE YOU BOTHERING TO COLLECT THE GARBAGE AND PUT IT IN THE TRASH?
THE BASTARD WHO VIOLATED MY DAUGHTER IS AMONG THE PRISONERS YOU'RE ESCORTING.
MY DAUGHTER HANGED HERSELF...
...AND MY WIFE IS STILL IN THE HOSPITAL FROM THE SHOCK.
THAT ANIMAL WILL BE LOOSE ON THE STREETS IN A FEW YEARS, WITH NO FURTHER CONSEQUENCES...
HOW CAN I SLEEP AT NIGHT, KNOWING THAT?
I UNDERSTAND.
DON'T WORRY— I CAN PROVIDE YOU A SERVICE WELL WORTH THREE BILLION WON.

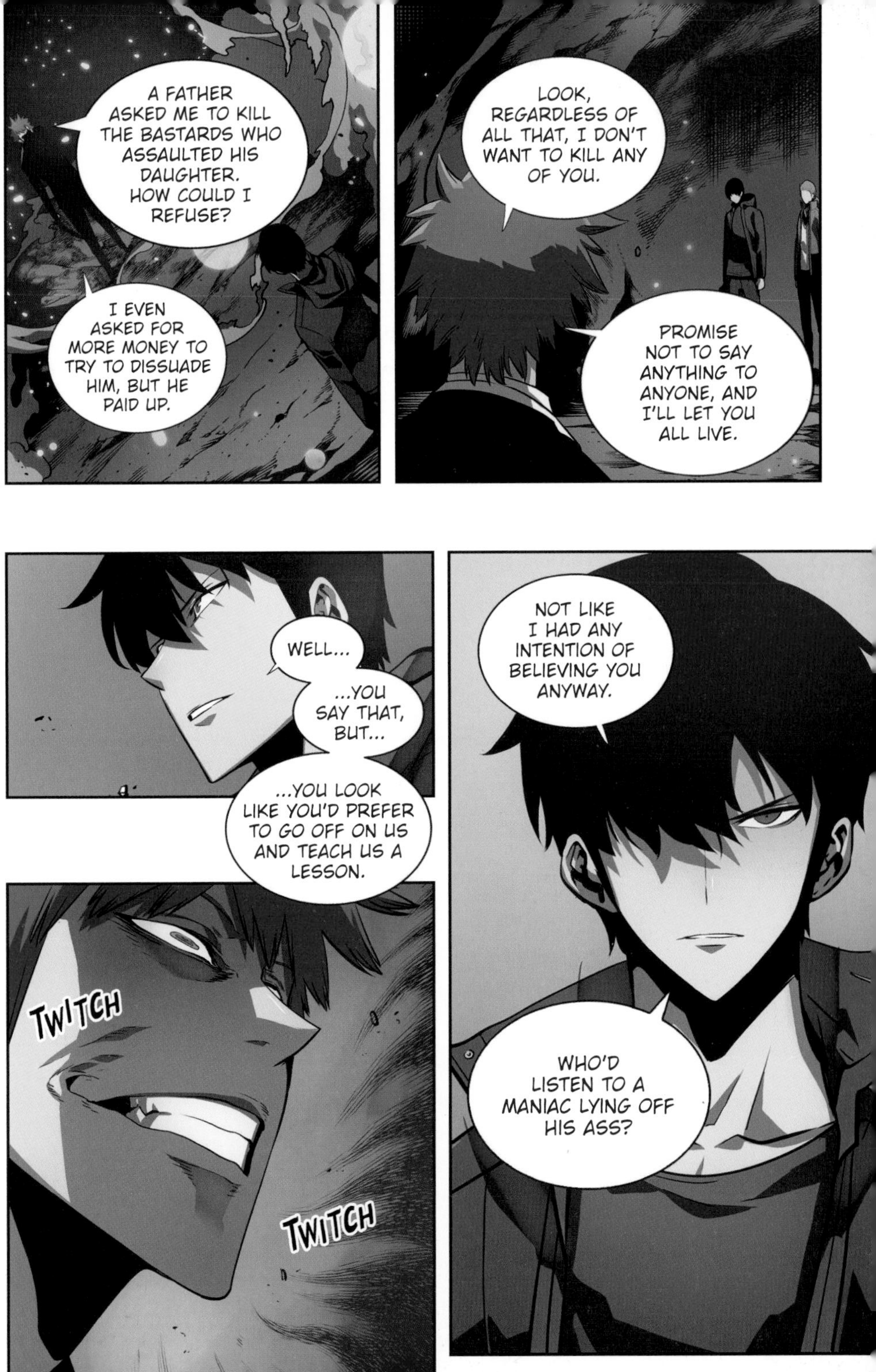
A FATHER ASKED ME TO KILL THE BASTARDS WHO ASSAULTED HIS DAUGHTER. HOW COULD I REFUSE?
I EVEN ASKED FOR MORE MONEY TO TRY TO DISSUADE HIM, BUT HE PAID UP.
LOOK, REGARDLESS OF ALL THAT, I DON'T WANT TO KILL ANY OF YOU.
PROMISE NOT TO SAY ANYTHING TO ANYONE, AND I'LL LET YOU ALL LIVE.
WELL...
...YOU SAY THAT, BUT...
...YOU LOOK LIKE YOU'D PREFER TO GO OFF ON US AND TEACH US A LESSON.
TWITCH
TWITCH
NOT LIKE I HAD ANY INTENTION OF BELIEVING YOU ANYWAY.
WHO'D LISTEN TO A MANIAC LYING OFF HIS ASS?

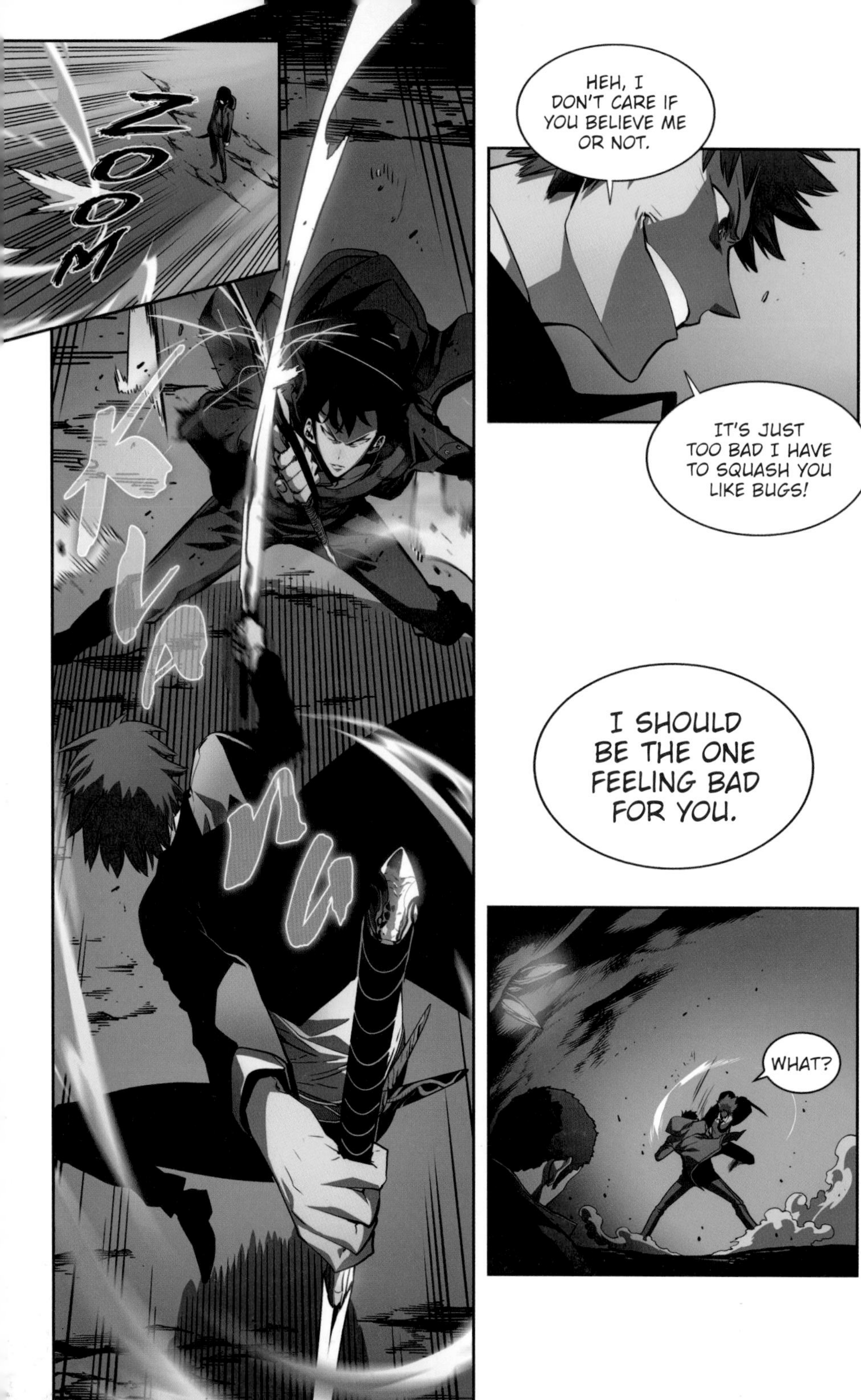
ZOOM
HEH, I DON'T CARE IF YOU BELIEVE ME OR NOT.
IT'S JUST TOO BAD I HAVE TO SQUASH YOU LIKE BUGS!
I SHOULD BE THE ONE FEELING BAD FOR YOU.
WHAT?

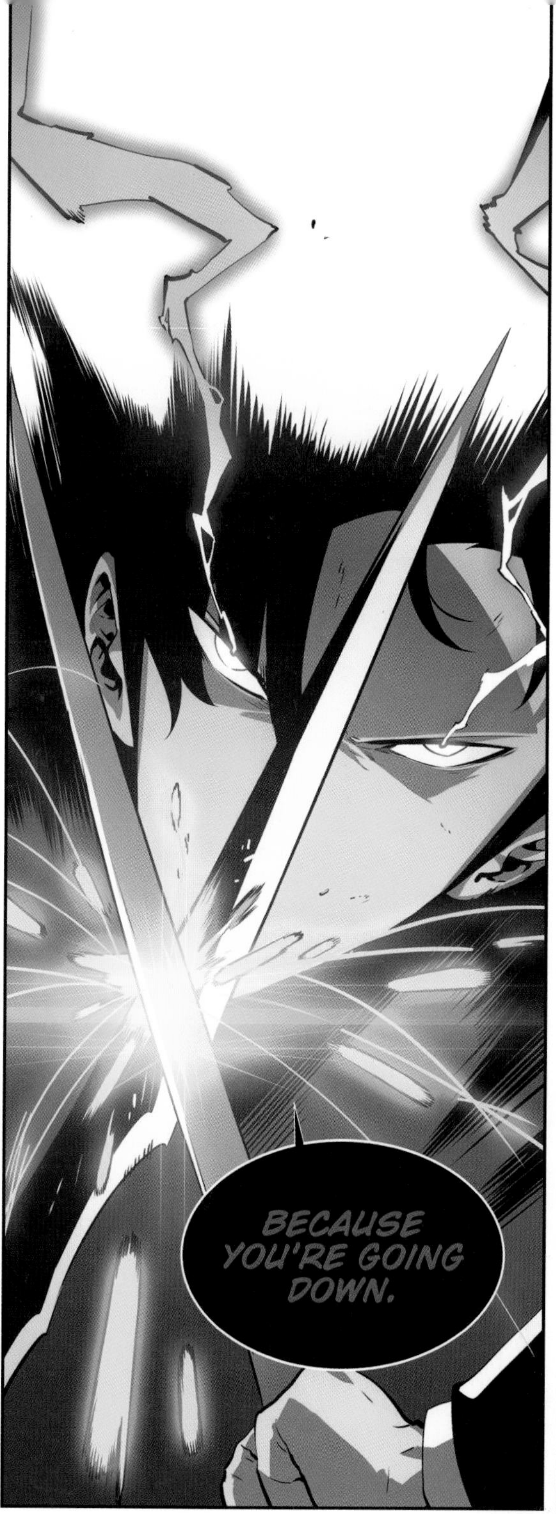
BECAUSE YOU'RE GOING DOWN.

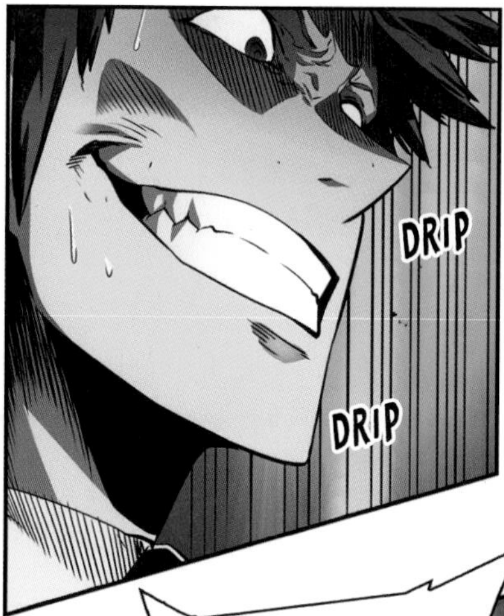
DRIP
DRIP

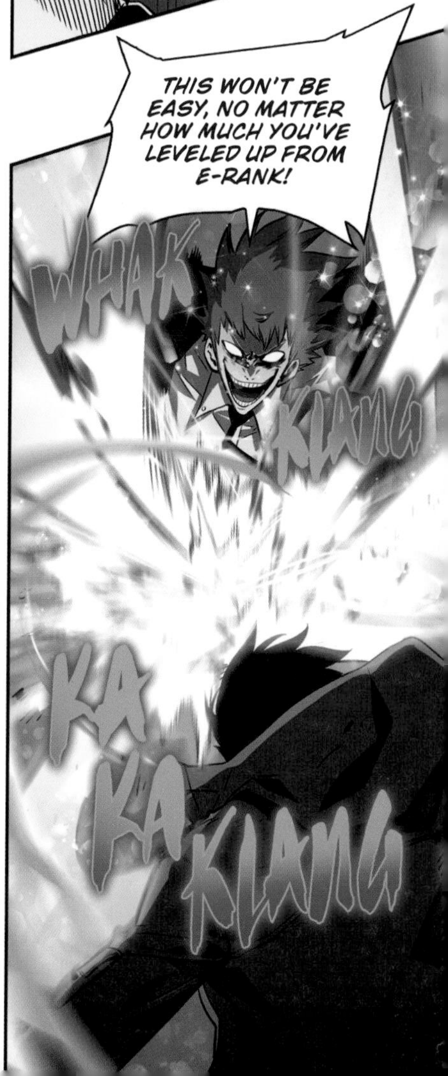
THIS WON'T BE EASY, NO MATTER HOW MUCH YOU'VE LEVELED UP FROM E-RANK!
WHAK
KLANG
KA
KA
KLANG

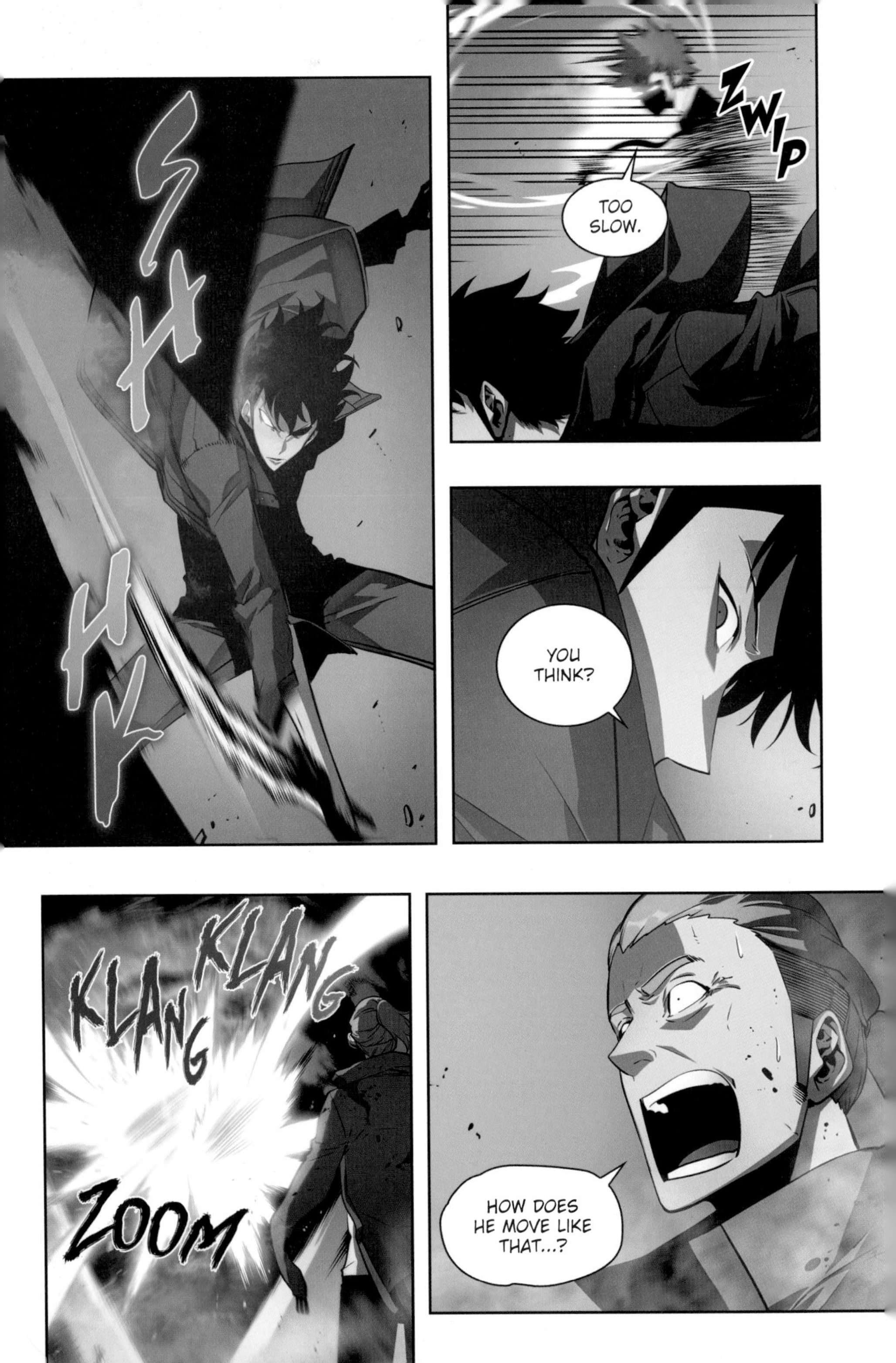
SHHK
ZWIP
TOO SLOW.
YOU THINK?
KLANG KLANG
ZOOM
HOW DOES HE MOVE LIKE THAT...?

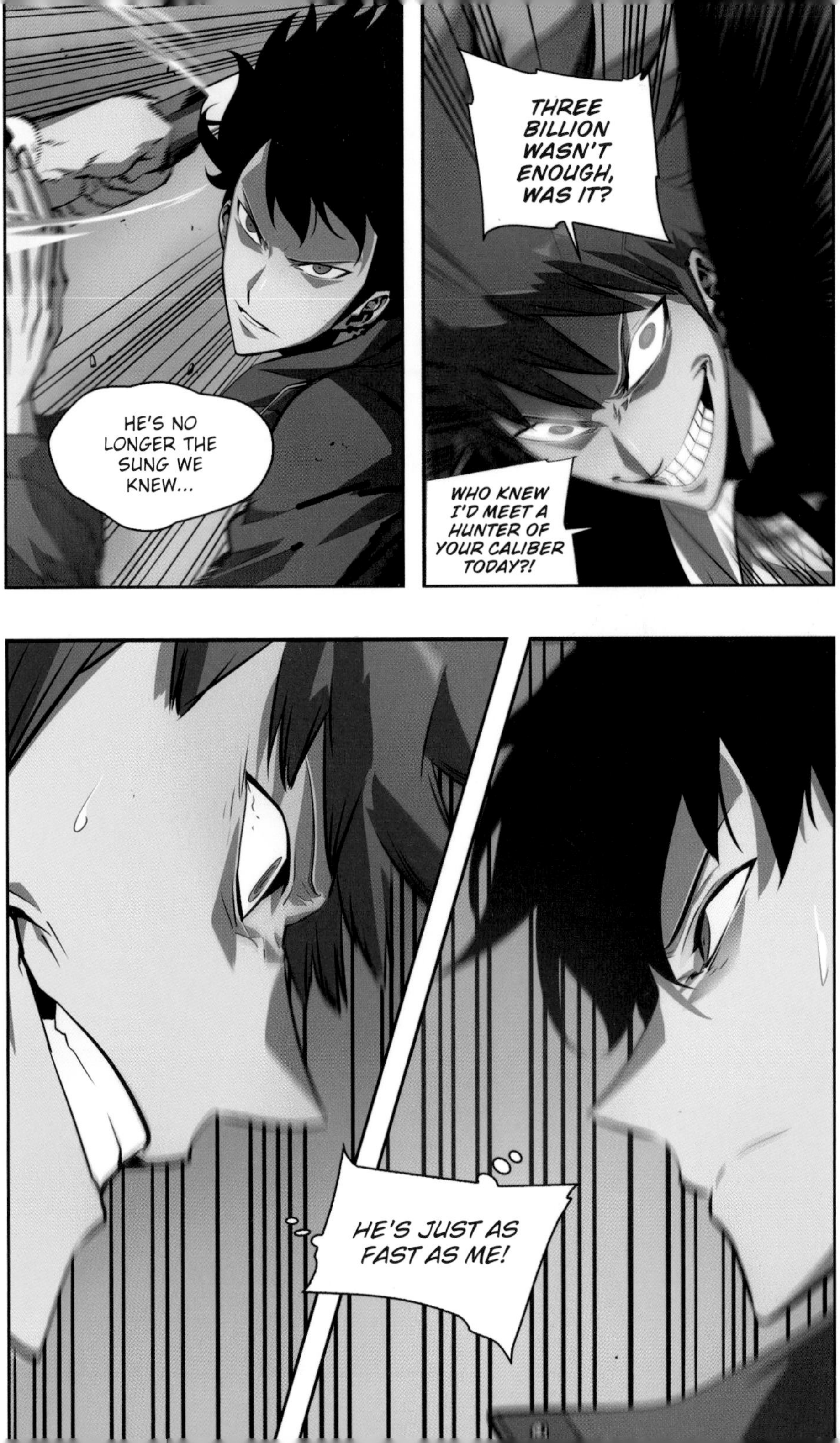
HE'S NO LONGER THE SUNG WE KNEW...
THREE BILLION WASN'T ENOUGH, WAS IT?
WHO KNEW I'D MEET A HUNTER OF YOUR CALIBER TODAY?!
HE'S JUST AS FAST AS ME!

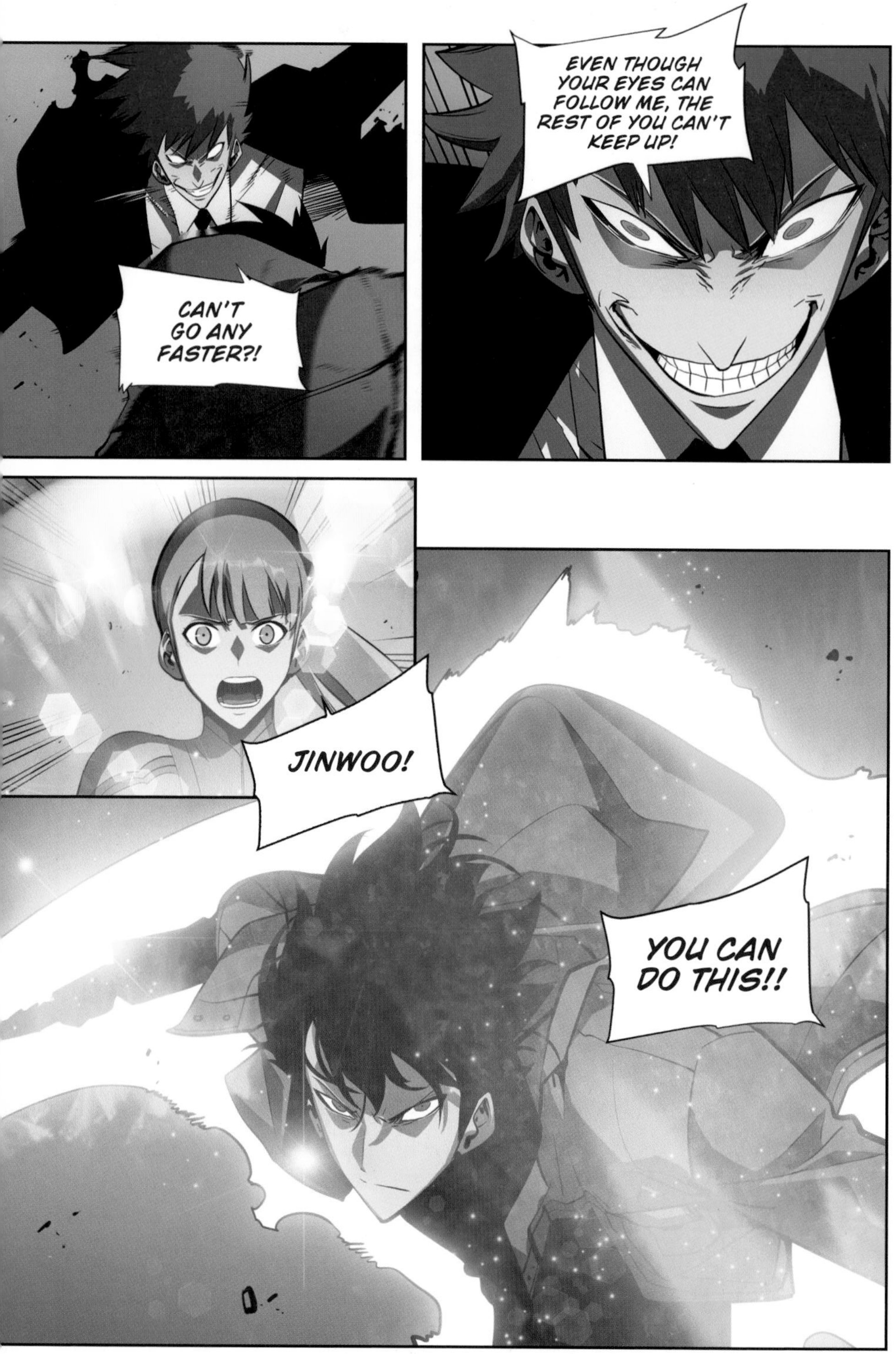
CAN'T GO ANY FASTER?!
EVEN THOUGH YOUR EYES CAN FOLLOW ME, THE REST OF YOU CAN'T KEEP UP!
JINWOO!
YOU CAN DO THIS!!

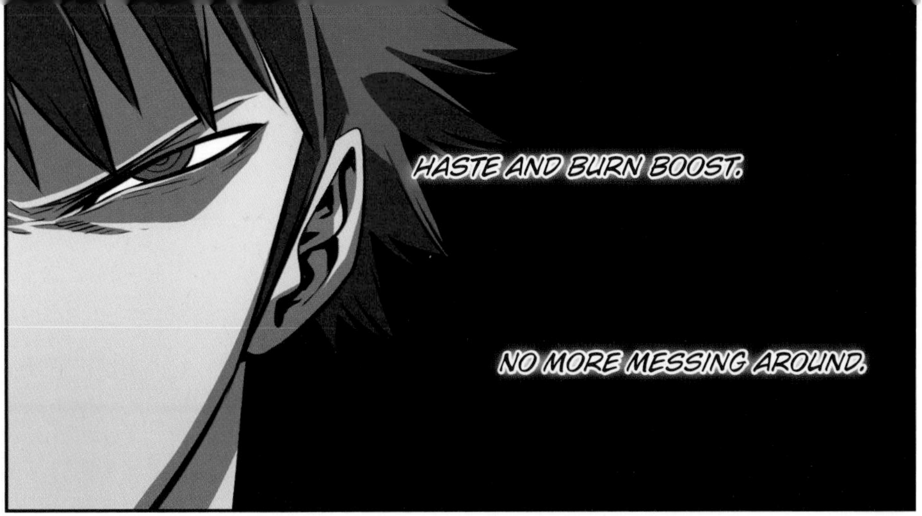
HASTE AND BURN BOOST.
NO MORE MESSING AROUND.
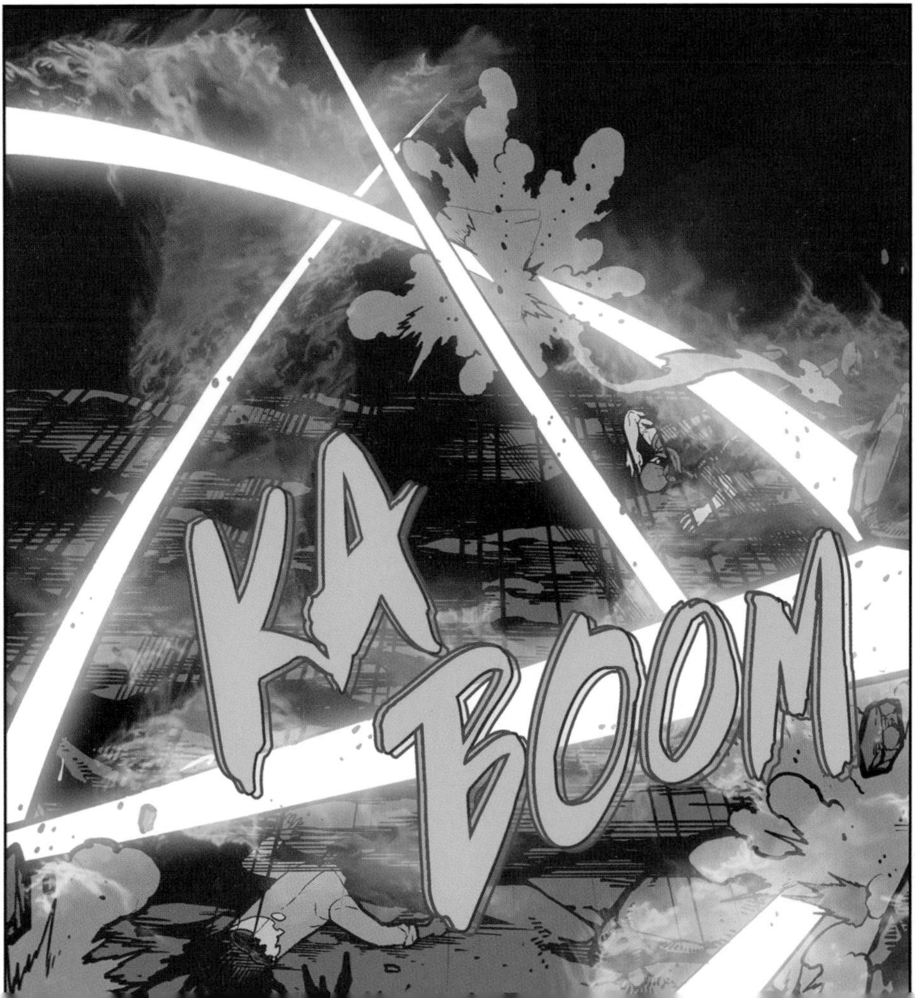
KA
BOOM

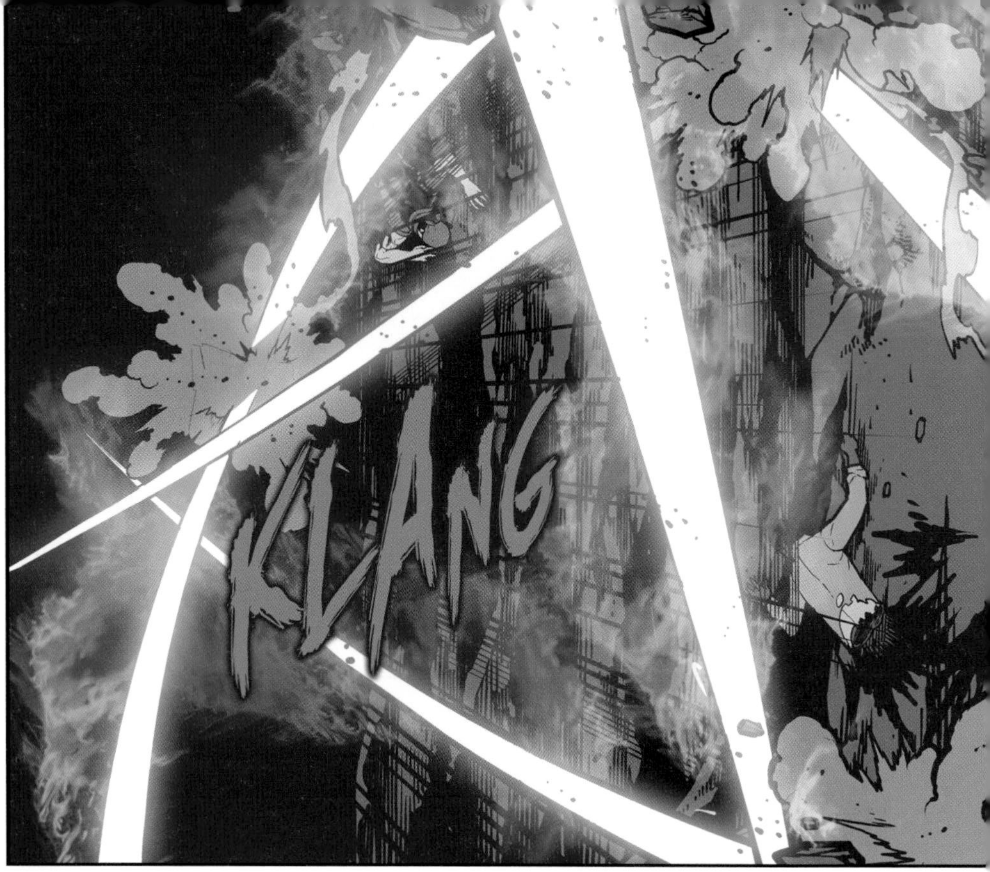
KLANG
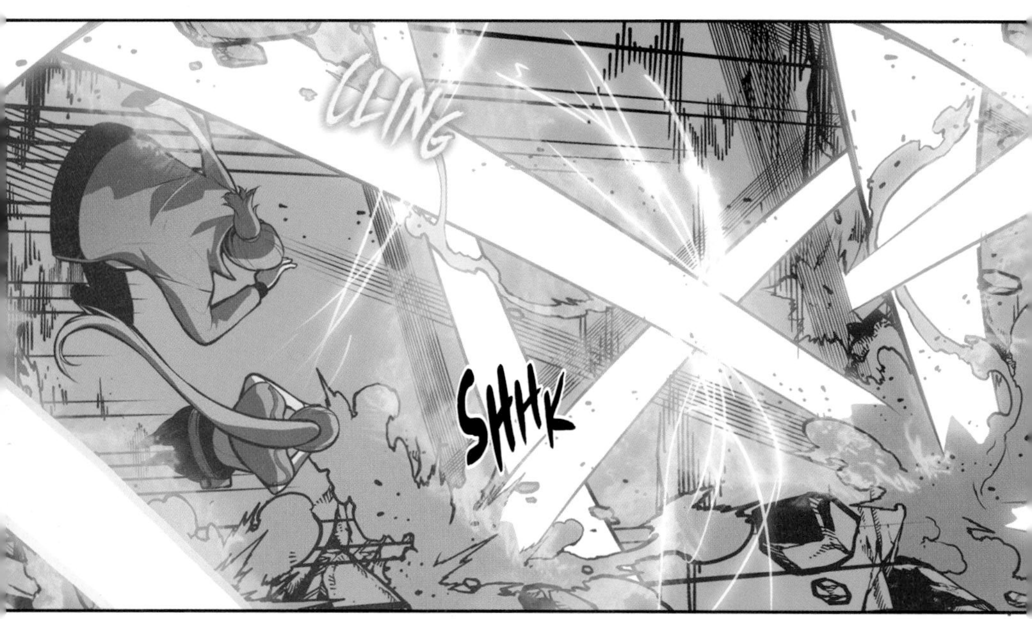
CLING
SHHK

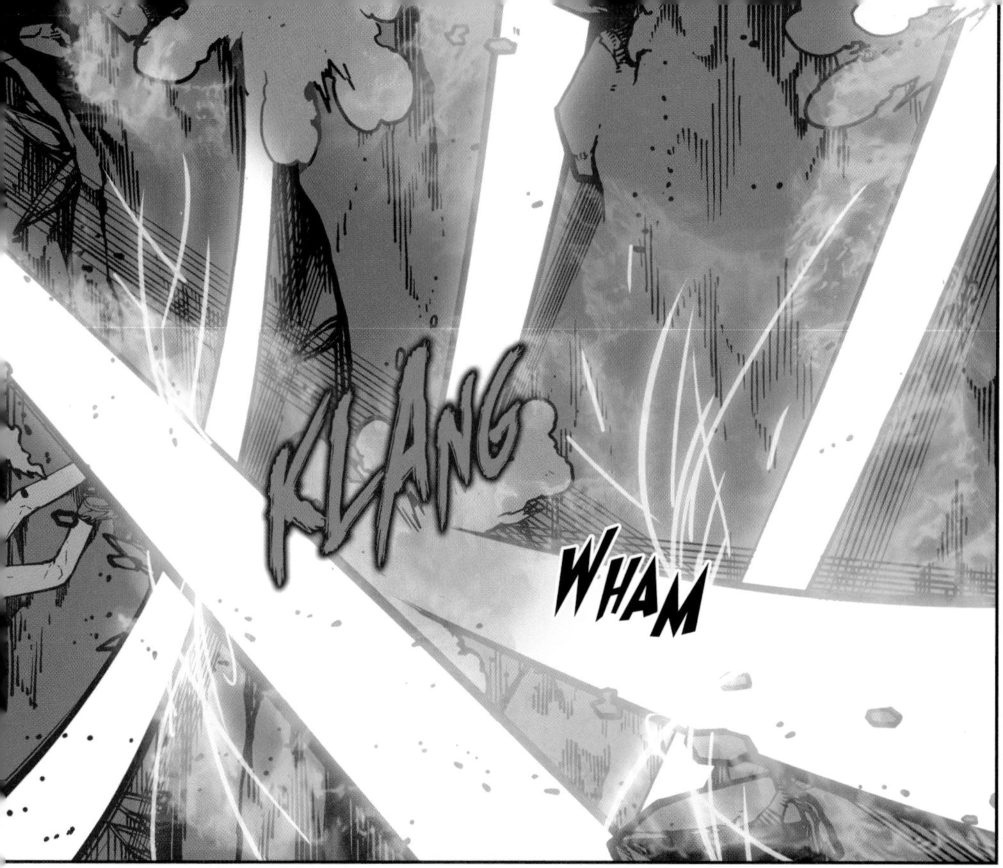
KLANG
WHAM
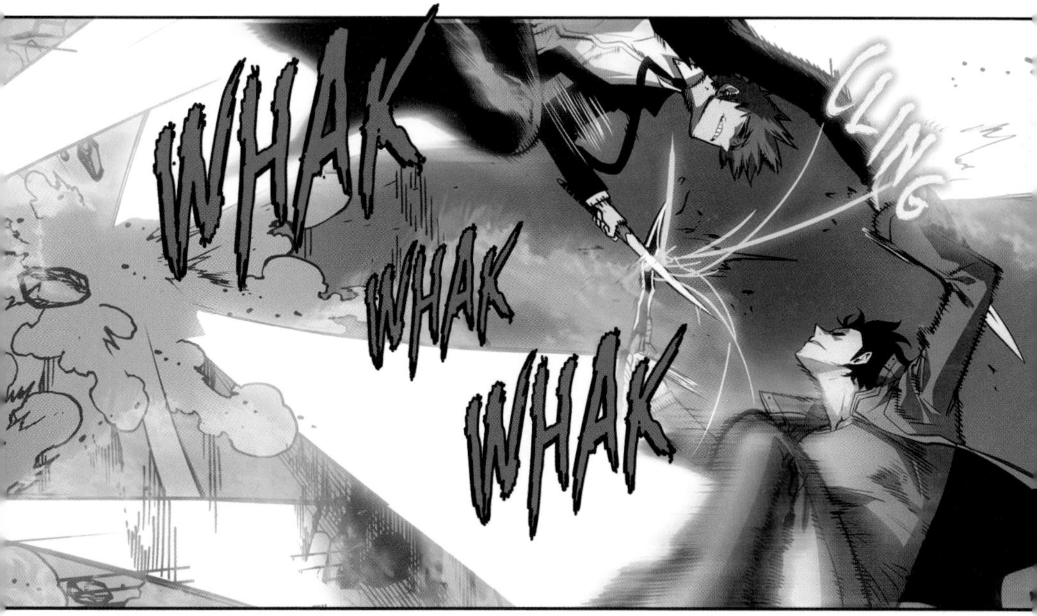
WHAK
WHAK
WHAK
CLING

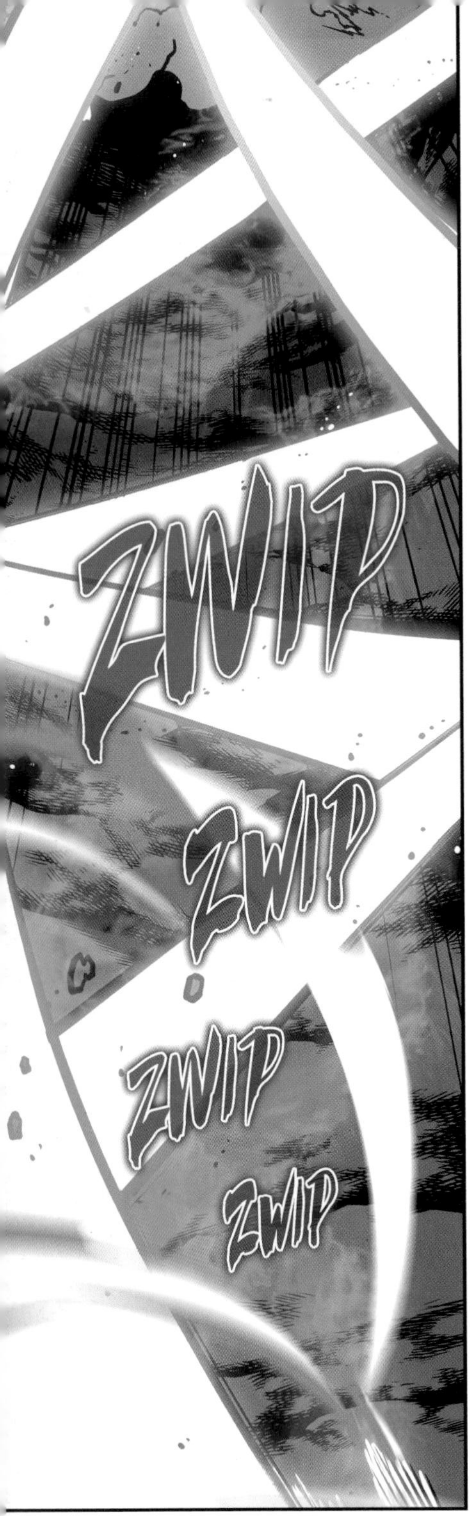
ZWIP
ZWIP
ZWIP
ZWIP

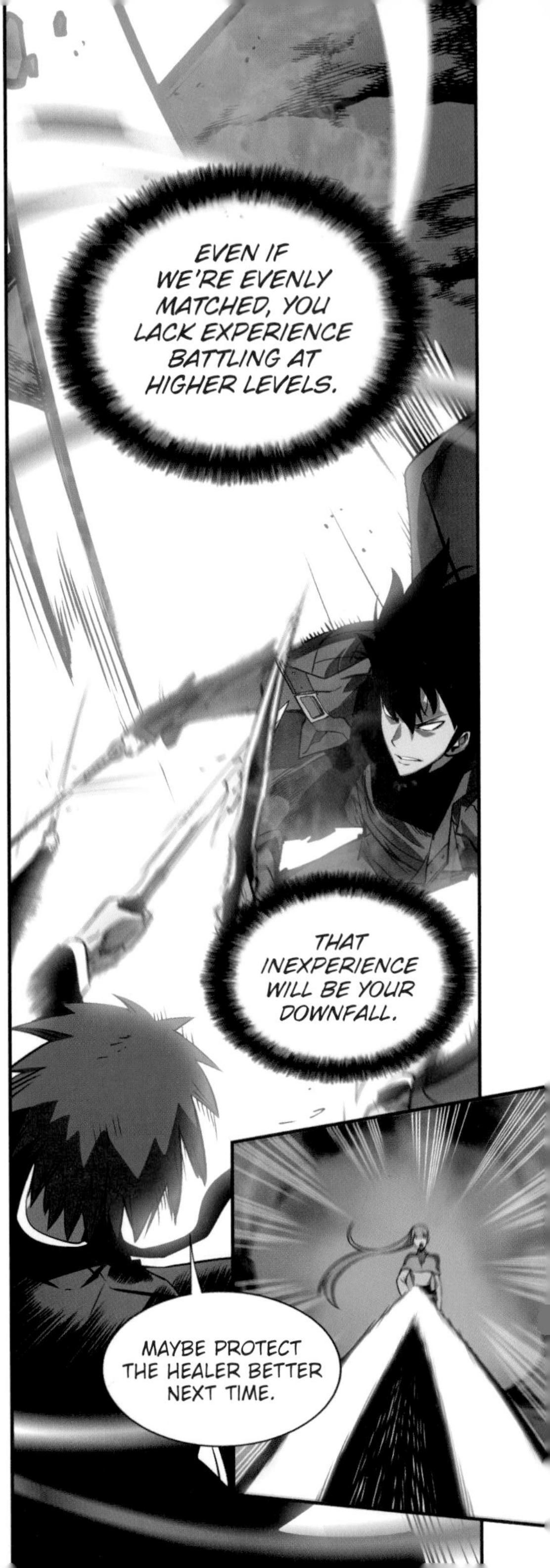
EVEN IF WE'RE EVENLY MATCHED, YOU LACK EXPERIENCE BATTLING AT HIGHER LEVELS.
THAT INEXPERIENCE WILL BE YOUR DOWNFALL.
MAYBE PROTECT THE HEALER BETTER NEXT TIME.

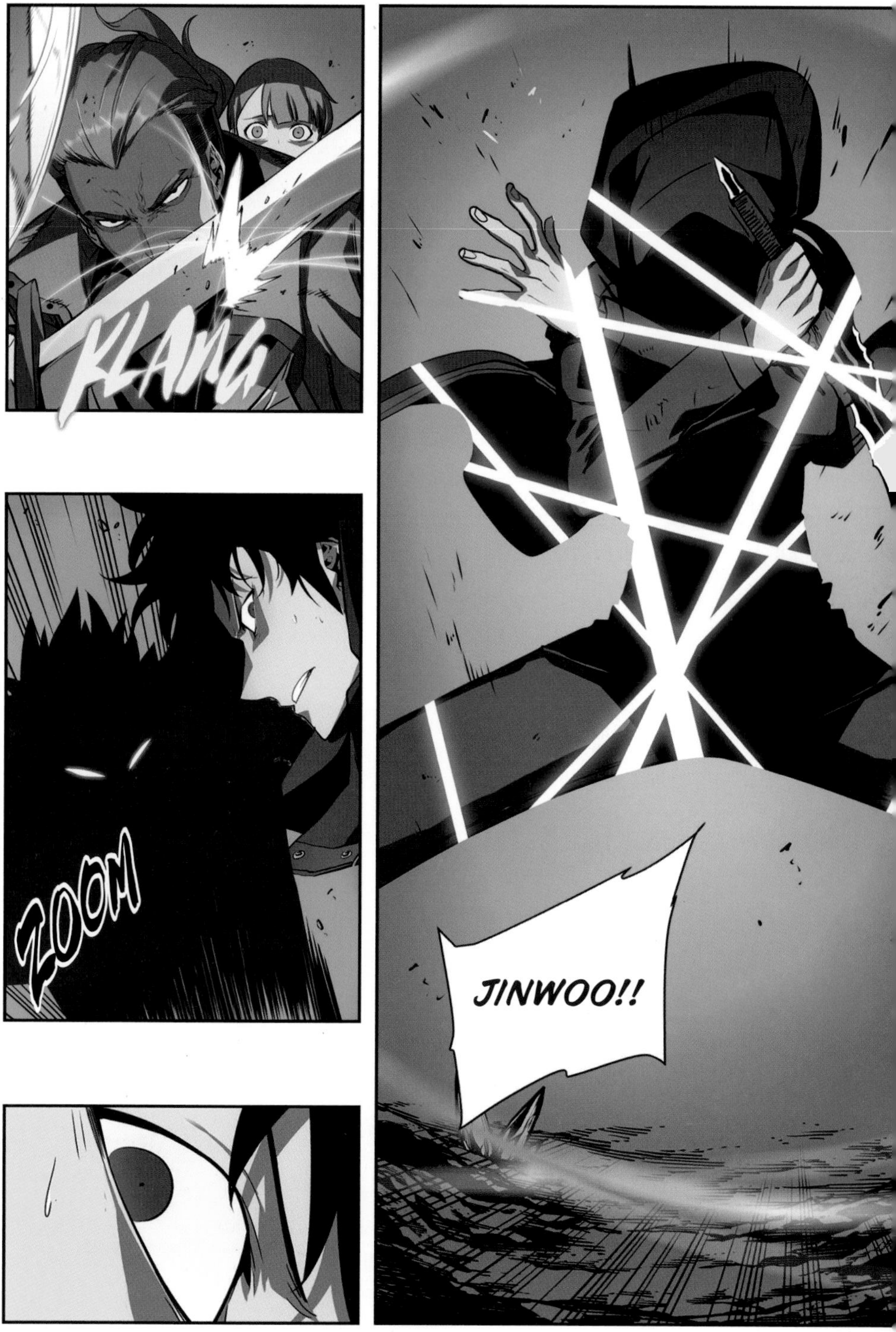
KLANG
ZOOM
JINWOO!!

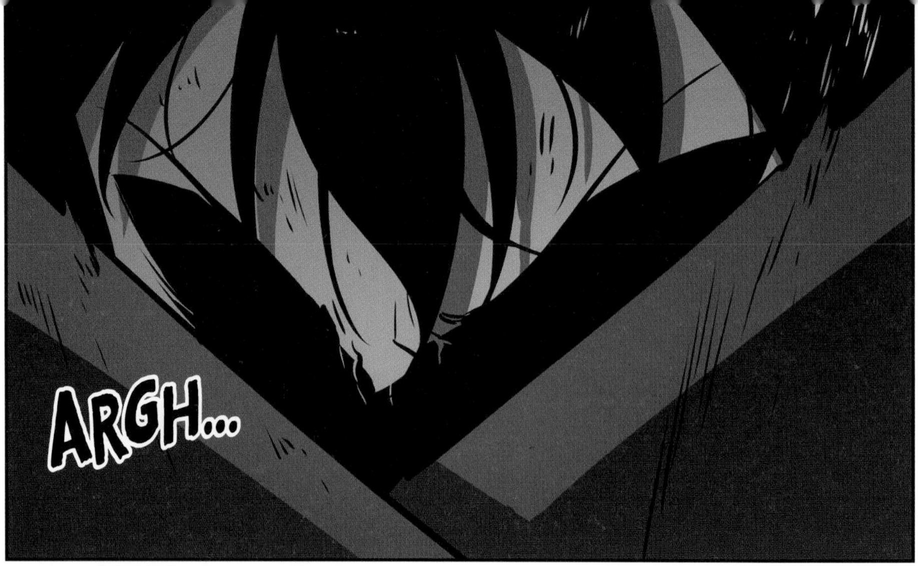
ARGH...

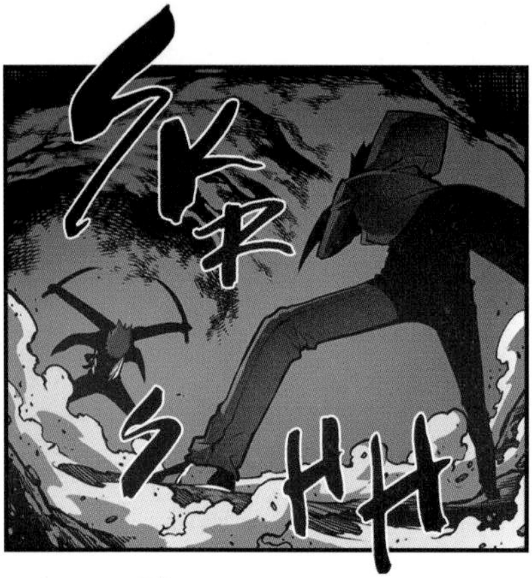
SKRSHH

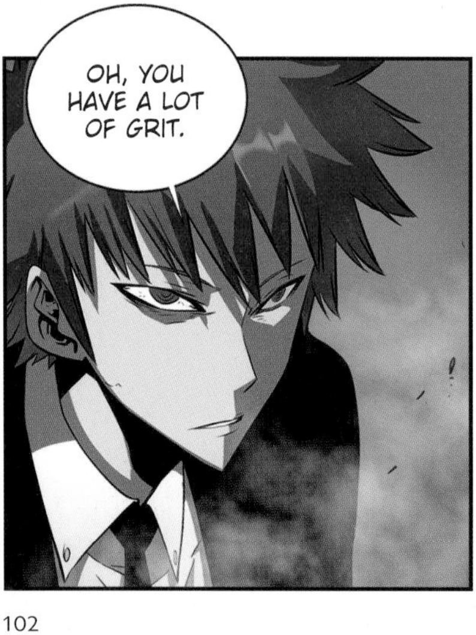
OH, YOU HAVE A LOT OF GRIT.

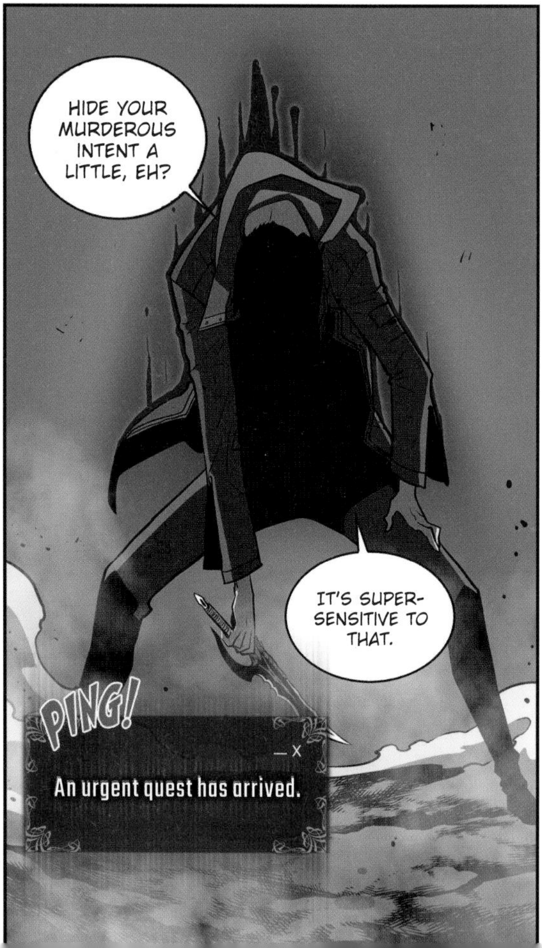
HIDE YOUR MURDEROUS INTENT A LITTLE, EH?
IT'S SUPER-SENSITIVE TO THAT.
PING!
— X
An urgent quest has arrived.

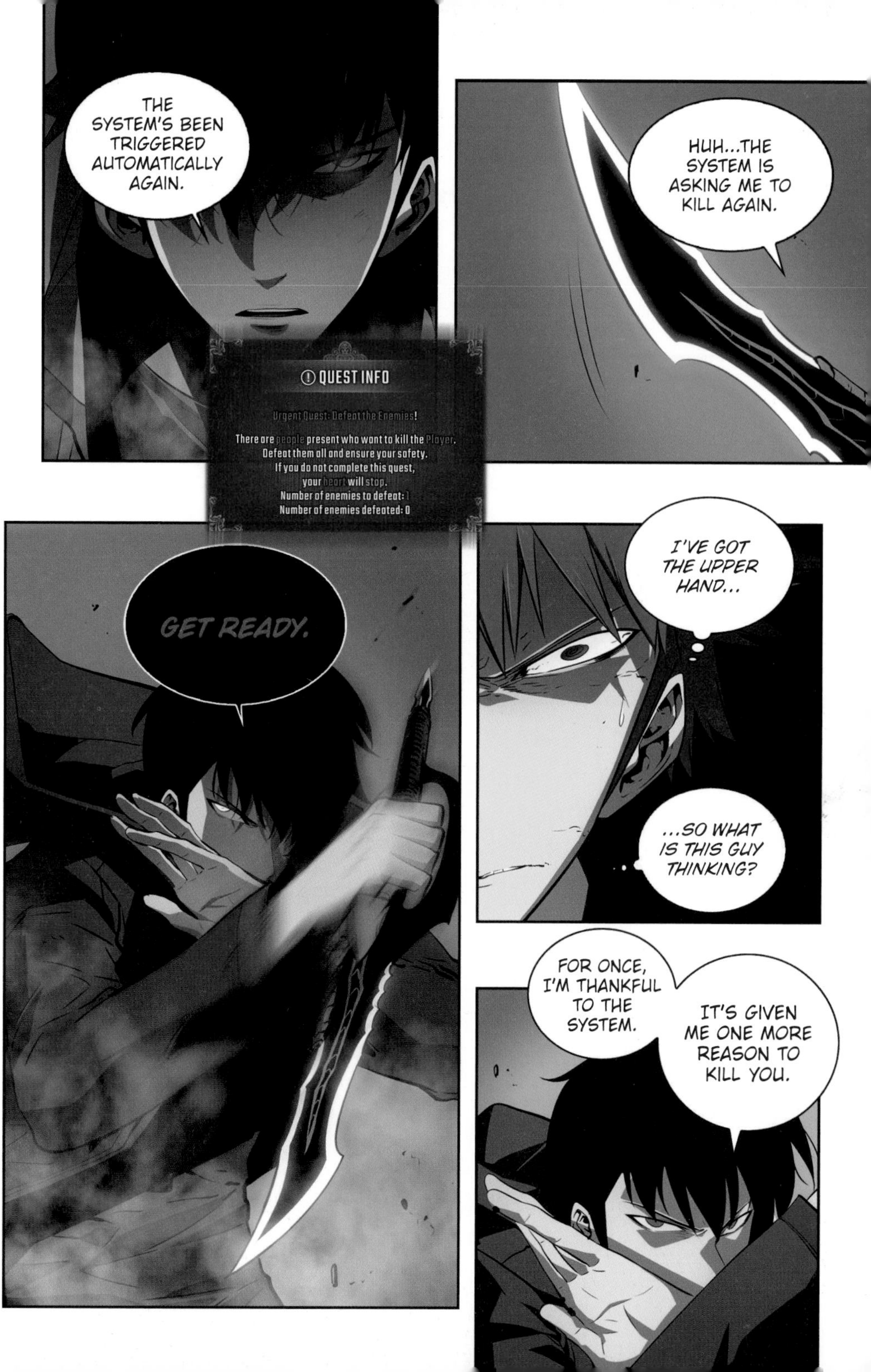
THE SYSTEM'S BEEN TRIGGERED AUTOMATICALLY AGAIN.
HUH...THE SYSTEM IS ASKING ME TO KILL AGAIN.
QUEST INFO
Urgent Quest: Defeat the Enemies!
There are people present who want to kill the Player. Defeat them all and ensure your safety. If you do not complete this quest, your heart will stop.
Number of enemies to defeat: 1
Number of enemies defeated: 0
GET READY.
I'VE GOT THE UPPER HAND...
...SO WHAT IS THIS GUY THINKING?
FOR ONCE, I'M THANKFUL TO THE SYSTEM.
IT'S GIVEN ME ONE MORE REASON TO KILL YOU.

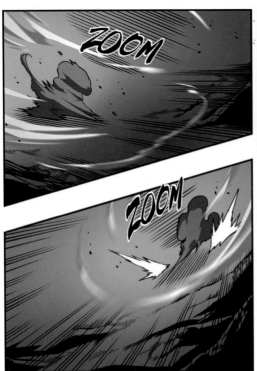

ZOOM

KLANG

ZOOM

A CLASS SPECIALIZING IN DAGGERS AND AGILITY!

KLANG

KLINK

AND AN ASSASSIN EXPERT IN DEALING CLOSE-RANGE DAMAGE!

KLINK

A PERFECT MATCH, WOULDN'T YOU SAY?

KLANG

WELL, I'M DEFINITELY LEARNING A LOT.

INCLUDING THE FACT THAT YOU TALK TOO MUCH.

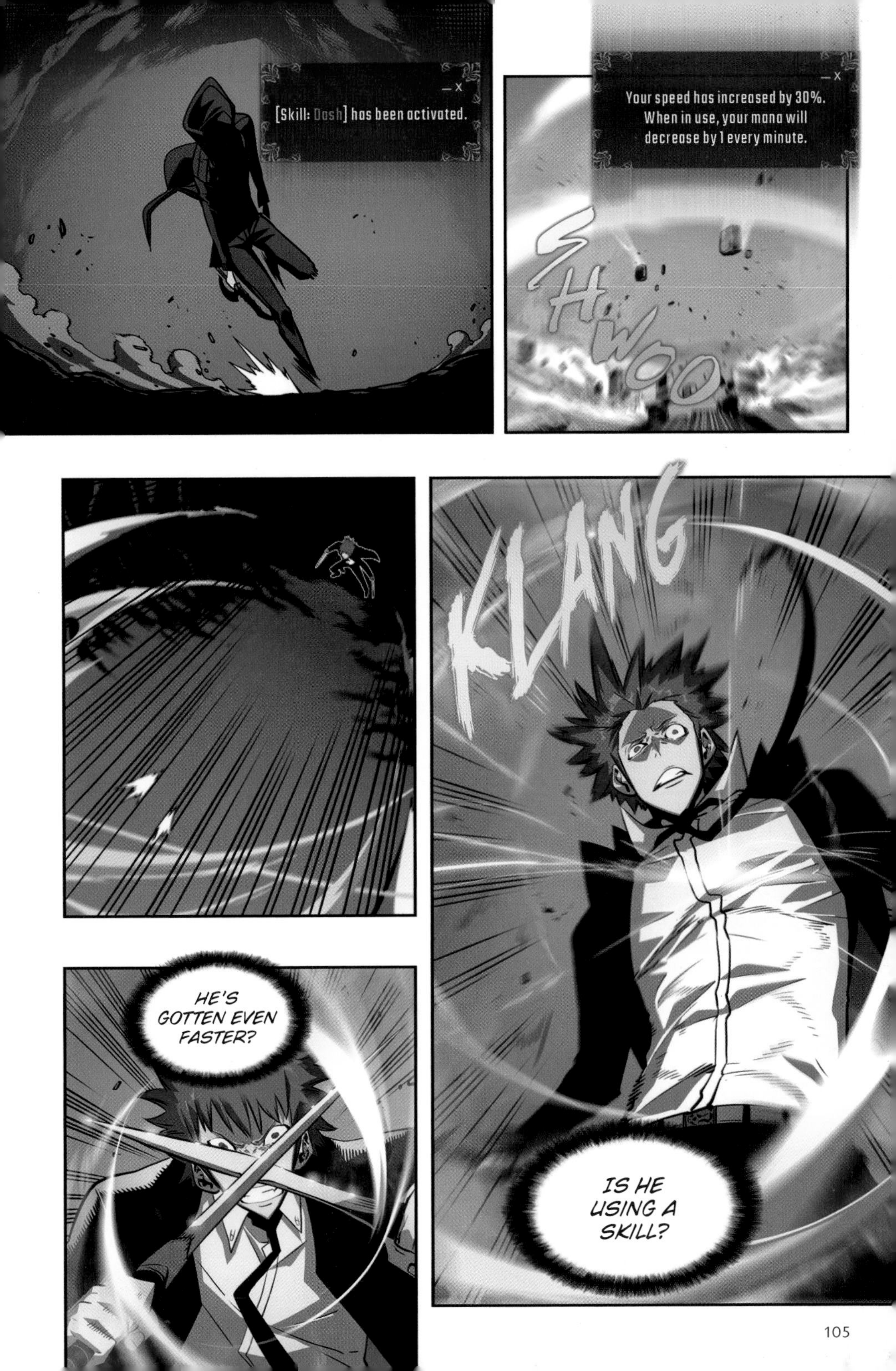
[Skill: Dash] has been activated.
Your speed has increased by 30%. When in use, your mana will decrease by 1 every minute.
SHWOOO
HE'S GOTTEN EVEN FASTER?
KLANG
IS HE USING A SKILL?

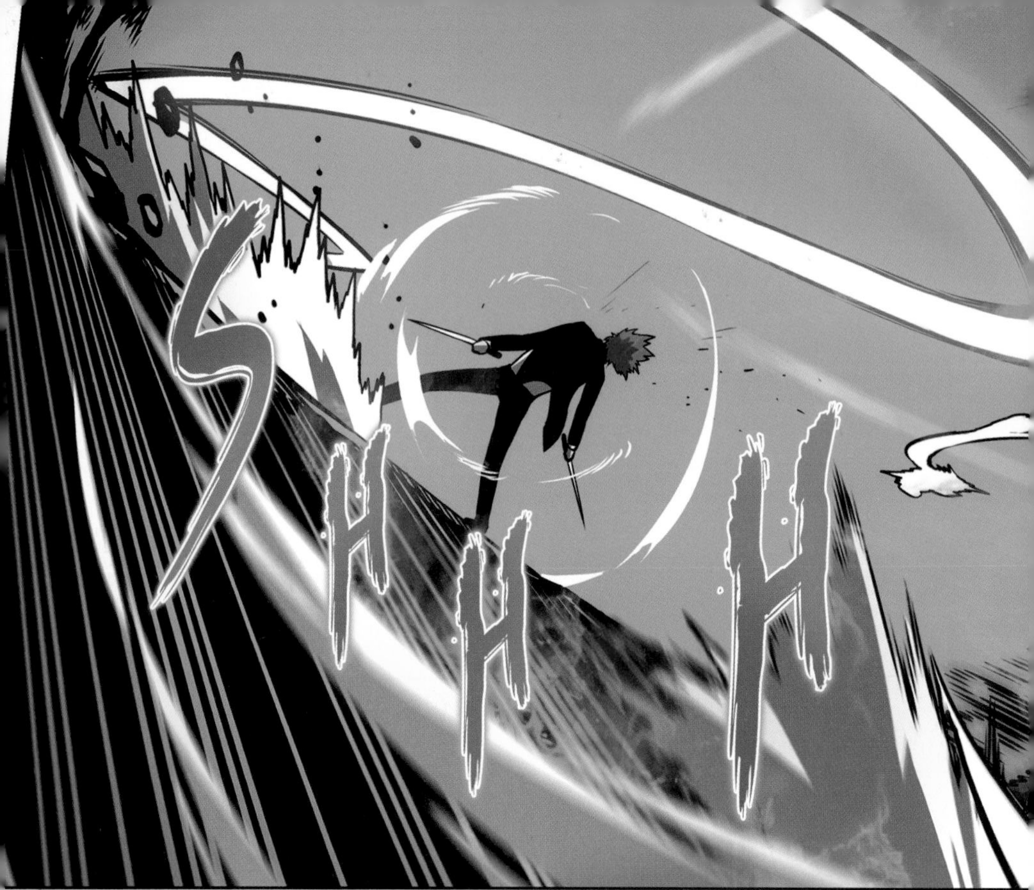
SHHH

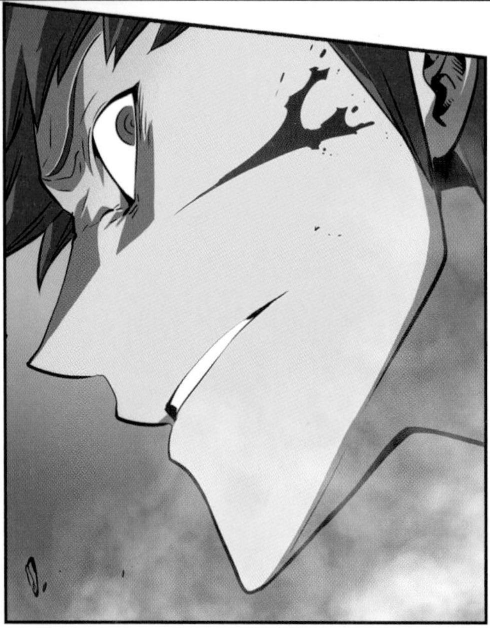

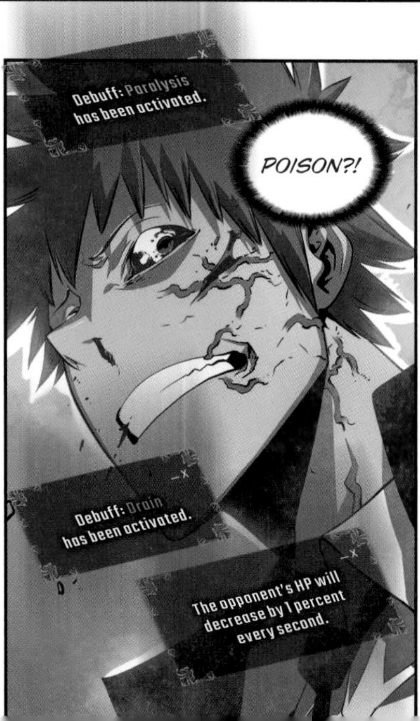
Debuff: Paralysis has been activated.
POISON?!
Debuff: Drain has been activated.
The opponent's HP will decrease by 1 percent every second.

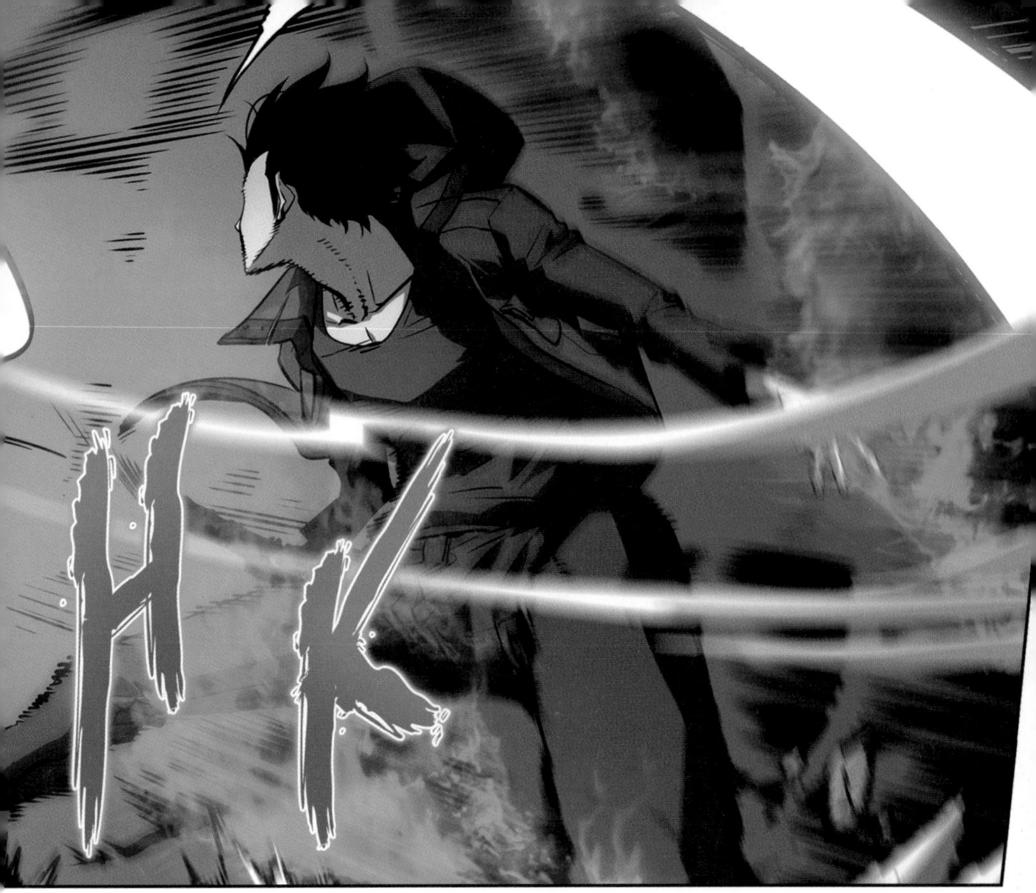
HK
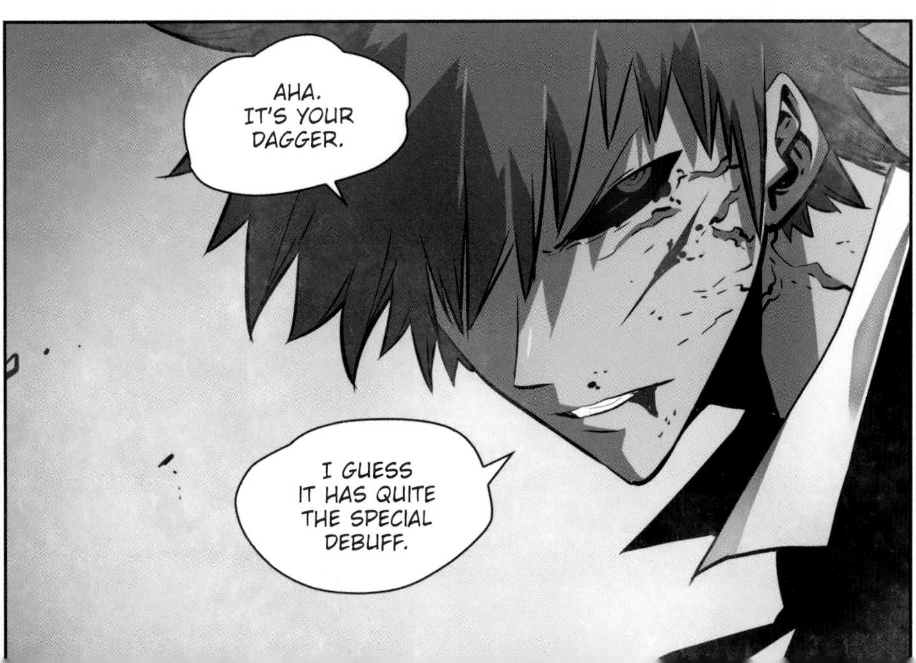
AHA. IT'S YOUR DAGGER.
I GUESS IT HAS QUITE THE SPECIAL DEBUFF.

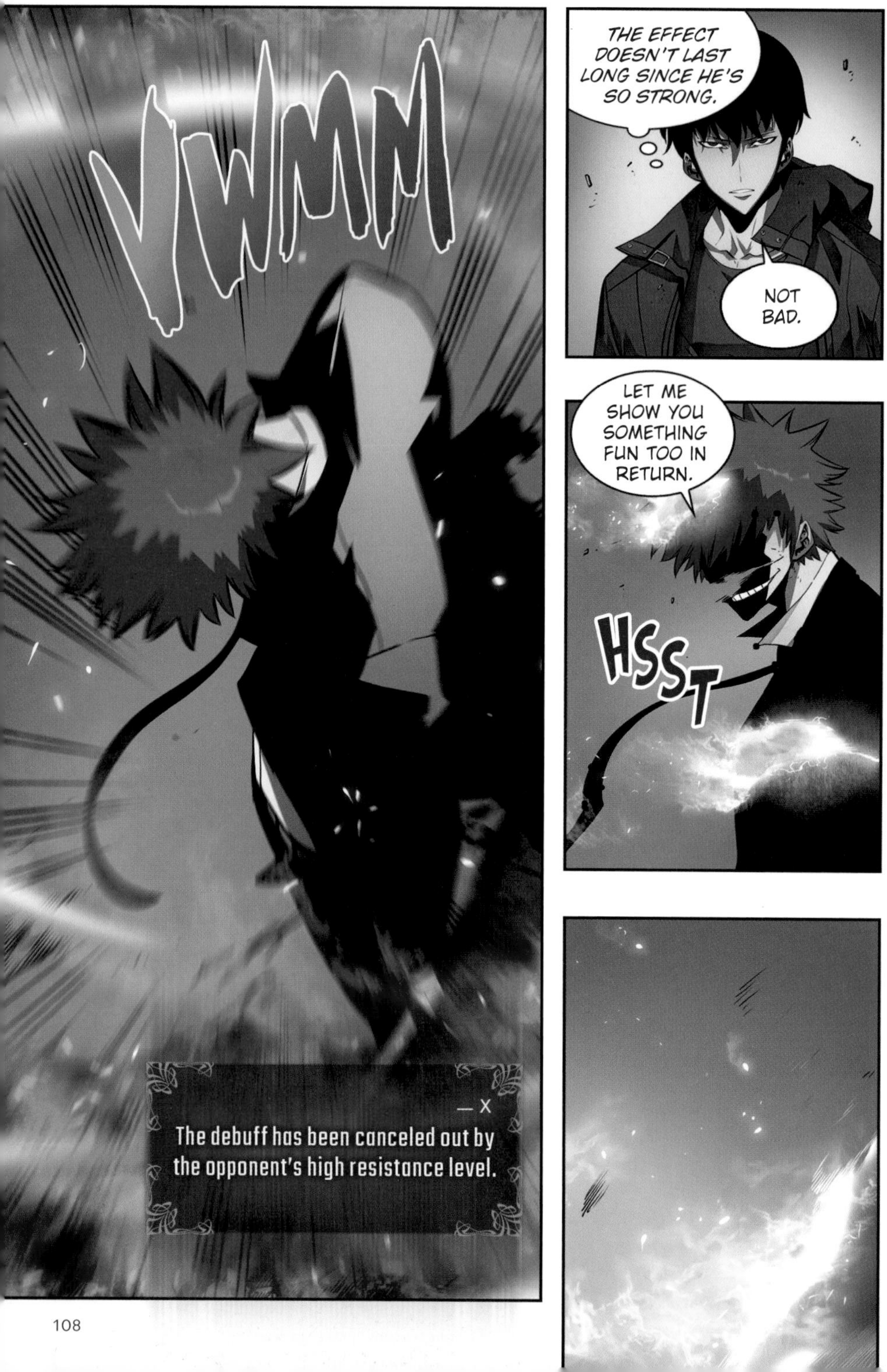
VWMM
— X
The debuff has been canceled out by the opponent's high resistance level.
THE EFFECT DOESN'T LAST LONG SINCE HE'S SO STRONG.
NOT BAD.
LET ME SHOW YOU SOMETHING FUN TOO IN RETURN.
HSST

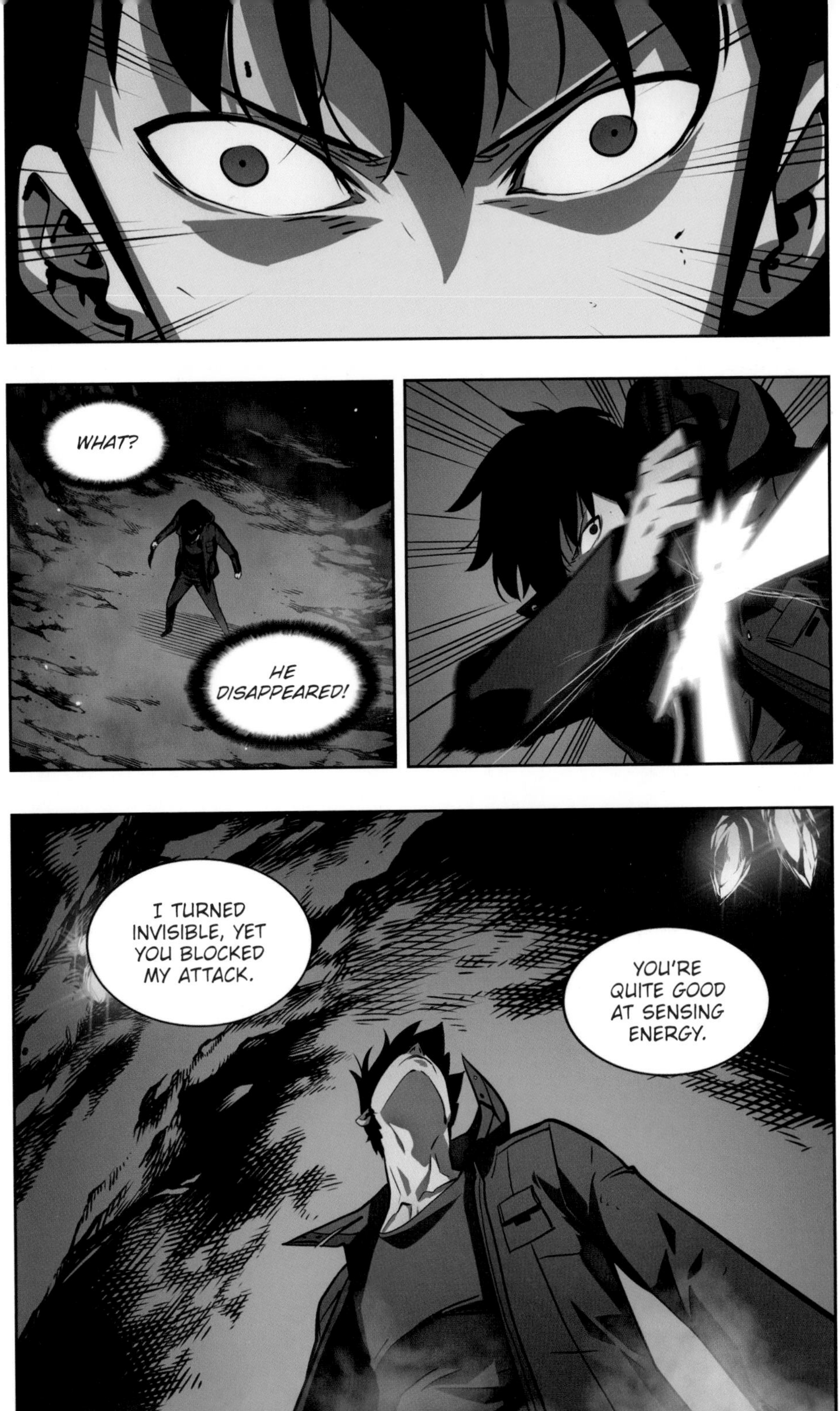
WHAT?
HE DISAPPEARED!
I TURNED INVISIBLE, YET YOU BLOCKED MY ATTACK.
YOU'RE QUITE GOOD AT SENSING ENERGY.

STEALTH SKILL.

I MUTE MY SOUND, SCENT, AND PRESENCE.

ONLY A SELECT FEW ASSASSIN HUNTERS CAN USE THIS.

OF COURSE, NO ONE KNOWS I HAVE IT.

AGH!!

SHHHK

ZOOM

BECAUSE...NO ONE'S LIVED LONG ENOUGH TO TELL THE TALE!

I SEVERED A TENDON.

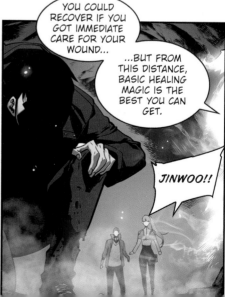

YOU COULD RECOVER IF YOU GOT IMMEDIATE CARE FOR YOUR WOUND...

...BUT FROM THIS DISTANCE, BASIC HEALING MAGIC IS THE BEST YOU CAN GET.

JINWOO!!

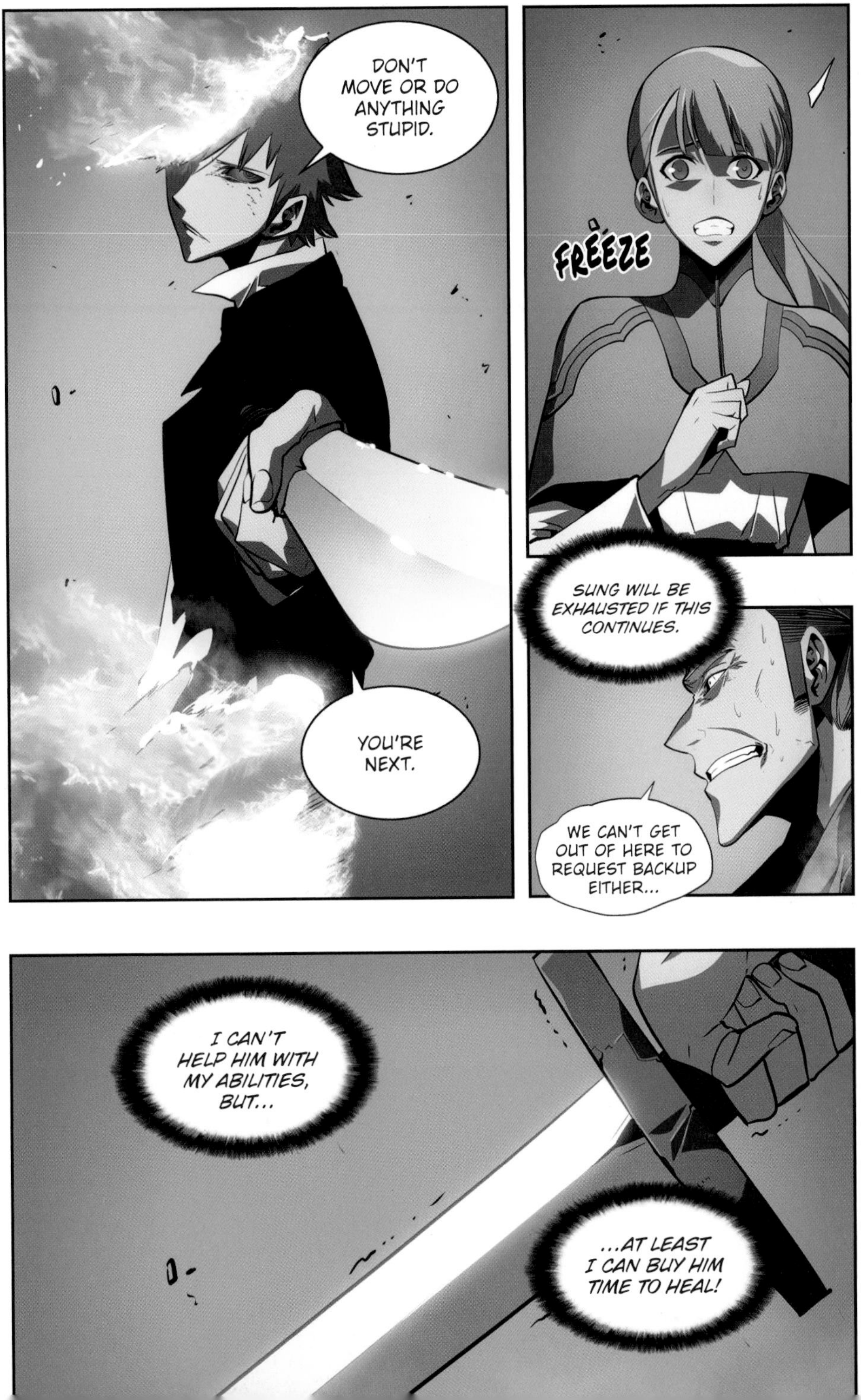
DON'T MOVE OR DO ANYTHING STUPID.
YOU'RE NEXT.
FREEZE
SUNG WILL BE EXHAUSTED IF THIS CONTINUES.
WE CAN'T GET OUT OF HERE TO REQUEST BACKUP EITHER...
I CAN'T HELP HIM WITH MY ABILITIES, BUT...
...AT LEAST I CAN BUY HIM TIME TO HEAL!

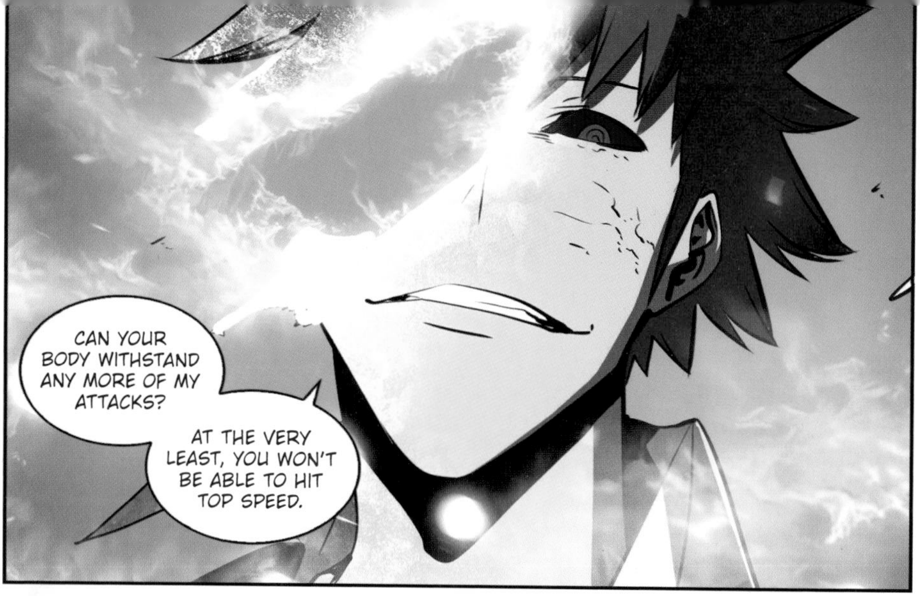
CAN YOUR BODY WITHSTAND ANY MORE OF MY ATTACKS?
AT THE VERY LEAST, YOU WON'T BE ABLE TO HIT TOP SPEED.
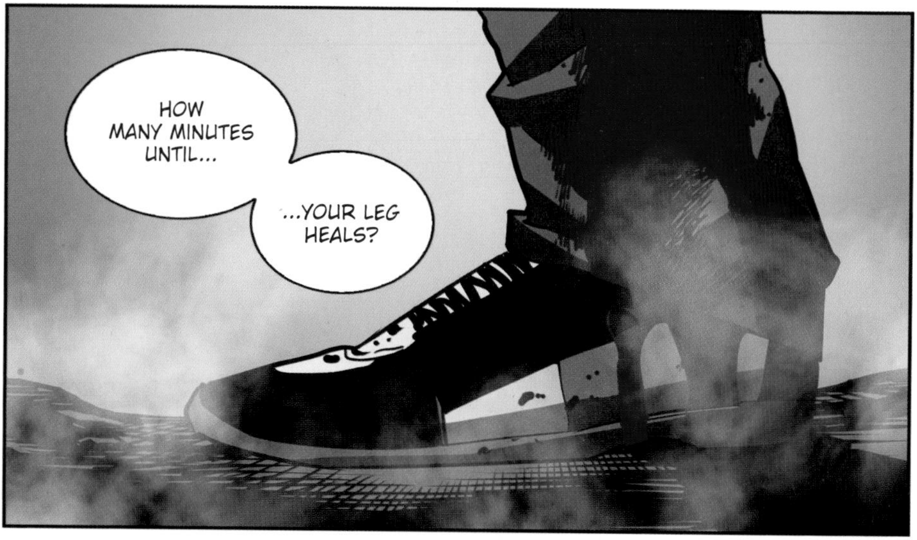
HOW MANY MINUTES UNTIL...
...YOUR LEG HEALS?
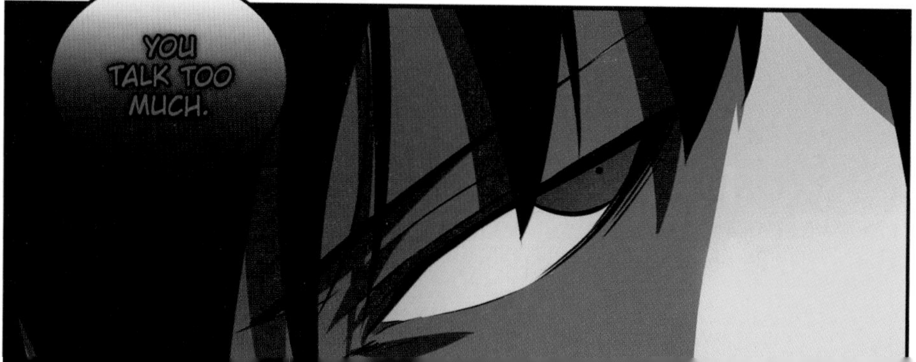
YOU TALK TOO MUCH.

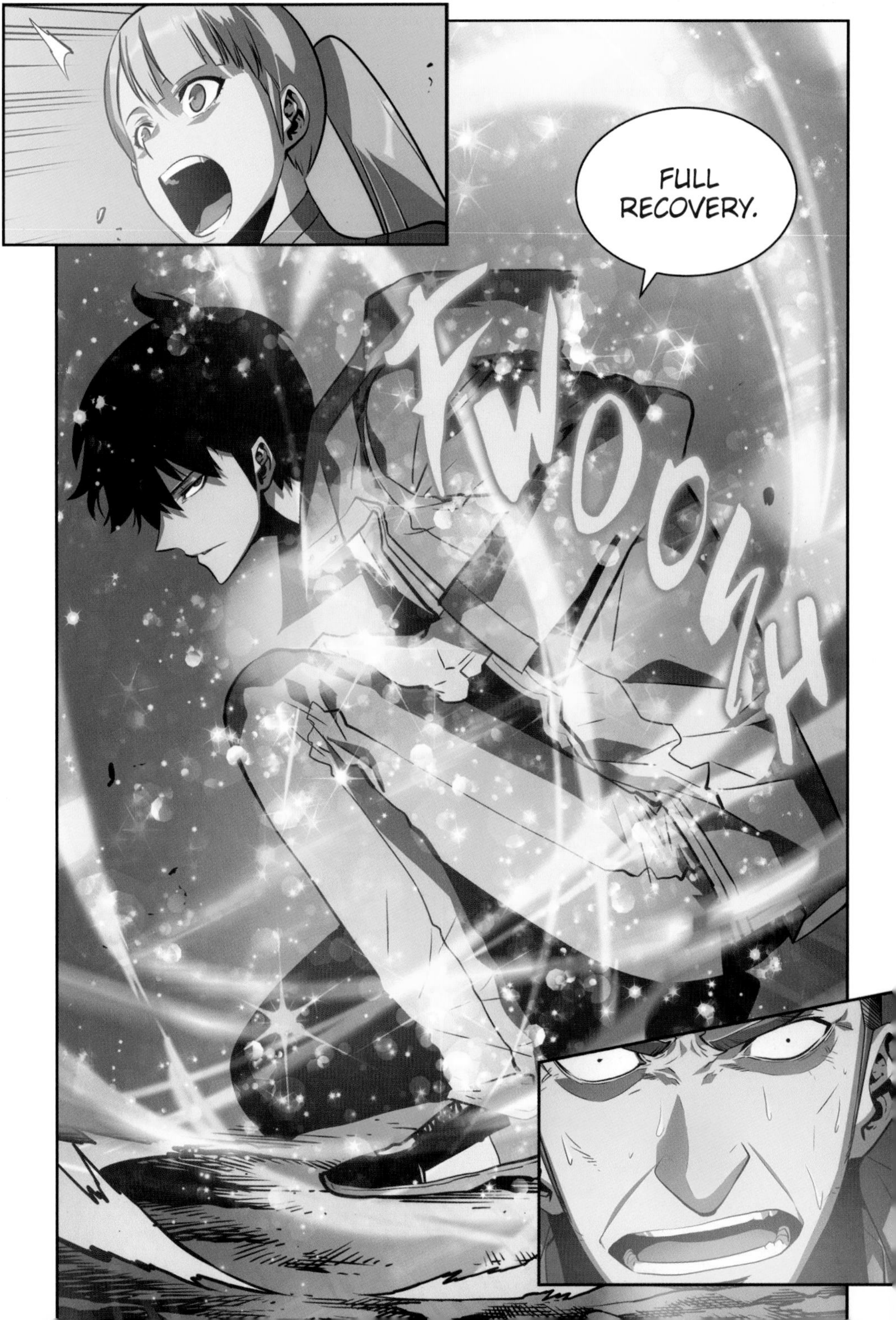
FULL RECOVERY.
FWOOOSH

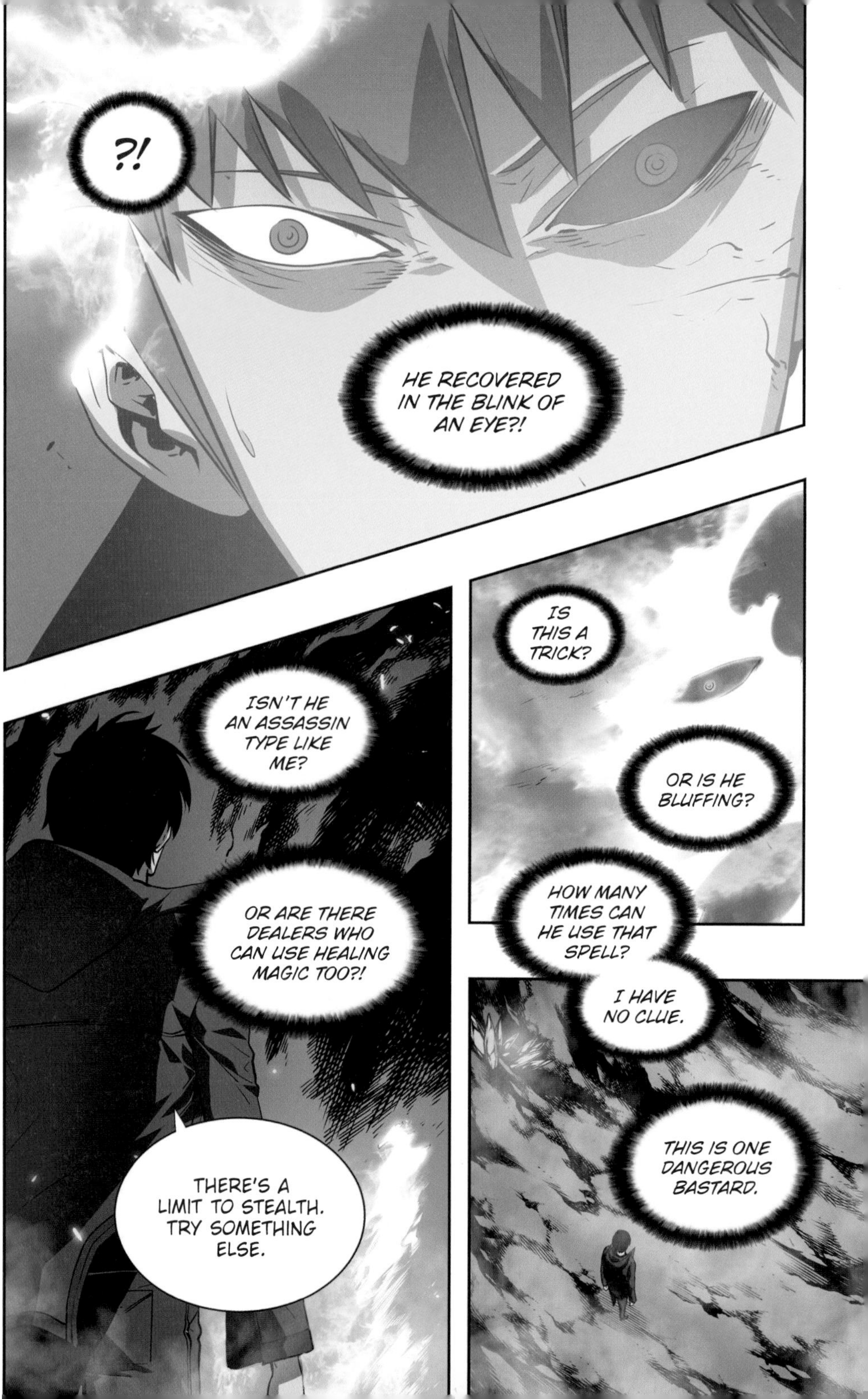
?!
HE RECOVERED IN THE BLINK OF AN EYE?!
ISN'T HE AN ASSASSIN TYPE LIKE ME?
OR ARE THERE DEALERS WHO CAN USE HEALING MAGIC TOO?!
THERE'S A LIMIT TO STEALTH. TRY SOMETHING ELSE.
IS THIS A TRICK?
OR IS HE BLUFFING?
HOW MANY TIMES CAN HE USE THAT SPELL?
I HAVE NO CLUE.
THIS IS ONE DANGEROUS BASTARD.

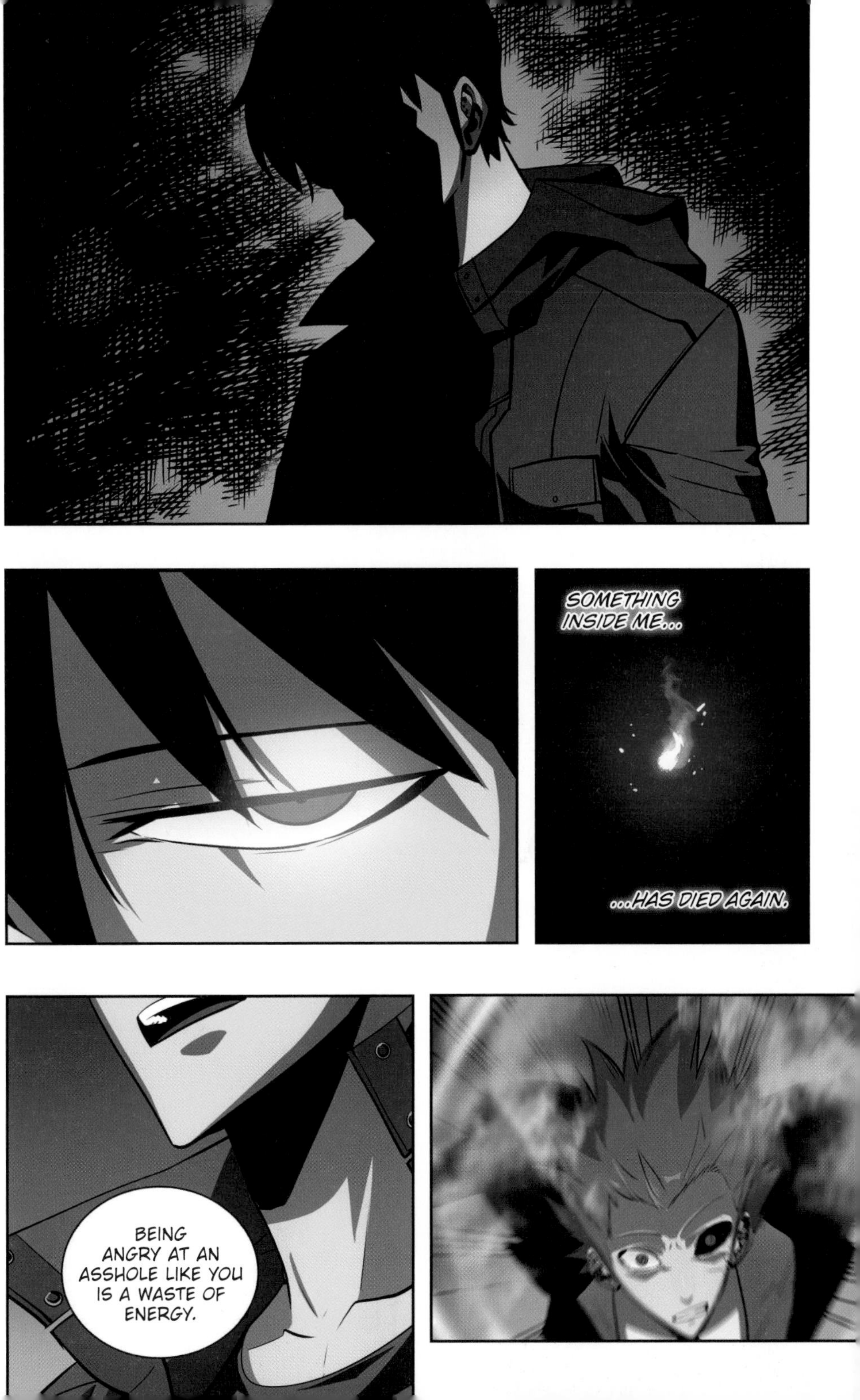
SOMETHING INSIDE ME...
...HAS DIED AGAIN.
BEING ANGRY AT AN ASSHOLE LIKE YOU IS A WASTE OF ENERGY.

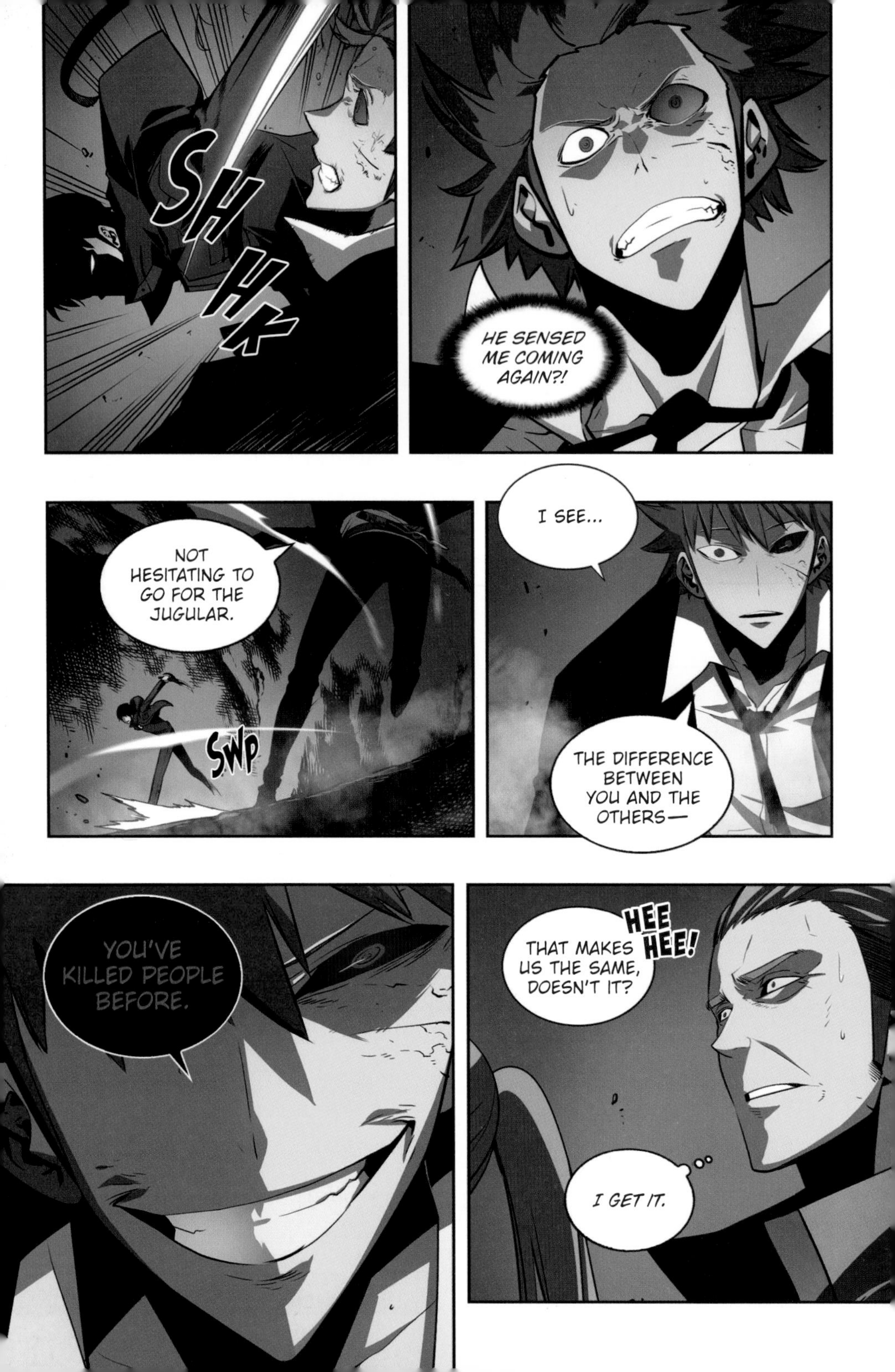
SHHK
HE SENSED ME COMING AGAIN?!
NOT HESITATING TO GO FOR THE JUGULAR.
SWP
I SEE...
THE DIFFERENCE BETWEEN YOU AND THE OTHERS—
YOU'VE KILLED PEOPLE BEFORE.
THAT MAKES US THE SAME, DOESN'T IT?
HEE HEE!
I GET IT.

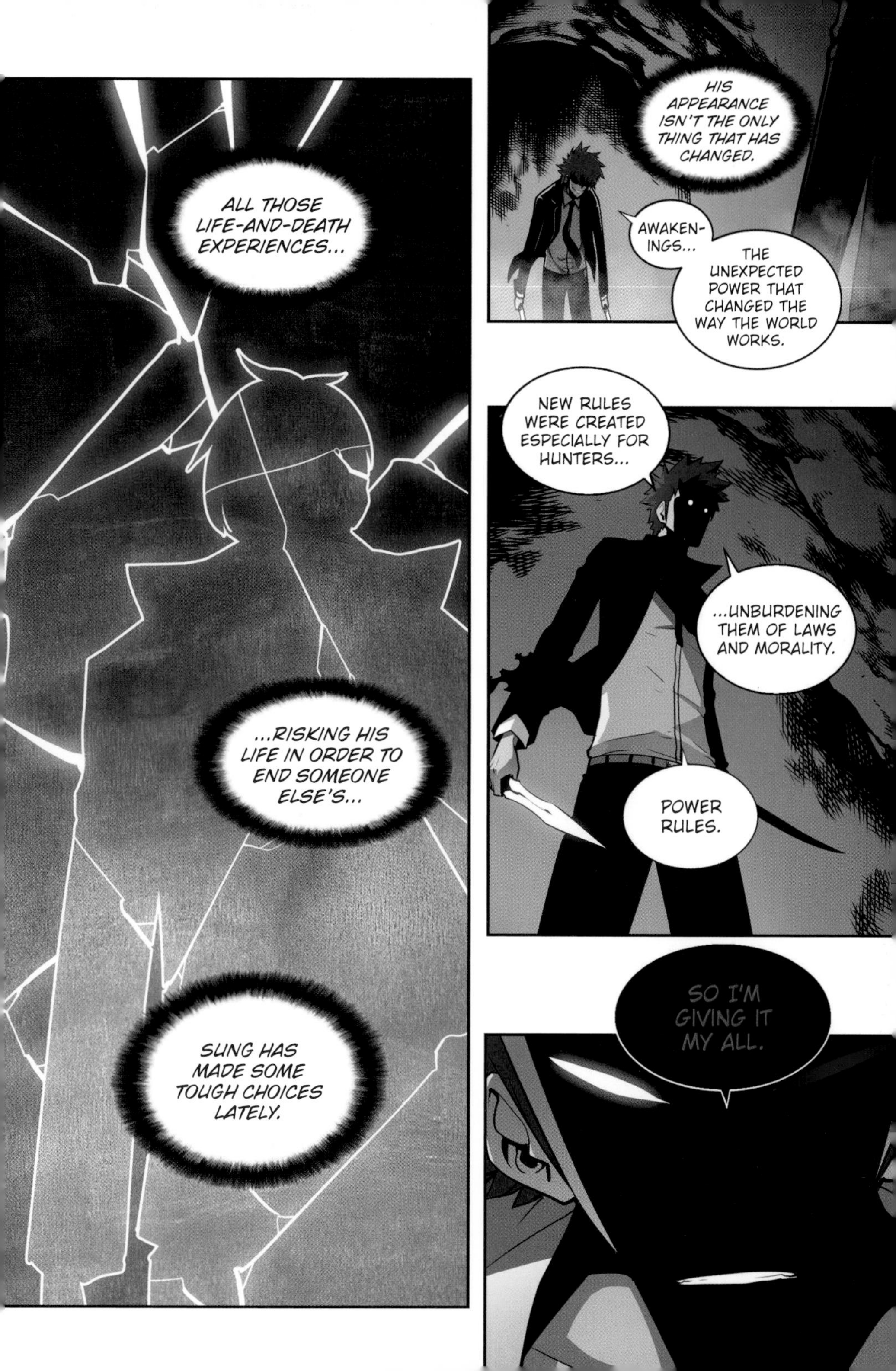
ALL THOSE LIFE-AND-DEATH EXPERIENCES...
...RISKING HIS LIFE IN ORDER TO END SOMEONE ELSE'S...
SUNG HAS MADE SOME TOUGH CHOICES LATELY.
HIS APPEARANCE ISN'T THE ONLY THING THAT HAS CHANGED.
AWAKEN-INGS...
THE UNEXPECTED POWER THAT CHANGED THE WAY THE WORLD WORKS.
NEW RULES WERE CREATED ESPECIALLY FOR HUNTERS...
...UNBURDENING THEM OF LAWS AND MORALITY.
POWER RULES.
SO I'M GIVING IT MY ALL.

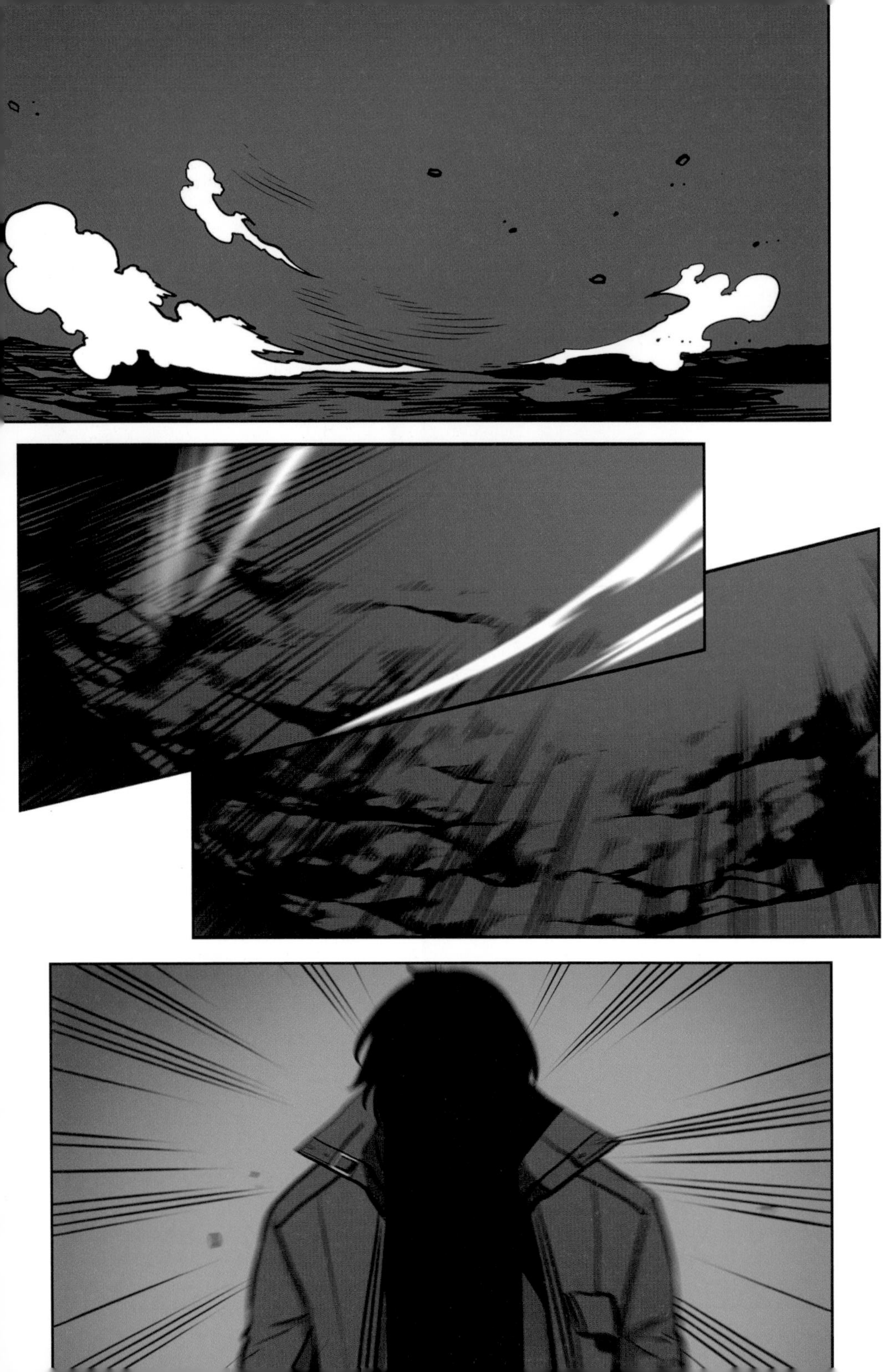

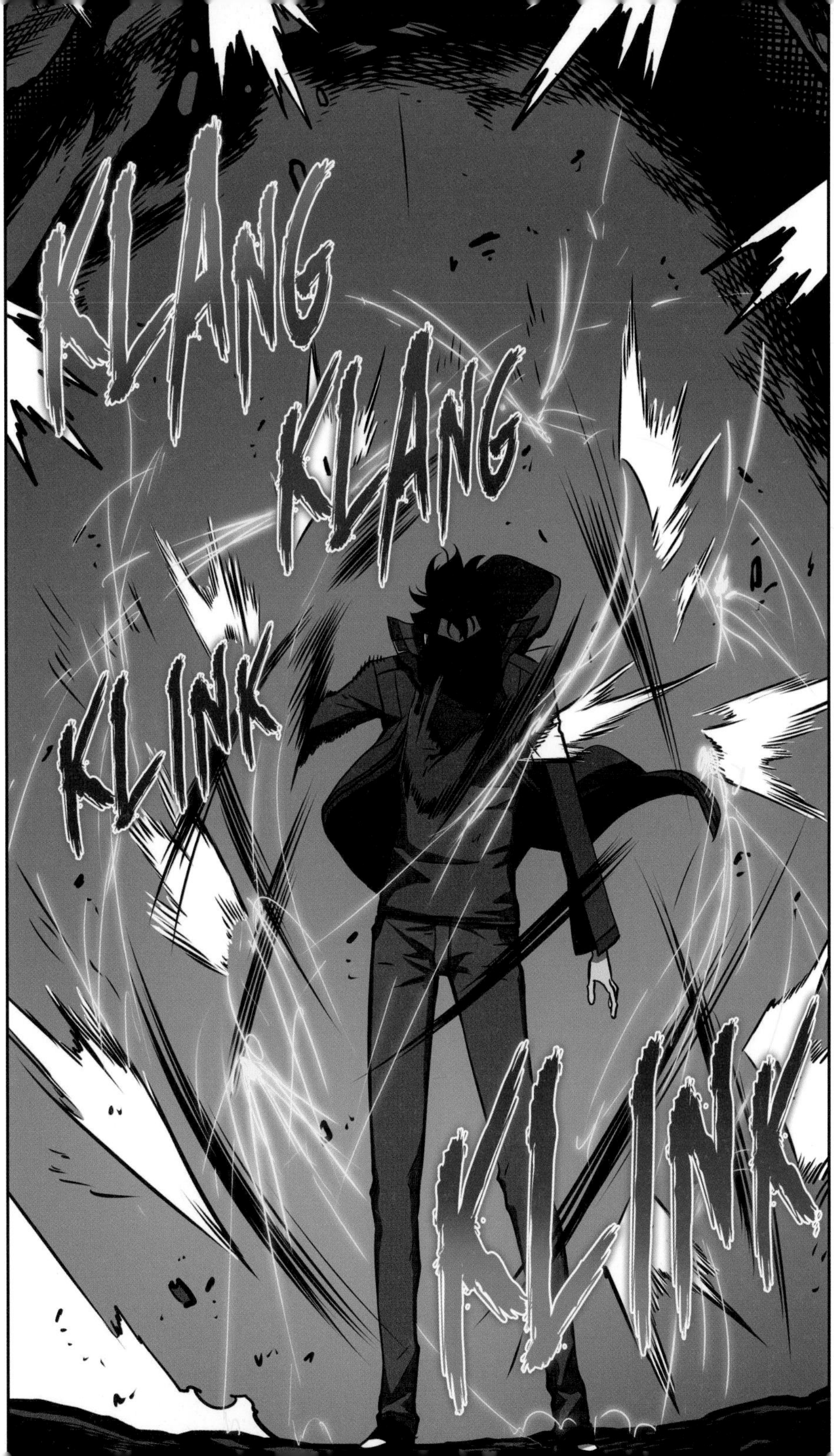
KLANG
KLANG
KLINK
KLINK

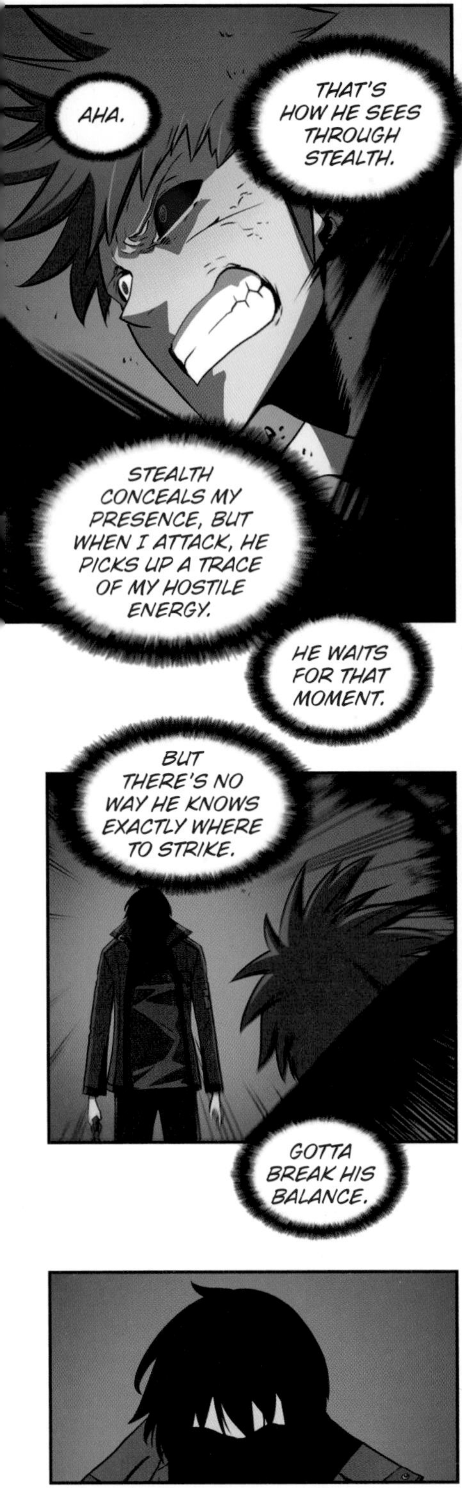
AHA.
THAT'S HOW HE SEES THROUGH STEALTH.
STEALTH CONCEALS MY PRESENCE, BUT WHEN I ATTACK, HE PICKS UP A TRACE OF MY HOSTILE ENERGY.
HE WAITS FOR THAT MOMENT.
BUT THERE'S NO WAY HE KNOWS EXACTLY WHERE TO STRIKE.
GOTTA BREAK HIS BALANCE.
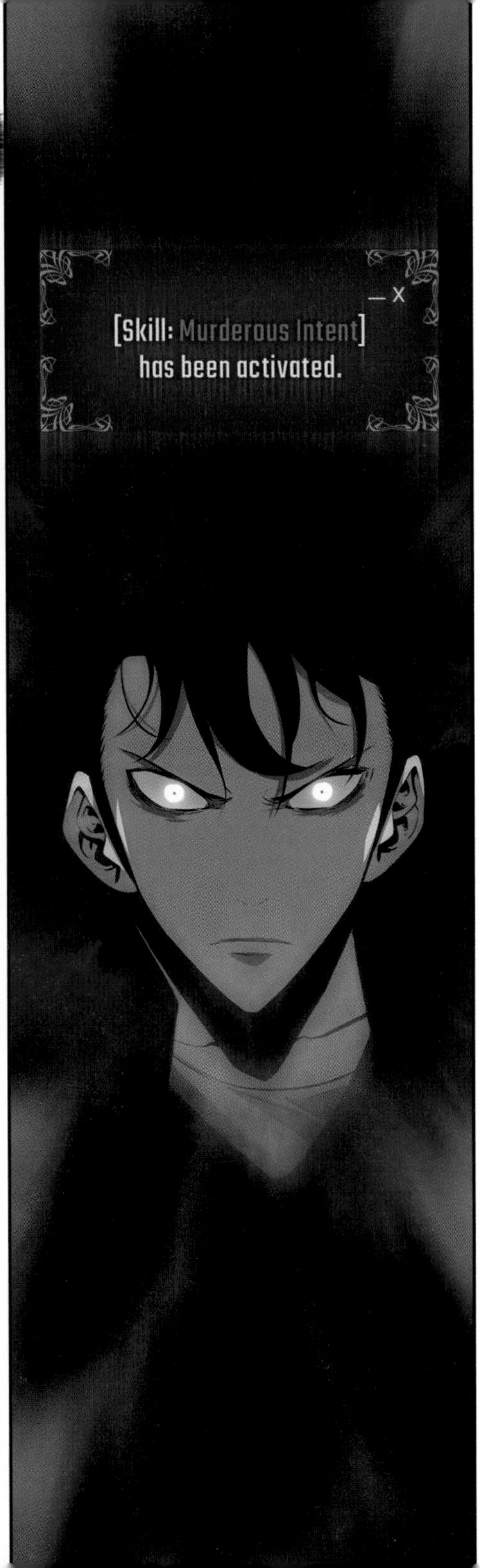
— X
[Skill: Murderous Intent]
has been activated.

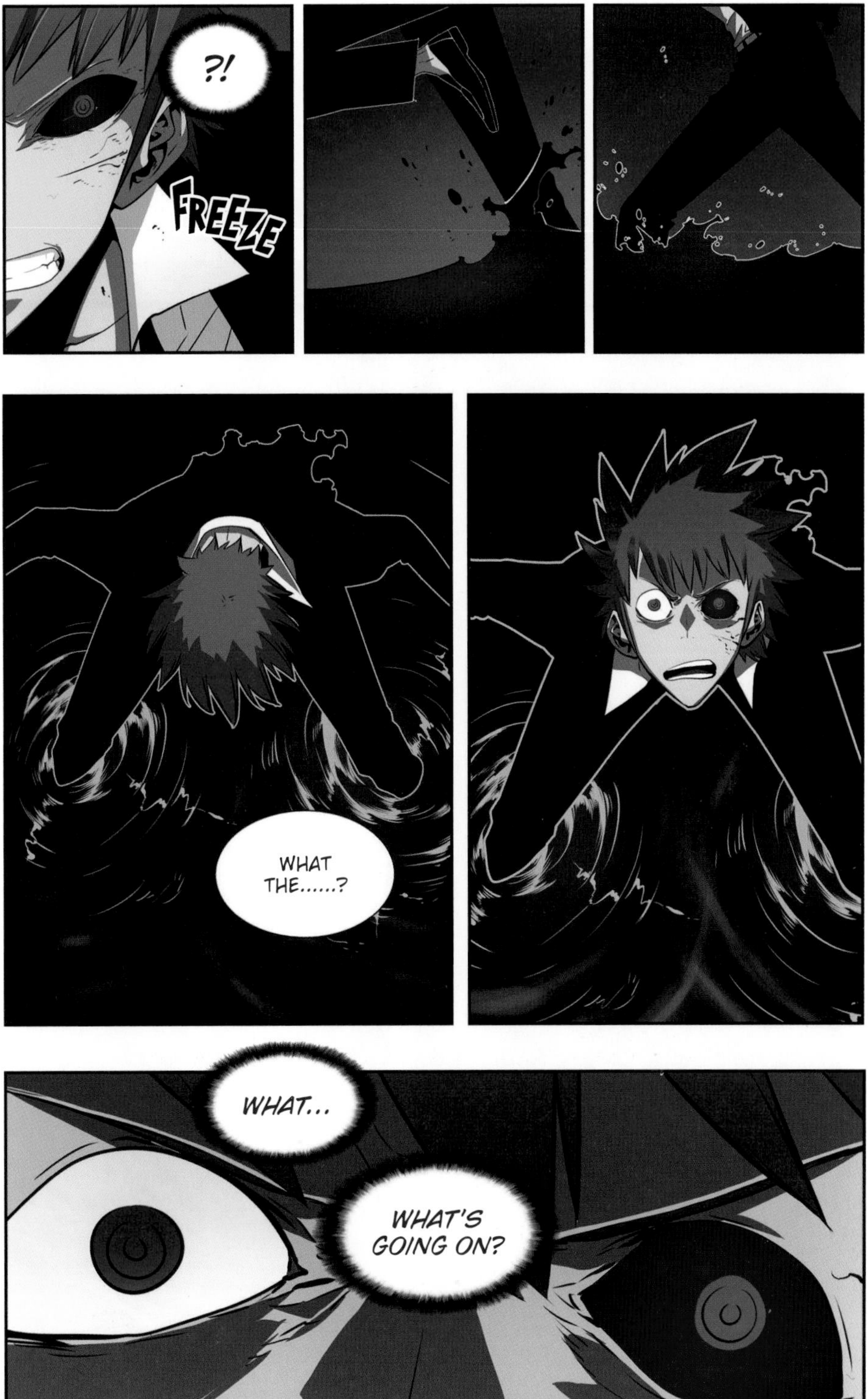
?!
FREEZE
WHAT THE......?
WHAT...
WHAT'S GOING ON?

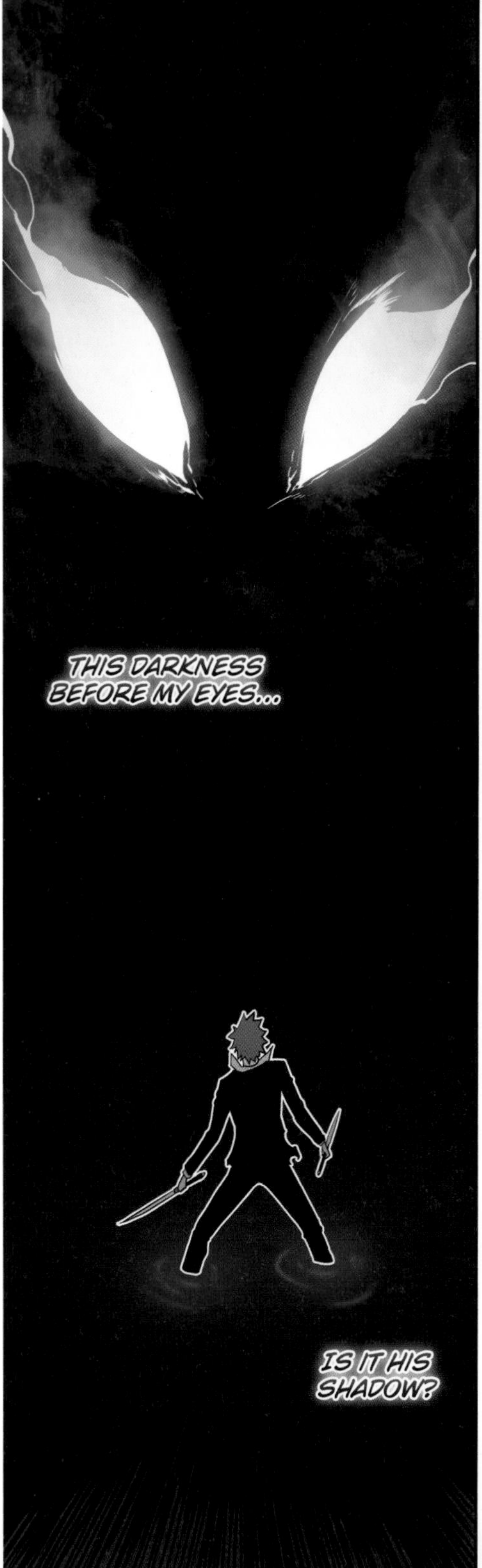
THIS DARKNESS BEFORE MY EYES...
IS IT HIS SHADOW?
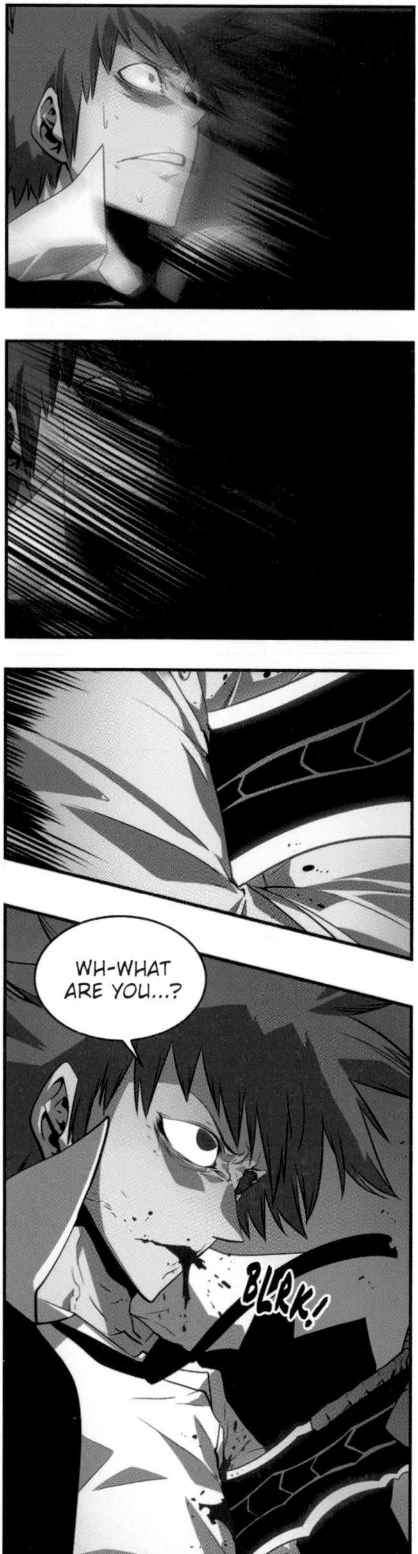
WH-WHAT ARE YOU...?
BLRK!

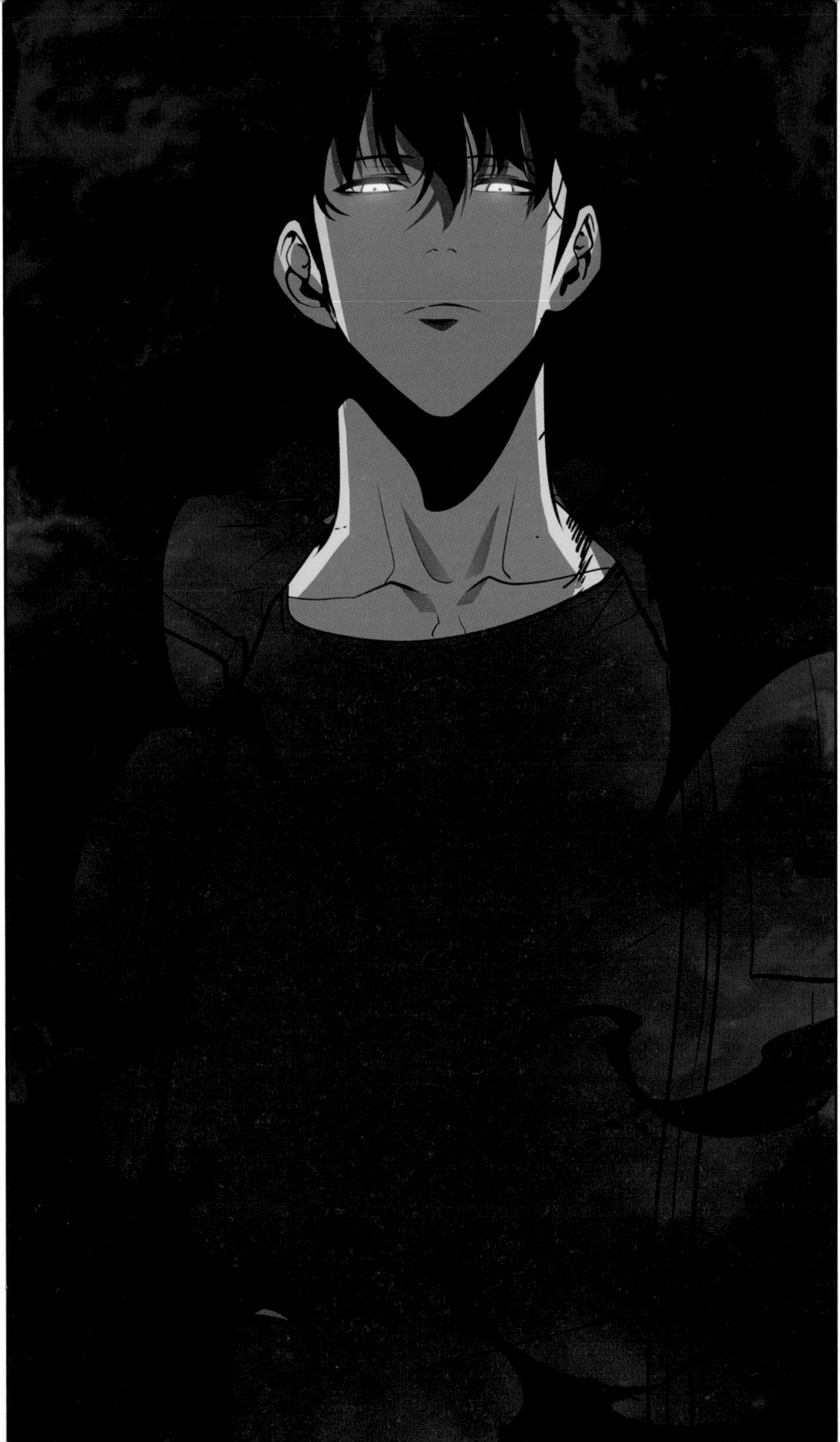

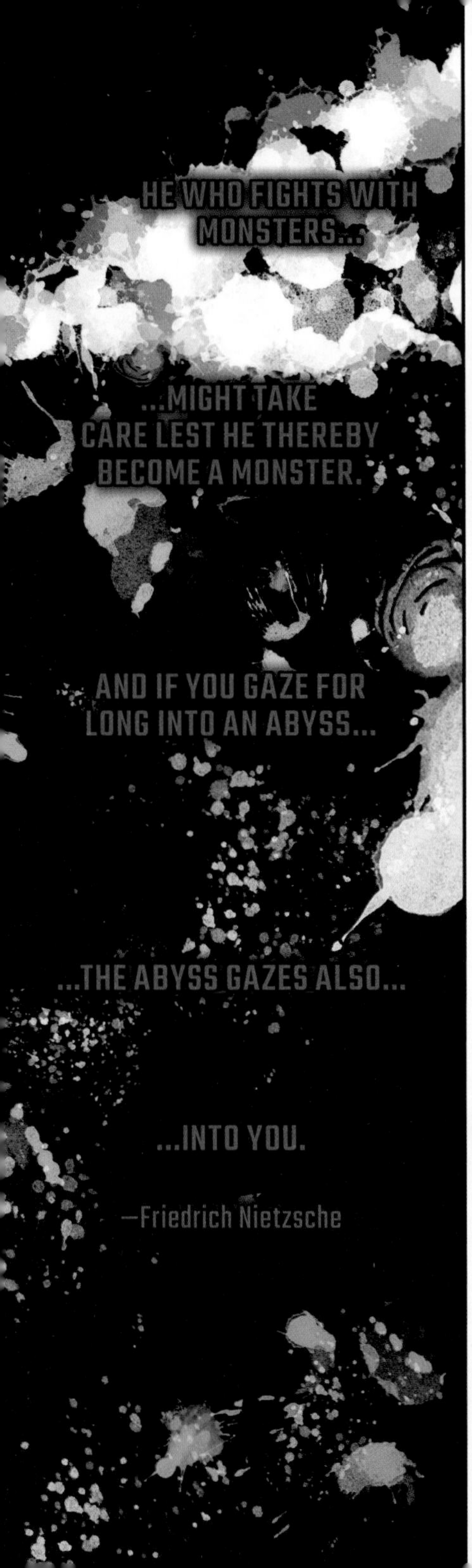
HE WHO FIGHTS WITH MONSTERS...
...MIGHT TAKE CARE LEST HE THEREBY BECOME A MONSTER.
AND IF YOU GAZE FOR LONG INTO AN ABYSS...
...THE ABYSS GAZES ALSO...
...INTO YOU.
—Friedrich Nietzsche
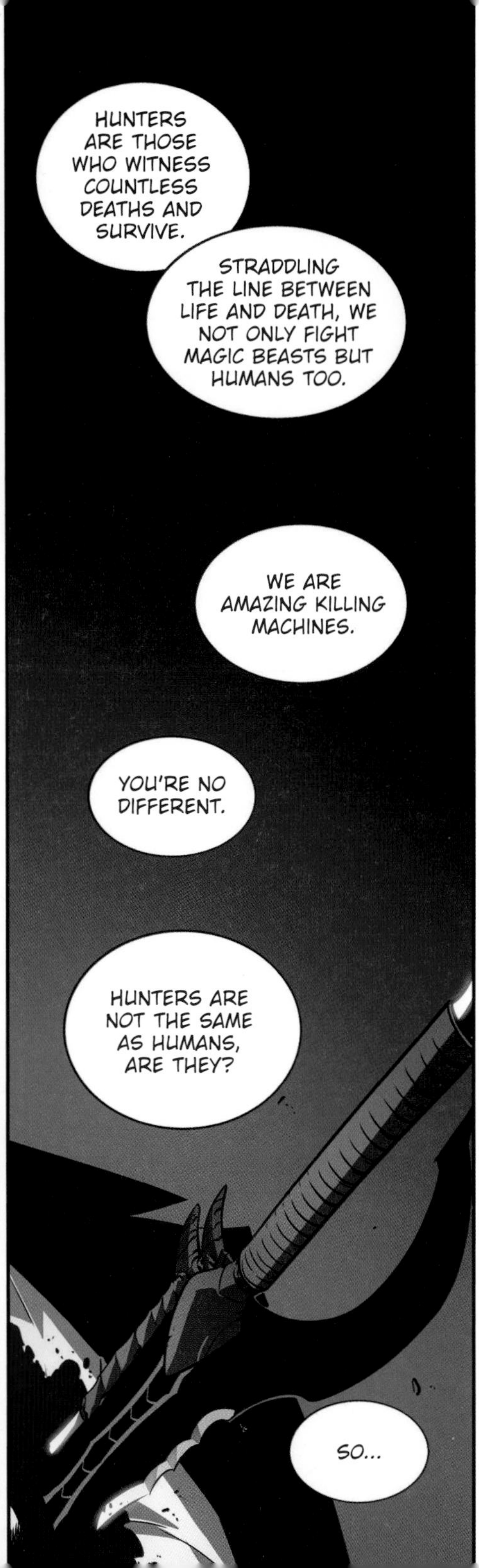
HUNTERS ARE THOSE WHO WITNESS COUNTLESS DEATHS AND SURVIVE.
STRADDLING THE LINE BETWEEN LIFE AND DEATH, WE NOT ONLY FIGHT MAGIC BEASTS BUT HUMANS TOO.
WE ARE AMAZING KILLING MACHINES.
YOU'RE NO DIFFERENT.
HUNTERS ARE NOT THE SAME AS HUMANS, ARE THEY?
SO...

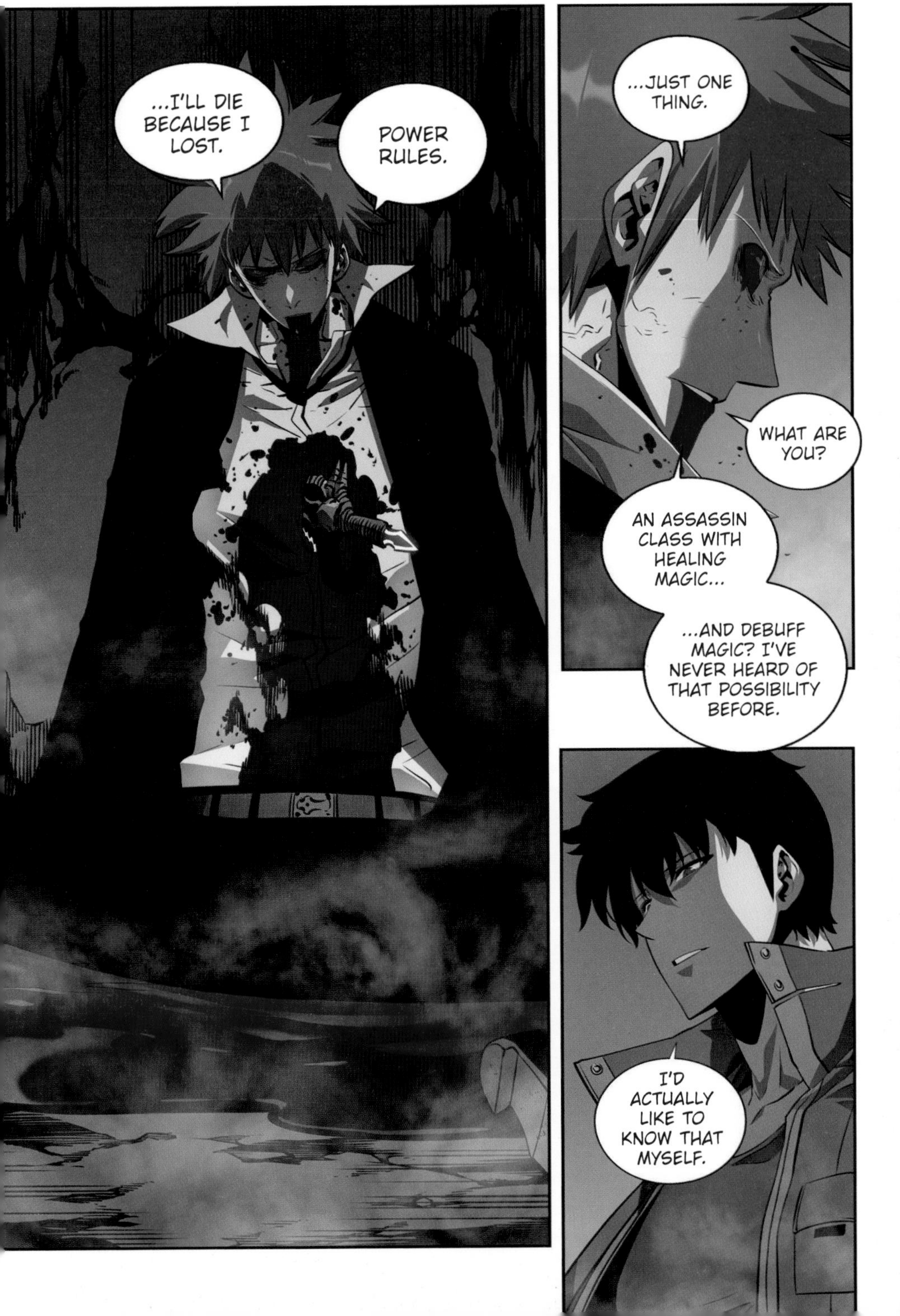
...I'LL DIE BECAUSE I LOST.
POWER RULES.
...JUST ONE THING.
WHAT ARE YOU?
AN ASSASSIN CLASS WITH HEALING MAGIC...
...AND DEBUFF MAGIC? I'VE NEVER HEARD OF THAT POSSIBILITY BEFORE.
I'D ACTUALLY LIKE TO KNOW THAT MYSELF.

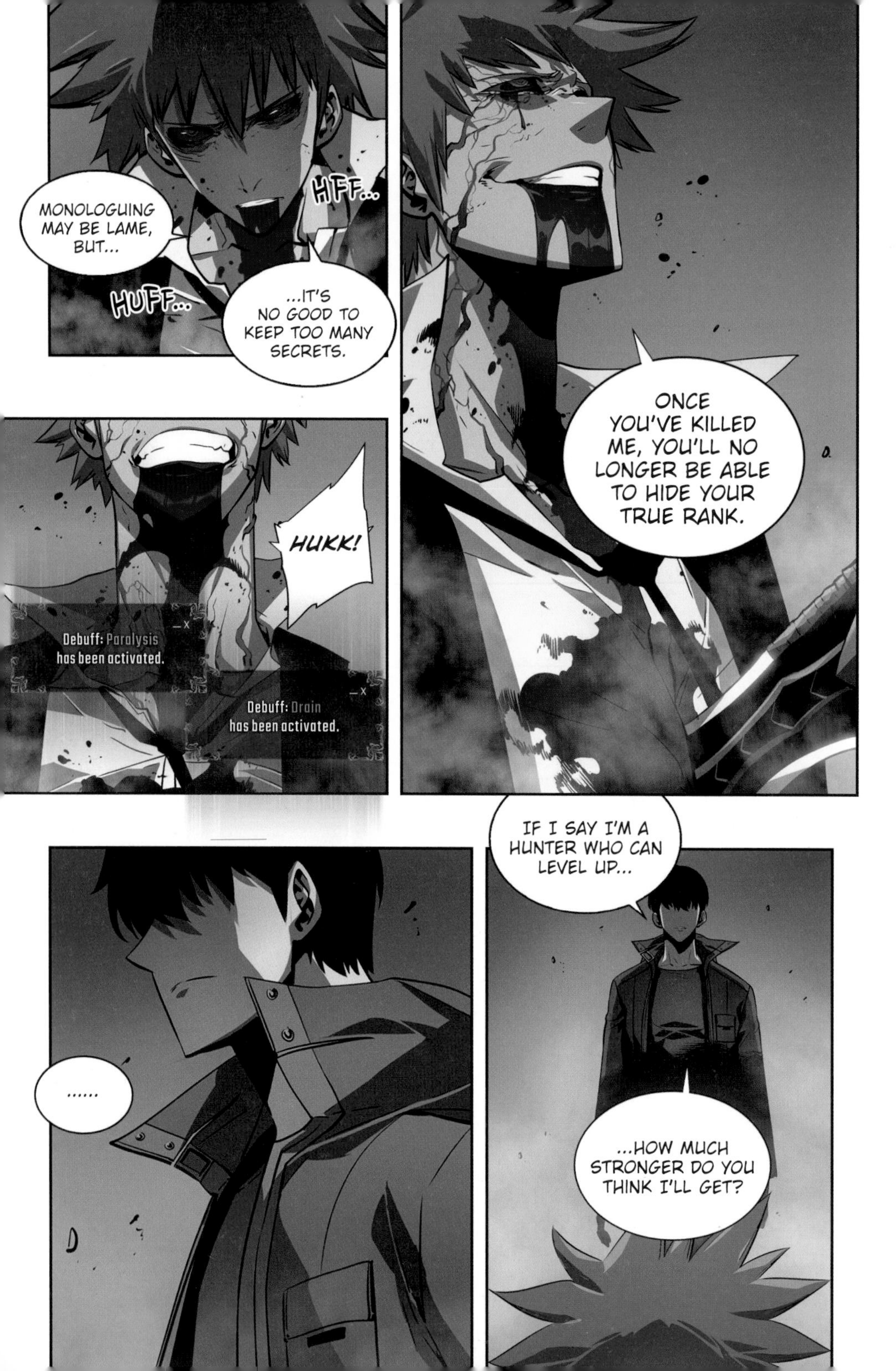
MONOLOGUING MAY BE LAME, BUT...
HFF...
HUFF...
...IT'S NO GOOD TO KEEP TOO MANY SECRETS.
HUKK!
Debuff: Paralysis has been activated.
Debuff: Drain has been activated.
ONCE YOU'VE KILLED ME, YOU'LL NO LONGER BE ABLE TO HIDE YOUR TRUE RANK.
......
IF I SAY I'M A HUNTER WHO CAN LEVEL UP...
...HOW MUCH STRONGER DO YOU THINK I'LL GET?

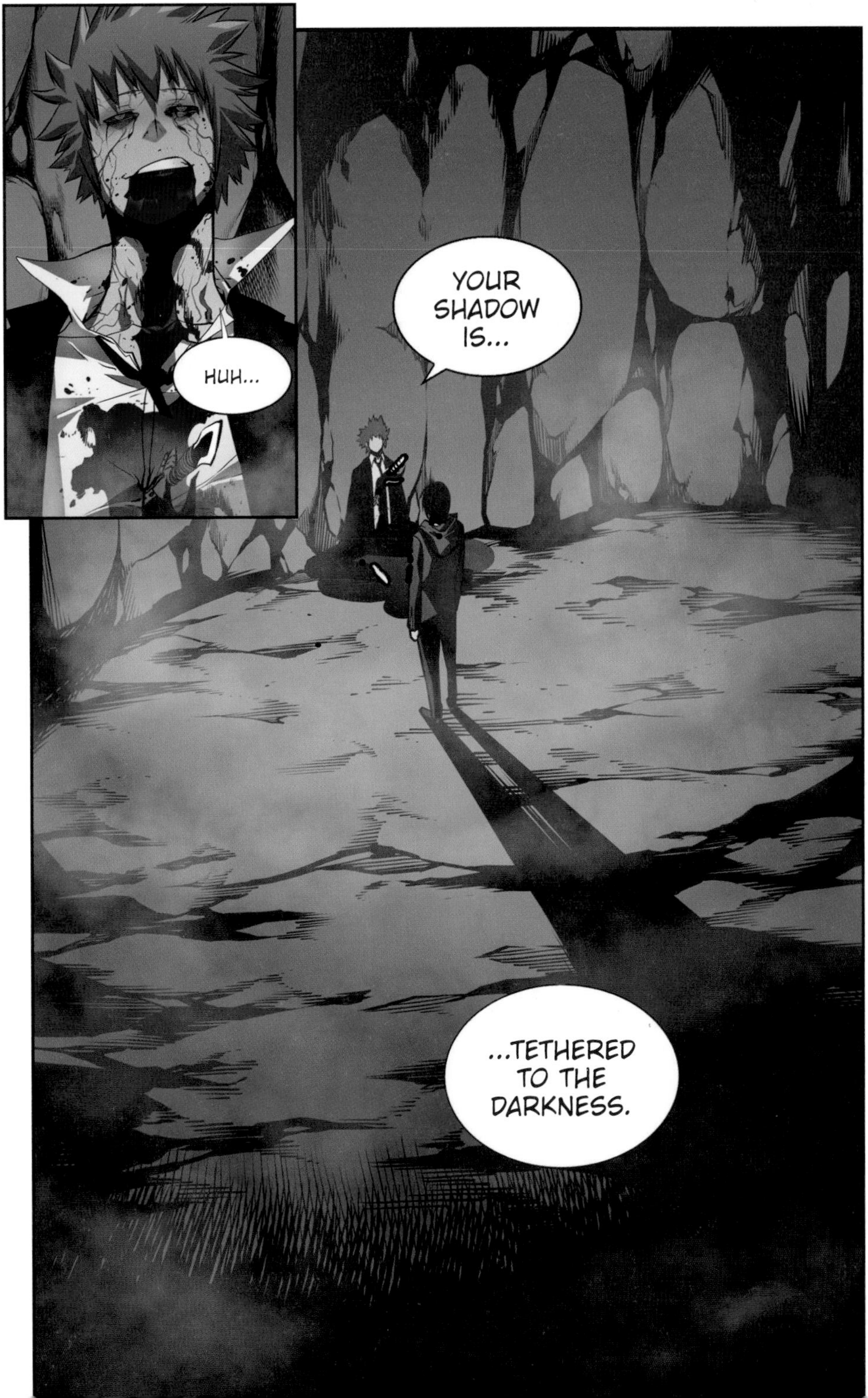
HUH...
YOUR SHADOW IS...
...TETHERED TO THE DARKNESS.

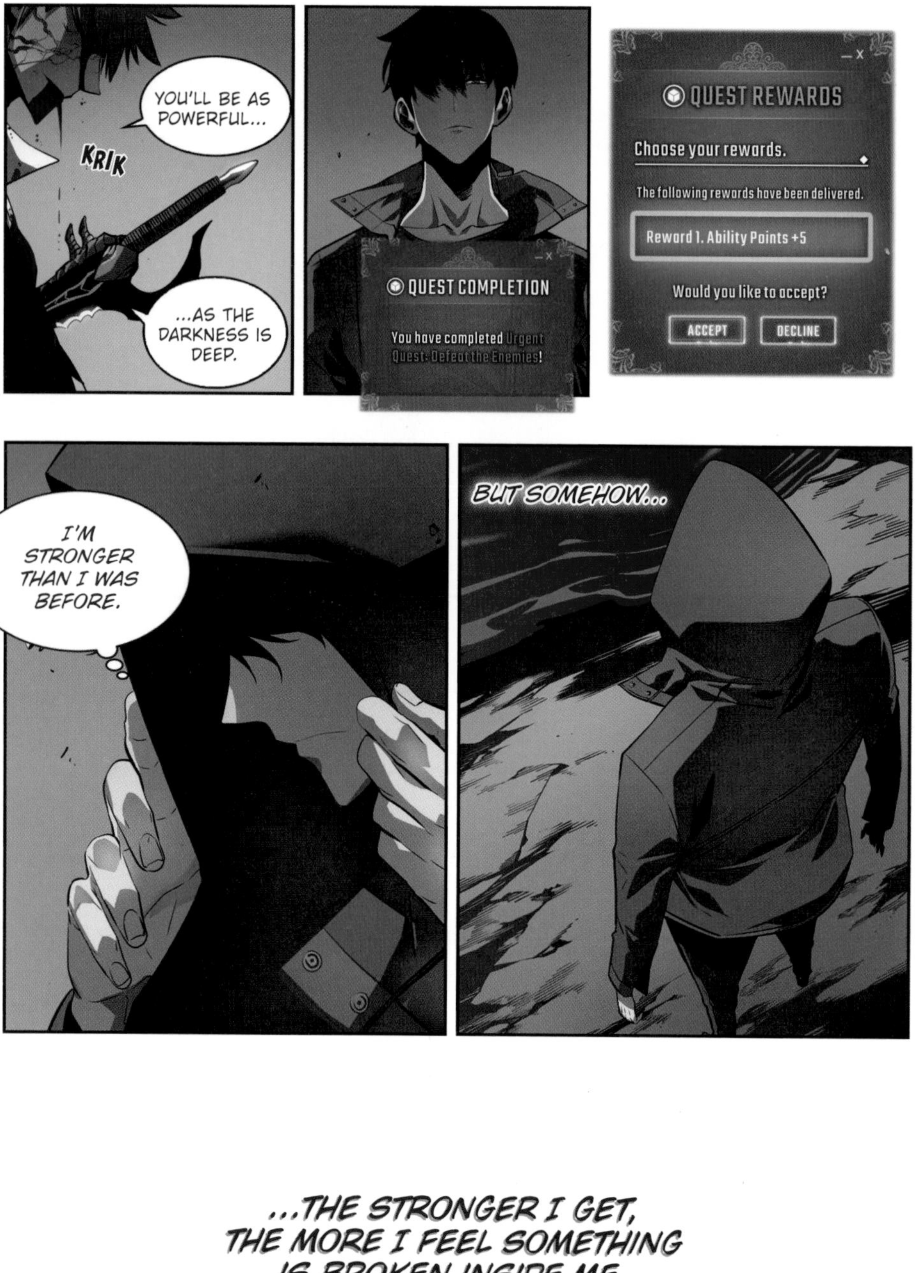
YOU'LL BE AS POWERFUL...
KRIK
...AS THE DARKNESS IS DEEP.
QUEST COMPLETION
You have completed Urgent Quest: Defeat the Enemies!
QUEST REWARDS
Choose your rewards.
The following rewards have been delivered.
Reward 1. Ability Points +5
Would you like to accept?
ACCEPT
DECLINE
I'M STRONGER THAN I WAS BEFORE.
BUT SOMEHOW...
...THE STRONGER I GET, THE MORE I FEEL SOMETHING IS BROKEN INSIDE ME.

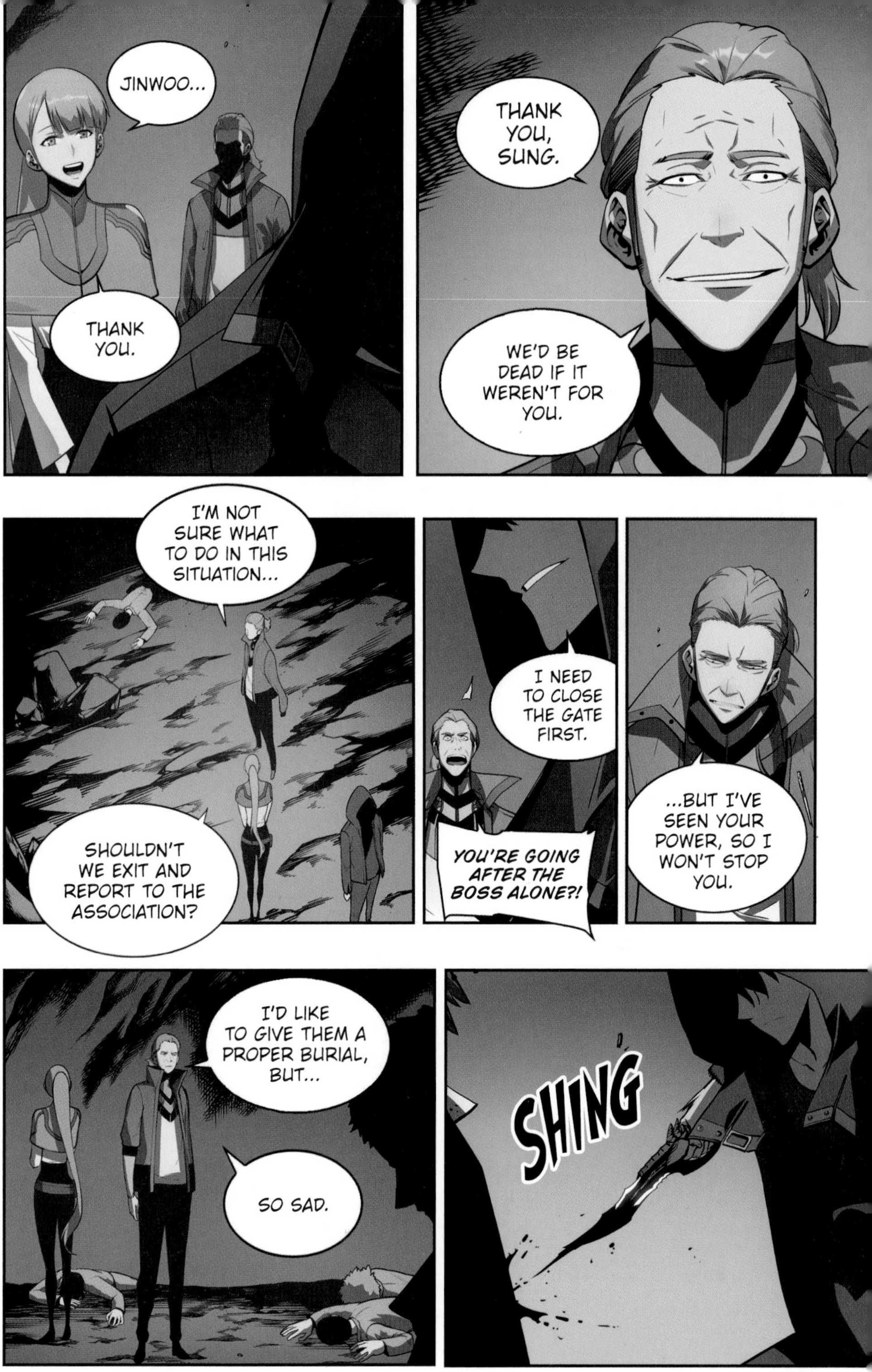
JINWOO...
THANK YOU.
THANK YOU, SUNG.
WE'D BE DEAD IF IT WEREN'T FOR YOU.
I'M NOT SURE WHAT TO DO IN THIS SITUATION...
SHOULDN'T WE EXIT AND REPORT TO THE ASSOCIATION?
I NEED TO CLOSE THE GATE FIRST.
YOU'RE GOING AFTER THE BOSS ALONE?!
...BUT I'VE SEEN YOUR POWER, SO I WON'T STOP YOU.
I'D LIKE TO GIVE THEM A PROPER BURIAL, BUT...
SO SAD.
SHING

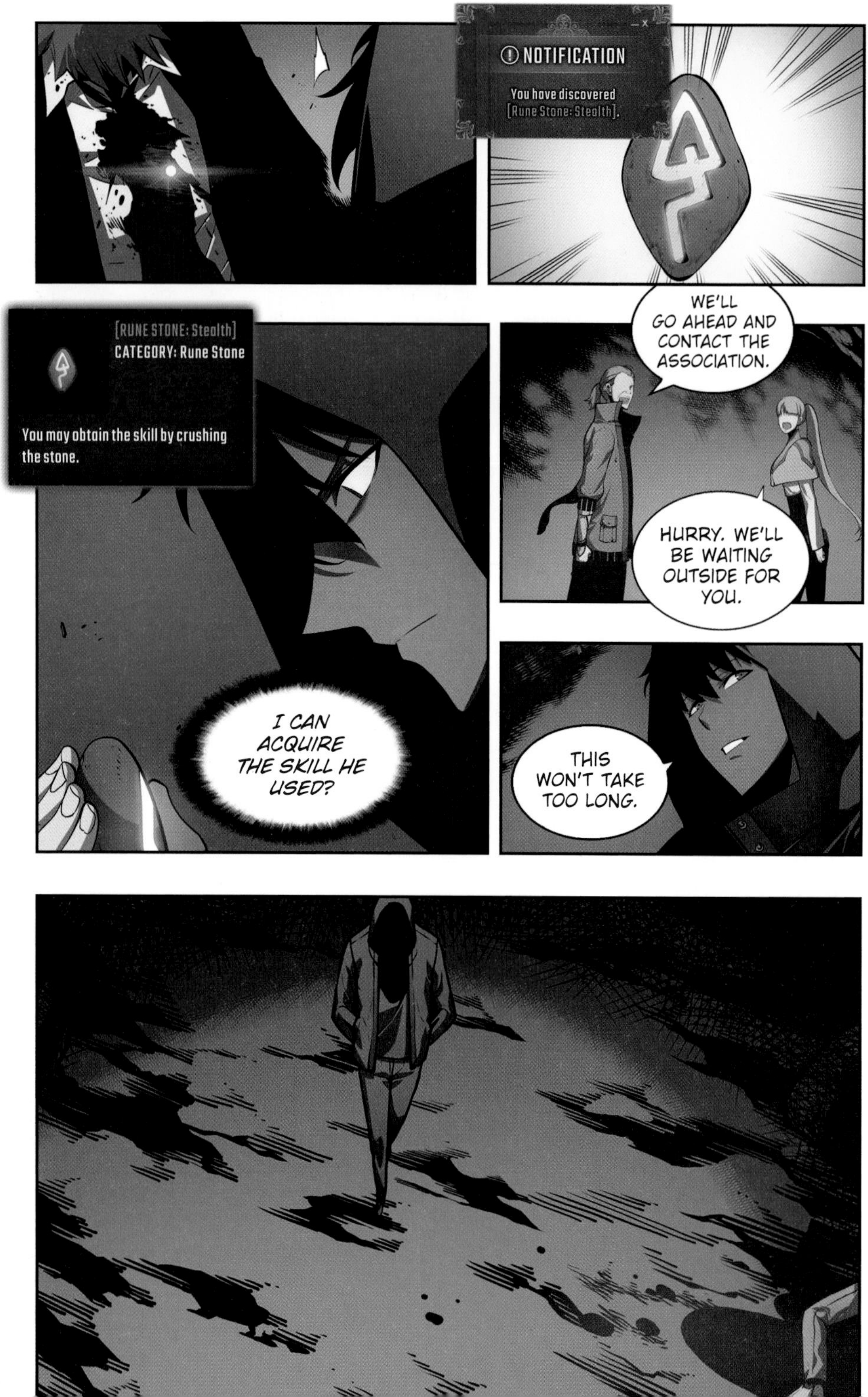
NOTIFICATION
You have discovered [Rune Stone: Stealth].
[RUNE STONE: Stealth]
CATEGORY: Rune Stone
You may obtain the skill by crushing the stone.
I CAN ACQUIRE THE SKILL HE USED?
WE'LL GO AHEAD AND CONTACT THE ASSOCIATION.
HURRY. WE'LL BE WAITING OUTSIDE FOR YOU.
THIS WON'T TAKE TOO LONG.

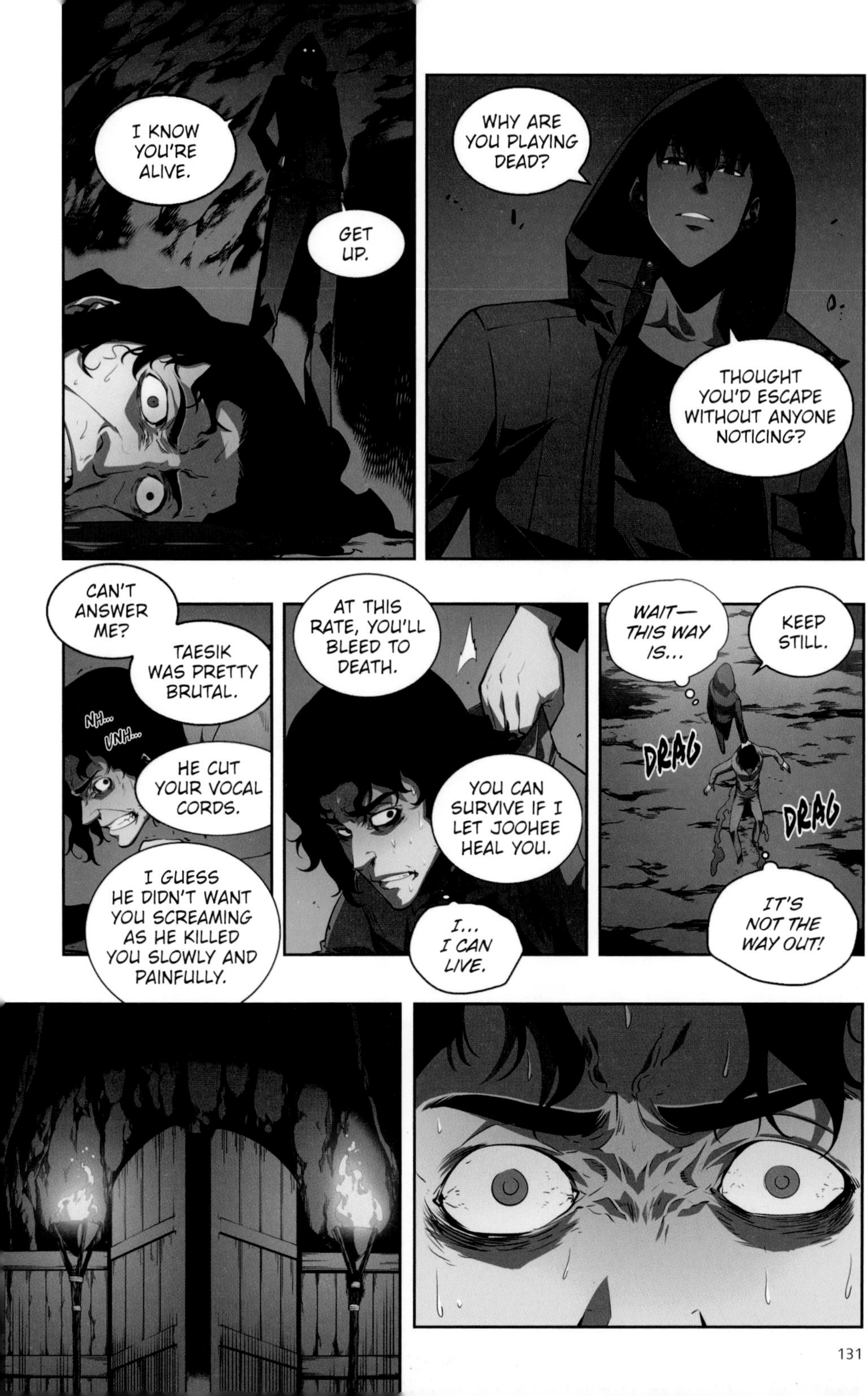
I KNOW YOU'RE ALIVE.
GET UP.
WHY ARE YOU PLAYING DEAD?
THOUGHT YOU'D ESCAPE WITHOUT ANYONE NOTICING?
CAN'T ANSWER ME?
TAESIK WAS PRETTY BRUTAL.
NH... UNH...
HE CUT YOUR VOCAL CORDS.
I GUESS HE DIDN'T WANT YOU SCREAMING AS HE KILLED YOU SLOWLY AND PAINFULLY.
AT THIS RATE, YOU'LL BLEED TO DEATH.
YOU CAN SURVIVE IF I LET JOOHEE HEAL YOU.
I... I CAN LIVE.
WAIT— THIS WAY IS...
KEEP STILL.
DRAG
DRAG
IT'S NOT THE WAY OUT!

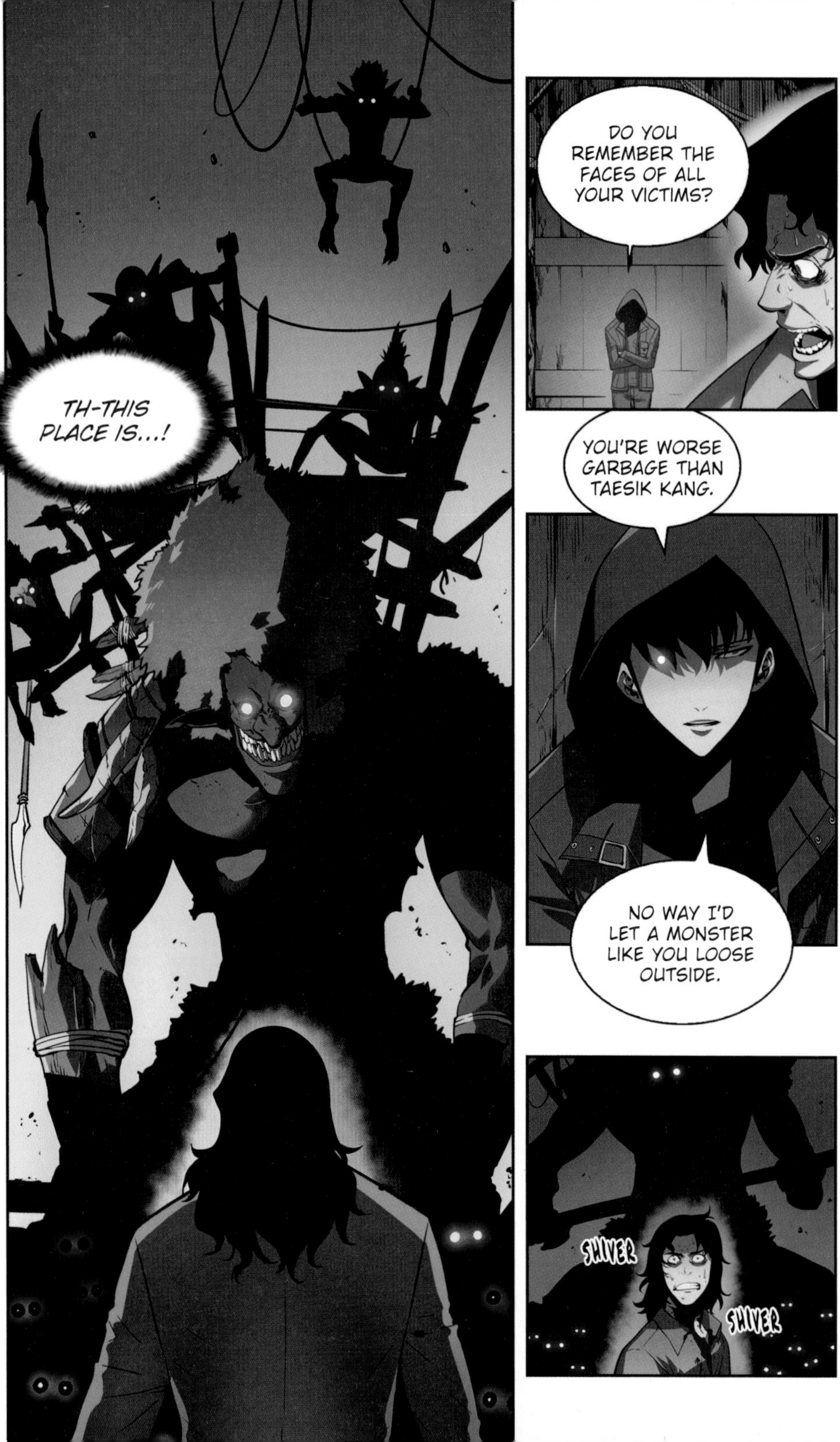
TH-THIS PLACE IS...!
DO YOU REMEMBER THE FACES OF ALL YOUR VICTIMS?
YOU'RE WORSE GARBAGE THAN TAESIK KANG.
NO WAY I'D LET A MONSTER LIKE YOU LOOSE OUTSIDE.
SHIVER
SHIVER

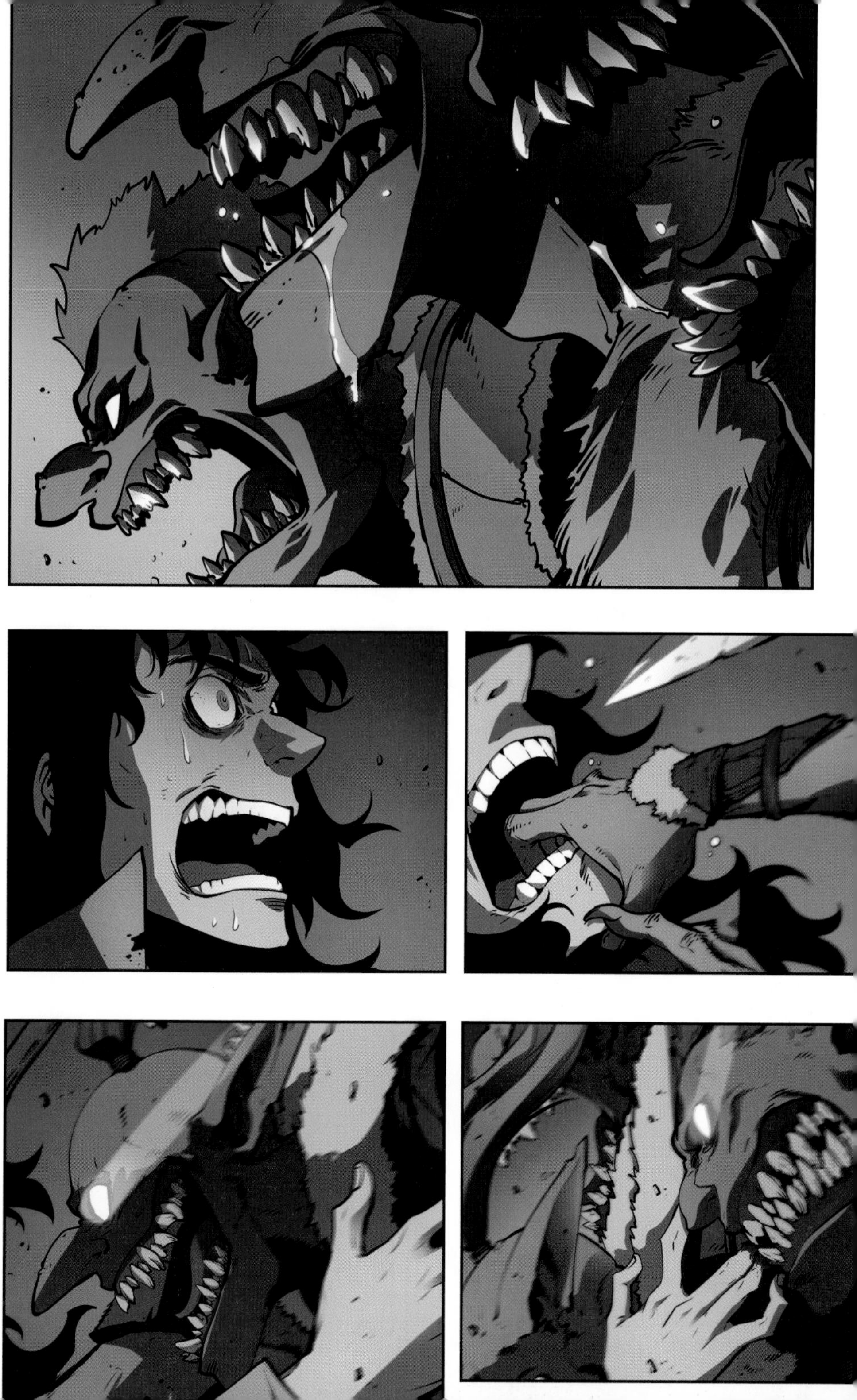

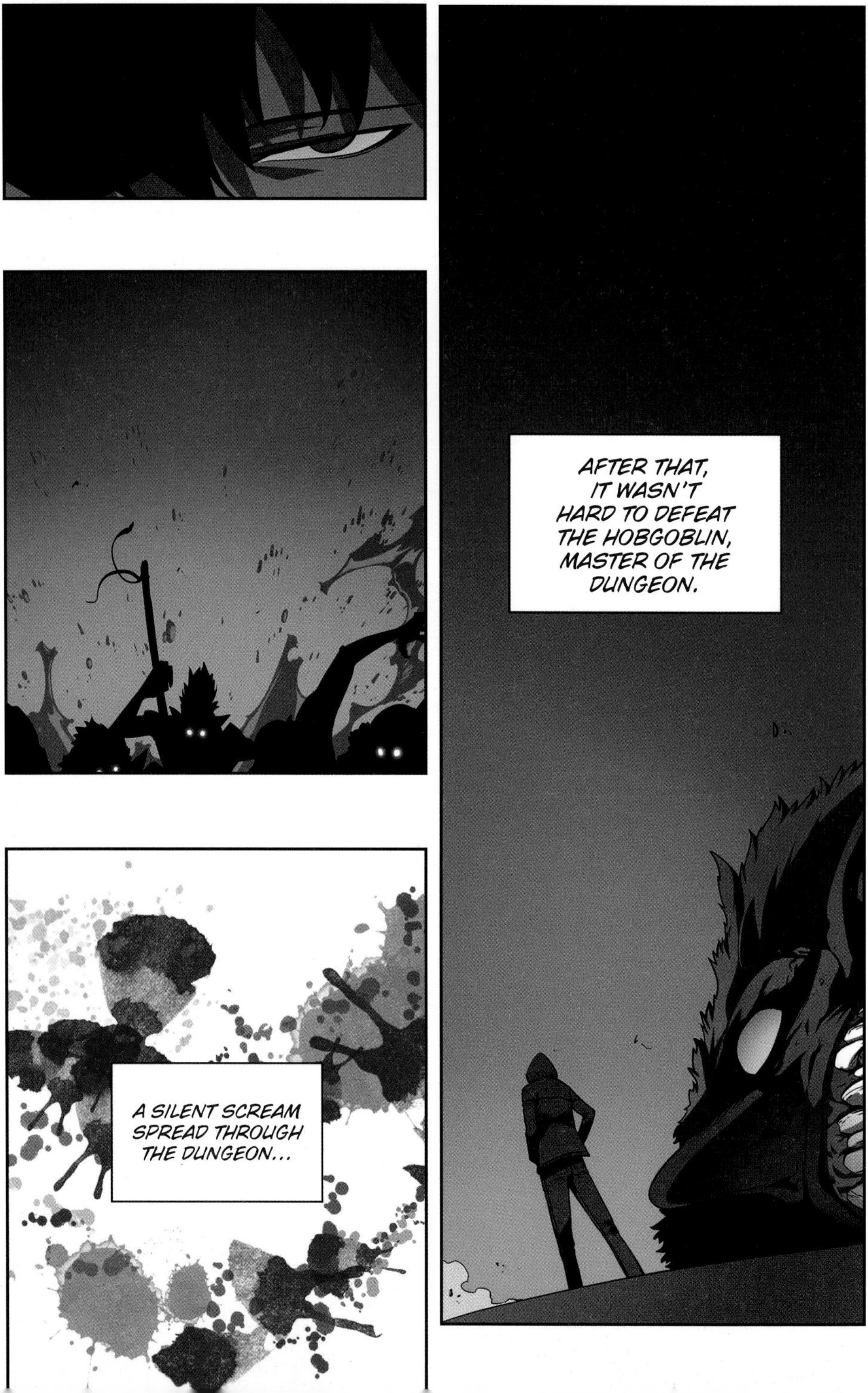
A SILENT SCREAM SPREAD THROUGH THE DUNGEON...
AFTER THAT, IT WASN'T HARD TO DEFEAT THE HOBGOBLIN, MASTER OF THE DUNGEON.

CHAPTER 7

The Strange Raids

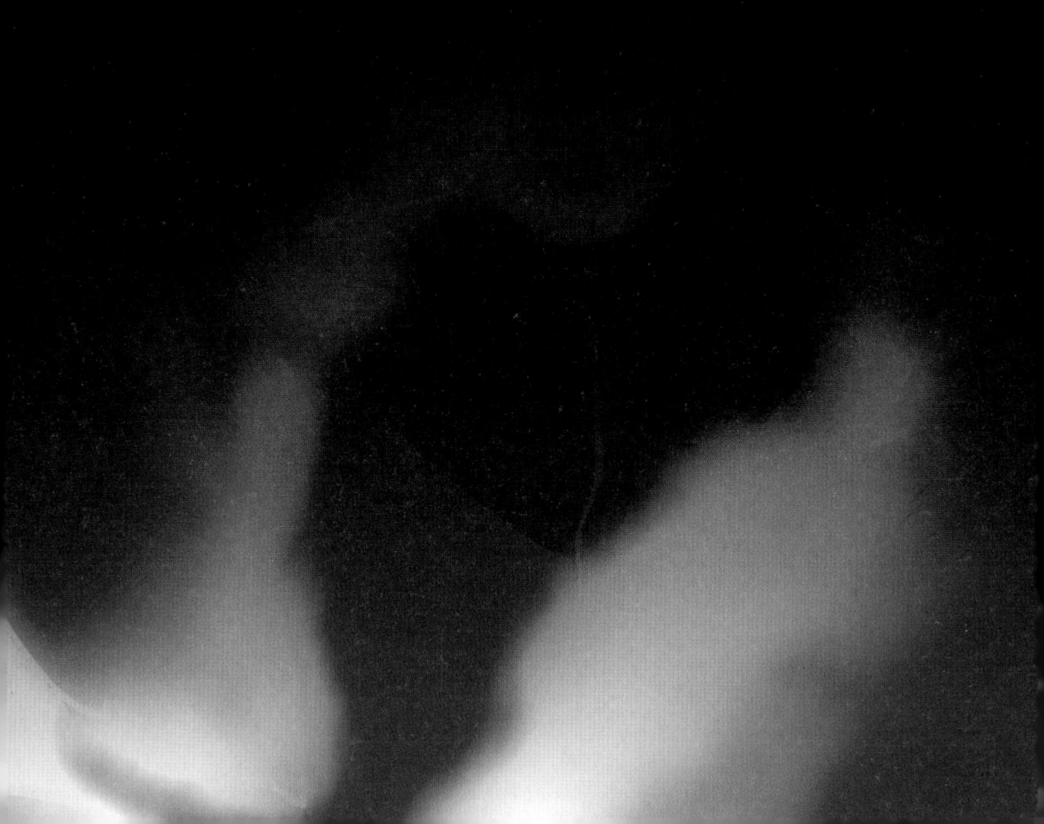

Solo Leveling

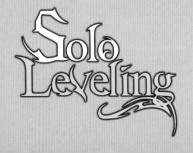

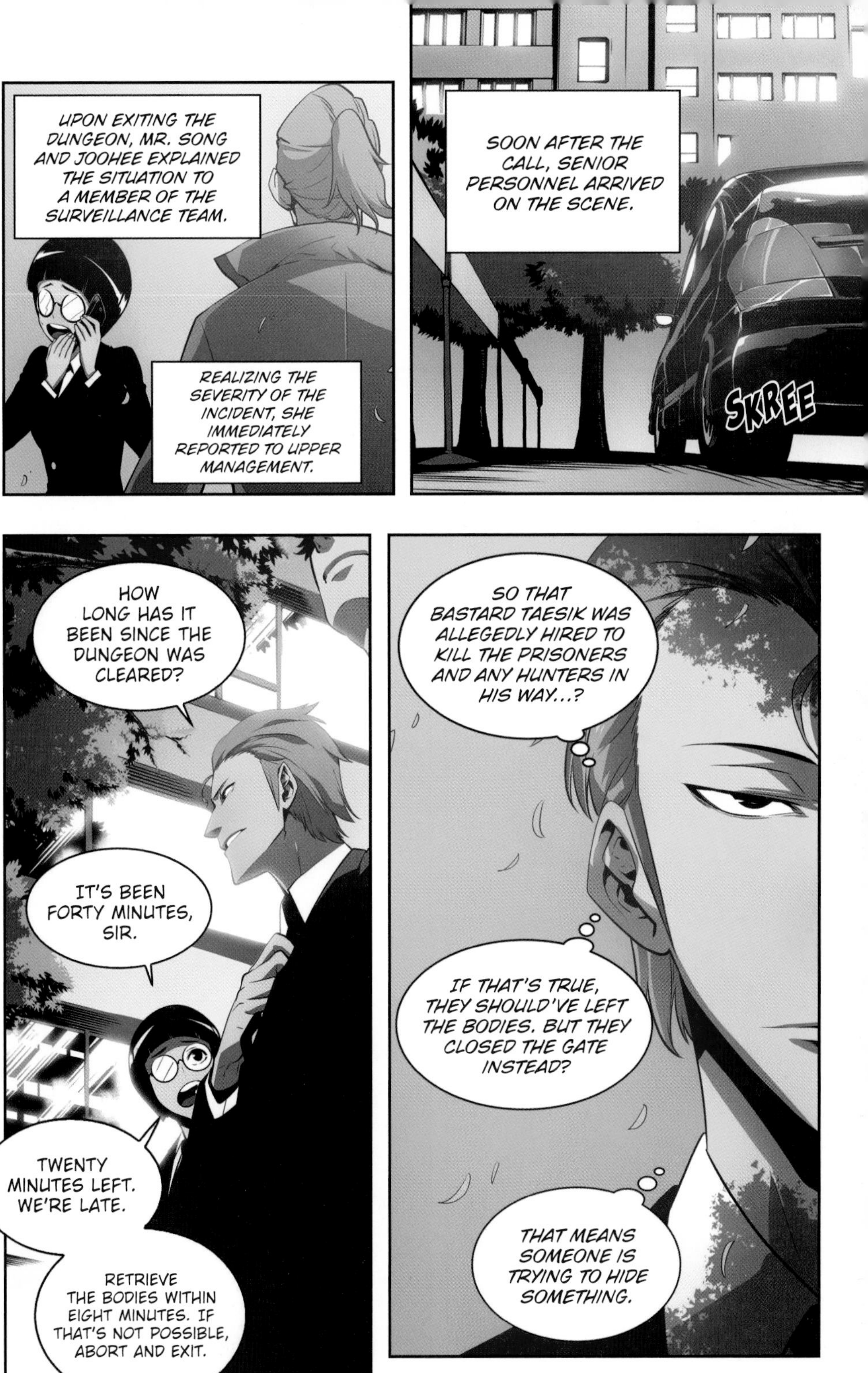
UPON EXITING THE DUNGEON, MR. SONG AND JOOHEE EXPLAINED THE SITUATION TO A MEMBER OF THE SURVEILLANCE TEAM.
REALIZING THE SEVERITY OF THE INCIDENT, SHE IMMEDIATELY REPORTED TO UPPER MANAGEMENT.
SOON AFTER THE CALL, SENIOR PERSONNEL ARRIVED ON THE SCENE.
SKREE
HOW LONG HAS IT BEEN SINCE THE DUNGEON WAS CLEARED?
IT'S BEEN FORTY MINUTES, SIR.
TWENTY MINUTES LEFT. WE'RE LATE.
RETRIEVE THE BODIES WITHIN EIGHT MINUTES. IF THAT'S NOT POSSIBLE, ABORT AND EXIT.
SO THAT BASTARD TAESIK WAS ALLEGEDLY HIRED TO KILL THE PRISONERS AND ANY HUNTERS IN HIS WAY...?
IF THAT'S TRUE, THEY SHOULD'VE LEFT THE BODIES. BUT THEY CLOSED THE GATE INSTEAD?
THAT MEANS SOMEONE IS TRYING TO HIDE SOMETHING.

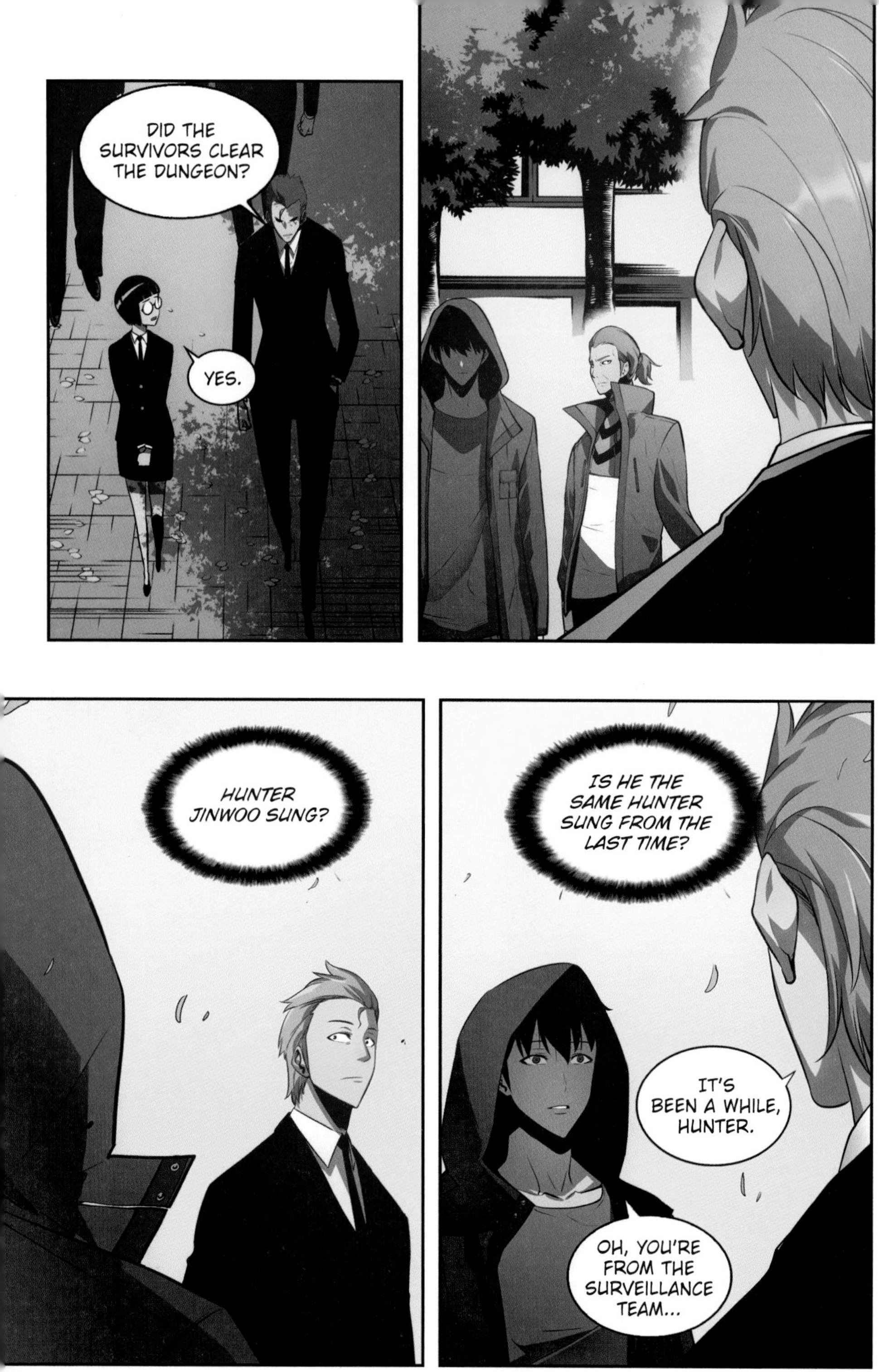
DID THE SURVIVORS CLEAR THE DUNGEON?
YES.
HUNTER JINWOO SUNG?
IS HE THE SAME HUNTER SUNG FROM THE LAST TIME?
IT'S BEEN A WHILE, HUNTER.
OH, YOU'RE FROM THE SURVEILLANCE TEAM...

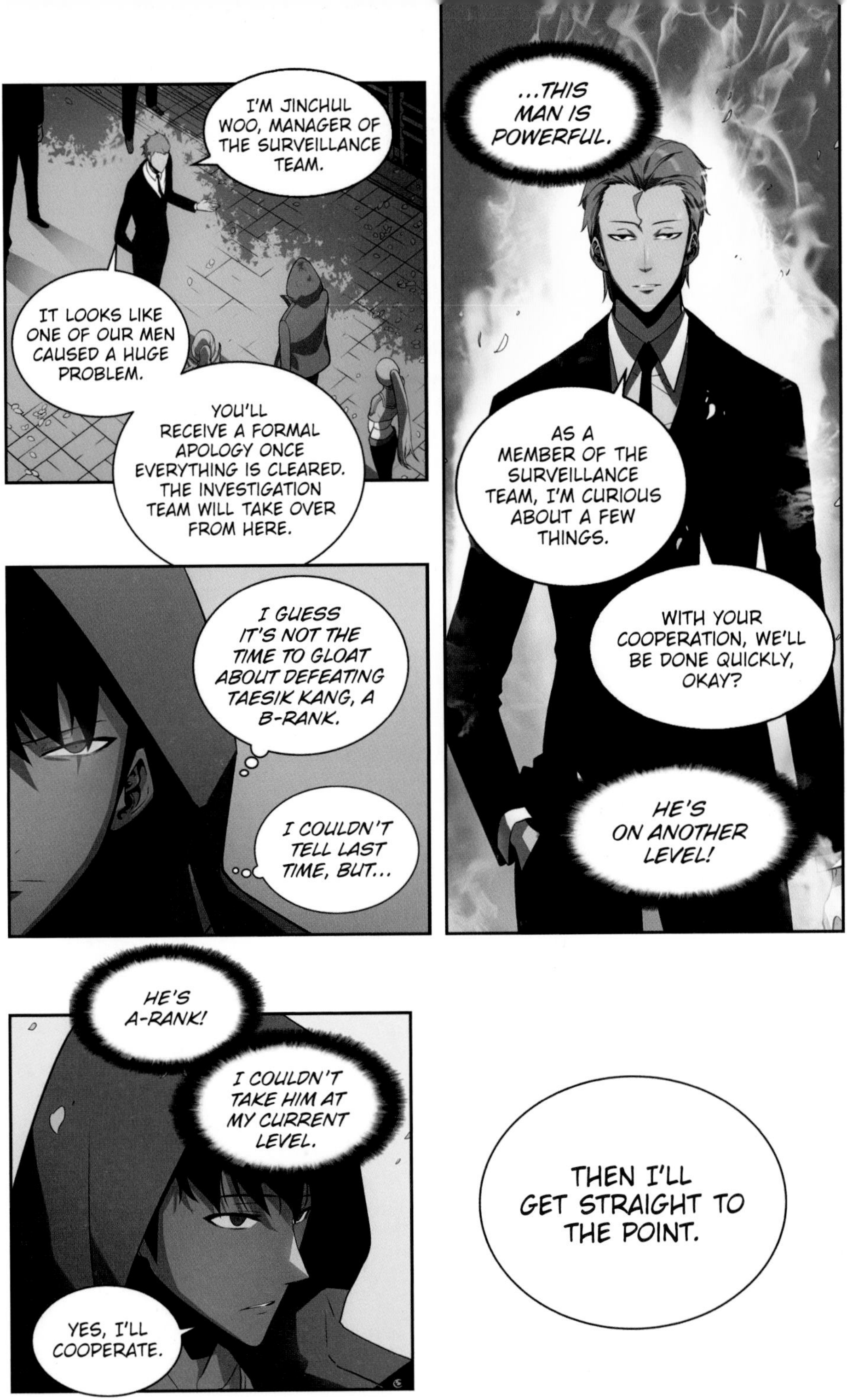
I'M JINCHUL WOO, MANAGER OF THE SURVEILLANCE TEAM.
IT LOOKS LIKE ONE OF OUR MEN CAUSED A HUGE PROBLEM.
YOU'LL RECEIVE A FORMAL APOLOGY ONCE EVERYTHING IS CLEARED. THE INVESTIGATION TEAM WILL TAKE OVER FROM HERE.
I GUESS IT'S NOT THE TIME TO GLOAT ABOUT DEFEATING TAESIK KANG, A B-RANK.
I COULDN'T TELL LAST TIME, BUT...
...THIS MAN IS POWERFUL.
AS A MEMBER OF THE SURVEILLANCE TEAM, I'M CURIOUS ABOUT A FEW THINGS.
WITH YOUR COOPERATION, WE'LL BE DONE QUICKLY, OKAY?
HE'S ON ANOTHER LEVEL!
HE'S A-RANK!
I COULDN'T TAKE HIM AT MY CURRENT LEVEL.
YES, I'LL COOPERATE.
THEN I'LL GET STRAIGHT TO THE POINT.

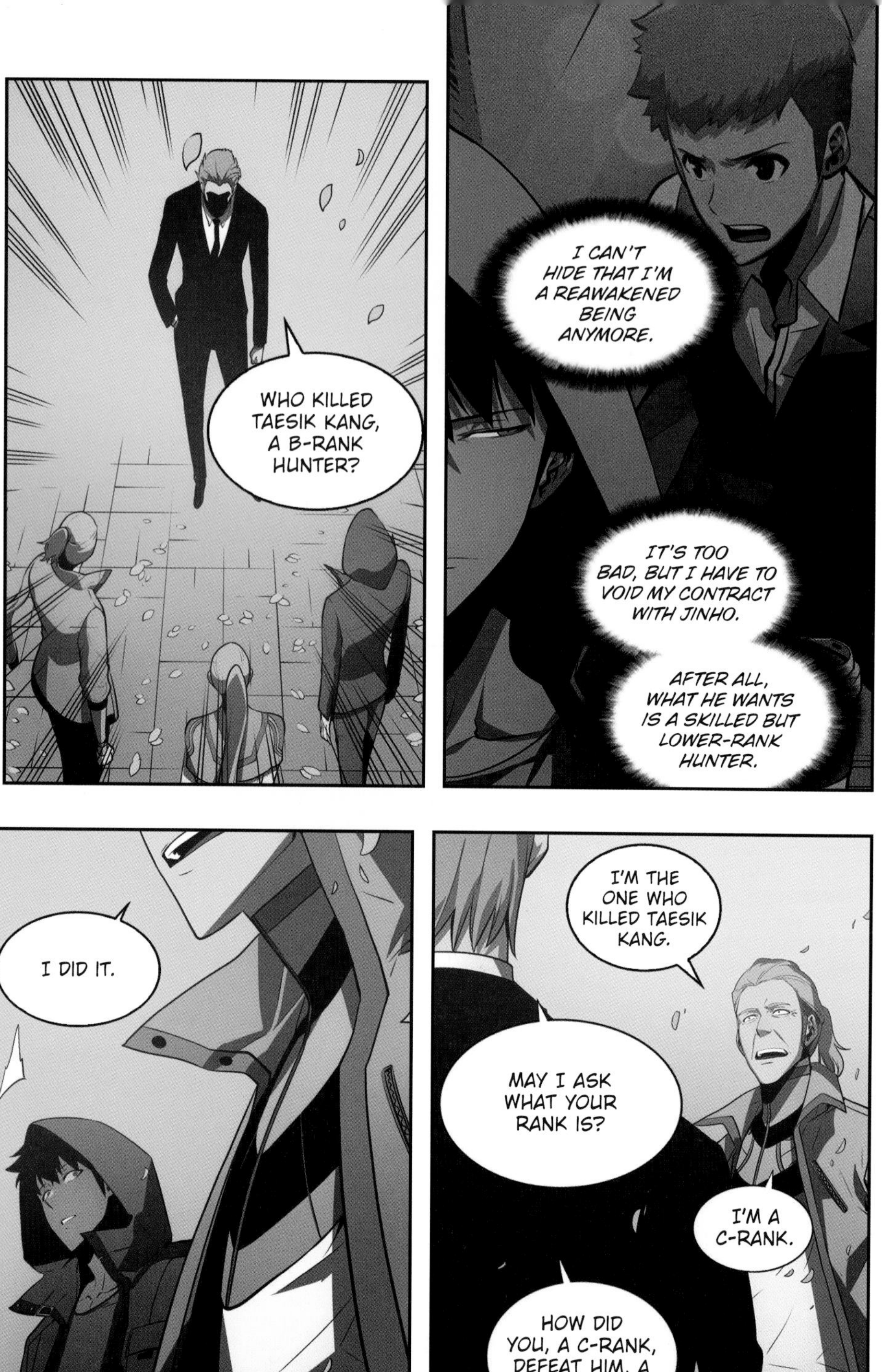
WHO KILLED TAESIK KANG, A B-RANK HUNTER?
I CAN'T HIDE THAT I'M A REAWAKENED BEING ANYMORE.
IT'S TOO BAD, BUT I HAVE TO VOID MY CONTRACT WITH JINHO.
AFTER ALL, WHAT HE WANTS IS A SKILLED BUT LOWER-RANK HUNTER.
I DID IT.
I'M THE ONE WHO KILLED TAESIK KANG.
MAY I ASK WHAT YOUR RANK IS?
I'M A C-RANK.
HOW DID YOU, A C-RANK, DEFEAT HIM, A B-RANK...?

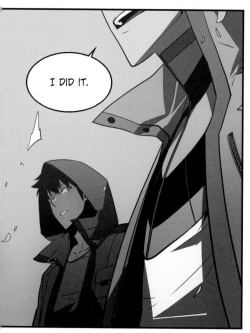

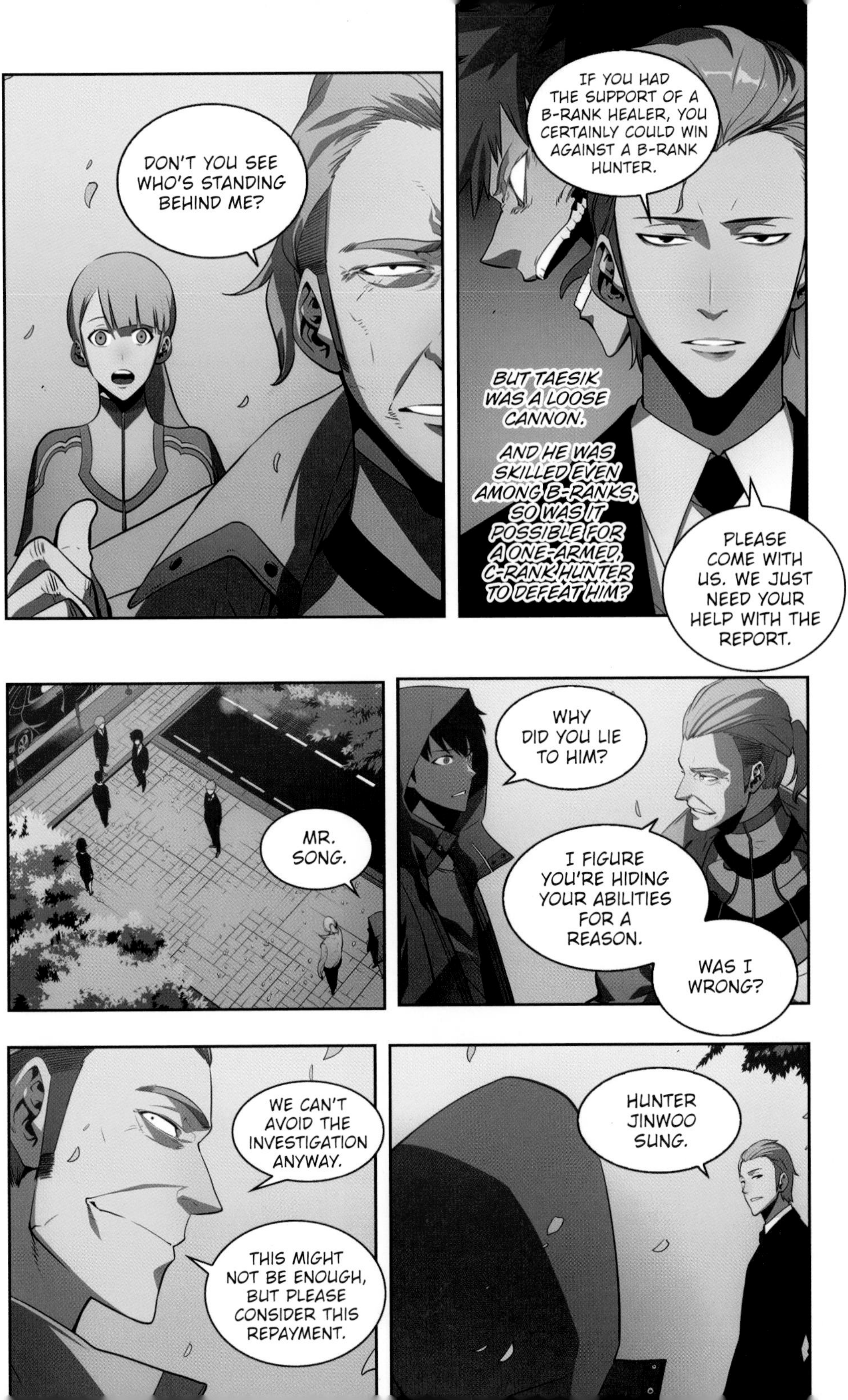
DON'T YOU SEE WHO'S STANDING BEHIND ME?
IF YOU HAD THE SUPPORT OF A B-RANK HEALER, YOU CERTAINLY COULD WIN AGAINST A B-RANK HUNTER.
BUT TAESIK WAS A LOOSE CANNON.
AND HE WAS SKILLED EVEN AMONG B-RANKS, SO WAS IT POSSIBLE FOR A ONE-ARMED, C-RANK HUNTER TO DEFEAT HIM?
PLEASE COME WITH US. WE JUST NEED YOUR HELP WITH THE REPORT.
MR. SONG.
WHY DID YOU LIE TO HIM?
I FIGURE YOU'RE HIDING YOUR ABILITIES FOR A REASON.
WAS I WRONG?
WE CAN'T AVOID THE INVESTIGATION ANYWAY.
THIS MIGHT NOT BE ENOUGH, BUT PLEASE CONSIDER THIS REPAYMENT.
HUNTER JINWOO SUNG.

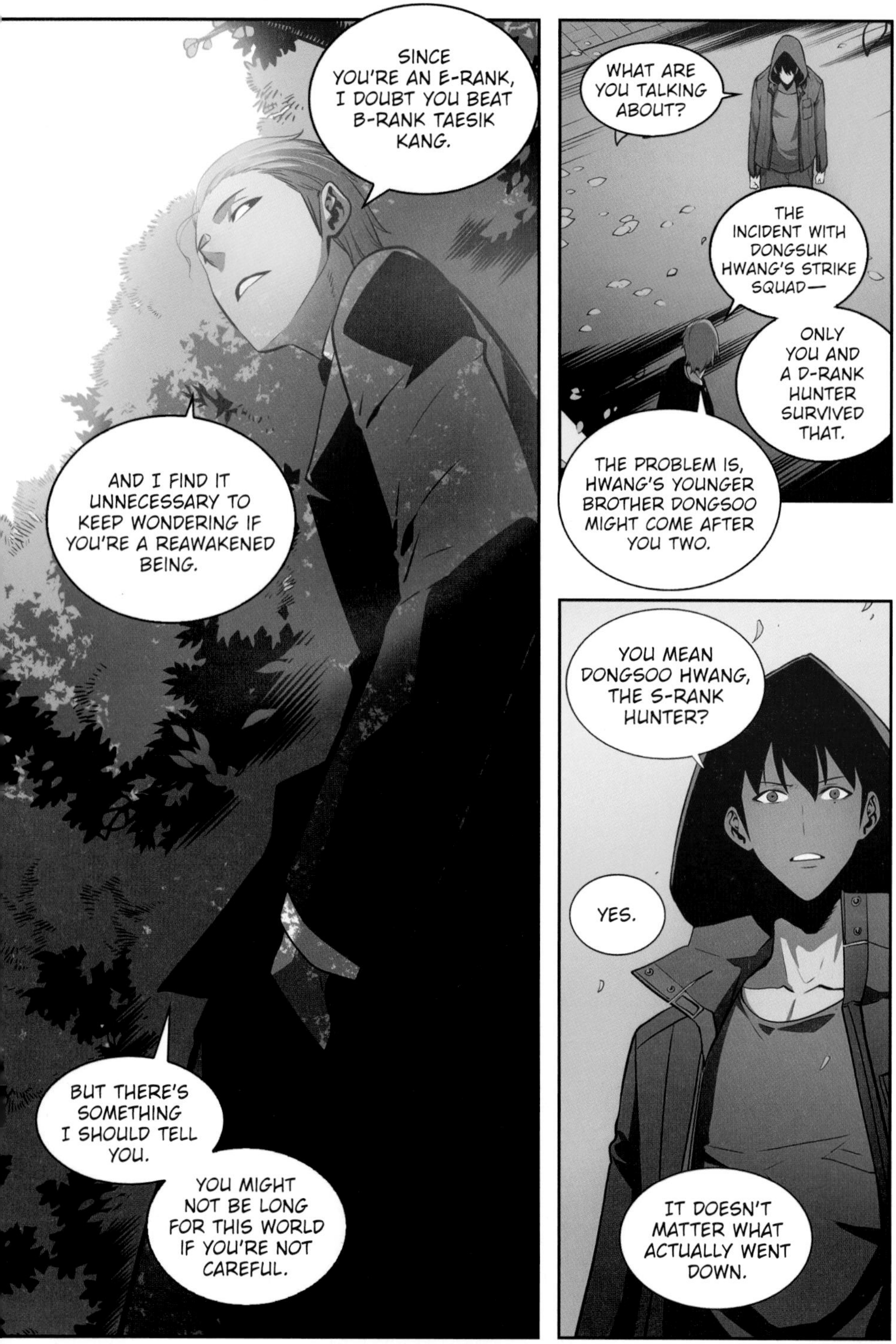
SINCE YOU'RE AN E-RANK, I DOUBT YOU BEAT B-RANK TAESIK KANG.
AND I FIND IT UNNECESSARY TO KEEP WONDERING IF YOU'RE A REAWAKENED BEING.
BUT THERE'S SOMETHING I SHOULD TELL YOU.
YOU MIGHT NOT BE LONG FOR THIS WORLD IF YOU'RE NOT CAREFUL.
WHAT ARE YOU TALKING ABOUT?
THE INCIDENT WITH DONGSUK HWANG'S STRIKE SQUAD—
ONLY YOU AND A D-RANK HUNTER SURVIVED THAT.
THE PROBLEM IS, HWANG'S YOUNGER BROTHER DONGSOO MIGHT COME AFTER YOU TWO.
YOU MEAN DONGSOO HWANG, THE S-RANK HUNTER?
YES.
IT DOESN'T MATTER WHAT ACTUALLY WENT DOWN.

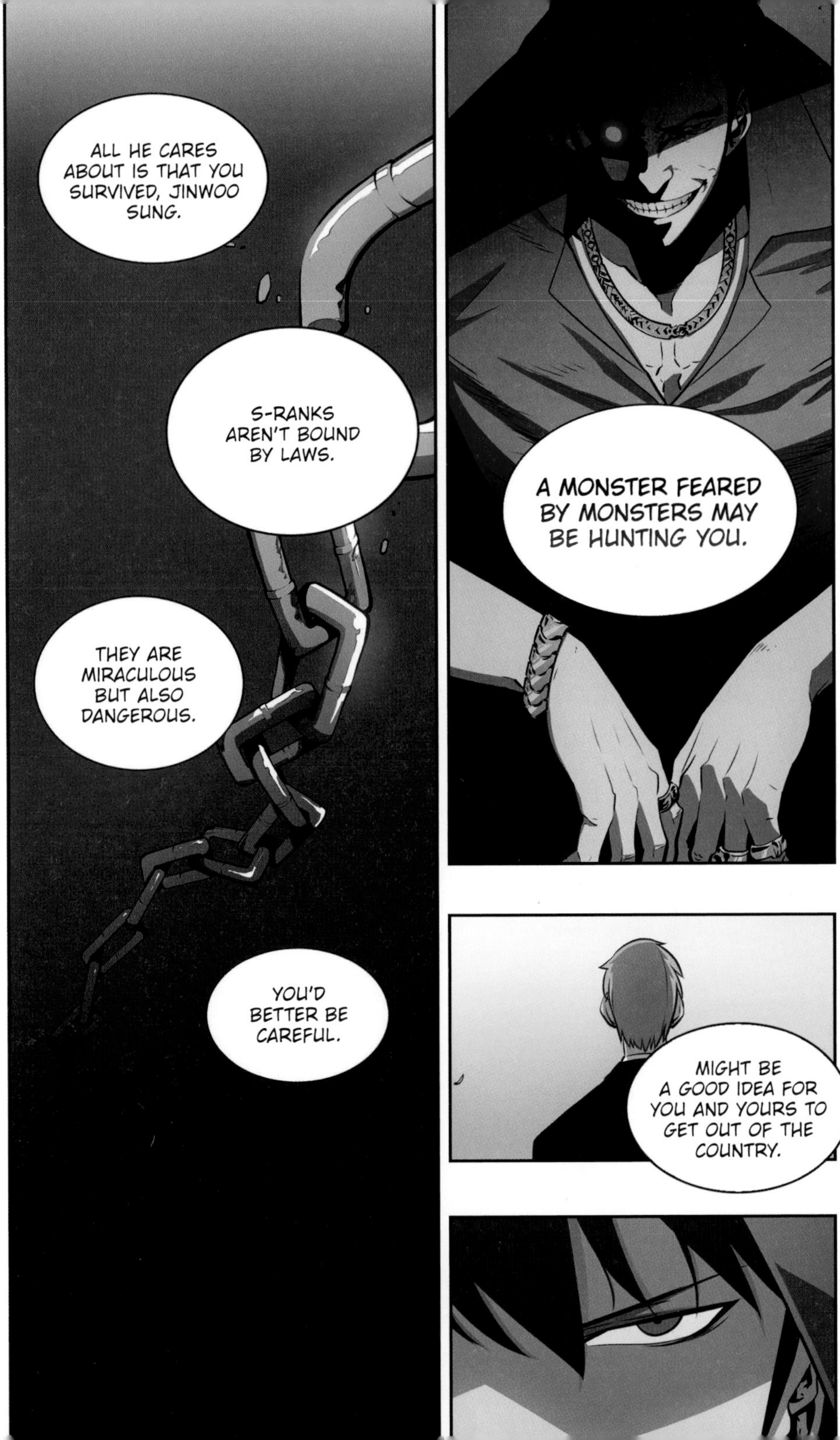
ALL HE CARES ABOUT IS THAT YOU SURVIVED, JINWOO SUNG.
S-RANKS AREN'T BOUND BY LAWS.
THEY ARE MIRACULOUS BUT ALSO DANGEROUS.
YOU'D BETTER BE CAREFUL.
A MONSTER FEARED BY MONSTERS MAY BE HUNTING YOU.
MIGHT BE A GOOD IDEA FOR YOU AND YOURS TO GET OUT OF THE COUNTRY.

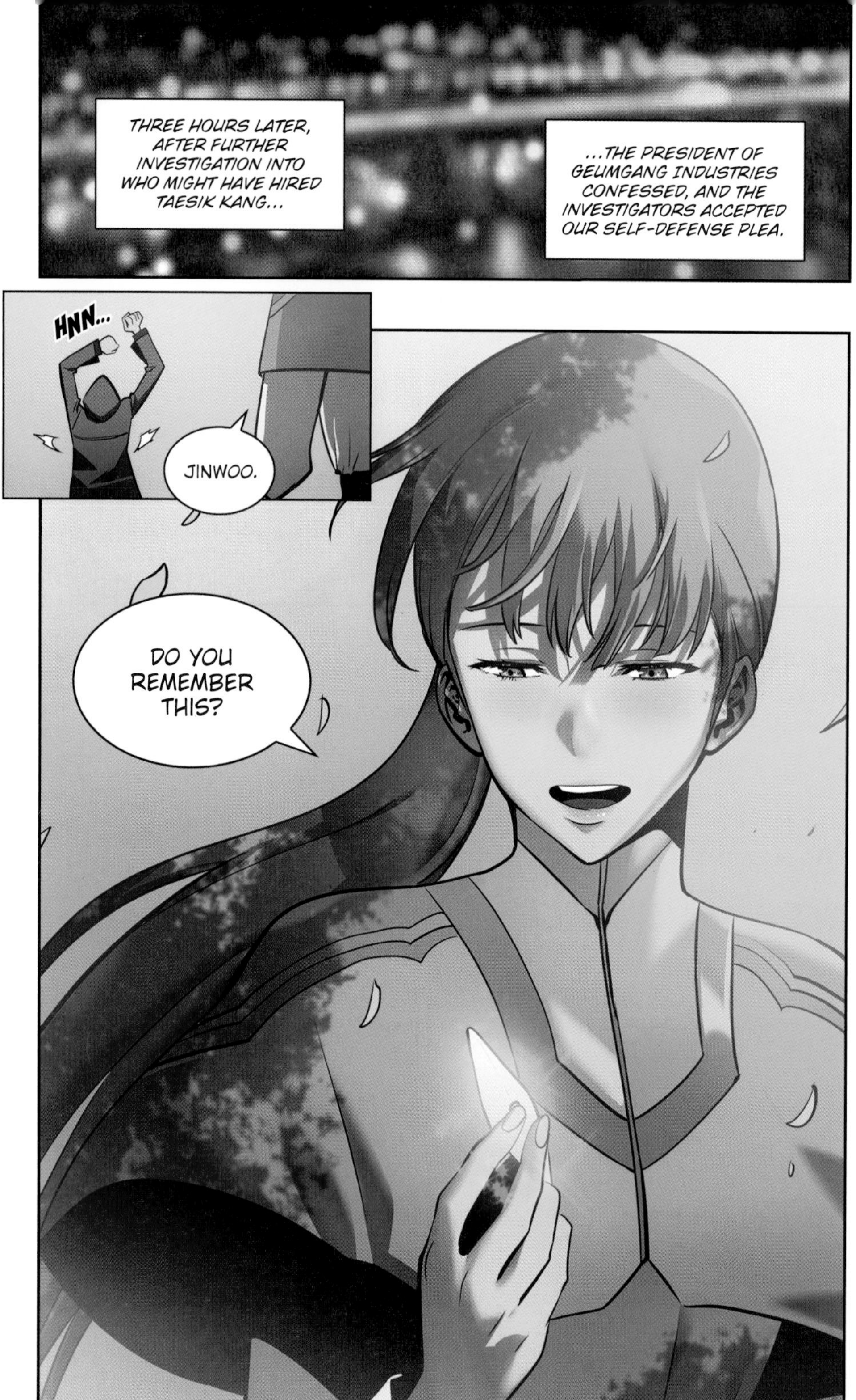
THREE HOURS LATER, AFTER FURTHER INVESTIGATION INTO WHO MIGHT HAVE HIRED TAESIK KANG...
...THE PRESIDENT OF GEUMGANG INDUSTRIES CONFESSED, AND THE INVESTIGATORS ACCEPTED OUR SELF-DEFENSE PLEA.
HNN...
JINWOO.
DO YOU REMEMBER THIS?

STATUS

NAME: Jinwoo Sung   LEVEL: 27
JOB: None   FATIGUE: 0
TITLE: Wolf Assassin

HP: 5114

MP: 548

STRENGTH: 72 ◦   STAMINA: 43 ◦
AGILITY: 82 ◦   INTELLECT: 39 ◦
PERCEPTION: 69 ◦

Physical Damage Decrease: 20% Activated

Available points: 5

⊕ SKILLS

[Passive Skill]

? (Unknown)   MAX

🧍 Willpower   Lv. 1

[Active Skill]

🏃 Dash   Lv. 1

Murderous Intent   Lv. 1

[ITEM: Warden's Collar]
ACQUISITION DIFFICULTY: A
CATEGORY: Collar
EQUIPPED

Agility +20, Perception +20

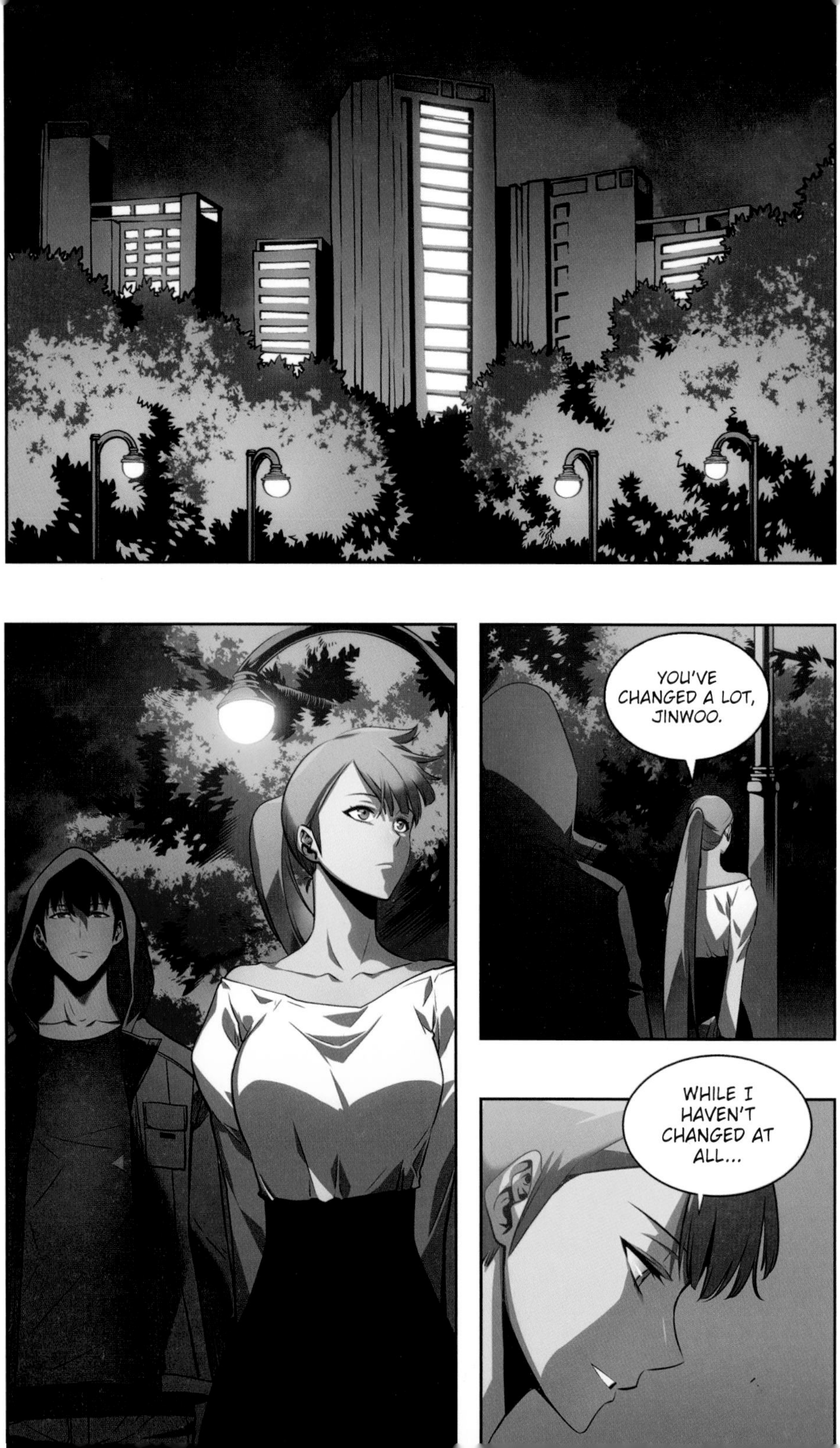
YOU'VE CHANGED A LOT, JINWOO.
WHILE I HAVEN'T CHANGED AT ALL...

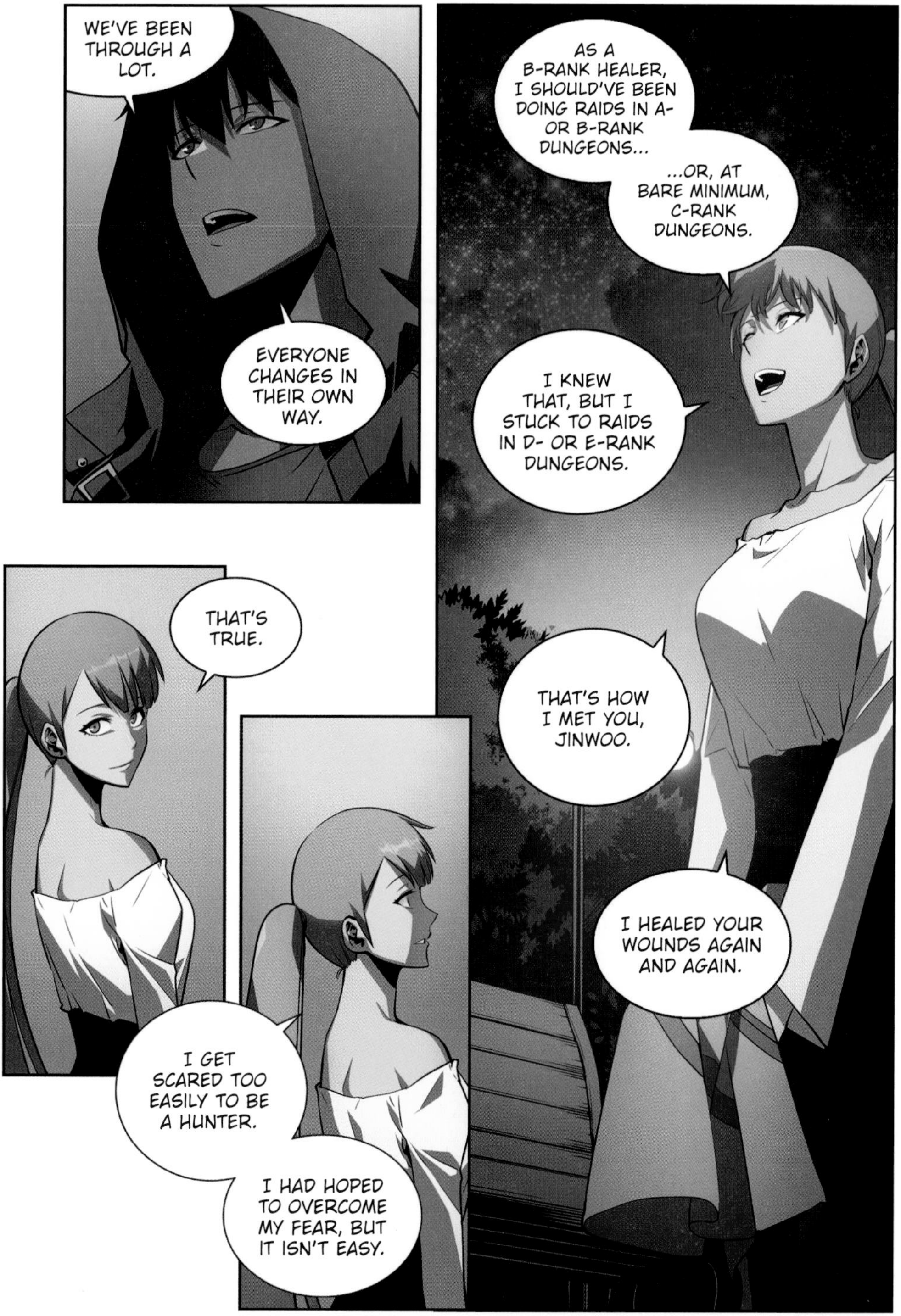
WE'VE BEEN THROUGH A LOT.
EVERYONE CHANGES IN THEIR OWN WAY.
THAT'S TRUE.
I GET SCARED TOO EASILY TO BE A HUNTER.
I HAD HOPED TO OVERCOME MY FEAR, BUT IT ISN'T EASY.
AS A B-RANK HEALER, I SHOULD'VE BEEN DOING RAIDS IN A- OR B-RANK DUNGEONS...
...OR, AT BARE MINIMUM, C-RANK DUNGEONS.
I KNEW THAT, BUT I STUCK TO RAIDS IN D- OR E-RANK DUNGEONS.
THAT'S HOW I MET YOU, JINWOO.
I HEALED YOUR WOUNDS AGAIN AND AGAIN.

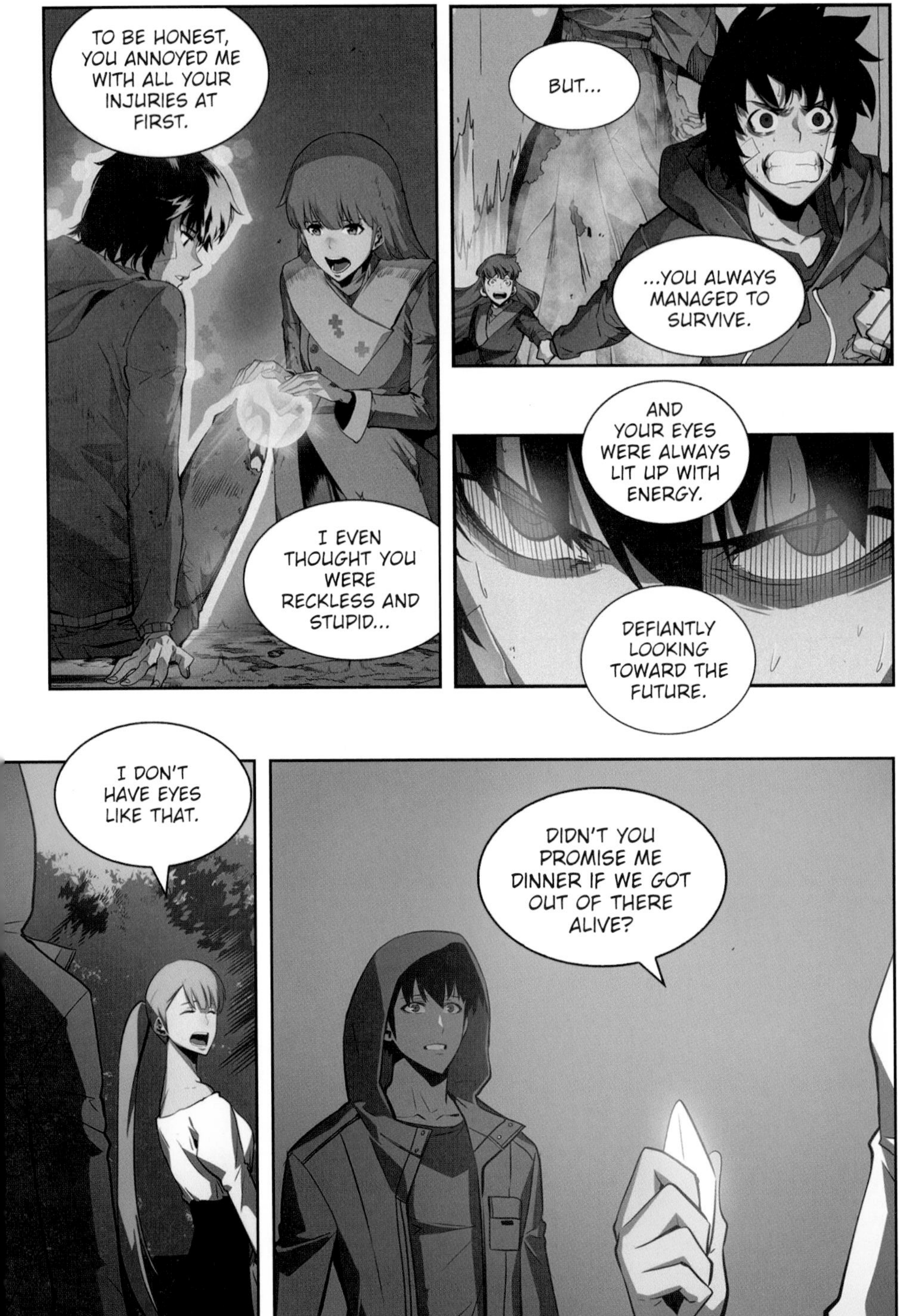
TO BE HONEST, YOU ANNOYED ME WITH ALL YOUR INJURIES AT FIRST.
I EVEN THOUGHT YOU WERE RECKLESS AND STUPID...
BUT...
...YOU ALWAYS MANAGED TO SURVIVE.
AND YOUR EYES WERE ALWAYS LIT UP WITH ENERGY.
DEFIANTLY LOOKING TOWARD THE FUTURE.
I DON'T HAVE EYES LIKE THAT.
DIDN'T YOU PROMISE ME DINNER IF WE GOT OUT OF THERE ALIVE?

HERE...
TAKE THIS
BACK.

WAIT...

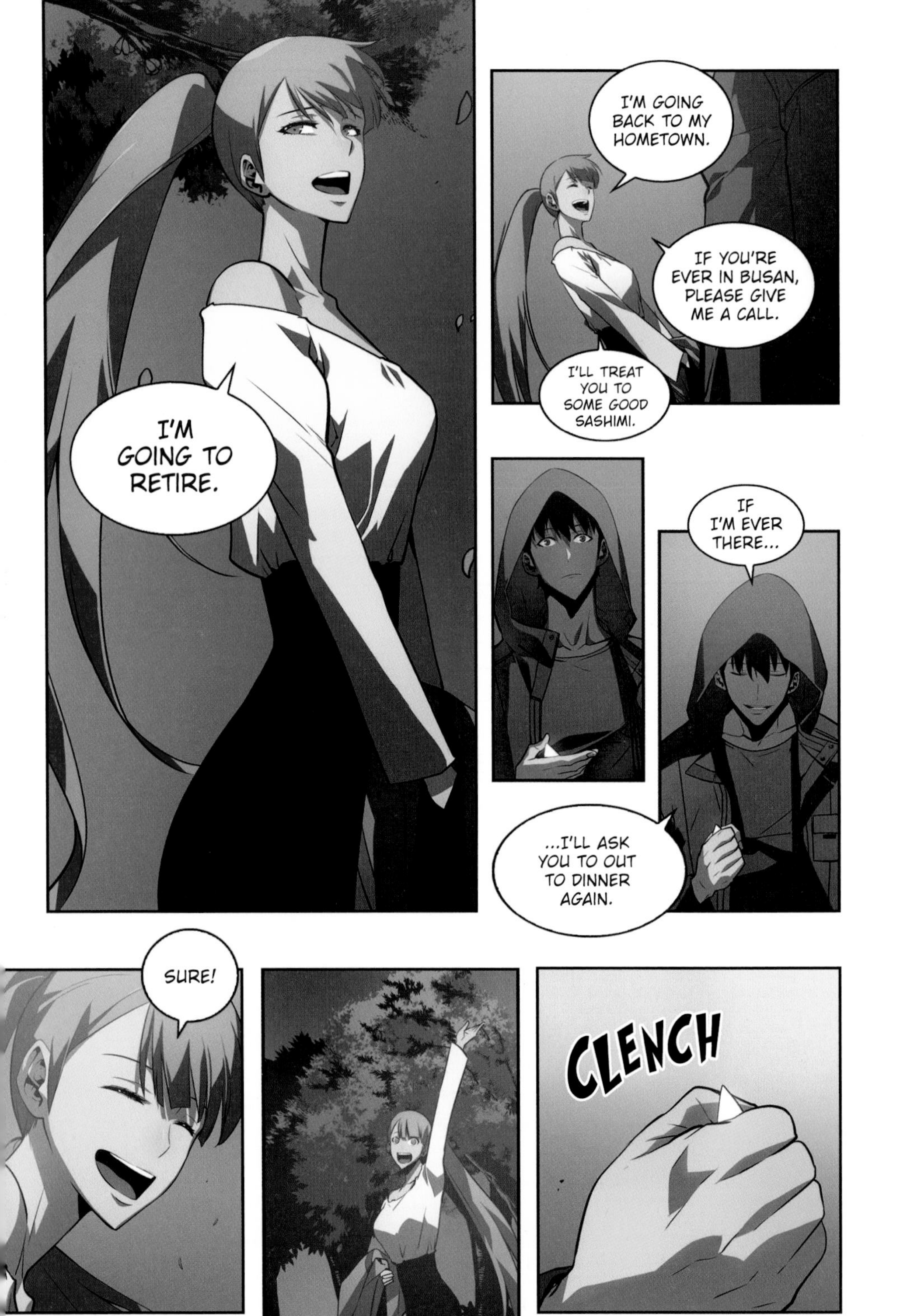
I'M GOING TO RETIRE.
I'M GOING BACK TO MY HOMETOWN.
IF YOU'RE EVER IN BUSAN, PLEASE GIVE ME A CALL.
I'LL TREAT YOU TO SOME GOOD SASHIMI.
IF I'M EVER THERE...
...I'LL ASK YOU TO OUT TO DINNER AGAIN.
SURE!
CLENCH

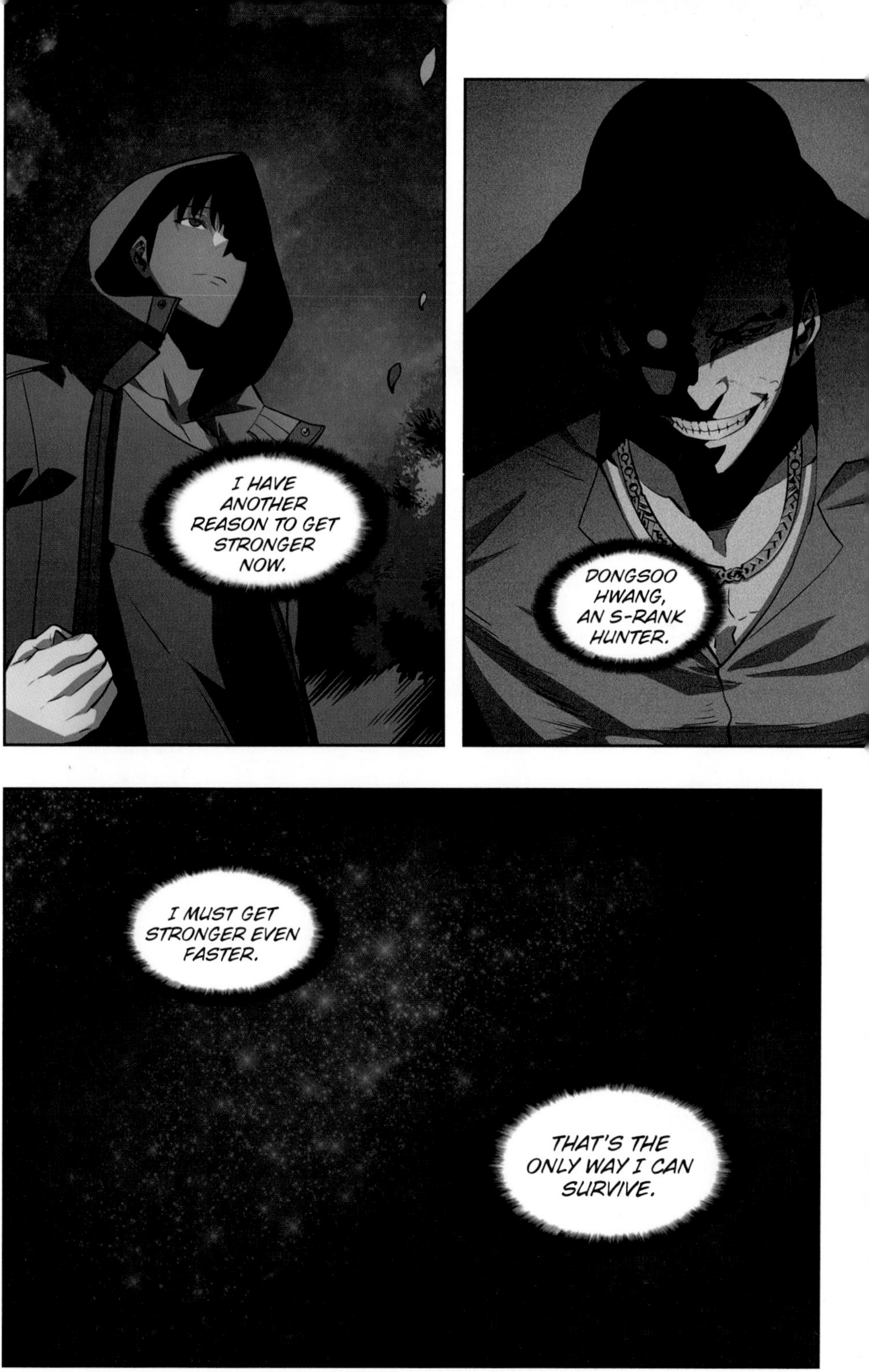
I HAVE ANOTHER REASON TO GET STRONGER NOW.
DONGSOO HWANG, AN S-RANK HUNTER.
I MUST GET STRONGER EVEN FASTER.
THAT'S THE ONLY WAY I CAN SURVIVE.

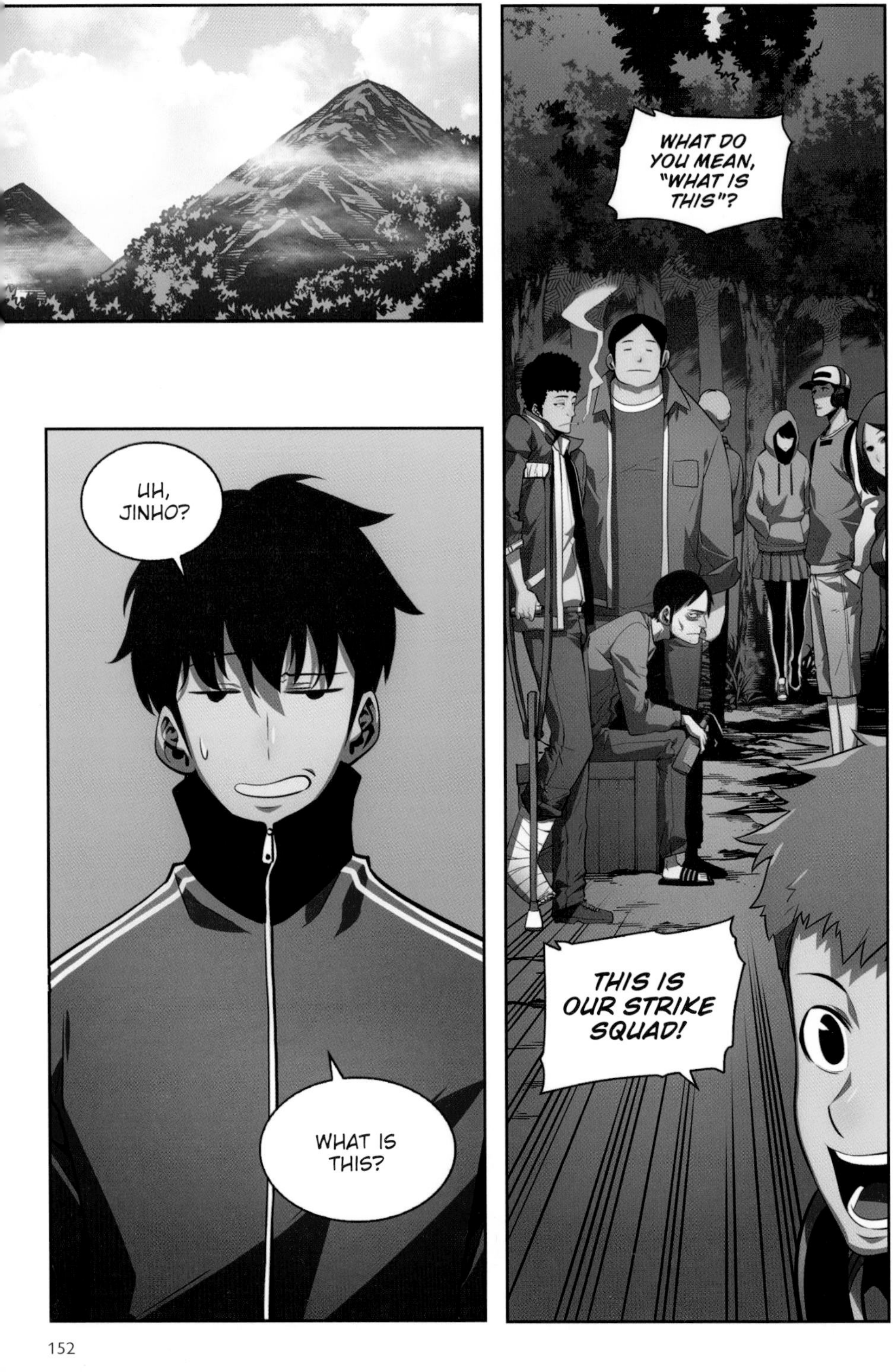
UH, JINHO?
WHAT IS THIS?
WHAT DO YOU MEAN, "WHAT IS THIS"?
THIS IS OUR STRIKE SQUAD!

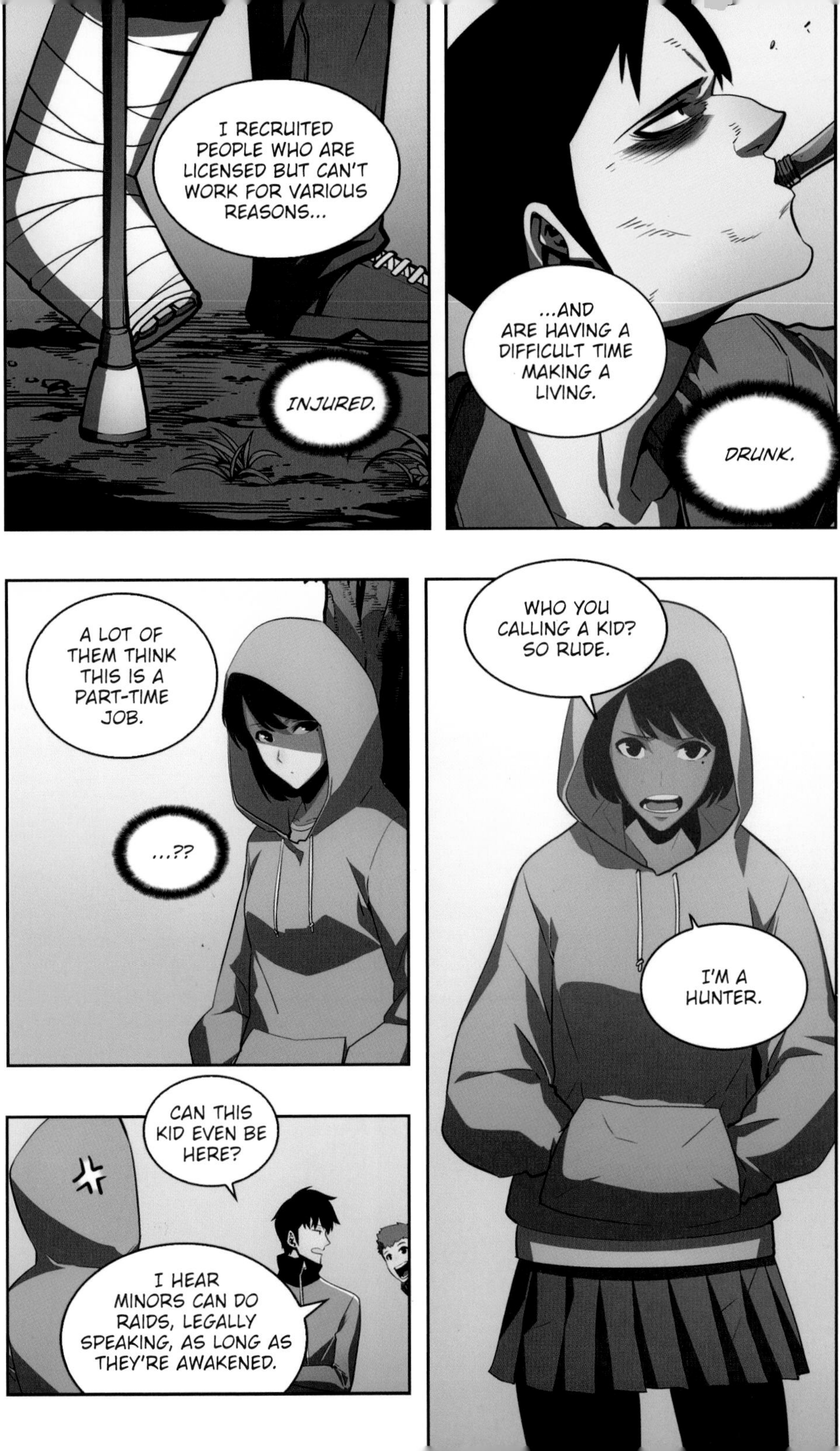
I RECRUITED PEOPLE WHO ARE LICENSED BUT CAN'T WORK FOR VARIOUS REASONS...
INJURED.
...AND ARE HAVING A DIFFICULT TIME MAKING A LIVING.
DRUNK.
A LOT OF THEM THINK THIS IS A PART-TIME JOB.
...??
CAN THIS KID EVEN BE HERE?
I HEAR MINORS CAN DO RAIDS, LEGALLY SPEAKING, AS LONG AS THEY'RE AWAKENED.
WHO YOU CALLING A KID? SO RUDE.
I'M A HUNTER.

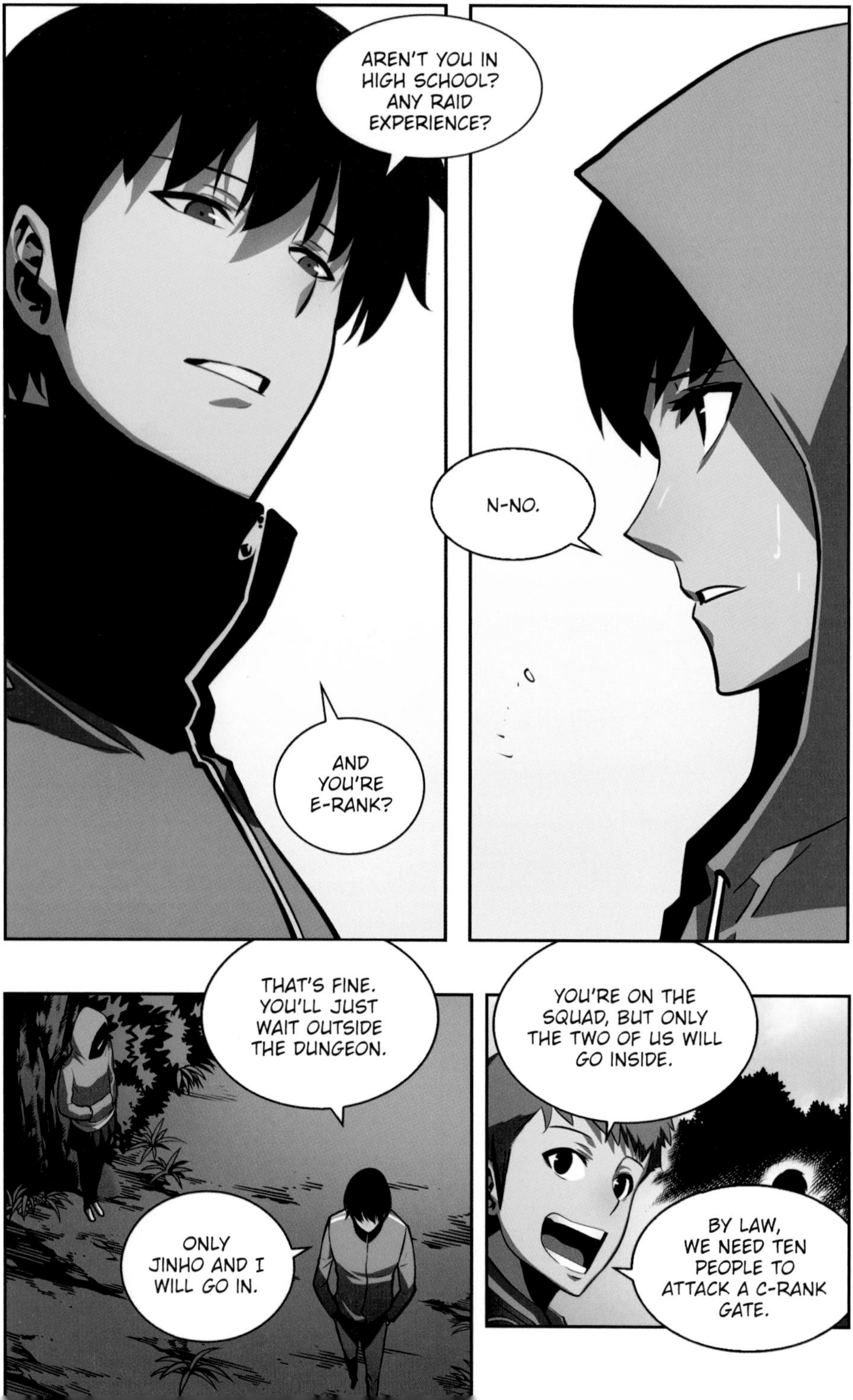
AREN'T YOU IN HIGH SCHOOL? ANY RAID EXPERIENCE?
AND YOU'RE E-RANK?
N-NO.
THAT'S FINE. YOU'LL JUST WAIT OUTSIDE THE DUNGEON.
ONLY JINHO AND I WILL GO IN.
YOU'RE ON THE SQUAD, BUT ONLY THE TWO OF US WILL GO INSIDE.
BY LAW, WE NEED TEN PEOPLE TO ATTACK A C-RANK GATE.

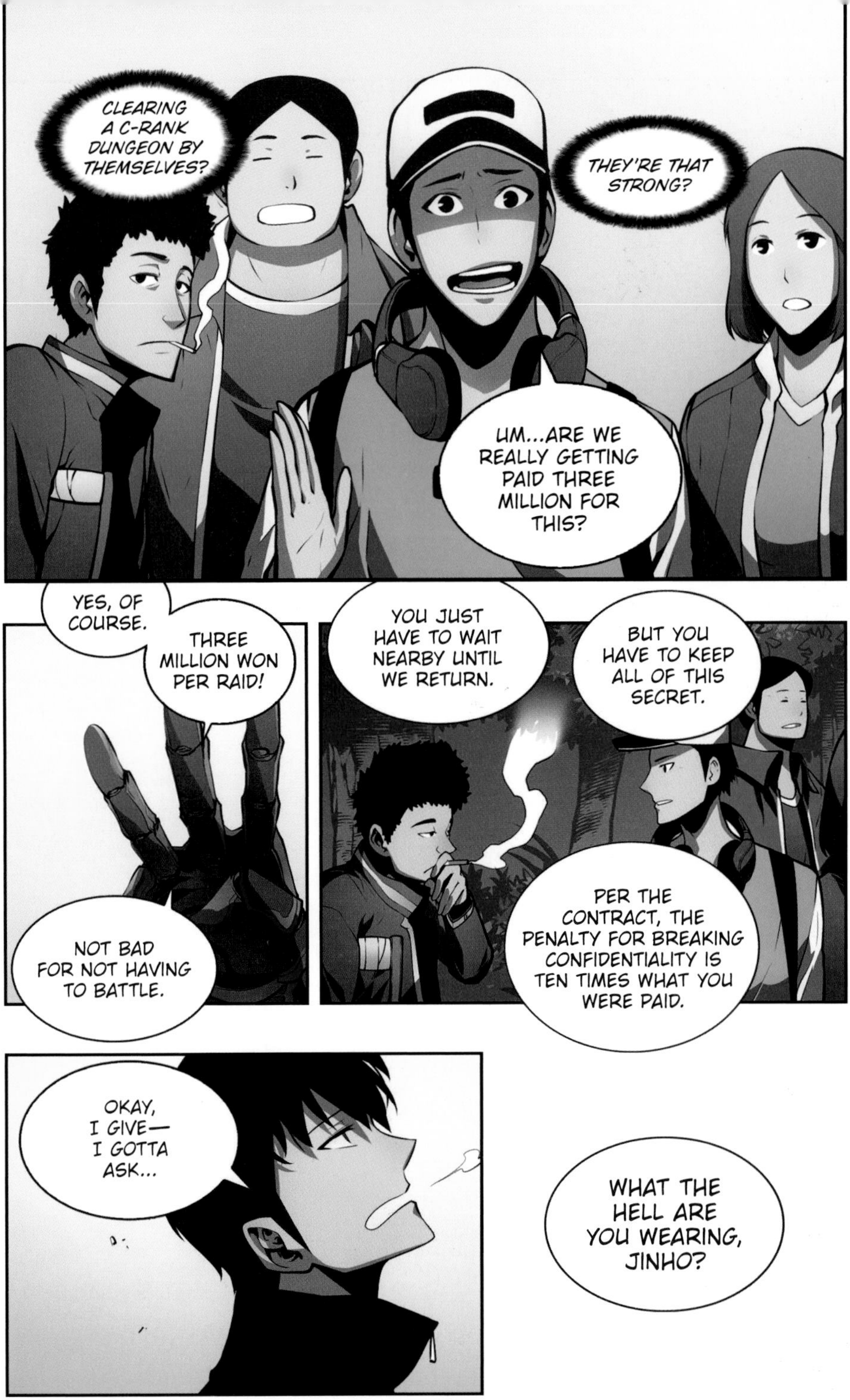
CLEARING A C-RANK DUNGEON BY THEMSELVES?
THEY'RE THAT STRONG?
UM...ARE WE REALLY GETTING PAID THREE MILLION FOR THIS?
YES, OF COURSE.
THREE MILLION WON PER RAID!
NOT BAD FOR NOT HAVING TO BATTLE.
YOU JUST HAVE TO WAIT NEARBY UNTIL WE RETURN.
BUT YOU HAVE TO KEEP ALL OF THIS SECRET.
PER THE CONTRACT, THE PENALTY FOR BREAKING CONFIDENTIALITY IS TEN TIMES WHAT YOU WERE PAID.
OKAY, I GIVE— I GOTTA ASK...
WHAT THE HELL ARE YOU WEARING, JINHO?

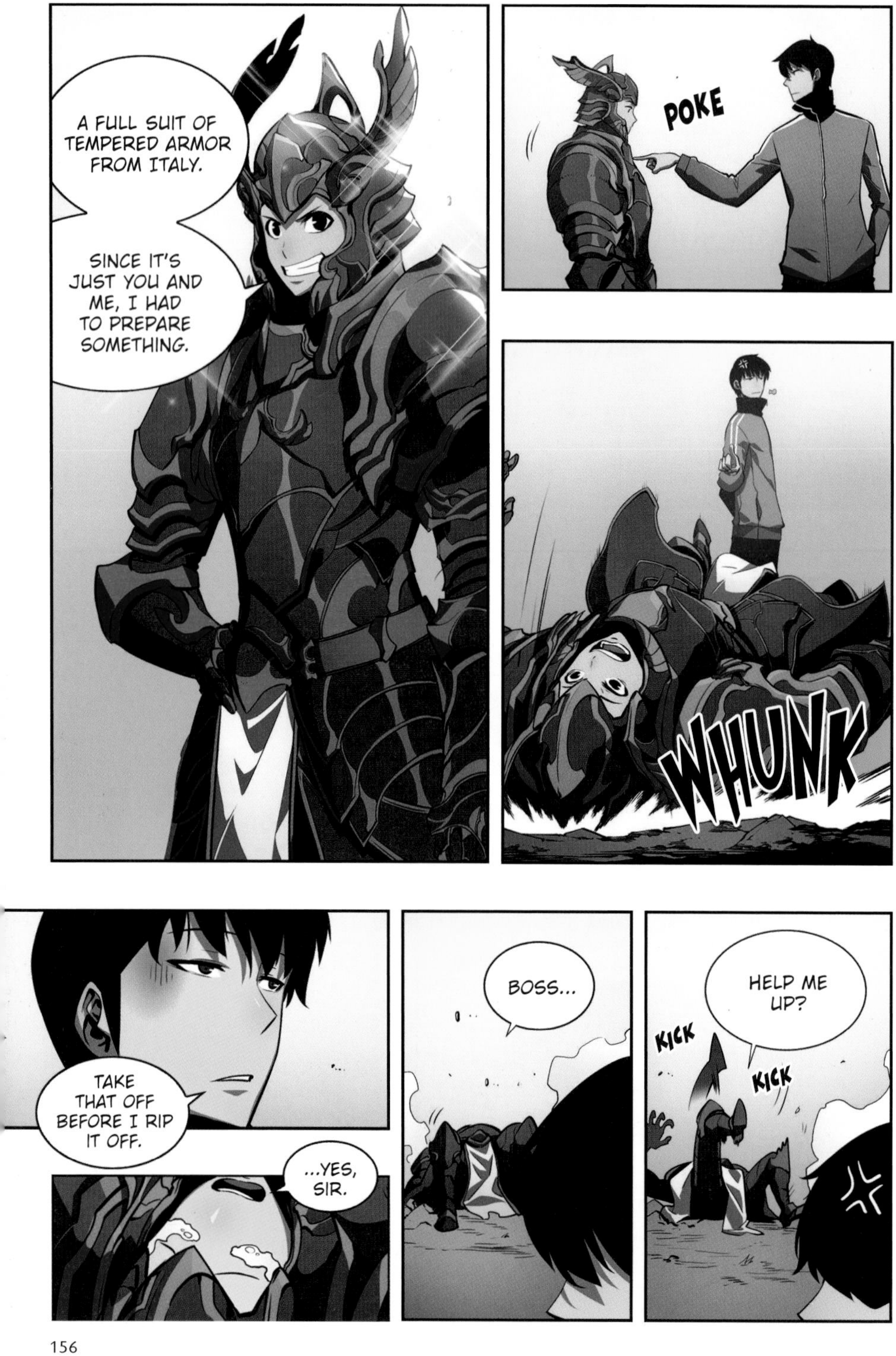
A FULL SUIT OF TEMPERED ARMOR FROM ITALY.
SINCE IT'S JUST YOU AND ME, I HAD TO PREPARE SOMETHING.
POKE
WHUNK
TAKE THAT OFF BEFORE I RIP IT OFF.
...YES, SIR.
BOSS...
KICK
KICK
HELP ME UP?

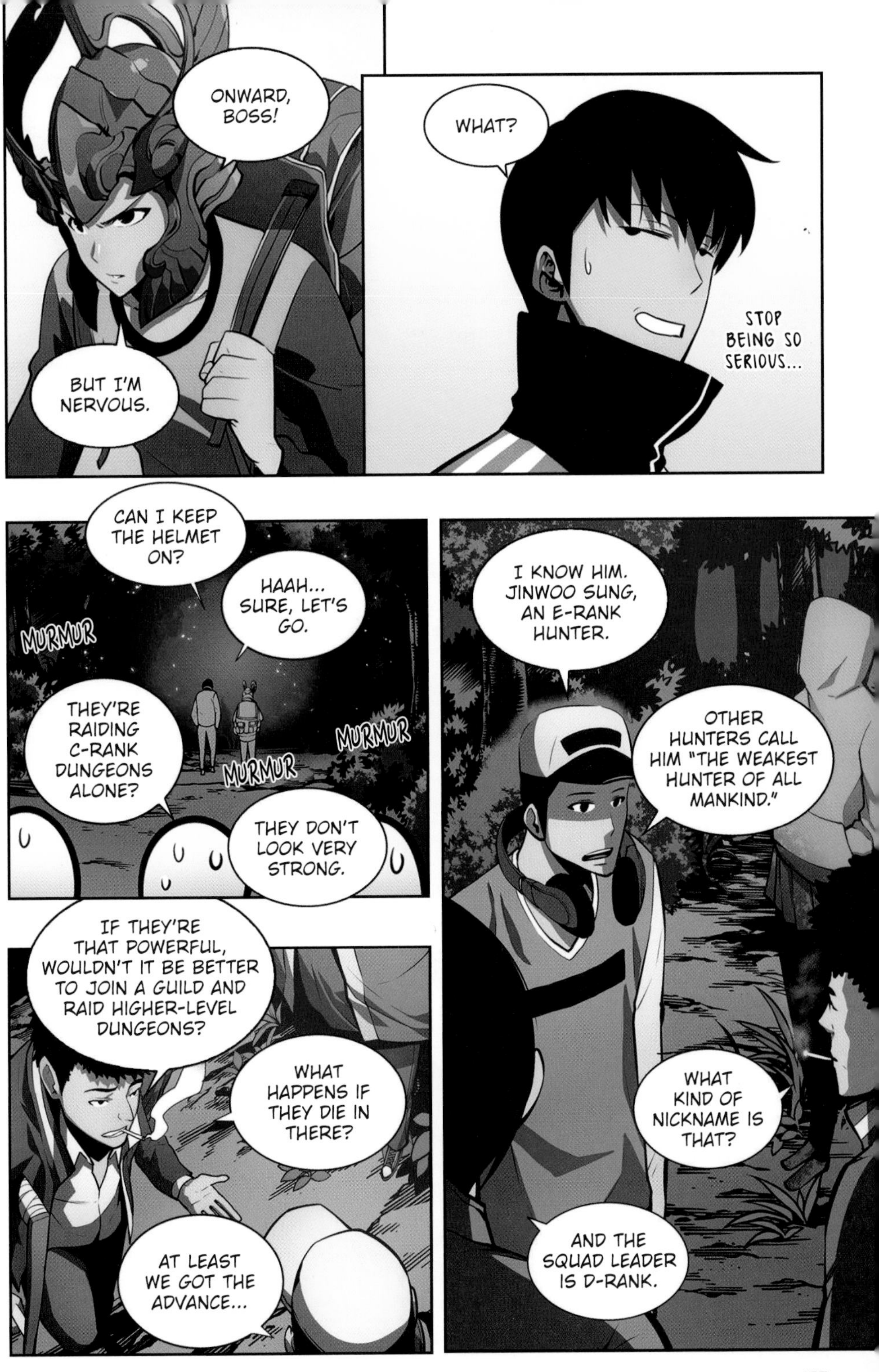
ONWARD, BOSS!
BUT I'M NERVOUS.
WHAT?
STOP BEING SO SERIOUS...
CAN I KEEP THE HELMET ON?
HAAH... SURE, LET'S GO.
MURMUR
THEY'RE RAIDING C-RANK DUNGEONS ALONE?
MURMUR
MURMUR
THEY DON'T LOOK VERY STRONG.
IF THEY'RE THAT POWERFUL, WOULDN'T IT BE BETTER TO JOIN A GUILD AND RAID HIGHER-LEVEL DUNGEONS?
WHAT HAPPENS IF THEY DIE IN THERE?
AT LEAST WE GOT THE ADVANCE...
I KNOW HIM. JINWOO SUNG, AN E-RANK HUNTER.
OTHER HUNTERS CALL HIM "THE WEAKEST HUNTER OF ALL MANKIND."
WHAT KIND OF NICKNAME IS THAT?
AND THE SQUAD LEADER IS D-RANK.

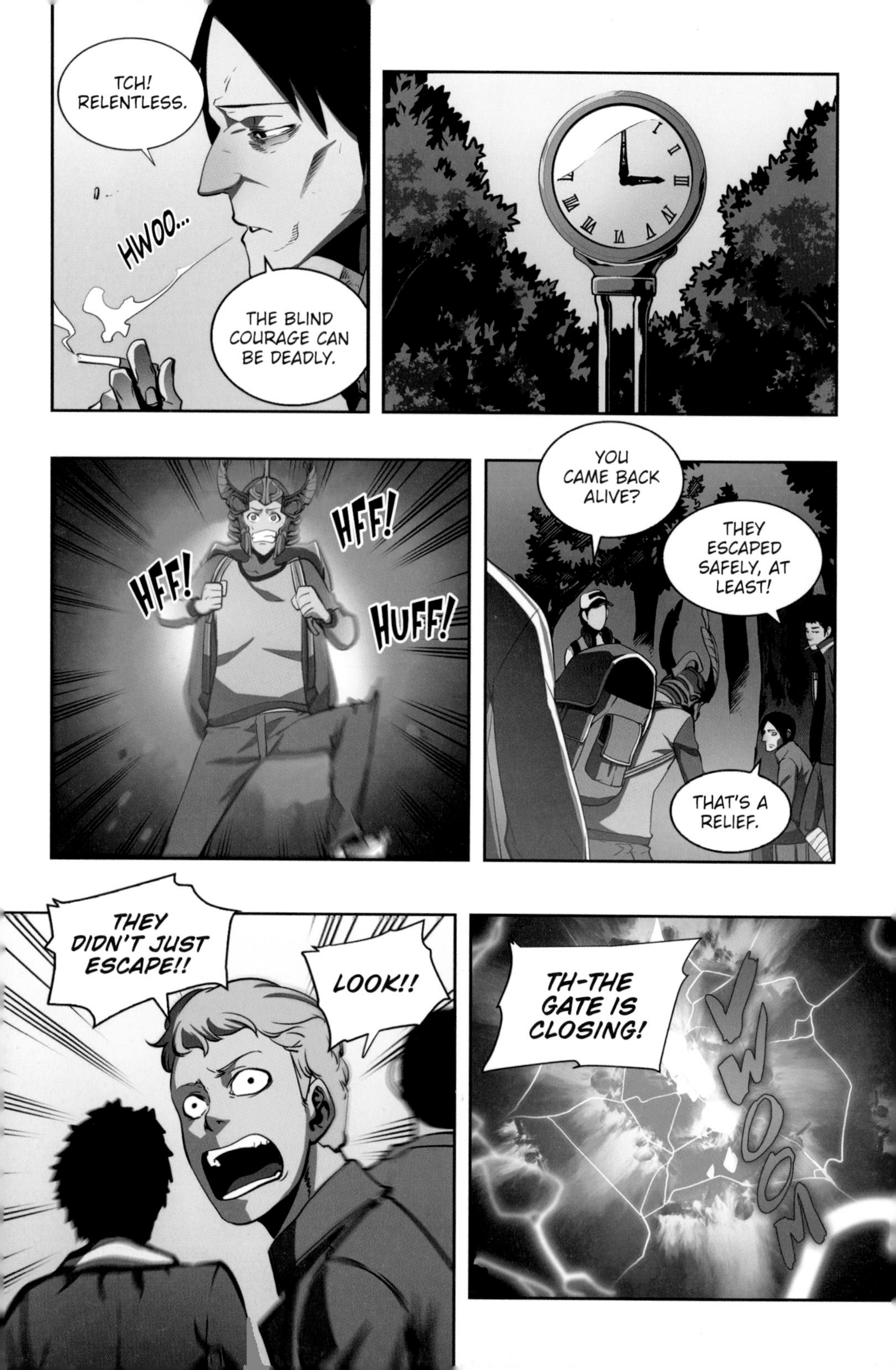
TCH! RELENTLESS.
HWOO...
THE BLIND COURAGE CAN BE DEADLY.
HFF!
HFF!
HUFF!
YOU CAME BACK ALIVE?
THEY ESCAPED SAFELY, AT LEAST!
THAT'S A RELIEF.
THEY DIDN'T JUST ESCAPE!!
LOOK!!
TH-THE GATE IS CLOSING!
VWOOM

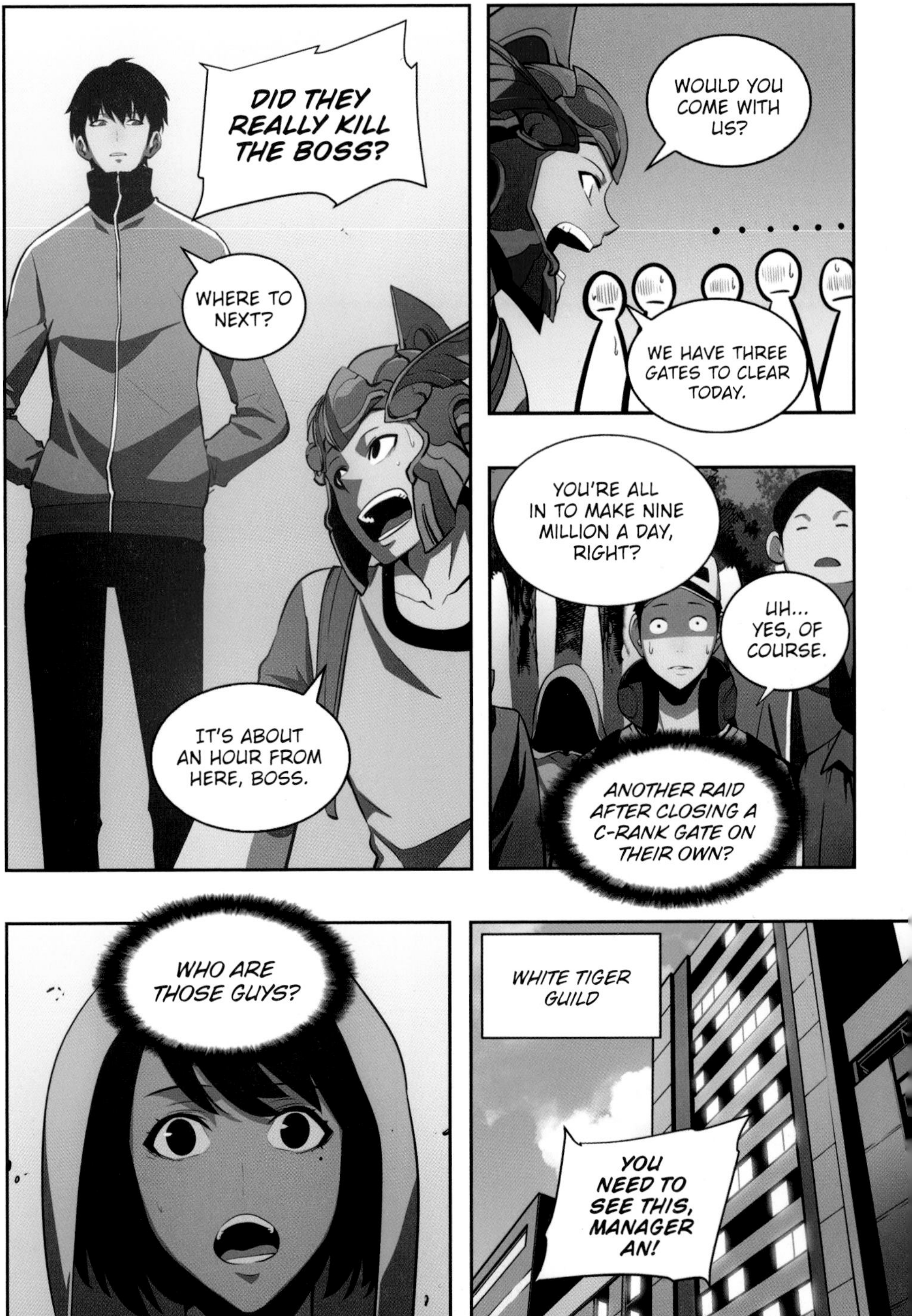
DID THEY REALLY KILL THE BOSS?
WHERE TO NEXT?
IT'S ABOUT AN HOUR FROM HERE, BOSS.
WOULD YOU COME WITH US?
WE HAVE THREE GATES TO CLEAR TODAY.
YOU'RE ALL IN TO MAKE NINE MILLION A DAY, RIGHT?
UH... YES, OF COURSE.
ANOTHER RAID AFTER CLOSING A C-RANK GATE ON THEIR OWN?
WHO ARE THOSE GUYS?
WHITE TIGER GUILD
YOU NEED TO SEE THIS, MANAGER AN!

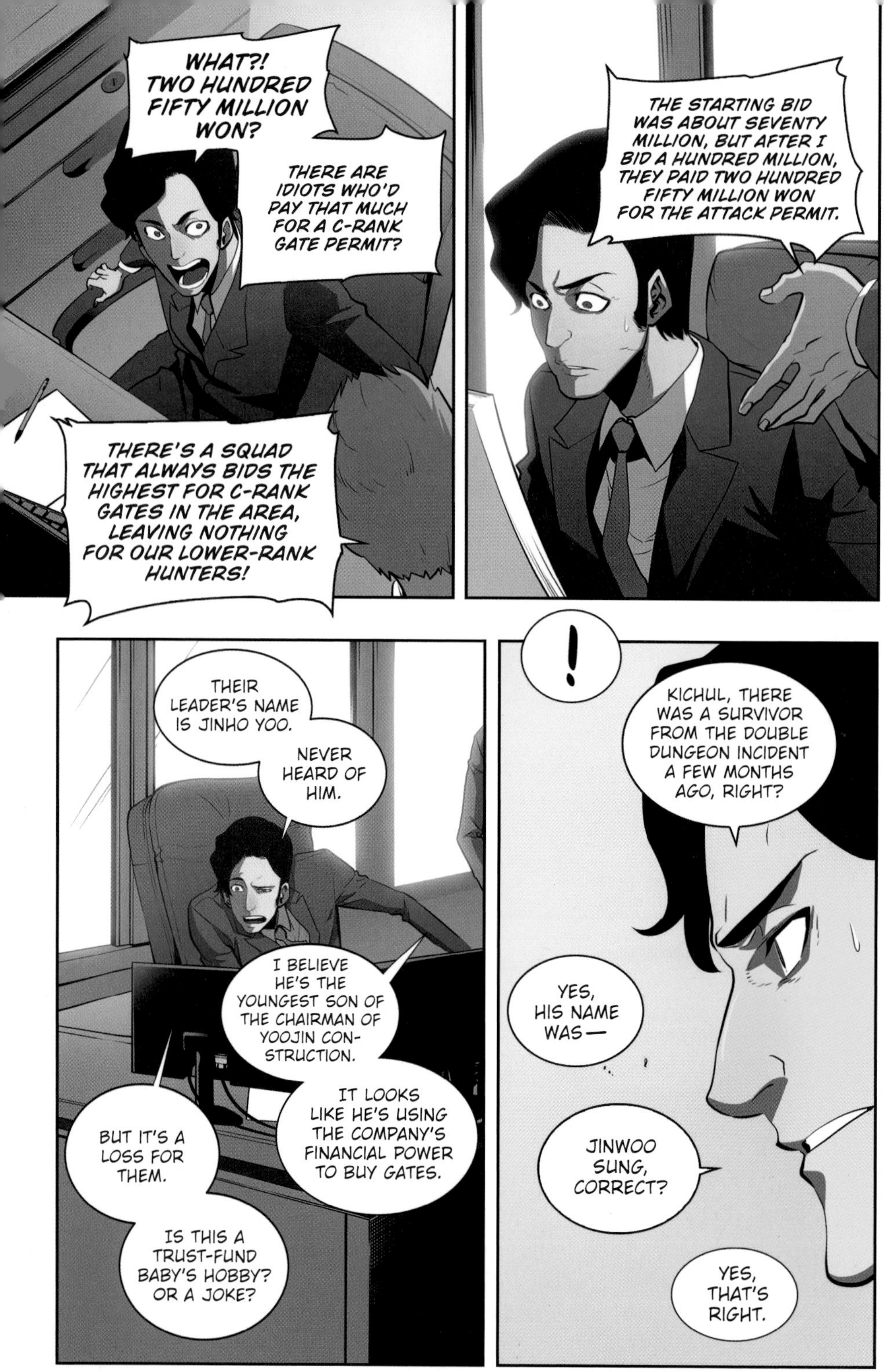
WHAT?! TWO HUNDRED FIFTY MILLION WON?
THERE ARE IDIOTS WHO'D PAY THAT MUCH FOR A C-RANK GATE PERMIT?
THERE'S A SQUAD THAT ALWAYS BIDS THE HIGHEST FOR C-RANK GATES IN THE AREA, LEAVING NOTHING FOR OUR LOWER-RANK HUNTERS!
THE STARTING BID WAS ABOUT SEVENTY MILLION, BUT AFTER I BID A HUNDRED MILLION, THEY PAID TWO HUNDRED FIFTY MILLION WON FOR THE ATTACK PERMIT.
THEIR LEADER'S NAME IS JINHO YOO.
NEVER HEARD OF HIM.
I BELIEVE HE'S THE YOUNGEST SON OF THE CHAIRMAN OF YOOJIN CONSTRUCTION.
BUT IT'S A LOSS FOR THEM.
IT LOOKS LIKE HE'S USING THE COMPANY'S FINANCIAL POWER TO BUY GATES.
IS THIS A TRUST-FUND BABY'S HOBBY? OR A JOKE?
!
KICHUL, THERE WAS A SURVIVOR FROM THE DOUBLE DUNGEON INCIDENT A FEW MONTHS AGO, RIGHT?
YES, HIS NAME WAS—
JINWOO SUNG, CORRECT?
YES, THAT'S RIGHT.

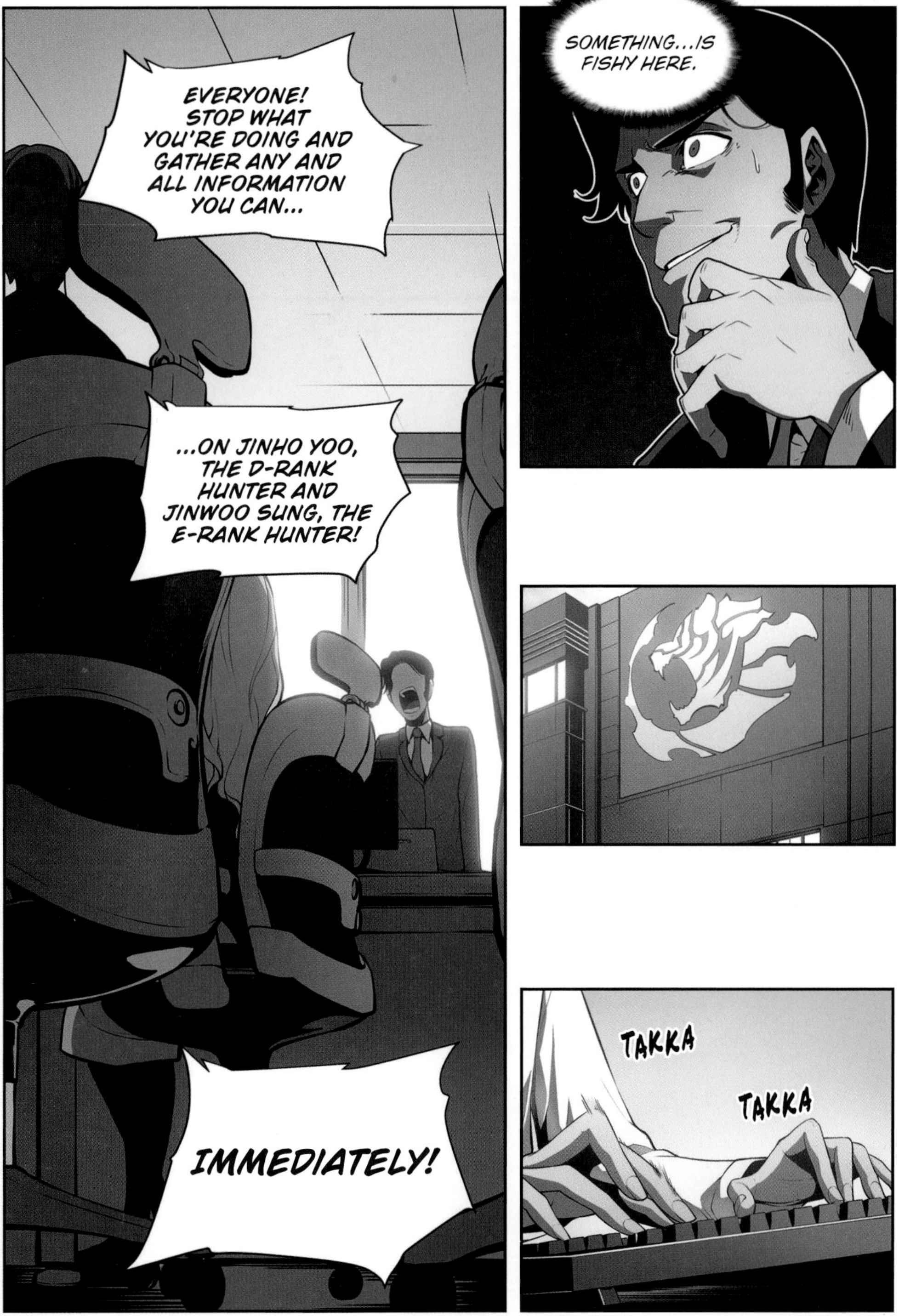
EVERYONE! STOP WHAT YOU'RE DOING AND GATHER ANY AND ALL INFORMATION YOU CAN...
...ON JINHO YOO, THE D-RANK HUNTER AND JINWOO SUNG, THE E-RANK HUNTER!
IMMEDIATELY!
SOMETHING...IS FISHY HERE.
TAKKA
TAKKA

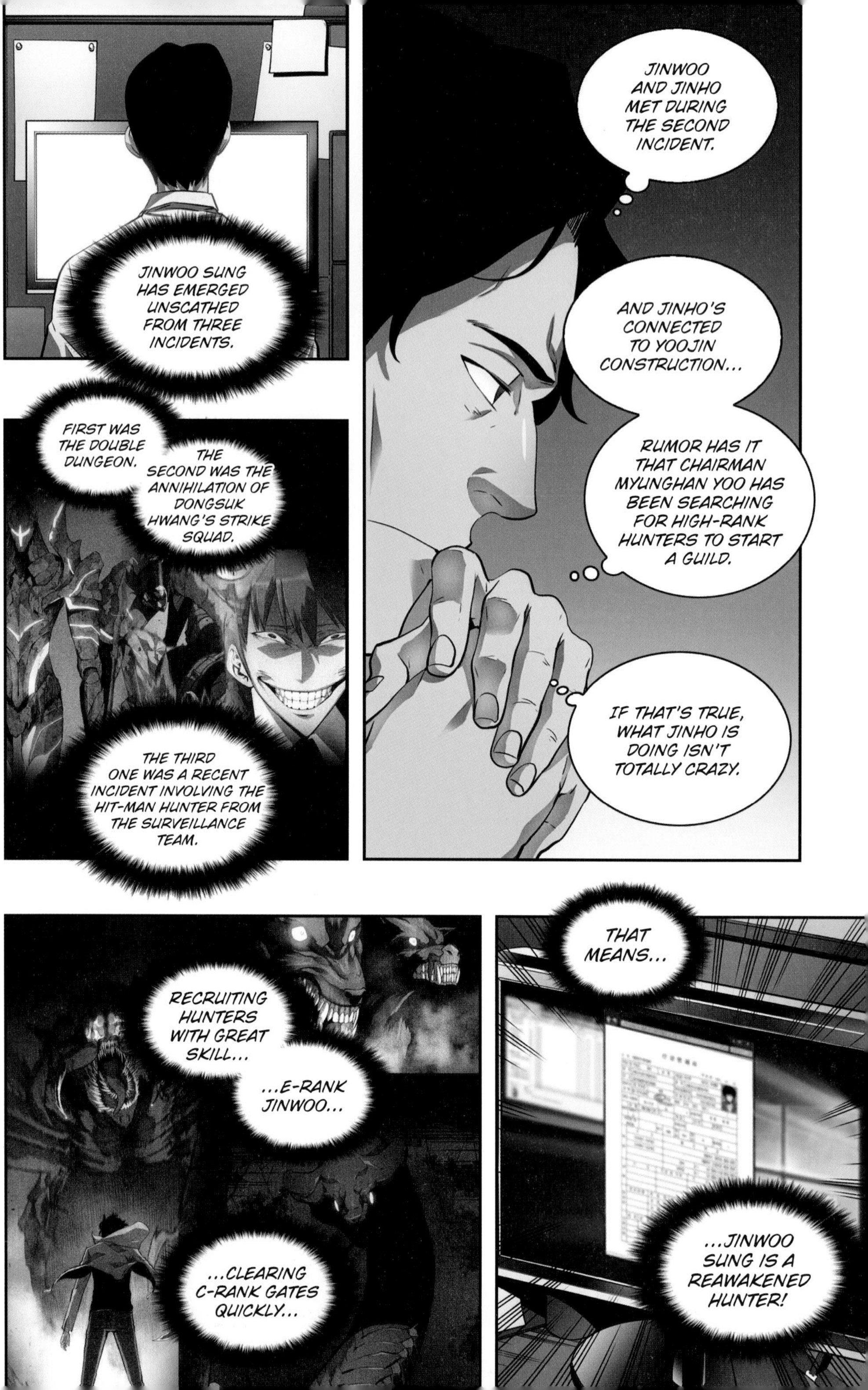
JINWOO SUNG HAS EMERGED UNSCATHED FROM THREE INCIDENTS.
FIRST WAS THE DOUBLE DUNGEON.
THE SECOND WAS THE ANNIHILATION OF DONGSUK HWANG'S STRIKE SQUAD.
THE THIRD ONE WAS A RECENT INCIDENT INVOLVING THE HIT-MAN HUNTER FROM THE SURVEILLANCE TEAM.
JINWOO AND JINHO MET DURING THE SECOND INCIDENT.
AND JINHO'S CONNECTED TO YOOJIN CONSTRUCTION...
RUMOR HAS IT THAT CHAIRMAN MYUNGHAN YOO HAS BEEN SEARCHING FOR HIGH-RANK HUNTERS TO START A GUILD.
IF THAT'S TRUE, WHAT JINHO IS DOING ISN'T TOTALLY CRAZY.
RECRUITING HUNTERS WITH GREAT SKILL...
...E-RANK JINWOO...
...CLEARING C-RANK GATES QUICKLY...
THAT MEANS...
...JINWOO SUNG IS A REAWAKENED HUNTER!

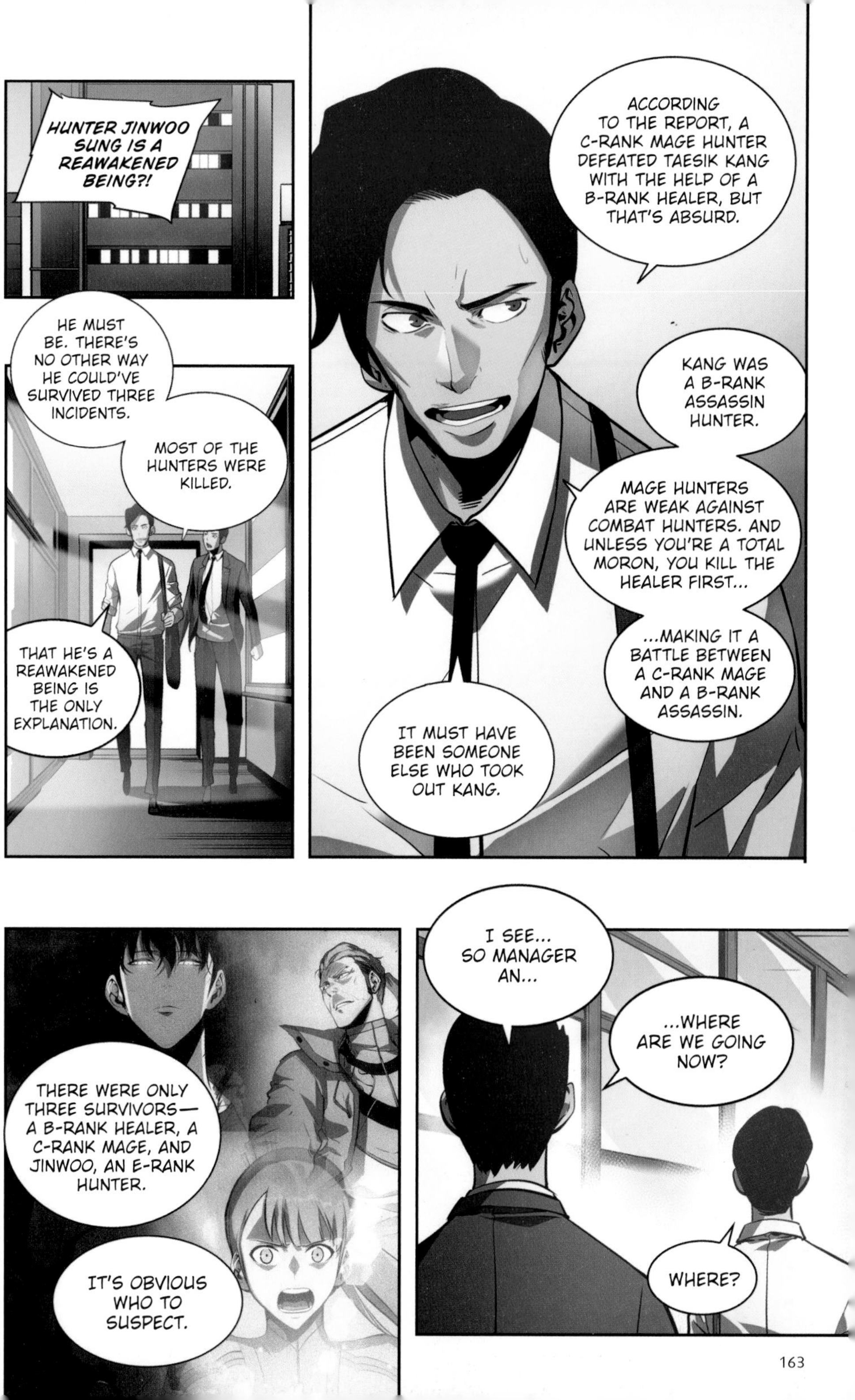
HUNTER JINWOO SUNG IS A REAWAKENED BEING?!
HE MUST BE. THERE'S NO OTHER WAY HE COULD'VE SURVIVED THREE INCIDENTS.
MOST OF THE HUNTERS WERE KILLED.
THAT HE'S A REAWAKENED BEING IS THE ONLY EXPLANATION.
ACCORDING TO THE REPORT, A C-RANK MAGE HUNTER DEFEATED TAESIK KANG WITH THE HELP OF A B-RANK HEALER, BUT THAT'S ABSURD.
KANG WAS A B-RANK ASSASSIN HUNTER.
MAGE HUNTERS ARE WEAK AGAINST COMBAT HUNTERS. AND UNLESS YOU'RE A TOTAL MORON, YOU KILL THE HEALER FIRST...
...MAKING IT A BATTLE BETWEEN A C-RANK MAGE AND A B-RANK ASSASSIN.
IT MUST HAVE BEEN SOMEONE ELSE WHO TOOK OUT KANG.
THERE WERE ONLY THREE SURVIVORS—A B-RANK HEALER, A C-RANK MAGE, AND JINWOO, AN E-RANK HUNTER.
IT'S OBVIOUS WHO TO SUSPECT.
I SEE... SO MANAGER AN...
...WHERE ARE WE GOING NOW?
WHERE?

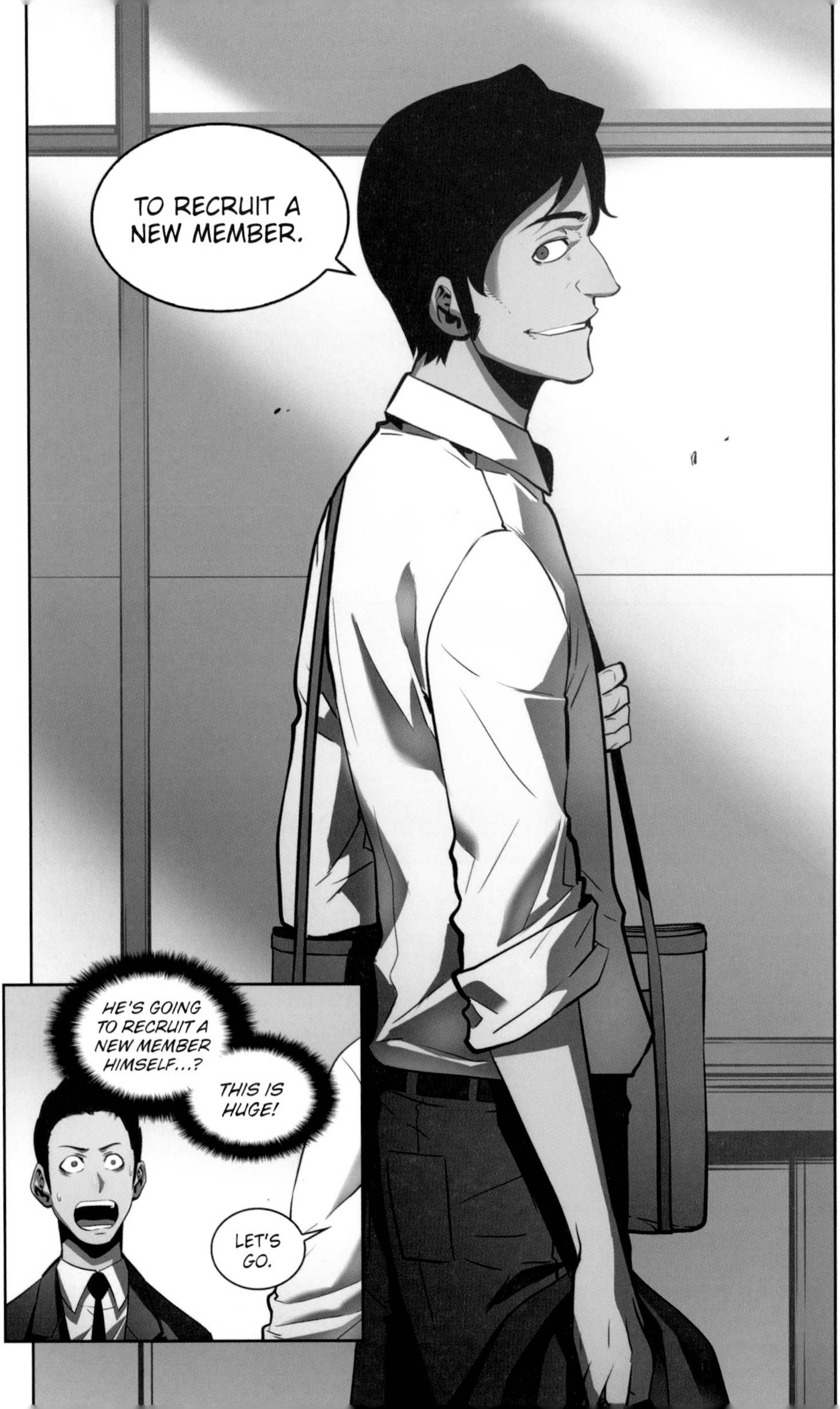
TO RECRUIT A NEW MEMBER.
HE'S GOING TO RECRUIT A NEW MEMBER HIMSELF...?
THIS IS HUGE!
LET'S GO.

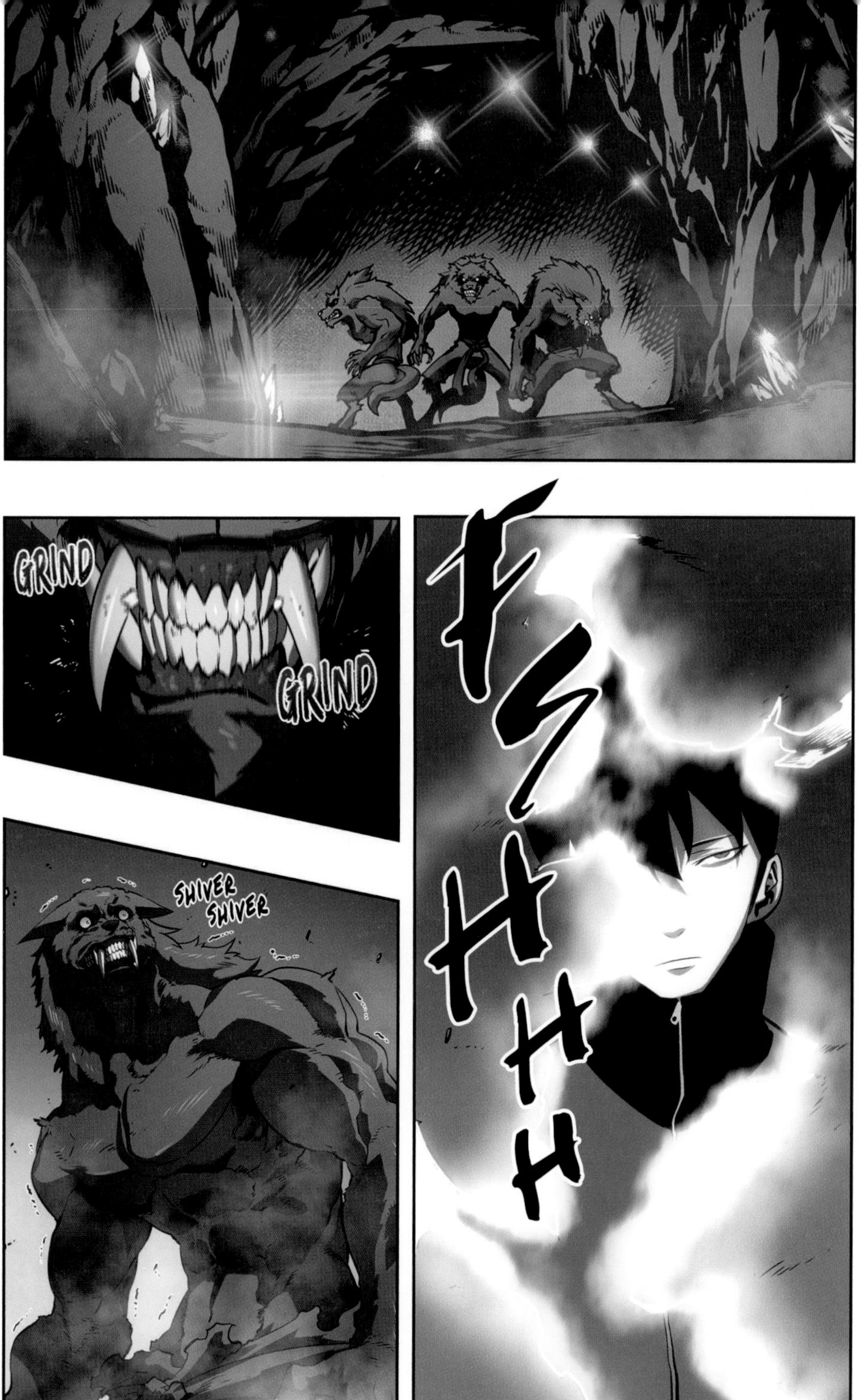
GRIND
GRIND
FSSHHHH
SHIVER SHIVER

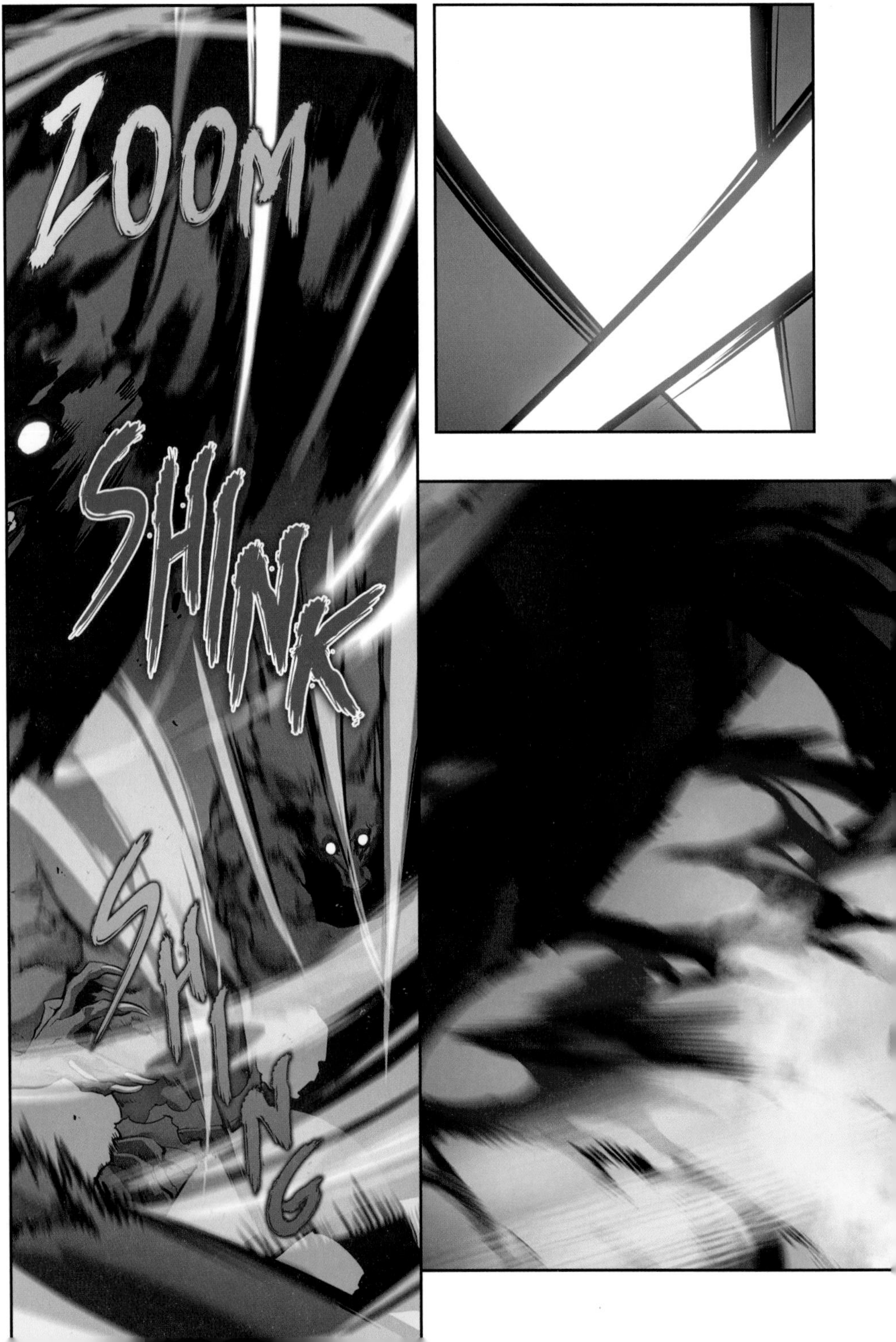
ZOOM
SHINK
SHING

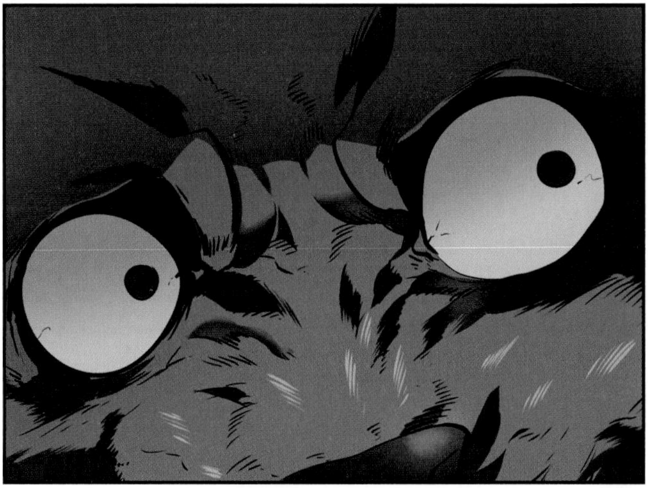

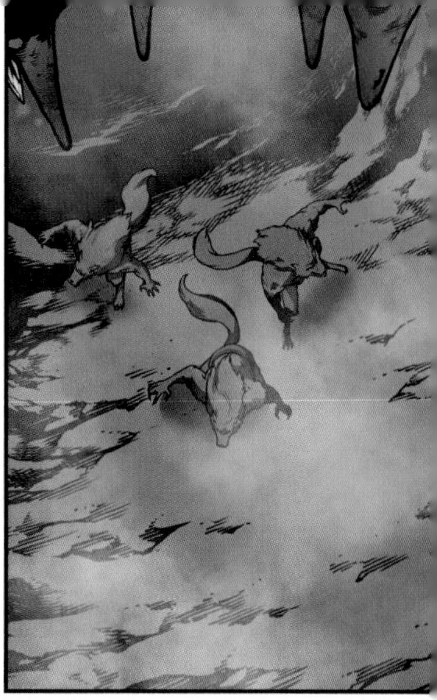

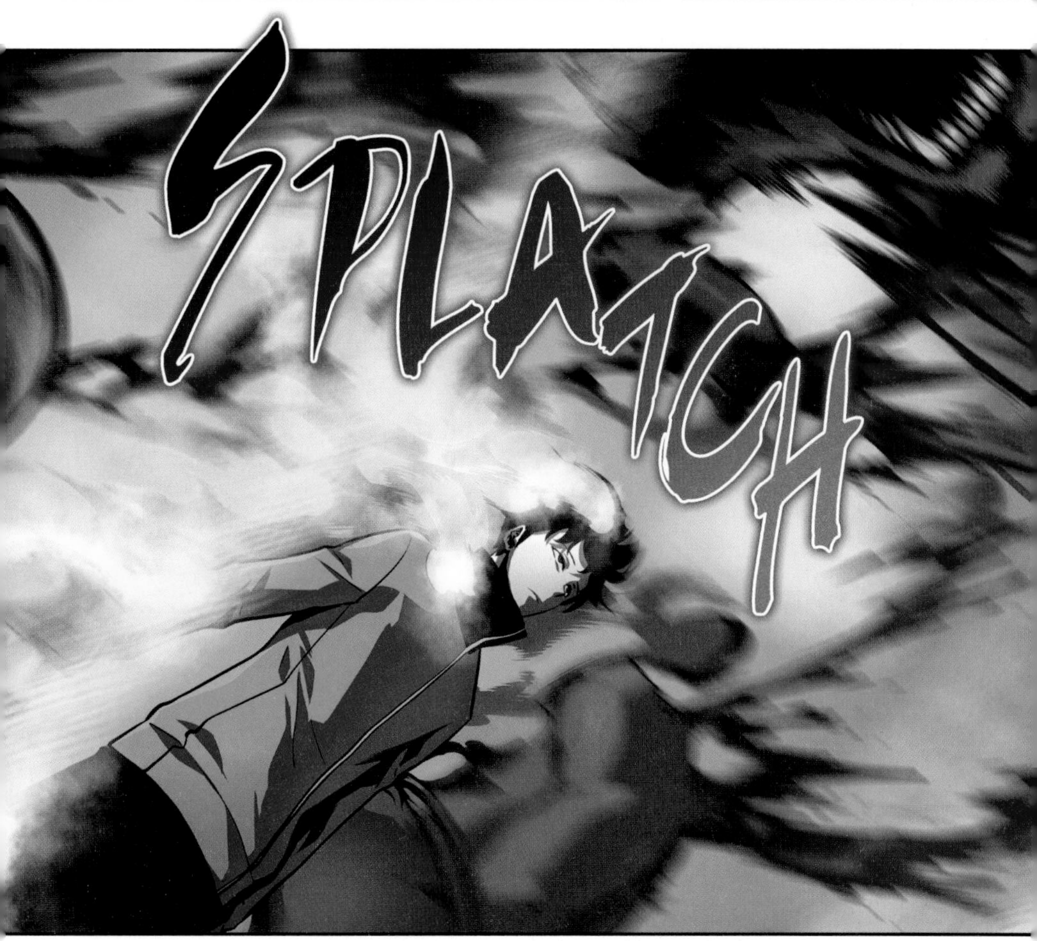
SPLATCH

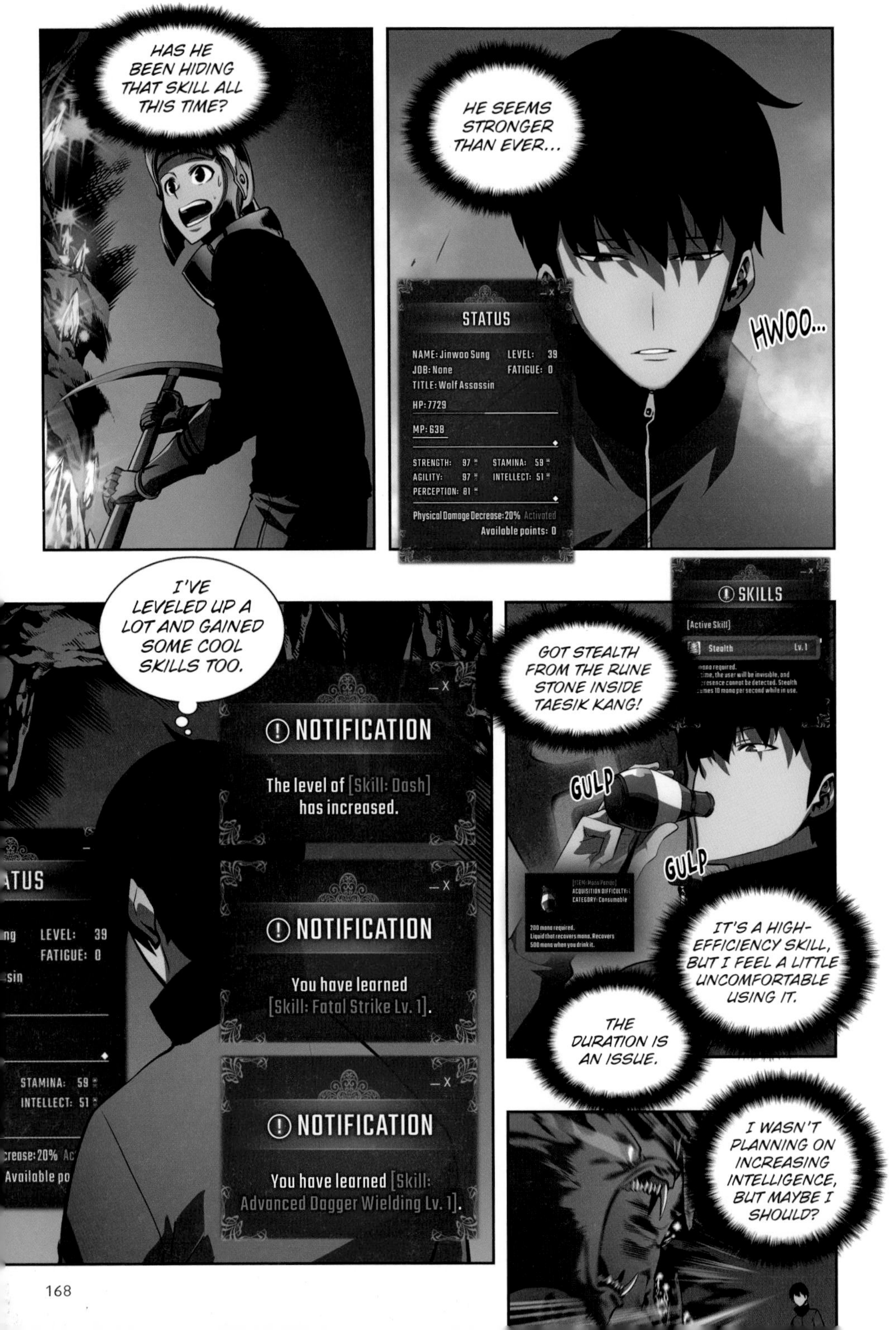
HAS HE BEEN HIDING THAT SKILL ALL THIS TIME?
HE SEEMS STRONGER THAN EVER...
STATUS
NAME: Jinwoo Sung LEVEL: 39
JOB: None FATIGUE: 0
TITLE: Wolf Assassin
HP: 7729
MP: 638
STRENGTH: 97 STAMINA: 59
AGILITY: 97 INTELLECT: 51
PERCEPTION: 81
Physical Damage Decrease: 20% Activated
Available points: 0
HWOO...
I'VE LEVELED UP A LOT AND GAINED SOME COOL SKILLS TOO.
NOTIFICATION
The level of [Skill: Dash] has increased.
NOTIFICATION
You have learned [Skill: Fatal Strike Lv. 1].
NOTIFICATION
You have learned [Skill: Advanced Dagger Wielding Lv. 1].
SKILLS
[Active Skill]
Stealth Lv. 1
GOT STEALTH FROM THE RUNE STONE INSIDE TAESIK KANG!
GULP
GULP
ACQUISITION DIFFICULTY:
CATEGORY: Consumable
200 mana required.
Liquid that recovers mana. Recovers 500 mana when you drink it.
IT'S A HIGH-EFFICIENCY SKILL, BUT I FEEL A LITTLE UNCOMFORTABLE USING IT.
THE DURATION IS AN ISSUE.
I WASN'T PLANNING ON INCREASING INTELLIGENCE, BUT MAYBE I SHOULD?

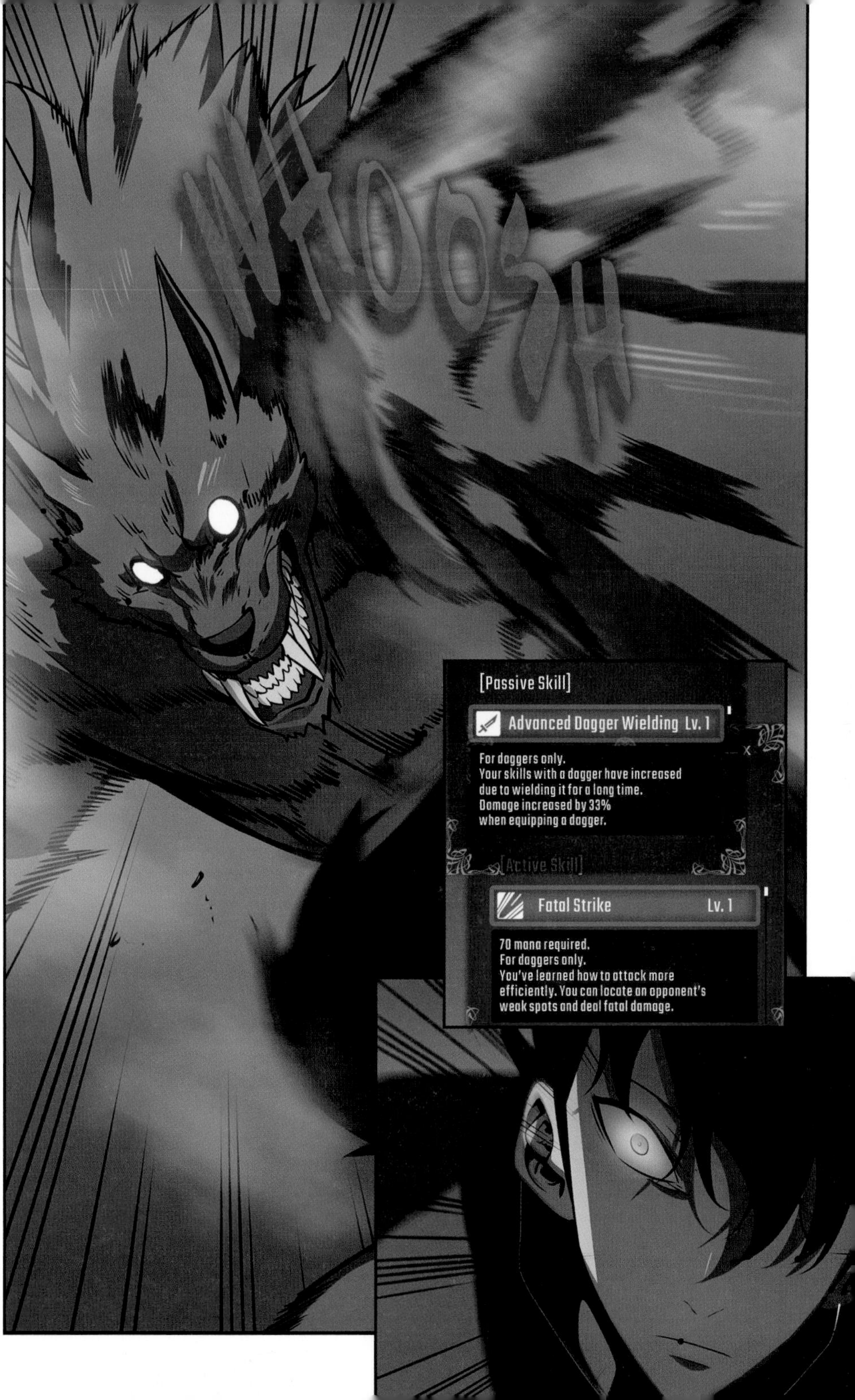
WHOOSH
[Passive Skill]
Advanced Dagger Wielding Lv. 1
For daggers only.
Your skills with a dagger have increased
due to wielding it for a long time.
Damage increased by 33%
when equipping a dagger.
[Active Skill]
Fatal Strike Lv. 1
70 mana required.
For daggers only.
You've learned how to attack more
efficiently. You can locate an opponent's
weak spots and deal fatal damage.

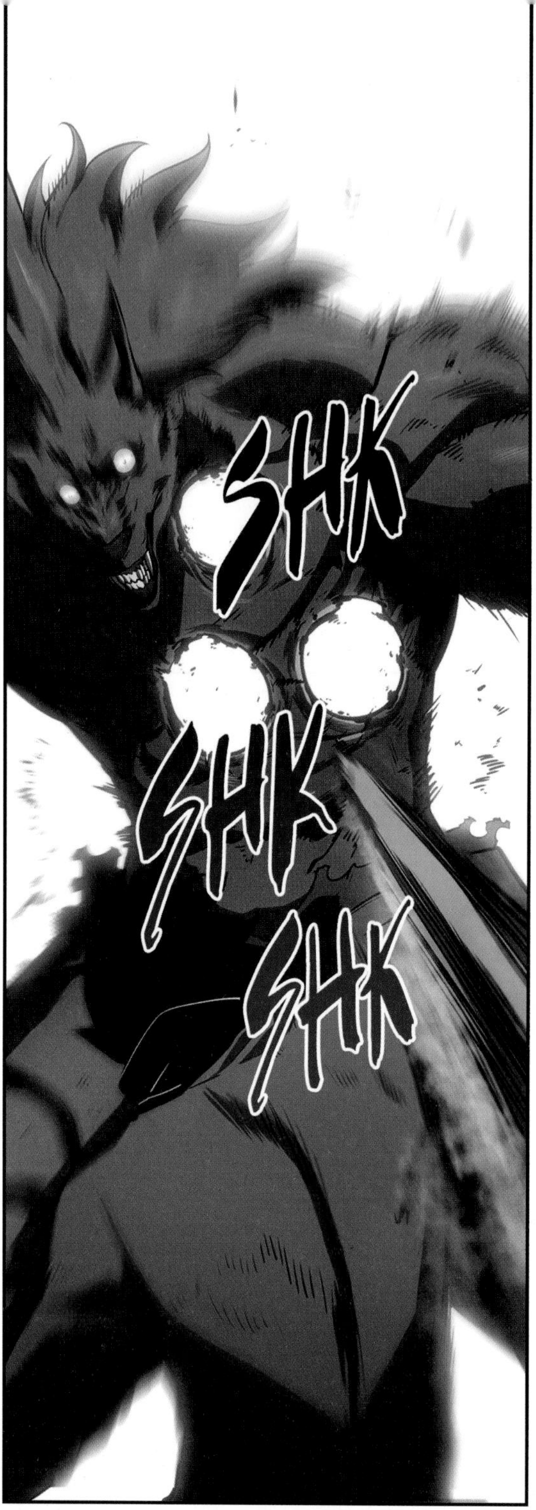
SHK
SHK
SHK

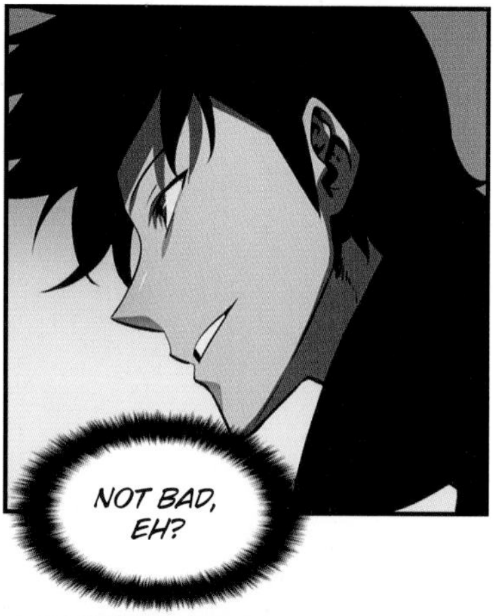
NOT BAD, EH?

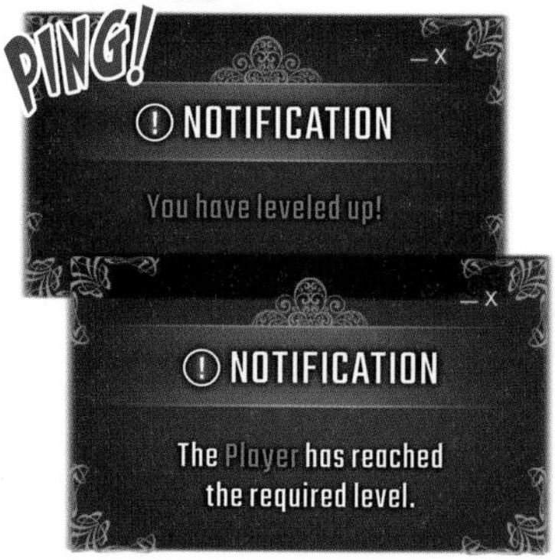
PING!
NOTIFICATION
You have leveled up!
NOTIFICATION
The Player has reached the required level.

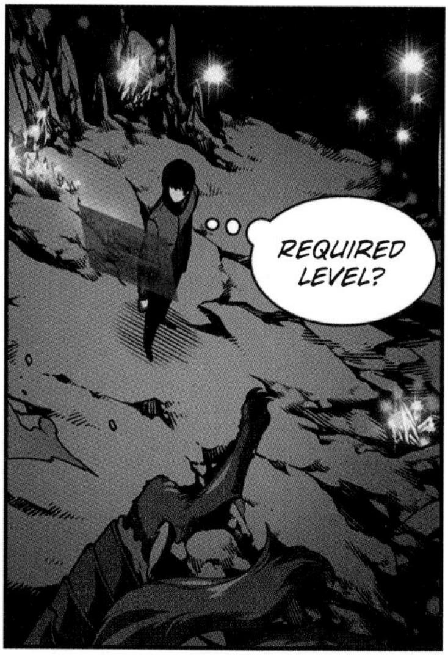
REQUIRED LEVEL?

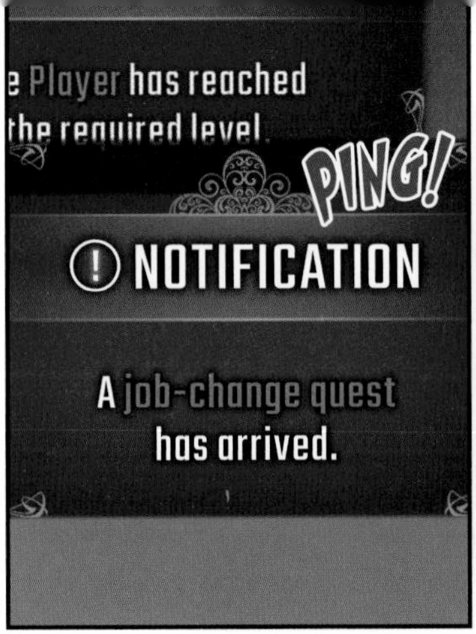
e Player has reached
the required level.
PING!
NOTIFICATION
A job-change quest
has arrived.
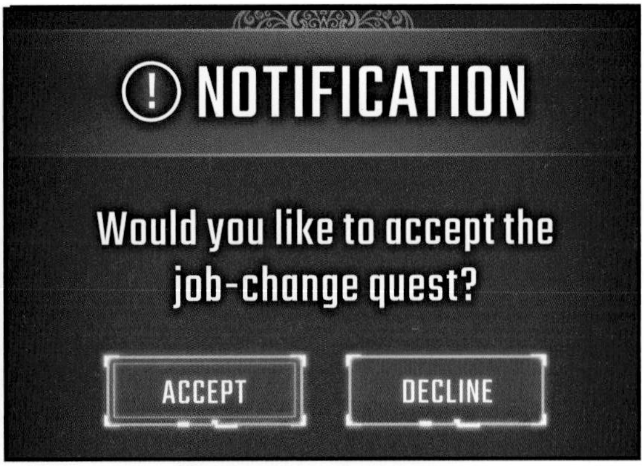
NOTIFICATION
Would you like to accept the
job-change quest?
ACCEPT
DECLINE
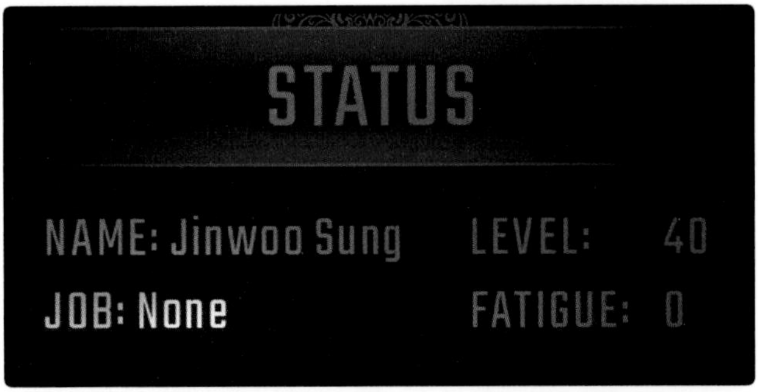
STATUS
NAME: Jinwoo Sung
LEVEL: 40
JOB: None
FATIGUE: 0
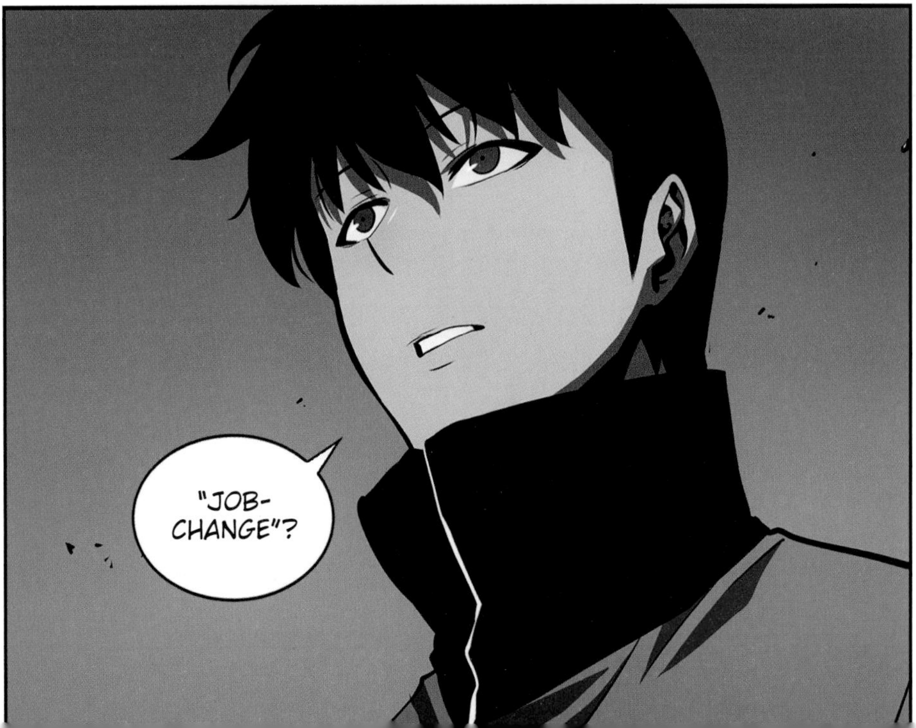
"JOB-CHANGE"?

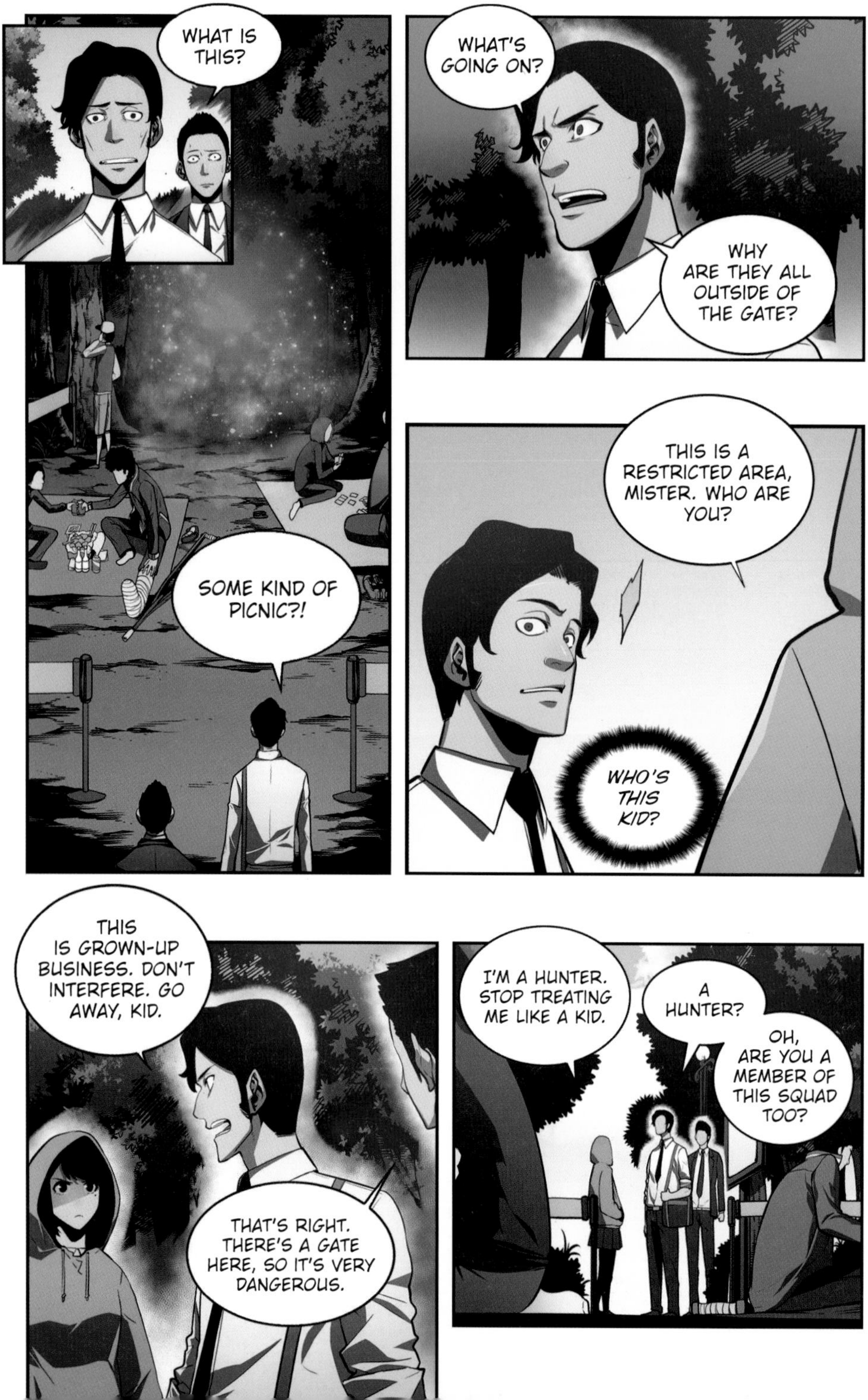
WHAT IS THIS?
SOME KIND OF PICNIC?!
WHAT'S GOING ON?
WHY ARE THEY ALL OUTSIDE OF THE GATE?
THIS IS A RESTRICTED AREA, MISTER. WHO ARE YOU?
WHO'S THIS KID?
THIS IS GROWN-UP BUSINESS. DON'T INTERFERE. GO AWAY, KID.
THAT'S RIGHT. THERE'S A GATE HERE, SO IT'S VERY DANGEROUS.
I'M A HUNTER. STOP TREATING ME LIKE A KID.
A HUNTER?
OH, ARE YOU A MEMBER OF THIS SQUAD TOO?

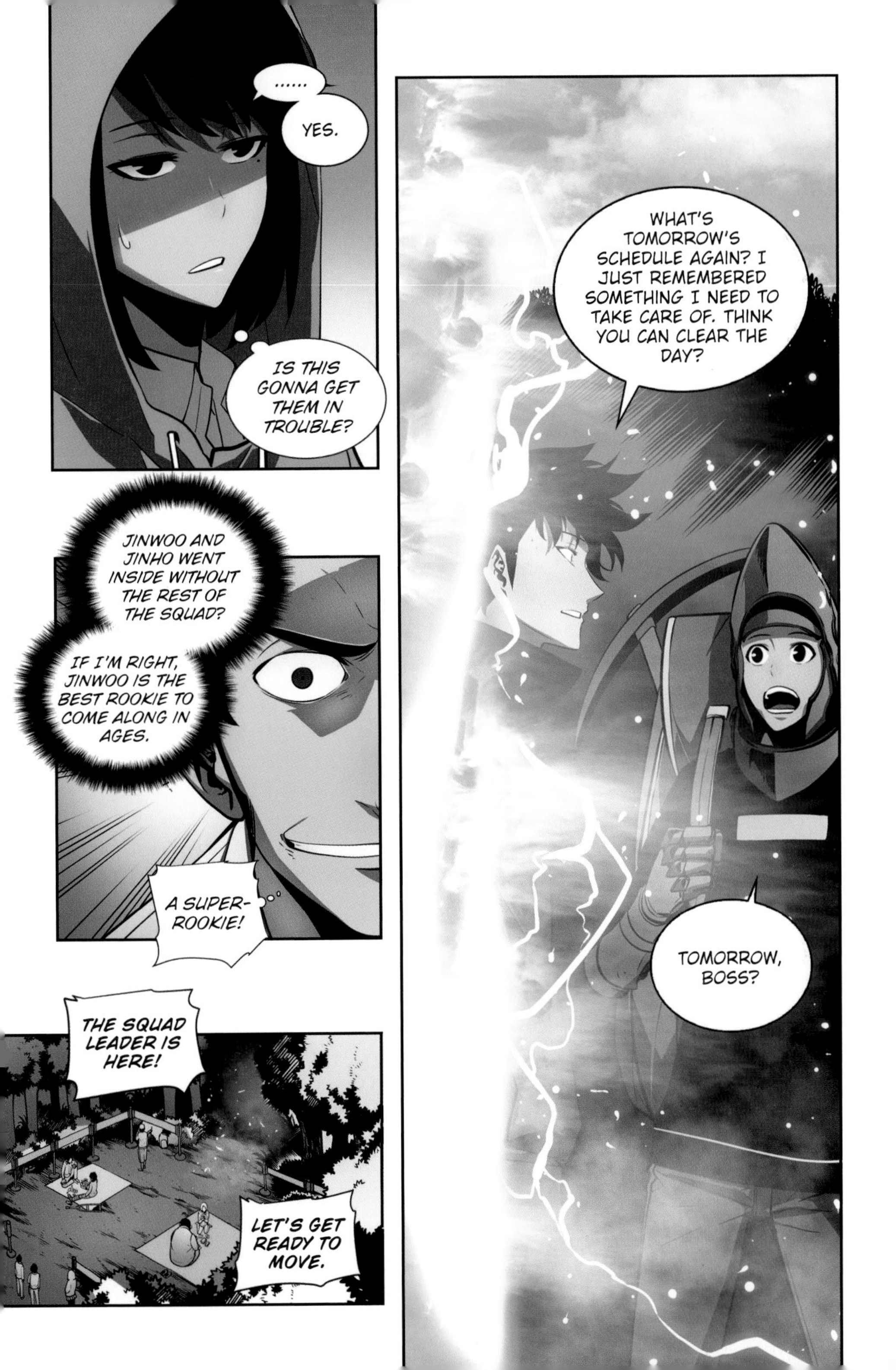
......
YES.
IS THIS GONNA GET THEM IN TROUBLE?
JINWOO AND JINHO WENT INSIDE WITHOUT THE REST OF THE SQUAD?
IF I'M RIGHT, JINWOO IS THE BEST ROOKIE TO COME ALONG IN AGES.
A SUPER-ROOKIE!
THE SQUAD LEADER IS HERE!
LET'S GET READY TO MOVE.
WHAT'S TOMORROW'S SCHEDULE AGAIN? I JUST REMEMBERED SOMETHING I NEED TO TAKE CARE OF. THINK YOU CAN CLEAR THE DAY?
TOMORROW, BOSS?

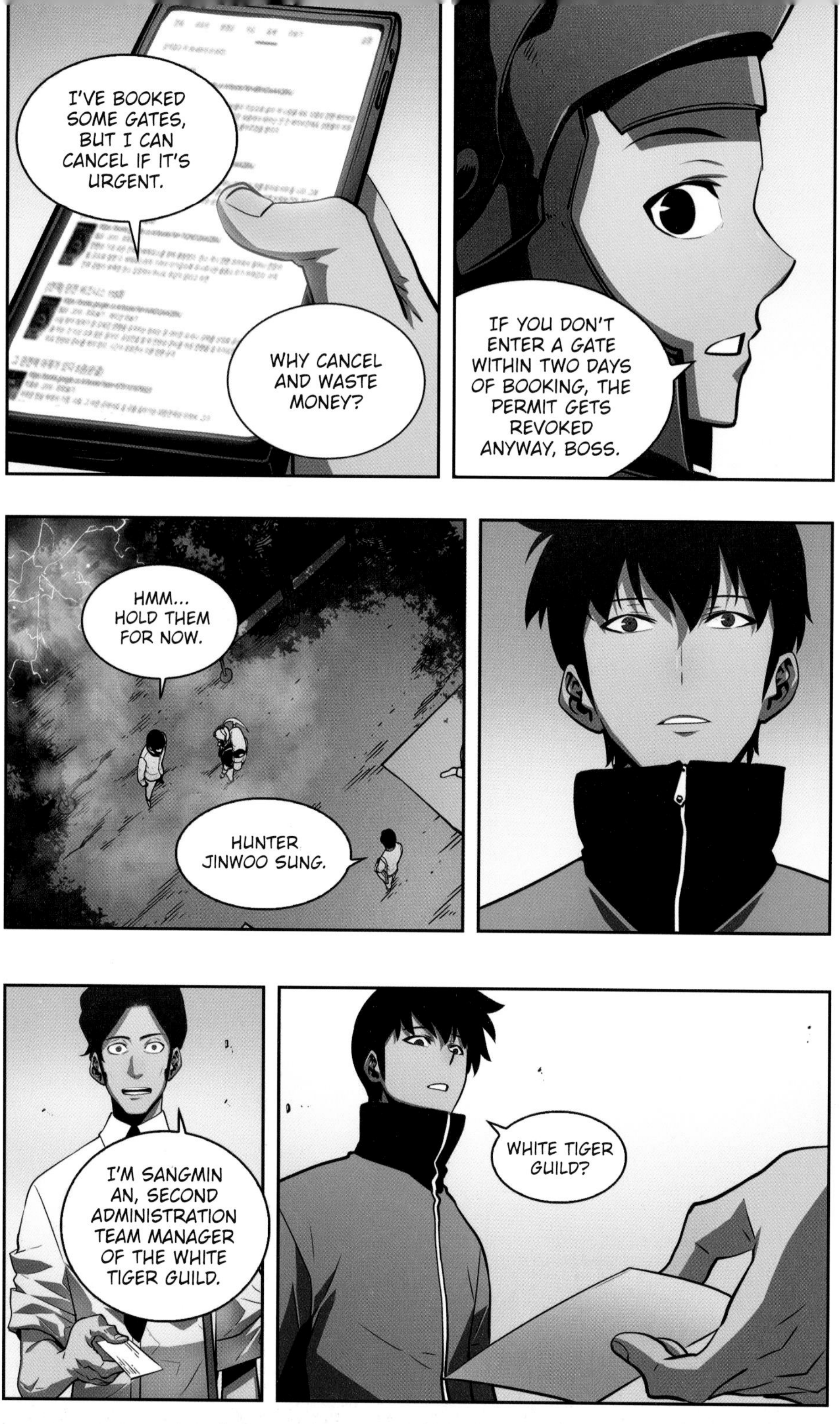
I'VE BOOKED SOME GATES, BUT I CAN CANCEL IF IT'S URGENT.
WHY CANCEL AND WASTE MONEY?
IF YOU DON'T ENTER A GATE WITHIN TWO DAYS OF BOOKING, THE PERMIT GETS REVOKED ANYWAY, BOSS.
HMM... HOLD THEM FOR NOW.
HUNTER JINWOO SUNG.
I'M SANGMIN AN, SECOND ADMINISTRATION TEAM MANAGER OF THE WHITE TIGER GUILD.
WHITE TIGER GUILD?

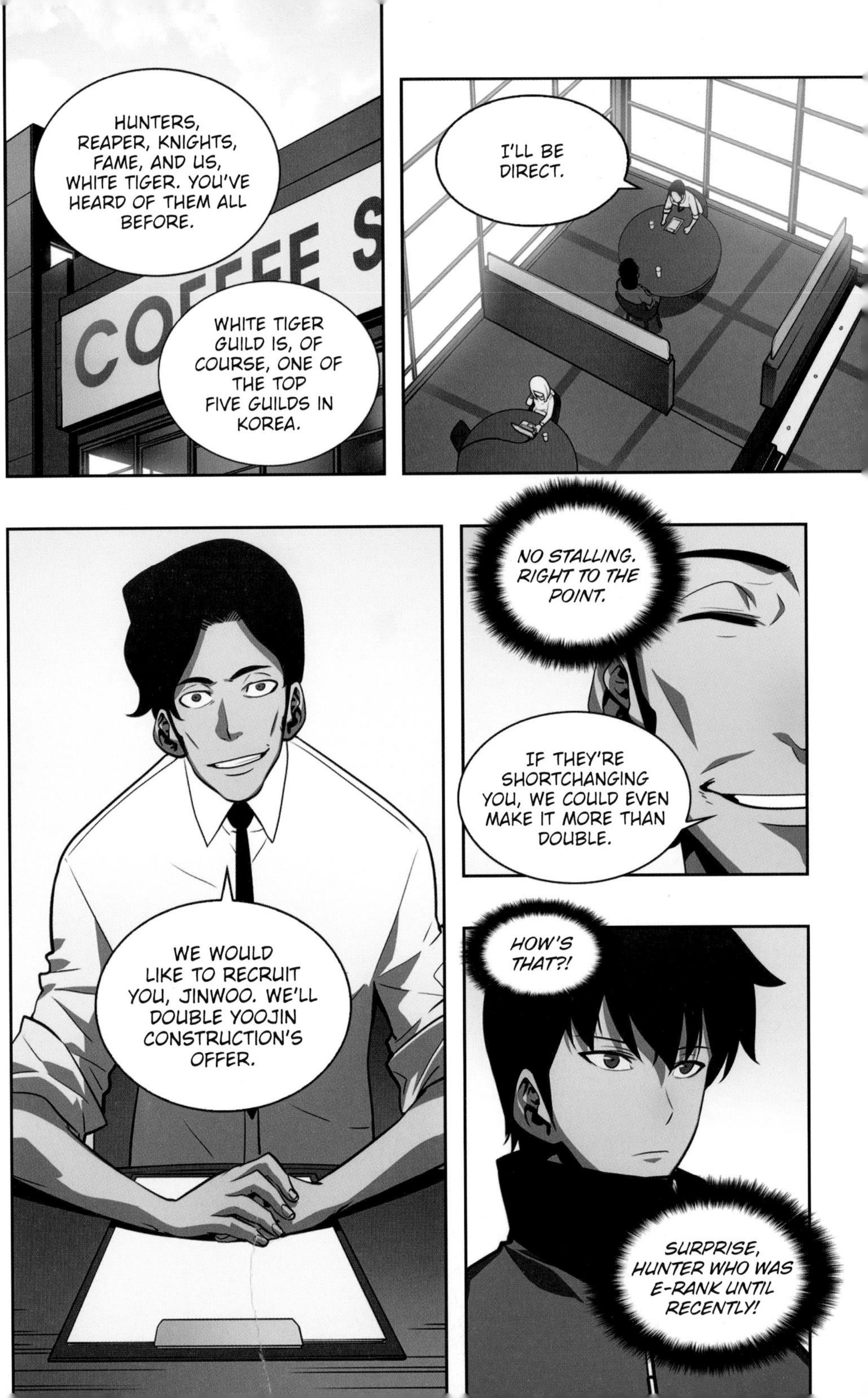
HUNTERS, REAPER, KNIGHTS, FAME, AND US, WHITE TIGER. YOU'VE HEARD OF THEM ALL BEFORE.
COFFEE S
WHITE TIGER GUILD IS, OF COURSE, ONE OF THE TOP FIVE GUILDS IN KOREA.
I'LL BE DIRECT.
WE WOULD LIKE TO RECRUIT YOU, JINWOO. WE'LL DOUBLE YOOJIN CONSTRUCTION'S OFFER.
NO STALLING. RIGHT TO THE POINT.
IF THEY'RE SHORTCHANGING YOU, WE COULD EVEN MAKE IT MORE THAN DOUBLE.
HOW'S THAT?!
SURPRISE, HUNTER WHO WAS E-RANK UNTIL RECENTLY!

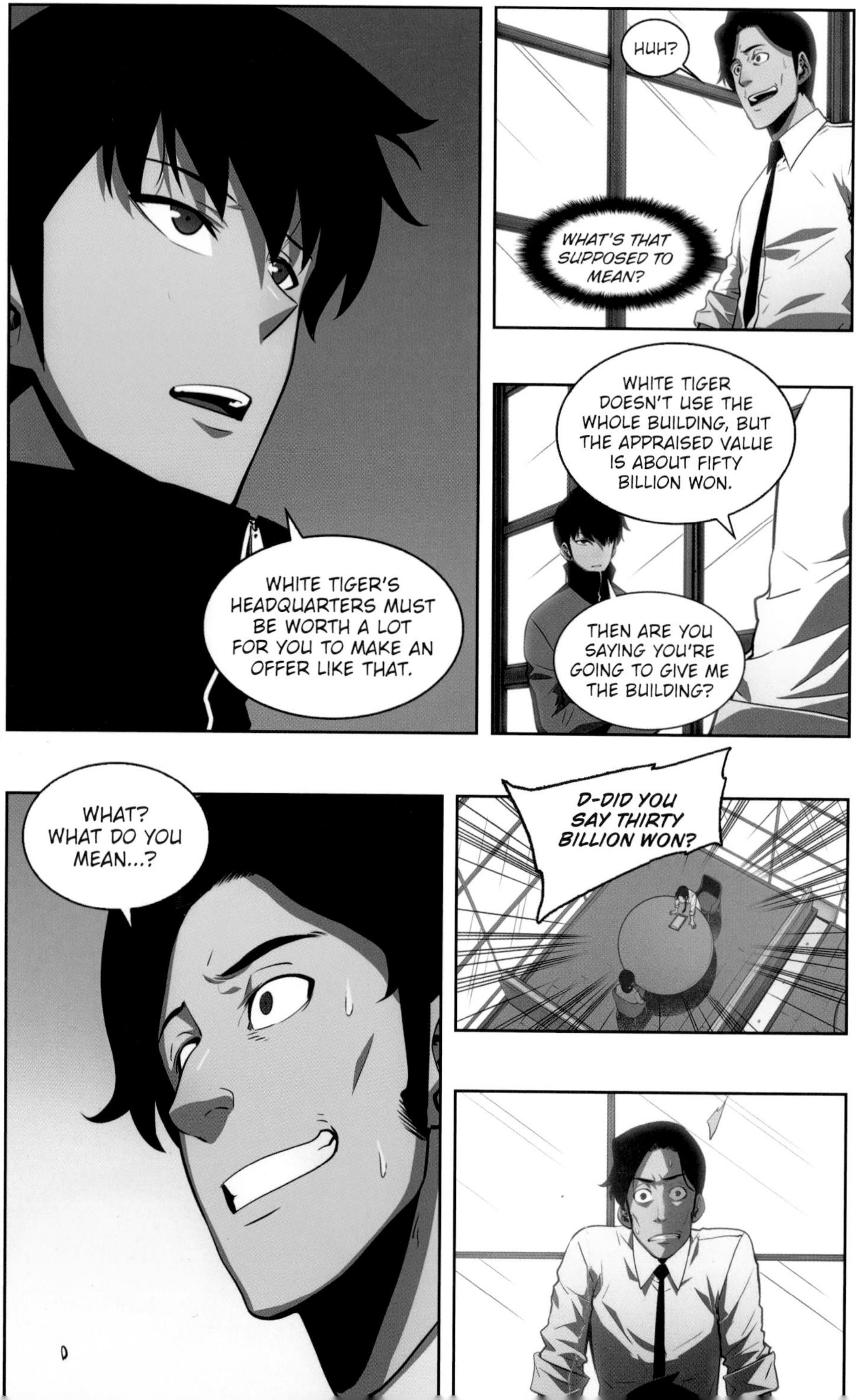
WHITE TIGER'S HEADQUARTERS MUST BE WORTH A LOT FOR YOU TO MAKE AN OFFER LIKE THAT.
HUH?
WHAT'S THAT SUPPOSED TO MEAN?
WHITE TIGER DOESN'T USE THE WHOLE BUILDING, BUT THE APPRAISED VALUE IS ABOUT FIFTY BILLION WON.
THEN ARE YOU SAYING YOU'RE GOING TO GIVE ME THE BUILDING?
WHAT? WHAT DO YOU MEAN...?
D-DID YOU SAY THIRTY BILLION WON?

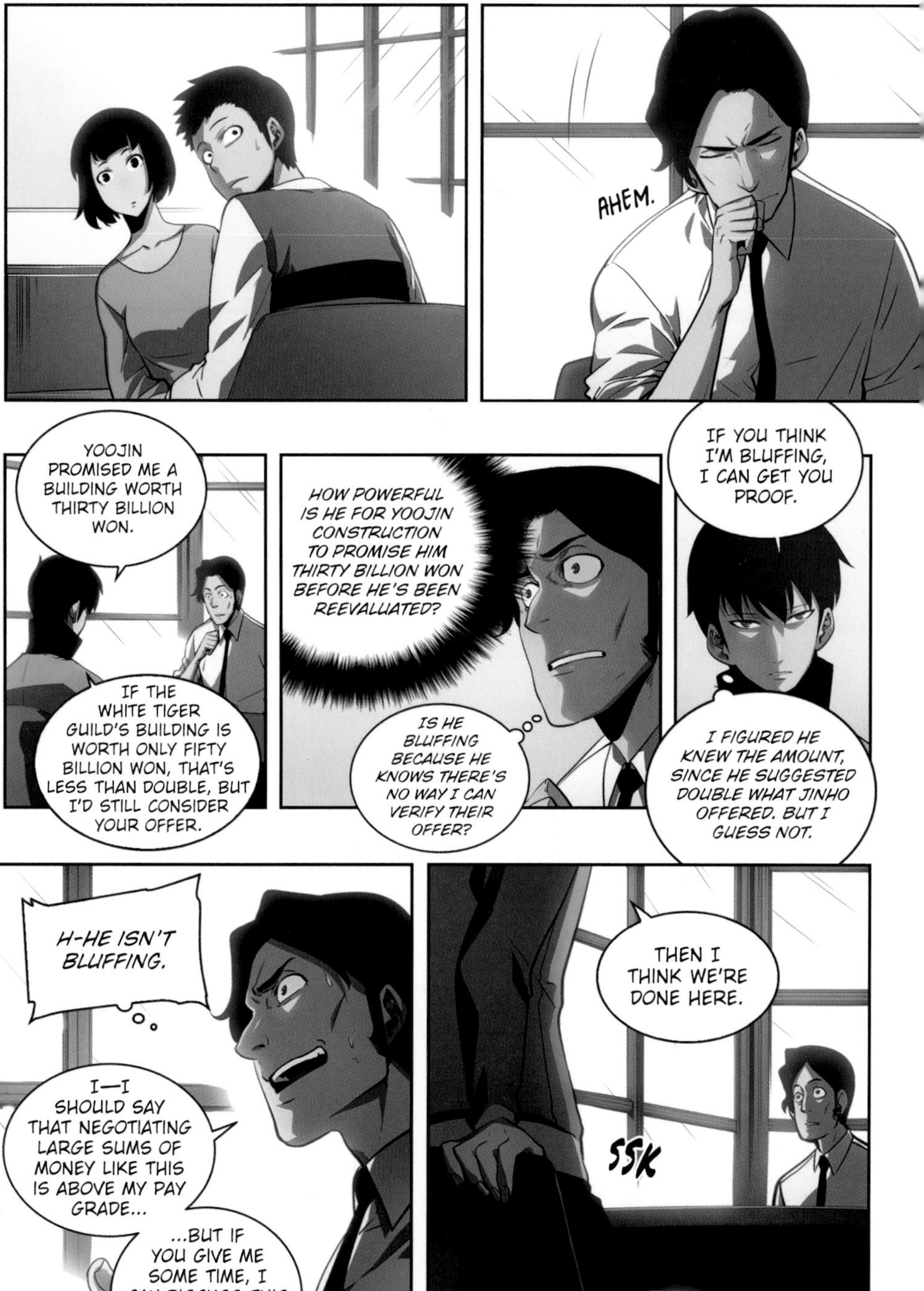

AHEM.
YOOJIN PROMISED ME A BUILDING WORTH THIRTY BILLION WON.
IF THE WHITE TIGER GUILD'S BUILDING IS WORTH ONLY FIFTY BILLION WON, THAT'S LESS THAN DOUBLE, BUT I'D STILL CONSIDER YOUR OFFER.
HOW POWERFUL IS HE FOR YOOJIN CONSTRUCTION TO PROMISE HIM THIRTY BILLION WON BEFORE HE'S BEEN REEVALUATED?
IS HE BLUFFING BECAUSE HE KNOWS THERE'S NO WAY I CAN VERIFY THEIR OFFER?
IF YOU THINK I'M BLUFFING, I CAN GET YOU PROOF.
I FIGURED HE KNEW THE AMOUNT, SINCE HE SUGGESTED DOUBLE WHAT JINHO OFFERED. BUT I GUESS NOT.
H-HE ISN'T BLUFFING.
I—I SHOULD SAY THAT NEGOTIATING LARGE SUMS OF MONEY LIKE THIS IS ABOVE MY PAY GRADE...
...BUT IF YOU GIVE ME SOME TIME, I CAN DISCUSS THIS WITH UPPER MANAGE—
THEN I THINK WE'RE DONE HERE.
SSK

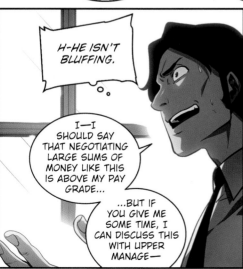

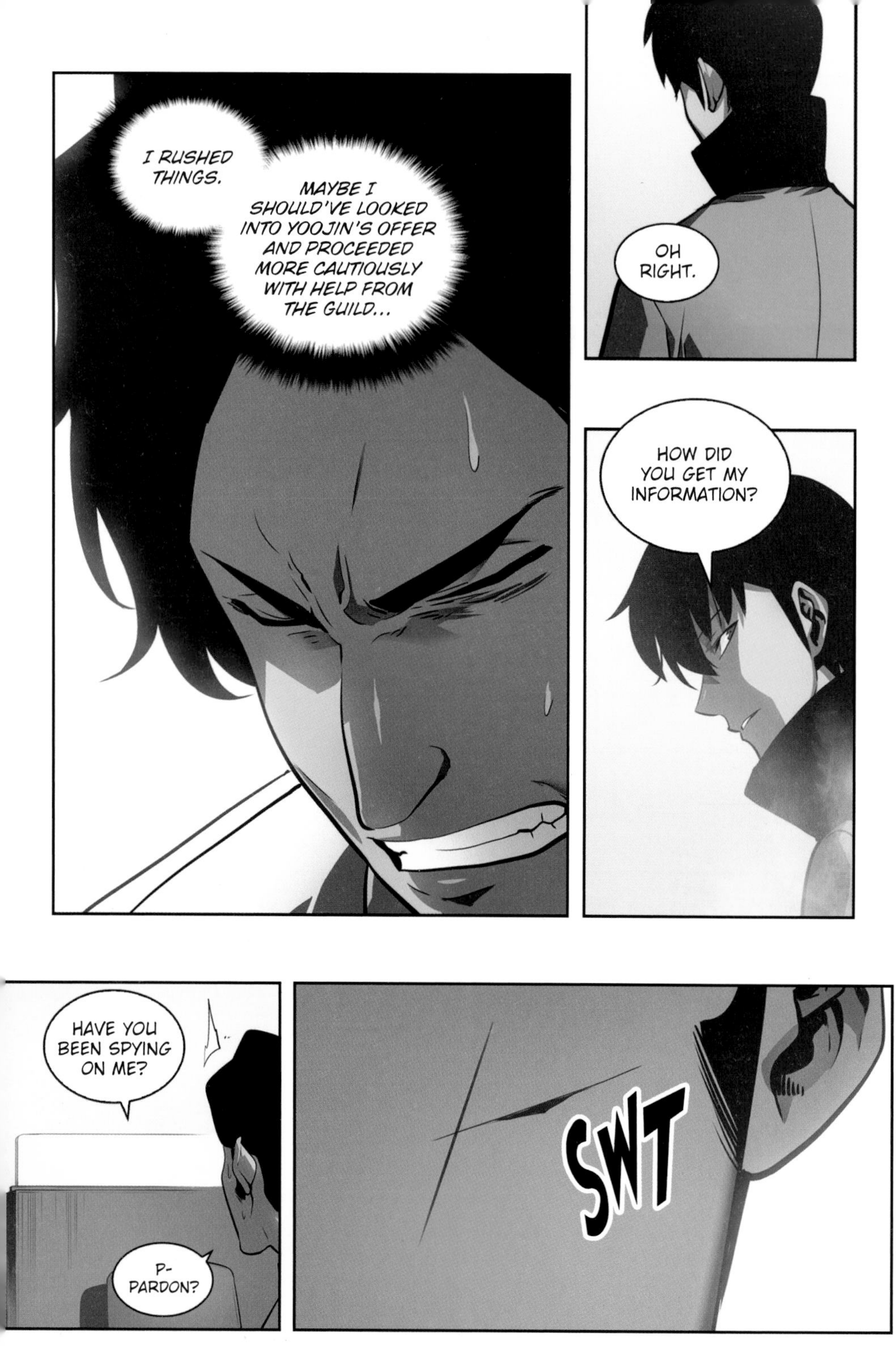
I RUSHED THINGS.
MAYBE I SHOULD'VE LOOKED INTO YOOJIN'S OFFER AND PROCEEDED MORE CAUTIOUSLY WITH HELP FROM THE GUILD...
OH RIGHT.
HOW DID YOU GET MY INFORMATION?
HAVE YOU BEEN SPYING ON ME?
P-PARDON?
SWT

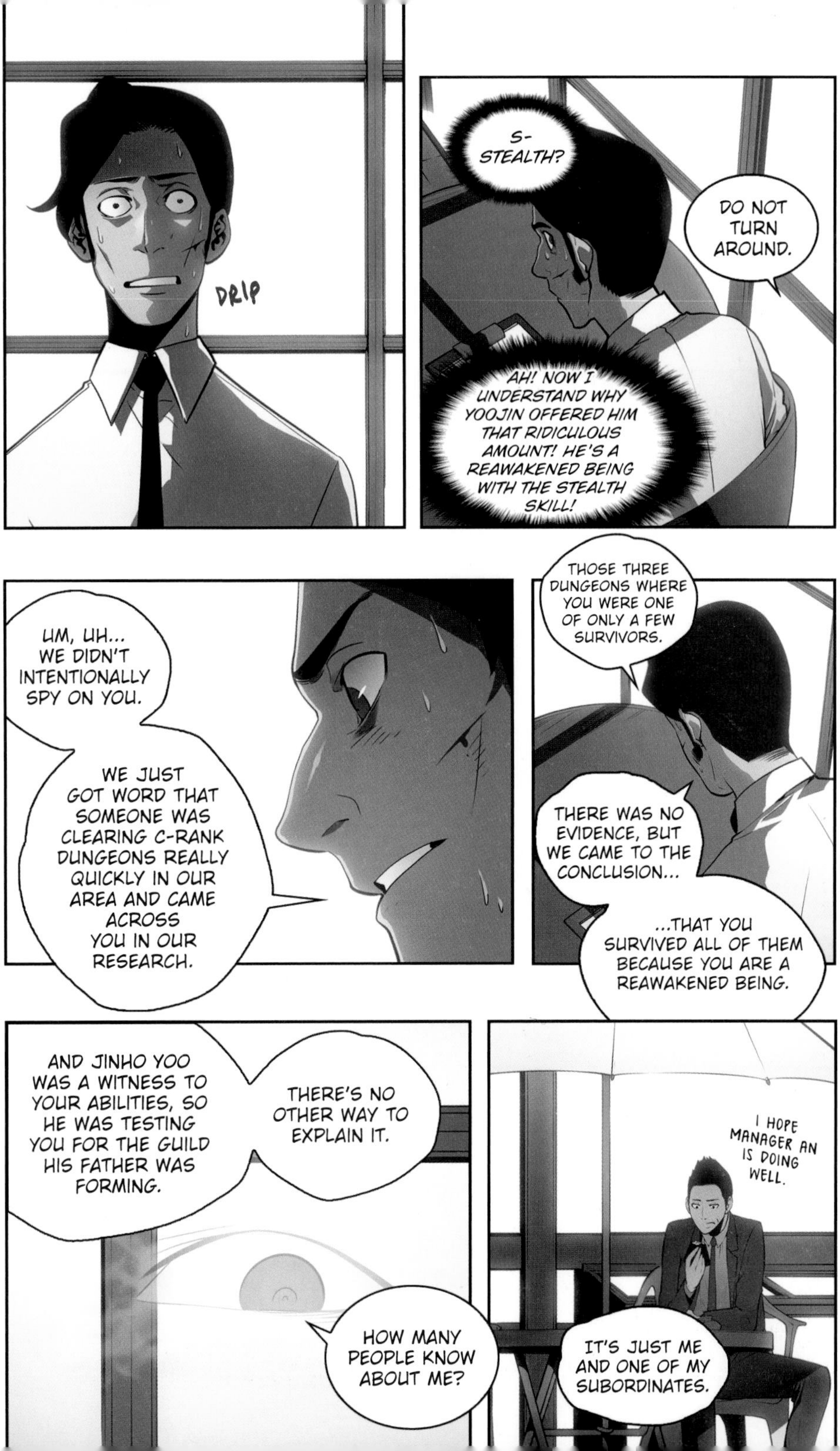
DRIP
S- STEALTH?
DO NOT TURN AROUND.
AH! NOW I UNDERSTAND WHY YOOJIN OFFERED HIM THAT RIDICULOUS AMOUNT! HE'S A REAWAKENED BEING WITH THE STEALTH SKILL!
UM, UH... WE DIDN'T INTENTIONALLY SPY ON YOU.
WE JUST GOT WORD THAT SOMEONE WAS CLEARING C-RANK DUNGEONS REALLY QUICKLY IN OUR AREA AND CAME ACROSS YOU IN OUR RESEARCH.
THOSE THREE DUNGEONS WHERE YOU WERE ONE OF ONLY A FEW SURVIVORS.
THERE WAS NO EVIDENCE, BUT WE CAME TO THE CONCLUSION...
...THAT YOU SURVIVED ALL OF THEM BECAUSE YOU ARE A REAWAKENED BEING.
AND JINHO YOO WAS A WITNESS TO YOUR ABILITIES, SO HE WAS TESTING YOU FOR THE GUILD HIS FATHER WAS FORMING.
THERE'S NO OTHER WAY TO EXPLAIN IT.
HOW MANY PEOPLE KNOW ABOUT ME?
I HOPE MANAGER AN IS DOING WELL.
IT'S JUST ME AND ONE OF MY SUBORDINATES.

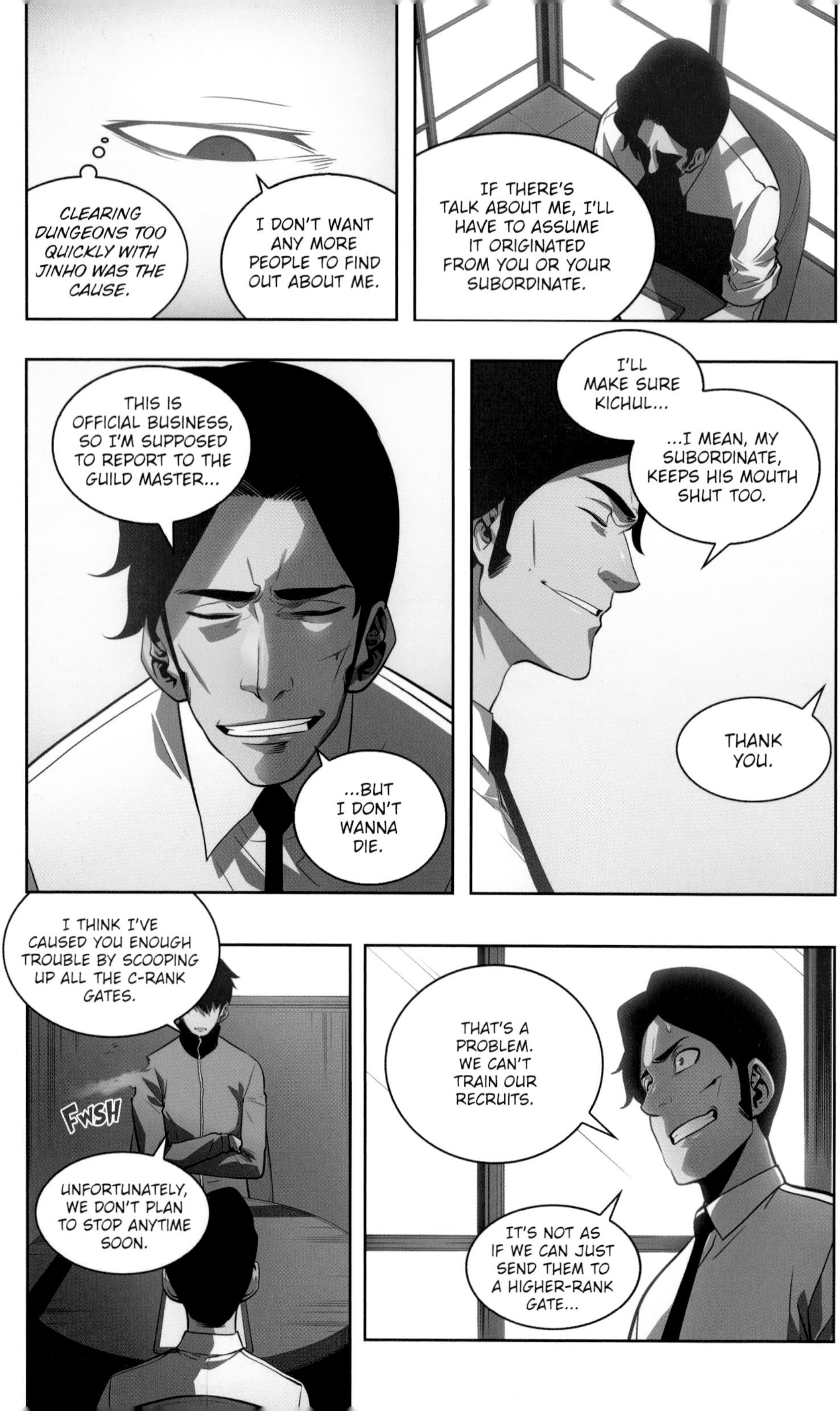
CLEARING DUNGEONS TOO QUICKLY WITH JINHO WAS THE CAUSE.
I DON'T WANT ANY MORE PEOPLE TO FIND OUT ABOUT ME.
IF THERE'S TALK ABOUT ME, I'LL HAVE TO ASSUME IT ORIGINATED FROM YOU OR YOUR SUBORDINATE.
THIS IS OFFICIAL BUSINESS, SO I'M SUPPOSED TO REPORT TO THE GUILD MASTER...
...BUT I DON'T WANNA DIE.
I'LL MAKE SURE KICHUL...
...I MEAN, MY SUBORDINATE, KEEPS HIS MOUTH SHUT TOO.
THANK YOU.
I THINK I'VE CAUSED YOU ENOUGH TROUBLE BY SCOOPING UP ALL THE C-RANK GATES.
FWSH
UNFORTUNATELY, WE DON'T PLAN TO STOP ANYTIME SOON.
THAT'S A PROBLEM. WE CAN'T TRAIN OUR RECRUITS.
IT'S NOT AS IF WE CAN JUST SEND THEM TO A HIGHER-RANK GATE...

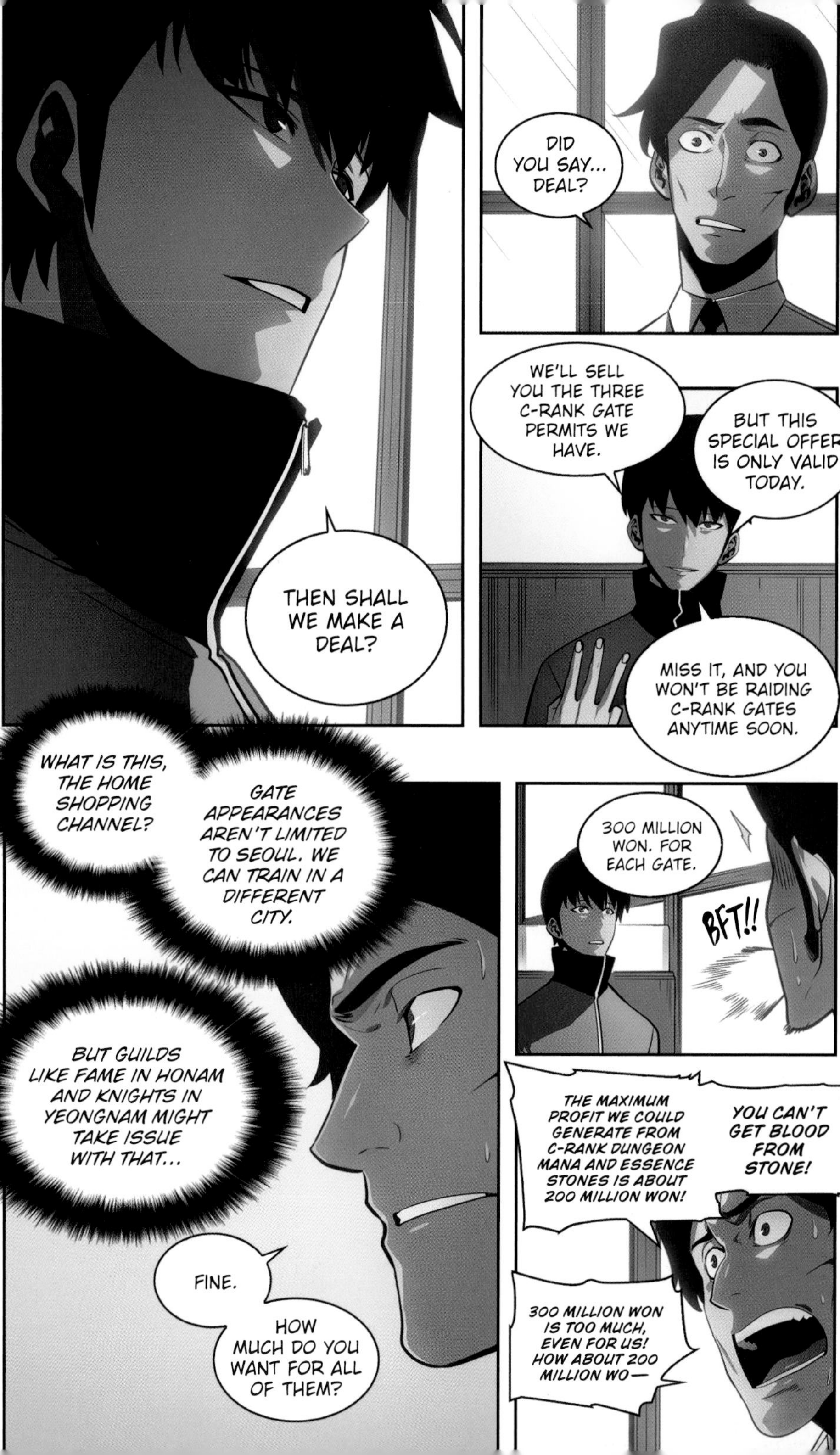
THEN SHALL WE MAKE A DEAL?
DID YOU SAY... DEAL?
WE'LL SELL YOU THE THREE C-RANK GATE PERMITS WE HAVE.
BUT THIS SPECIAL OFFER IS ONLY VALID TODAY.
MISS IT, AND YOU WON'T BE RAIDING C-RANK GATES ANYTIME SOON.
WHAT IS THIS, THE HOME SHOPPING CHANNEL?
GATE APPEARANCES AREN'T LIMITED TO SEOUL. WE CAN TRAIN IN A DIFFERENT CITY.
BUT GUILDS LIKE FAME IN HONAM AND KNIGHTS IN YEONGNAM MIGHT TAKE ISSUE WITH THAT...
FINE.
HOW MUCH DO YOU WANT FOR ALL OF THEM?
300 MILLION WON. FOR EACH GATE.
BFT!!
THE MAXIMUM PROFIT WE COULD GENERATE FROM C-RANK DUNGEON MANA AND ESSENCE STONES IS ABOUT 200 MILLION WON!
YOU CAN'T GET BLOOD FROM STONE!
300 MILLION WON IS TOO MUCH, EVEN FOR US! HOW ABOUT 200 MILLION WO—

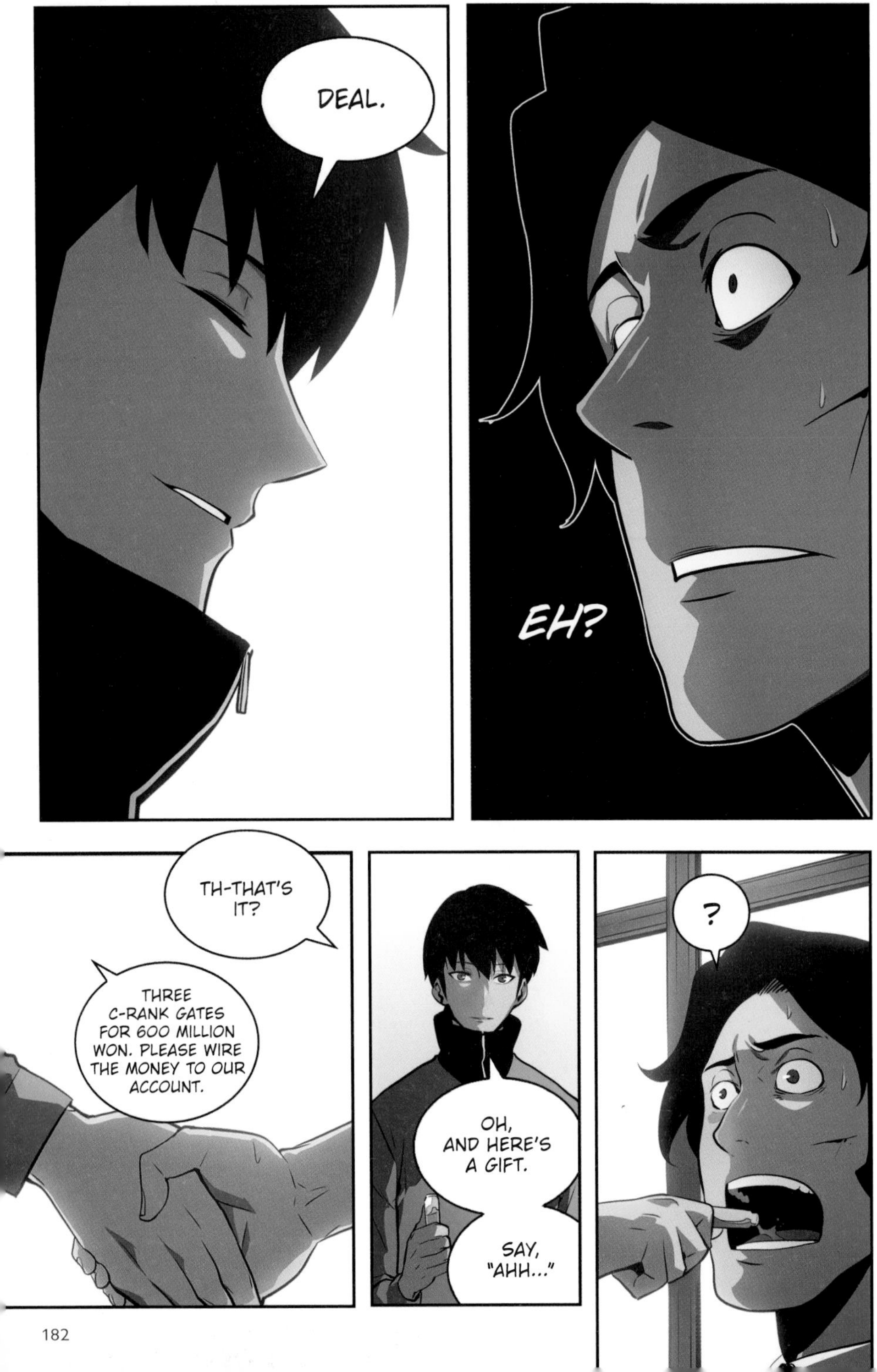
DEAL.
EH?
TH-THAT'S IT?
THREE C-RANK GATES FOR 600 MILLION WON. PLEASE WIRE THE MONEY TO OUR ACCOUNT.
OH, AND HERE'S A GIFT.
SAY, "AHH..."
?

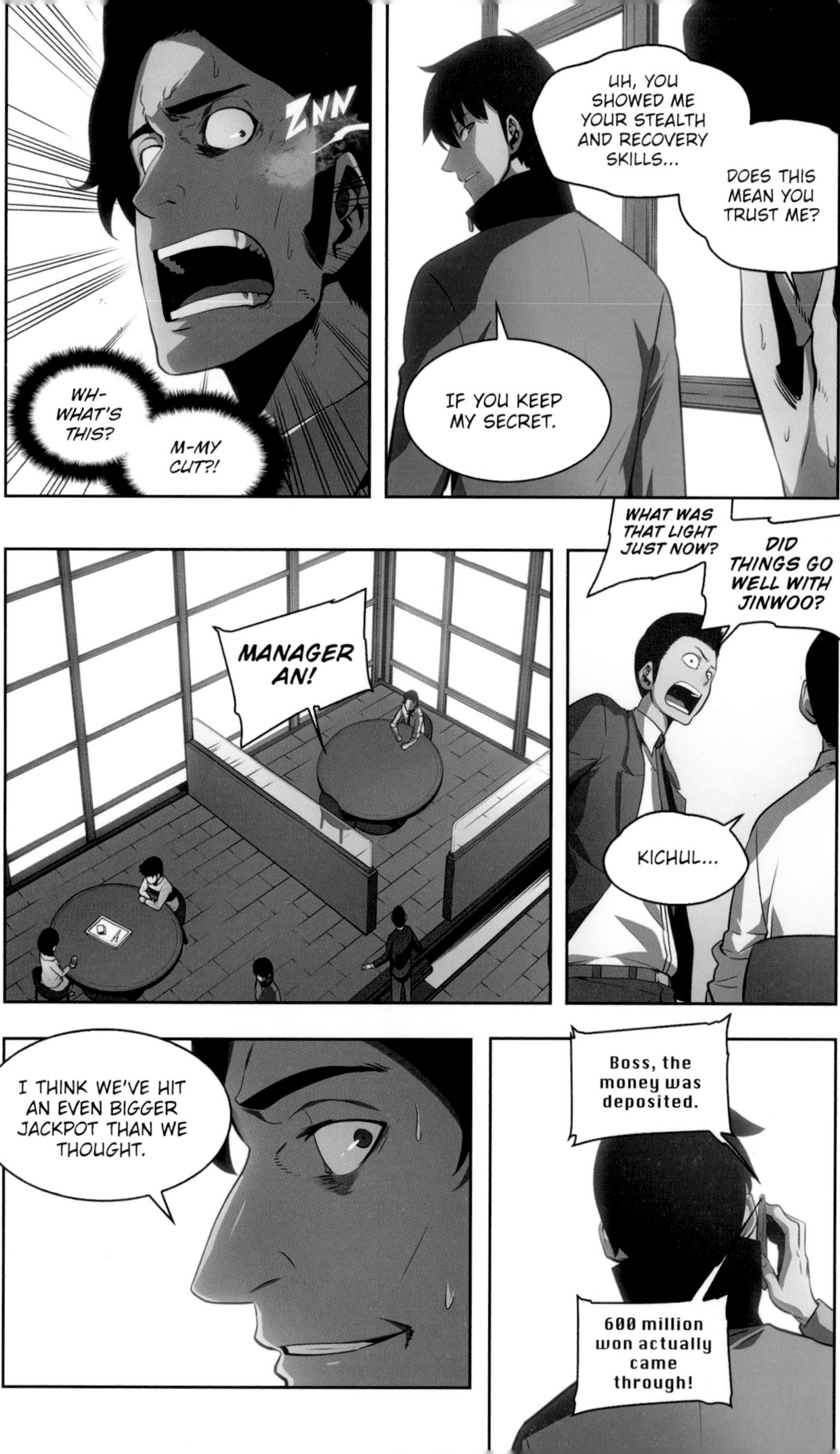
ZNN
WH- WHAT'S THIS?
M-MY CUT?!
UH, YOU SHOWED ME YOUR STEALTH AND RECOVERY SKILLS...
DOES THIS MEAN YOU TRUST ME?
IF YOU KEEP MY SECRET.
MANAGER AN!
WHAT WAS THAT LIGHT JUST NOW?
DID THINGS GO WELL WITH JINWOO?
KICHUL...
I THINK WE'VE HIT AN EVEN BIGGER JACKPOT THAN WE THOUGHT.
Boss, the money was deposited.
600 million won actually came through!

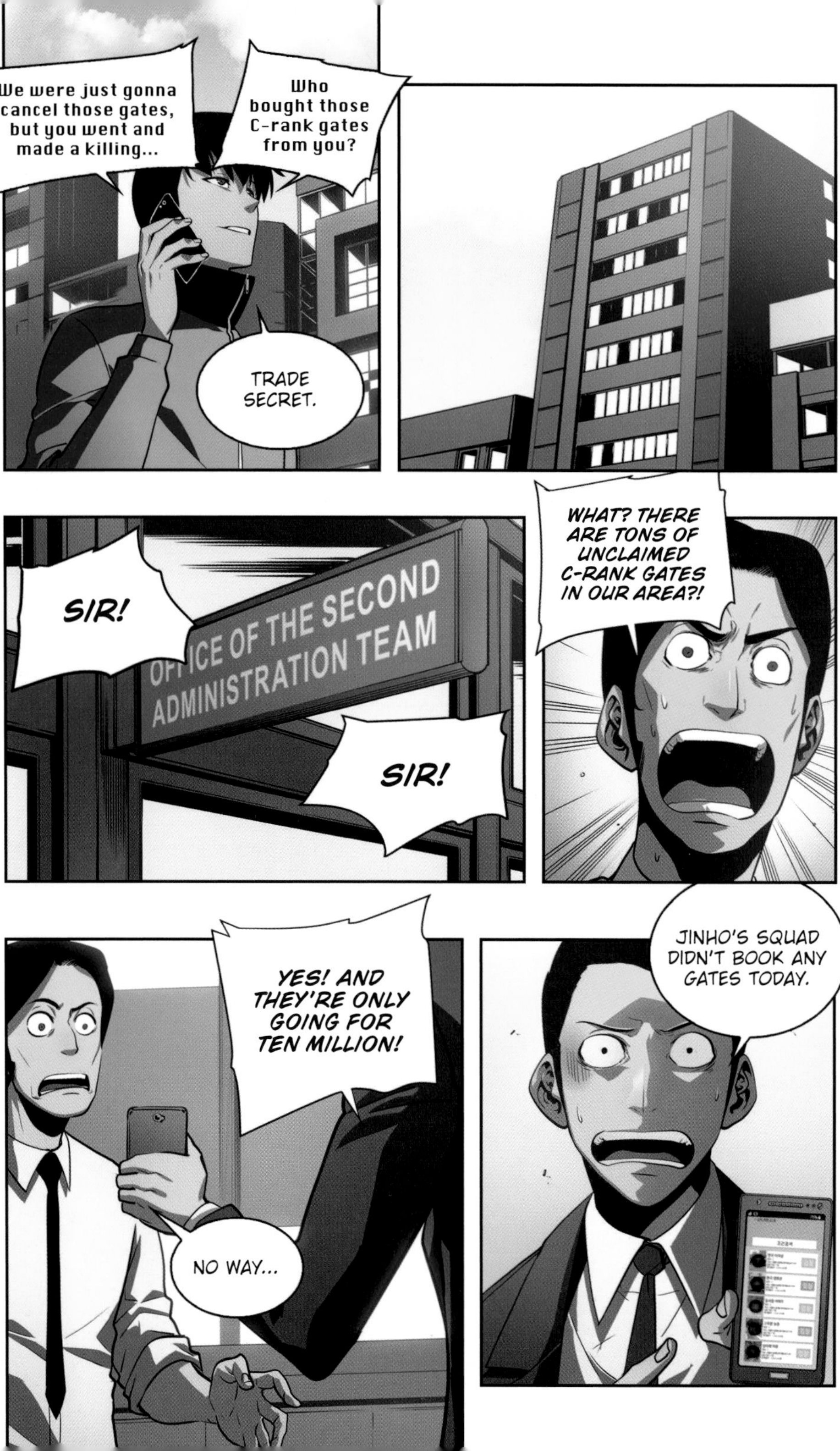
We were just gonna cancel those gates, but you went and made a killing...
Who bought those C-rank gates from you?
TRADE SECRET.
SIR!
OFFICE OF THE SECOND ADMINISTRATION TEAM
SIR!
WHAT? THERE ARE TONS OF UNCLAIMED C-RANK GATES IN OUR AREA?!
YES! AND THEY'RE ONLY GOING FOR TEN MILLION!
NO WAY...
JINHO'S SQUAD DIDN'T BOOK ANY GATES TODAY.

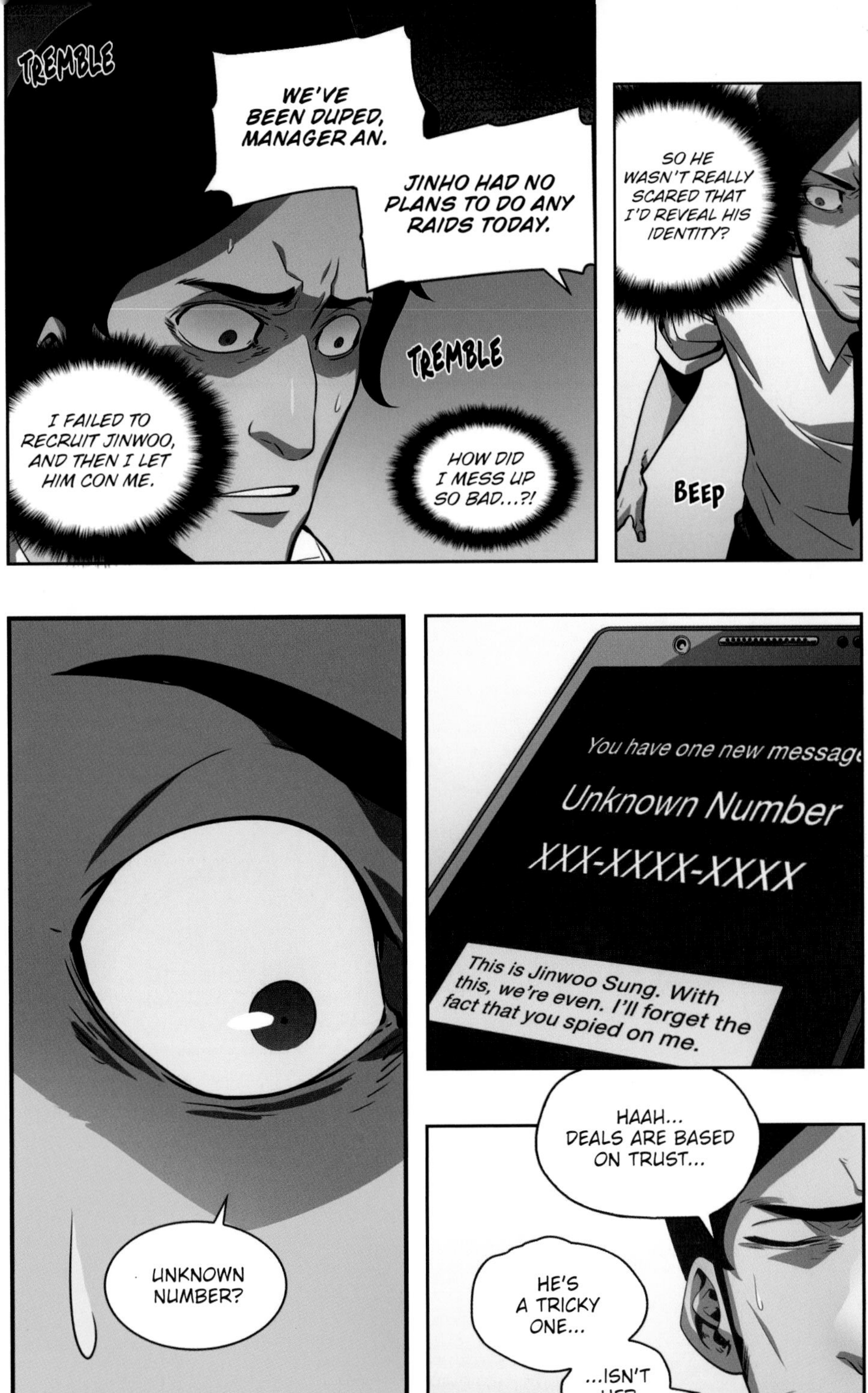
TREMBLE
WE'VE BEEN DUPED, MANAGER AN.
JINHO HAD NO PLANS TO DO ANY RAIDS TODAY.
TREMBLE
I FAILED TO RECRUIT JINWOO, AND THEN I LET HIM CON ME.
HOW DID I MESS UP SO BAD...?!
SO HE WASN'T REALLY SCARED THAT I'D REVEAL HIS IDENTITY?
BEEP
UNKNOWN NUMBER?
You have one new messag
Unknown Number
XXX-XXXX-XXXX
This is Jinwoo Sung. With this, we're even. I'll forget the fact that you spied on me.
HAAH... DEALS ARE BASED ON TRUST...
HE'S A TRICKY ONE...
...ISN'T HE?

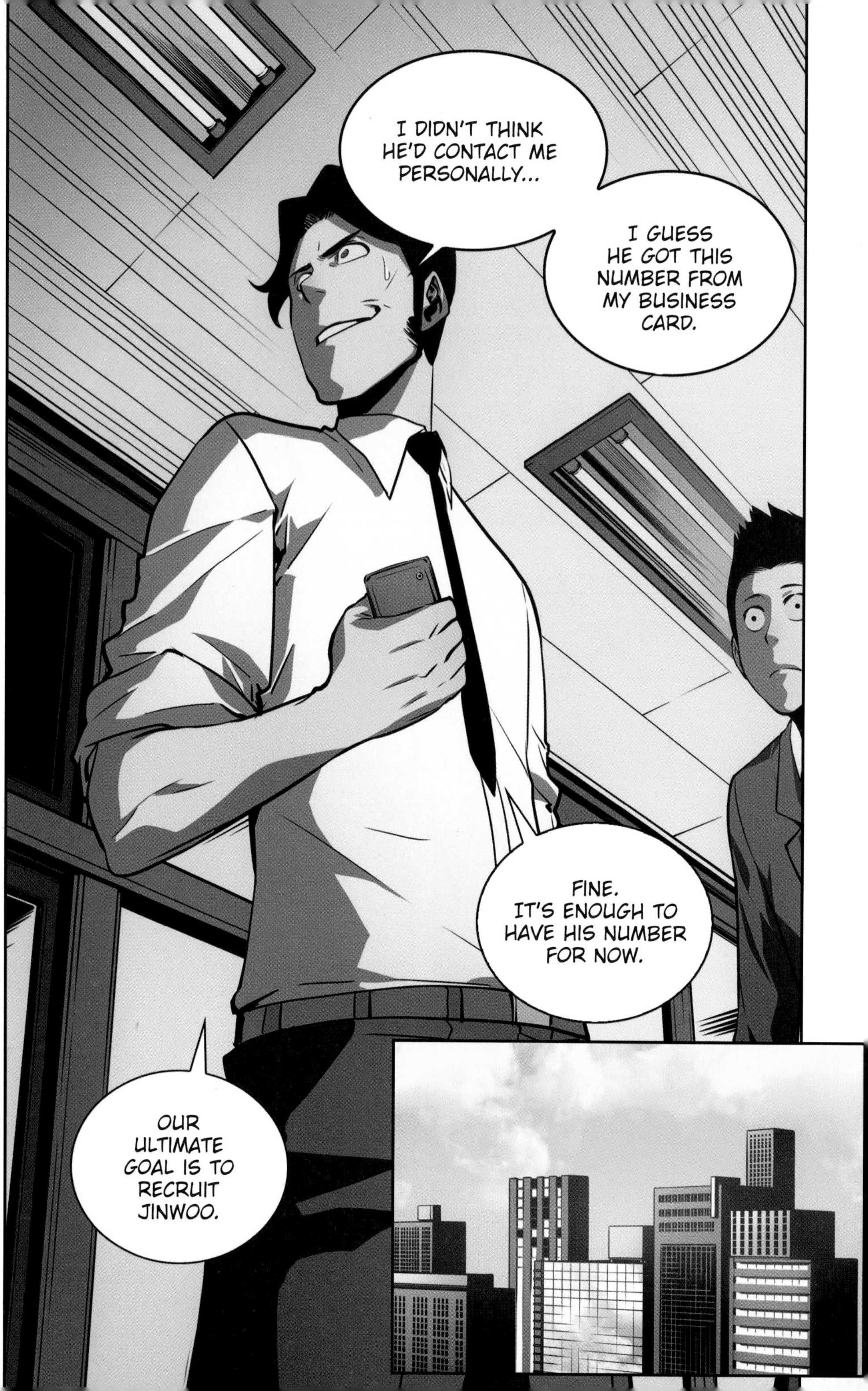
I DIDN'T THINK HE'D CONTACT ME PERSONALLY...
I GUESS HE GOT THIS NUMBER FROM MY BUSINESS CARD.
FINE. IT'S ENOUGH TO HAVE HIS NUMBER FOR NOW.
OUR ULTIMATE GOAL IS TO RECRUIT JINWOO.

CHAPTER 8

Job-Change Quest

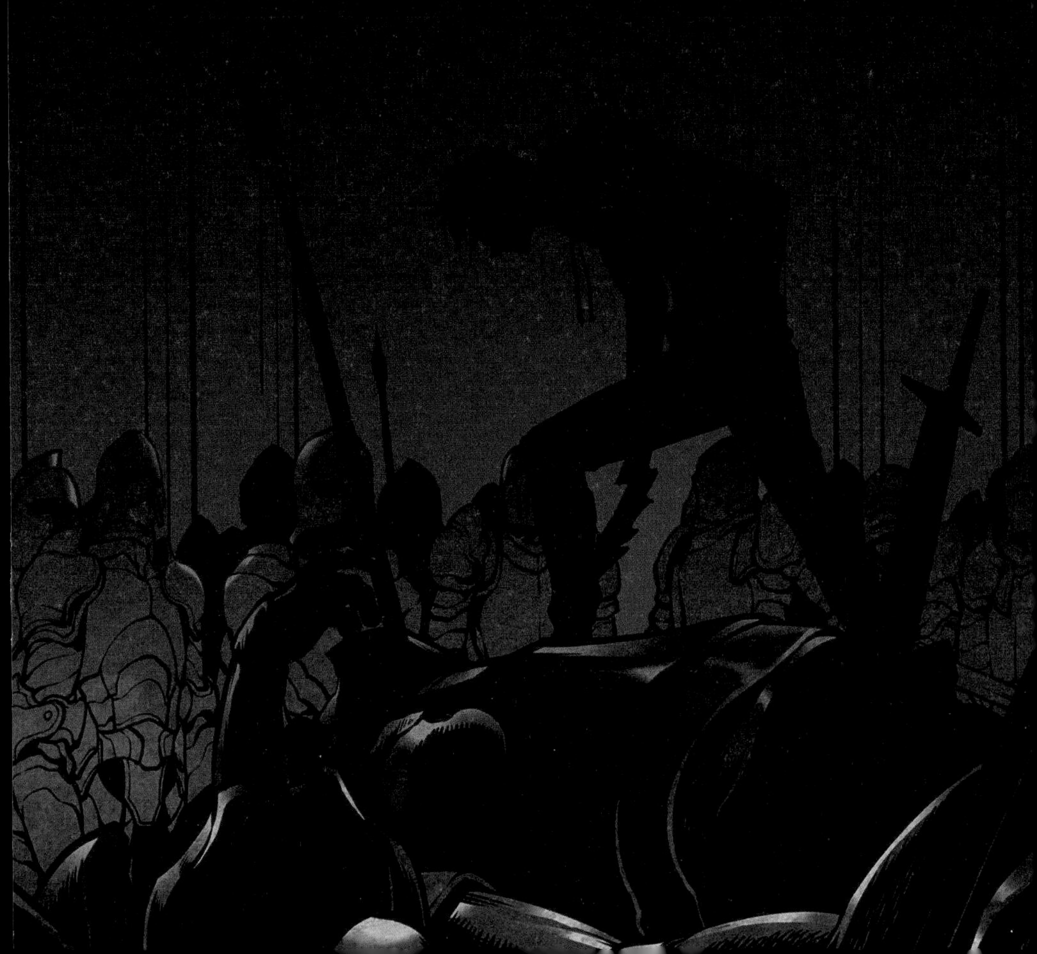

Solo Leveling

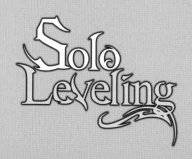

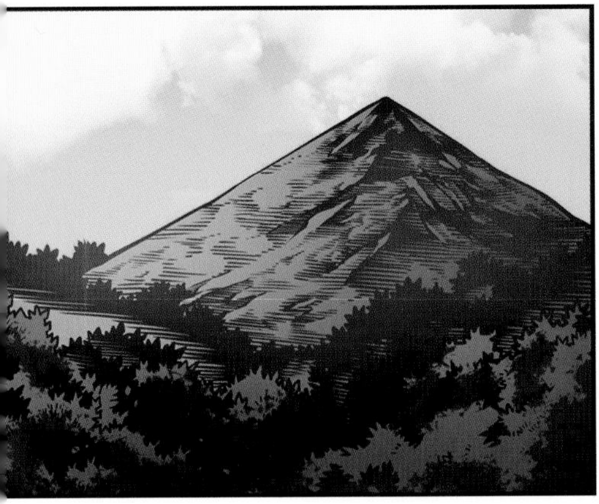

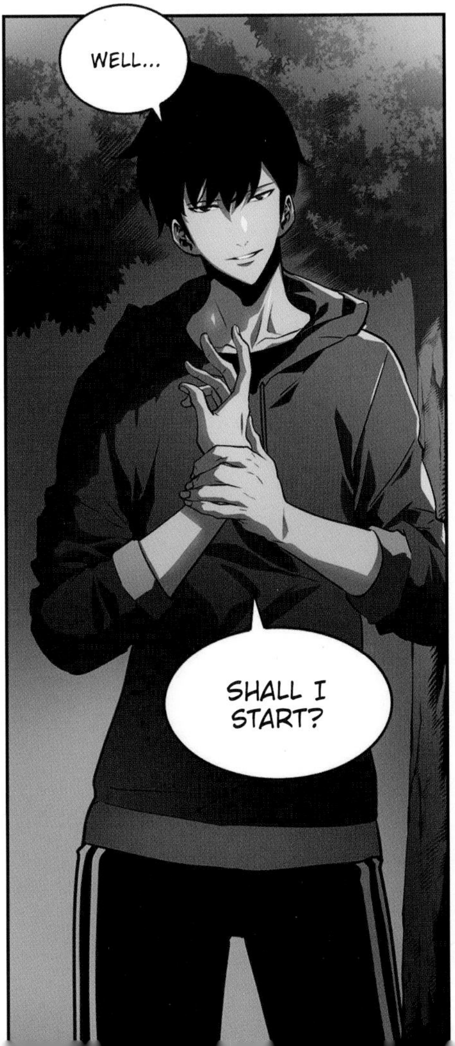
WELL...
SHALL I START?

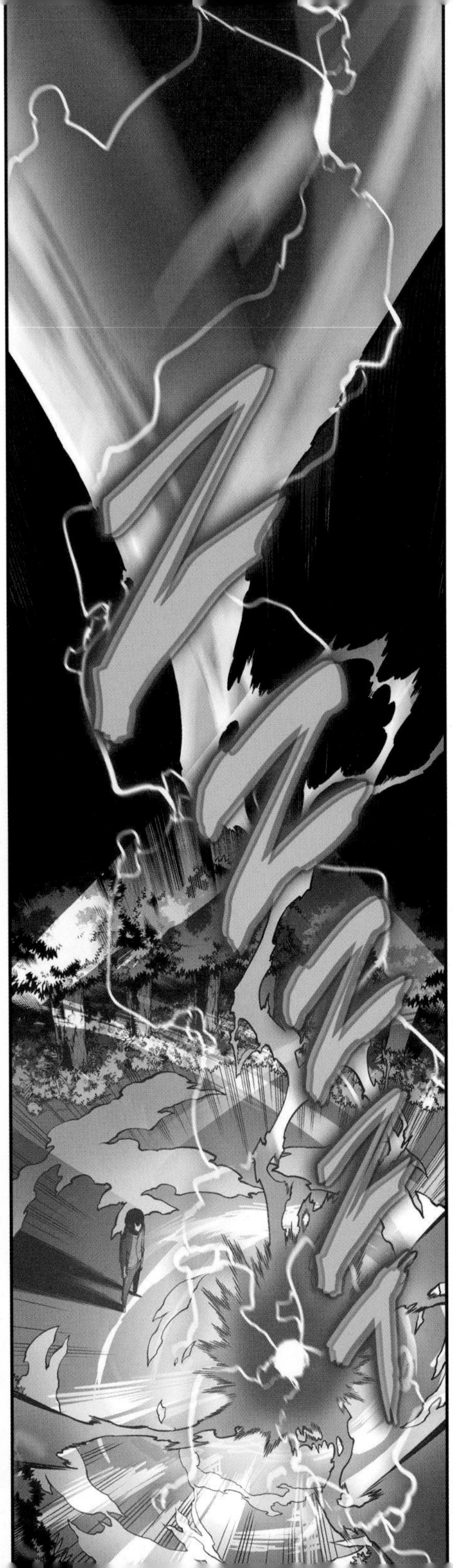

"JOB-CHANGE"...

...SOUNDS INTERESTING.

I WONDER WHAT KIND OF MONSTERS ARE IN HERE.

FINALLY, THIS GAME...

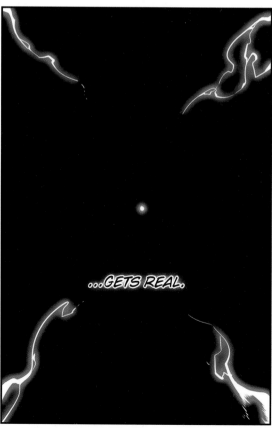

...GETS REAL.

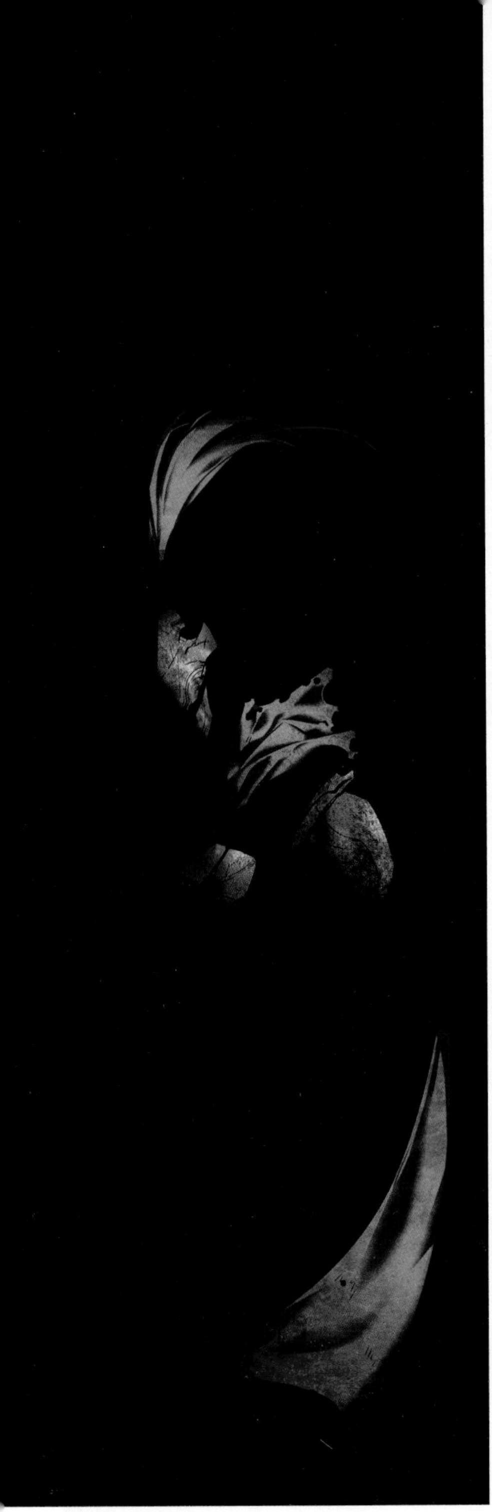
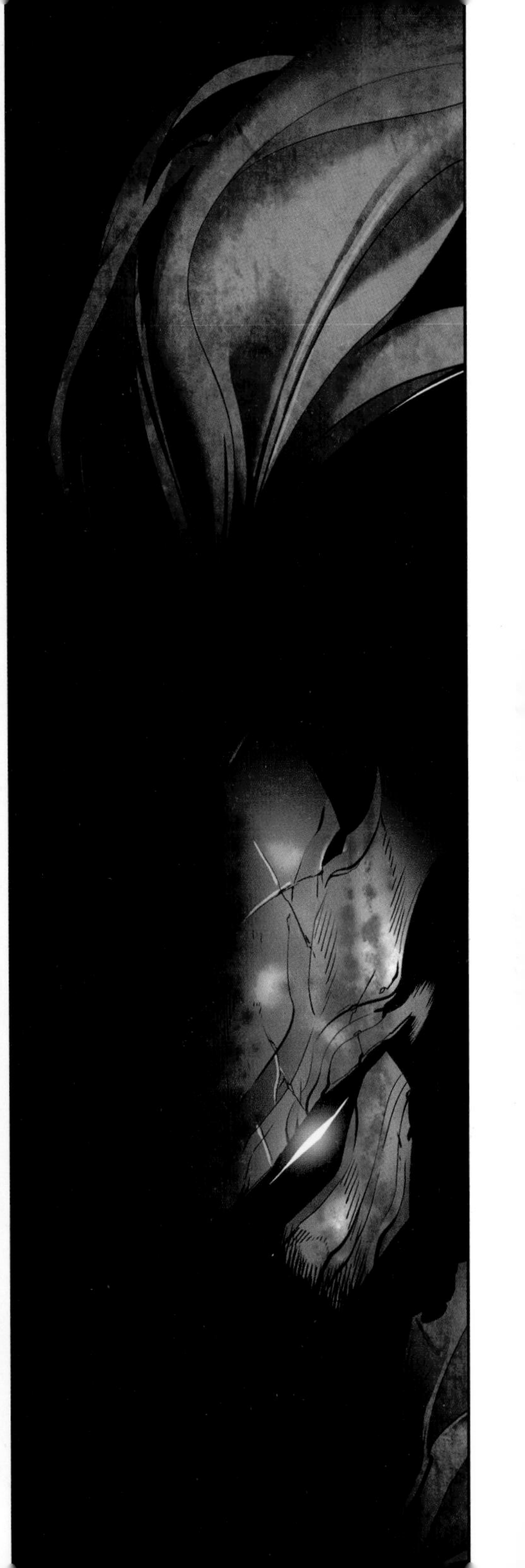

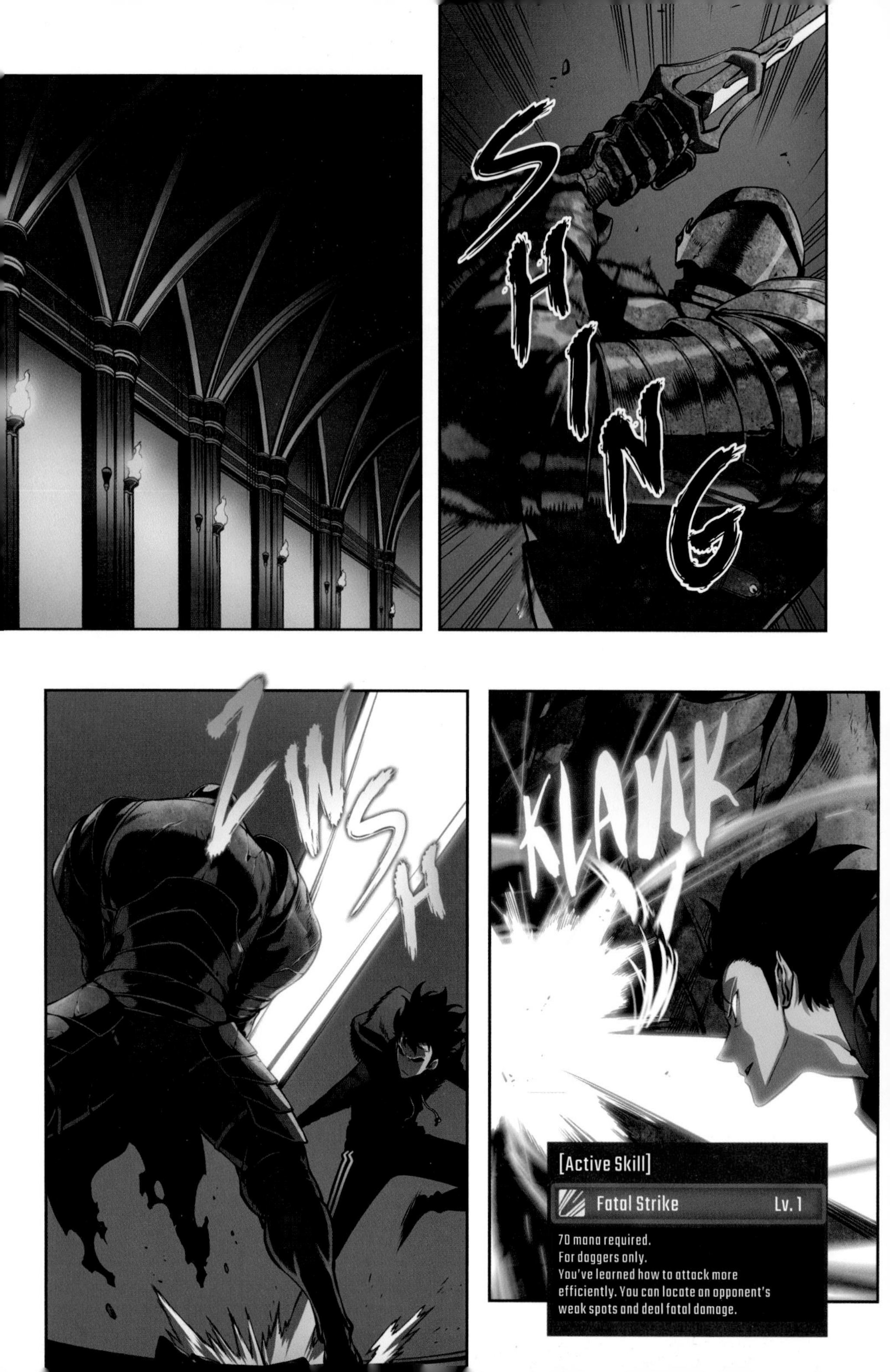
SHING
ZWISH
KLANK
[Active Skill]
Fatal Strike
Lv. 1
70 mana required.
For daggers only.
You've learned how to attack more efficiently. You can locate an opponent's weak spots and deal fatal damage.

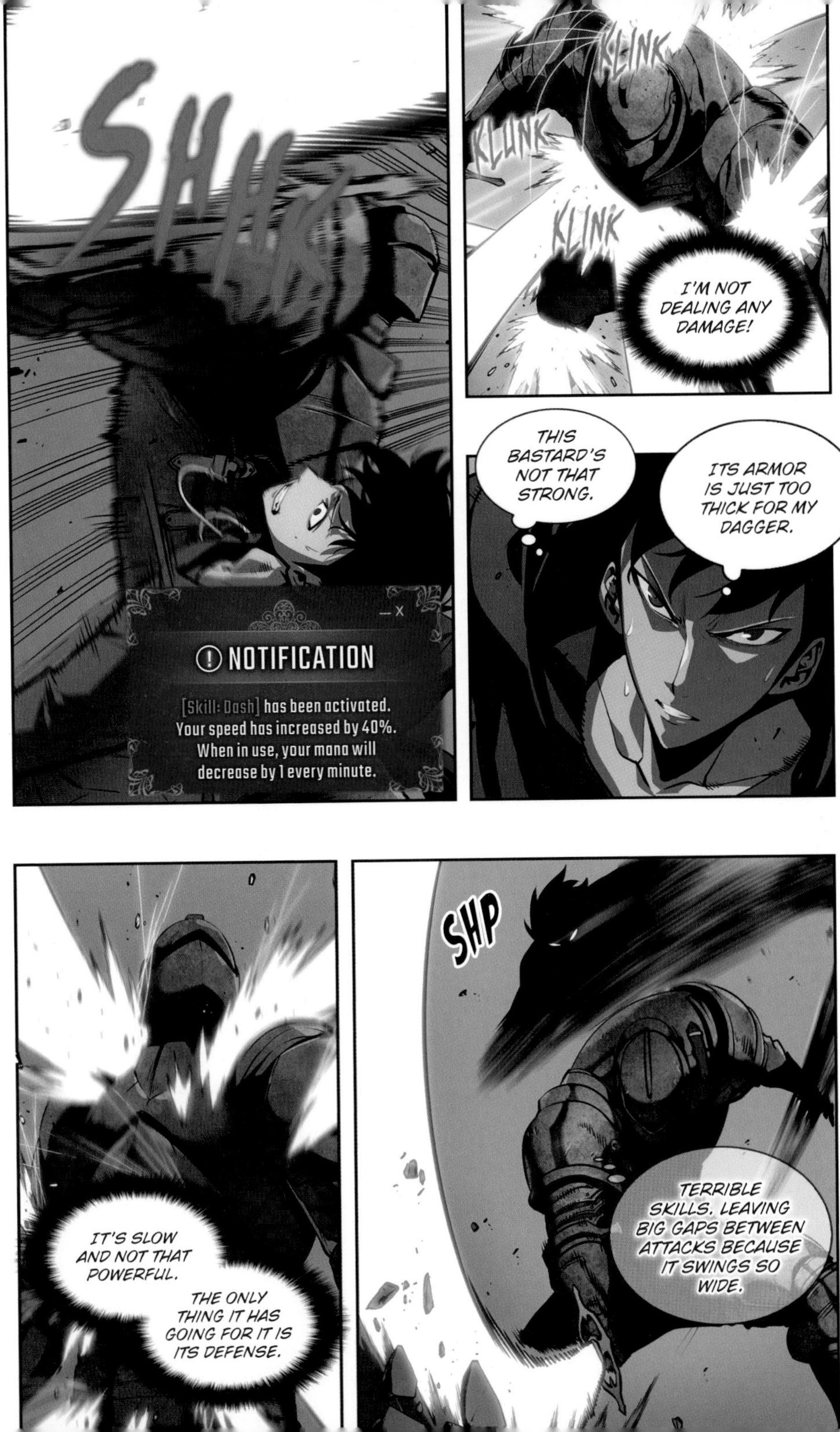
NOTIFICATION
[Skill: Dash] has been activated.
Your speed has increased by 40%.
When in use, your mana will
decrease by 1 every minute.
KLINK
KLUNK
KLINK
I'M NOT DEALING ANY DAMAGE!
THIS BASTARD'S NOT THAT STRONG.
ITS ARMOR IS JUST TOO THICK FOR MY DAGGER.
IT'S SLOW AND NOT THAT POWERFUL.
THE ONLY THING IT HAS GOING FOR IT IS ITS DEFENSE.
SHP
TERRIBLE SKILLS. LEAVING BIG GAPS BETWEEN ATTACKS BECAUSE IT SWINGS SO WIDE.

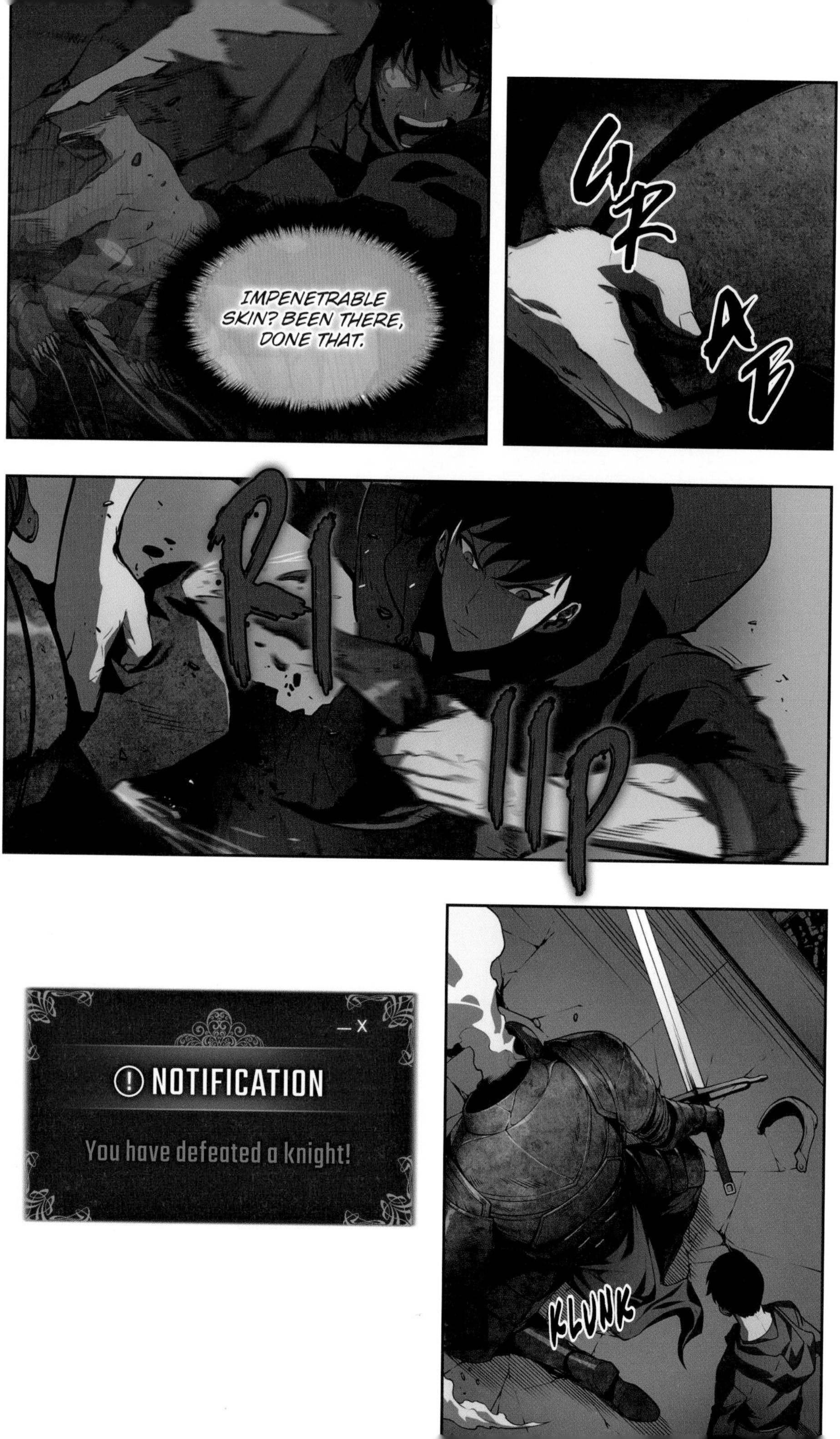
IMPENETRABLE SKIN? BEEN THERE, DONE THAT.
GRAB
RIIIP
— X
NOTIFICATION
You have defeated a knight!
KLUNK

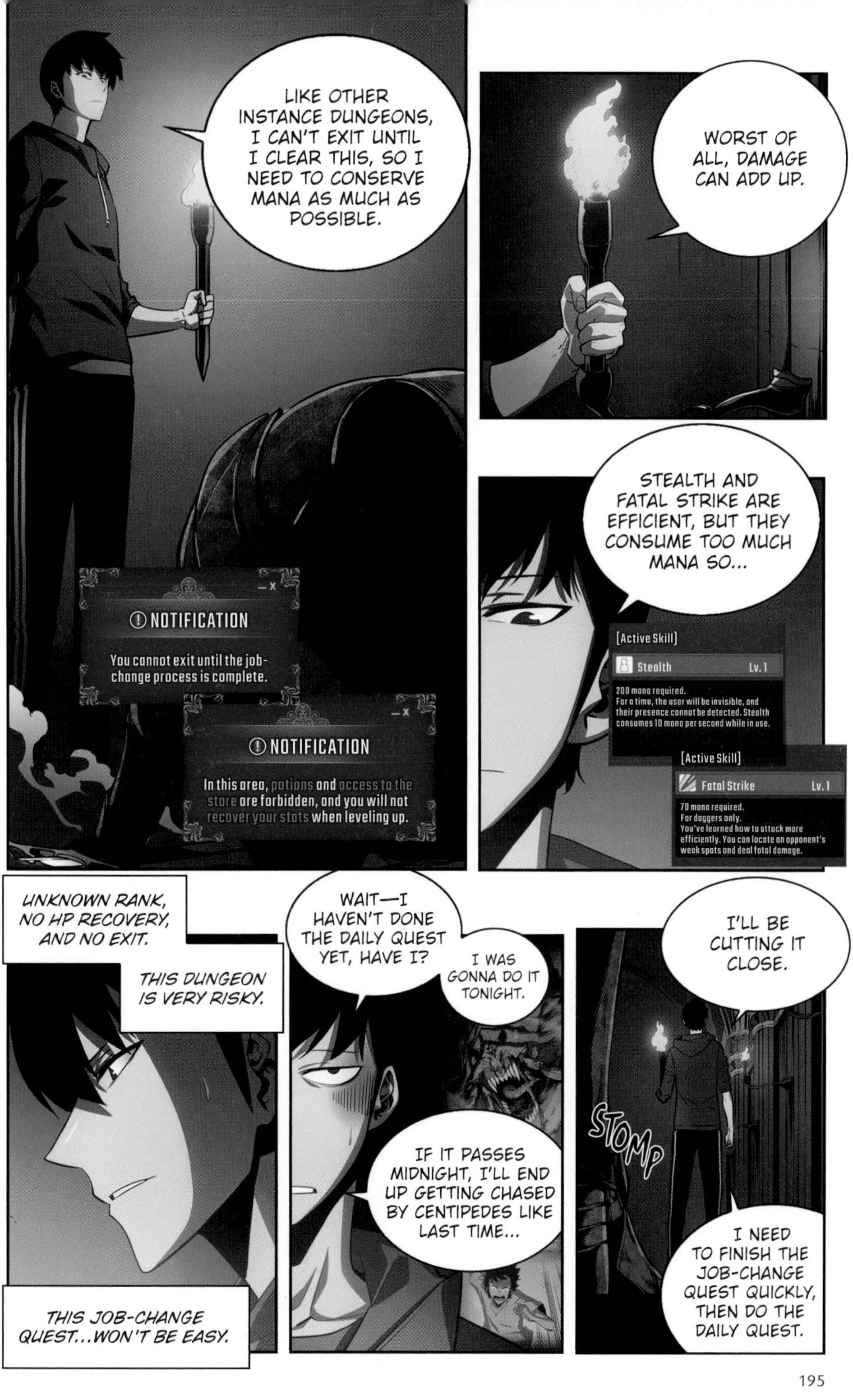
LIKE OTHER INSTANCE DUNGEONS, I CAN'T EXIT UNTIL I CLEAR THIS, SO I NEED TO CONSERVE MANA AS MUCH AS POSSIBLE.
NOTIFICATION
You cannot exit until the job-change process is complete.
NOTIFICATION
In this area, potions and access to the store are forbidden, and you will not recover your stats when leveling up.
WORST OF ALL, DAMAGE CAN ADD UP.
STEALTH AND FATAL STRIKE ARE EFFICIENT, BUT THEY CONSUME TOO MUCH MANA SO...
[Active Skill]
Stealth Lv. 1
200 mana required.
For a time, the user will be invisible, and their presence cannot be detected. Stealth consumes 10 mana per second while in use.
[Active Skill]
Fatal Strike Lv. 1
70 mana required.
For daggers only.
You've learned how to attack more efficiently. You can locate an opponent's weak spots and deal fatal damage.
UNKNOWN RANK, NO HP RECOVERY, AND NO EXIT.
THIS DUNGEON IS VERY RISKY.
THIS JOB-CHANGE QUEST...WON'T BE EASY.
WAIT—I HAVEN'T DONE THE DAILY QUEST YET, HAVE I?
I WAS GONNA DO IT TONIGHT.
IF IT PASSES MIDNIGHT, I'LL END UP GETTING CHASED BY CENTIPEDES LIKE LAST TIME...
I'LL BE CUTTING IT CLOSE.
STOMP
I NEED TO FINISH THE JOB-CHANGE QUEST QUICKLY, THEN DO THE DAILY QUEST.

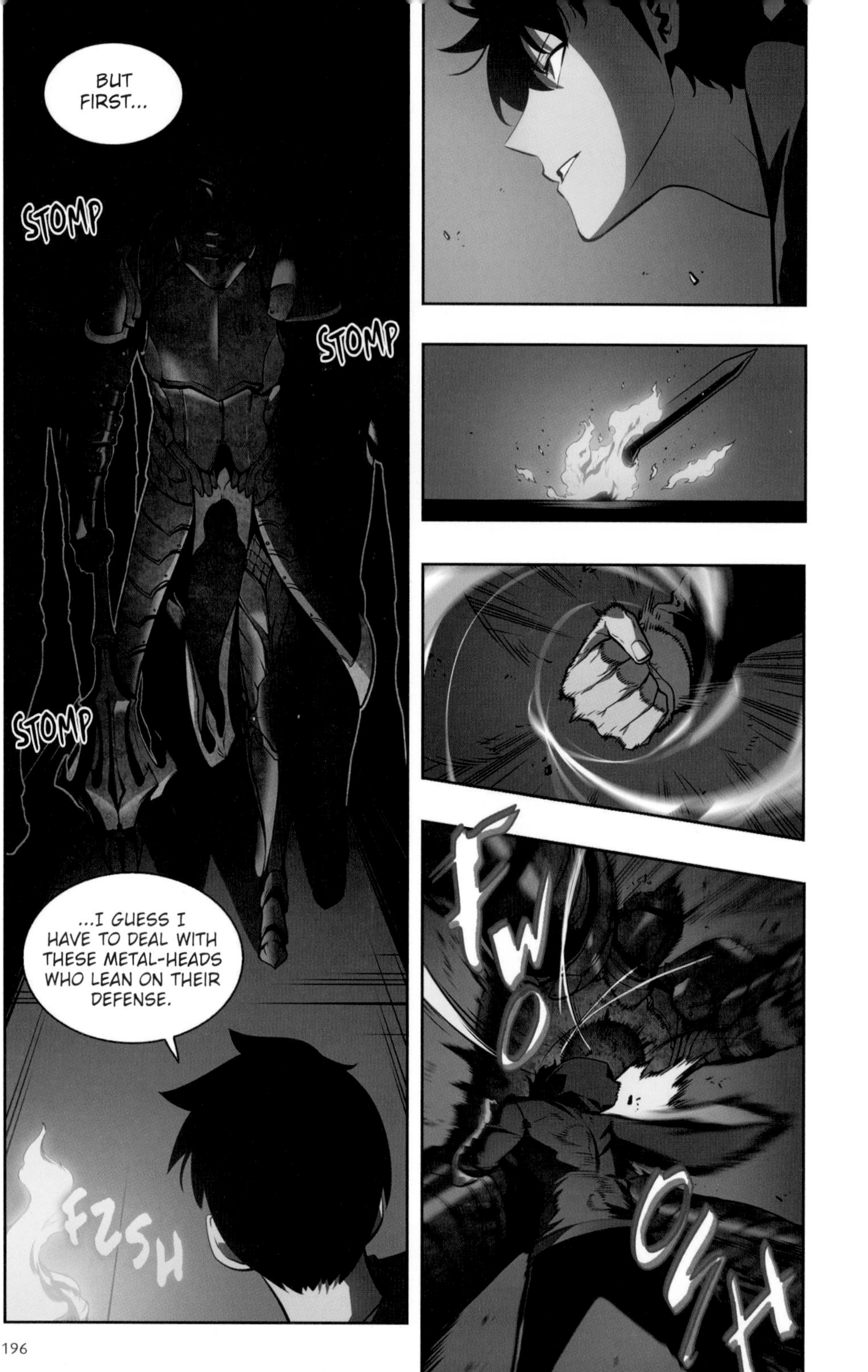
BUT FIRST...
STOMP
STOMP
STOMP
...I GUESS I HAVE TO DEAL WITH THESE METAL-HEADS WHO LEAN ON THEIR DEFENSE.
FZSH
FWO

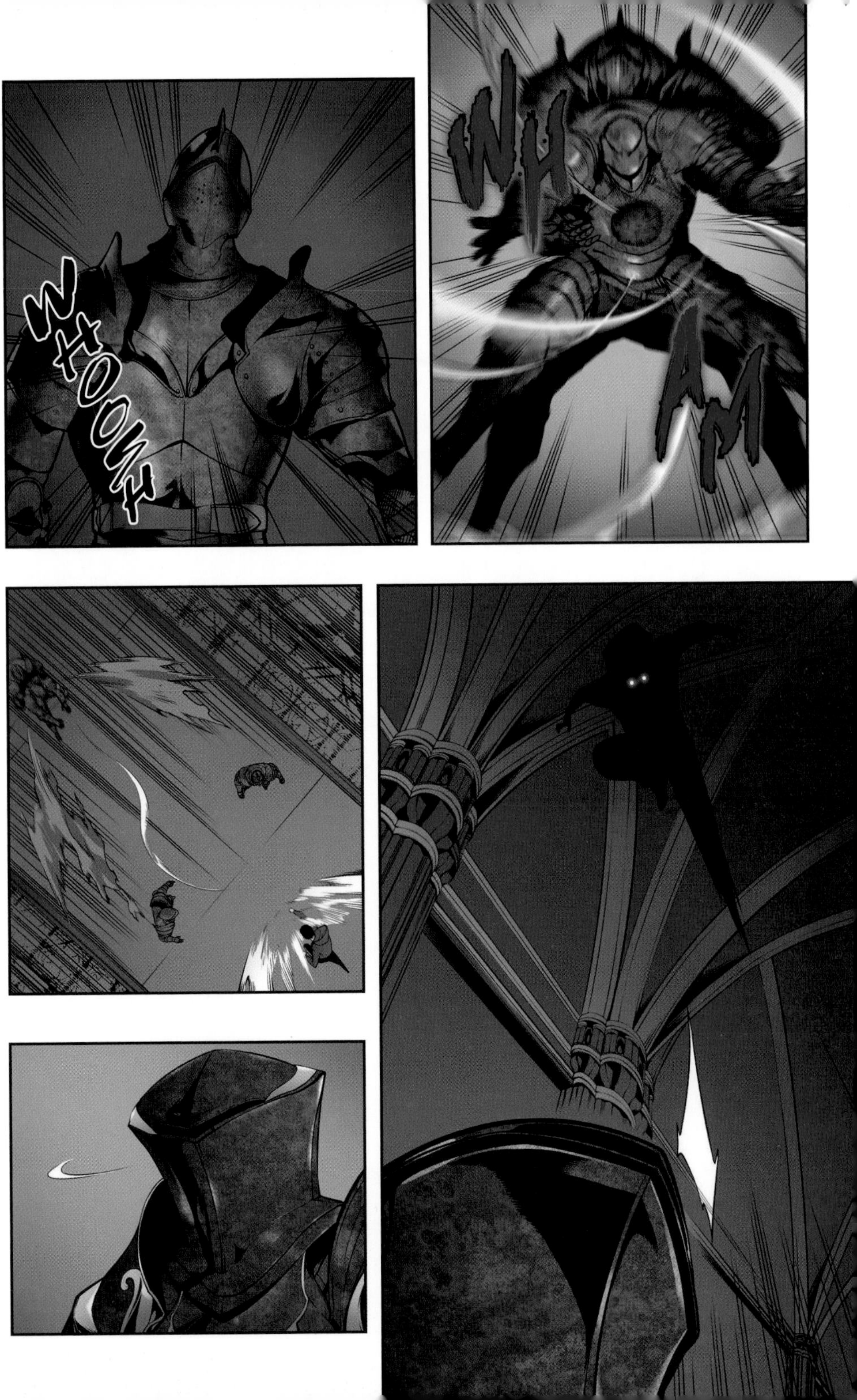
WHOOMH
WHAM

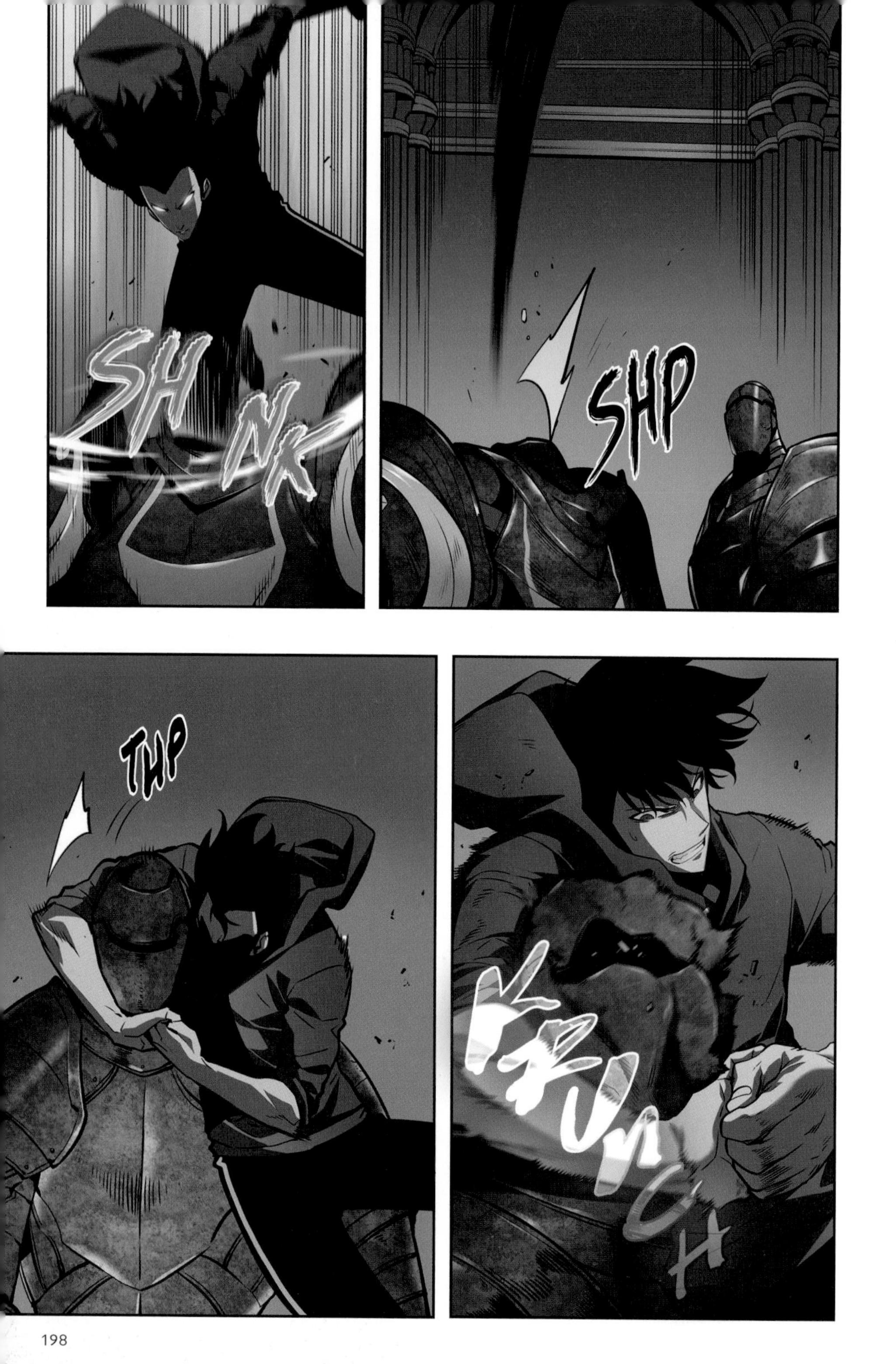
SHNK
SHP
THP
KRUNCH

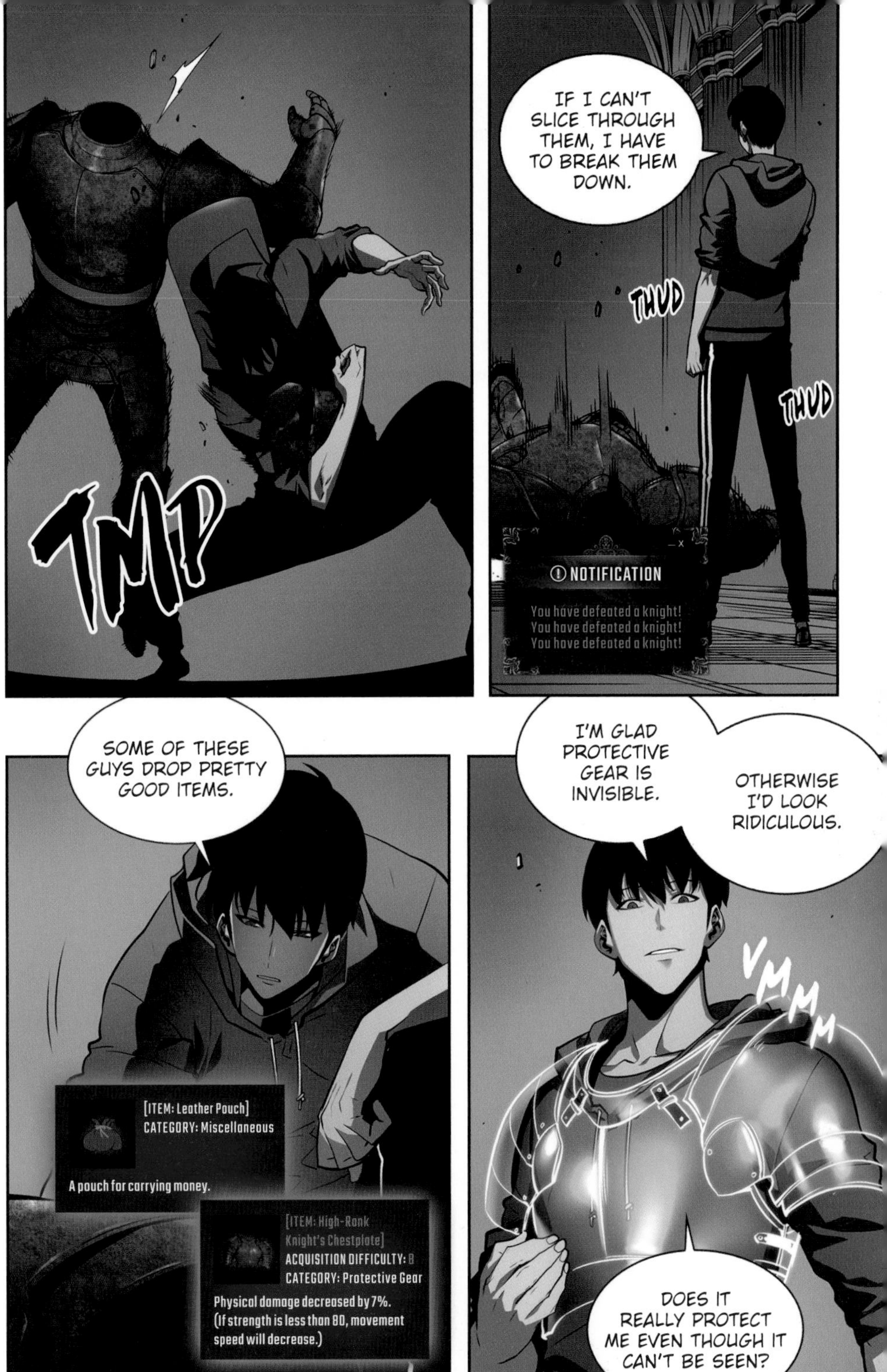
TMP
IF I CAN'T SLICE THROUGH THEM, I HAVE TO BREAK THEM DOWN.
THUD
THUD
NOTIFICATION
You have defeated a knight!
You have defeated a knight!
You have defeated a knight!
SOME OF THESE GUYS DROP PRETTY GOOD ITEMS.
[ITEM: Leather Pouch]
CATEGORY: Miscellaneous
A pouch for carrying money.
[ITEM: High-Rank Knight's Chestplate]
ACQUISITION DIFFICULTY: B
CATEGORY: Protective Gear
Physical damage decreased by 7%.
(If strength is less than 80, movement speed will decrease.)
I'M GLAD PROTECTIVE GEAR IS INVISIBLE.
OTHERWISE I'D LOOK RIDICULOUS.
VMMM
DOES IT REALLY PROTECT ME EVEN THOUGH IT CAN'T BE SEEN?

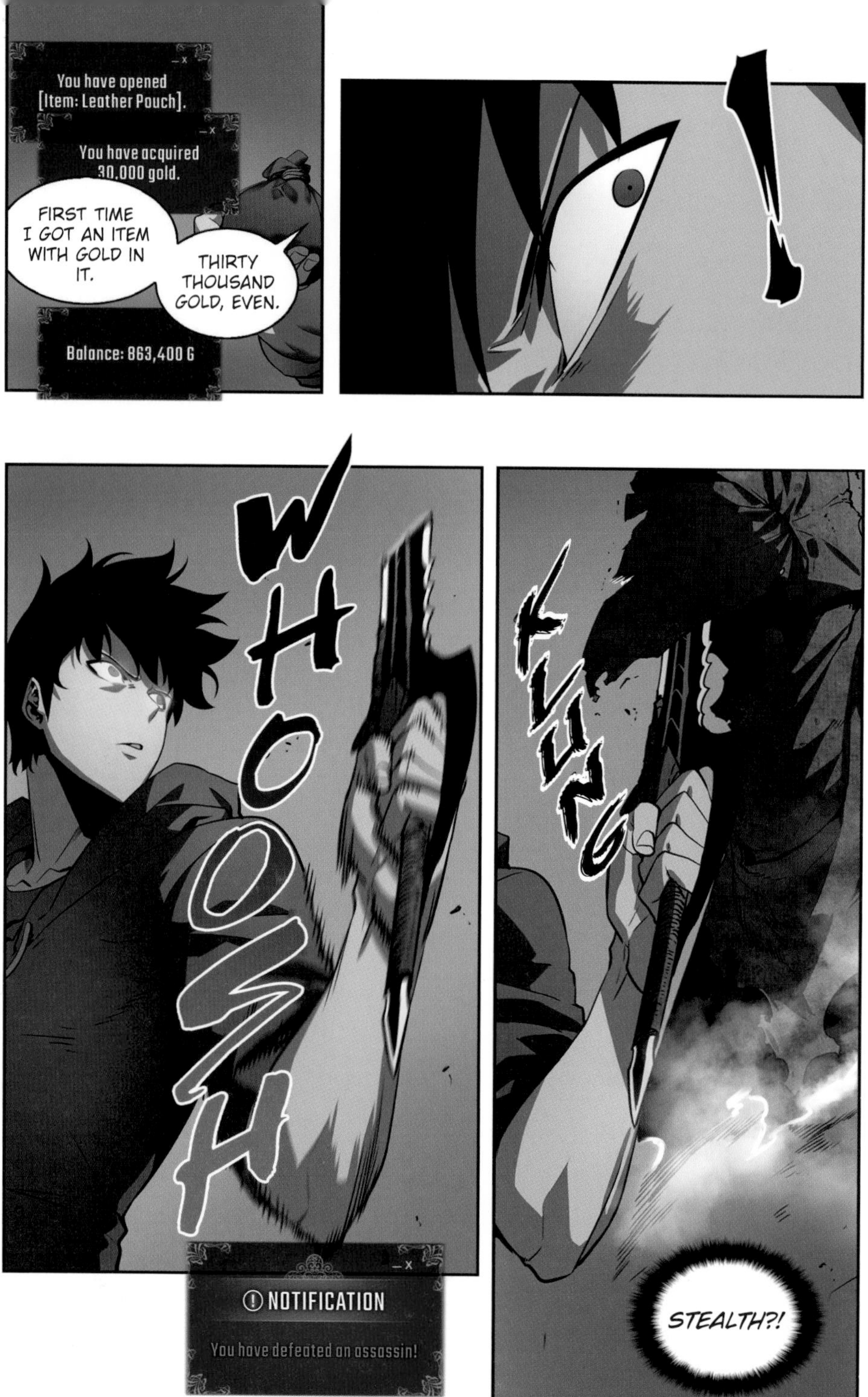

You have opened [Item: Leather Pouch].
You have acquired 30,000 gold.
FIRST TIME I GOT AN ITEM WITH GOLD IN IT.
THIRTY THOUSAND GOLD, EVEN.
Balance: 863,400 G
!
WHOOSH
KLUNG
NOTIFICATION
You have defeated an assassin!
STEALTH?!

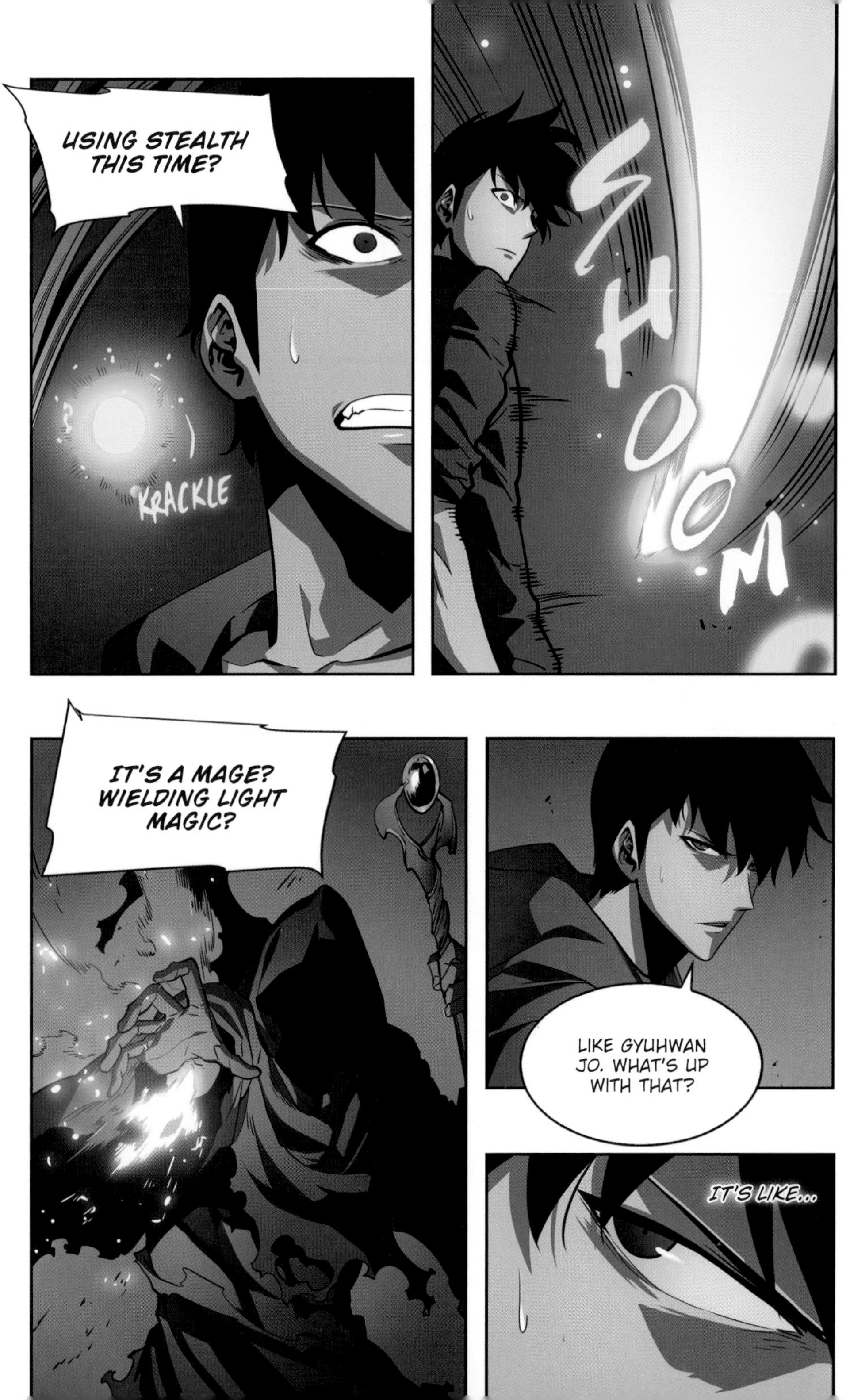
USING STEALTH THIS TIME?
KRACKLE
SHOOOM
IT'S A MAGE? WIELDING LIGHT MAGIC?
LIKE GYUHWAN JO. WHAT'S UP WITH THAT?
IT'S LIKE...

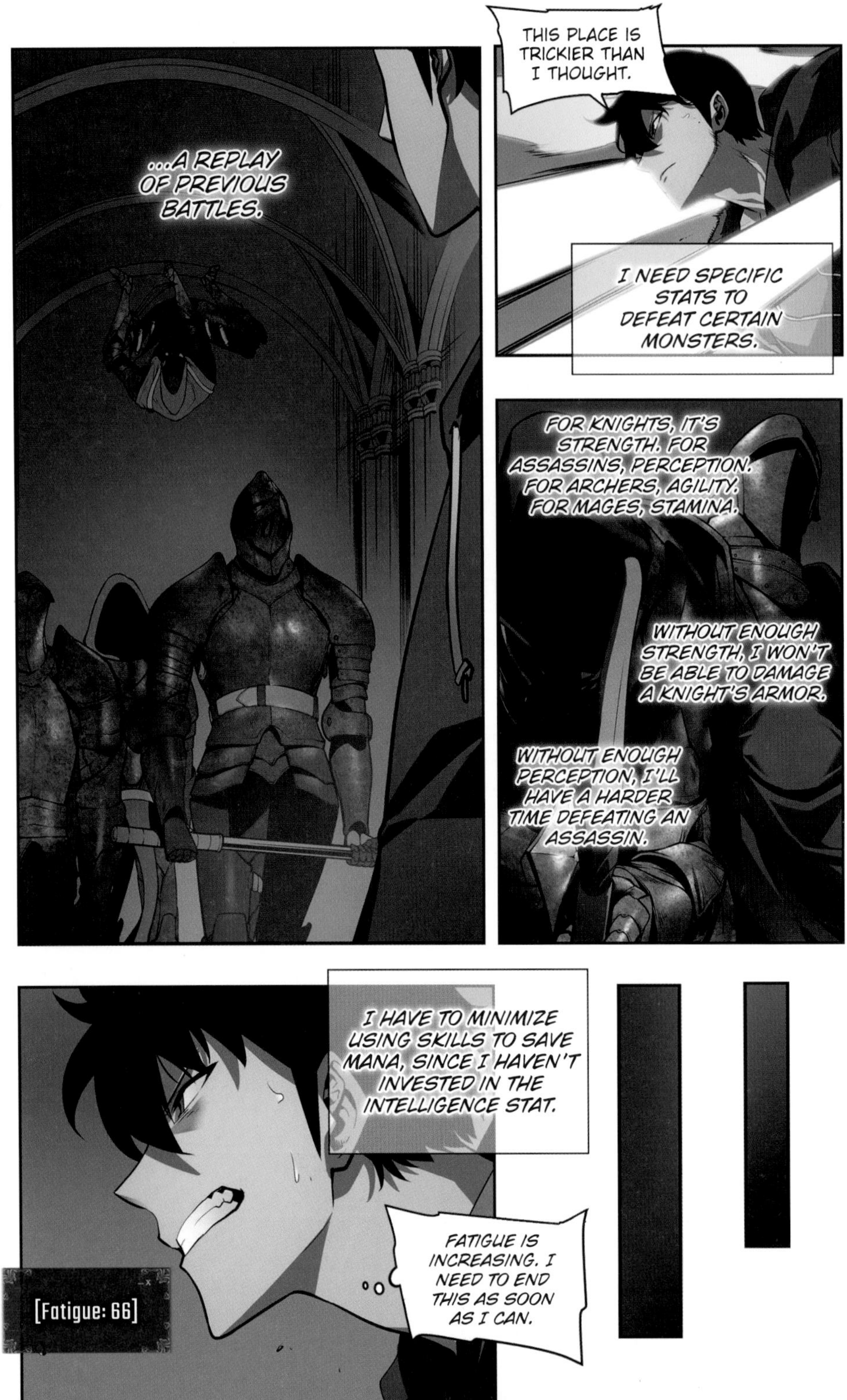
...A REPLAY OF PREVIOUS BATTLES.
THIS PLACE IS TRICKIER THAN I THOUGHT.
I NEED SPECIFIC STATS TO DEFEAT CERTAIN MONSTERS.
FOR KNIGHTS, IT'S STRENGTH. FOR ASSASSINS, PERCEPTION. FOR ARCHERS, AGILITY. FOR MAGES, STAMINA.
WITHOUT ENOUGH STRENGTH, I WON'T BE ABLE TO DAMAGE A KNIGHT'S ARMOR.
WITHOUT ENOUGH PERCEPTION, I'LL HAVE A HARDER TIME DEFEATING AN ASSASSIN.
I HAVE TO MINIMIZE USING SKILLS TO SAVE MANA, SINCE I HAVEN'T INVESTED IN THE INTELLIGENCE STAT.
[Fatigue: 66]
FATIGUE IS INCREASING. I NEED TO END THIS AS SOON AS I CAN.

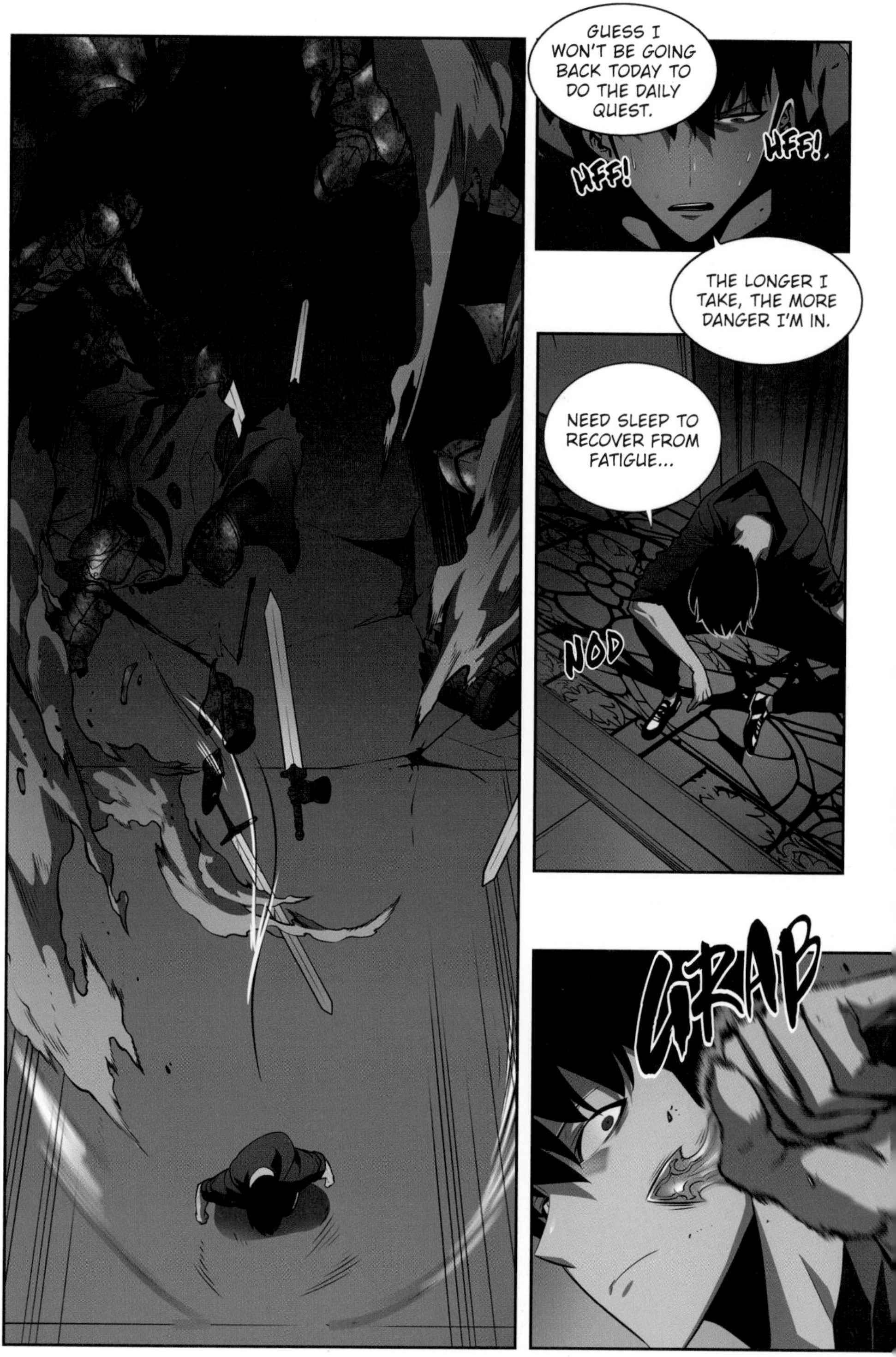
GUESS I WON'T BE GOING BACK TODAY TO DO THE DAILY QUEST.
HFF!
HFF!
THE LONGER I TAKE, THE MORE DANGER I'M IN.
NEED SLEEP TO RECOVER FROM FATIGUE...
NOD
GRAB

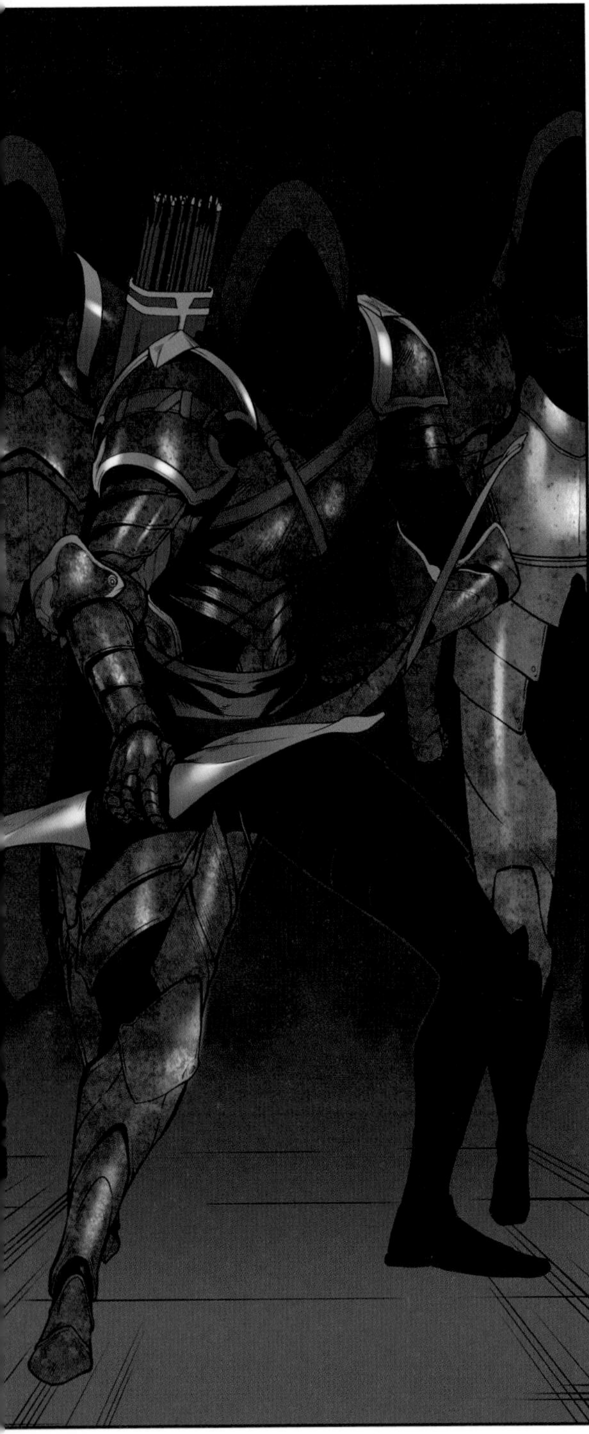

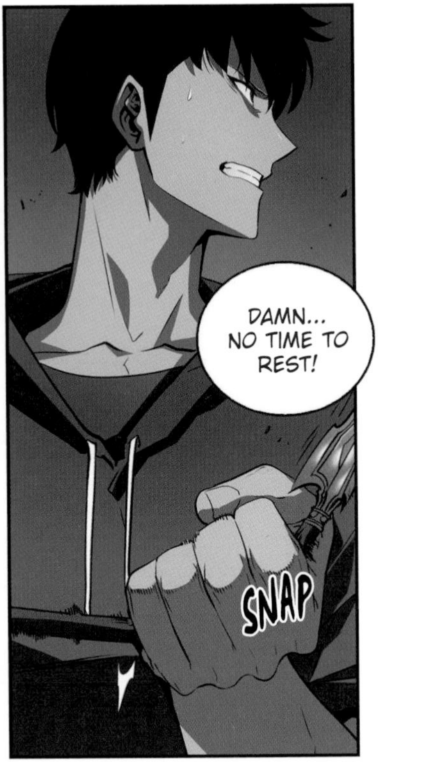
DAMN... NO TIME TO REST!
SNAP

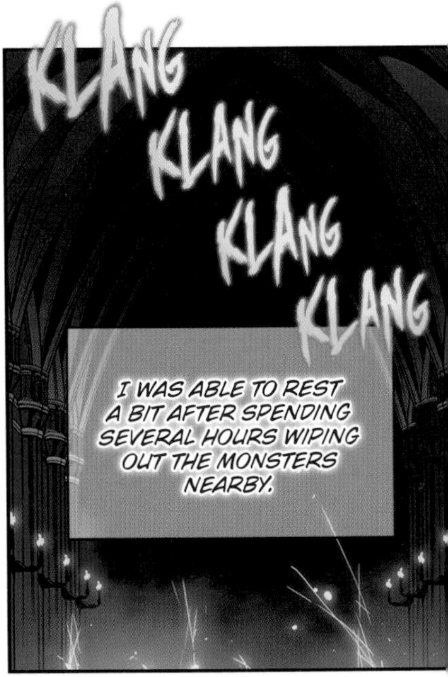
KLANG
KLANG
KLANG
KLANG
I WAS ABLE TO REST A BIT AFTER SPENDING SEVERAL HOURS WIPING OUT THE MONSTERS NEARBY.

You have opened [Item: Leather Pouch].

GULP

GULP

You have acquired 20,000 gold and a canteen of lukewarm water.

HWOO...

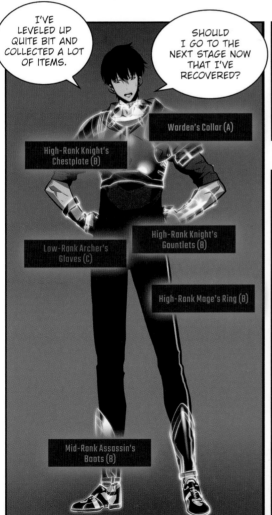

I'VE LEVELED UP QUITE BIT AND COLLECTED A LOT OF ITEMS.

SHOULD I GO TO THE NEXT STAGE NOW THAT I'VE RECOVERED?

Warden's Collar (A)

High-Rank Knight's Chestplate (B)

High-Rank Knight's Gauntlets (B)

Low-Rank Archer's Gloves (C)

High-Rank Mage's Ring (B)

Mid-Rank Assassin's Boots (B)

BUT EVEN THOUGH I'VE LEVELED UP THIS MUCH, I STILL CAN'T TELL...

...WHAT DANGER WAITS FOR ME ON THE OTHER SIDE OF THESE DOORS.

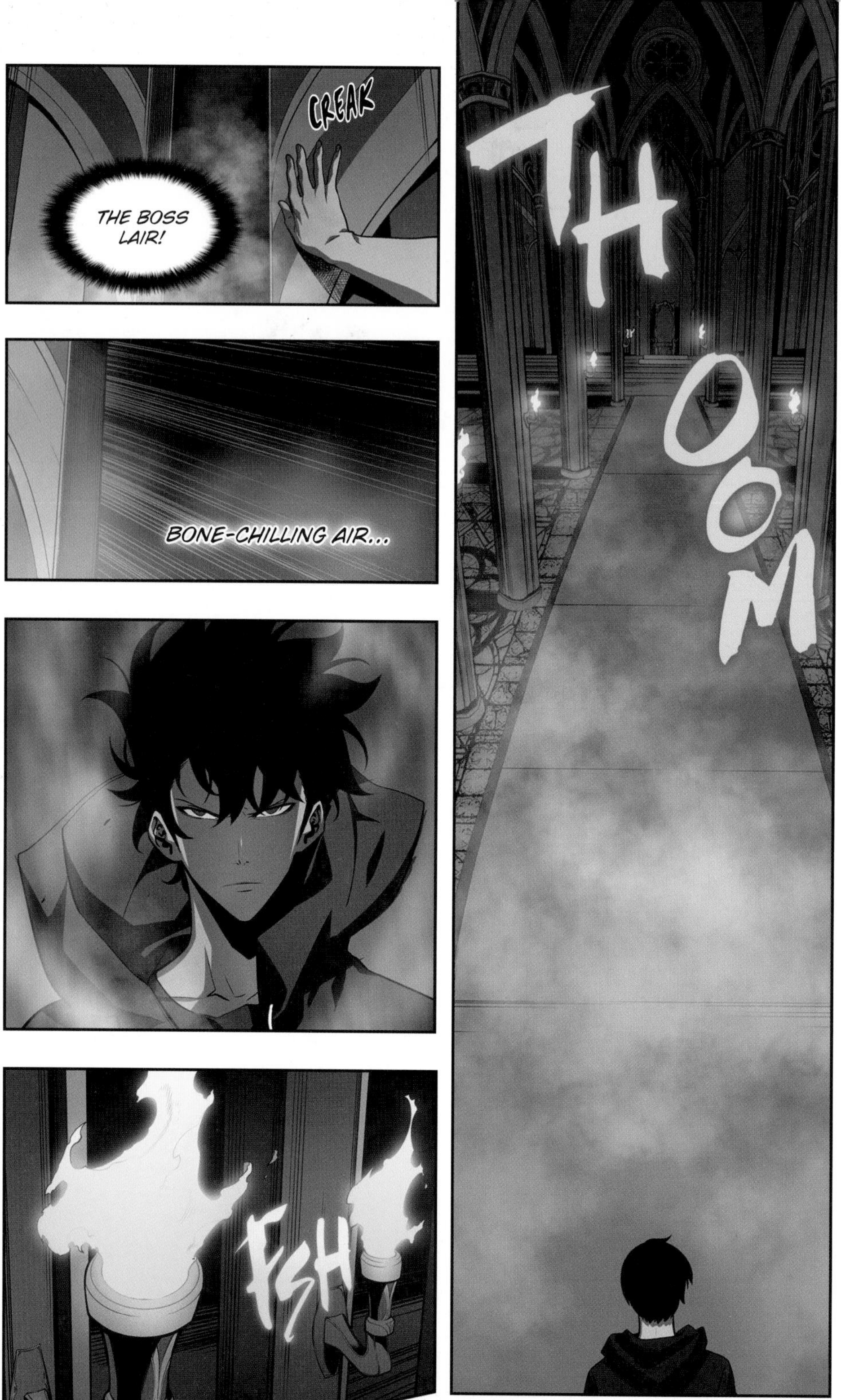
THE BOSS LAIR!
CREAK
BONE-CHILLING AIR...
FSH
THOOOM

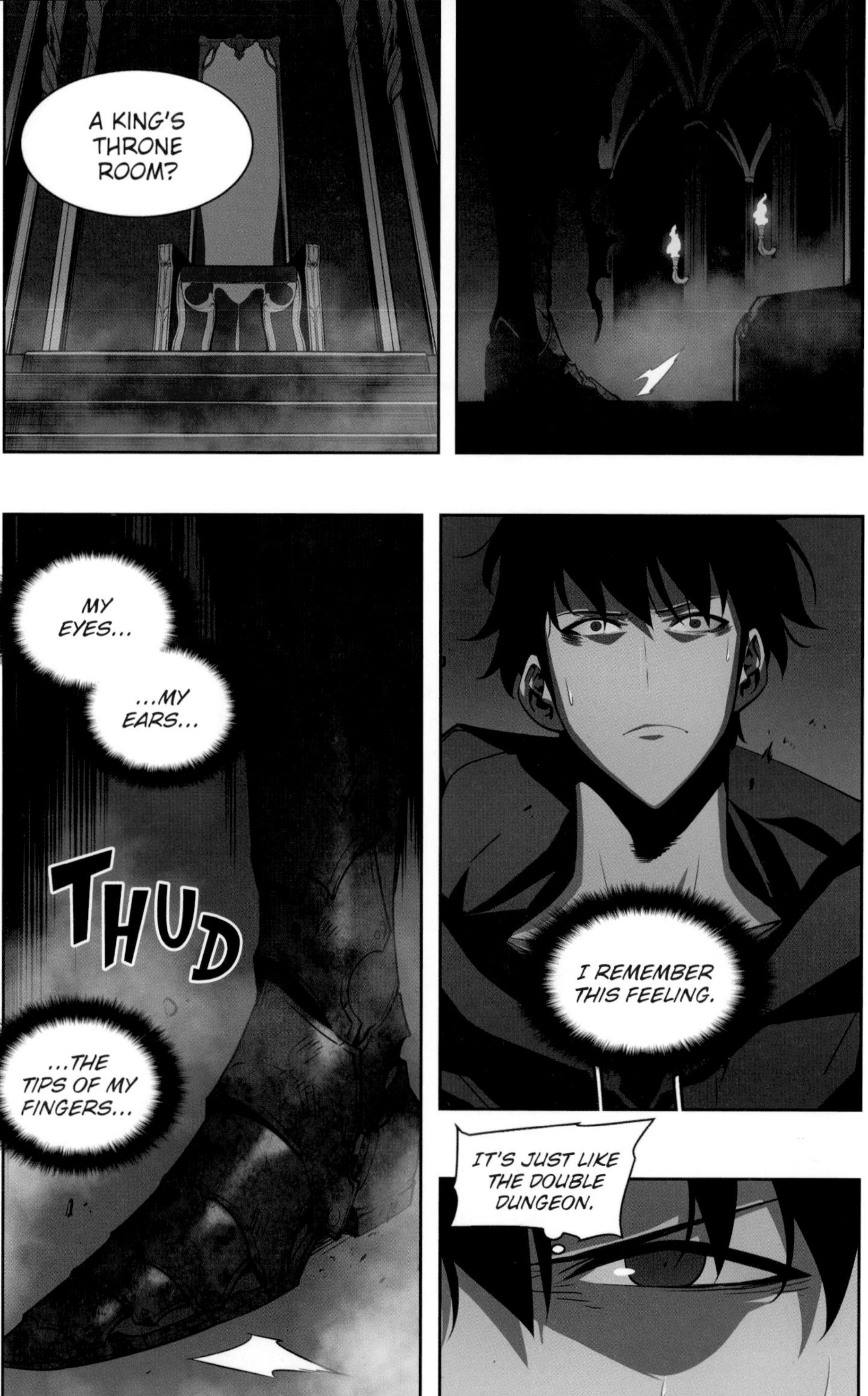
A KING'S THRONE ROOM?
MY EYES...
...MY EARS...
THUD
...THE TIPS OF MY FINGERS...
I REMEMBER THIS FEELING.
IT'S JUST LIKE THE DOUBLE DUNGEON.

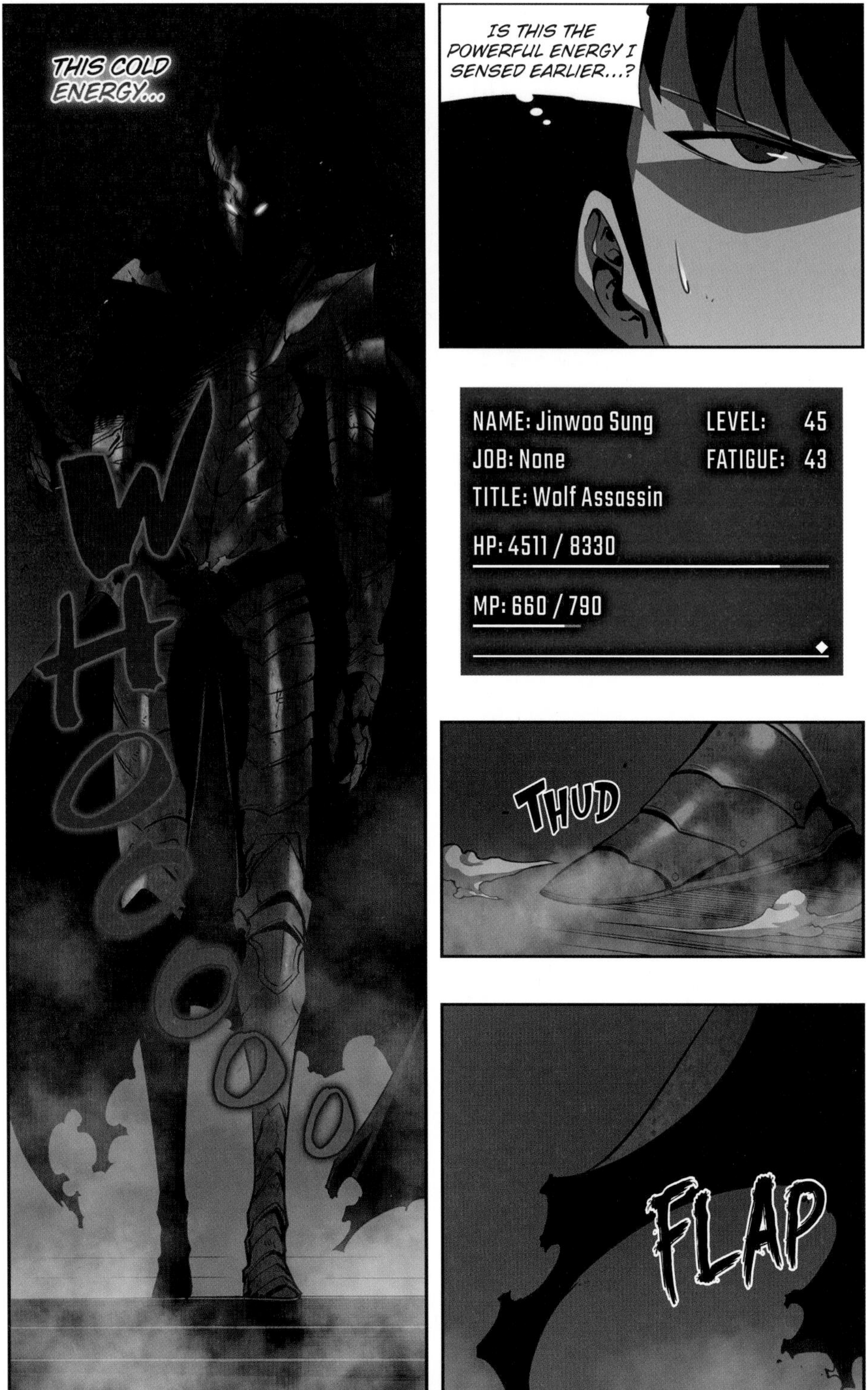
THIS COLD ENERGY...
WHOOOOO
IS THIS THE POWERFUL ENERGY I SENSED EARLIER...?
NAME: Jinwoo Sung LEVEL: 45
JOB: None FATIGUE: 43
TITLE: Wolf Assassin
HP: 4511 / 8330
MP: 660 / 790
THUD
FLAP

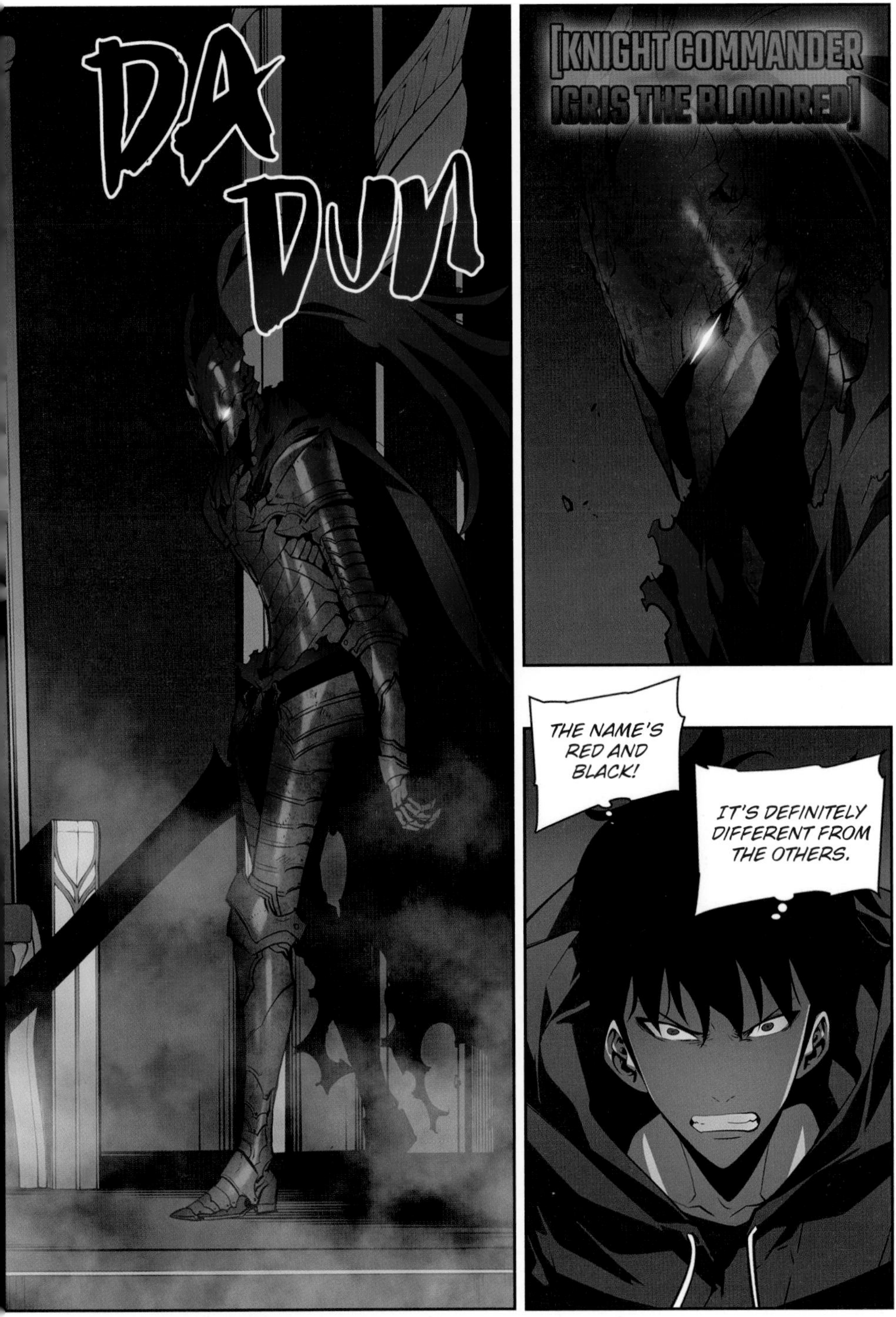
DA DUN
[KNIGHT COMMANDER IGRIS THE BLOODRED]
THE NAME'S RED AND BLACK!
IT'S DEFINITELY DIFFERENT FROM THE OTHERS.

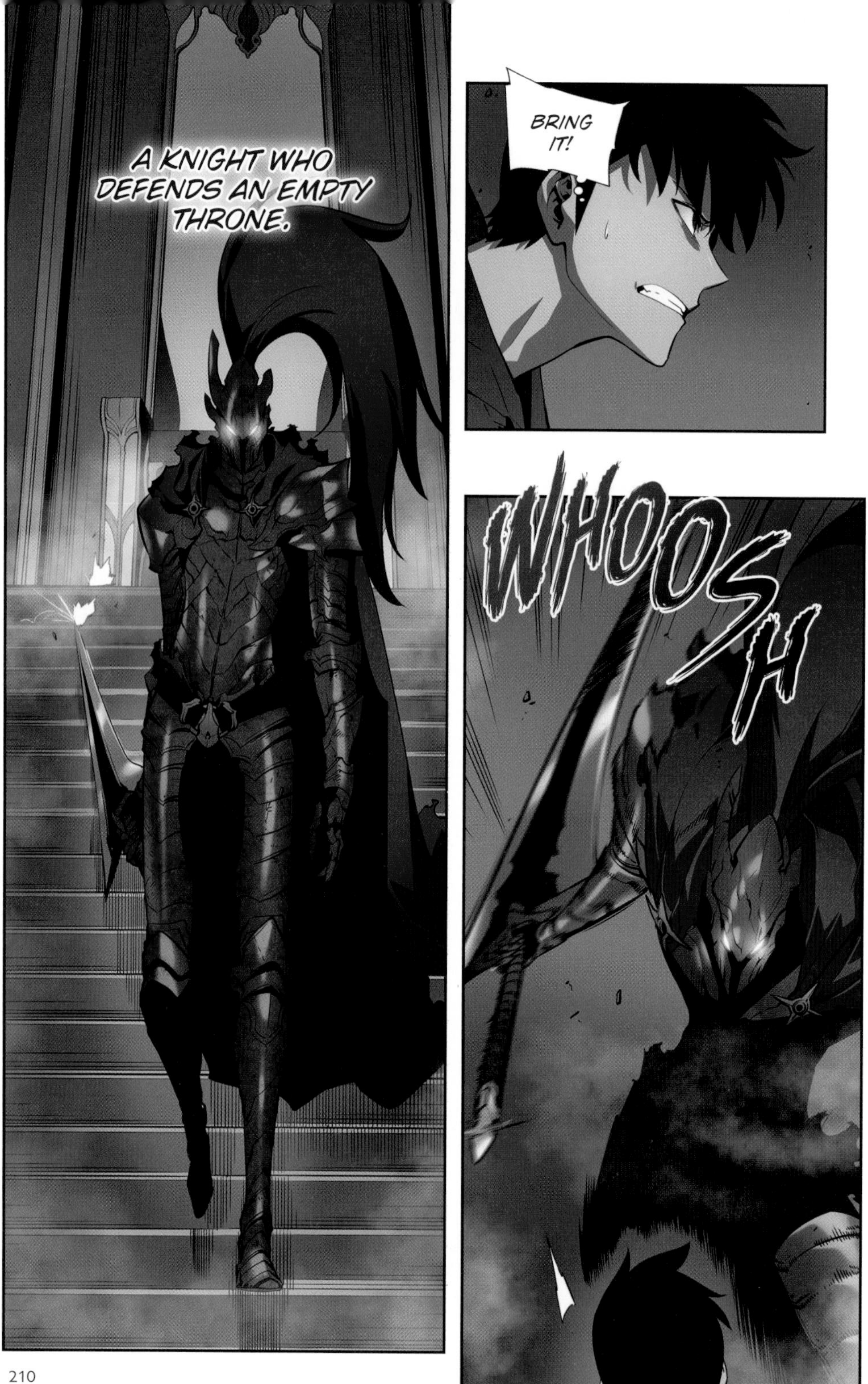
A KNIGHT WHO DEFENDS AN EMPTY THRONE.
BRING IT!
WHOOSH

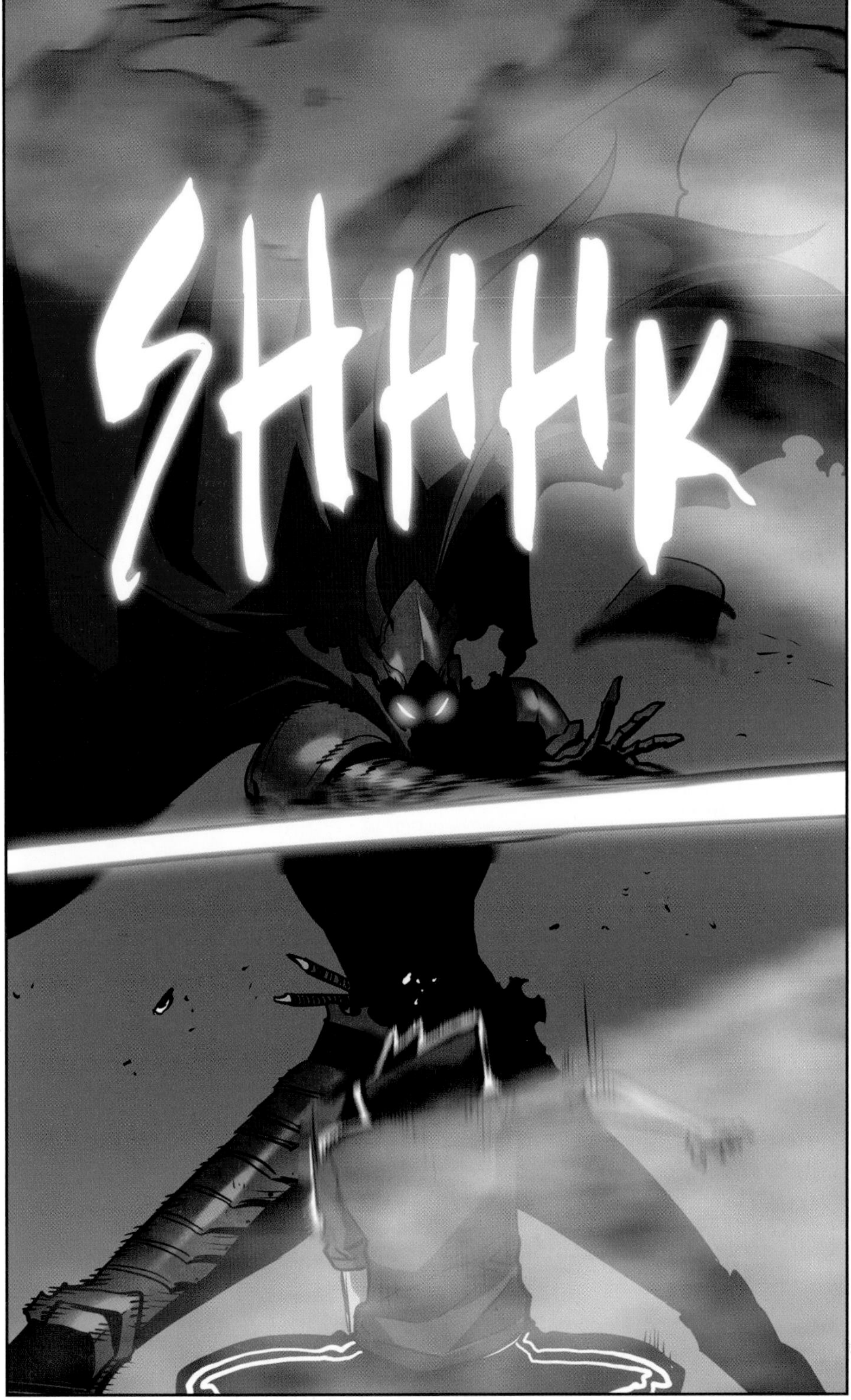
SHHHK

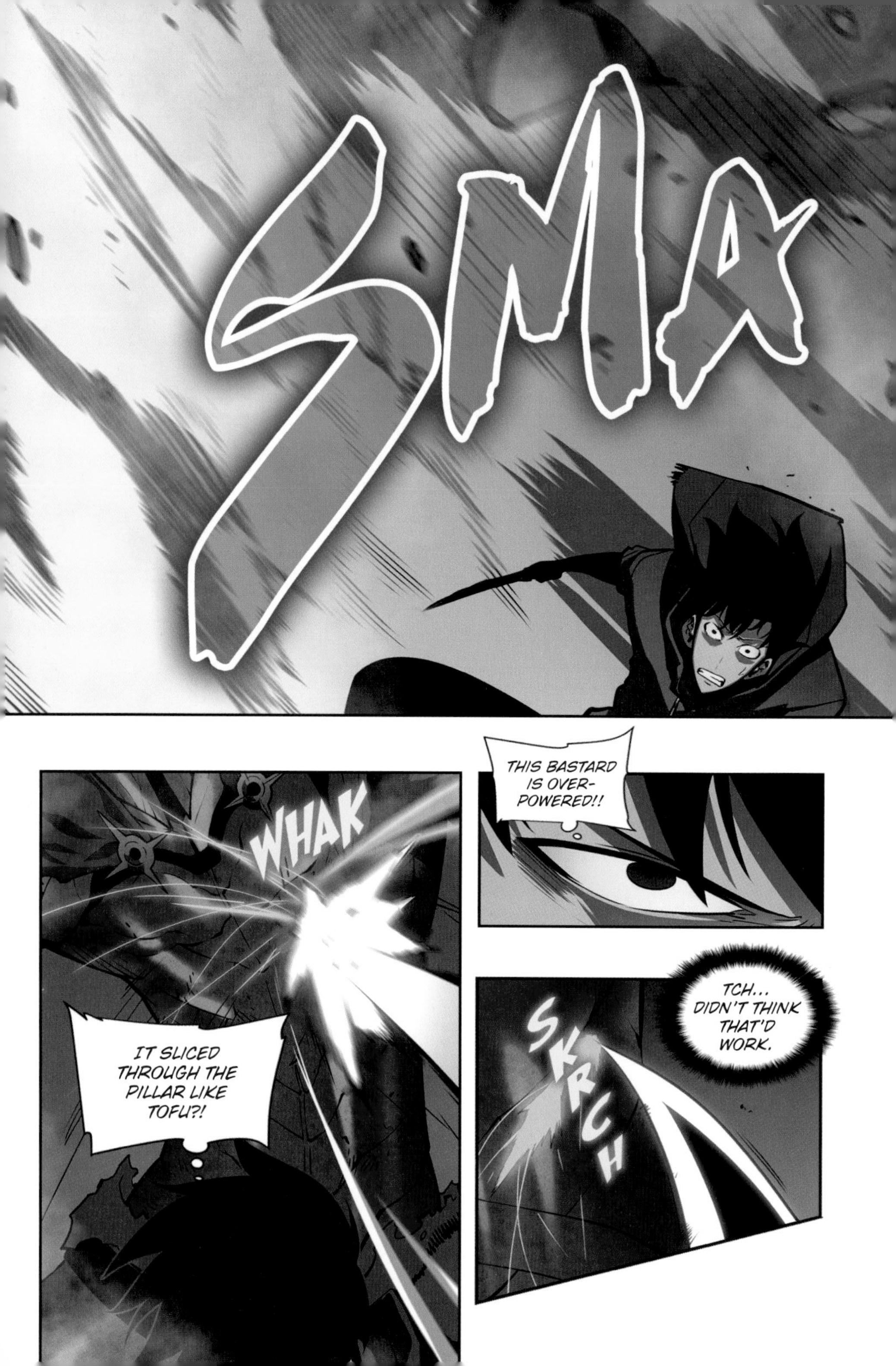
SMA
WHAK
IT SLICED THROUGH THE PILLAR LIKE TOFU?!
THIS BASTARD IS OVER-POWERED!!
SKRCH
TCH... DIDN'T THINK THAT'D WORK.

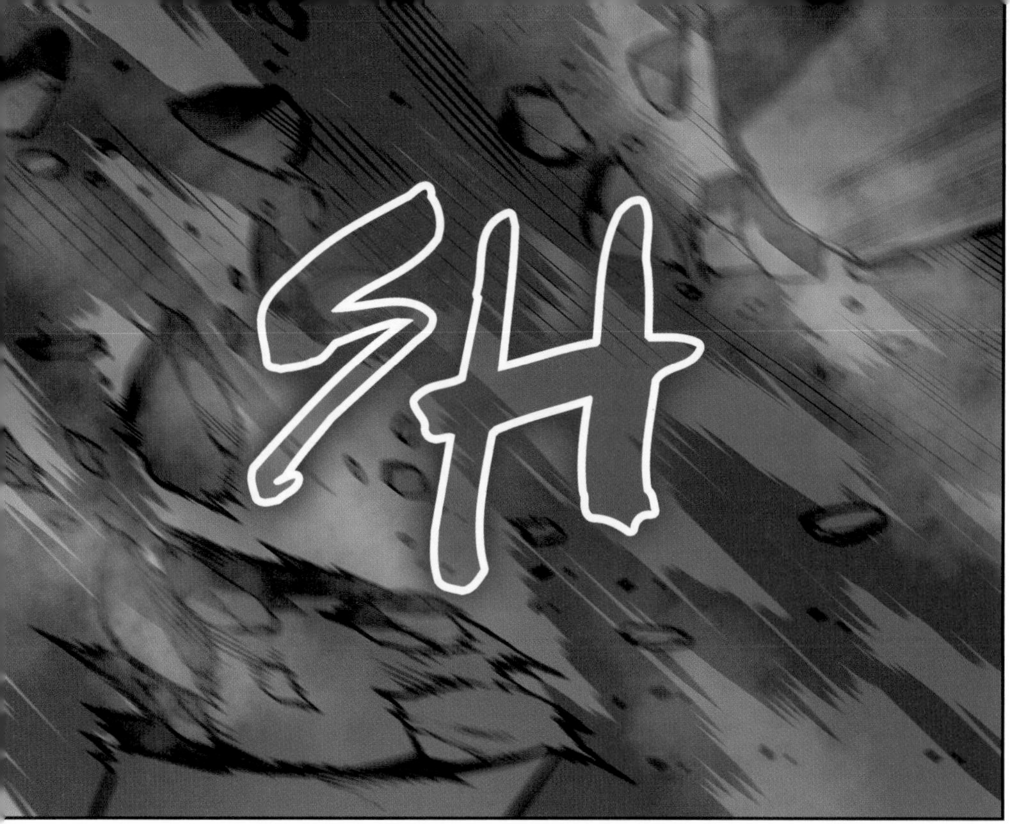
SH

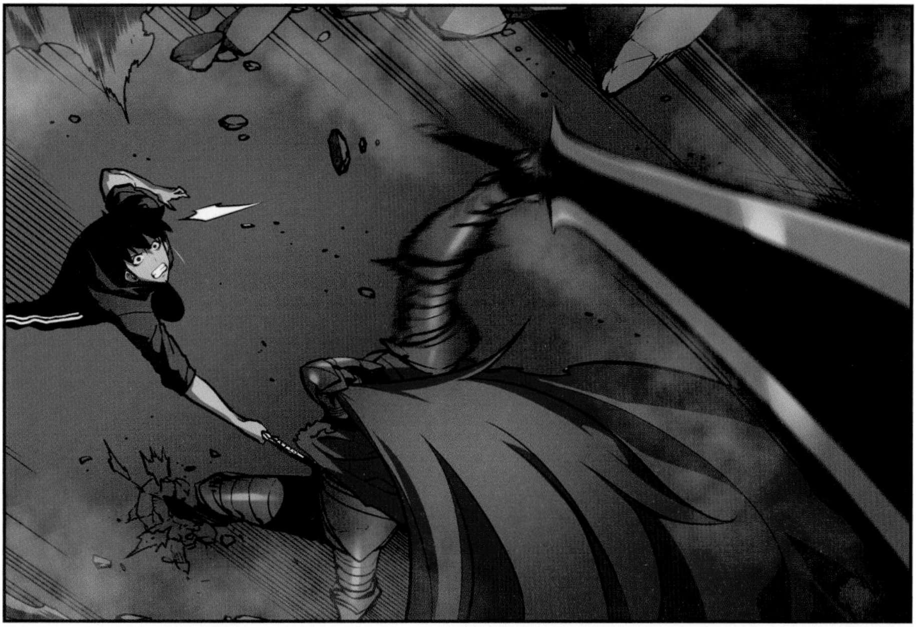

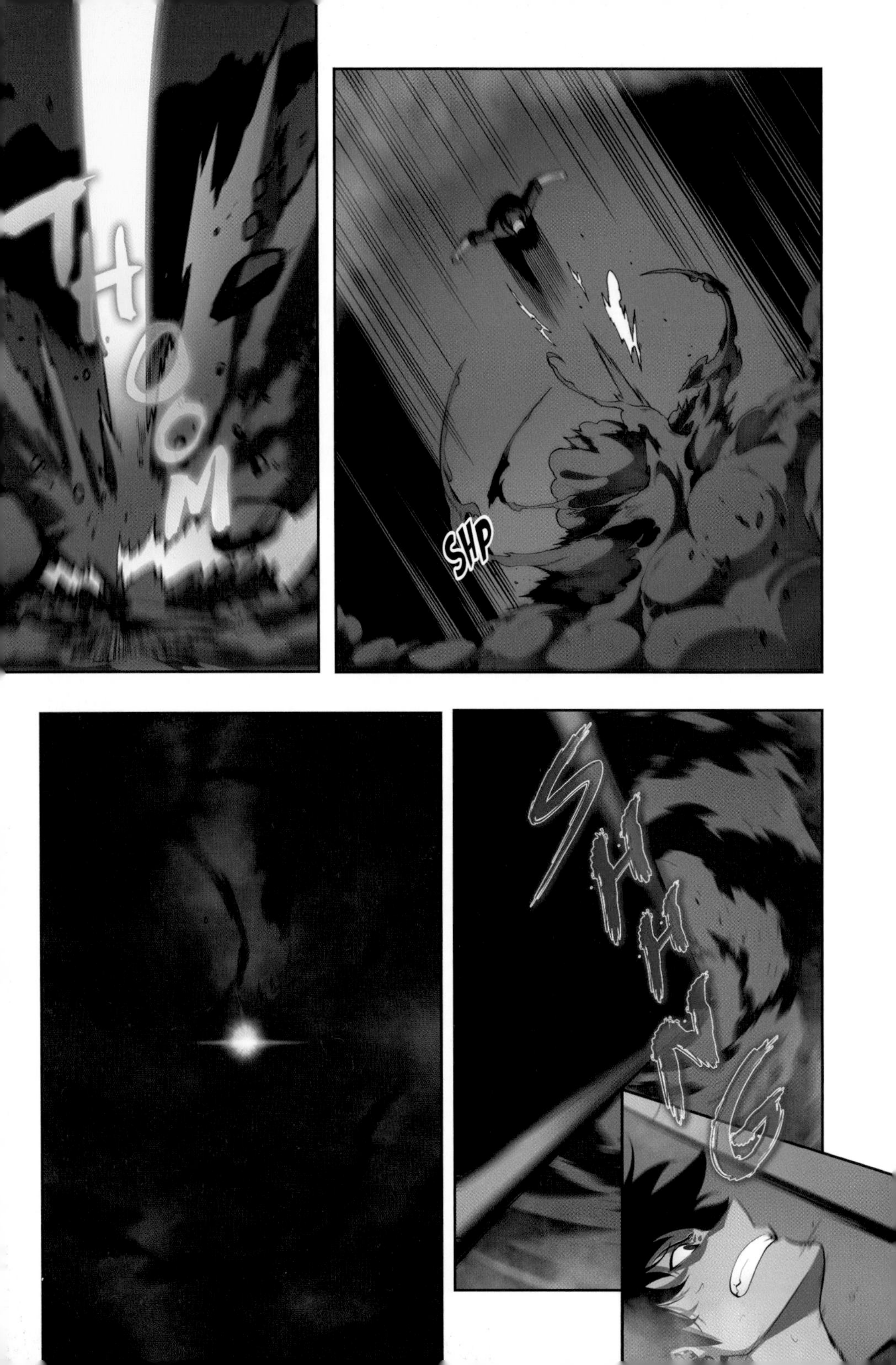
THOOOM
SHP
SHHNG

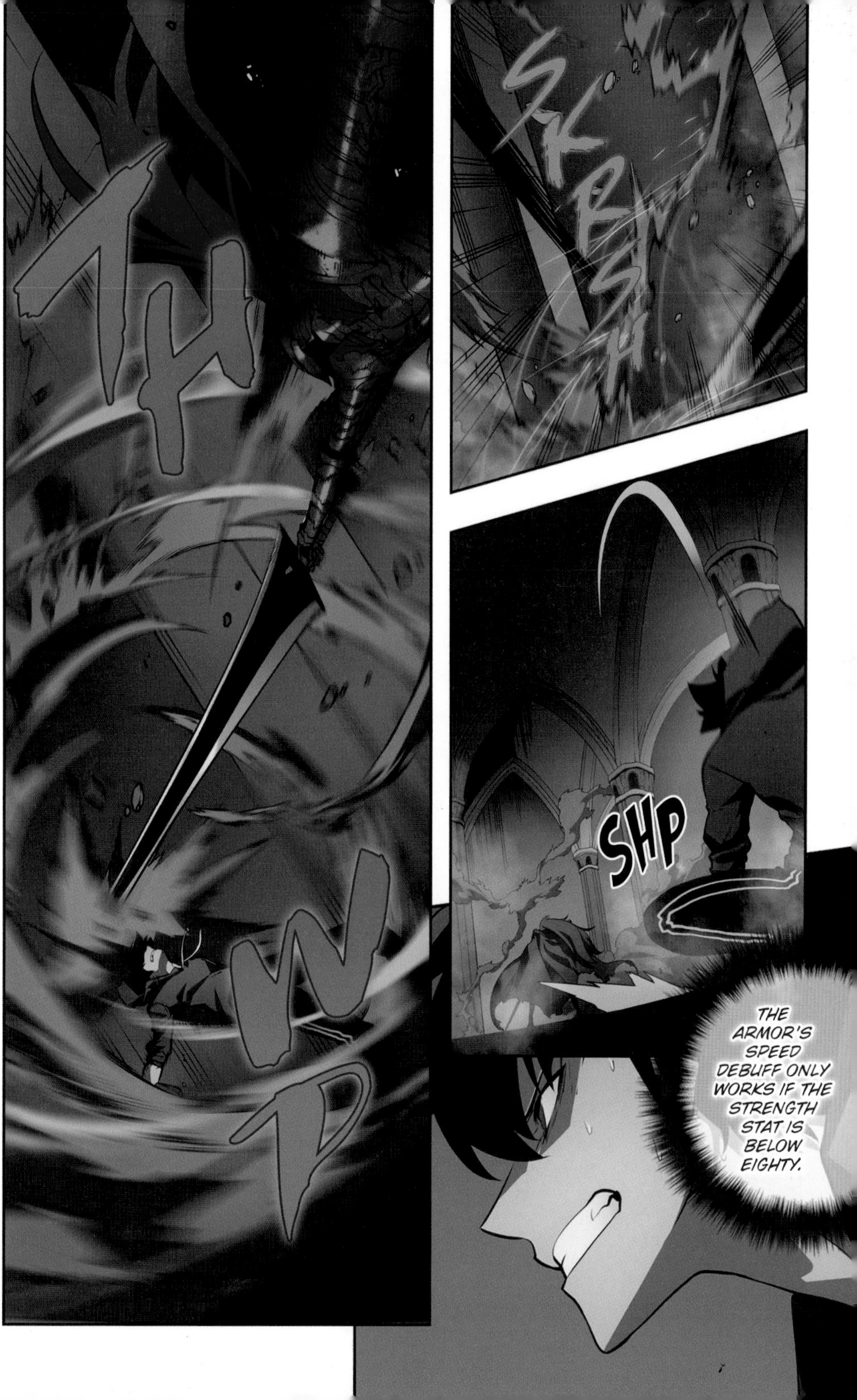
THWP
SKRSH
SHP
THE ARMOR'S SPEED DEBUFF ONLY WORKS IF THE STRENGTH STAT IS BELOW EIGHTY.

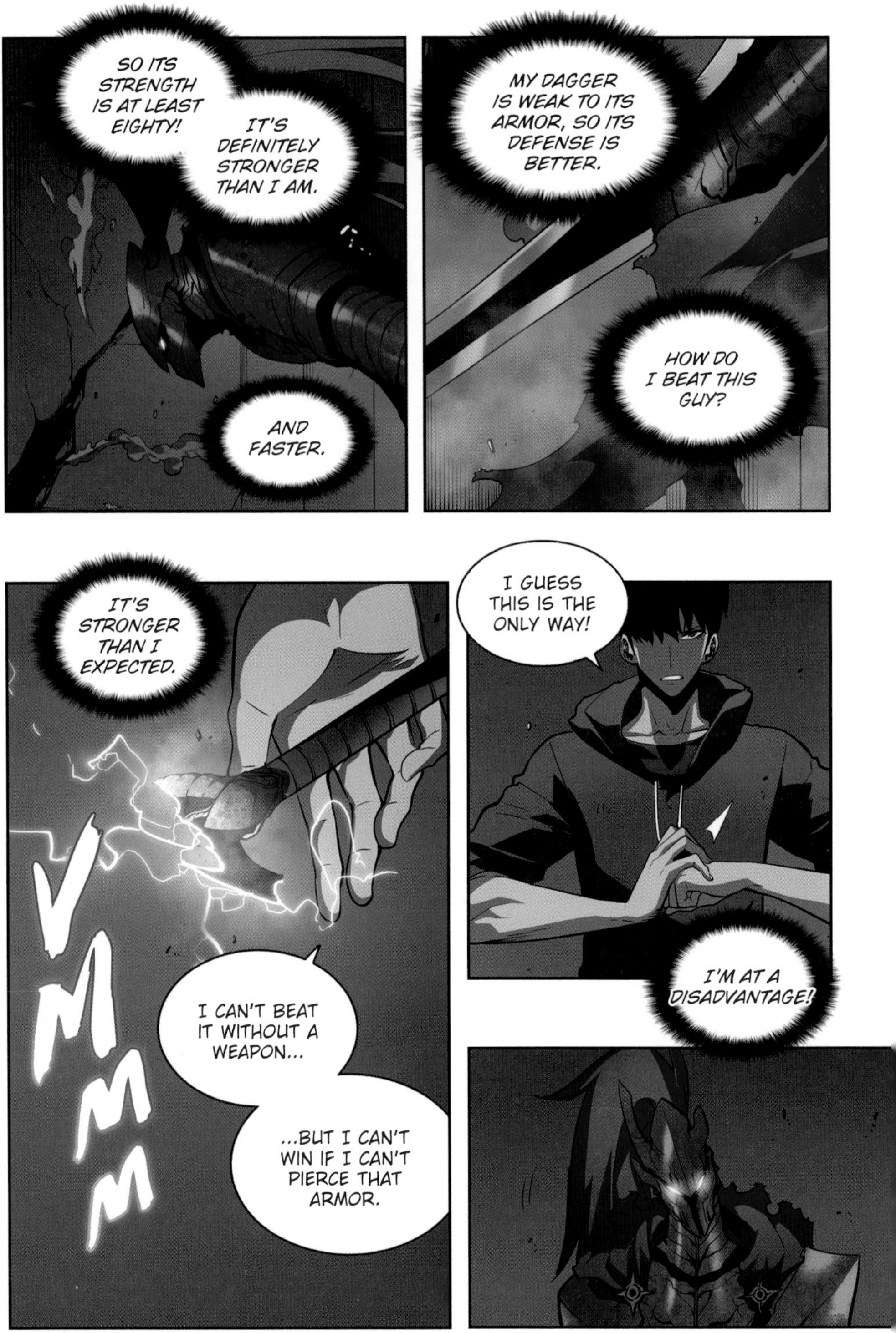
SO ITS STRENGTH IS AT LEAST EIGHTY!
IT'S DEFINITELY STRONGER THAN I AM.
AND FASTER.
MY DAGGER IS WEAK TO ITS ARMOR, SO ITS DEFENSE IS BETTER.
HOW DO I BEAT THIS GUY?
IT'S STRONGER THAN I EXPECTED.
VMMM
I CAN'T BEAT IT WITHOUT A WEAPON...
...BUT I CAN'T WIN IF I CAN'T PIERCE THAT ARMOR.
I GUESS THIS IS THE ONLY WAY!
I'M AT A DISADVANTAGE!

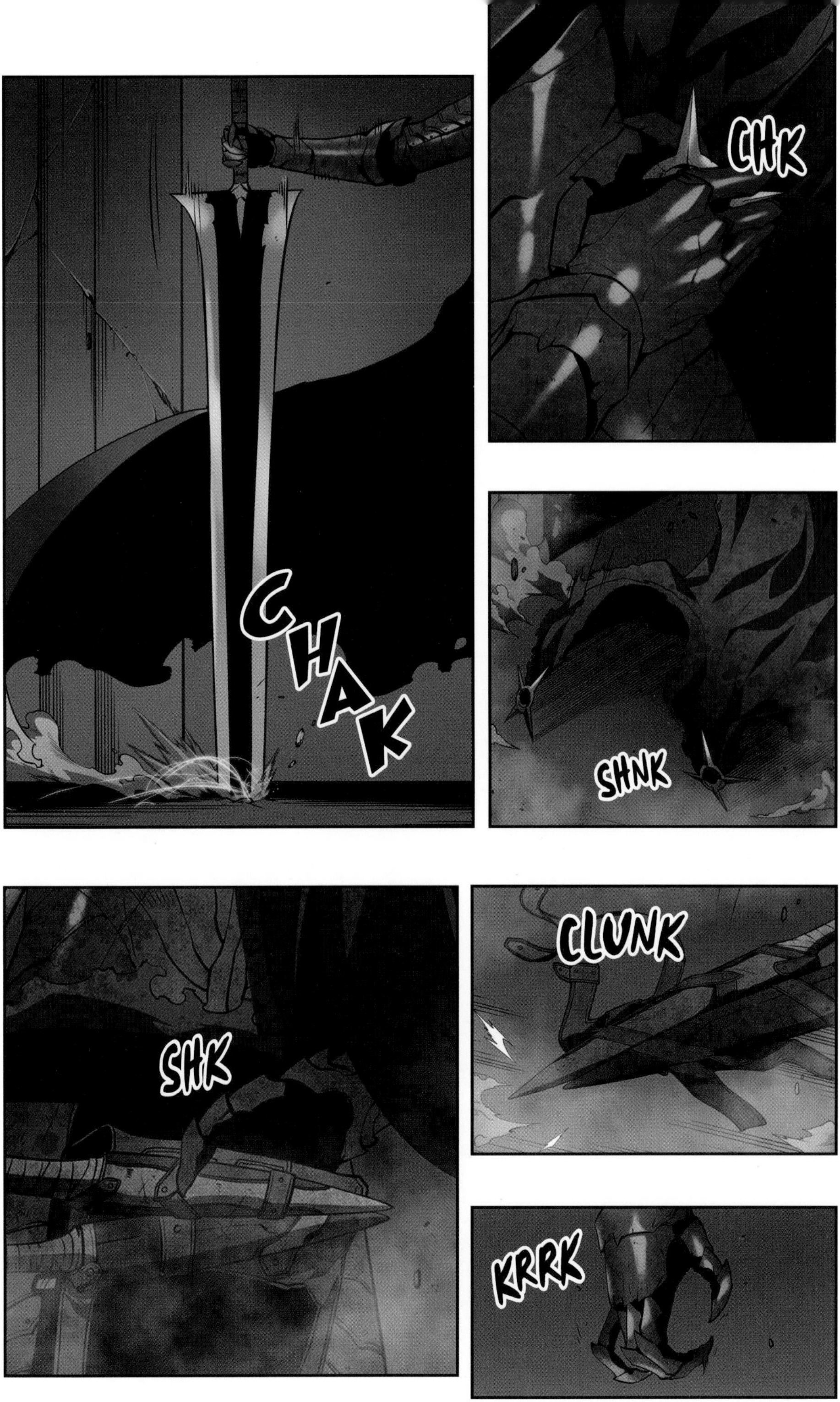
CHAK
CHK
SHNK
SHK
CLUNK
KRRK

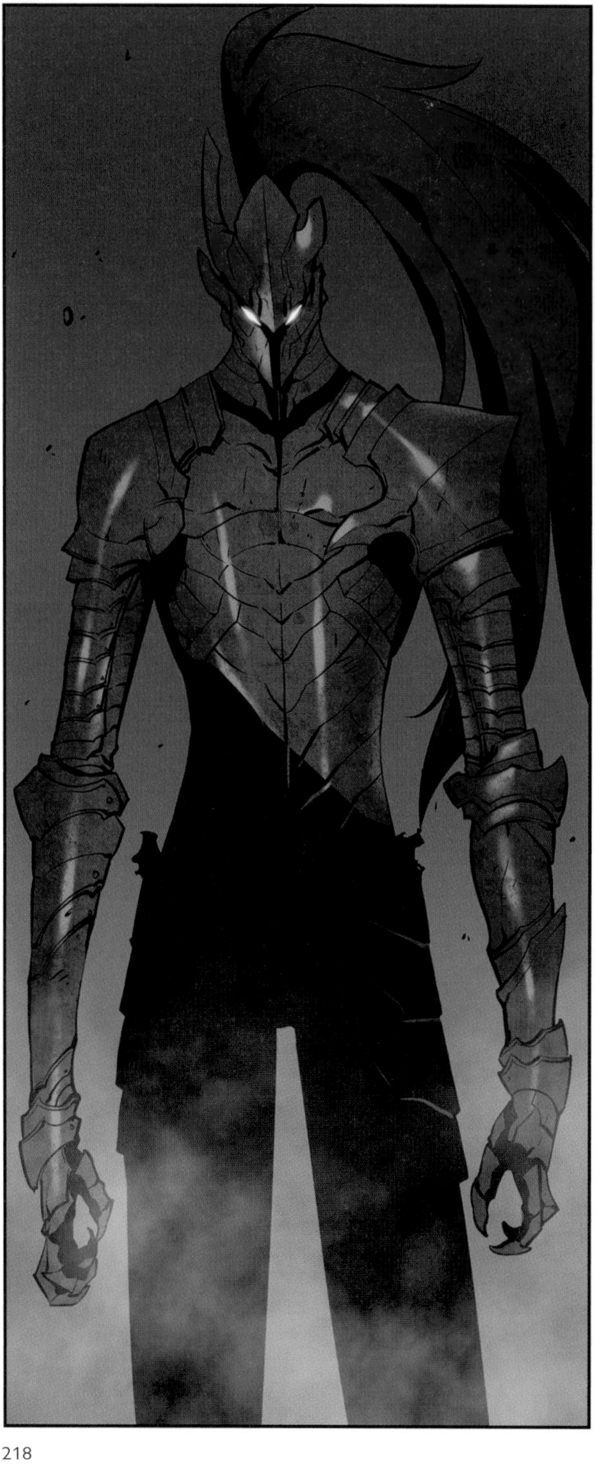

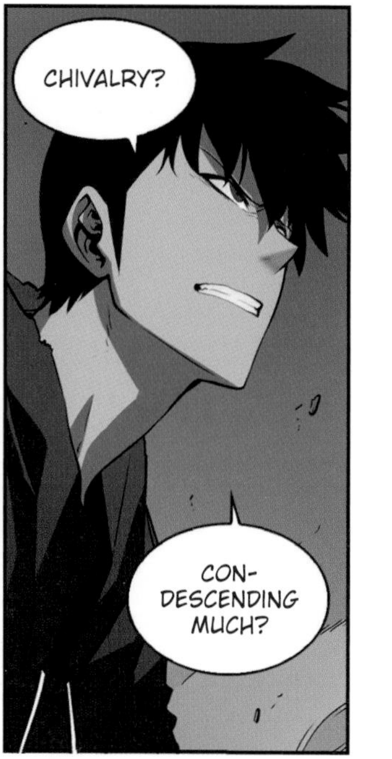
CHIVALRY?
CON-
DESCENDING
MUCH?

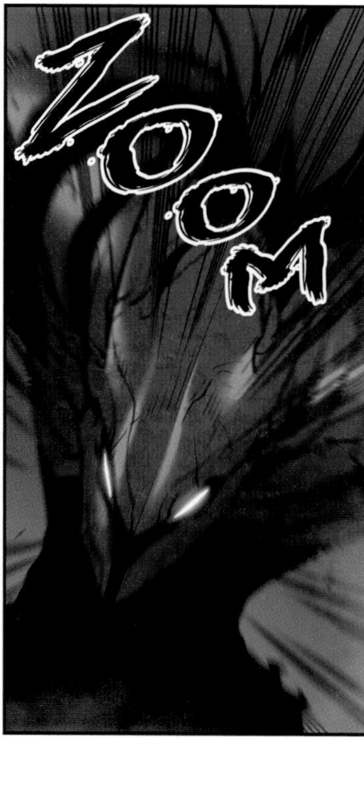
ZOOM

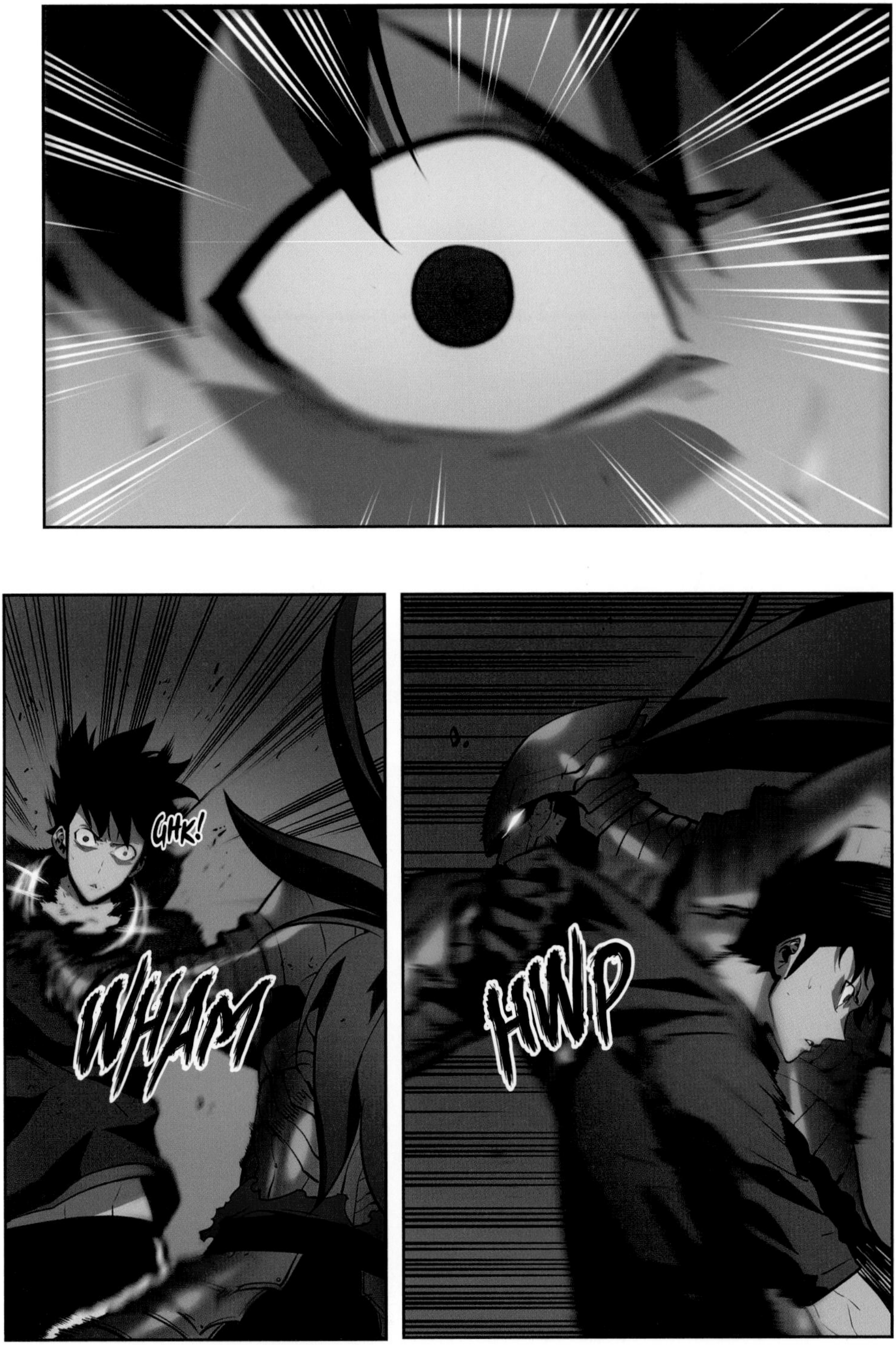
GHK!
WHAM
HWP

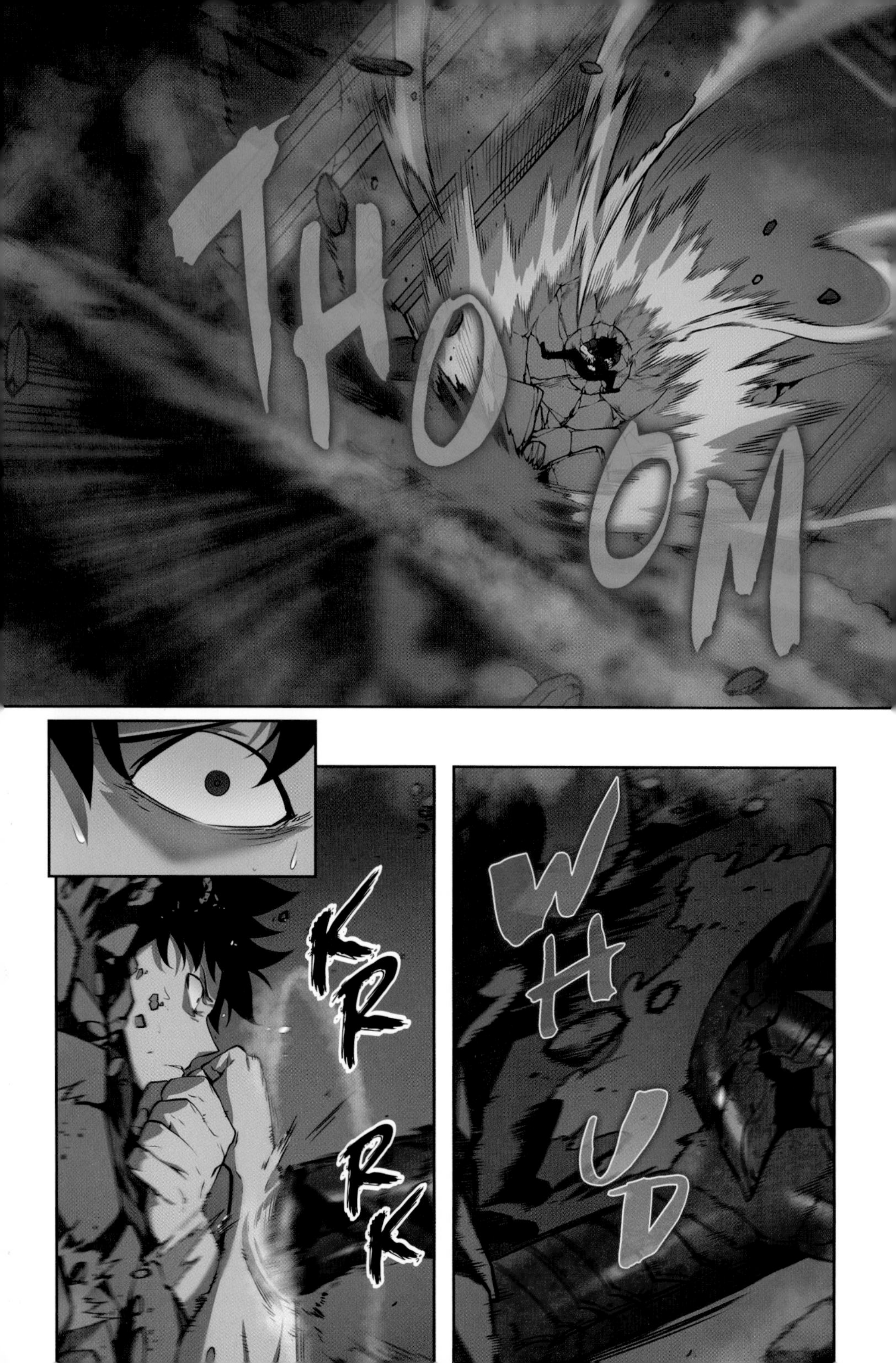
THOOM
KRRK
WHUD

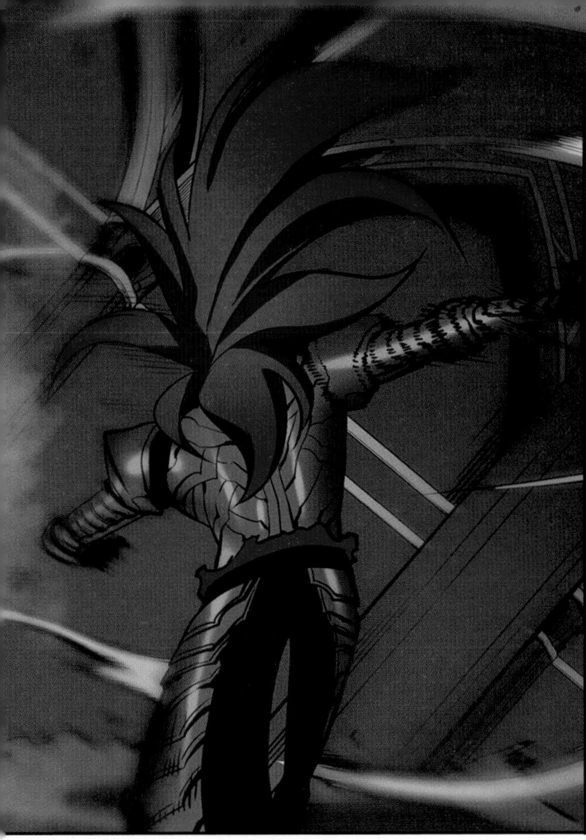

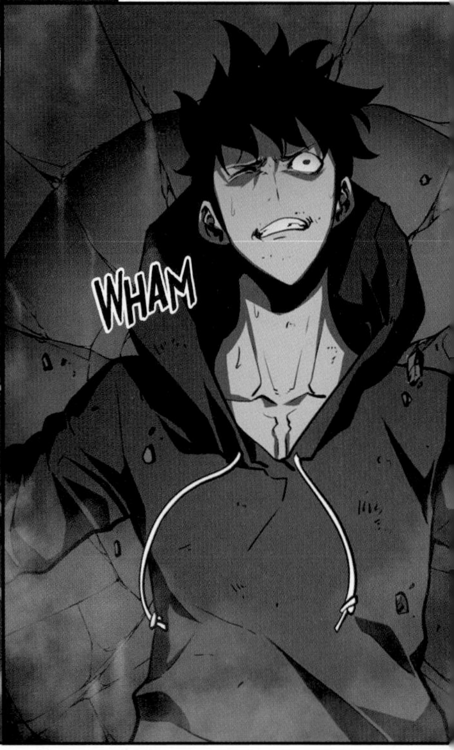

WHAM

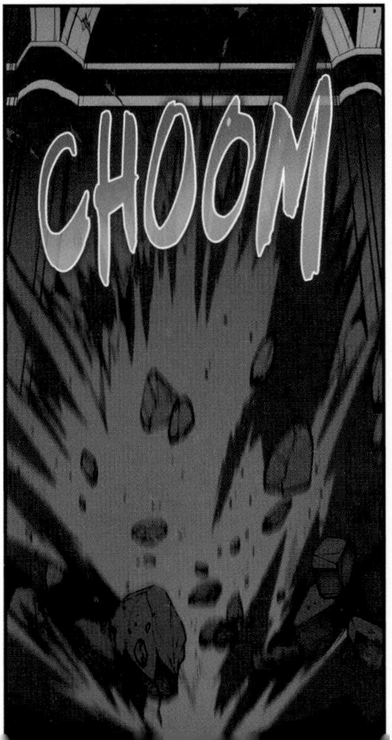

CHOOM

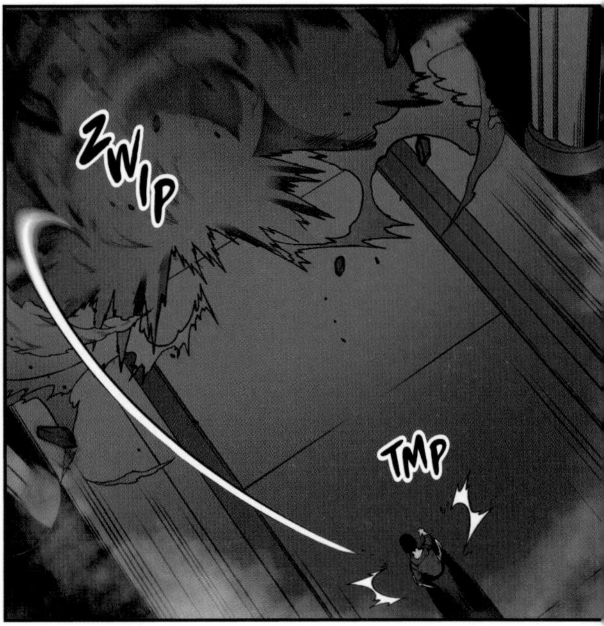

ZWIP
TMP

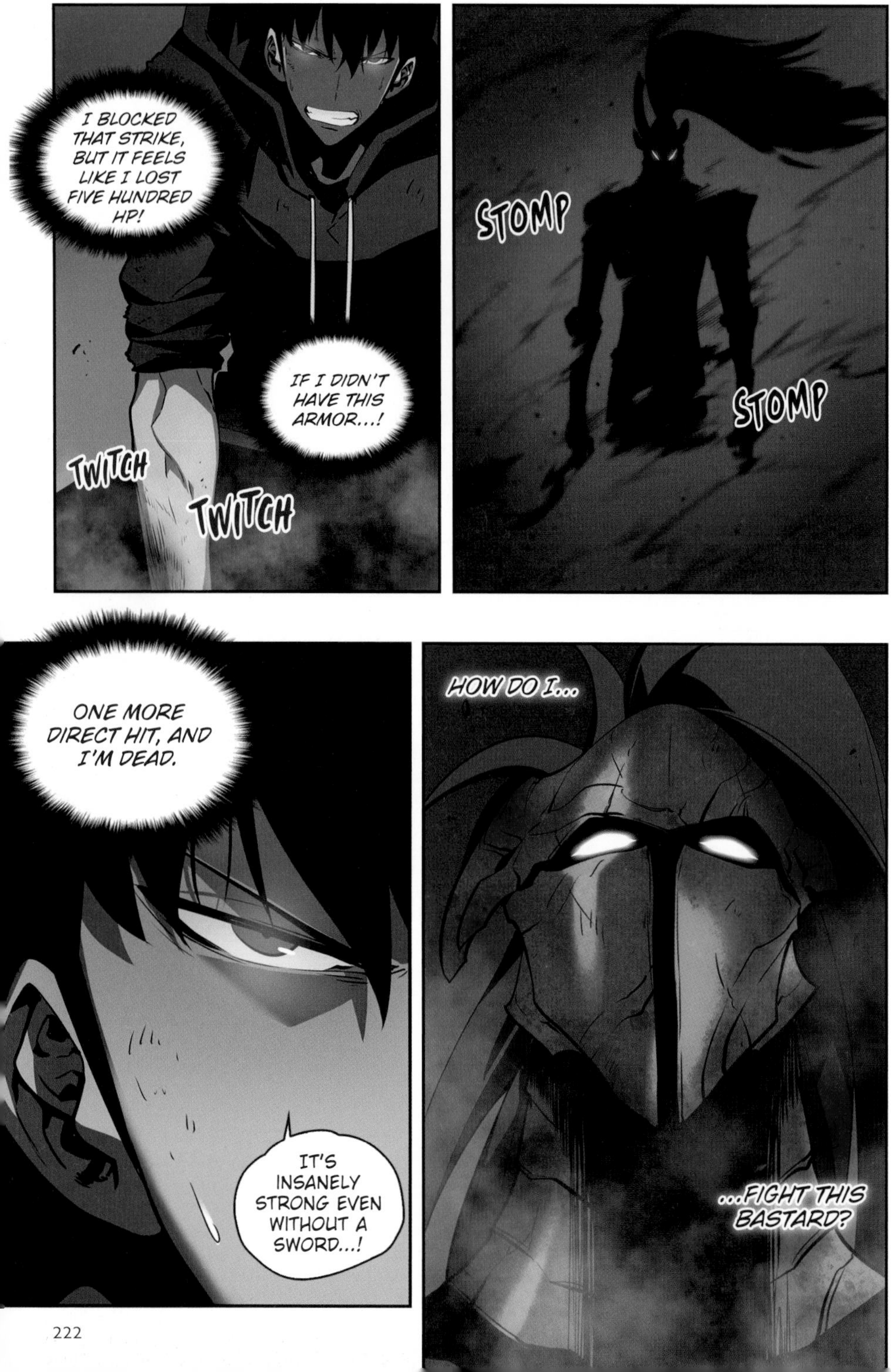
I BLOCKED THAT STRIKE, BUT IT FEELS LIKE I LOST FIVE HUNDRED HP!
IF I DIDN'T HAVE THIS ARMOR...!
TWITCH
TWITCH
STOMP
STOMP
ONE MORE DIRECT HIT, AND I'M DEAD.
IT'S INSANELY STRONG EVEN WITHOUT A SWORD...!
HOW DO I...
...FIGHT THIS BASTARD?

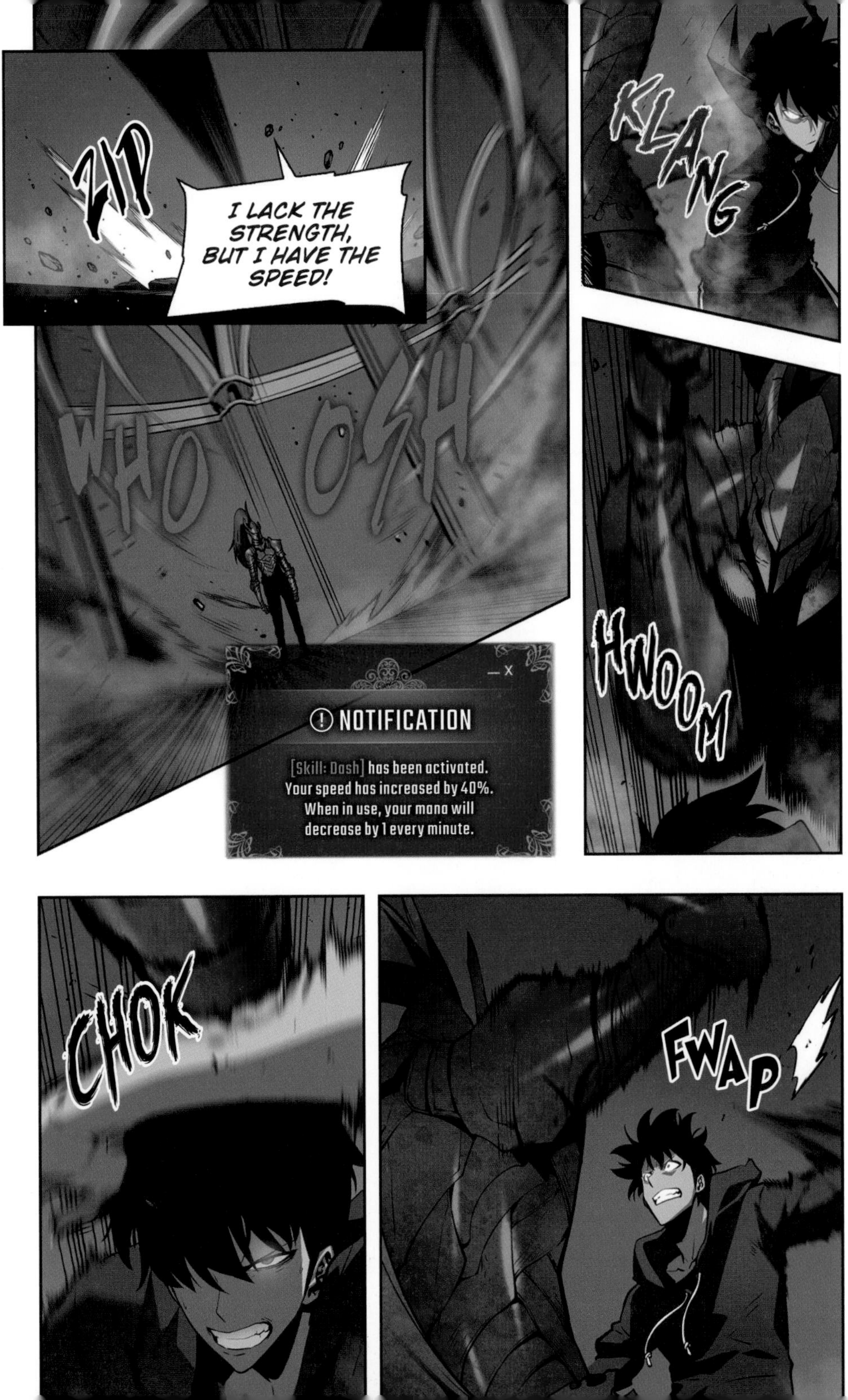
ZIP
I LACK THE STRENGTH, BUT I HAVE THE SPEED!
WHOOSH
NOTIFICATION
[Skill: Dash] has been activated. Your speed has increased by 40%. When in use, your mana will decrease by 1 every minute.
KLANG
HWOOM
CHOK
FWAP

THWP
WHAP
WHAP
WHAP
WHAP
WHAP
SHWOO

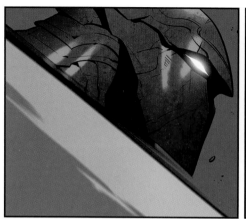

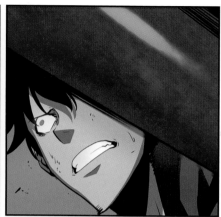

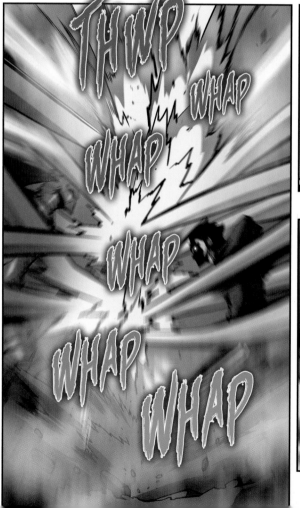

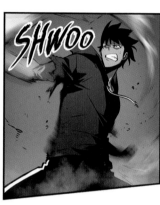

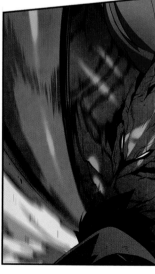

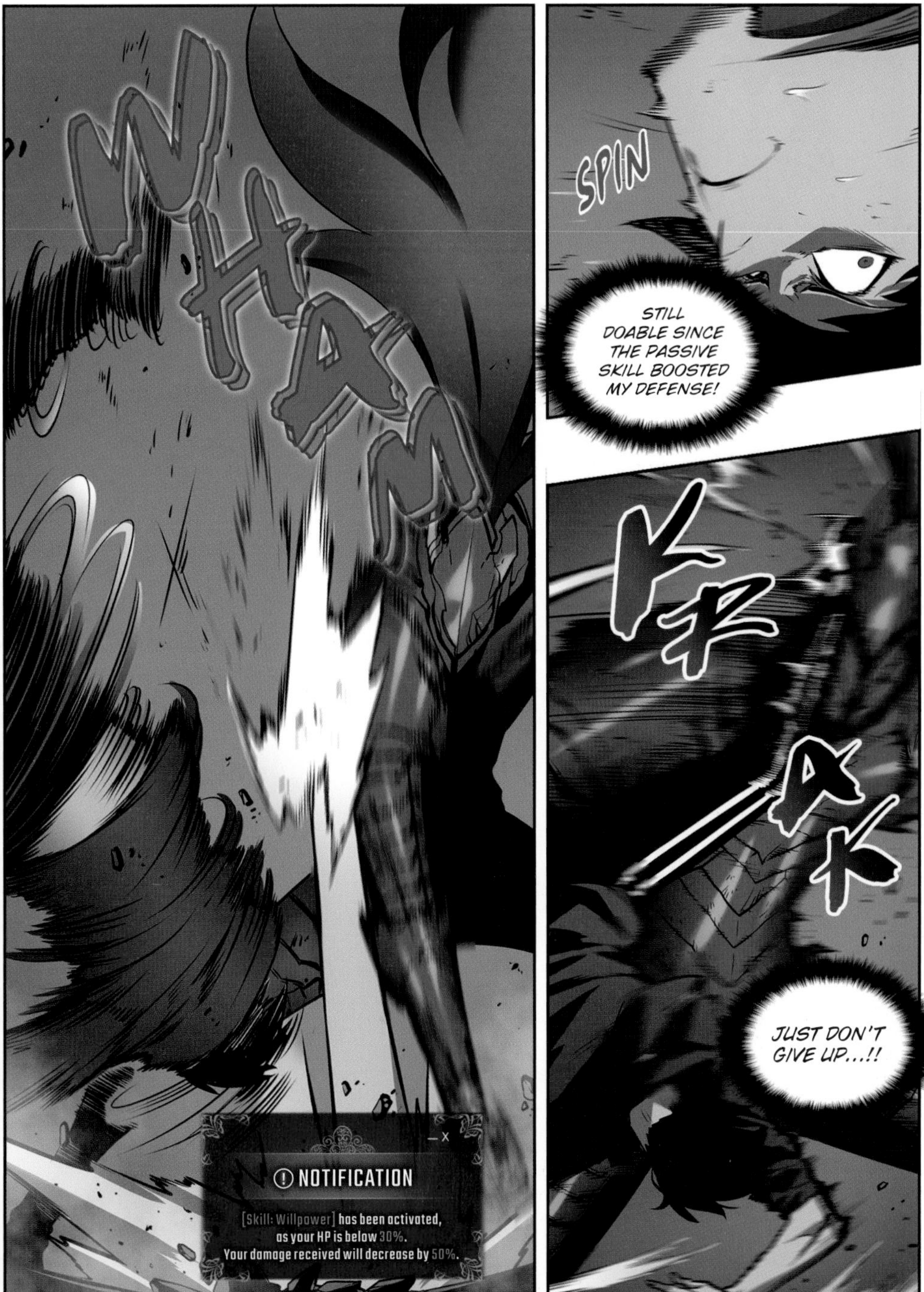
WHAM
NOTIFICATION
[Skill: Willpower] has been activated, as your HP is below 30%. Your damage received will decrease by 50%.
SPIN
STILL DOABLE SINCE THE PASSIVE SKILL BOOSTED MY DEFENSE!
KRAK
JUST DON'T GIVE UP...!!

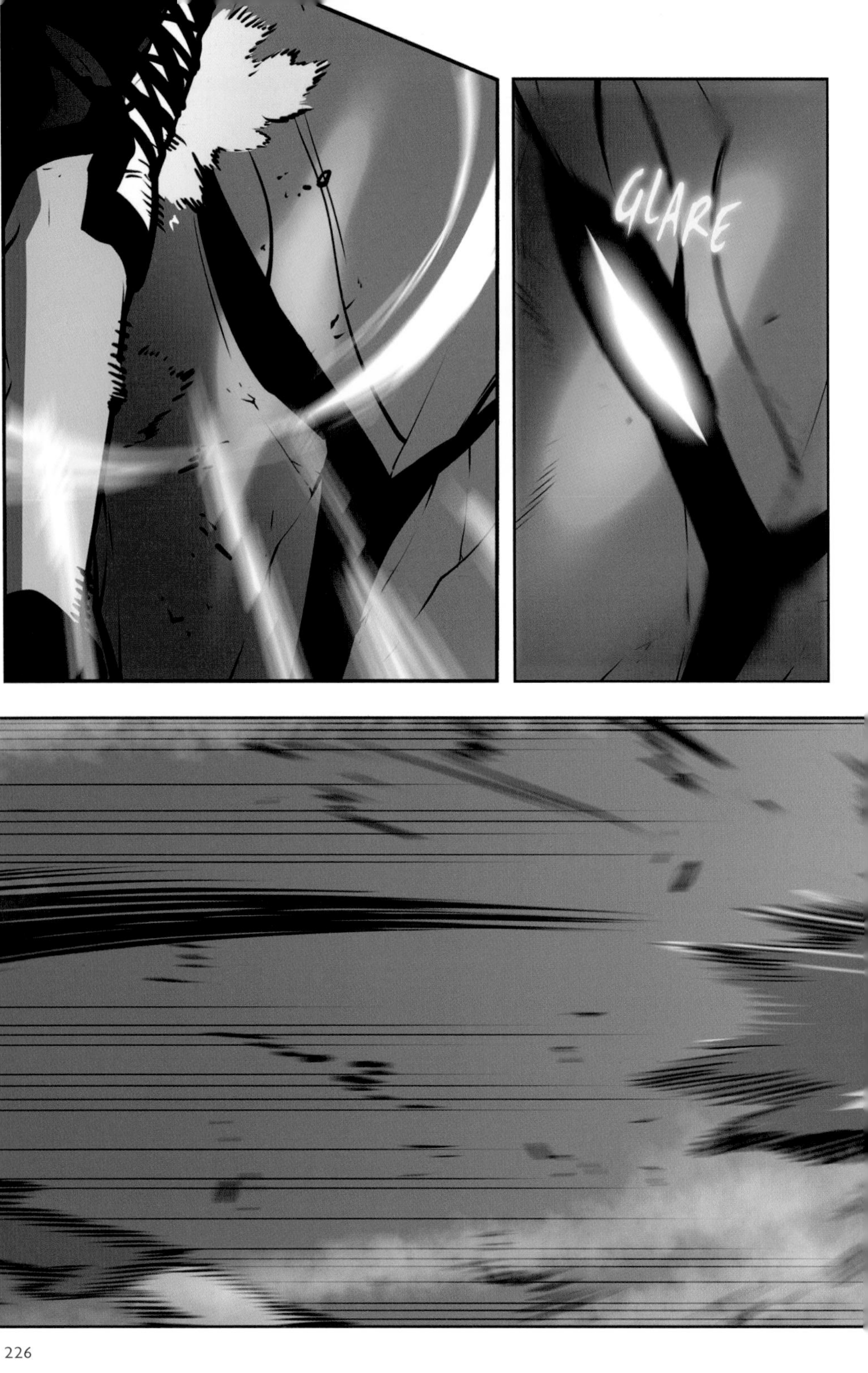
GLARE

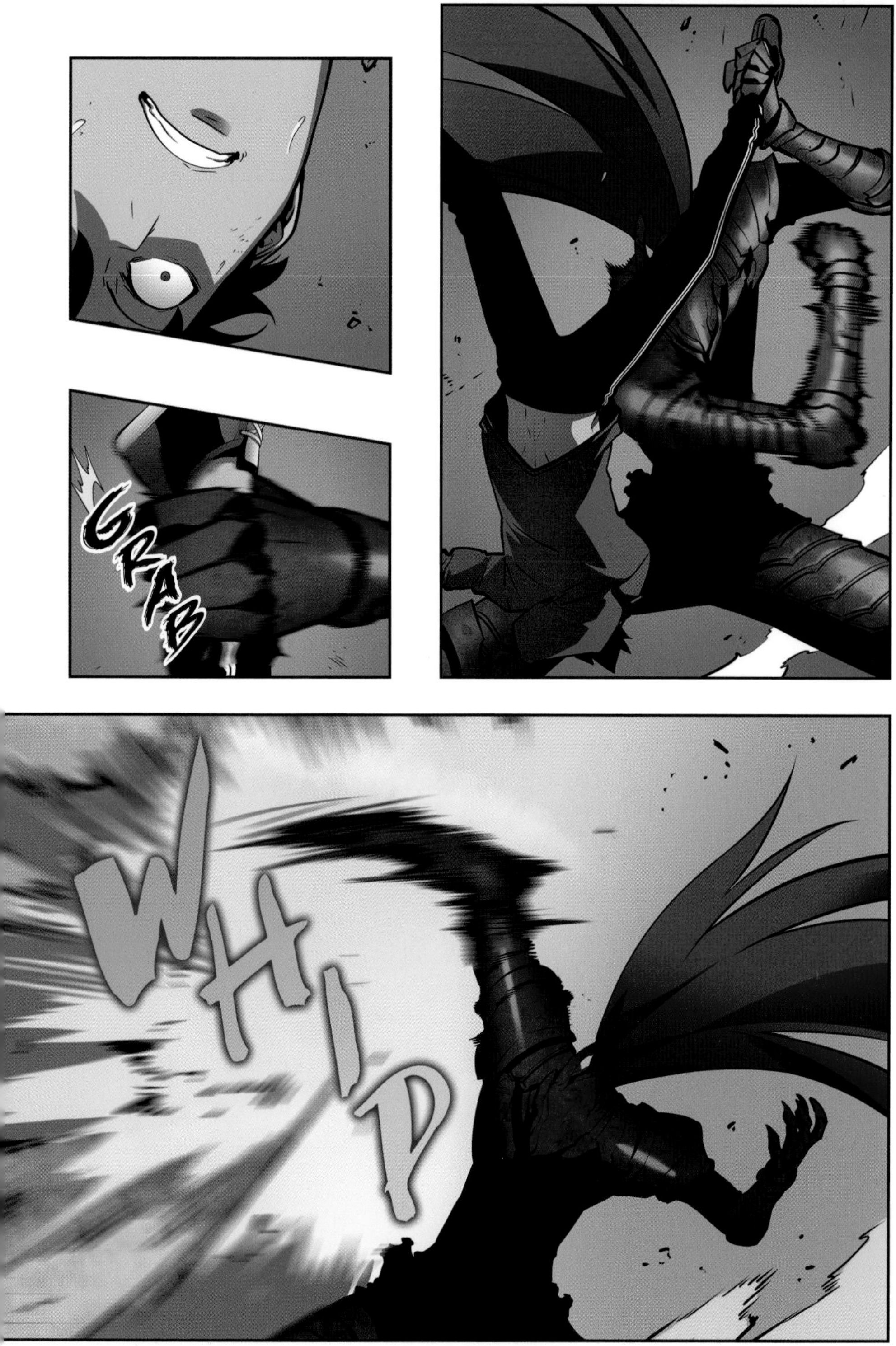
GRAB
WHID

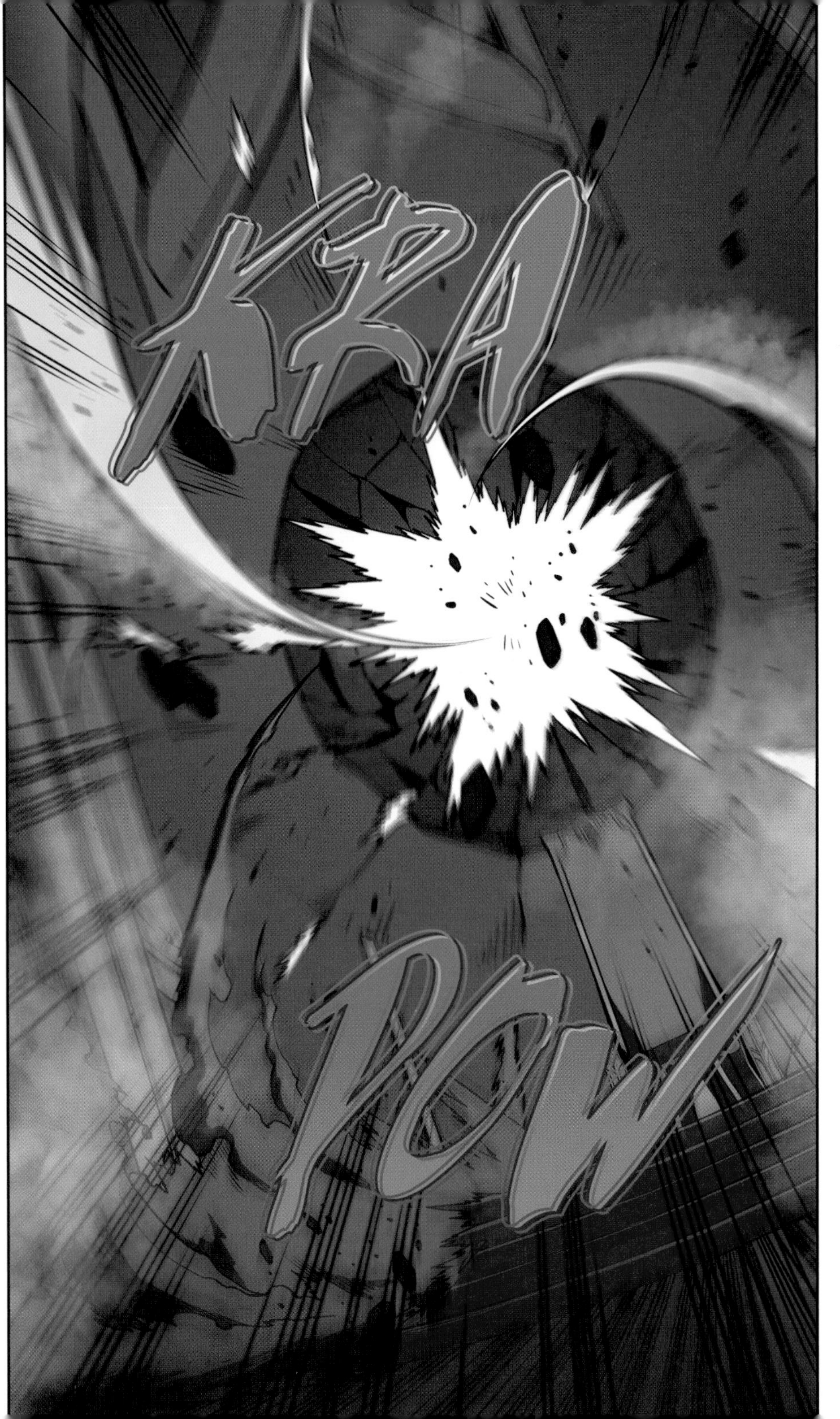
KRA
POW

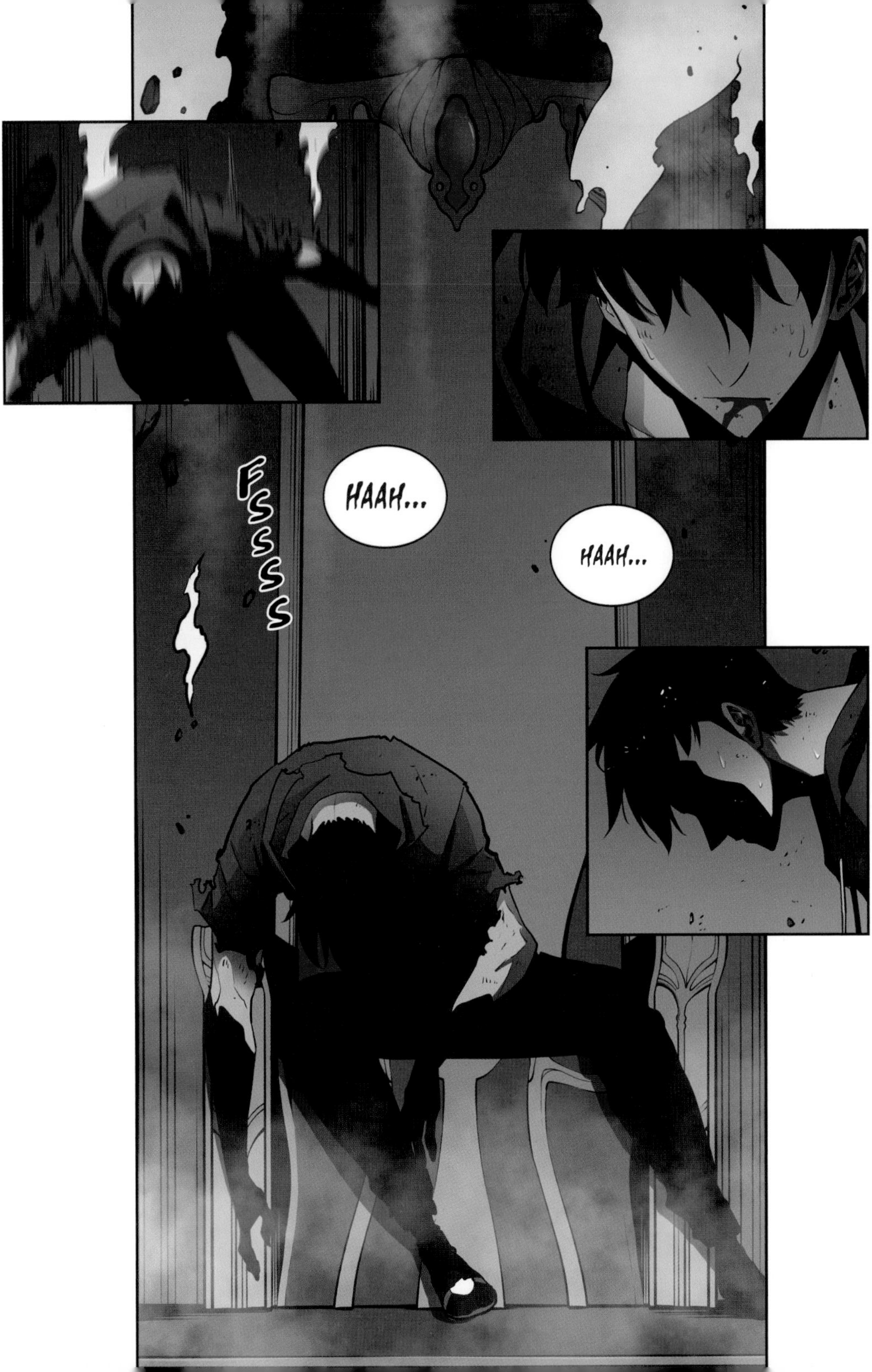
FSSSS
HAAH...
HAAH...

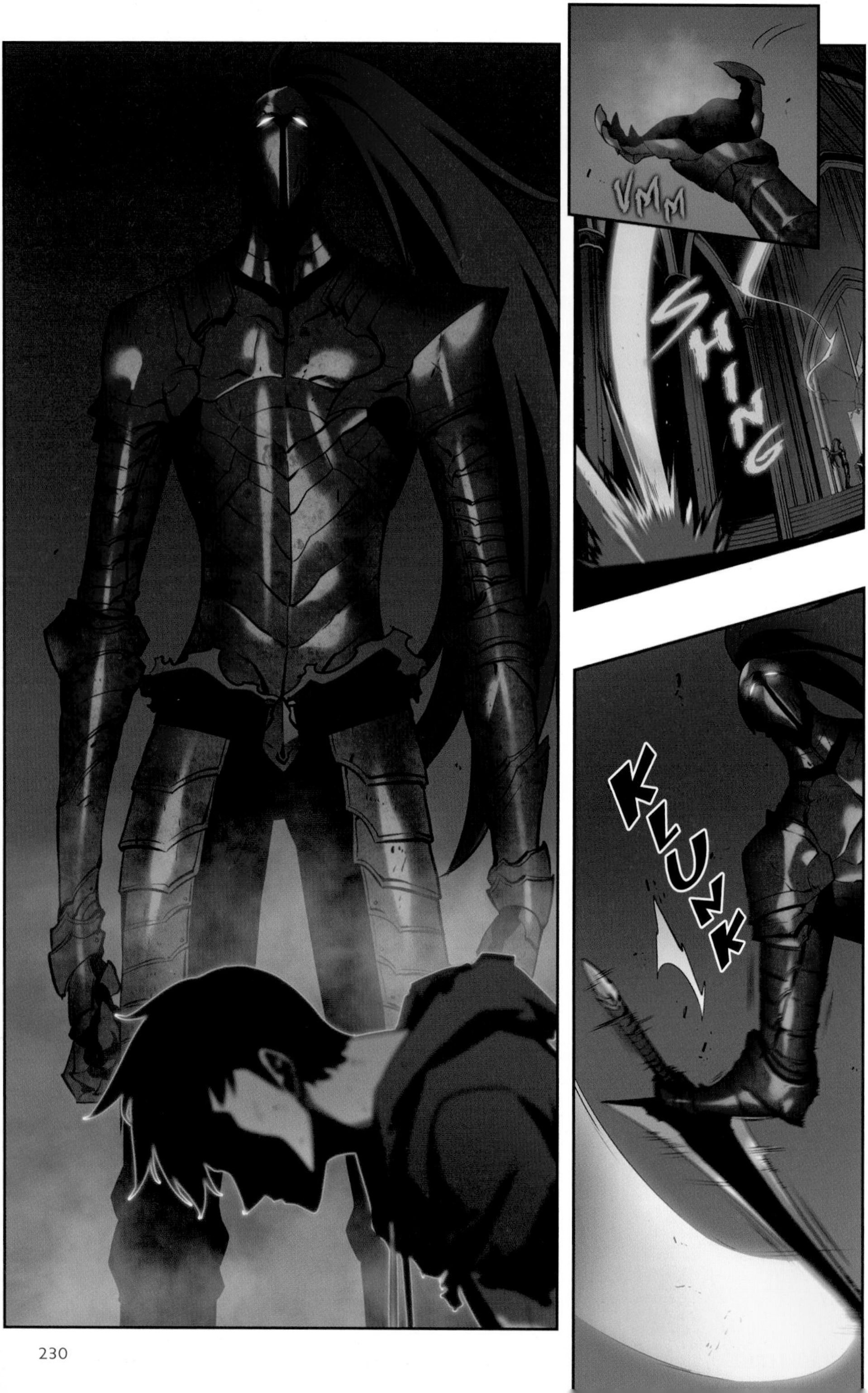
VMM
SHING
KLUNK

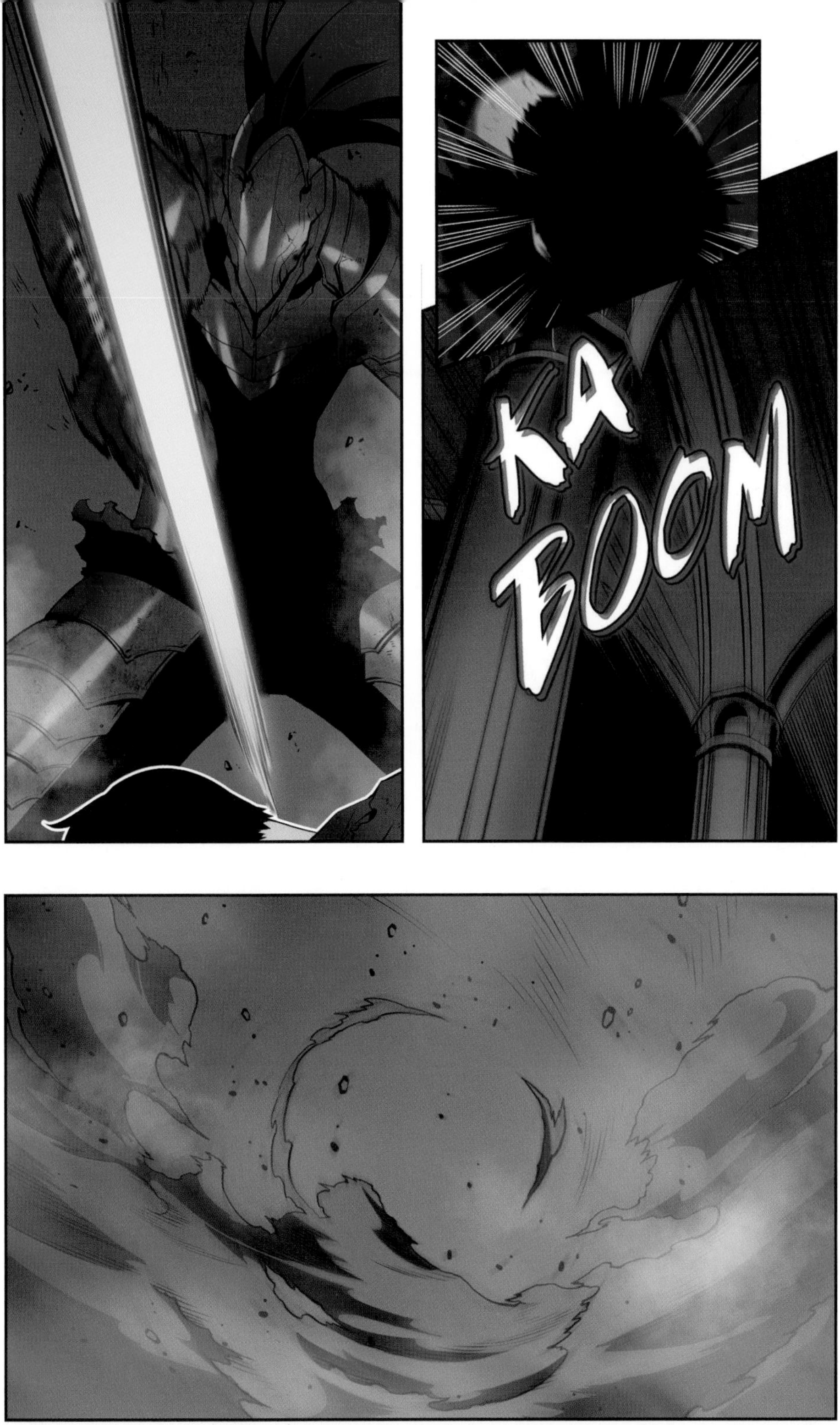
KA BOOM

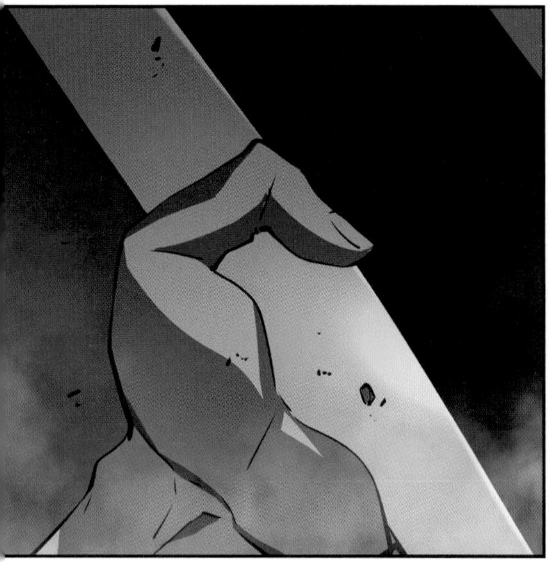

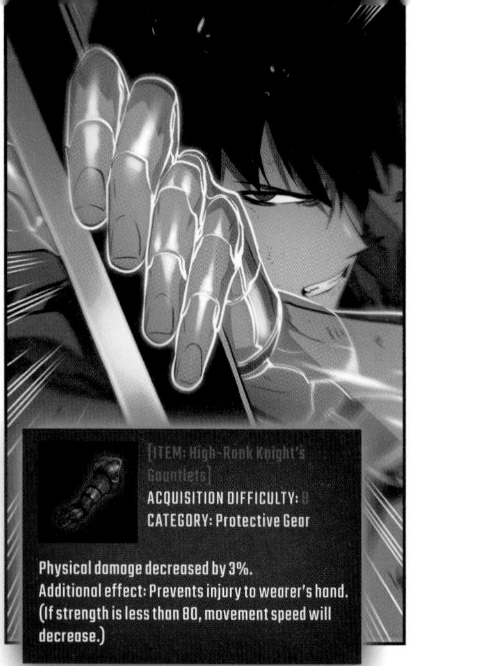
[ITEM: High-Rank Knight's Gauntlets]
ACQUISITION DIFFICULTY: B
CATEGORY: Protective Gear
Physical damage decreased by 3%.
Additional effect: Prevents injury to wearer's hand.
(If strength is less than 80, movement speed will decrease.)

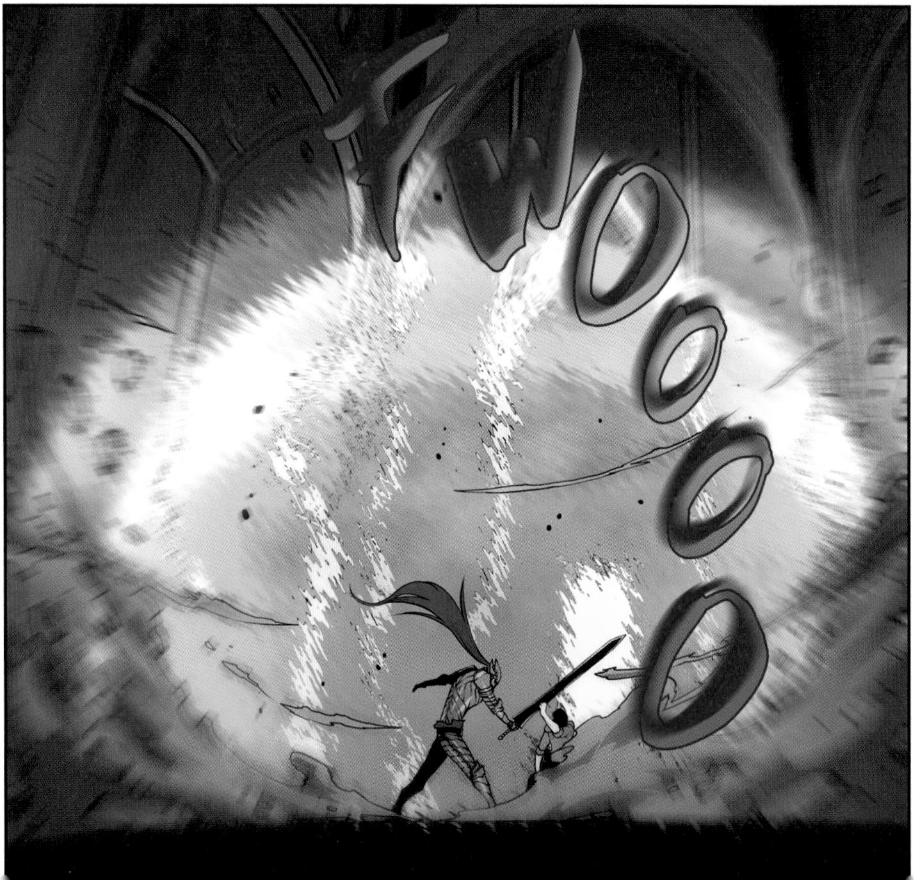
FWOOOO

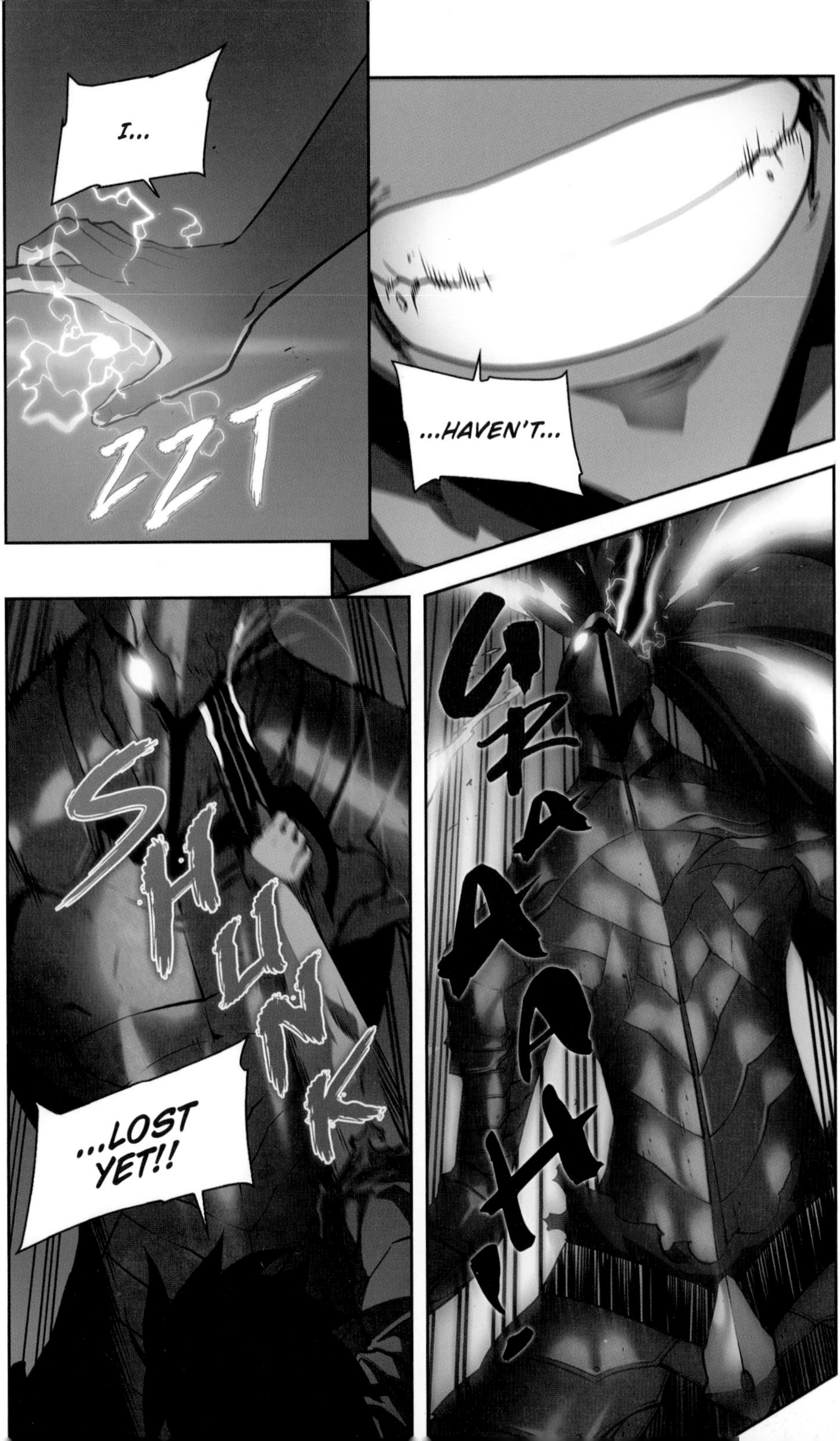
I...
ZZT
...HAVEN'T...
SHUNK
...LOST YET!!
URAAAH!

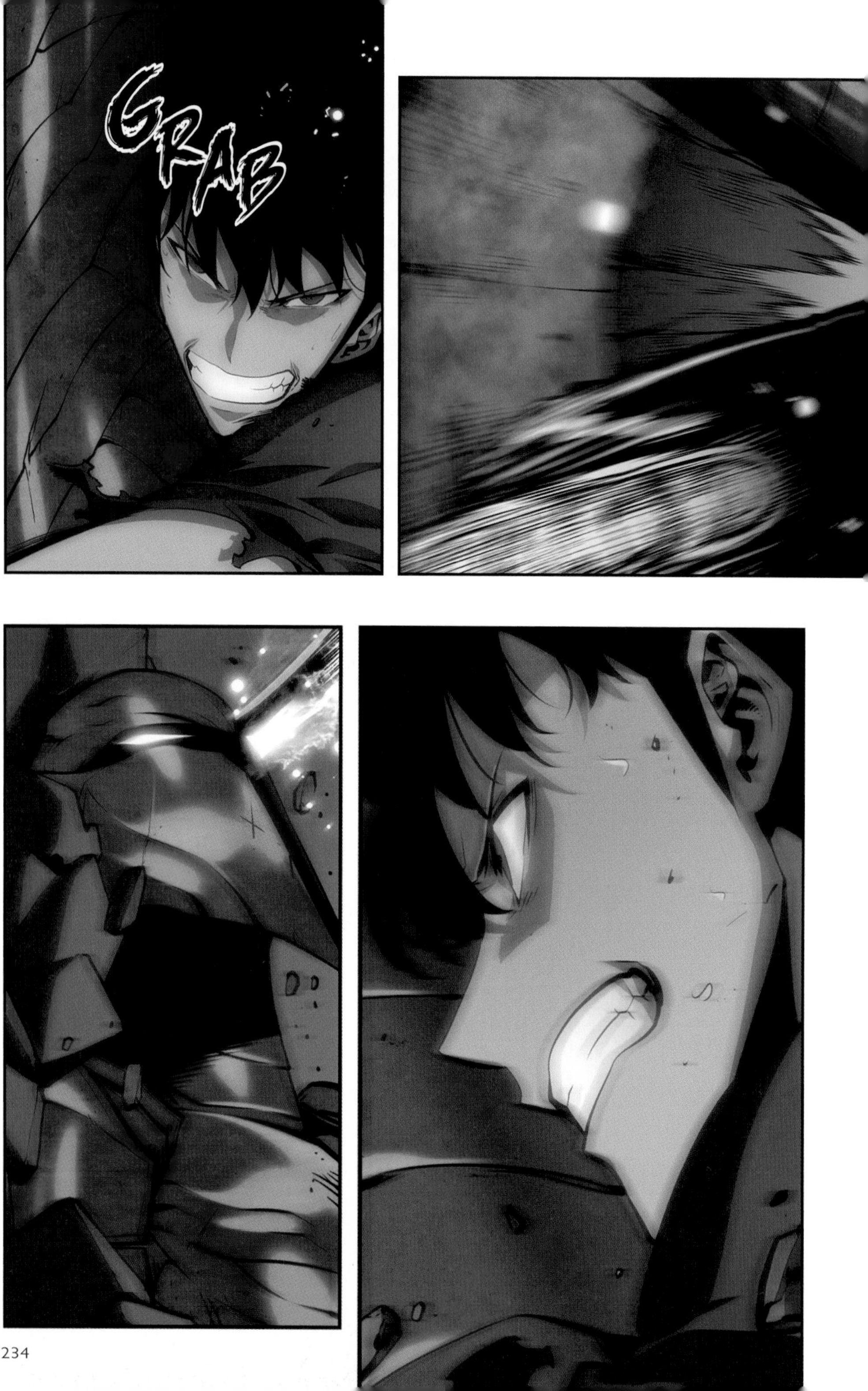
GRAB

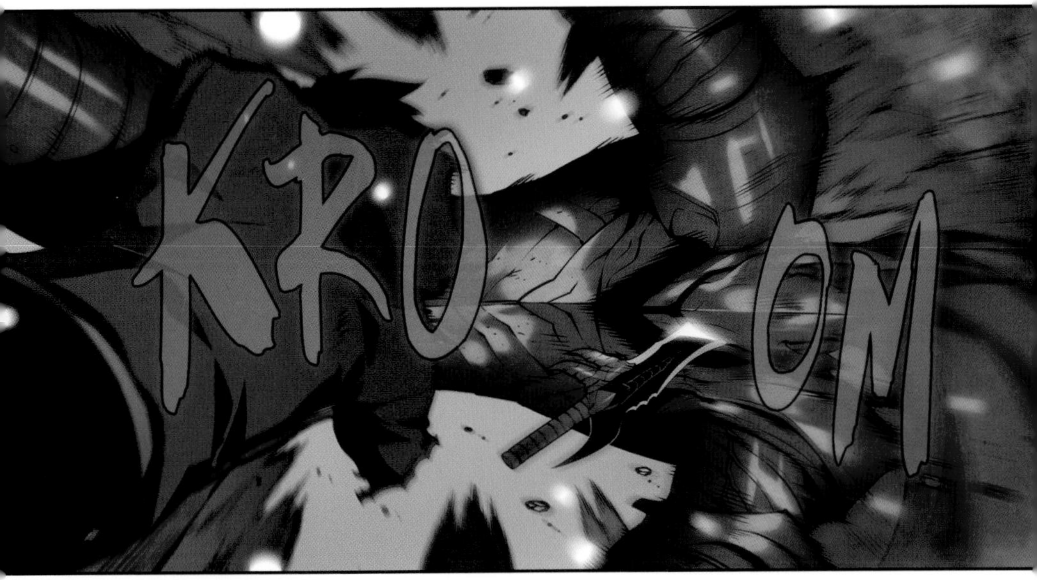
KRO-OM
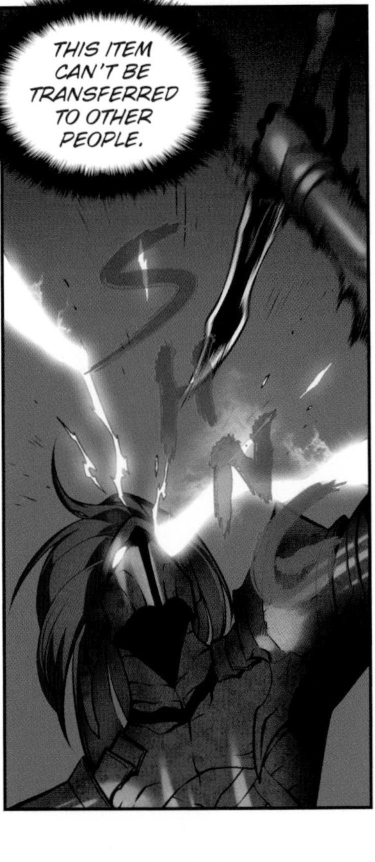
THIS ITEM CAN'T BE TRANSFERRED TO OTHER PEOPLE.
SHING
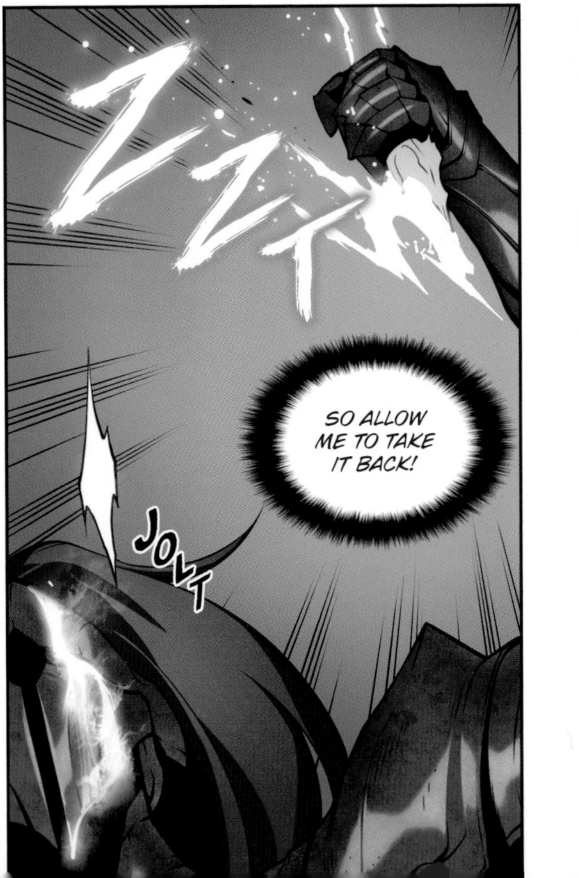
ZZZT
SO ALLOW ME TO TAKE IT BACK!
JOLT

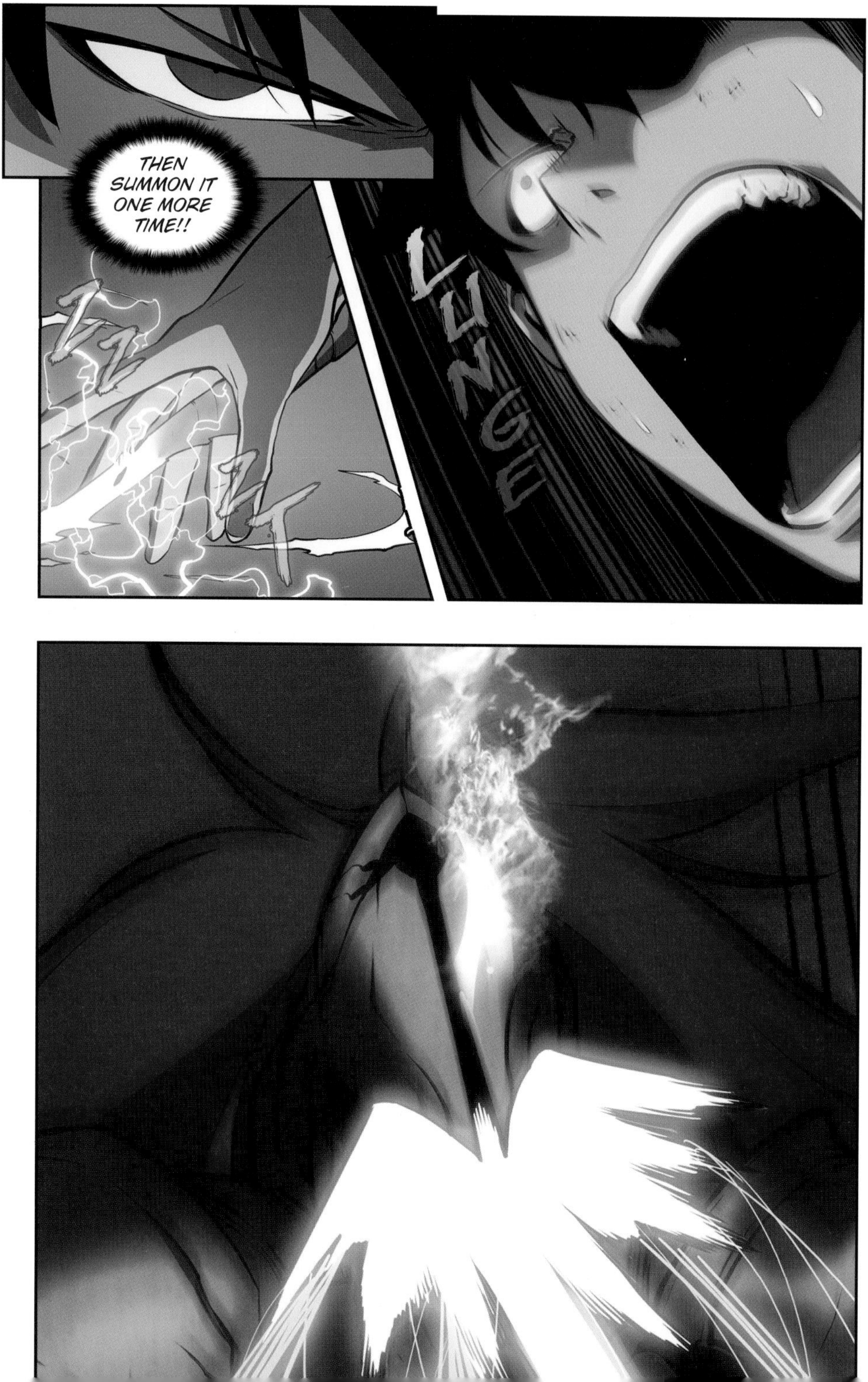
THEN SUMMON IT ONE MORE TIME!!
LUNGE

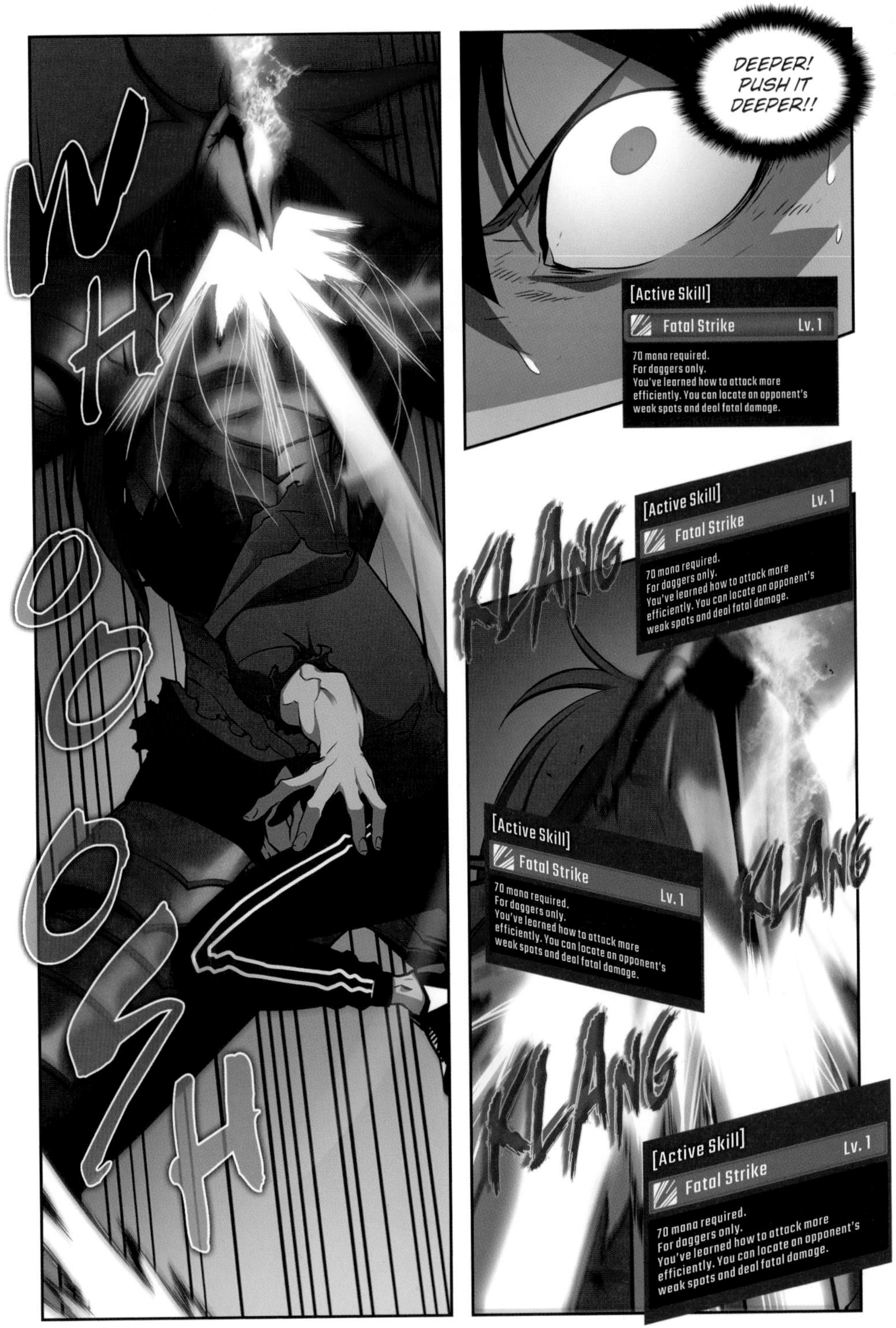
WHOOOOSH
DEEPER! PUSH IT DEEPER!!
[Active Skill]
Fatal Strike Lv. 1
70 mana required.
For daggers only.
You've learned how to attack more efficiently. You can locate an opponent's weak spots and deal fatal damage.
KLANG
[Active Skill]
Fatal Strike Lv. 1
70 mana required.
For daggers only.
You've learned how to attack more efficiently. You can locate an opponent's weak spots and deal fatal damage.
[Active Skill]
Fatal Strike Lv. 1
70 mana required.
For daggers only.
You've learned how to attack more efficiently. You can locate an opponent's weak spots and deal fatal damage.
KLANG
KLANG
[Active Skill]
Fatal Strike Lv. 1
70 mana required.
For daggers only.
You've learned how to attack more efficiently. You can locate an opponent's weak spots and deal fatal damage.

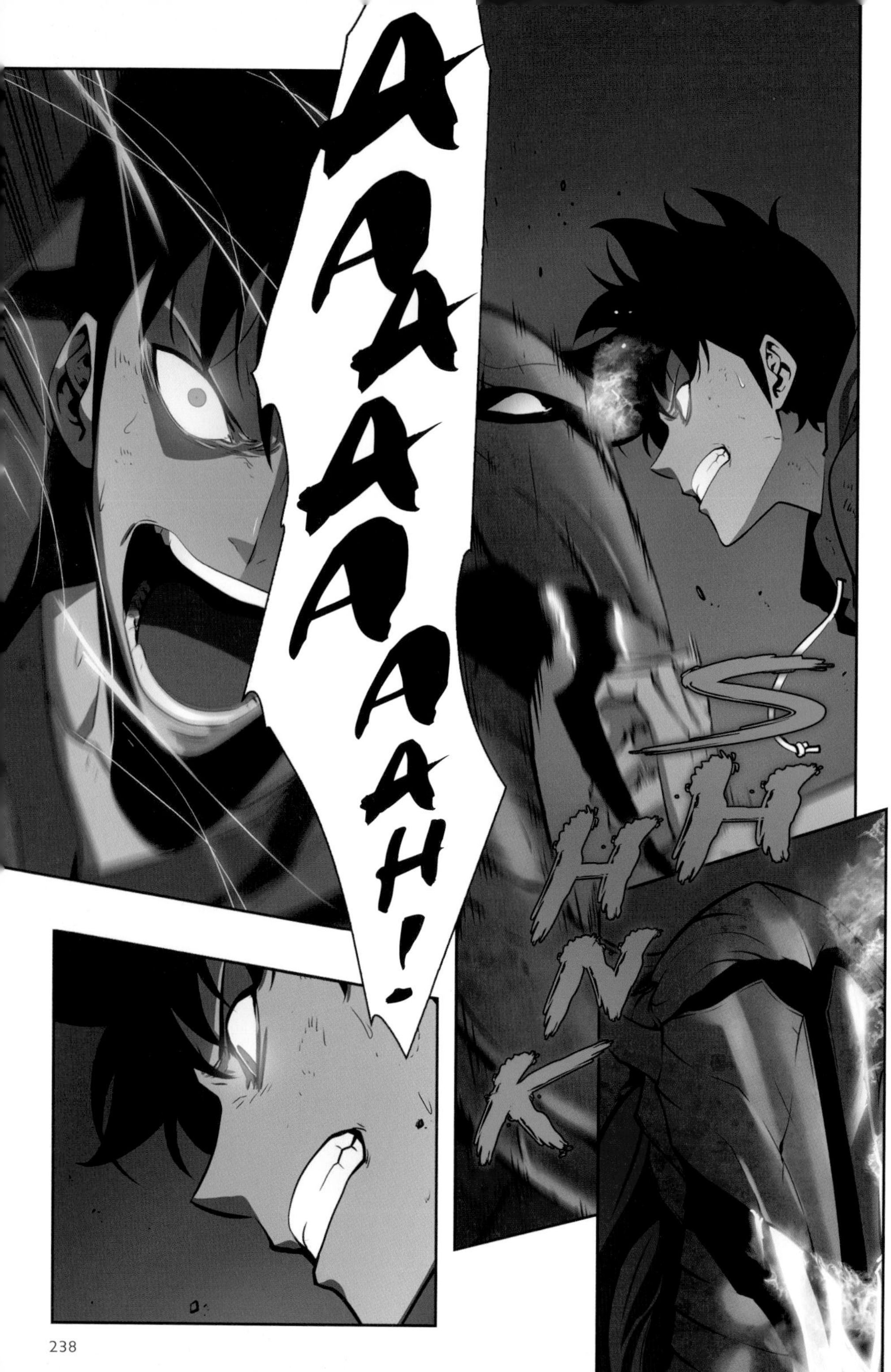

AAAAAAAH!
SHHNK

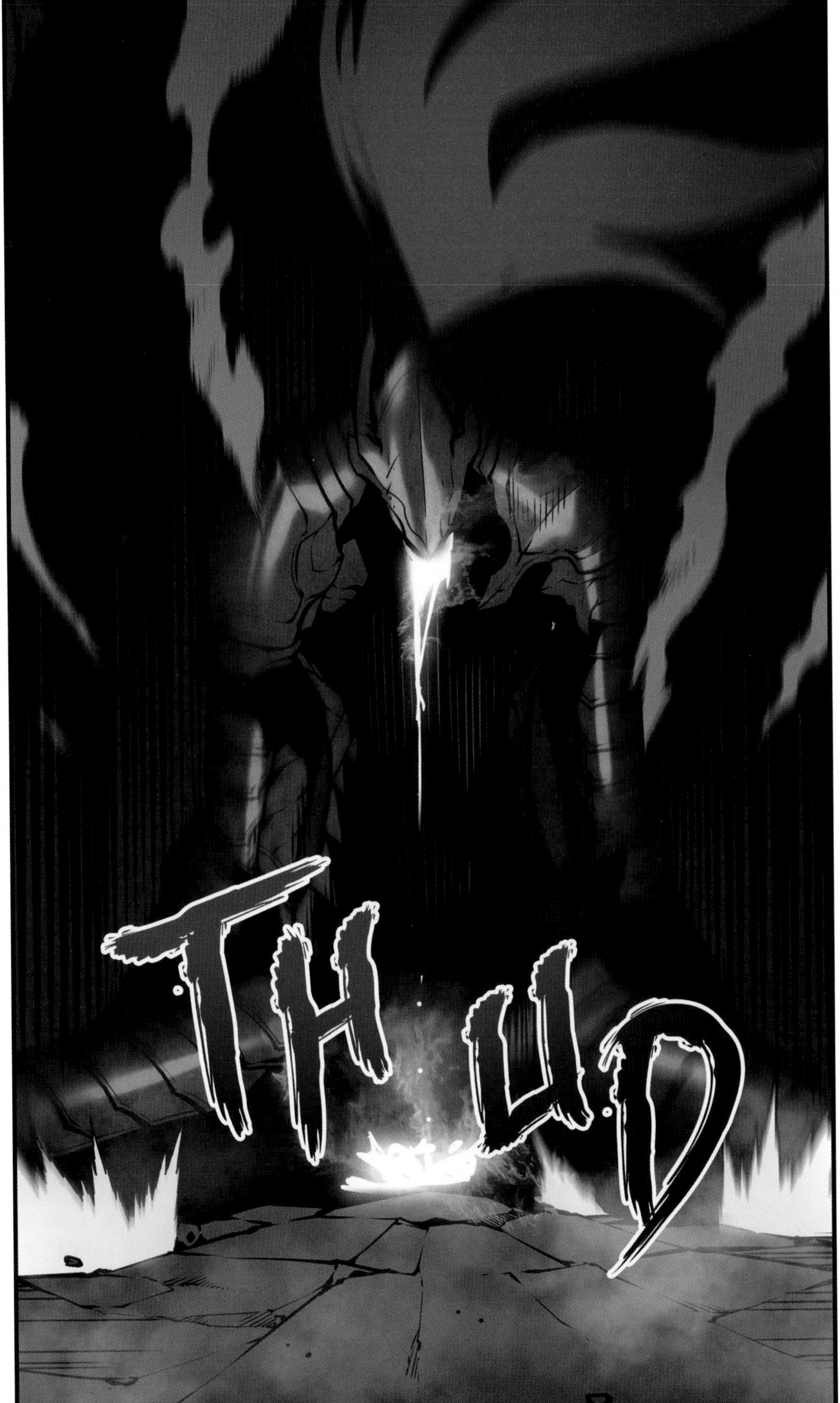
THUD

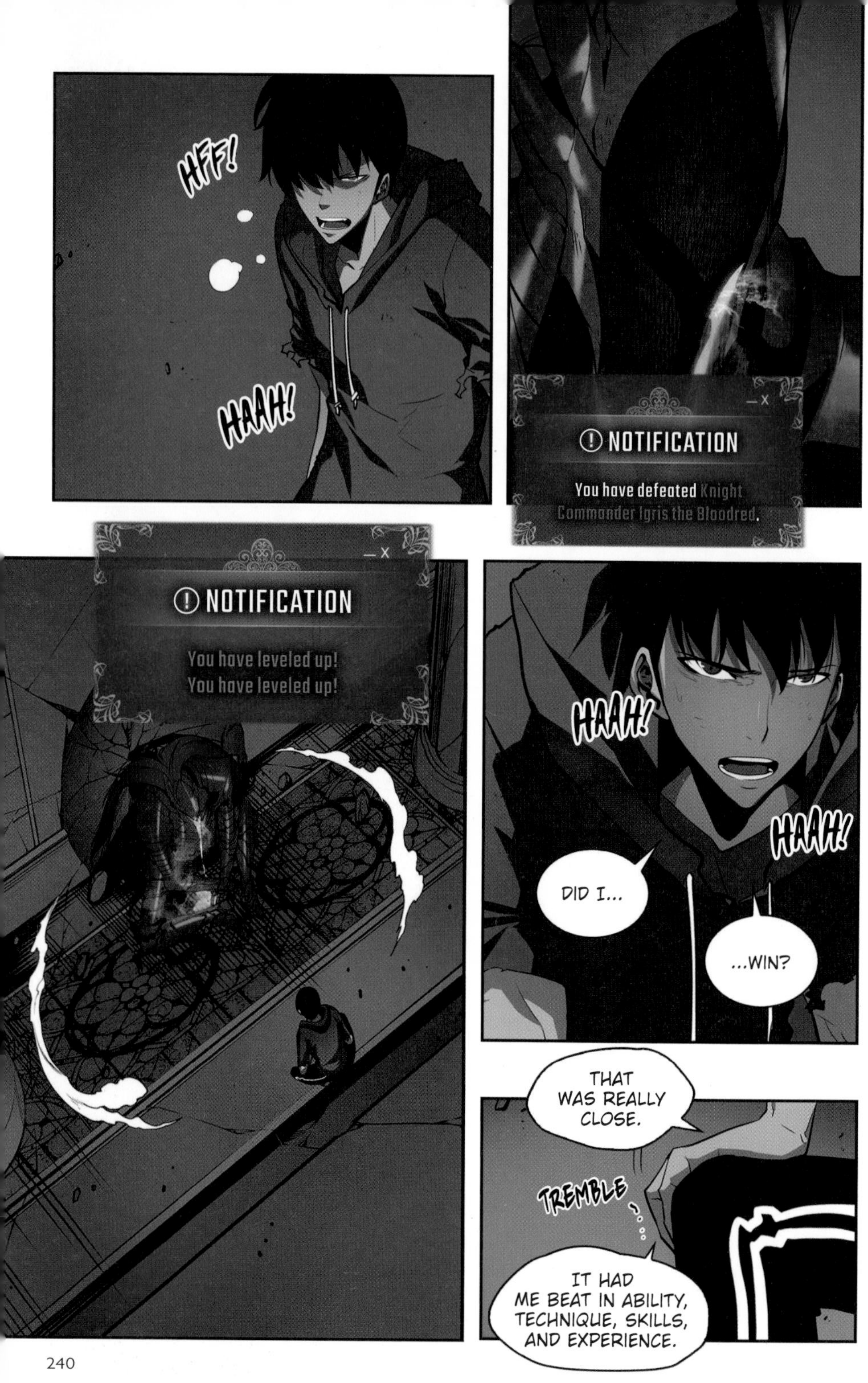
HFF!
HAAH!
NOTIFICATION
You have defeated Knight Commander Igris the Bloodred.
NOTIFICATION
You have leveled up!
You have leveled up!
HAAH!
HAAH!
DID I...
...WIN?
THAT WAS REALLY CLOSE.
TREMBLE
IT HAD ME BEAT IN ABILITY, TECHNIQUE, SKILLS, AND EXPERIENCE.

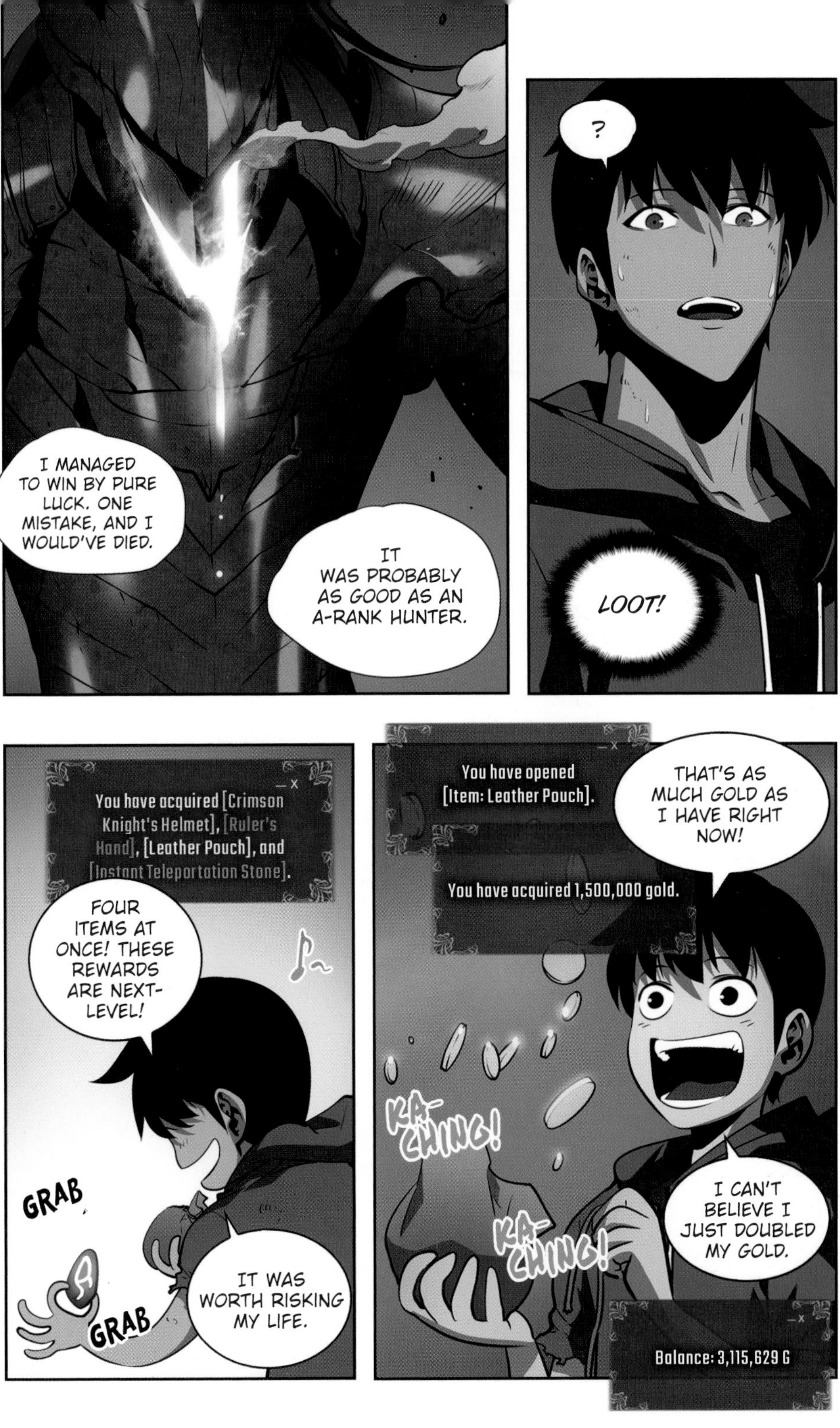
I MANAGED TO WIN BY PURE LUCK. ONE MISTAKE, AND I WOULD'VE DIED.
IT WAS PROBABLY AS GOOD AS AN A-RANK HUNTER.
?
LOOT!
You have acquired [Crimson Knight's Helmet], [Ruler's Hand], [Leather Pouch], and [Instant Teleportation Stone].
FOUR ITEMS AT ONCE! THESE REWARDS ARE NEXT-LEVEL!
GRAB
GRAB
IT WAS WORTH RISKING MY LIFE.
You have opened [Item: Leather Pouch].
You have acquired 1,500,000 gold.
THAT'S AS MUCH GOLD AS I HAVE RIGHT NOW!
KA-CHING!
KA-CHING!
I CAN'T BELIEVE I JUST DOUBLED MY GOLD.
Balance: 3,115,629 G

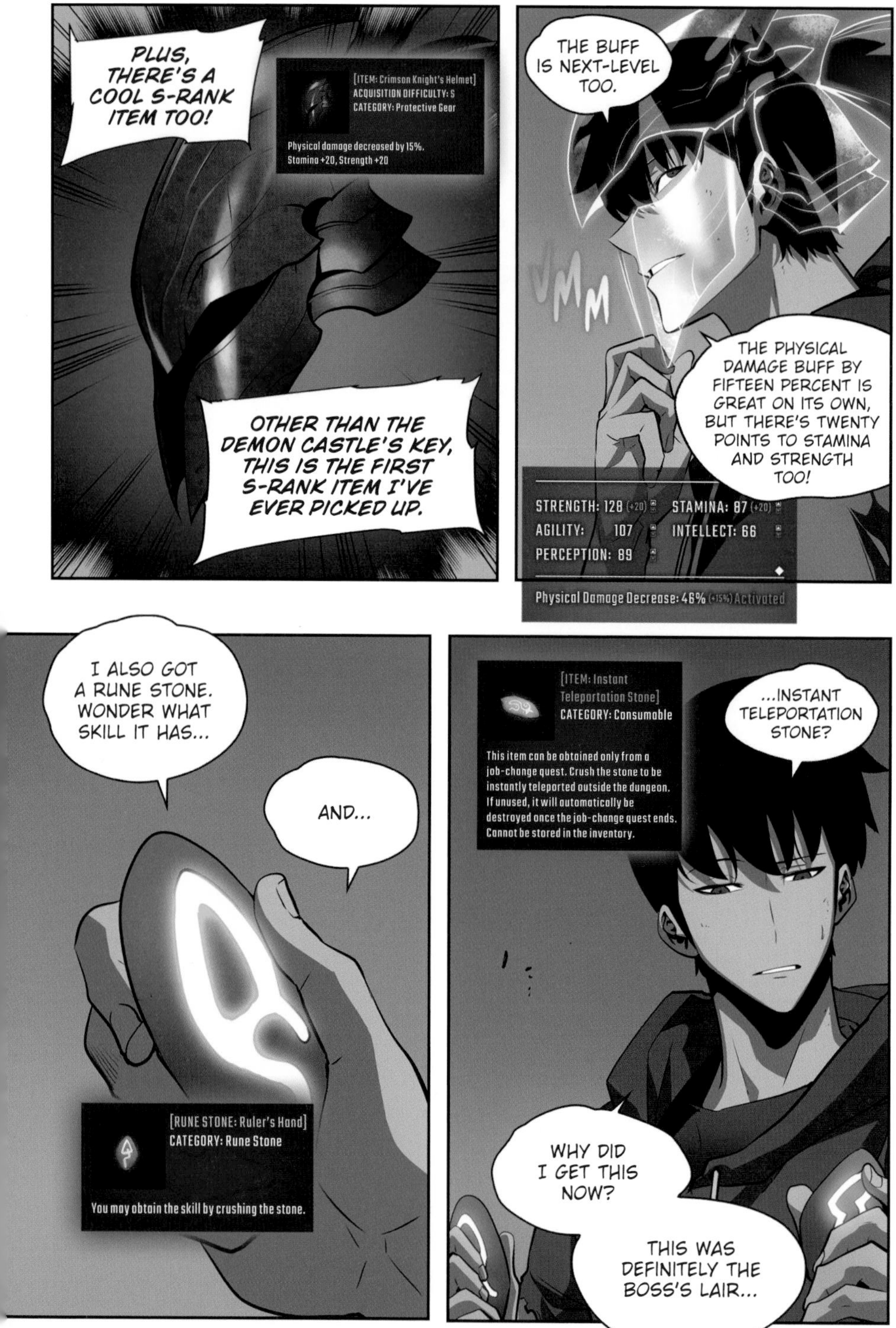
PLUS, THERE'S A COOL S-RANK ITEM TOO!
[ITEM: Crimson Knight's Helmet] ACQUISITION DIFFICULTY: S CATEGORY: Protective Gear
Physical damage decreased by 15%. Stamina +20, Strength +20
OTHER THAN THE DEMON CASTLE'S KEY, THIS IS THE FIRST S-RANK ITEM I'VE EVER PICKED UP.
THE BUFF IS NEXT-LEVEL TOO.
THE PHYSICAL DAMAGE BUFF BY FIFTEEN PERCENT IS GREAT ON ITS OWN, BUT THERE'S TWENTY POINTS TO STAMINA AND STRENGTH TOO!
STRENGTH: 128 (+20) STAMINA: 87 (+20)
AGILITY: 107 INTELLECT: 66
PERCEPTION: 89
Physical Damage Decrease: 46% (+15%) Activated
I ALSO GOT A RUNE STONE. WONDER WHAT SKILL IT HAS...
AND...
[RUNE STONE: Ruler's Hand] CATEGORY: Rune Stone
You may obtain the skill by crushing the stone.
[ITEM: Instant Teleportation Stone] CATEGORY: Consumable
This item can be obtained only from a job-change quest. Crush the stone to be instantly teleported outside the dungeon. If unused, it will automatically be destroyed once the job-change quest ends. Cannot be stored in the inventory.
...INSTANT TELEPORTATION STONE?
WHY DID I GET THIS NOW?
THIS WAS DEFINITELY THE BOSS'S LAIR...

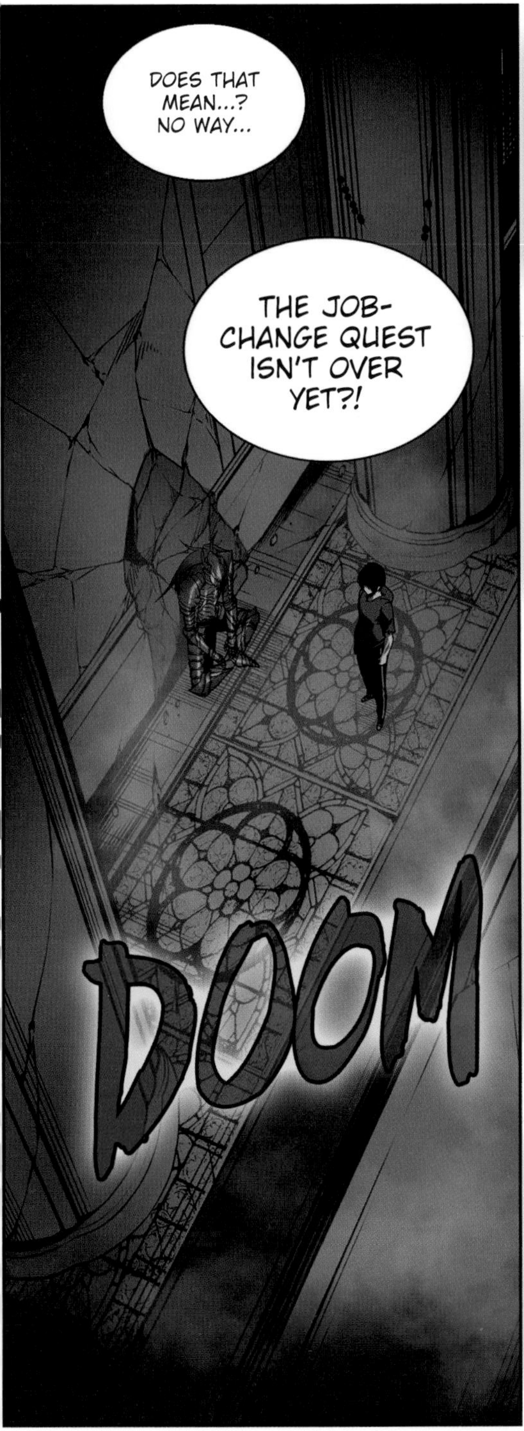
DOES THAT MEAN...? NO WAY...
THE JOB-CHANGE QUEST ISN'T OVER YET?!
DOOM

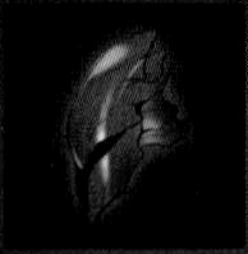

[ITEM: Crimson Knight's Helmet]
ACQUISITION DIFFICULTY: S
CATEGORY: Protective Gear

Physical damage decreased by 15%.
Stamina +20, Strength +20

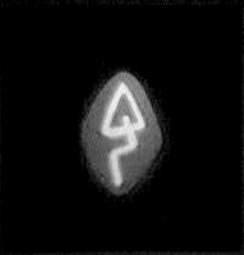

[RUNE STONE: Ruler's Hand]
CATEGORY: Rune Stone

You may obtain the skill by crushing the stone.

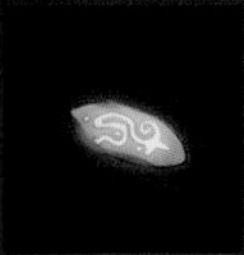

[ITEM: Instant Teleportation Stone]
CATEGORY: Consumable

This item can be obtained only from a job-change quest. Crush the stone to be instantly teleported outside the dungeon. If unused, it will automatically be destroyed once the job-change quest ends. Cannot be stored in the inventory.

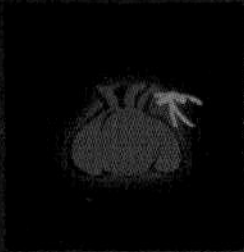

[ITEM: Leather Pouch]
CATEGORY: Miscellaneous

A pouch for carrying your belongings.
It contains 1,500,000 gold.

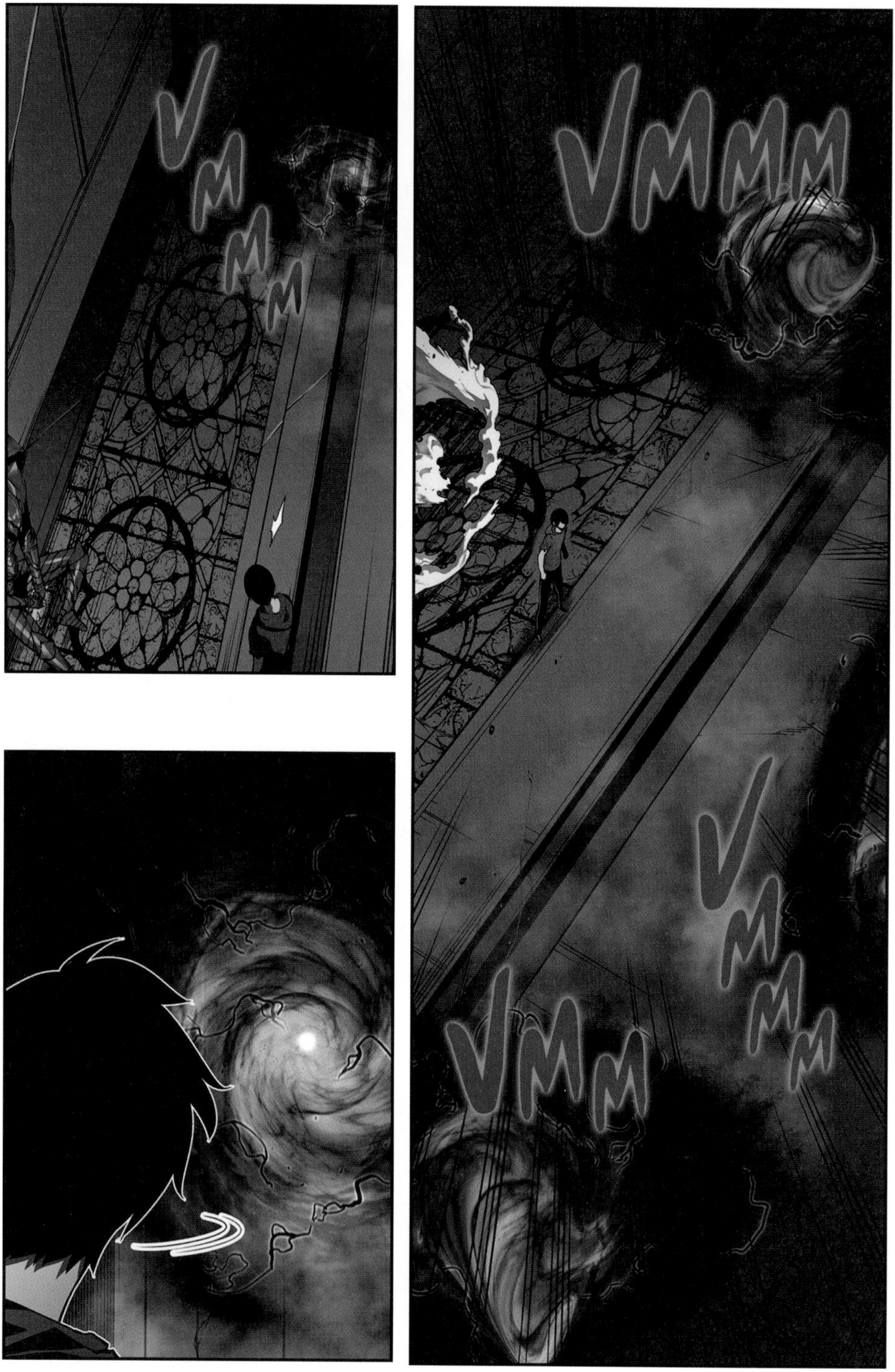
VMMMM
VMMMM
VMMMM
VMMM

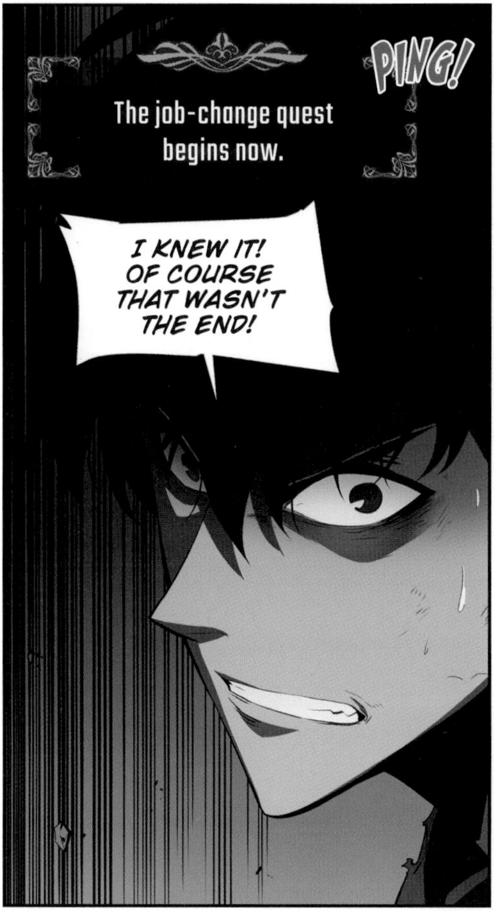
PING!
The job-change quest begins now.
I KNEW IT! OF COURSE THAT WASN'T THE END!

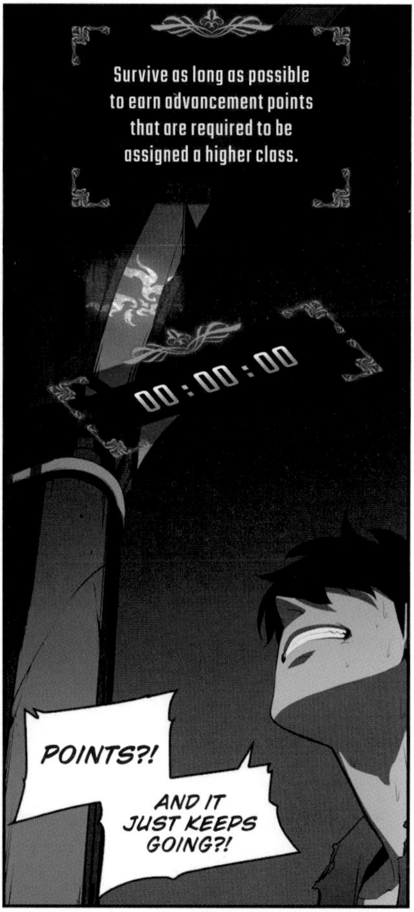
Survive as long as possible to earn advancement points that are required to be assigned a higher class.
00 : 00 : 00
POINTS?!
AND IT JUST KEEPS GOING?!

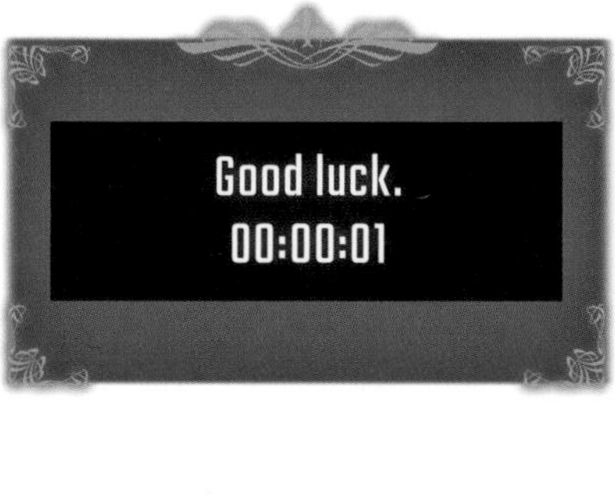
Good luck.
00:00:01

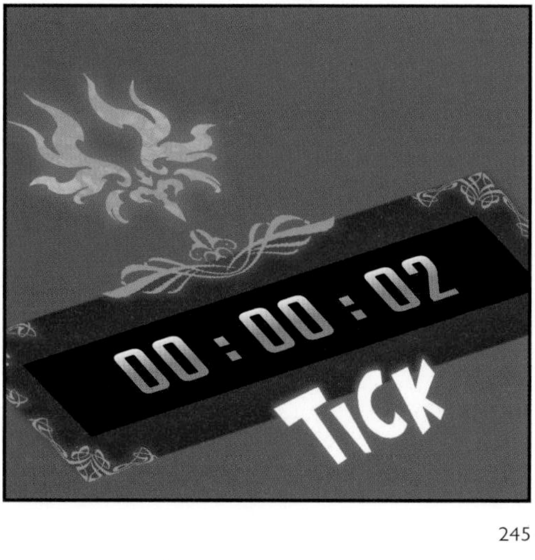
00 : 00 : 02
TICK

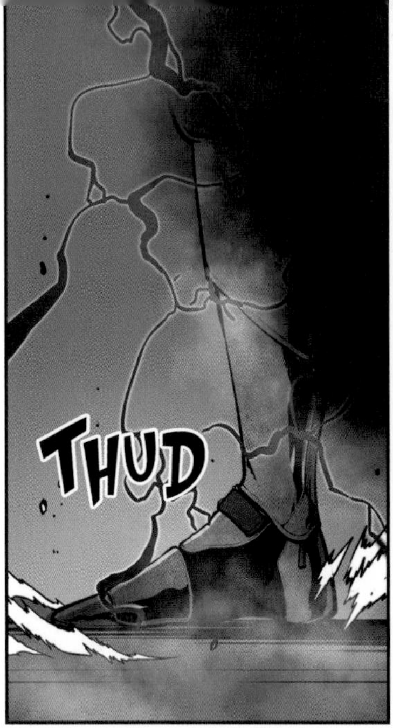
THUD
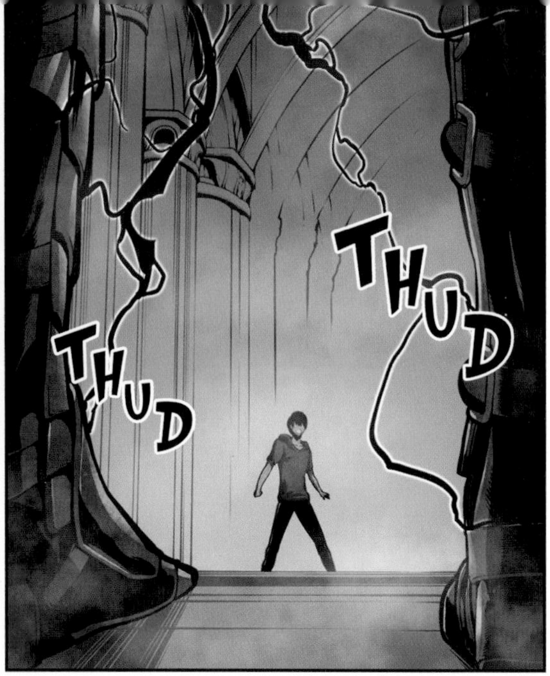
THUD
THUD
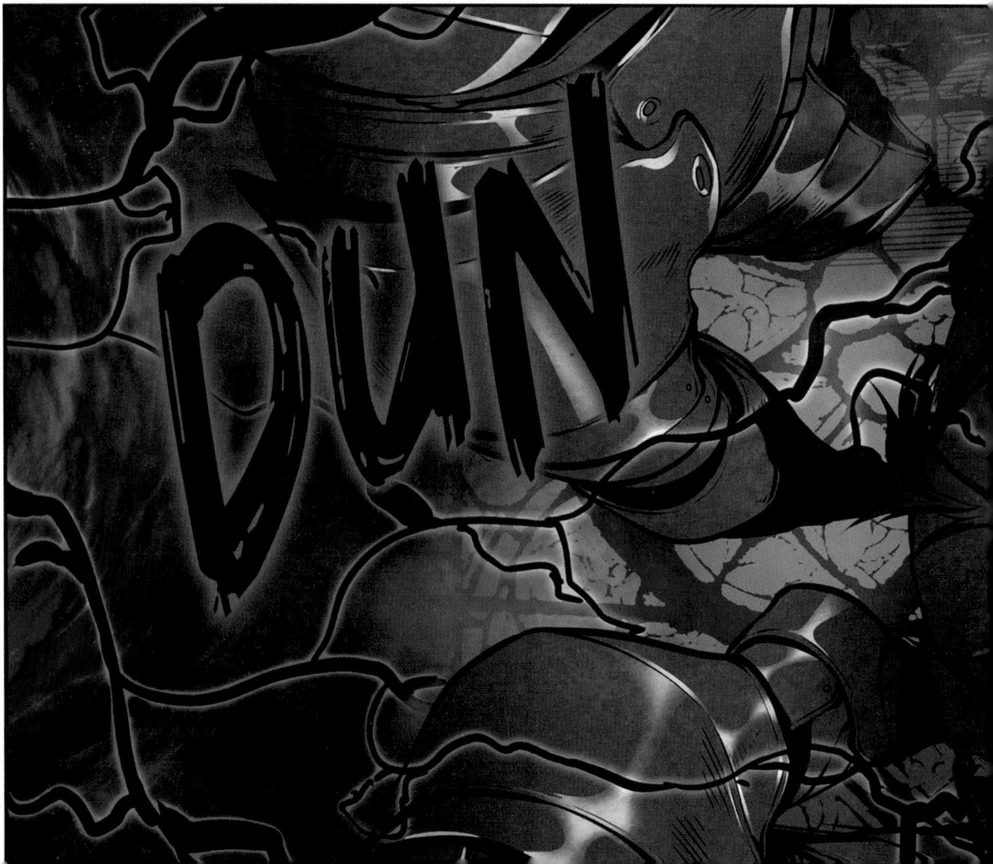
DUN

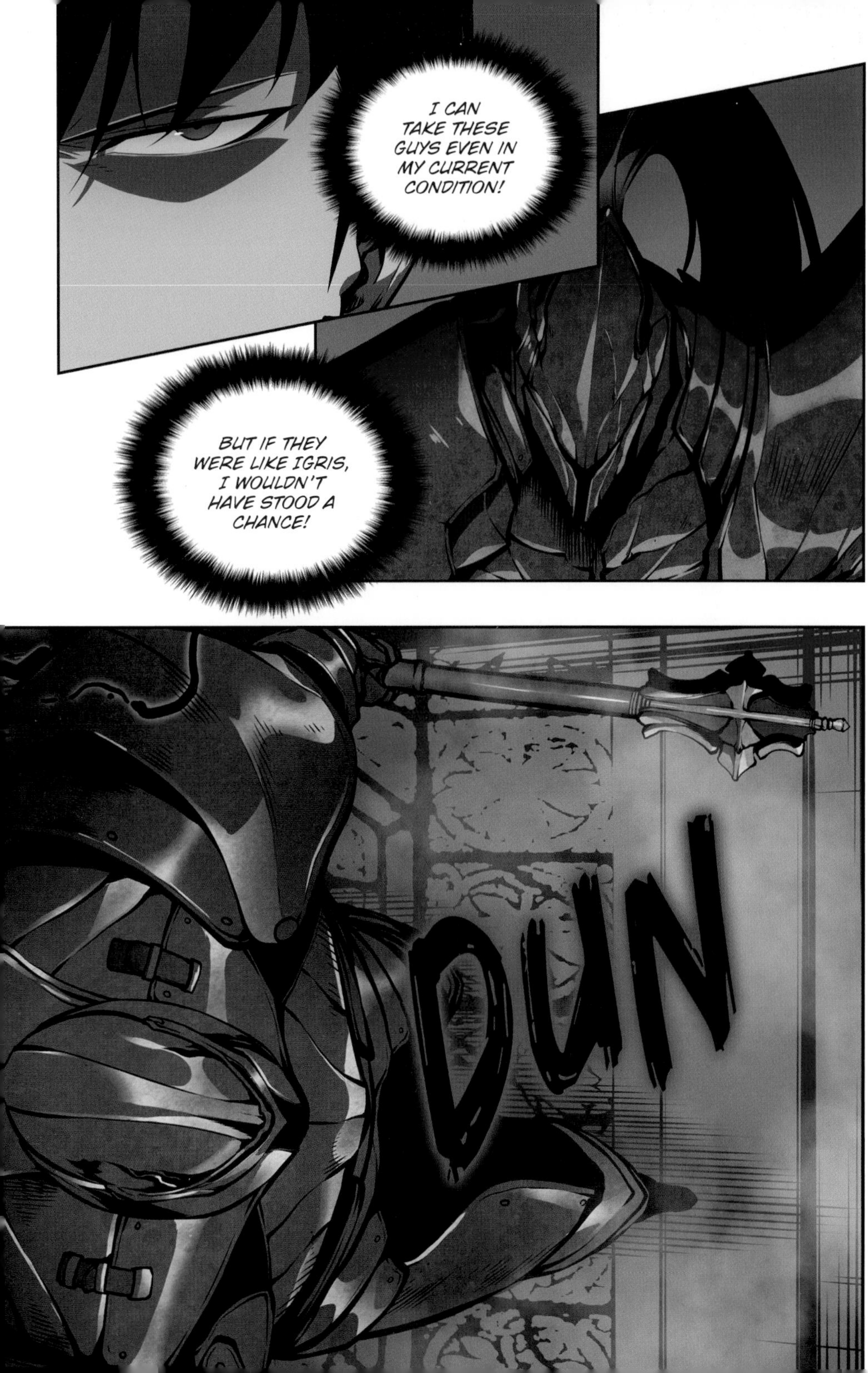
I CAN TAKE THESE GUYS EVEN IN MY CURRENT CONDITION!
BUT IF THEY WERE LIKE IGRIS, I WOULDN'T HAVE STOOD A CHANCE!
DUN

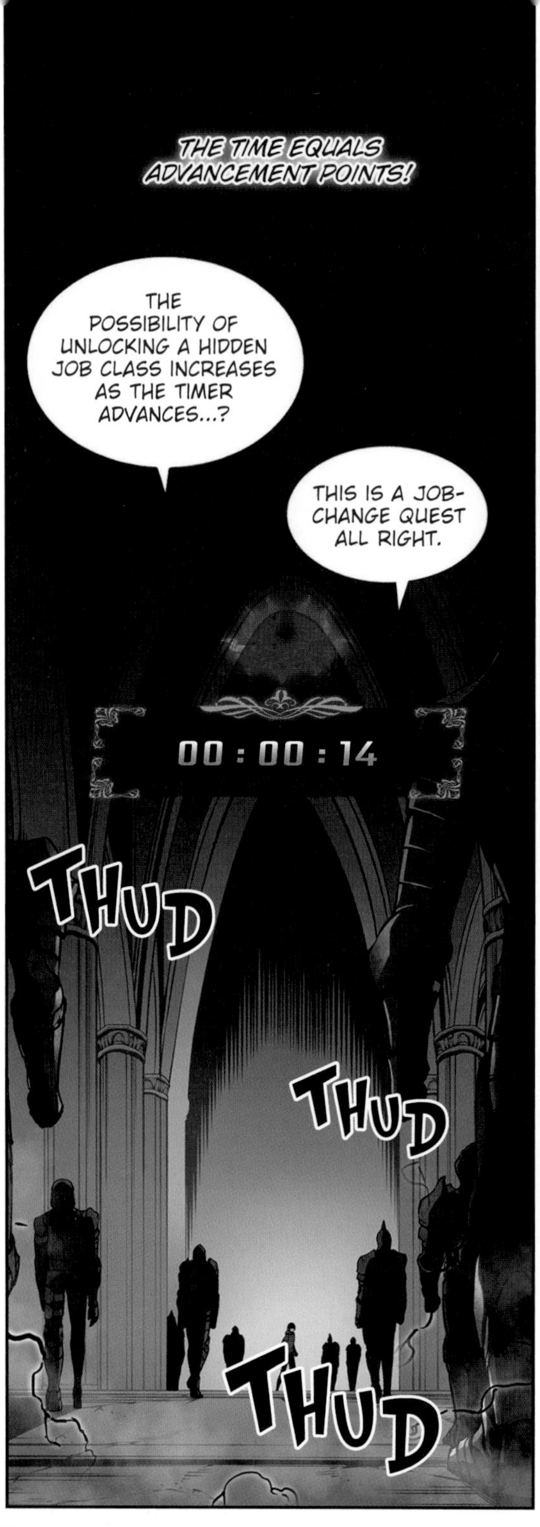
THE TIME EQUALS ADVANCEMENT POINTS!
THE POSSIBILITY OF UNLOCKING A HIDDEN JOB CLASS INCREASES AS THE TIMER ADVANCES...?
THIS IS A JOB-CHANGE QUEST ALL RIGHT.
00 : 00 : 14
THUD
THUD
THUD

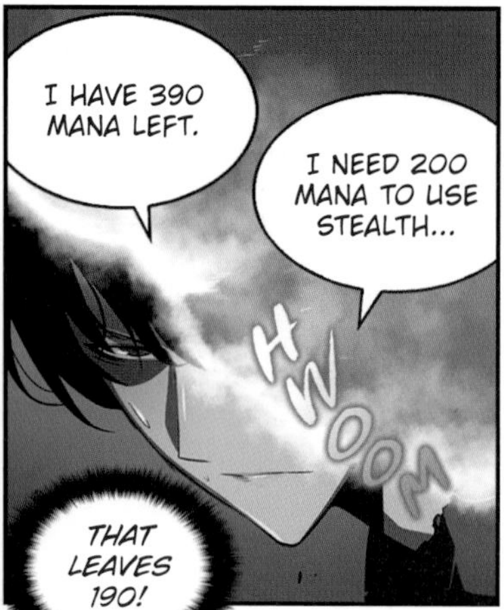
I HAVE 390 MANA LEFT.
I NEED 200 MANA TO USE STEALTH...
HWOOM
THAT LEAVES 190!

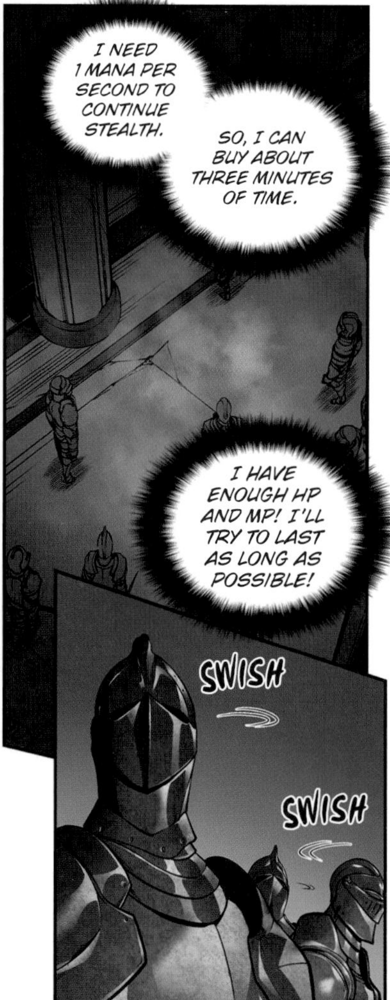
I NEED 1 MANA PER SECOND TO CONTINUE STEALTH.
SO, I CAN BUY ABOUT THREE MINUTES OF TIME.
I HAVE ENOUGH HP AND MP! I'LL TRY TO LAST AS LONG AS POSSIBLE!
SWISH
SWISH

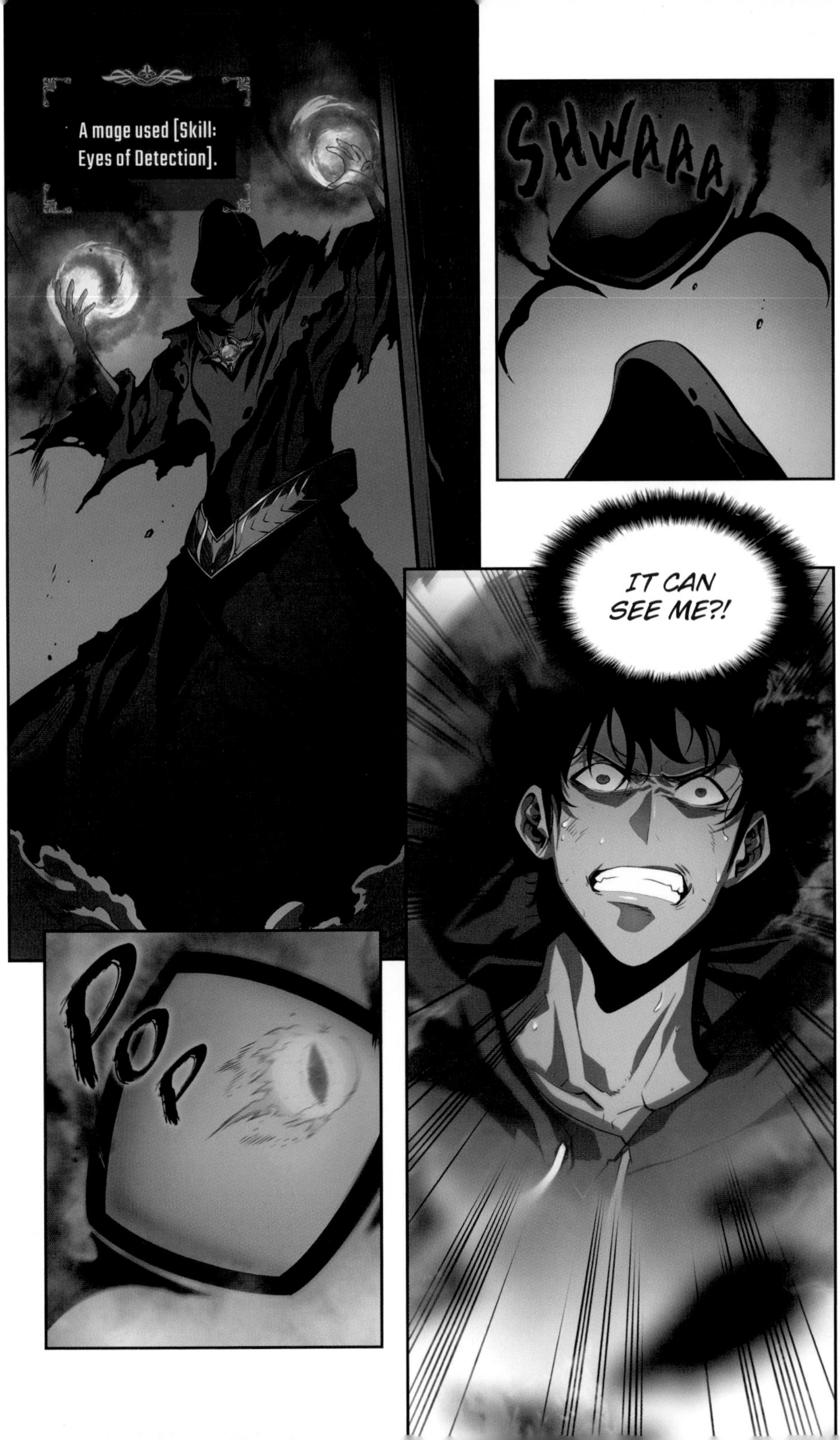
A mage used [Skill: Eyes of Detection].
SHWAAA
IT CAN SEE ME?!
POP

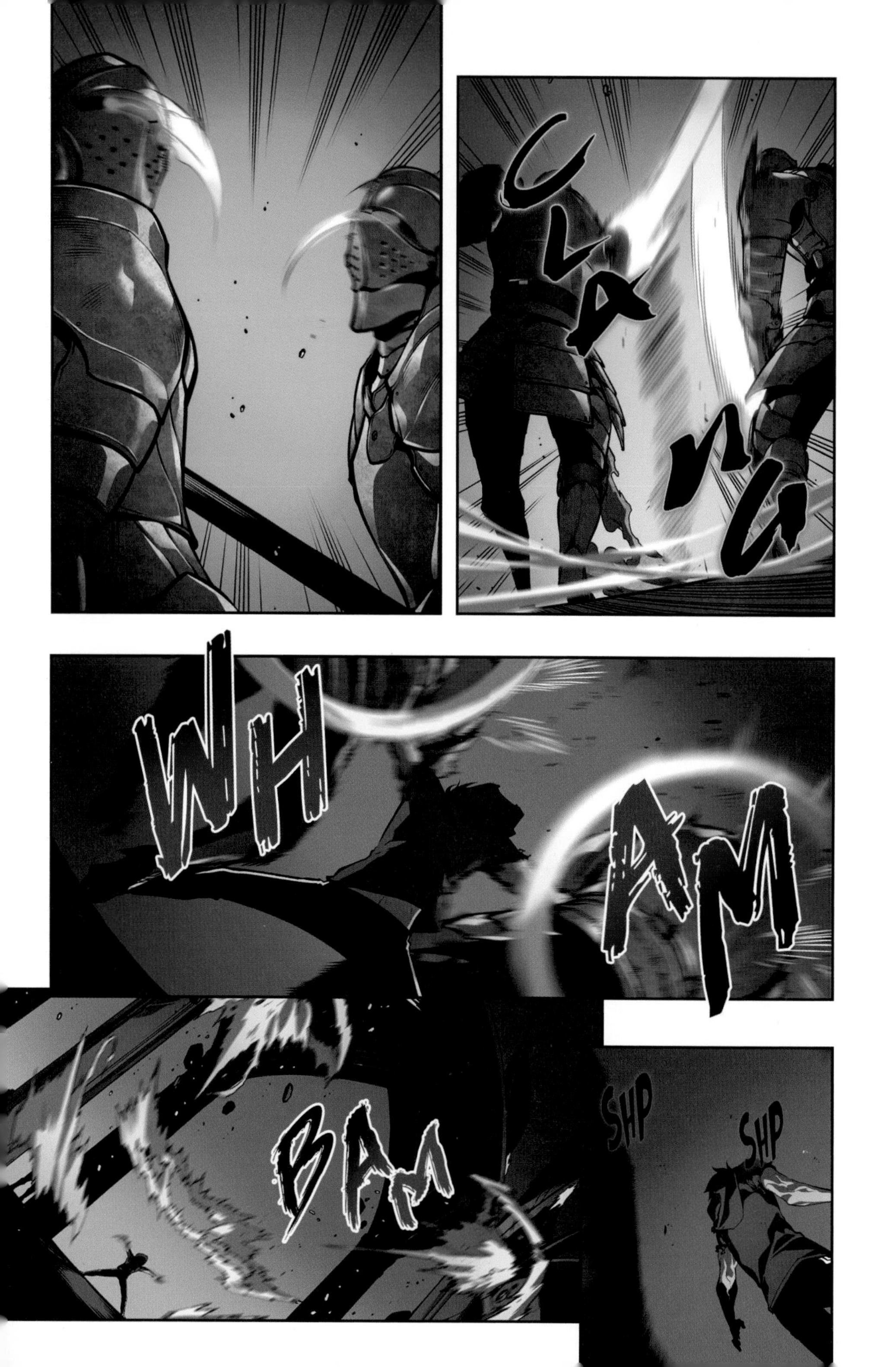
CLANG
WHAM
BAM
SHP
SHP

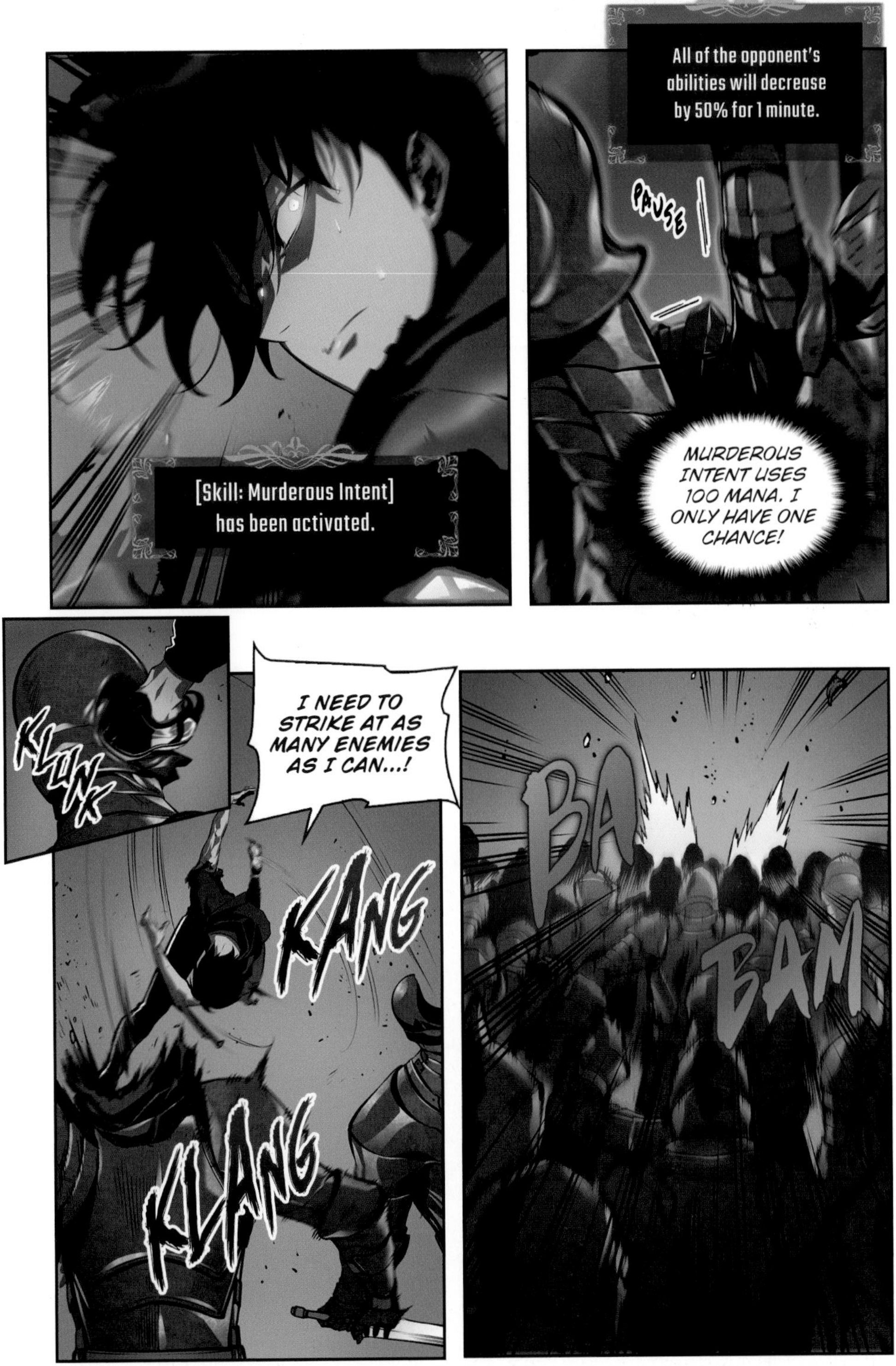
[Skill: Murderous Intent] has been activated.
All of the opponent's abilities will decrease by 50% for 1 minute.
PAUSE
MURDEROUS INTENT USES 100 MANA. I ONLY HAVE ONE CHANCE!
KLINK
I NEED TO STRIKE AT AS MANY ENEMIES AS I CAN...!
KANG
KLANG
BA
BAM

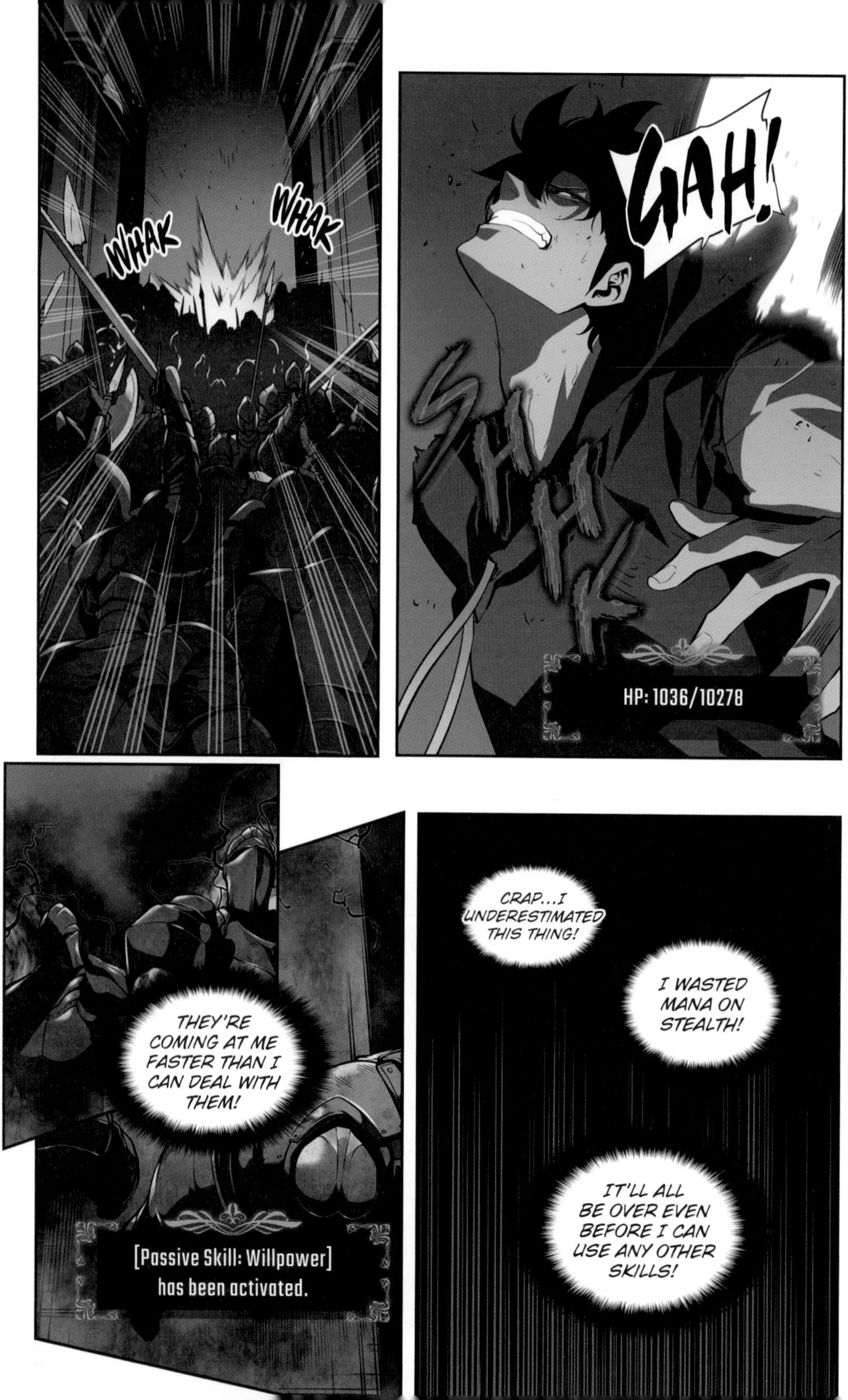
WHAK
WHAK
GAH!
SHHK
HP: 1036/10278
THEY'RE COMING AT ME FASTER THAN I CAN DEAL WITH THEM!
[Passive Skill: Willpower] has been activated.
CRAP...I UNDERESTIMATED THIS THING!
I WASTED MANA ON STEALTH!
IT'LL ALL BE OVER EVEN BEFORE I CAN USE ANY OTHER SKILLS!

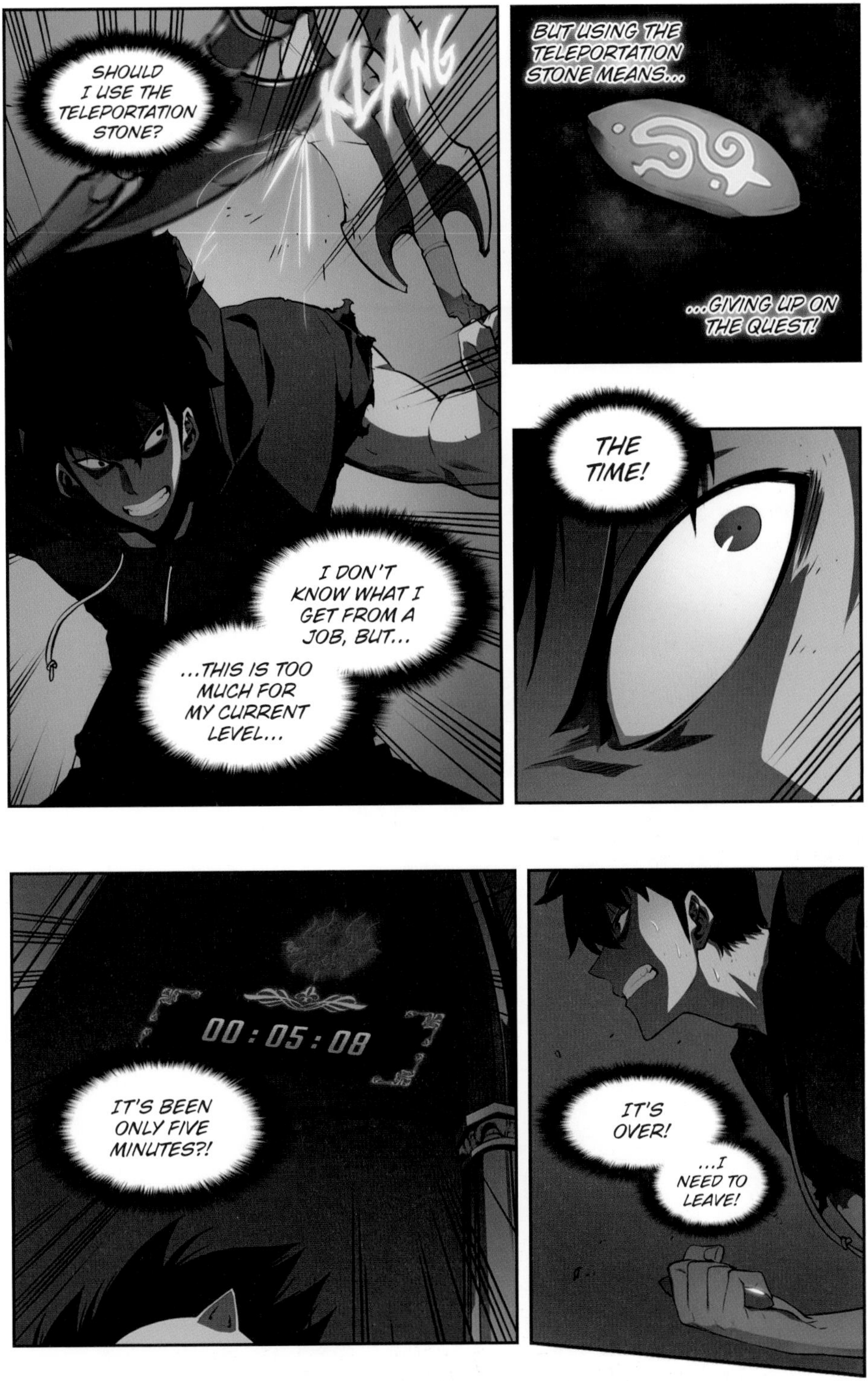
SHOULD I USE THE TELEPORTATION STONE?
KLANG
I DON'T KNOW WHAT I GET FROM A JOB, BUT...
...THIS IS TOO MUCH FOR MY CURRENT LEVEL...
BUT USING THE TELEPORTATION STONE MEANS...
...GIVING UP ON THE QUEST!
THE TIME!
00:05:08
IT'S BEEN ONLY FIVE MINUTES?!
IT'S OVER!
...I NEED TO LEAVE!

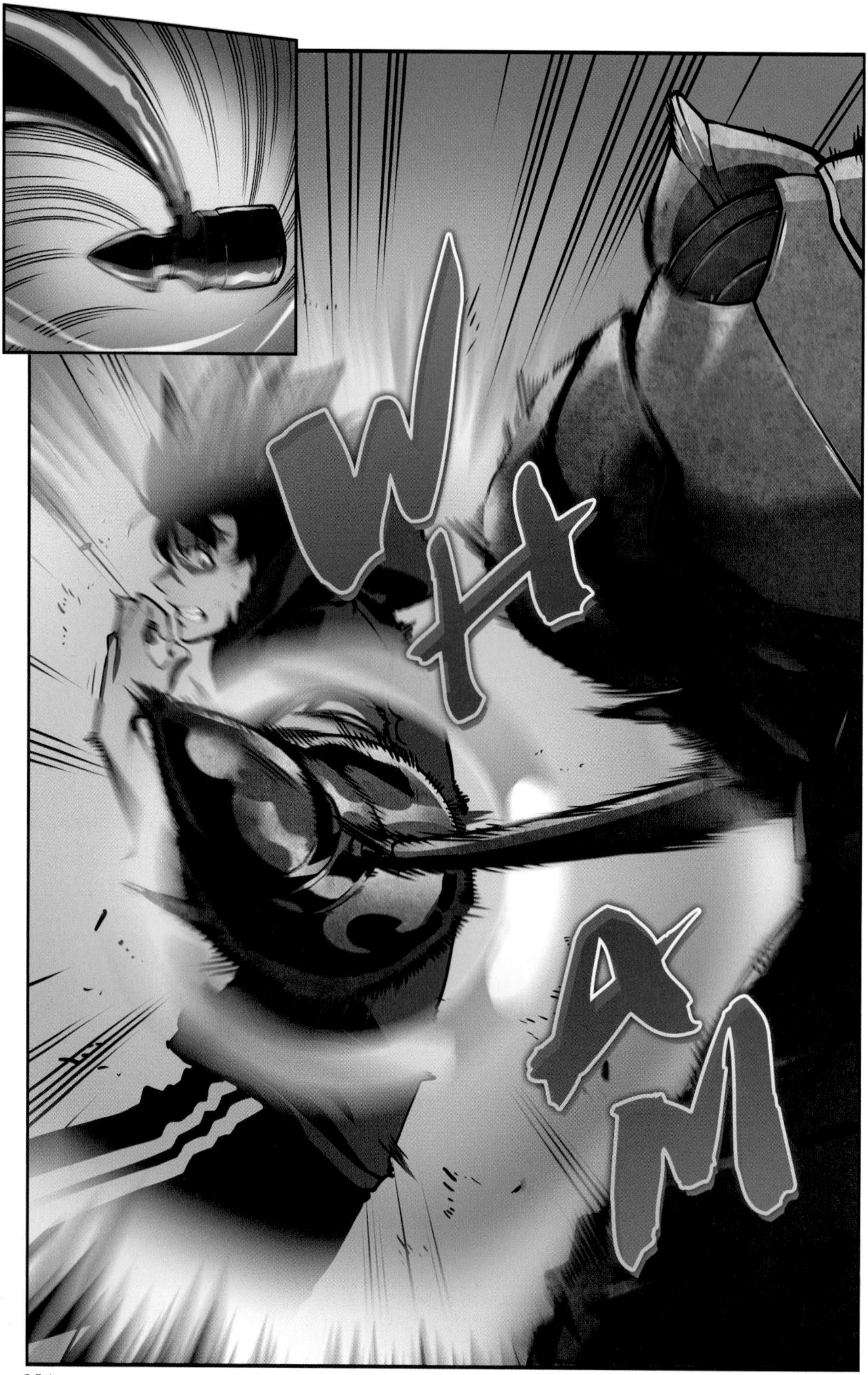
WHAM

KRRRK

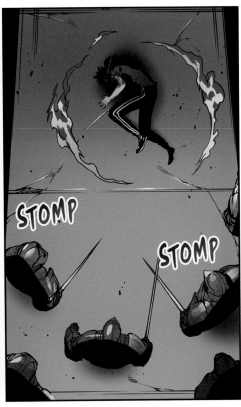

STOMP

STOMP

VRA BOOM

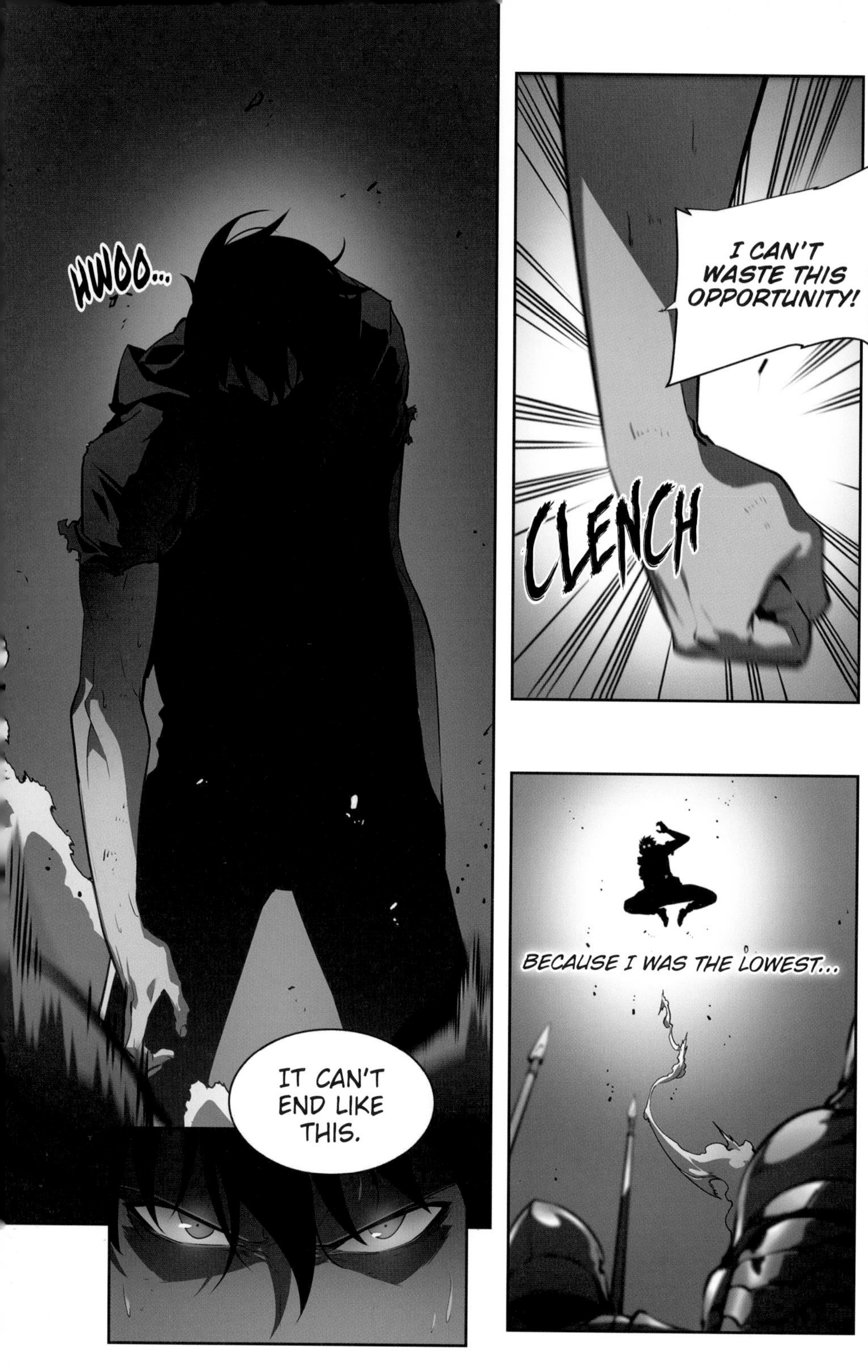
HWOO...
IT CAN'T END LIKE THIS.
I CAN'T WASTE THIS OPPORTUNITY!
CLENCH
BECAUSE I WAS THE LOWEST...

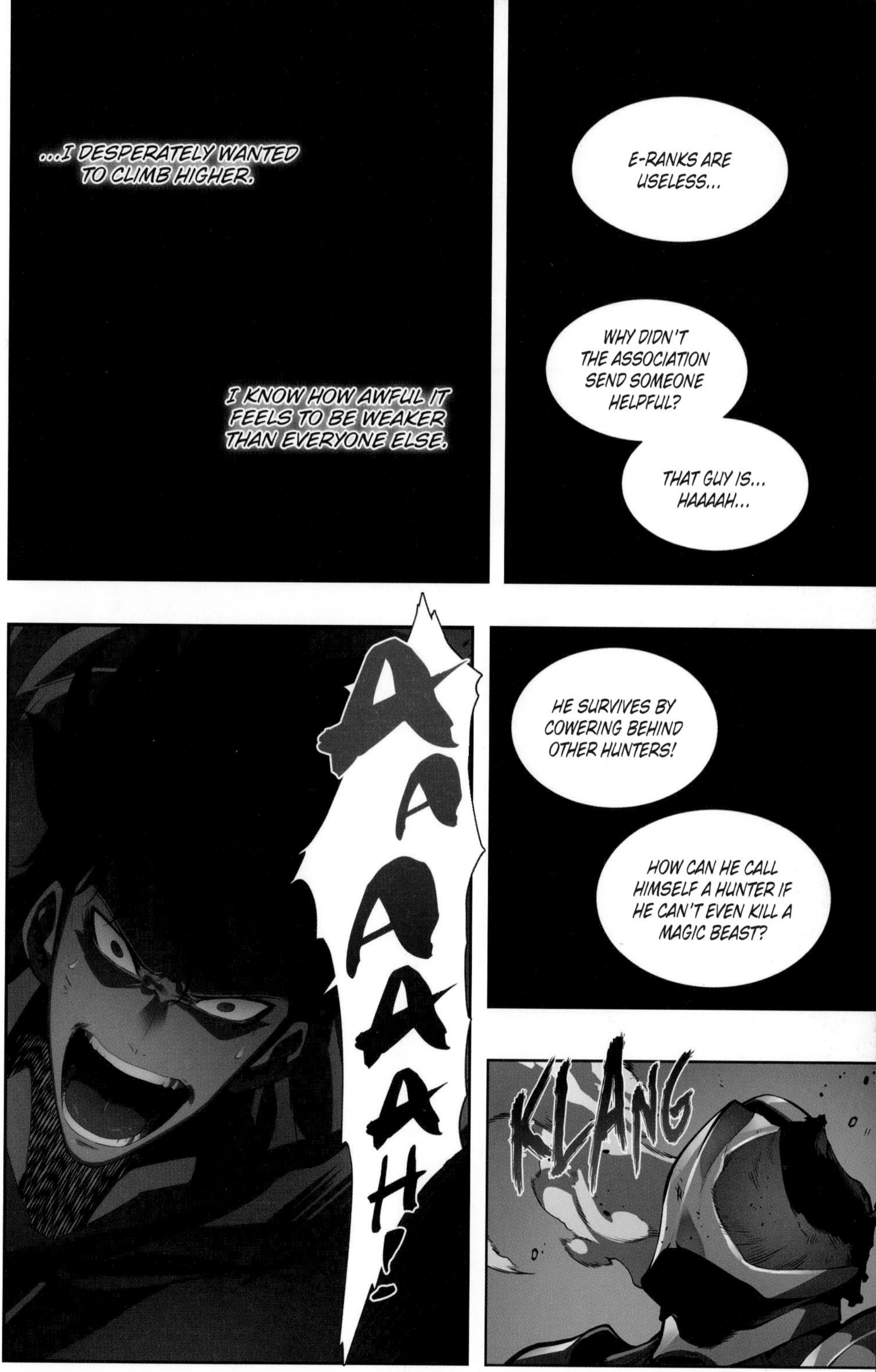

...I DESPERATELY WANTED TO CLIMB HIGHER.
I KNOW HOW AWFUL IT FEELS TO BE WEAKER THAN EVERYONE ELSE.
E-RANKS ARE USELESS...
WHY DIDN'T THE ASSOCIATION SEND SOMEONE HELPFUL?
THAT GUY IS... HAAAAH...
AAAAAAH!!
HE SURVIVES BY COWERING BEHIND OTHER HUNTERS!
HOW CAN HE CALL HIMSELF A HUNTER IF HE CAN'T EVEN KILL A MAGIC BEAST?
KLANG

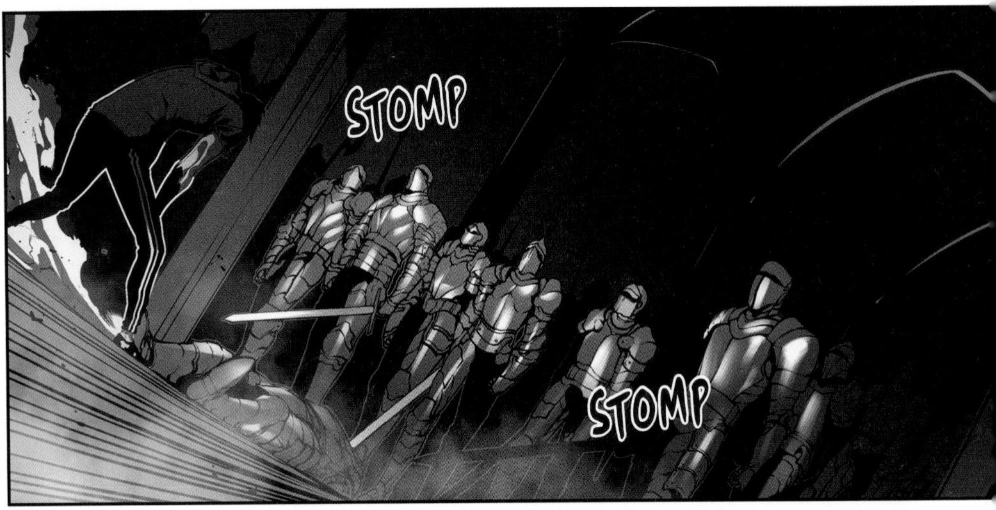
STOMP
STOMP

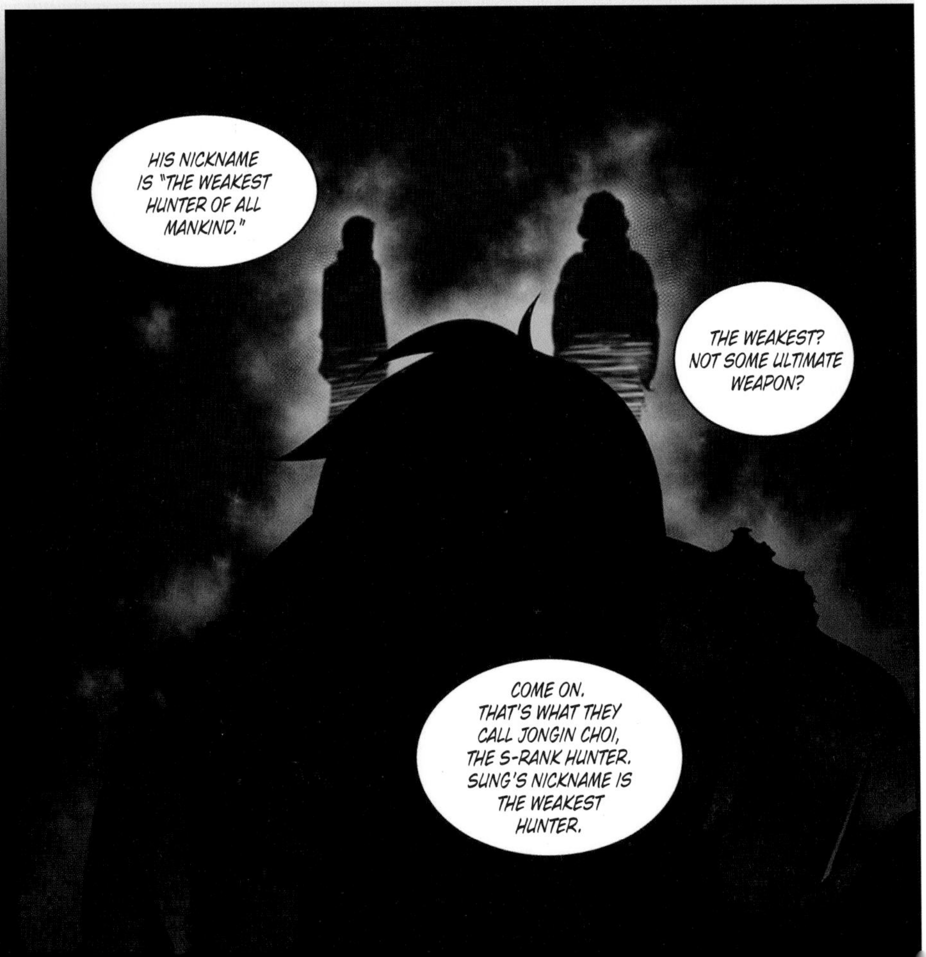
HIS NICKNAME IS "THE WEAKEST HUNTER OF ALL MANKIND."
THE WEAKEST? NOT SOME ULTIMATE WEAPON?
COME ON. THAT'S WHAT THEY CALL JONGIN CHOI, THE S-RANK HUNTER. SUNG'S NICKNAME IS THE WEAKEST HUNTER.

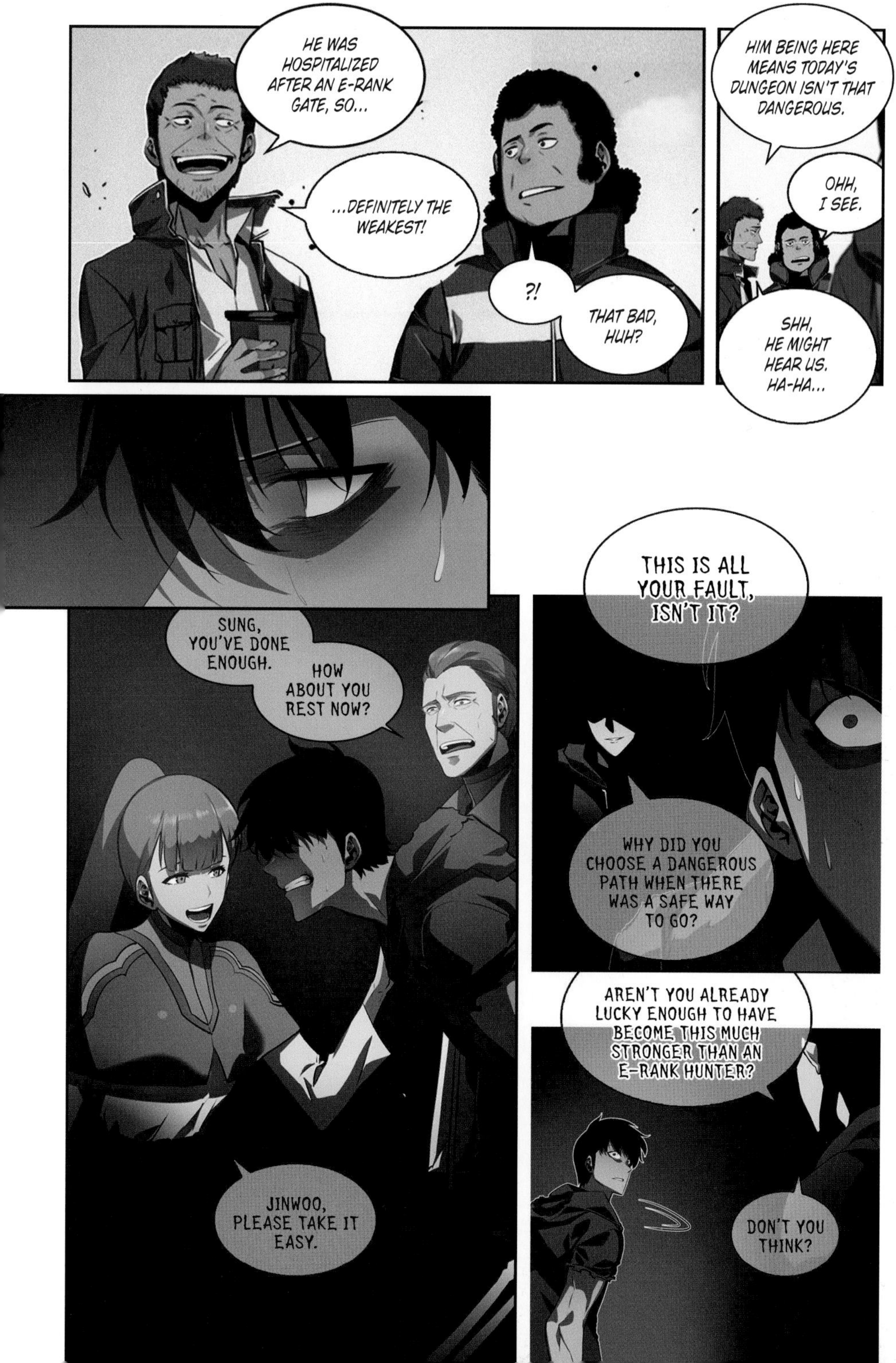
HE WAS HOSPITALIZED AFTER AN E-RANK GATE, SO...
...DEFINITELY THE WEAKEST!
?!
THAT BAD, HUH?
HIM BEING HERE MEANS TODAY'S DUNGEON ISN'T THAT DANGEROUS.
OHH, I SEE.
SHH, HE MIGHT HEAR US. HA-HA...
THIS IS ALL YOUR FAULT, ISN'T IT?
SUNG, YOU'VE DONE ENOUGH.
HOW ABOUT YOU REST NOW?
JINWOO, PLEASE TAKE IT EASY.
WHY DID YOU CHOOSE A DANGEROUS PATH WHEN THERE WAS A SAFE WAY TO GO?
AREN'T YOU ALREADY LUCKY ENOUGH TO HAVE BECOME THIS MUCH STRONGER THAN AN E-RANK HUNTER?
DON'T YOU THINK?

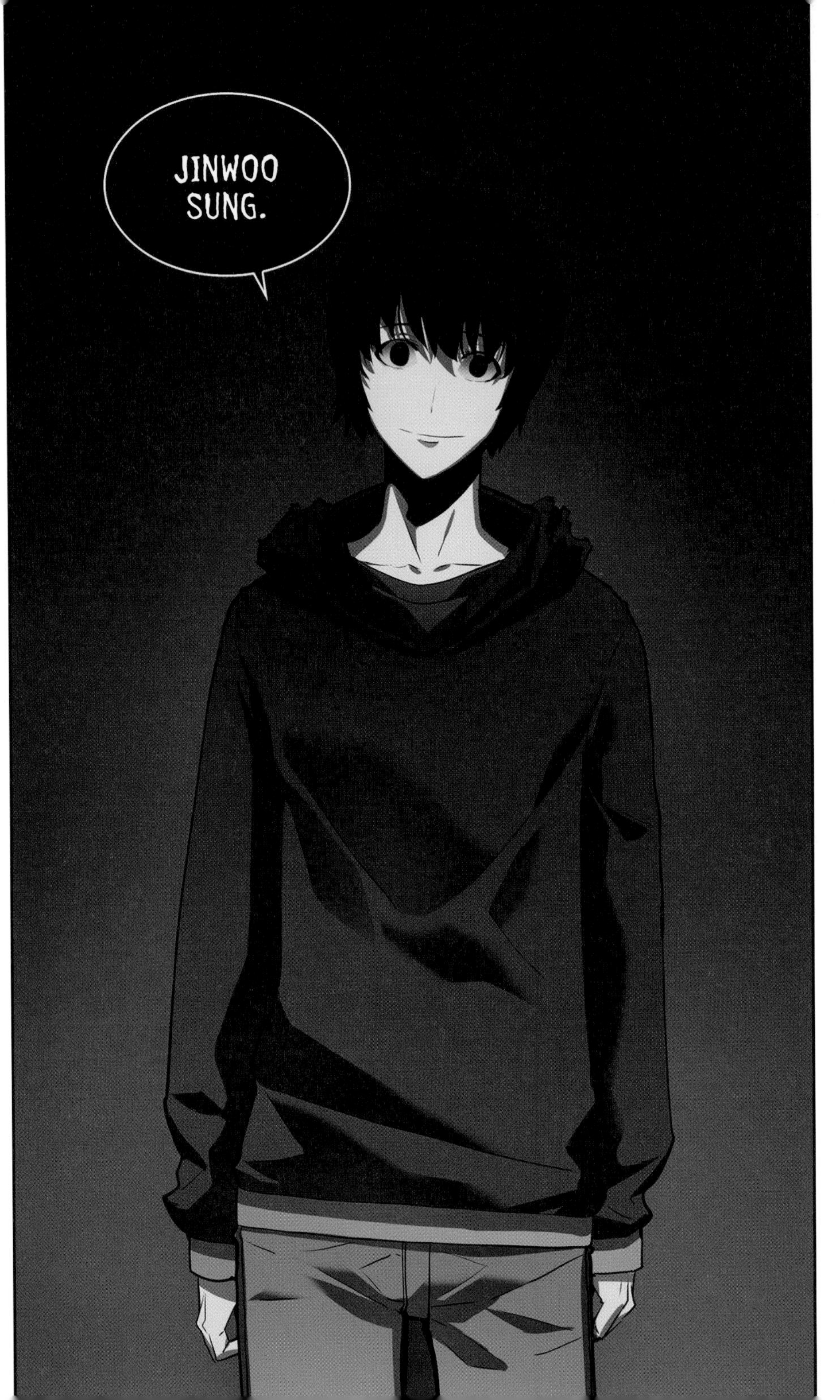
JINWOO SUNG.

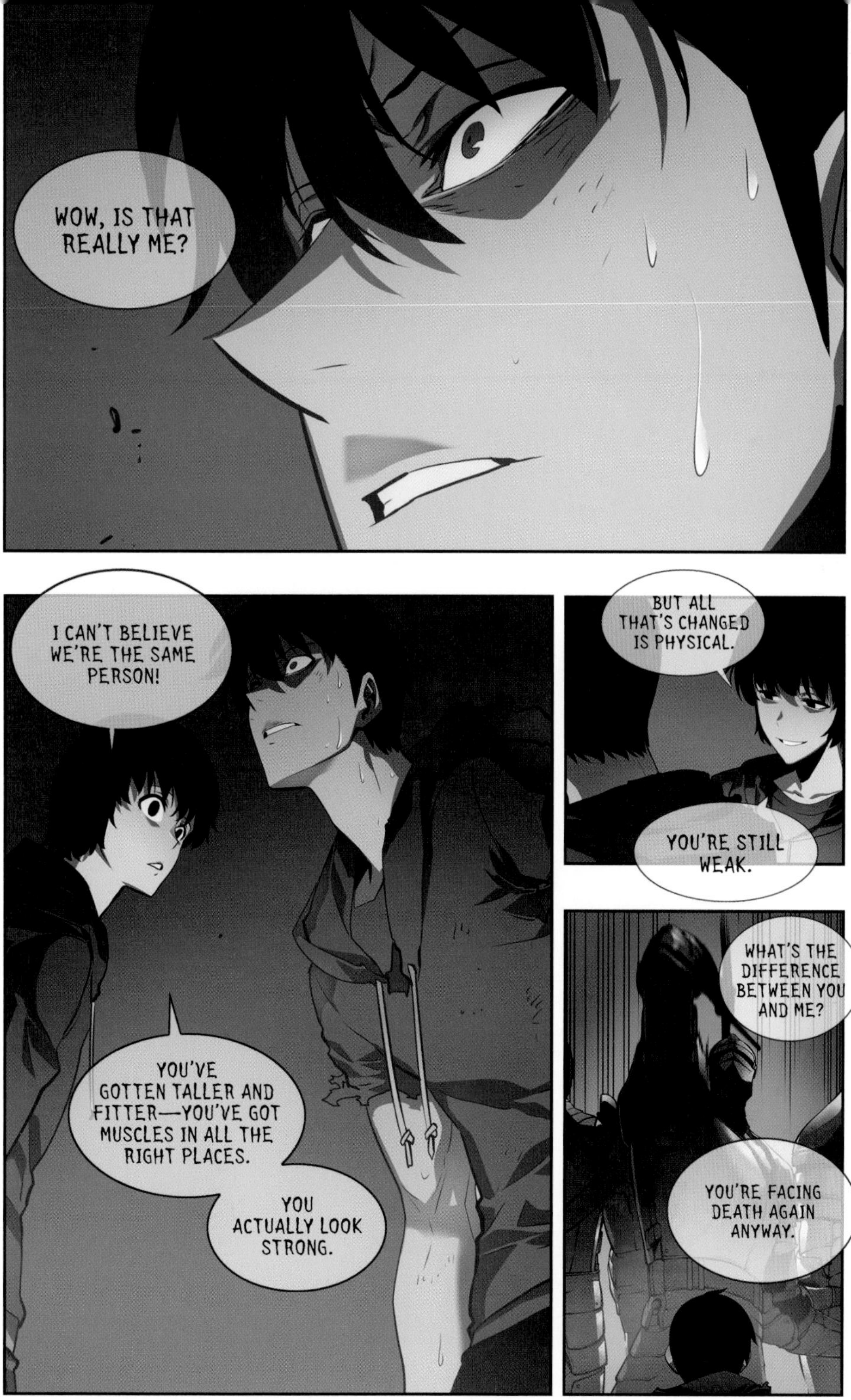
WOW, IS THAT REALLY ME?
I CAN'T BELIEVE WE'RE THE SAME PERSON!
YOU'VE GOTTEN TALLER AND FITTER—YOU'VE GOT MUSCLES IN ALL THE RIGHT PLACES.
YOU ACTUALLY LOOK STRONG.
BUT ALL THAT'S CHANGED IS PHYSICAL.
YOU'RE STILL WEAK.
WHAT'S THE DIFFERENCE BETWEEN YOU AND ME?
YOU'RE FACING DEATH AGAIN ANYWAY.

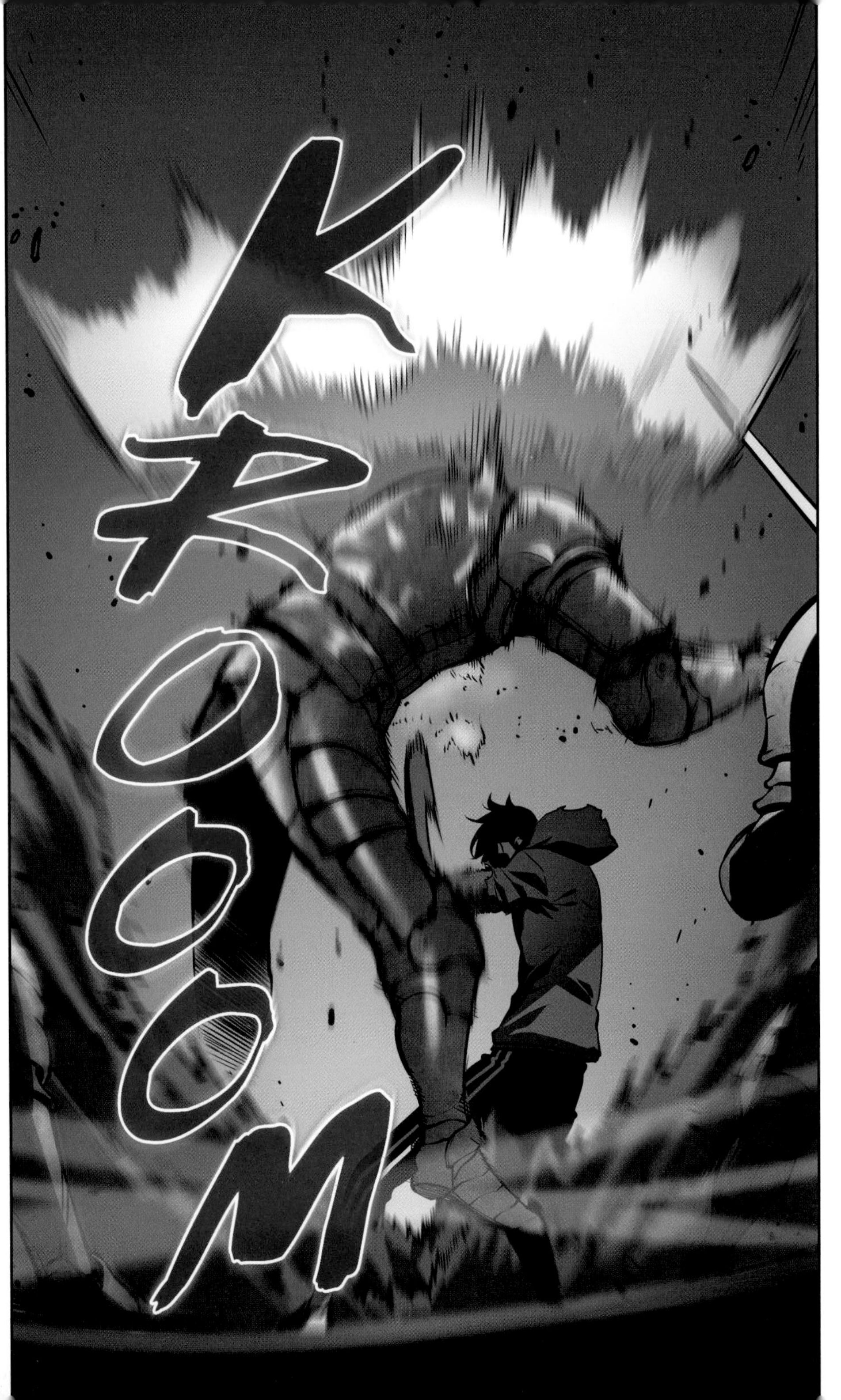
KRROOOM

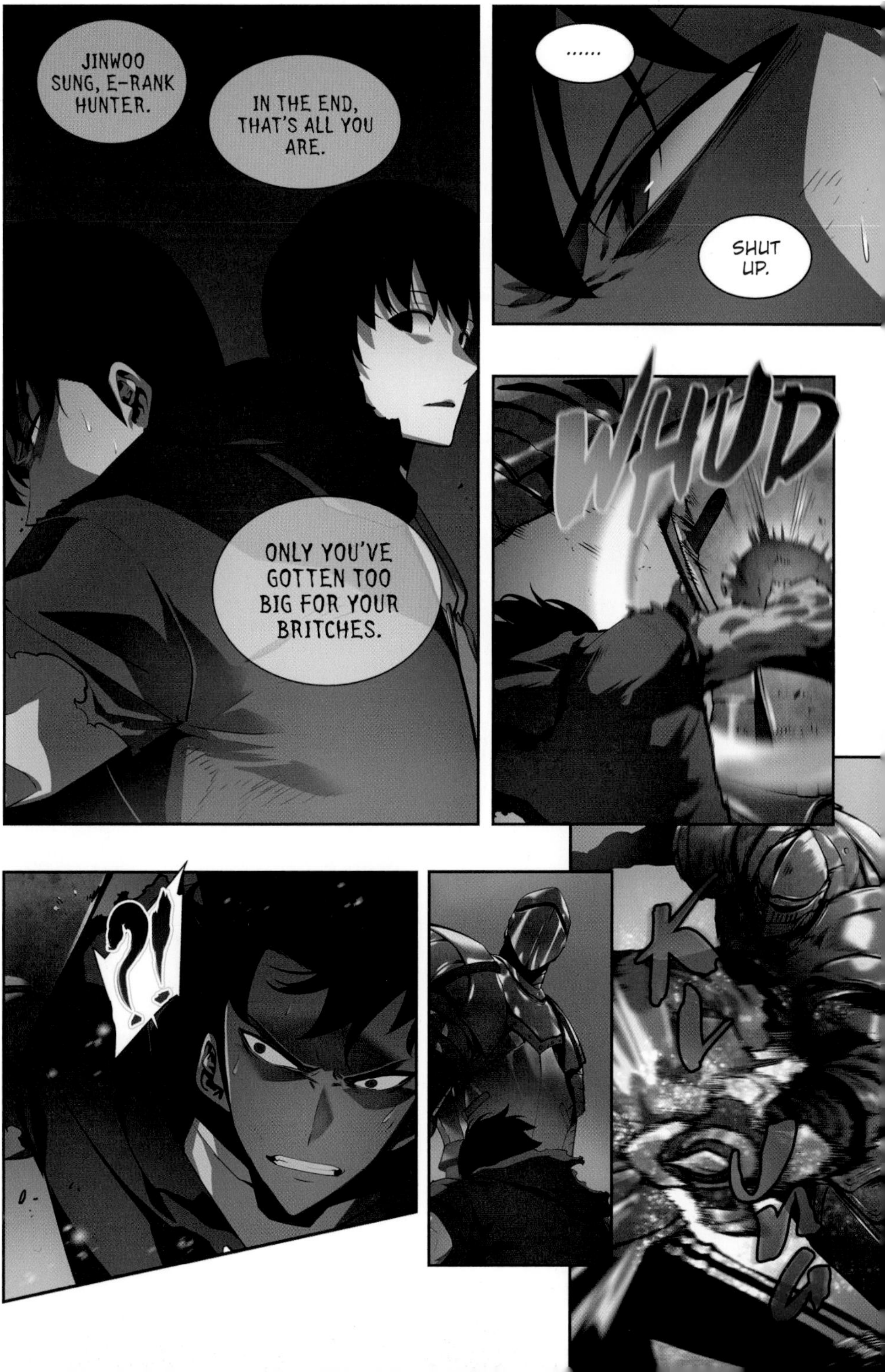
JINWOO SUNG, E-RANK HUNTER.
IN THE END, THAT'S ALL YOU ARE.
ONLY YOU'VE GOTTEN TOO BIG FOR YOUR BRITCHES.
......
SHUT UP.
WHUD
?!
O-

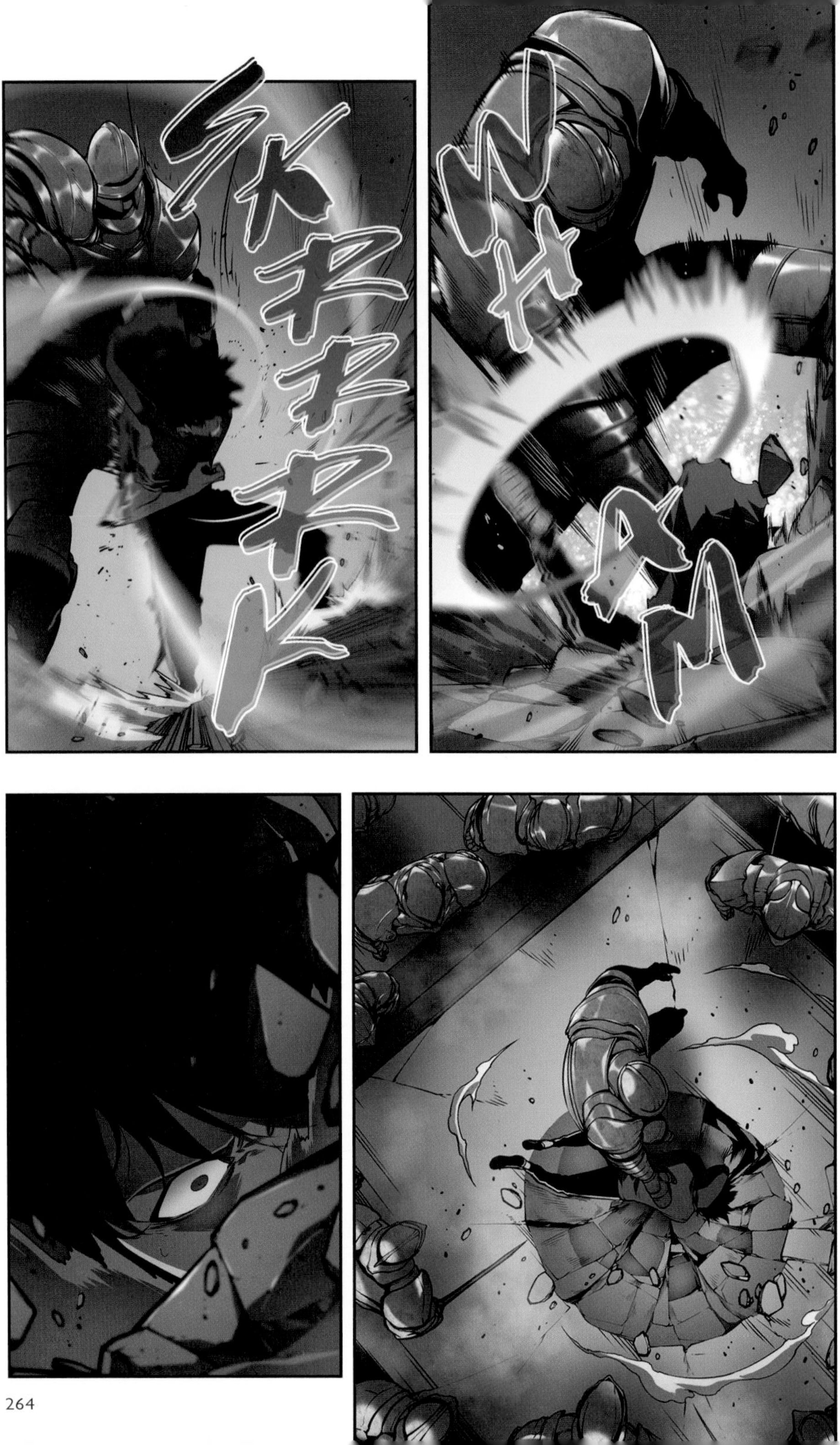
SKRRRK
WHAM

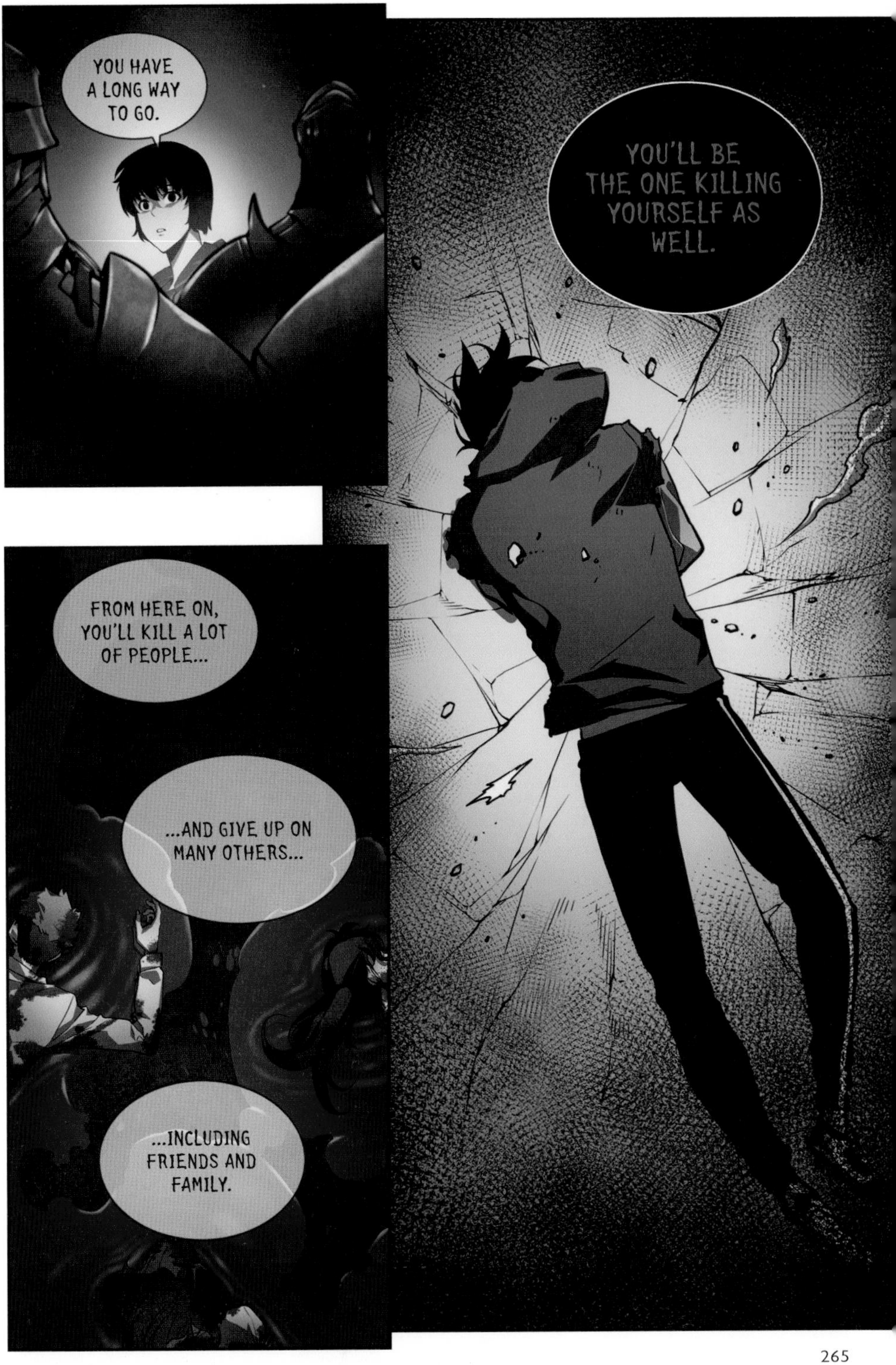
YOU HAVE A LONG WAY TO GO.
FROM HERE ON, YOU'LL KILL A LOT OF PEOPLE...
...AND GIVE UP ON MANY OTHERS...
...INCLUDING FRIENDS AND FAMILY.
YOU'LL BE THE ONE KILLING YOURSELF AS WELL.

WHAT...?

IT'S HAPPENING AGAIN.

BUT WHAT HAPPENS...

...NEXT?

I DON'T REMEMBER.

PING!

— X

ⓘ QUEST INFO

Daily Quest: Strength Training

GOAL

Push-ups	[0/100]
Sit-ups	[0/100]
Squats	[0/100]
Running	[0/10km]

WARNING
the daily quest will result in
an appropriate penalty.

WHAT'S HAPPENING?

Time remaining:
seconds

Time remaining:
seconds

Time remaining:
seconds

IS THE QUEST GOING TO BE OVER?

Time remaining:
seconds

DON'T PEOPLE SAY LUCK IS ALSO ONE OF YOUR ABILITIES?

LOOKS LIKE IT'S DECIDED THAT IT'D BE A WASTE TO LET YOU DIE HERE.

SEE YOU AGAIN.

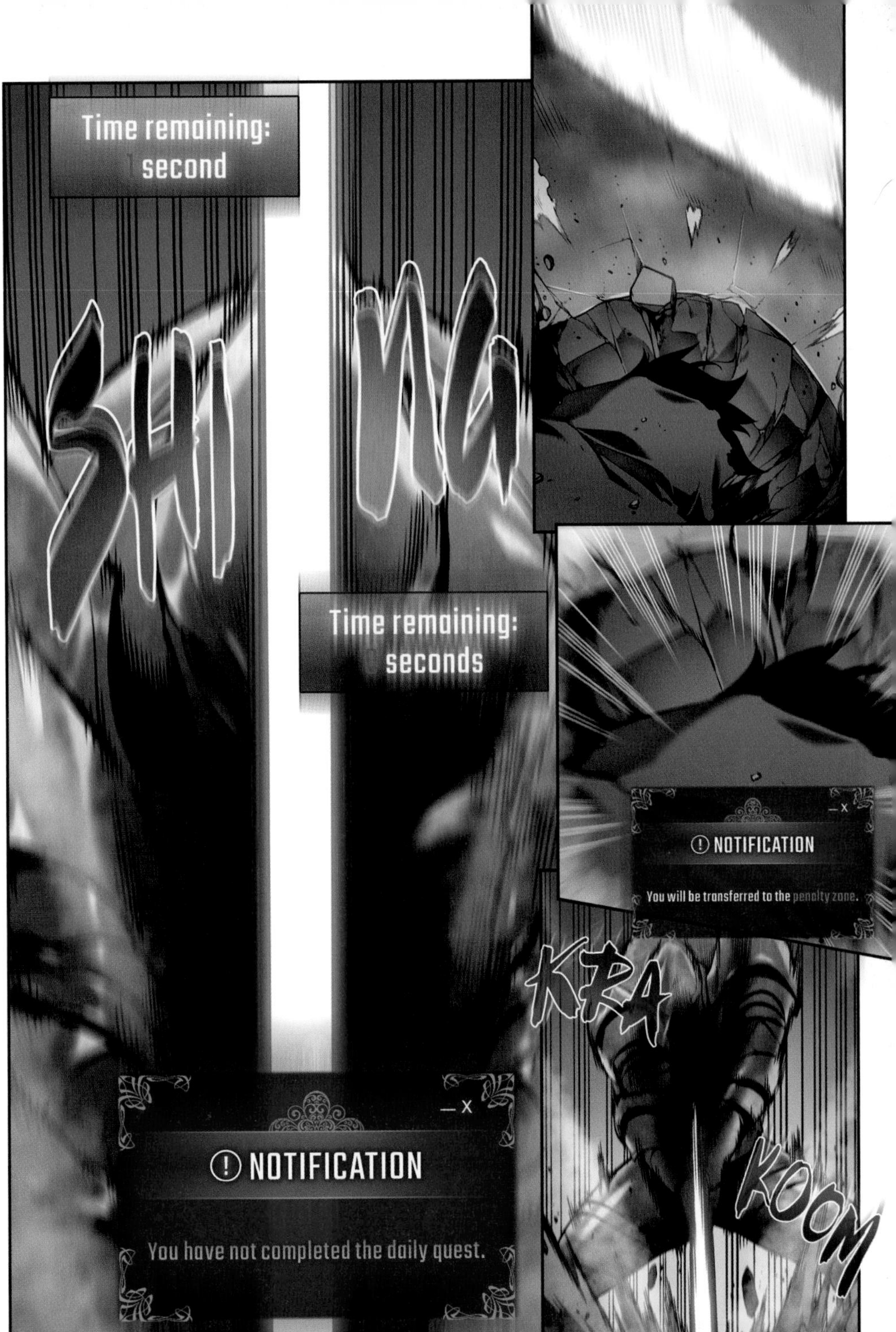
Time remaining:
1 second
SHI NG
Time remaining:
0 seconds
— x
! NOTIFICATION
You have not completed the daily quest.
— x
! NOTIFICATION
You will be transferred to the penalty zone.
KRA
KOOM

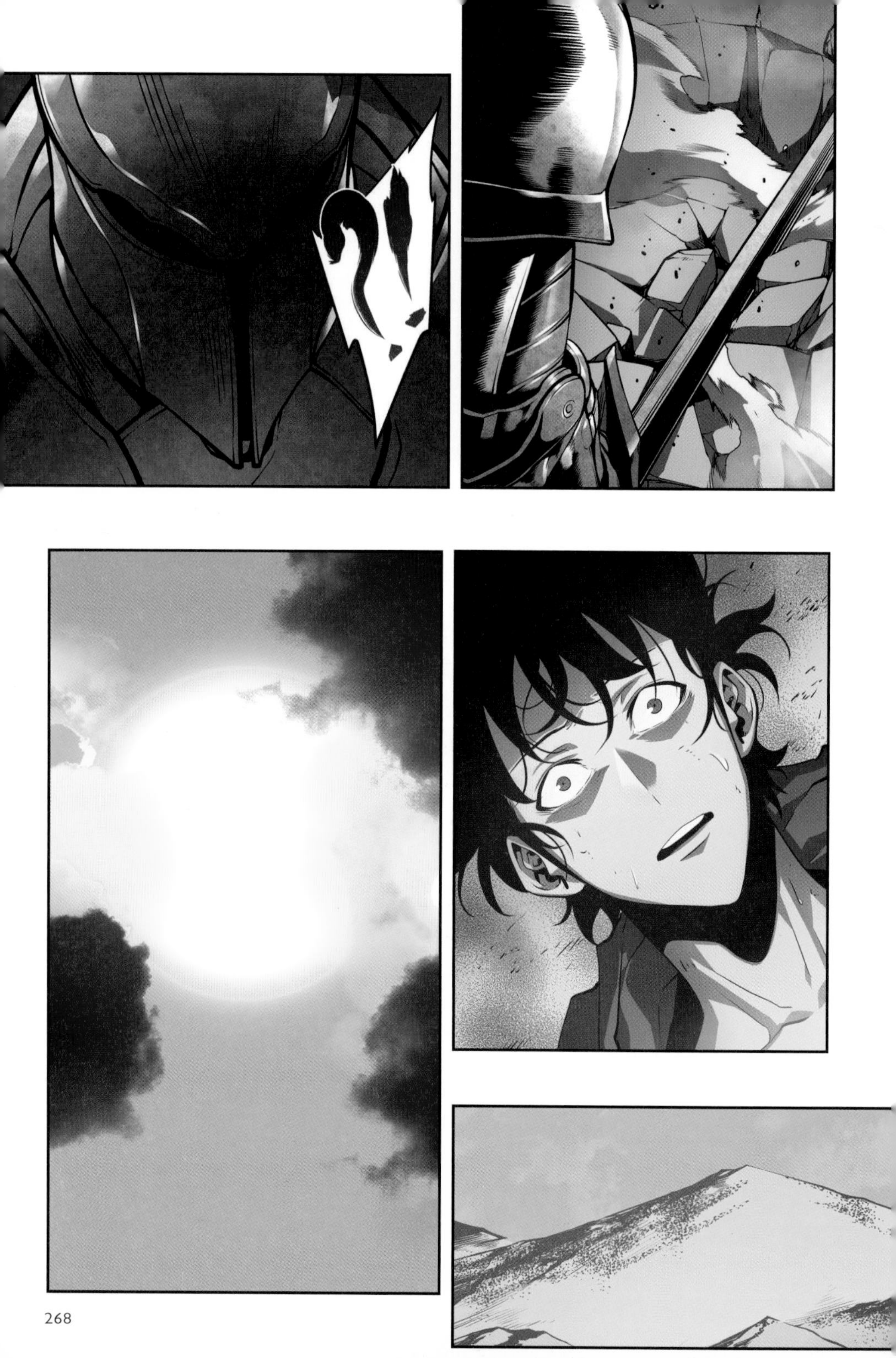
?!

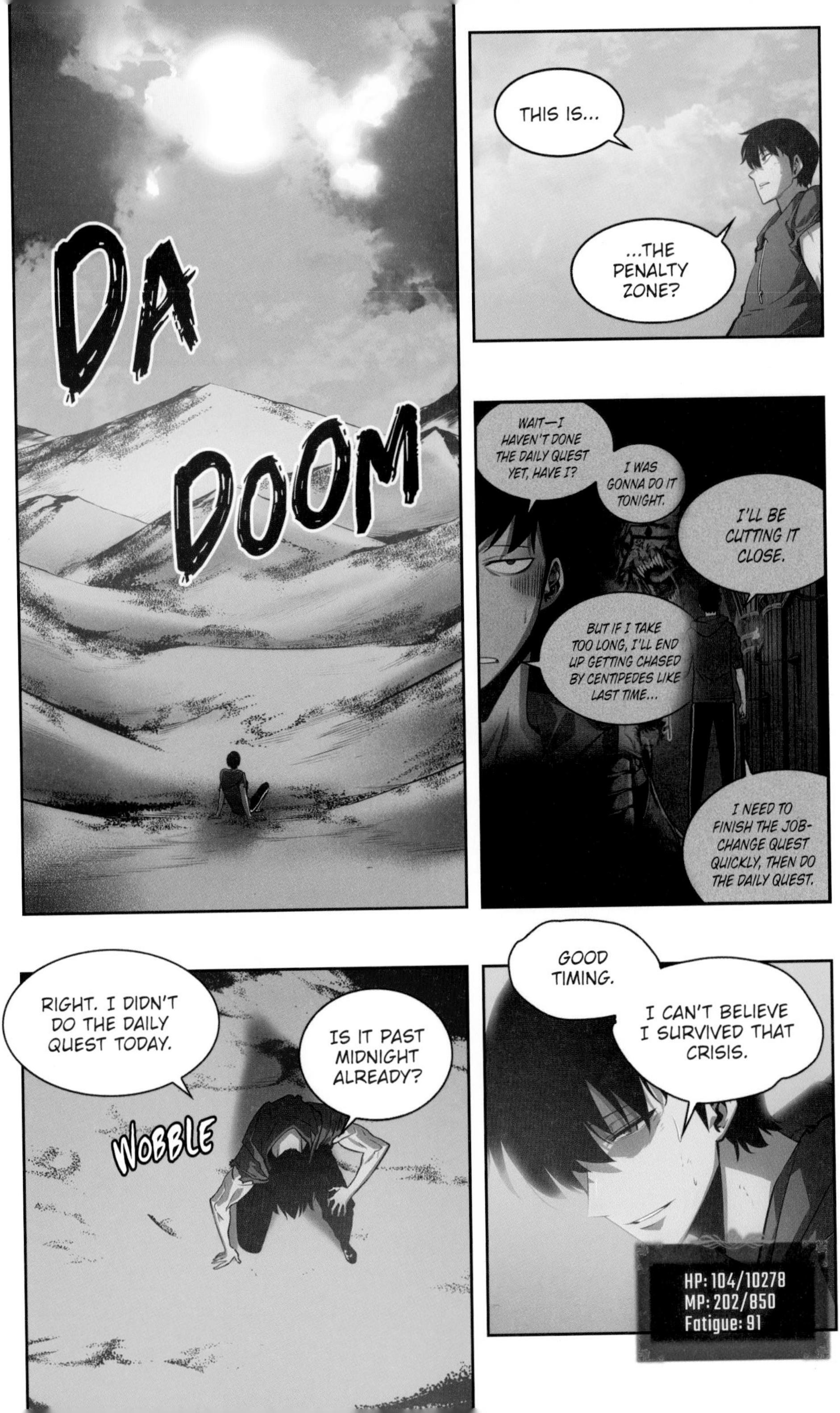
DA DOOM
THIS IS...
...THE PENALTY ZONE?
WAIT—I HAVEN'T DONE THE DAILY QUEST YET, HAVE I?
I WAS GONNA DO IT TONIGHT.
I'LL BE CUTTING IT CLOSE.
BUT IF I TAKE TOO LONG, I'LL END UP GETTING CHASED BY CENTIPEDES LIKE LAST TIME...
I NEED TO FINISH THE JOB-CHANGE QUEST QUICKLY, THEN DO THE DAILY QUEST.
RIGHT. I DIDN'T DO THE DAILY QUEST TODAY.
IS IT PAST MIDNIGHT ALREADY?
WOBBLE
GOOD TIMING.
I CAN'T BELIEVE I SURVIVED THAT CRISIS.
HP: 104/10278
MP: 202/850
Fatigue: 91

00:00:00

GOOD LUCK.

Survive as long as possible to earn advancement points that are required to be assigned a higher class.

POINTS?!

AND IT JUST KEEP GOING?!

Good luck.
00:00:01

WAS THE QUEST SO DIFFICULT THAT I NEEDED LUCK?

I PLANNED TO DO THE DAILY QUEST LATE AT NIGHT BECAUSE I THOUGHT THE JOB-CHANGE QUEST WOULD BE OVER QUICK.

00:00:02

TICK

IT DOESN'T MATTER... WHETHER YOU CALL IT LUCK OR COINCIDENCE.

PING!

SHOP.

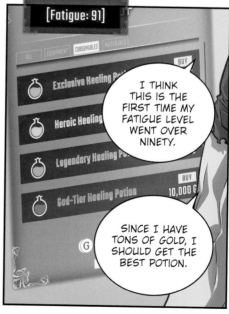

[Fatigue: 91]

ALL EQUIPMENT CONSUMABLES MATERIALS

BUY

Exclusive Healing Po

Heroic Healing

Legendary Healing P

BUY

God-Tier Healing Potion   10,000 G

I THINK THIS IS THE FIRST TIME MY FATIGUE LEVEL WENT OVER NINETY.

SINCE I HAVE TONS OF GOLD, I SHOULD GET THE BEST POTION.

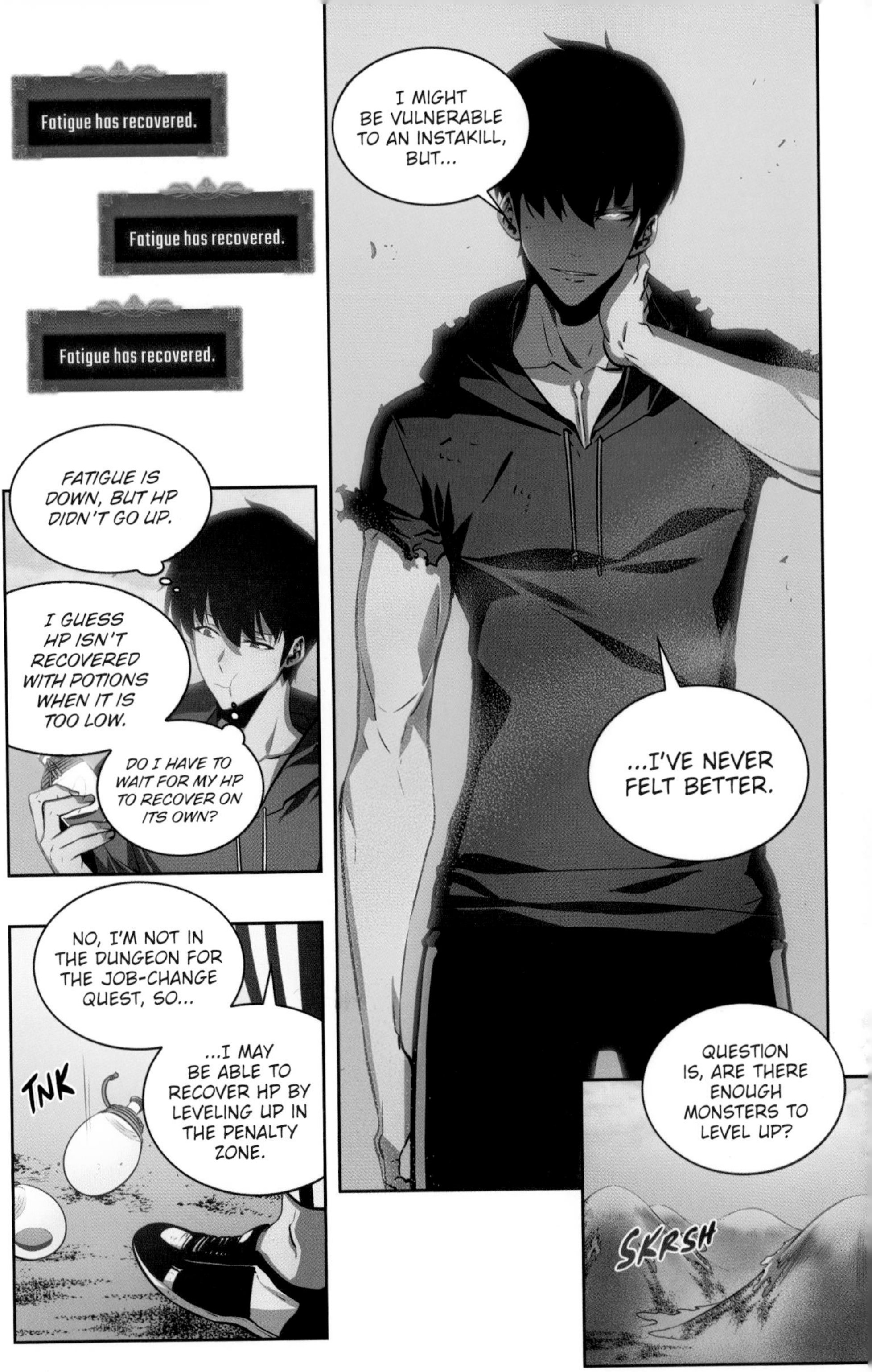
Fatigue has recovered.
Fatigue has recovered.
Fatigue has recovered.
FATIGUE IS DOWN, BUT HP DIDN'T GO UP.
I GUESS HP ISN'T RECOVERED WITH POTIONS WHEN IT IS TOO LOW.
DO I HAVE TO WAIT FOR MY HP TO RECOVER ON ITS OWN?
NO, I'M NOT IN THE DUNGEON FOR THE JOB-CHANGE QUEST, SO...
TNK
...I MAY BE ABLE TO RECOVER HP BY LEVELING UP IN THE PENALTY ZONE.
I MIGHT BE VULNERABLE TO AN INSTAKILL, BUT...
...I'VE NEVER FELT BETTER.
QUESTION IS, ARE THERE ENOUGH MONSTERS TO LEVEL UP?
SKRSH

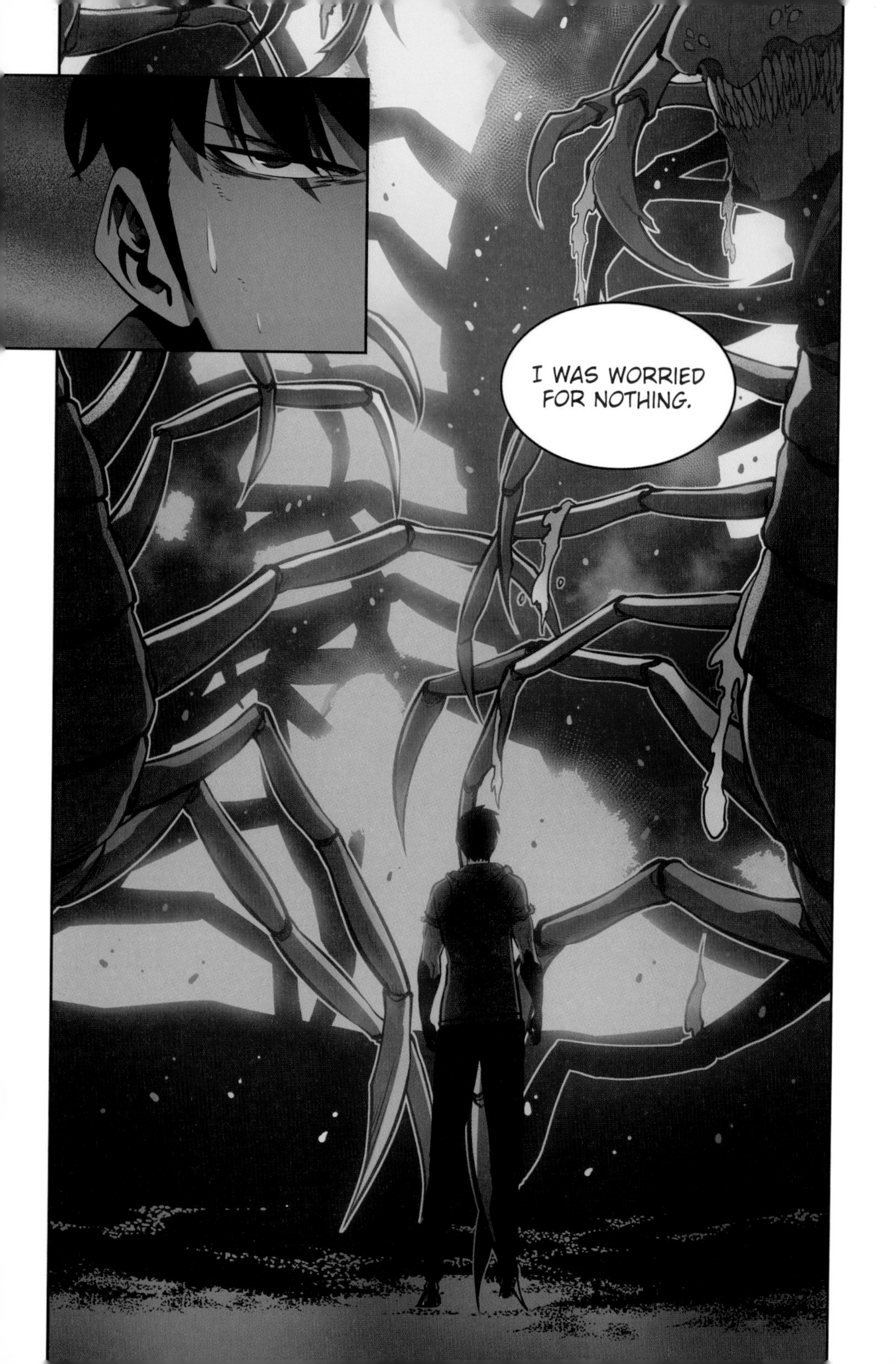
I WAS WORRIED FOR NOTHING.

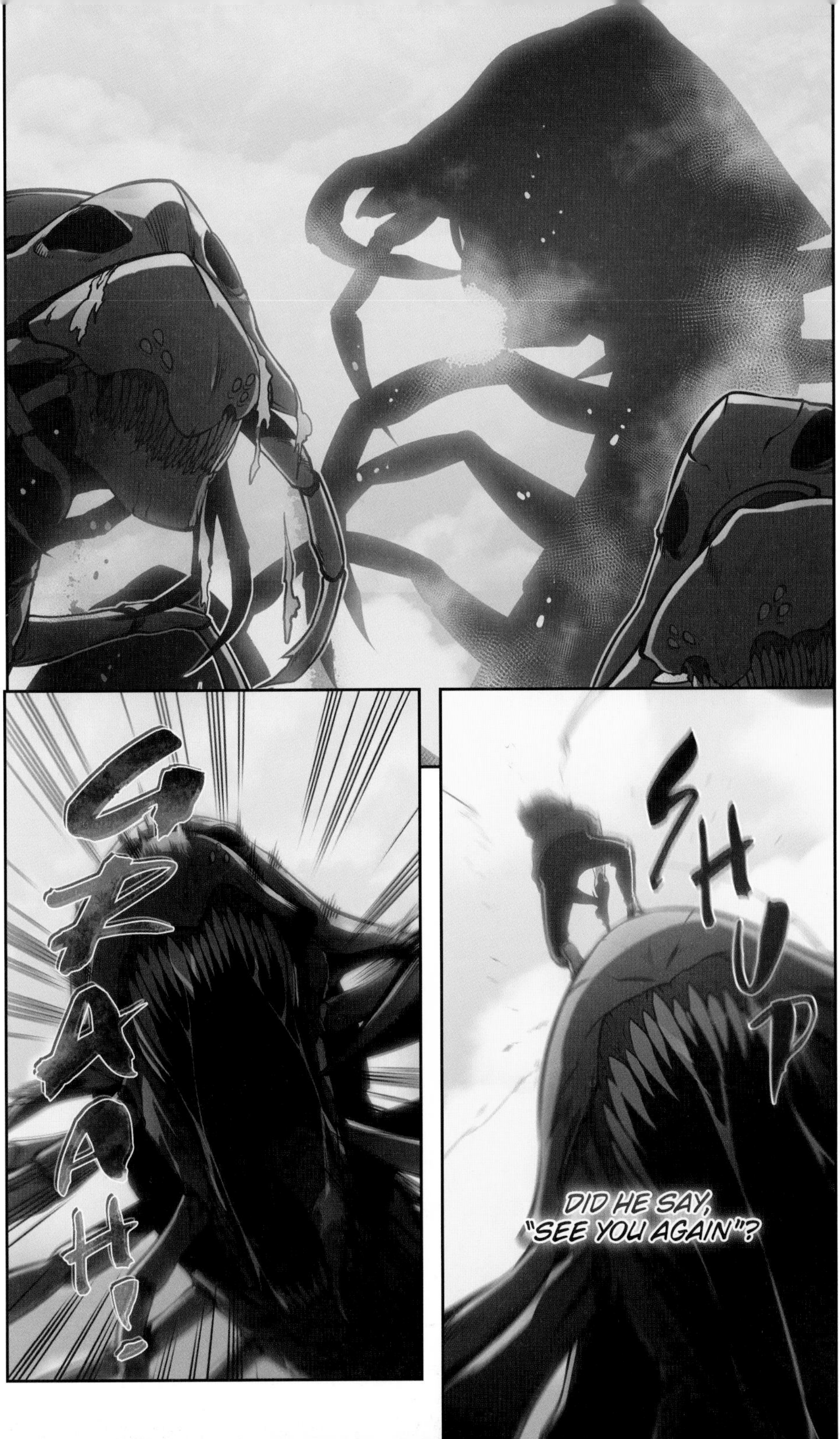
GRAAH!
SHUP
DID HE SAY,
"SEE YOU AGAIN"?

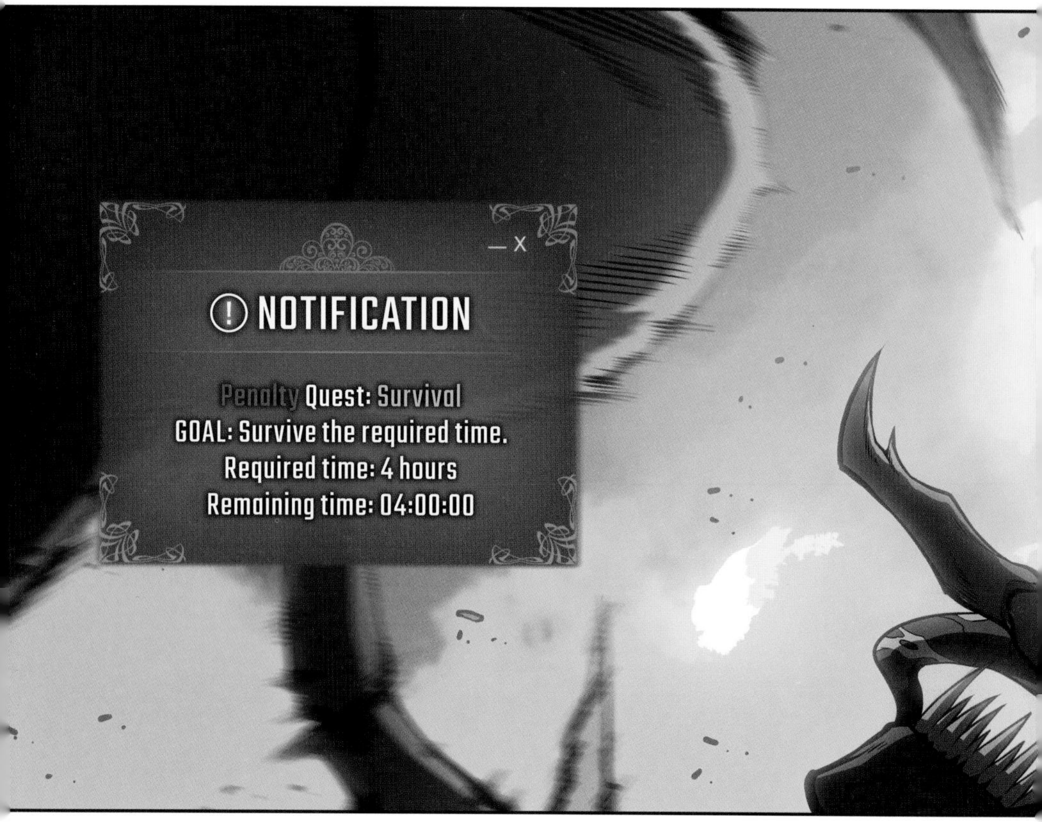
— X
NOTIFICATION
Penalty Quest: Survival
GOAL: Survive the required time.
Required time: 4 hours
Remaining time: 04:00:00

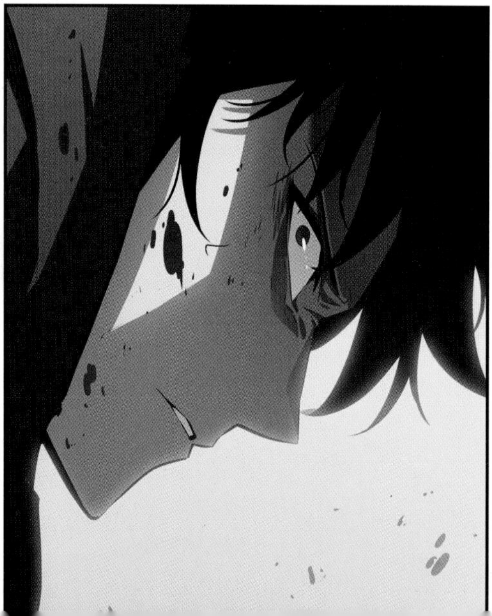

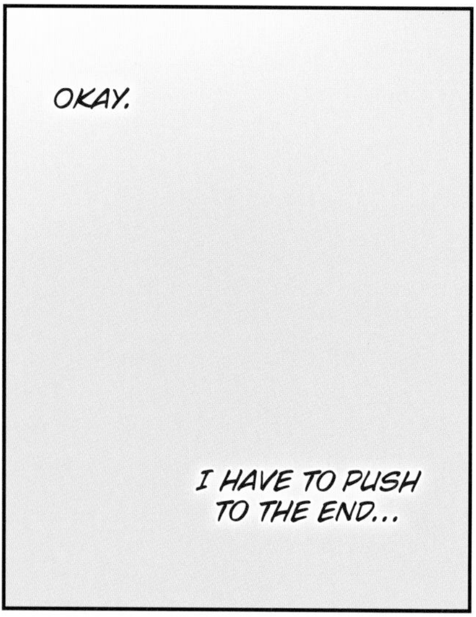
OKAY.
I HAVE TO PUSH TO THE END...

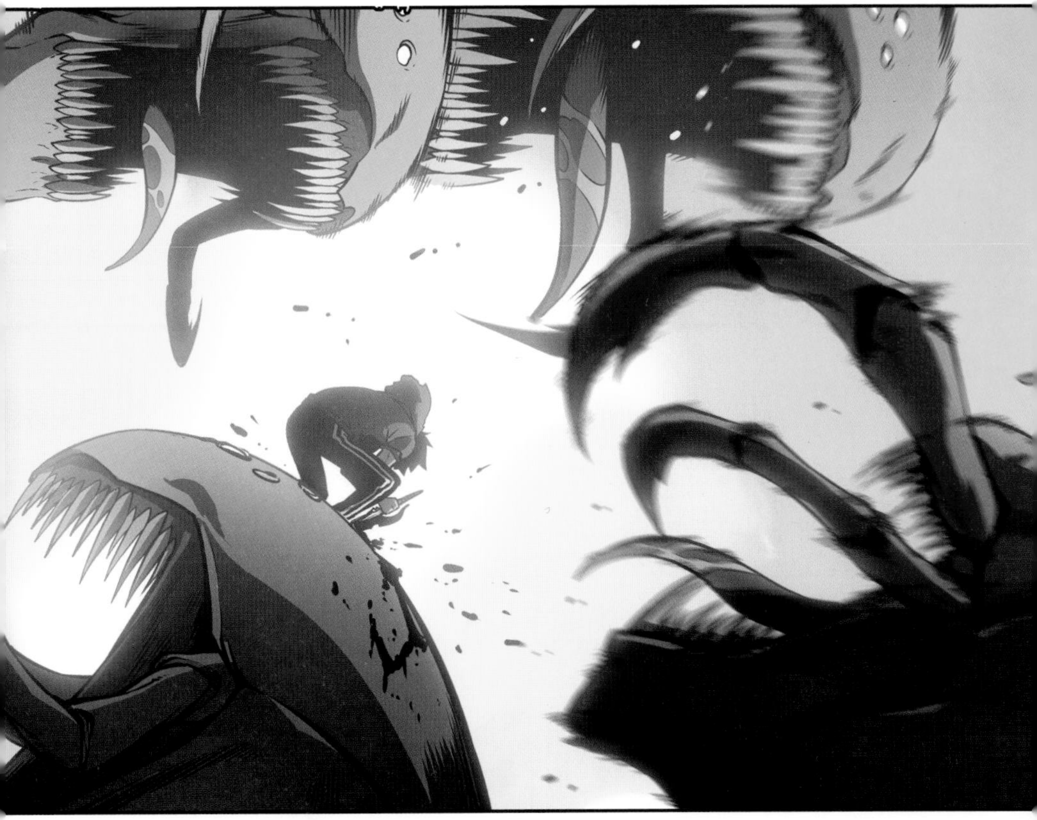
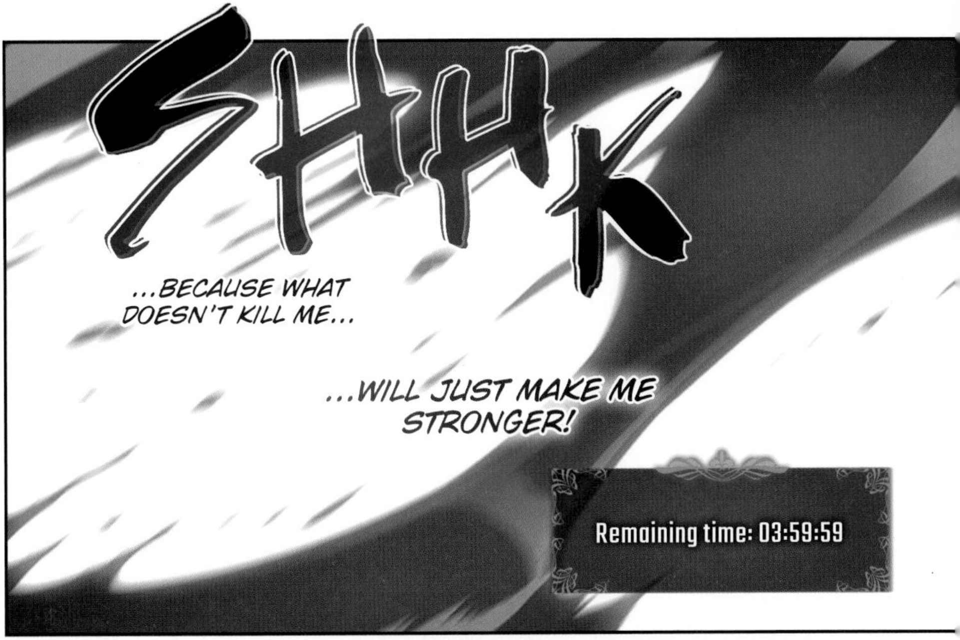
SHHK
...BECAUSE WHAT DOESN'T KILL ME...
...WILL JUST MAKE ME STRONGER!
Remaining time: 03:59:59

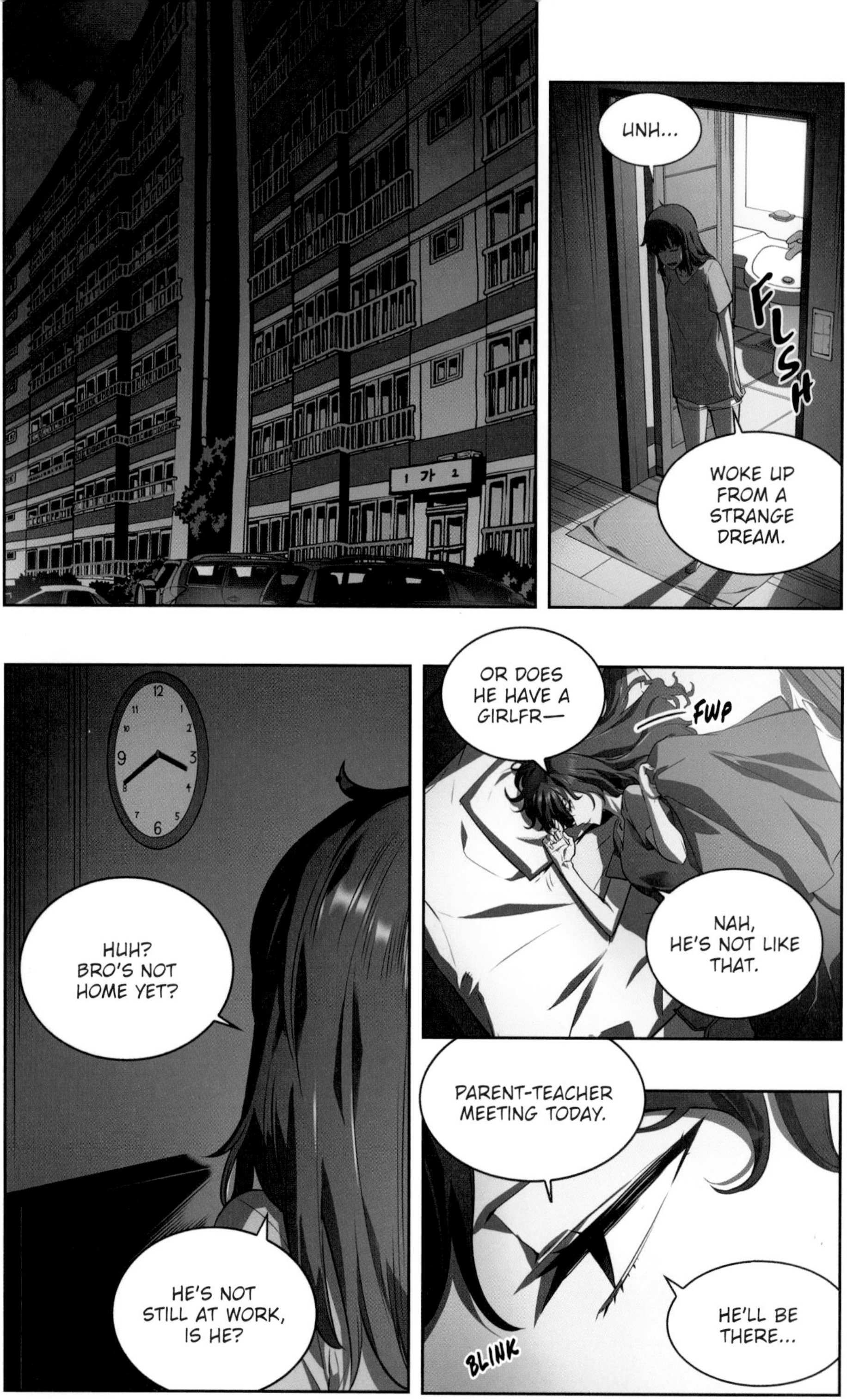
1 가 2
UNH...
FLSH
WOKE UP FROM A STRANGE DREAM.
HUH? BRO'S NOT HOME YET?
HE'S NOT STILL AT WORK, IS HE?
OR DOES HE HAVE A GIRLFR—
FWP
NAH, HE'S NOT LIKE THAT.
PARENT-TEACHER MEETING TODAY.
BLINK
HE'LL BE THERE...

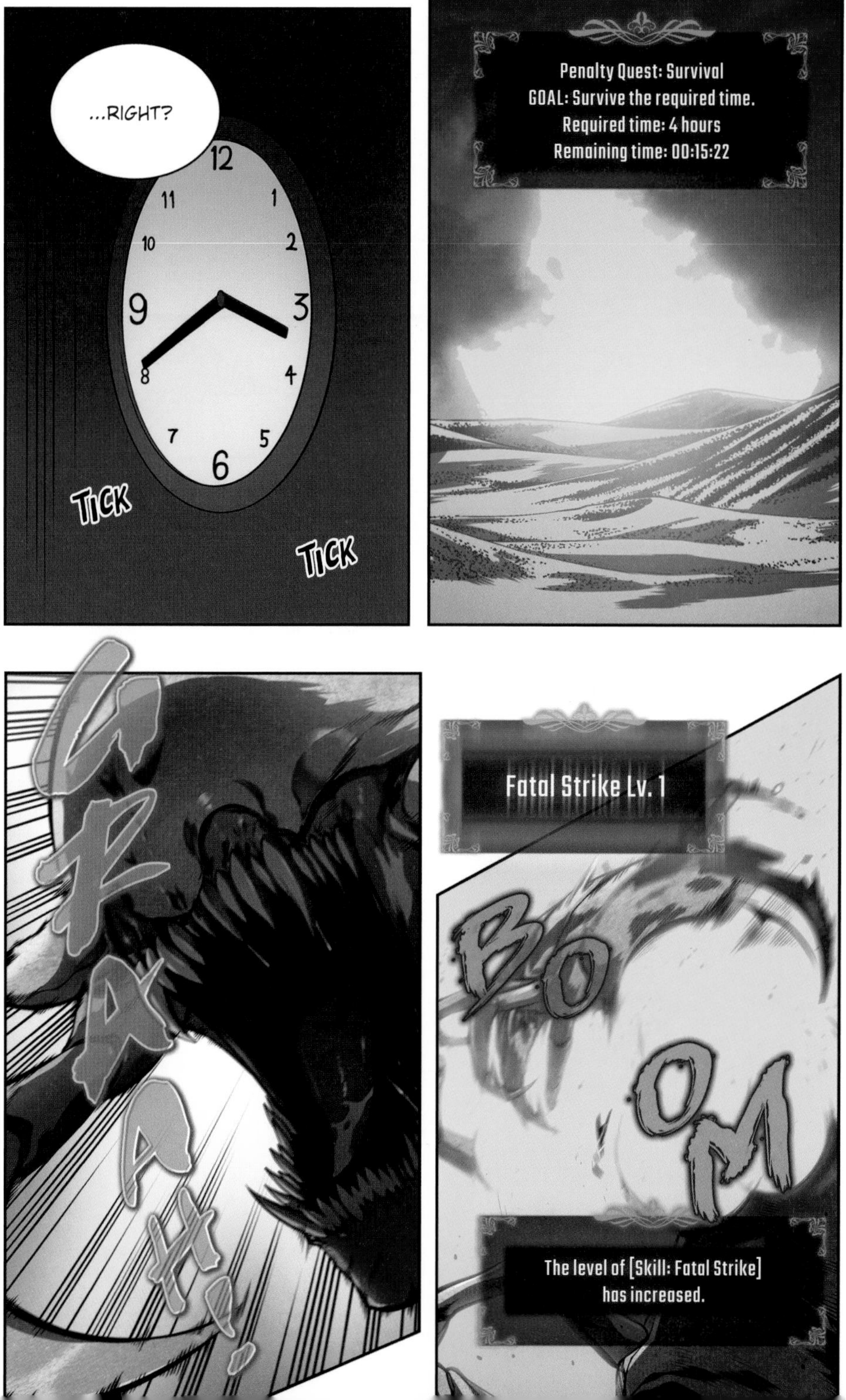
...RIGHT?
TICK
TICK
Penalty Quest: Survival
GOAL: Survive the required time.
Required time: 4 hours
Remaining time: 00:15:22
URAAH...
Fatal Strike Lv. 1
BOOM
The level of [Skill: Fatal Strike] has increased.

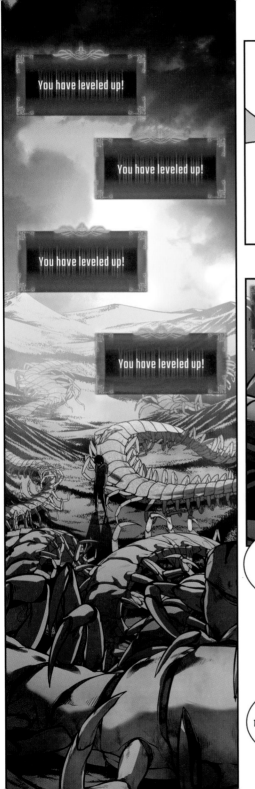

You have leveled up!

You have leveled up!

You have leveled up!

You have leveled up!

I KNEW IT! YOU HEAL WHEN YOU LEVEL UP IN THE PENALTY ZONE.

GLING!

GULP

GULP

I CAN RECOVER FATIGUE AND HP USING THE SHOP TOO.

NAME: Jinwoo Sung
LEVEL: 51
HP: 11035
MP: 1022
FATIGUE: 0

Penalty Quest: Survival
GOAL: Survive the required time.
Required time: 4 hours
Remaining time: 00:03:19

THREE MINUTES UNTIL I RETURN TO THE JOB-CHANGE QUEST...

I STILL HAVE TIME TO GET READY.

TOK

KASAKA'S VENOM FANG CAN'T PIERCE KNIGHTS' ARMOR.

ZZZZ

I NEED TO DO EVERYTHING I CAN.

I NEED A STRONGER WEAPON.

SHOP.

PING!

A DAGGER THAT CAN PENETRATE ARMOR...

EQUIPMENT		
Guardian Saber	BUY	890,000 G
Oracle Sword	BUY	1,300,000 G
Stone Ax	BUY	1,800,000 G
Knight Killer	BUY	2,800,000 G
G		3,102,629

BUY

THERE IT IS.

Stone Ax   00,000 G

BUY

Knight Killer   2,800,000 G

3,102,629

You have purchased Knight Killer.

2.8 MILLION GOLD.

IT'S A LITTLE EXPENSIVE, BUT...

ZZZT

...THIS SHOULD BE A GAME CHANGER.

ZZT

ZZT

ZZT

[ITEM: Knight Killer]
ACQUISITION DIFFICULTY: B
CATEGORY: Dagger
ATTACK POWER +75
—BUFF: Kill the Knights: Damage output increases by 25% when facing armored opponents.

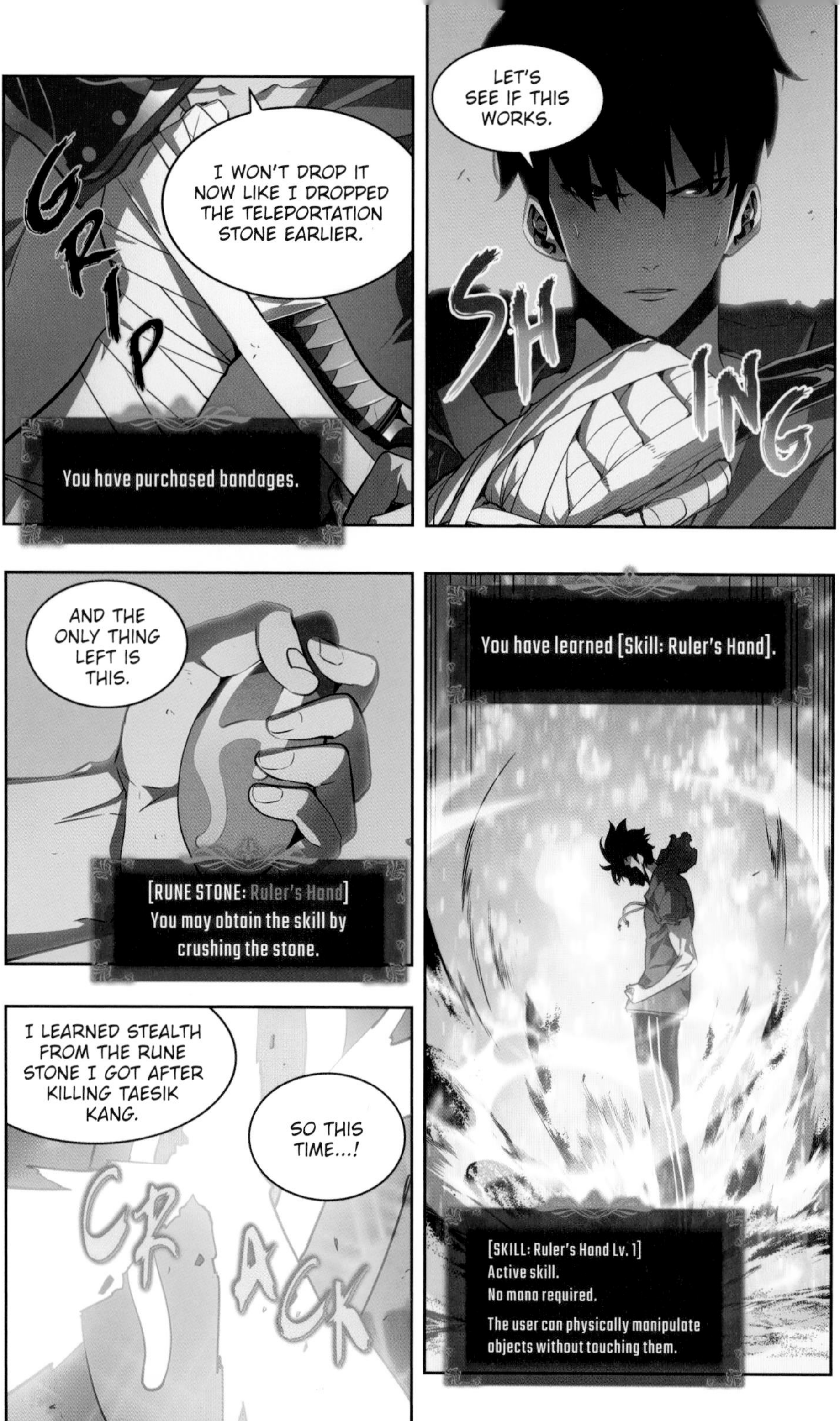
GRIP
I WON'T DROP IT NOW LIKE I DROPPED THE TELEPORTATION STONE EARLIER.
You have purchased bandages.
LET'S SEE IF THIS WORKS.
SHING
AND THE ONLY THING LEFT IS THIS.
[RUNE STONE: Ruler's Hand]
You may obtain the skill by crushing the stone.
I LEARNED STEALTH FROM THE RUNE STONE I GOT AFTER KILLING TAESIK KANG.
SO THIS TIME...!
CRACK
You have learned [Skill: Ruler's Hand].
[SKILL: Ruler's Hand Lv. 1]
Active skill.
No mana required.
The user can physically manipulate objects without touching them.

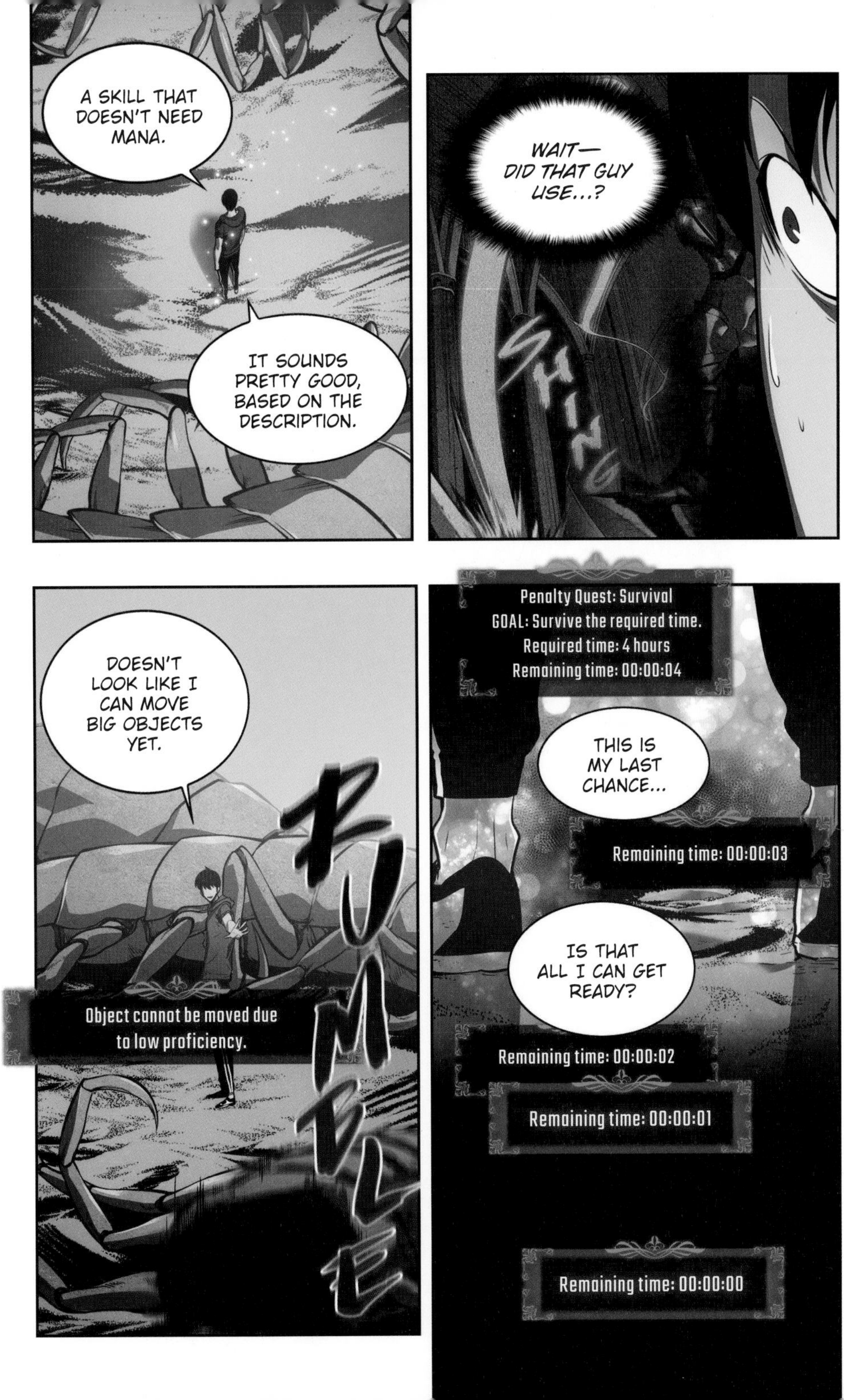
A SKILL THAT DOESN'T NEED MANA.
IT SOUNDS PRETTY GOOD, BASED ON THE DESCRIPTION.
WAIT— DID THAT GUY USE...?
SHING
DOESN'T LOOK LIKE I CAN MOVE BIG OBJECTS YET.
RUMBLE
Object cannot be moved due to low proficiency.
Penalty Quest: Survival
GOAL: Survive the required time.
Required time: 4 hours
Remaining time: 00:00:04
THIS IS MY LAST CHANCE...
Remaining time: 00:00:03
IS THAT ALL I CAN GET READY?
Remaining time: 00:00:02
Remaining time: 00:00:01
Remaining time: 00:00:00

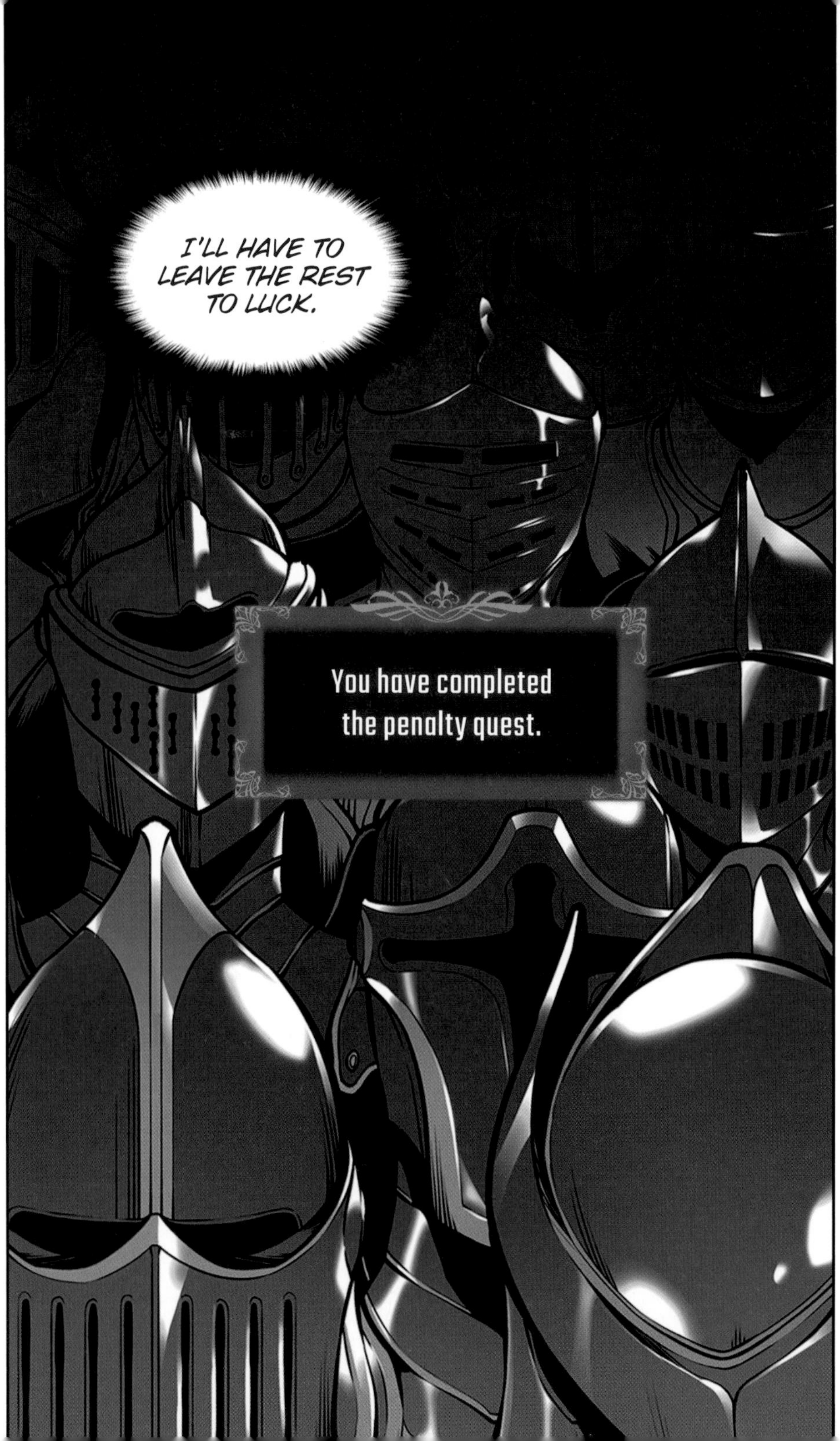
I'LL HAVE TO LEAVE THE REST TO LUCK.
You have completed the penalty quest.

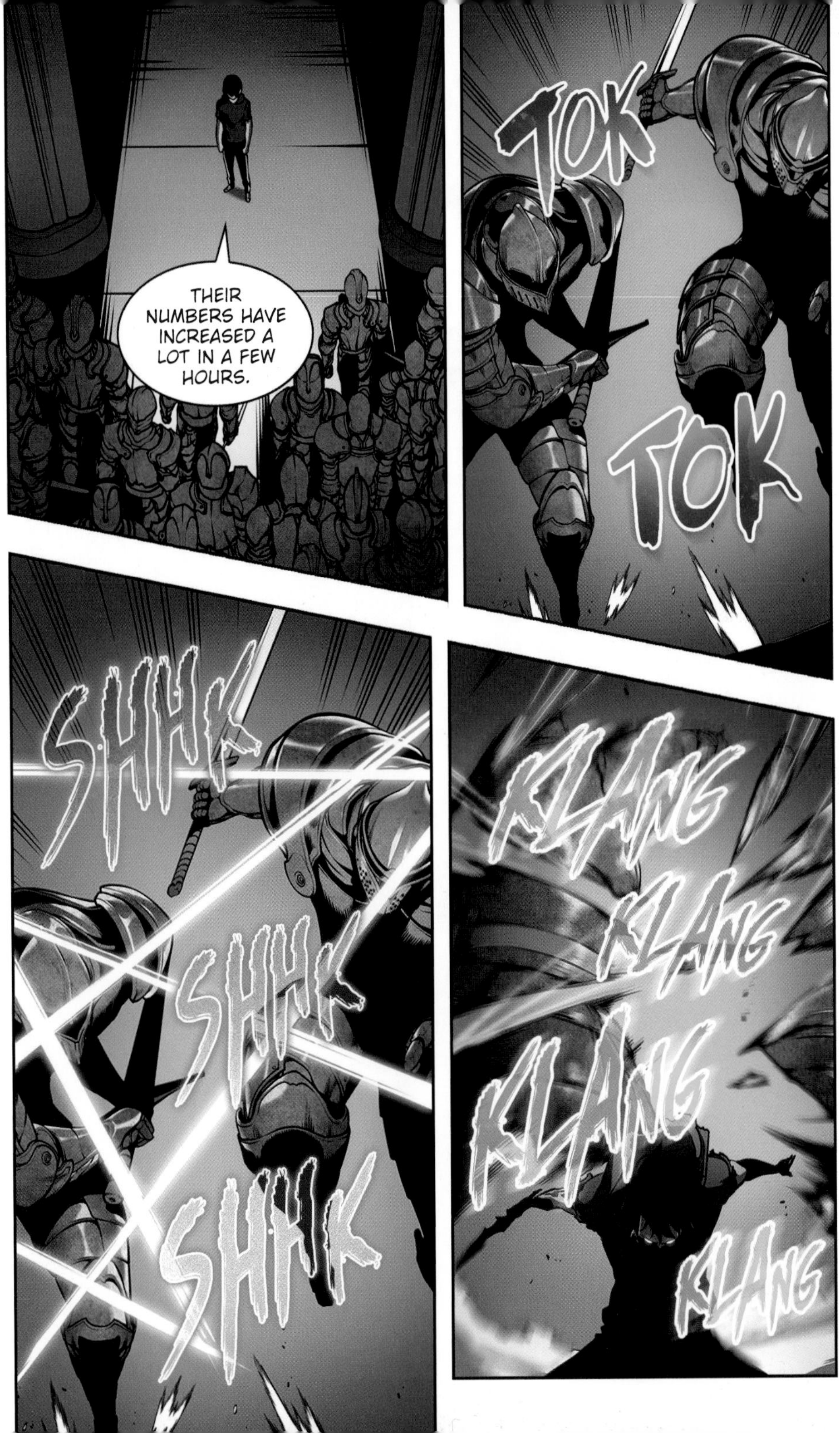
THEIR NUMBERS HAVE INCREASED A LOT IN A FEW HOURS.
TOK
TOK
SHHK
SHHK
SHHK
KLANG
KLANG
KLANG
KLANG

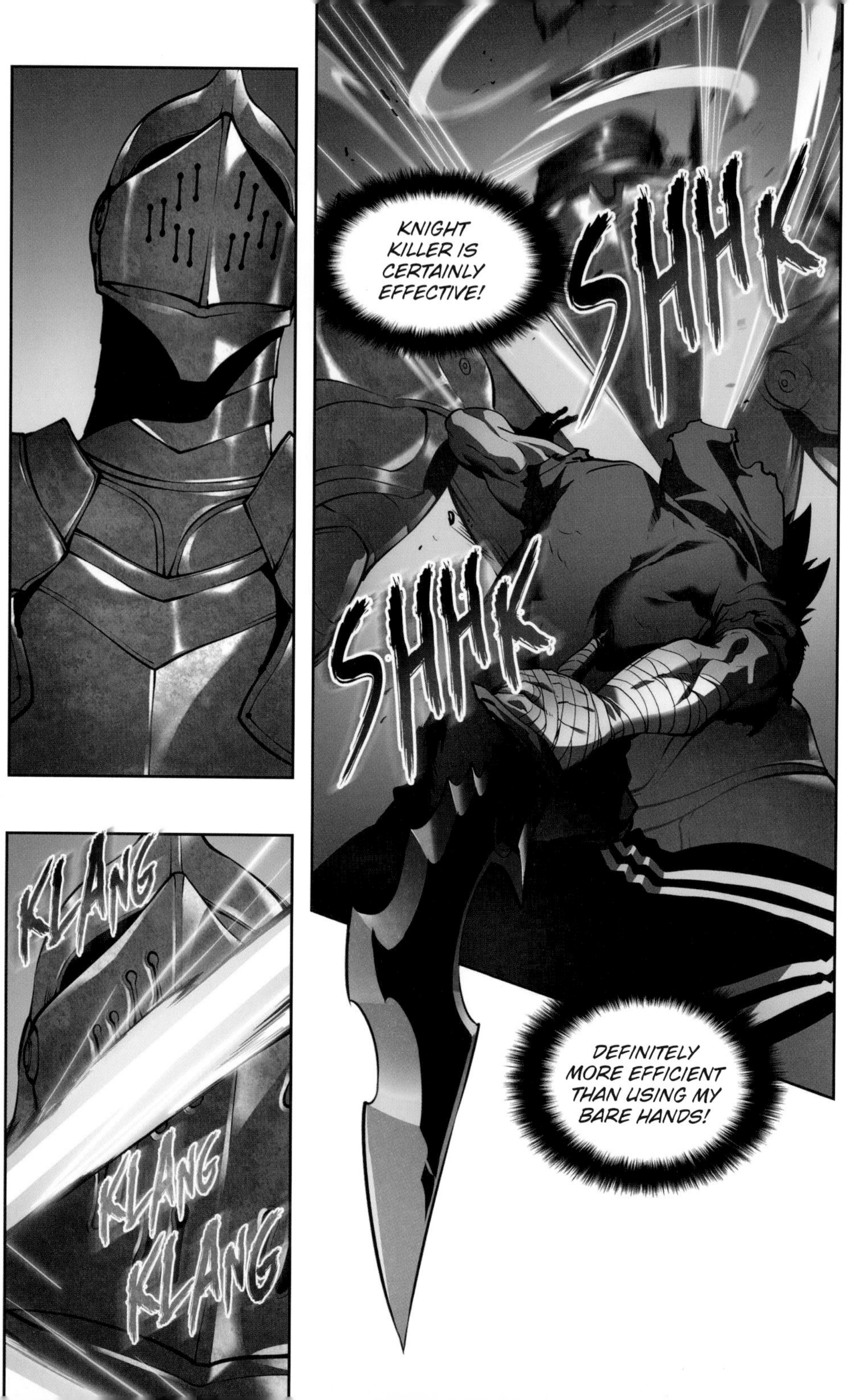
KLANG
KLANG
KLANG
KNIGHT KILLER IS CERTAINLY EFFECTIVE!
SHHK
SHHK
DEFINITELY MORE EFFICIENT THAN USING MY BARE HANDS!

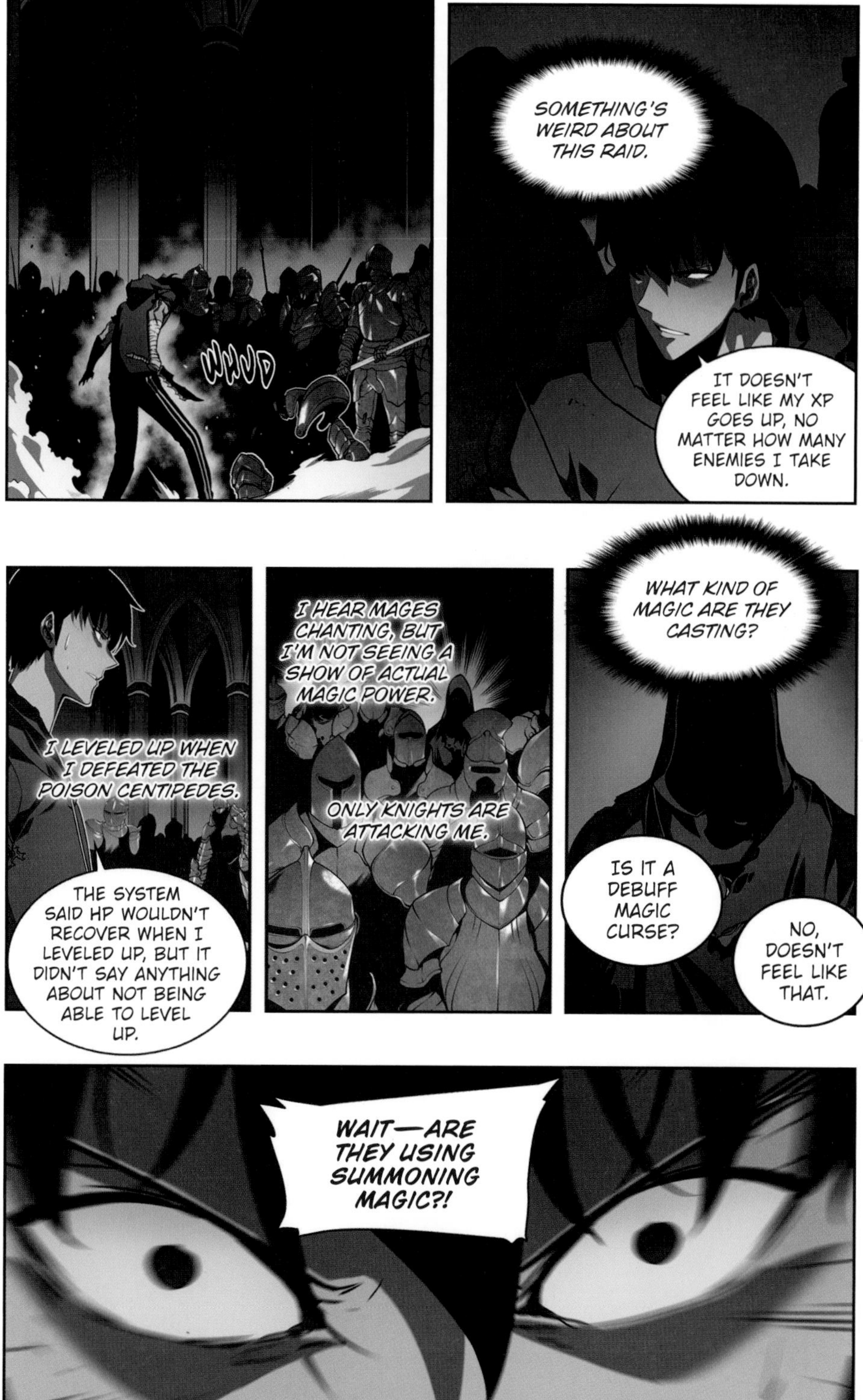
WHUD
SOMETHING'S WEIRD ABOUT THIS RAID.
IT DOESN'T FEEL LIKE MY XP GOES UP, NO MATTER HOW MANY ENEMIES I TAKE DOWN.
I LEVELED UP WHEN I DEFEATED THE POISON CENTIPEDES.
THE SYSTEM SAID HP WOULDN'T RECOVER WHEN I LEVELED UP, BUT IT DIDN'T SAY ANYTHING ABOUT NOT BEING ABLE TO LEVEL UP.
I HEAR MAGES CHANTING, BUT I'M NOT SEEING A SHOW OF ACTUAL MAGIC POWER.
ONLY KNIGHTS ARE ATTACKING ME.
WHAT KIND OF MAGIC ARE THEY CASTING?
IS IT A DEBUFF MAGIC CURSE?
NO, DOESN'T FEEL LIKE THAT.
WAIT—ARE THEY USING SUMMONING MAGIC?!

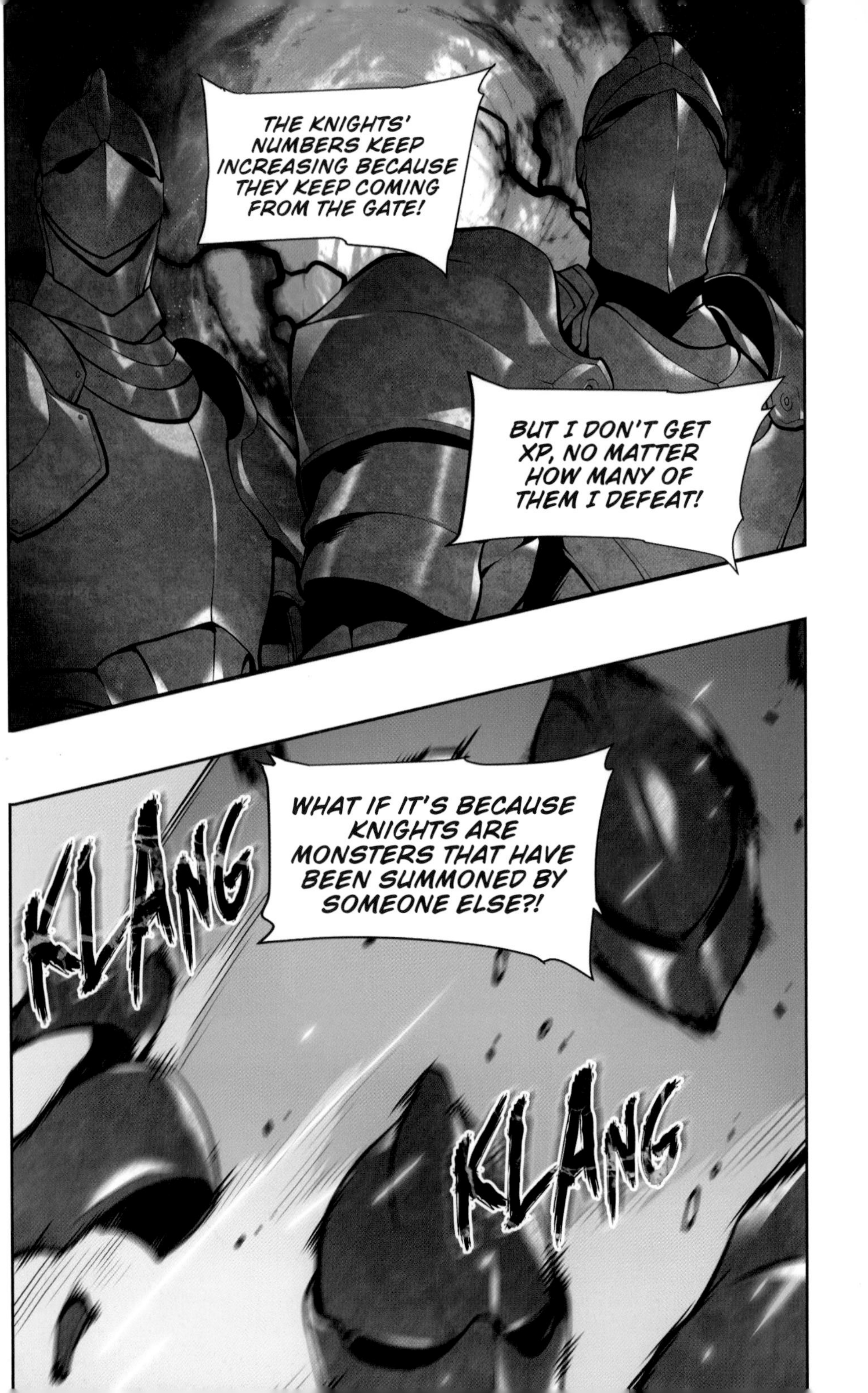
THE KNIGHTS' NUMBERS KEEP INCREASING BECAUSE THEY KEEP COMING FROM THE GATE!
BUT I DON'T GET XP, NO MATTER HOW MANY OF THEM I DEFEAT!
KLANG
WHAT IF IT'S BECAUSE KNIGHTS ARE MONSTERS THAT HAVE BEEN SUMMONED BY SOMEONE ELSE?!
KLANG

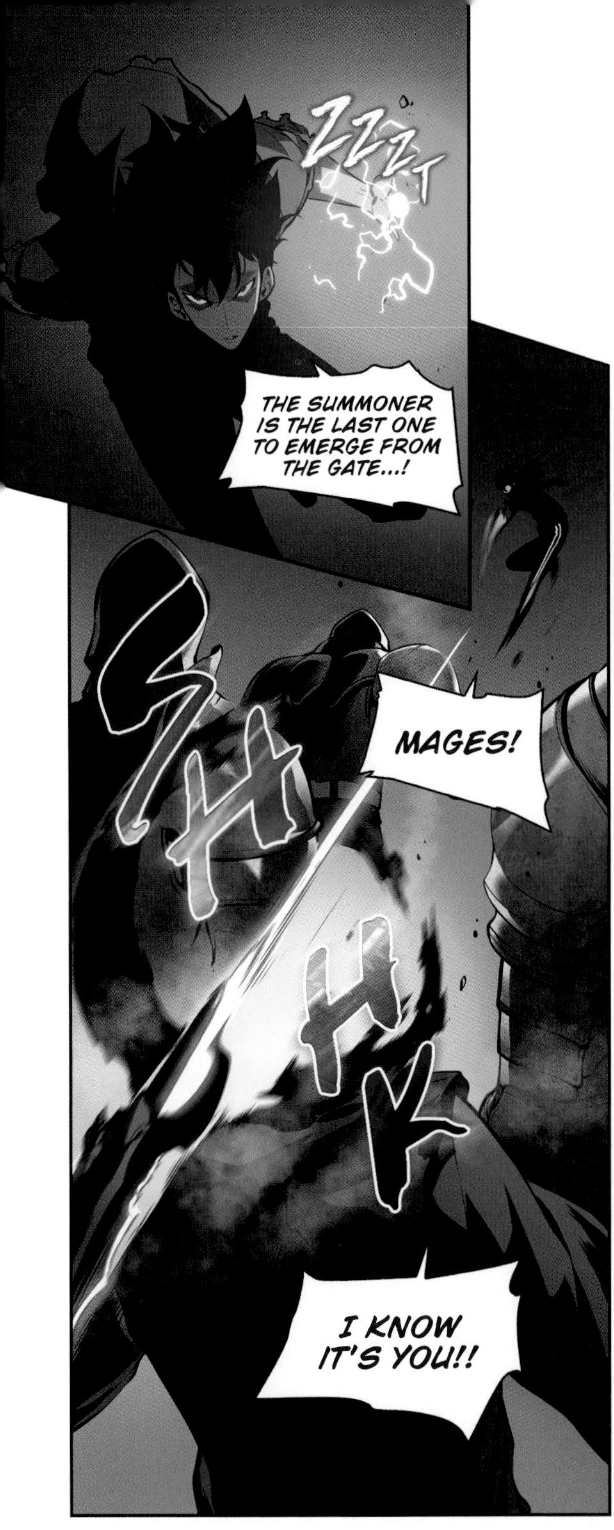
ZZZZT
THE SUMMONER IS THE LAST ONE TO EMERGE FROM THE GATE...!
SHHK
MAGES!
I KNOW IT'S YOU!!
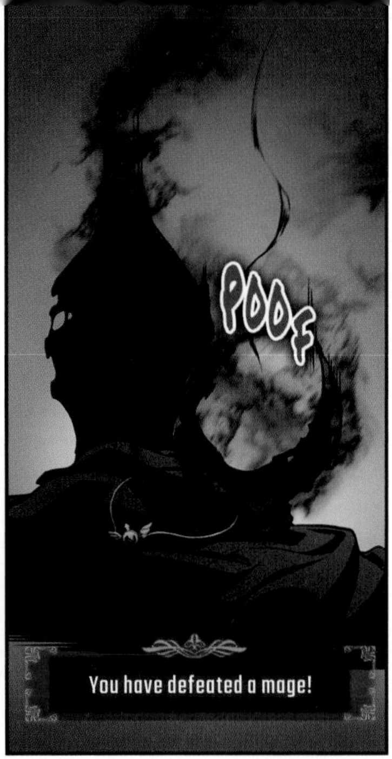
POOF
You have defeated a mage!
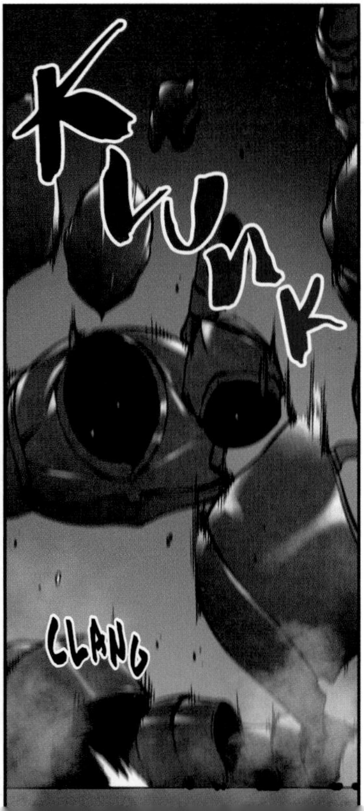
KLUNK
CLANG

You have learned [Skill: Dagger Throw].

THE KNIGHTS ARE MINIONS SUMMONED BY MAGES.

IT'S NOT OVER UNTIL I FIND THE REST OF THE MAGES!

VMMM

Skill: Stealth Lv. 1
Active skill.
200 mana required.

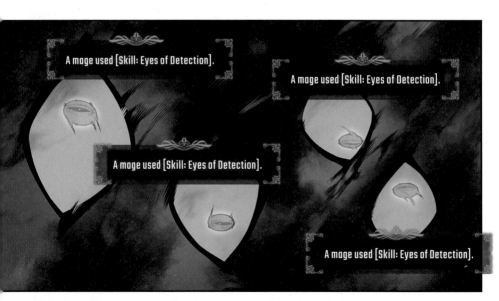

A mage used [Skill: Eyes of Detection].

A mage used [Skill: Eyes of Detection].

A mage used [Skill: Eyes of Detection].

A mage used [Skill: Eyes of Detection].

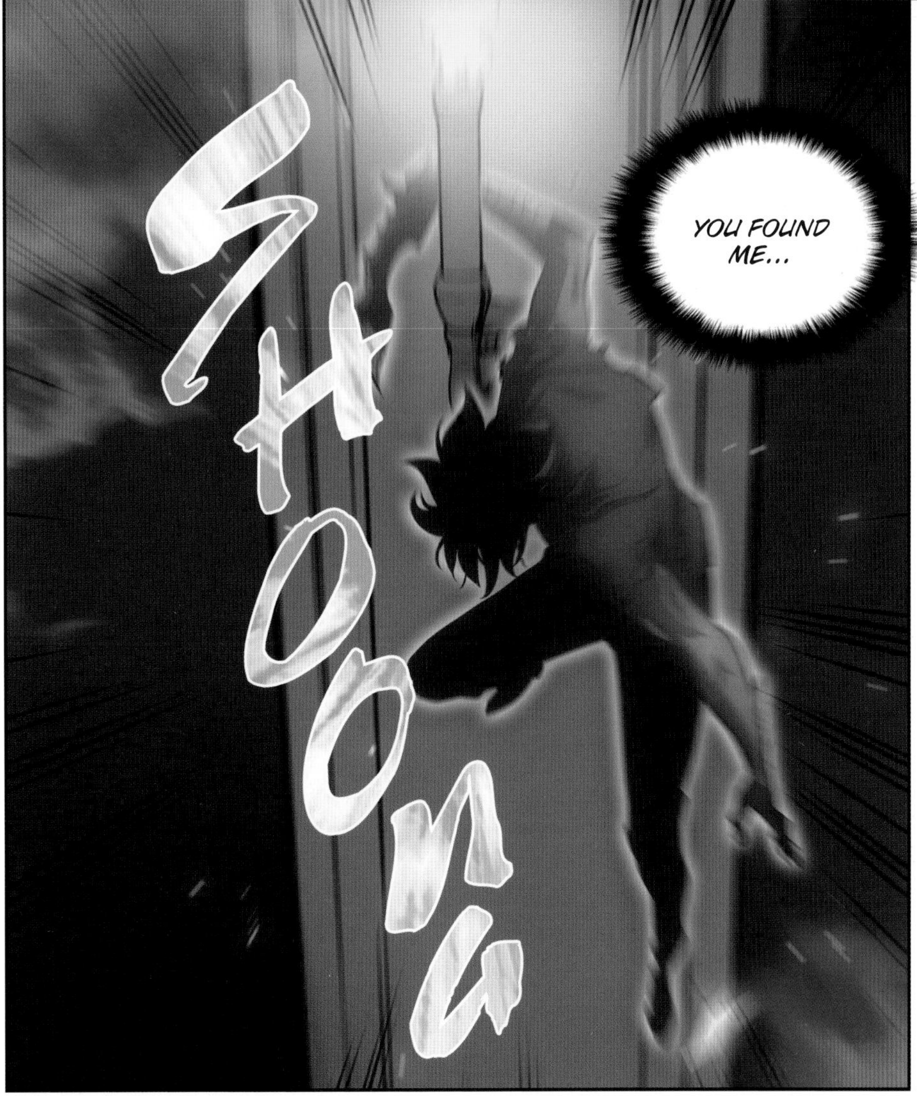
SHOOWU
YOU FOUND ME...
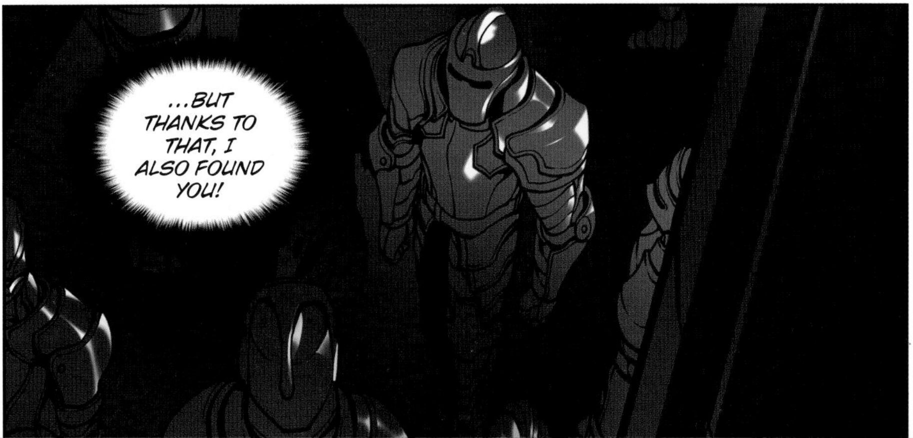
...BUT THANKS TO THAT, I ALSO FOUND YOU!

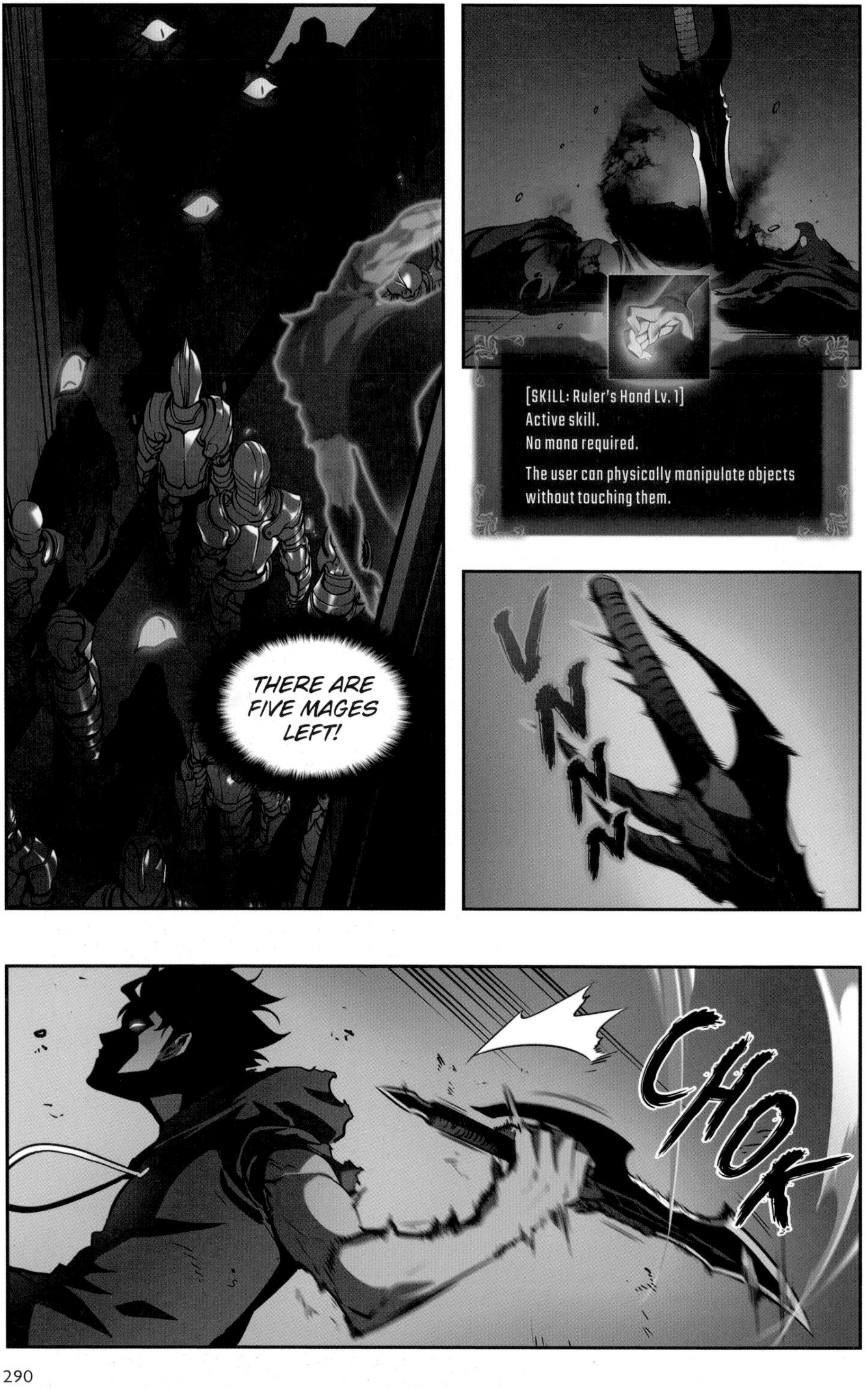
THERE ARE FIVE MAGES LEFT!
[SKILL: Ruler's Hand Lv. 1]
Active skill.
No mana required.
The user can physically manipulate objects without touching them.
VNNN
CHOK

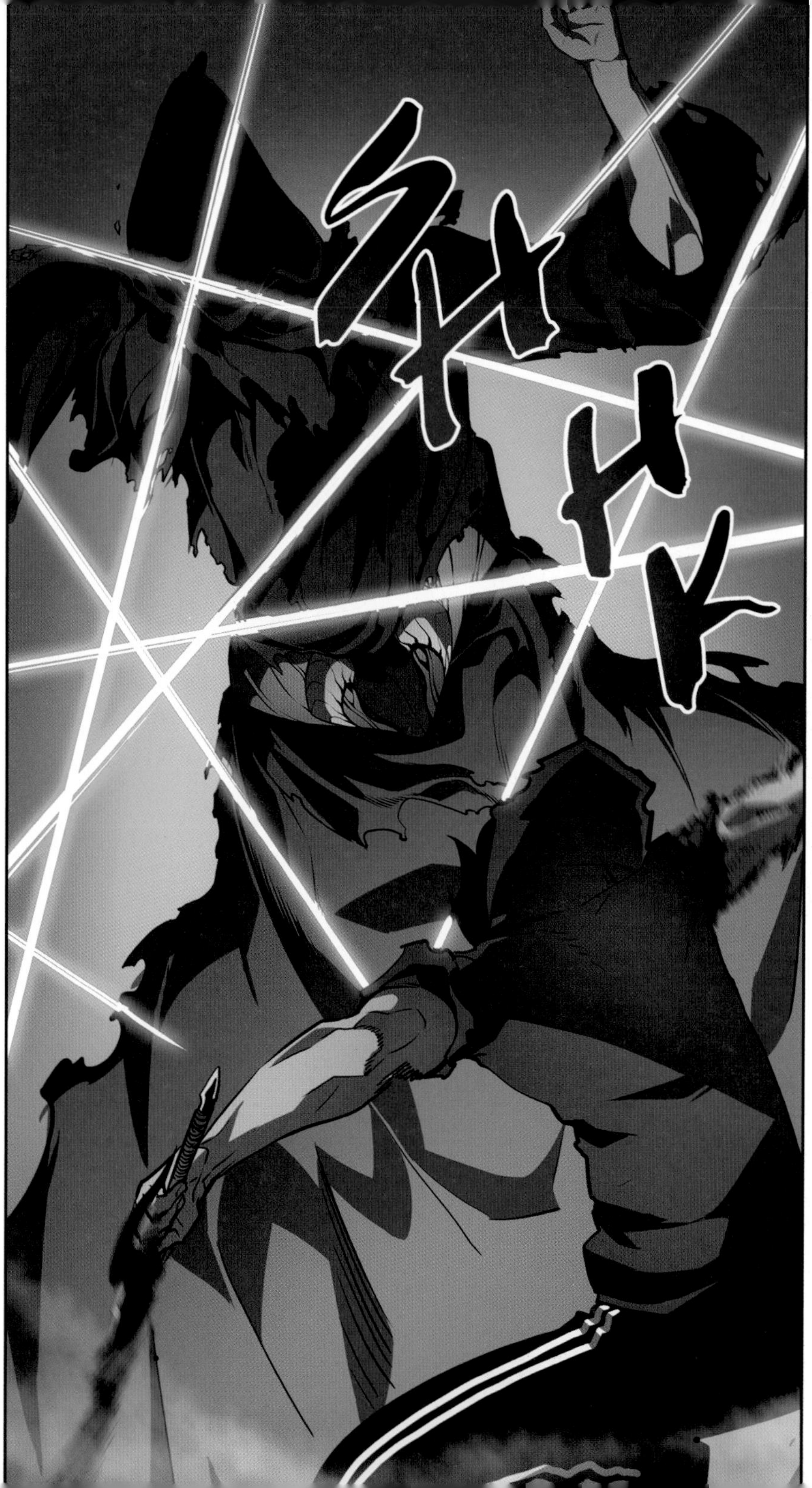
SHUK

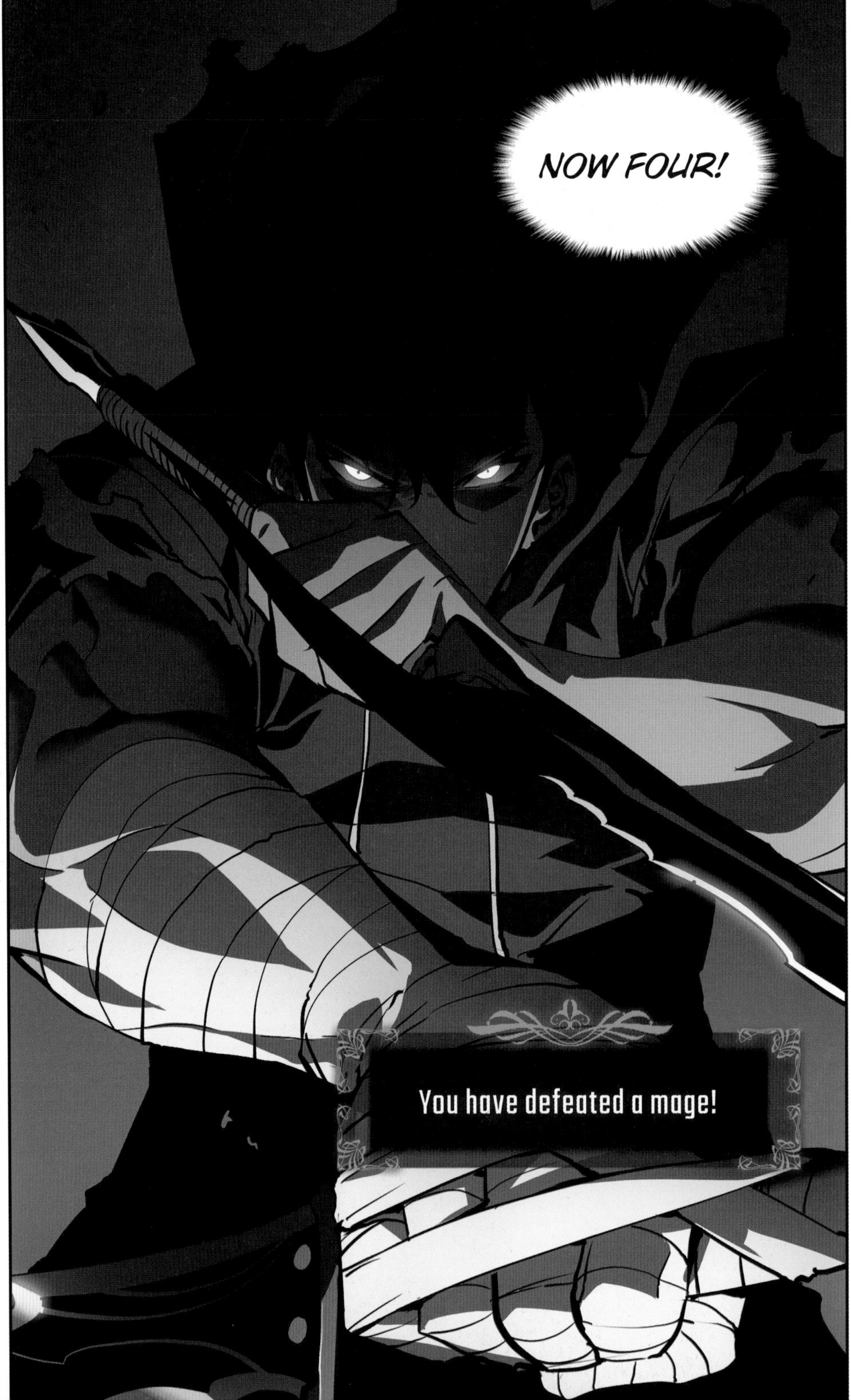
NOW FOUR!
You have defeated a mage!

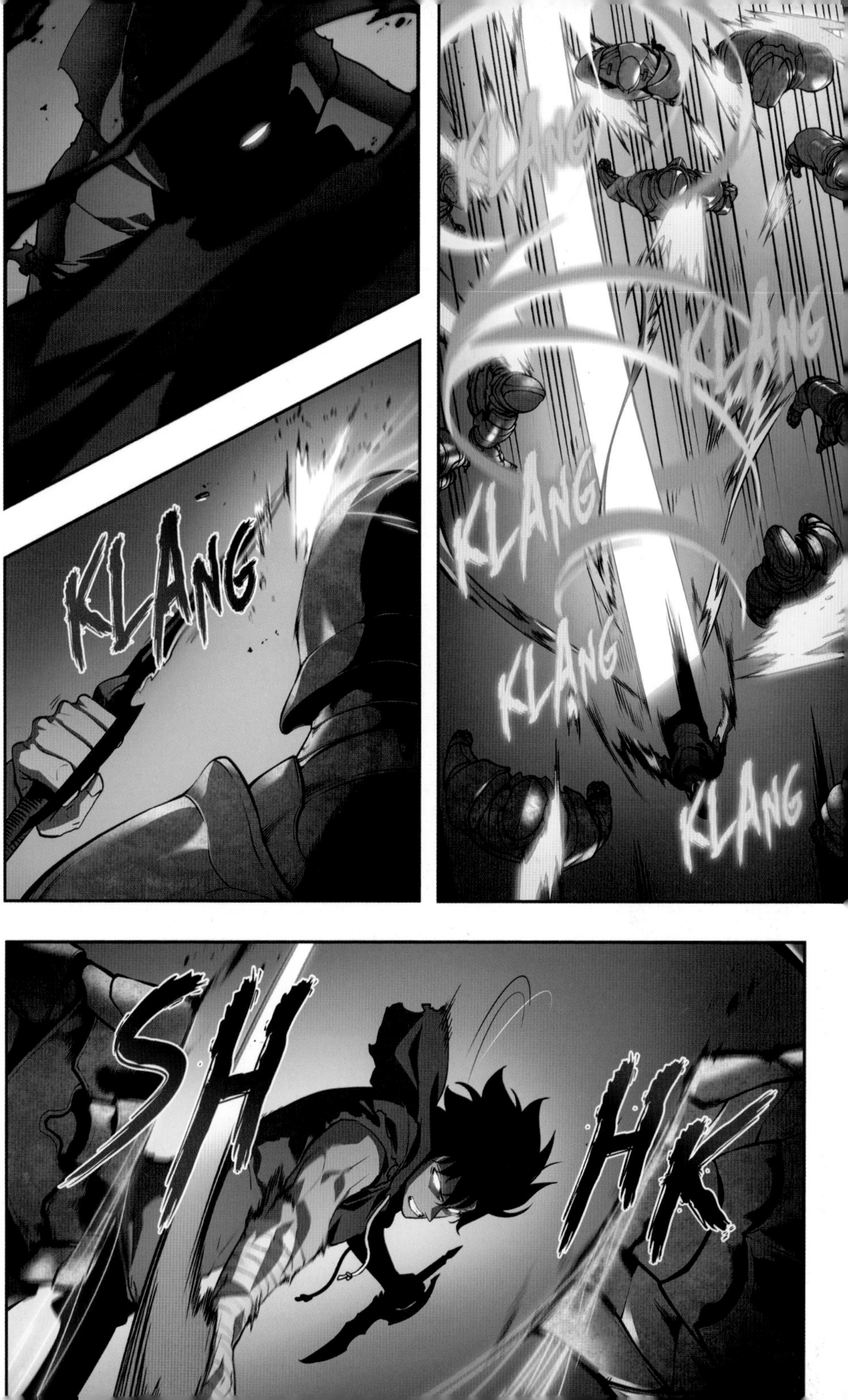
KLANG
KLANG
KLANG
KLANG
KLANG
KLANG
SH
HK

KRRNCH
Ruler's Hand Lv. 1

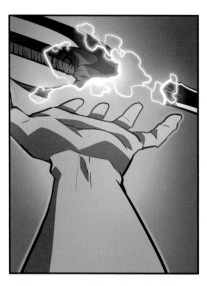

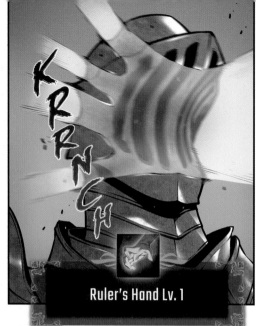

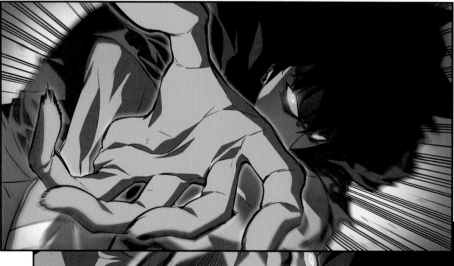

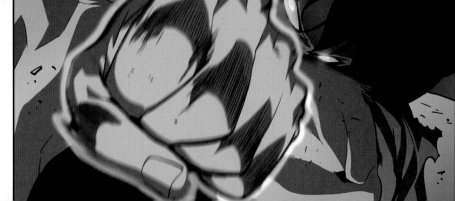

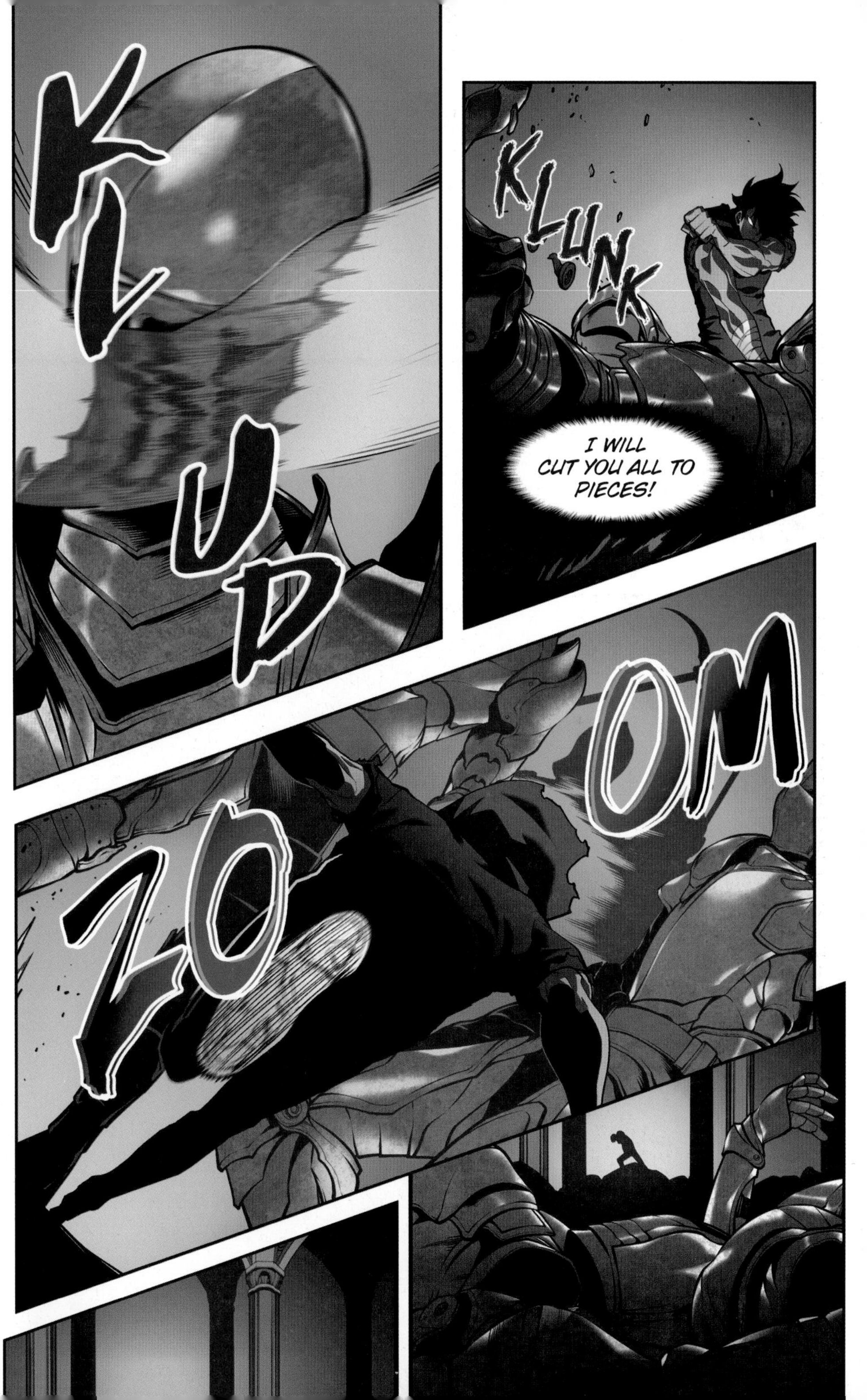
KLUD
KLUNK
I WILL CUT YOU ALL TO PIECES!
ZOOM

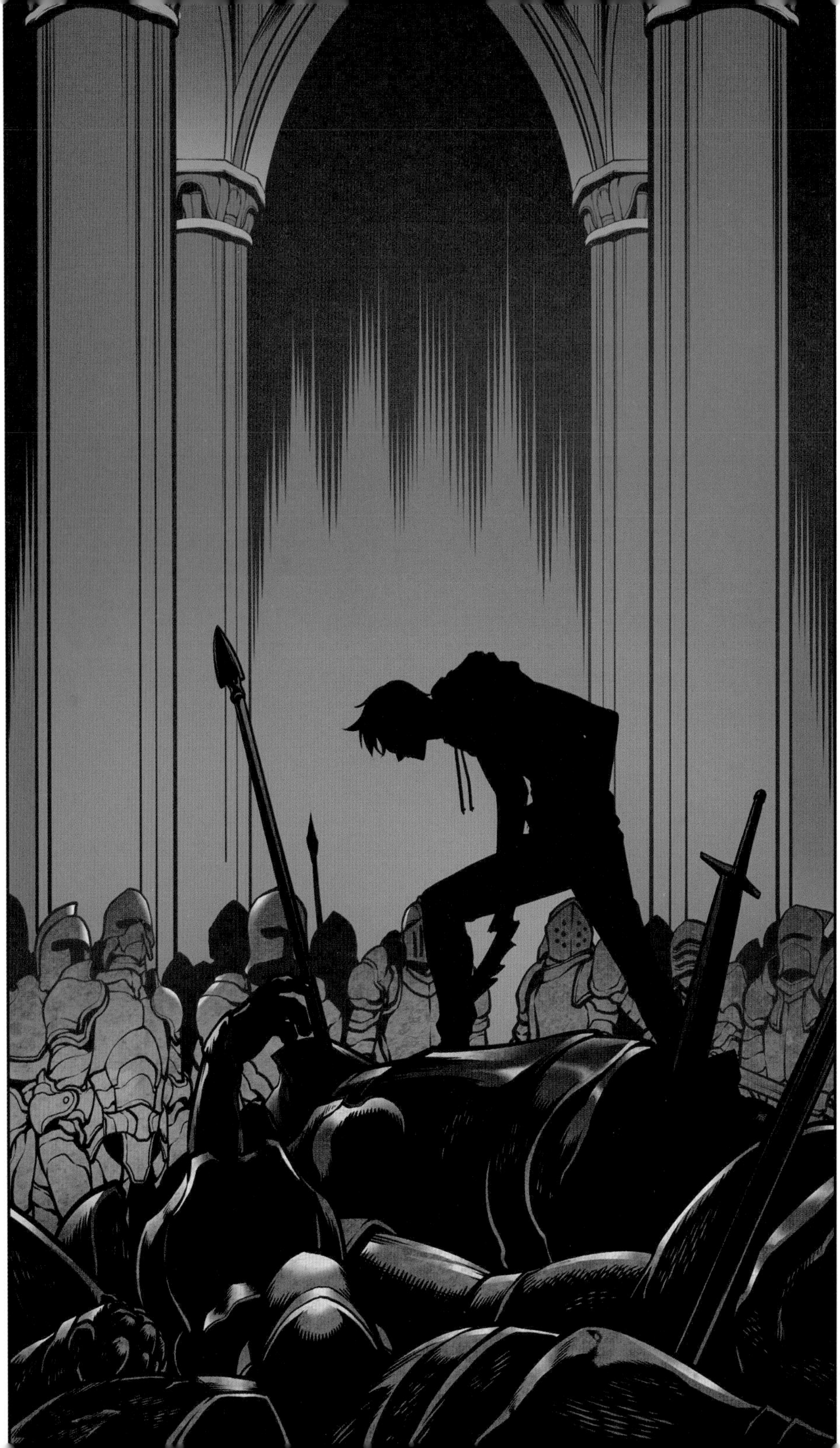

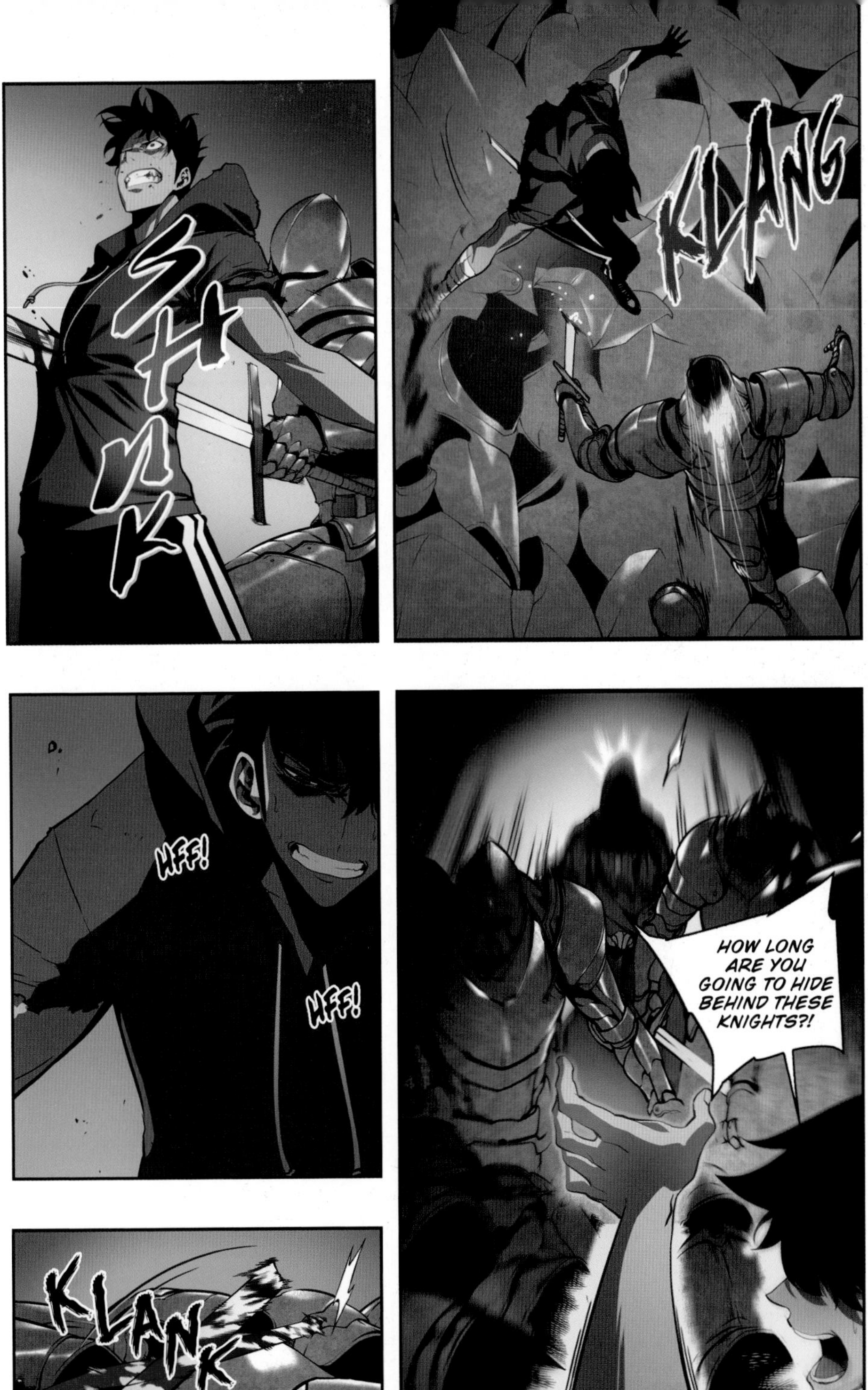
SHNK
KLANG
HFF!
HFF!
KLANK
HOW LONG ARE YOU GOING TO HIDE BEHIND THESE KNIGHTS?!

GRAB

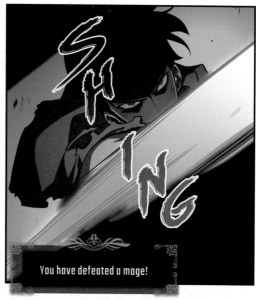

SHING

You have defeated a mage!

THREE TO GO!

KRAKOOM

CLONK
CLONK
A GOLEM?!
STOMP

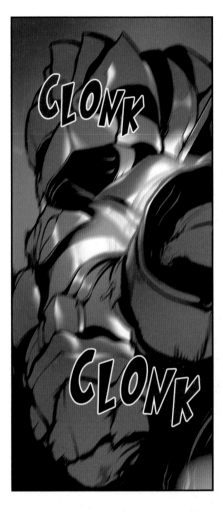

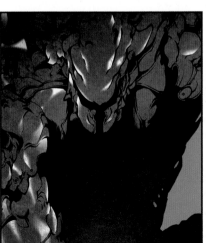

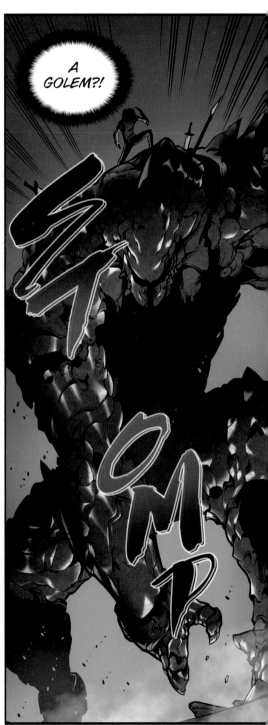

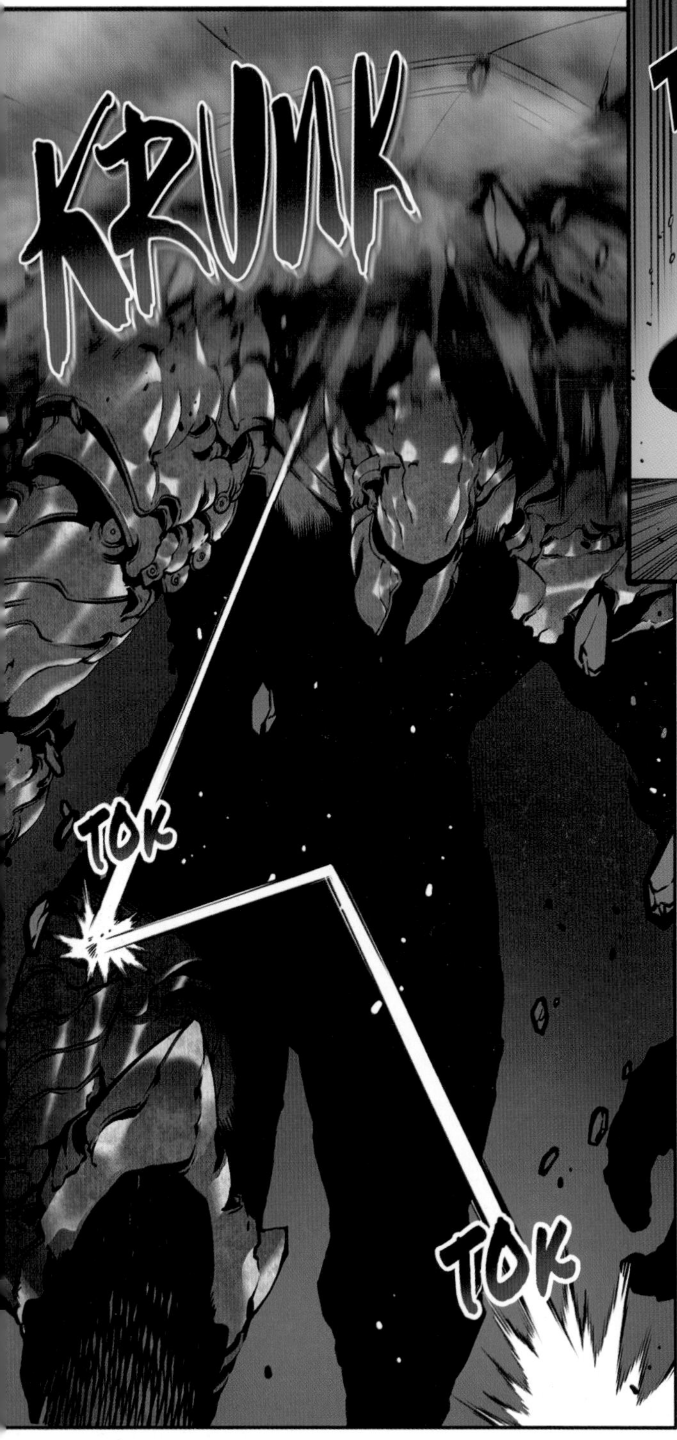
KRUNK
TOK
TOK
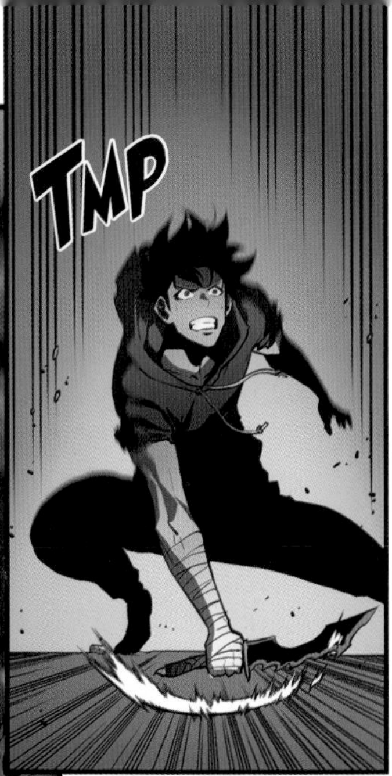
TMP
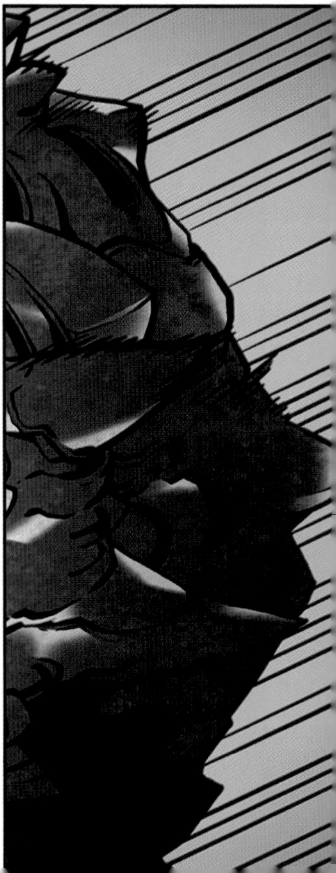

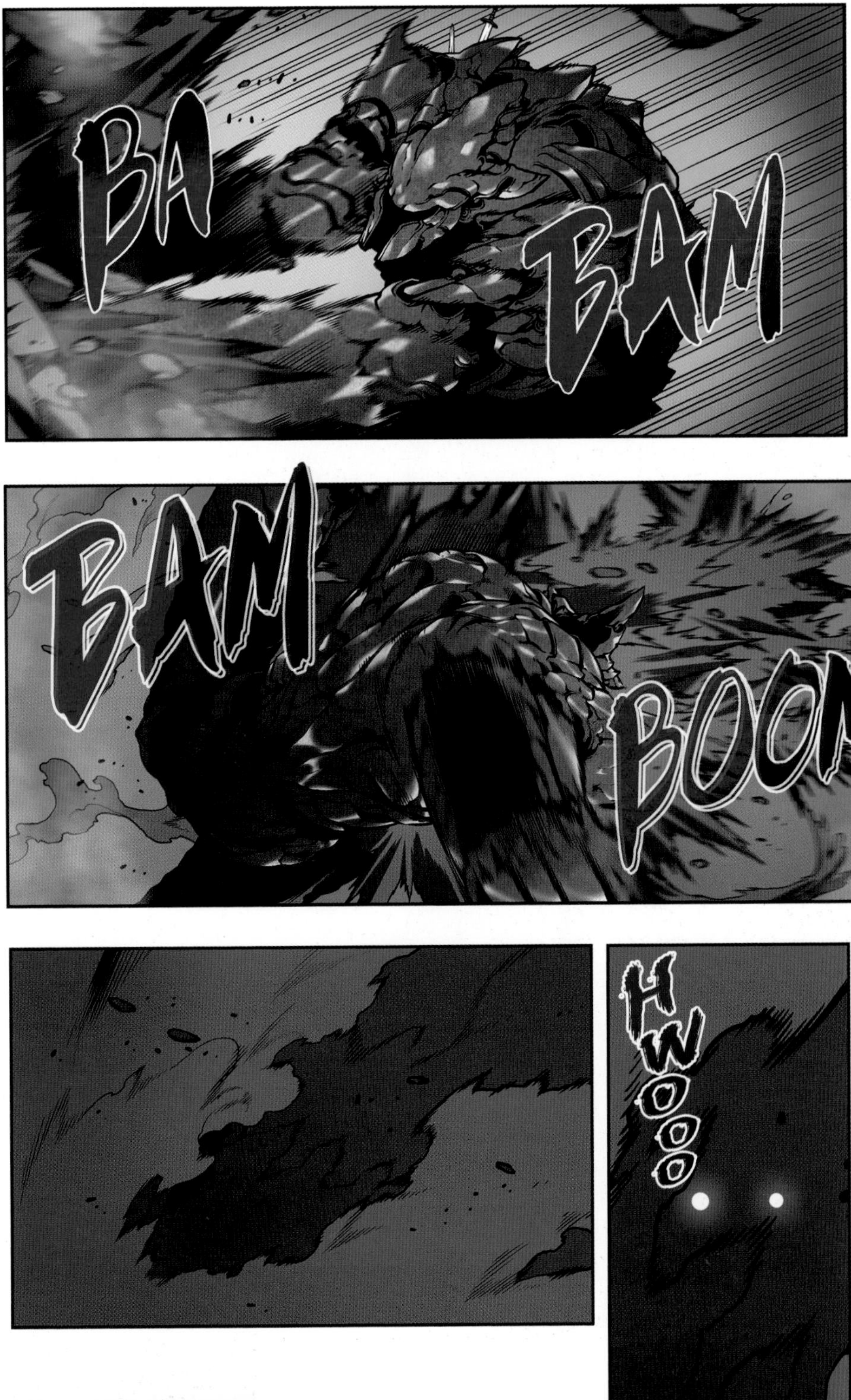
BA
BAM
BAM
BOOM
HWOOO

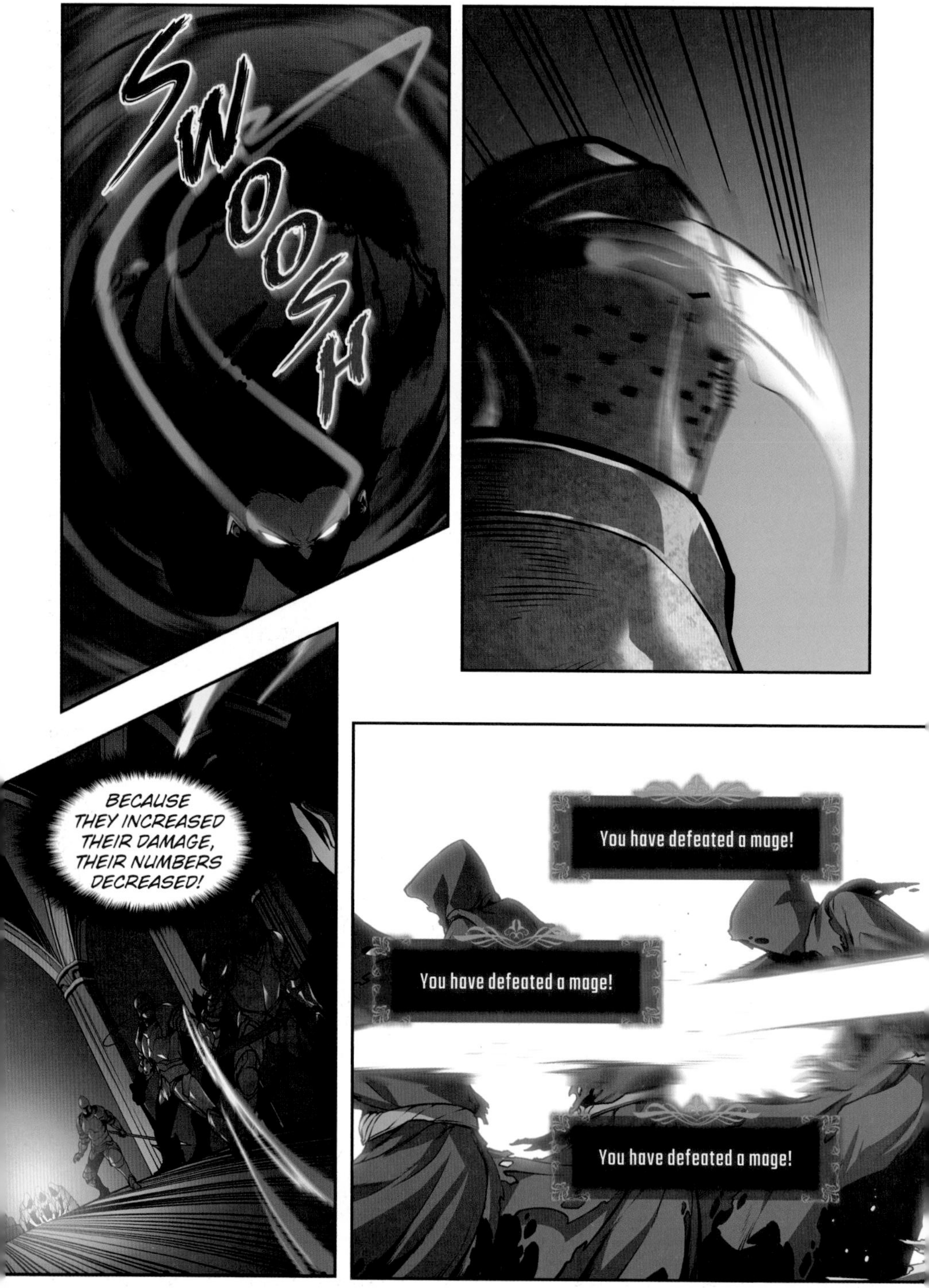
SWOOSH
BECAUSE THEY INCREASED THEIR DAMAGE, THEIR NUMBERS DECREASED!
You have defeated a mage!
You have defeated a mage!
You have defeated a mage!

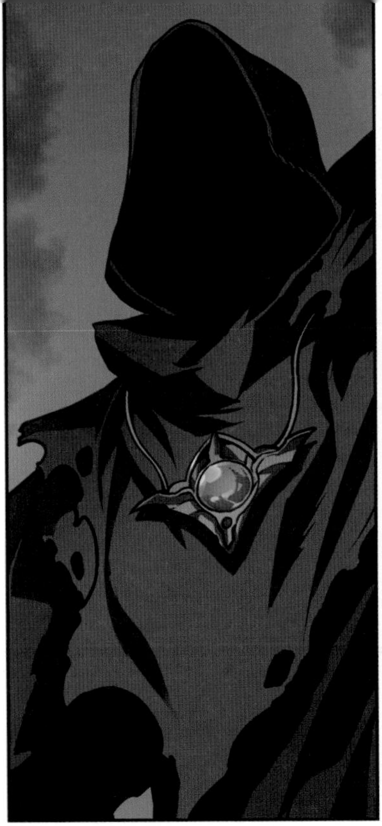

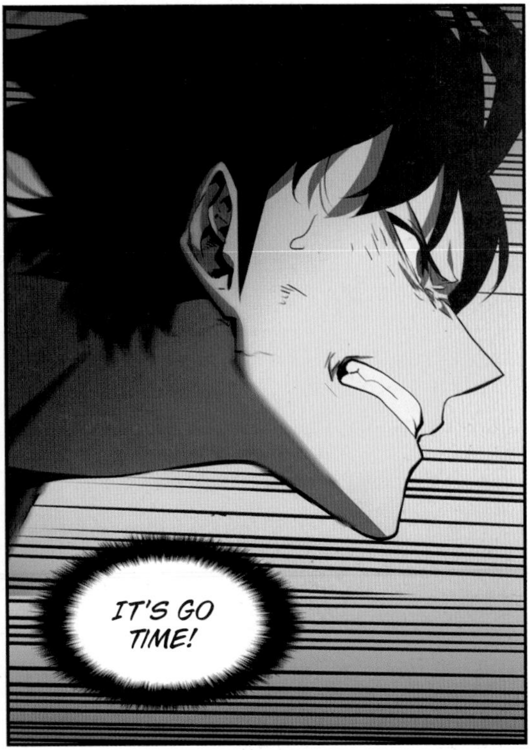
IT'S GO TIME!

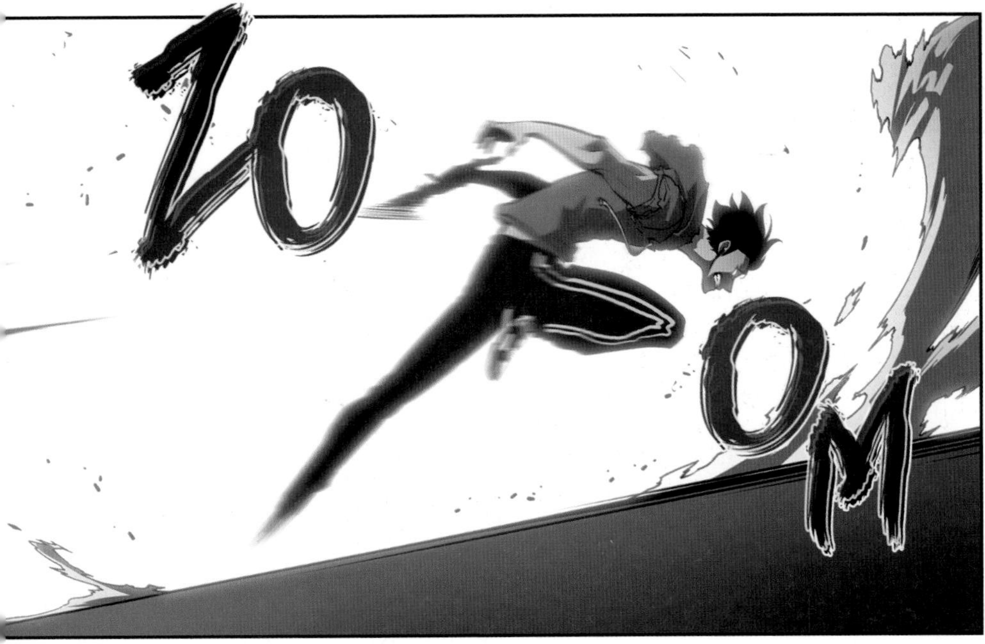
ZOOM

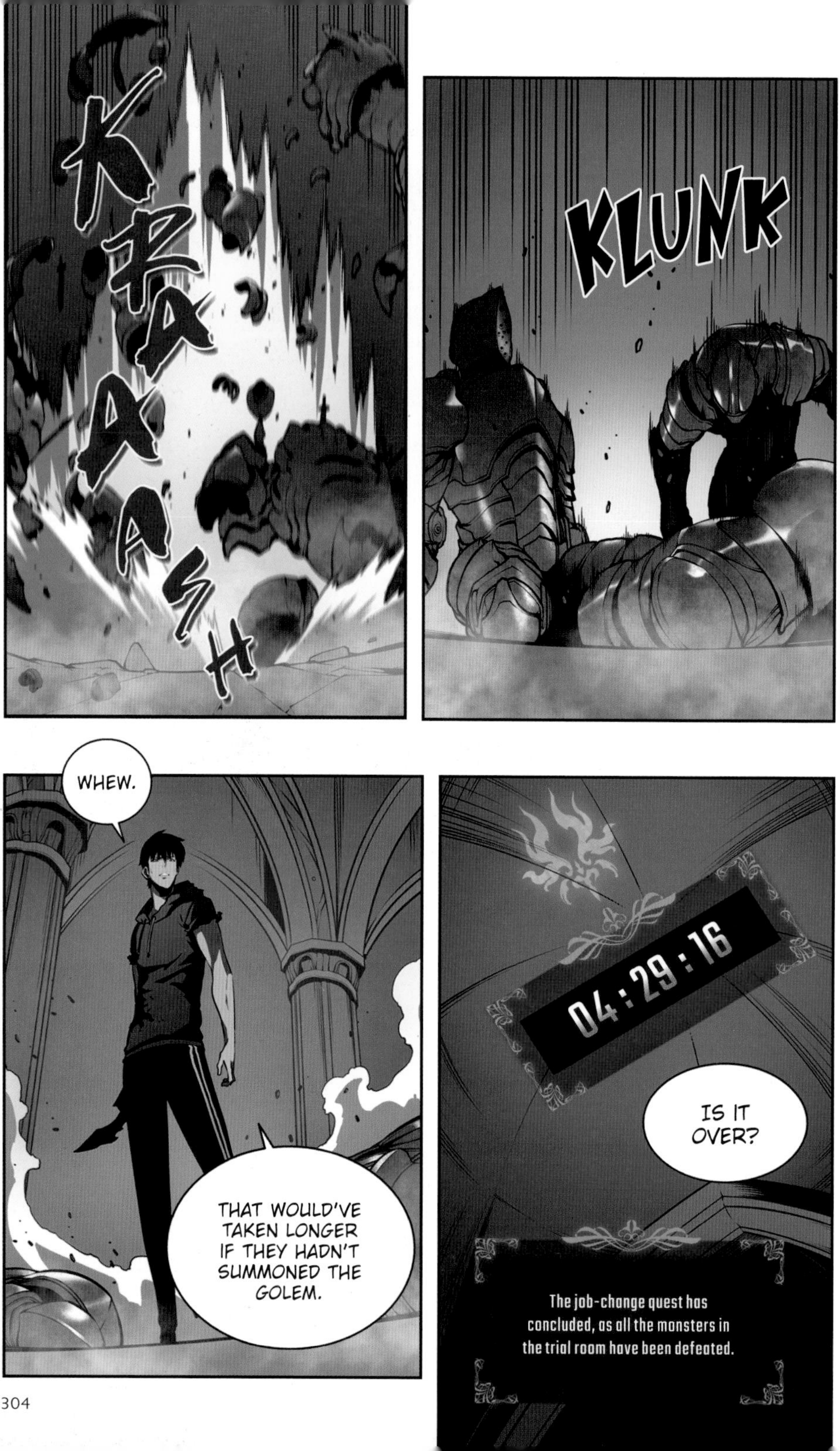

KRAAAASH
KLUNK
WHEW.
THAT WOULD'VE TAKEN LONGER IF THEY HADN'T SUMMONED THE GOLEM.
04:29:16
IS IT OVER?
The job-change quest has concluded, as all the monsters in the trial room have been defeated.

OR IS SOMETHING ELSE GONNA COME OUT...?

Depending on the advancement points acquired, you may progress to a higher class.

IT'S OVER. I'M FINALLY GETTING A JOB TITLE.

SINCE I USE DAGGERS, I SHOULD CHOOSE ASSASSIN, RIGHT?

The appropriate job will be assigned after analyzing the Player's actions.

ASSIGNED? I CAN'T CHOOSE?

I PUT ALL MY STATS IN STRENGTH AND AGILITY.

I COULD BE A WARRIOR WITH POWERFUL ATTACKS OR AN ASSASSIN WITH GREAT AGILITY.

OR MAYBE A TANK WITH LOTS OF STAMINA.

IT SHOULD BE ONE OF THOSE THREE.

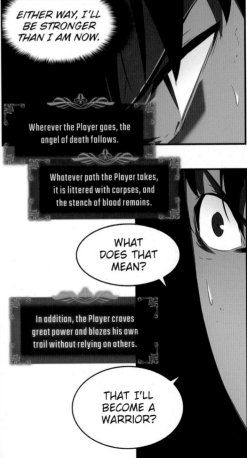

EITHER WAY, I'LL BE STRONGER THAN I AM NOW.

Wherever the Player goes, the angel of death follows.

Whatever path the Player takes, it is littered with corpses, and the stench of blood remains.

WHAT DOES THAT MEAN?

In addition, the Player craves great power and blazes his own trail without relying on others.

THAT I'LL BECOME A WARRIOR?

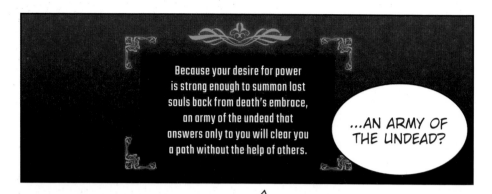

Because your desire for power is strong enough to summon lost souls back from death's embrace, an army of the undead that answers only to you will clear you a path without the help of others.

...AN ARMY OF THE UNDEAD?

...WHAT?

WAIT!

WHAT THE HELL...?

THIS IS...

...MY JOB?

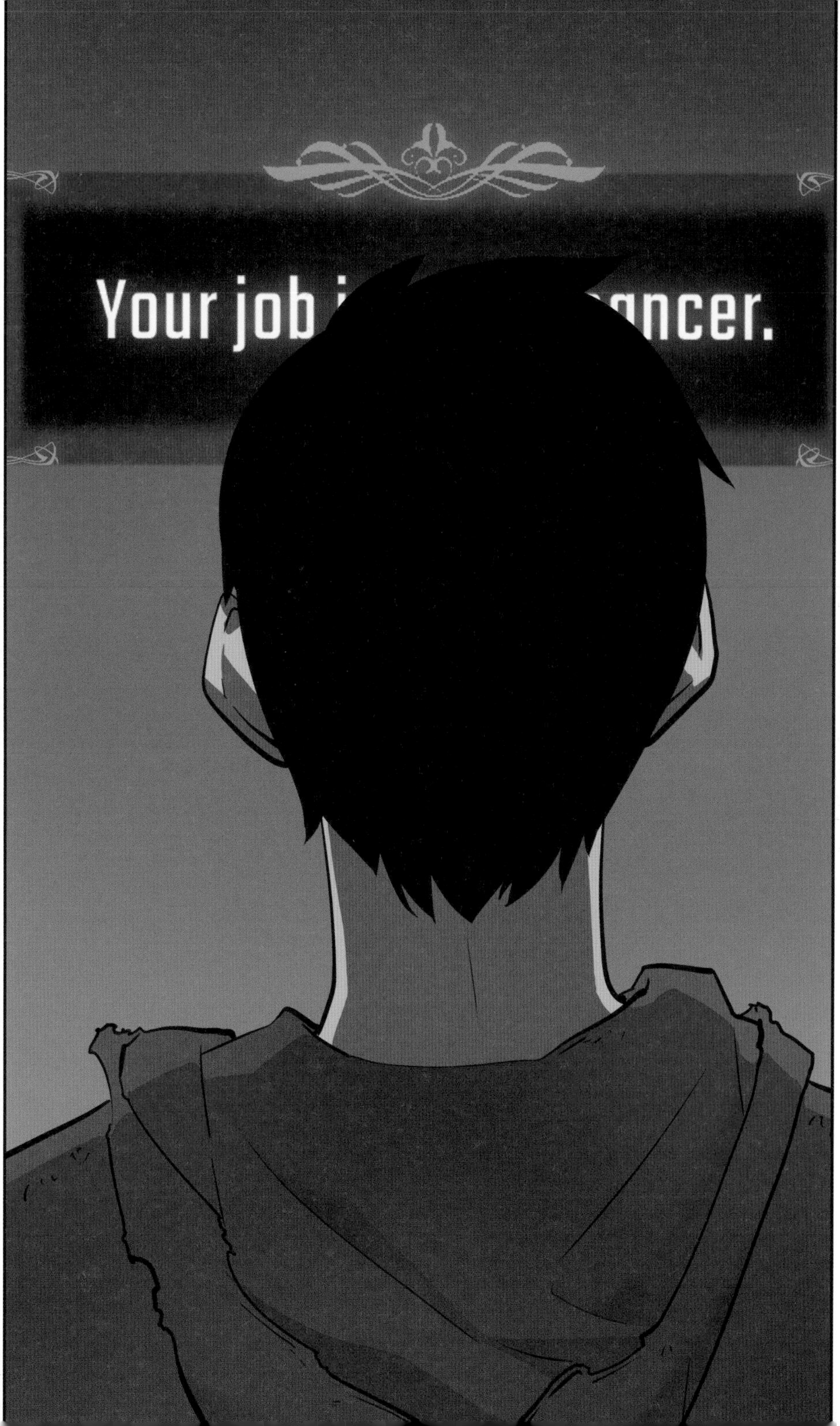
Your job i
ancer.

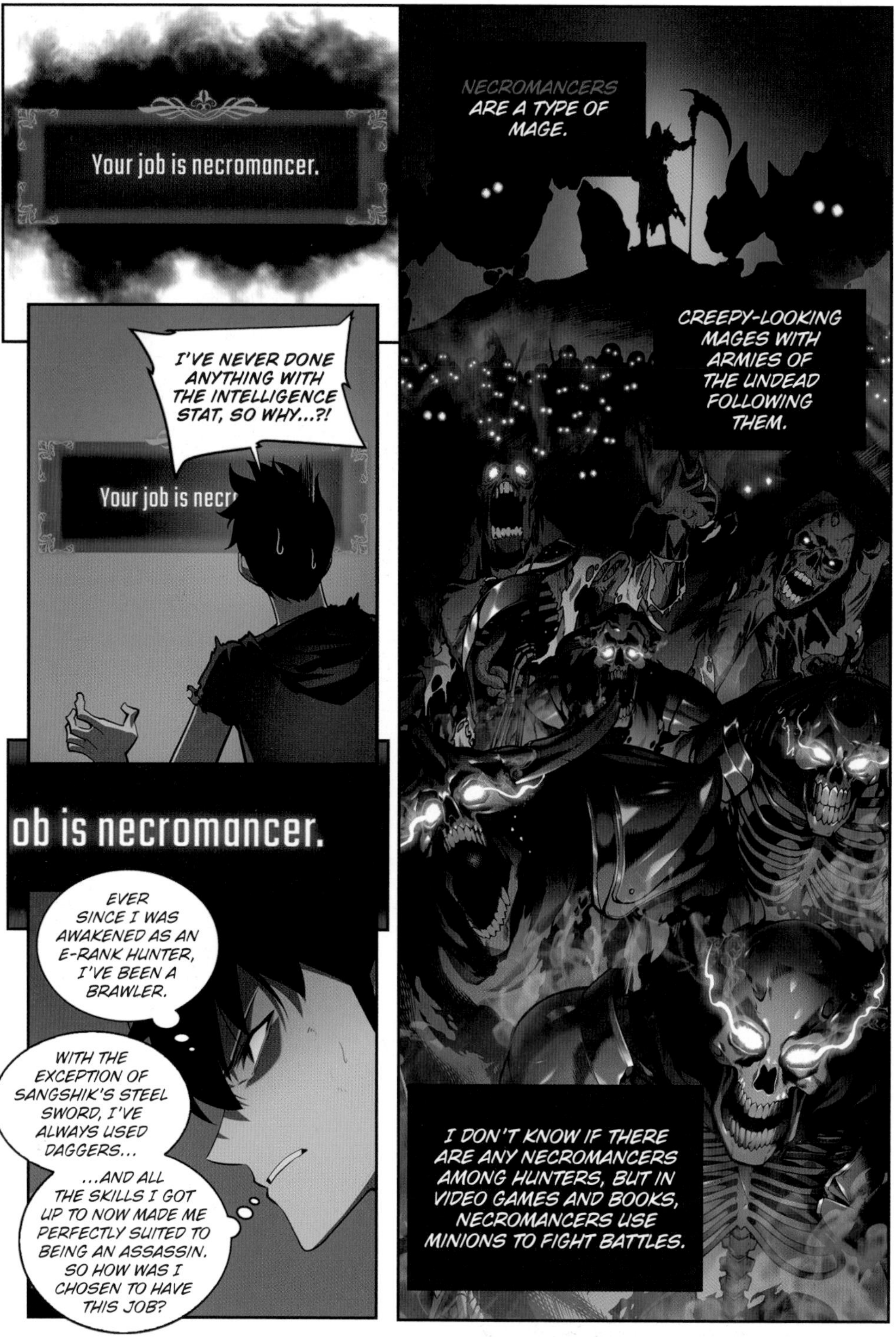
Your job is necromancer.
I'VE NEVER DONE ANYTHING WITH THE INTELLIGENCE STAT, SO WHY...?!
Your job is necr
ob is necromancer.
EVER SINCE I WAS AWAKENED AS AN E-RANK HUNTER, I'VE BEEN A BRAWLER.
WITH THE EXCEPTION OF SANGSHIK'S STEEL SWORD, I'VE ALWAYS USED DAGGERS...
...AND ALL THE SKILLS I GOT UP TO NOW MADE ME PERFECTLY SUITED TO BEING AN ASSASSIN. SO HOW WAS I CHOSEN TO HAVE THIS JOB?
NECROMANCERS ARE A TYPE OF MAGE.
CREEPY-LOOKING MAGES WITH ARMIES OF THE UNDEAD FOLLOWING THEM.
I DON'T KNOW IF THERE ARE ANY NECROMANCERS AMONG HUNTERS, BUT IN VIDEO GAMES AND BOOKS, NECROMANCERS USE MINIONS TO FIGHT BATTLES.

...I NEED TO CALM DOWN FIRST.

ON THE PLUS SIDE, BEING A NECROMANCER MEANS...

...I CAN COMMAND MY OWN ARMY, LIKE THE SYSTEM SAID?

BUT DO I GET STRONGER?

ARE ALL MY STATS USELESS NOW?

STATUS
Strength: 132
Stamina: 91
Agility: 111
Intellect: 70
Perception: 93

OH! AT LEAST I HAVE A CHOICE...

PING!

— X

⓪ NOTIFICATION

Will you accept this job?

ACCEPT   DECLINE

IF I DECLINE, I CAN STILL GET ANOTHER JOB, RIGHT...?

! NOTIFICATION

Will you accept this job?

DECLINE

DECLINE.

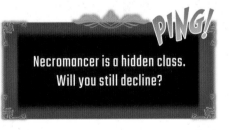

PING!

Necromancer is a hidden class.
Will you still decline?

HIDDEN... CLASS?

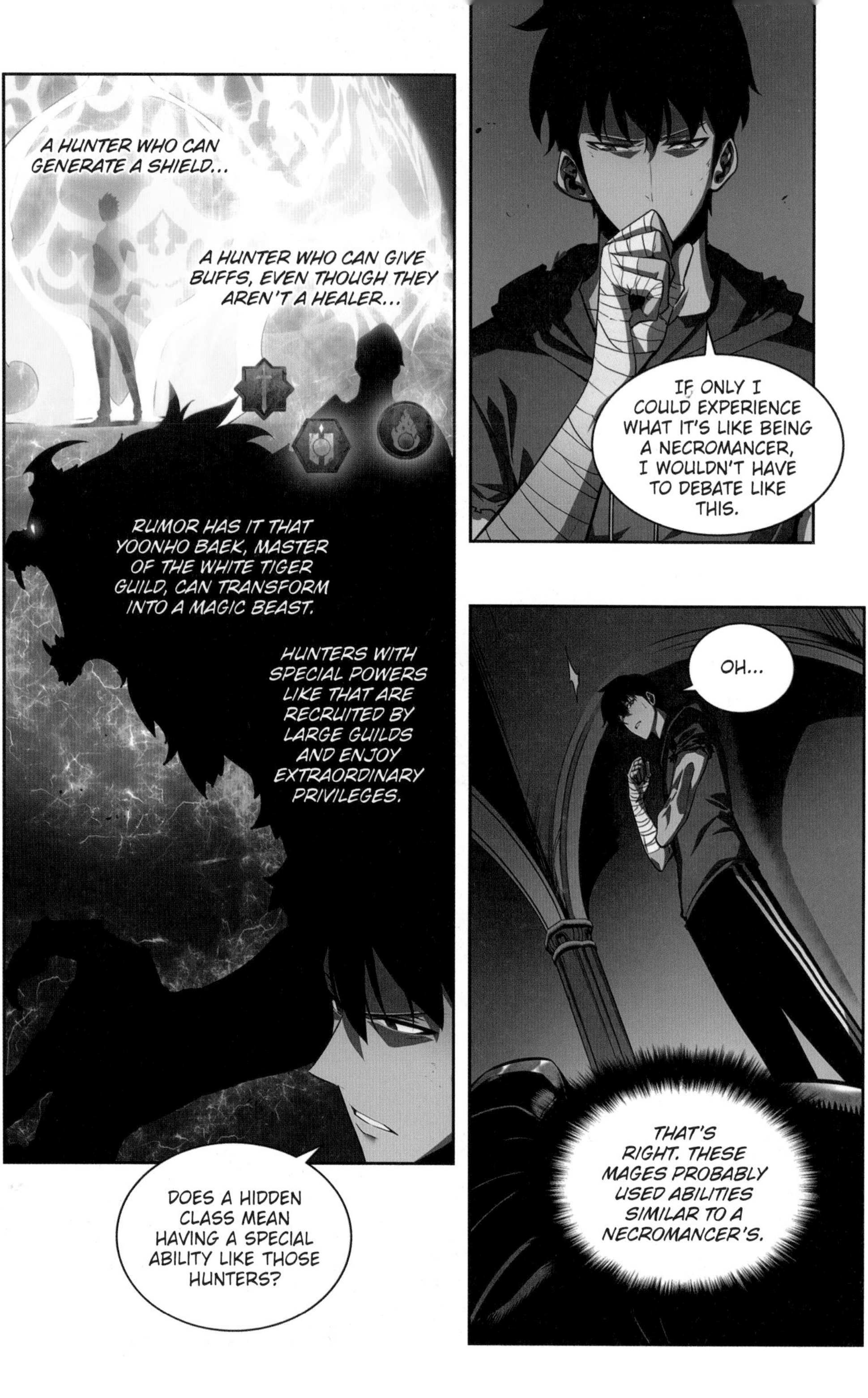
A HUNTER WHO CAN GENERATE A SHIELD...
A HUNTER WHO CAN GIVE BUFFS, EVEN THOUGH THEY AREN'T A HEALER...
RUMOR HAS IT THAT YOONHO BAEK, MASTER OF THE WHITE TIGER GUILD, CAN TRANSFORM INTO A MAGIC BEAST.
HUNTERS WITH SPECIAL POWERS LIKE THAT ARE RECRUITED BY LARGE GUILDS AND ENJOY EXTRAORDINARY PRIVILEGES.
DOES A HIDDEN CLASS MEAN HAVING A SPECIAL ABILITY LIKE THOSE HUNTERS?
IF ONLY I COULD EXPERIENCE WHAT IT'S LIKE BEING A NECROMANCER, I WOULDN'T HAVE TO DEBATE LIKE THIS.
OH...
THAT'S RIGHT. THESE MAGES PROBABLY USED ABILITIES SIMILAR TO A NECROMANCER'S.

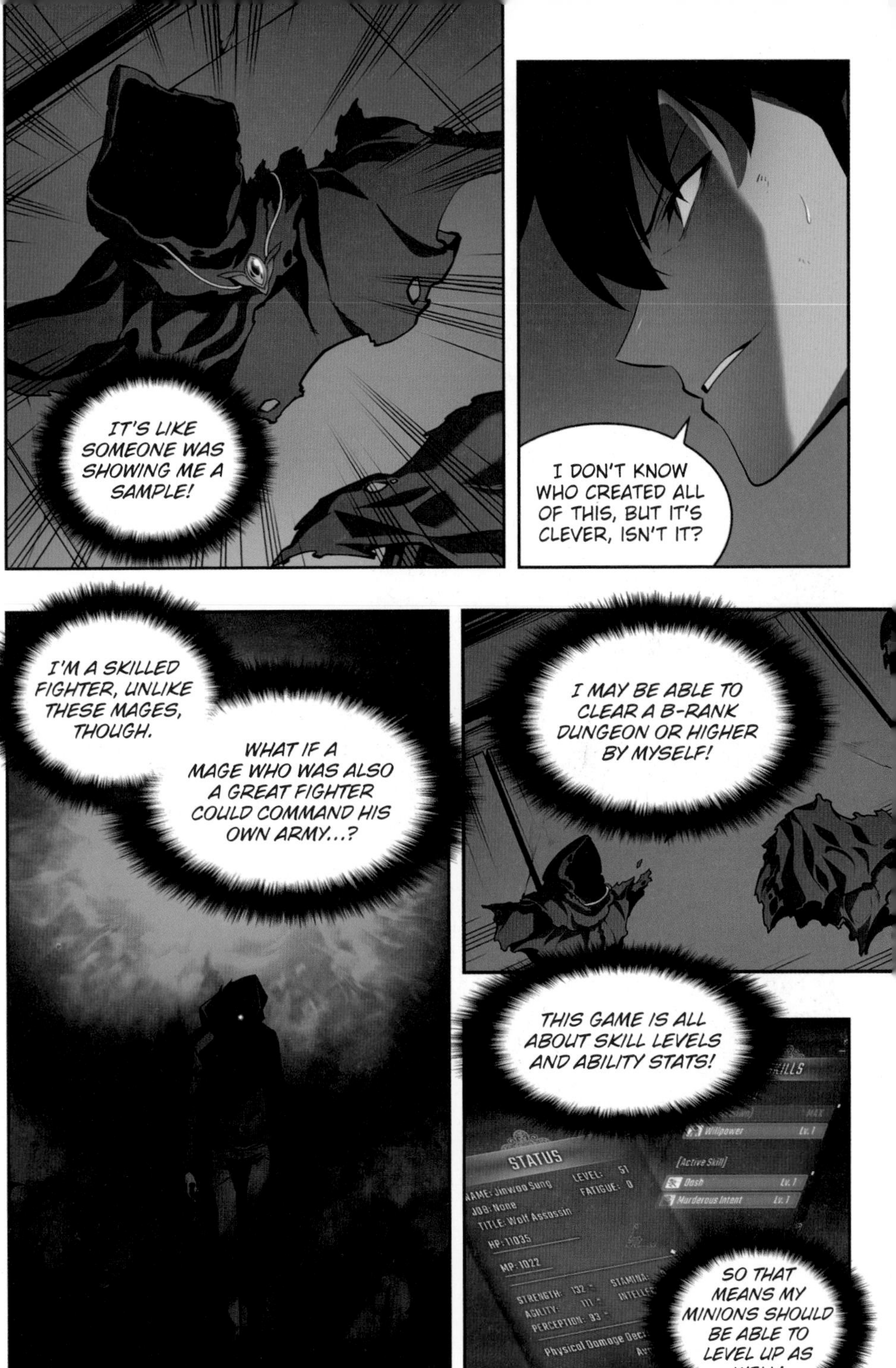
IT'S LIKE SOMEONE WAS SHOWING ME A SAMPLE!
I DON'T KNOW WHO CREATED ALL OF THIS, BUT IT'S CLEVER, ISN'T IT?
I'M A SKILLED FIGHTER, UNLIKE THESE MAGES, THOUGH.
WHAT IF A MAGE WHO WAS ALSO A GREAT FIGHTER COULD COMMAND HIS OWN ARMY...?
I MAY BE ABLE TO CLEAR A B-RANK DUNGEON OR HIGHER BY MYSELF!
THIS GAME IS ALL ABOUT SKILL LEVELS AND ABILITY STATS!
Willpower Lv. 1
[Active Skill]
Dash Lv. 1
Murderous Intent Lv. 1
STATUS
LEVEL: 51
FATIGUE: 0
JOB: None
TITLE: Wolf Assassin
HP: 11035
MP: 1022
STRENGTH: 132
AGILITY: 111
PERCEPTION: 93
SO THAT MEANS MY MINIONS SHOULD BE ABLE TO LEVEL UP AS WELL!

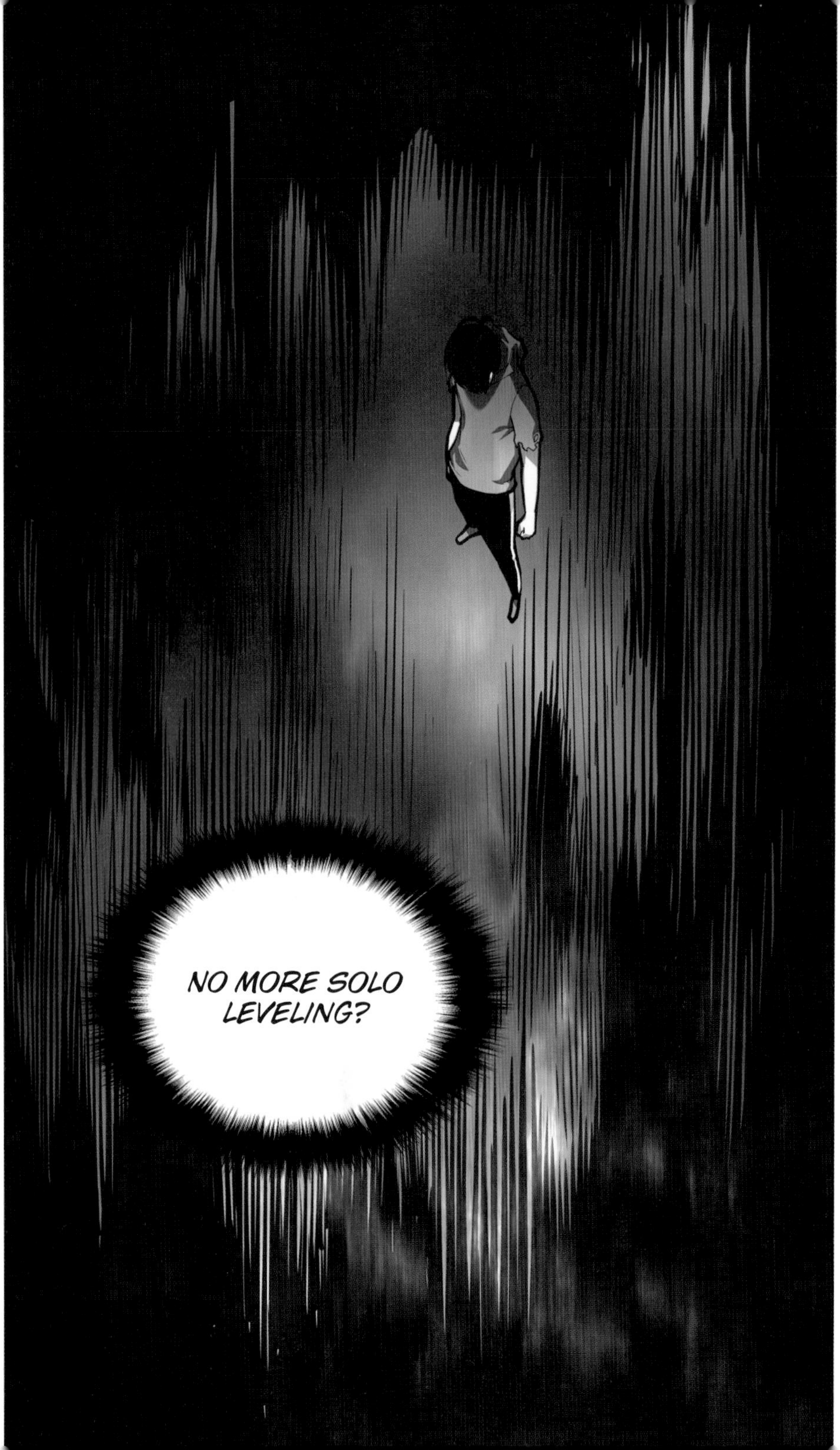
NO MORE SOLO LEVELING?

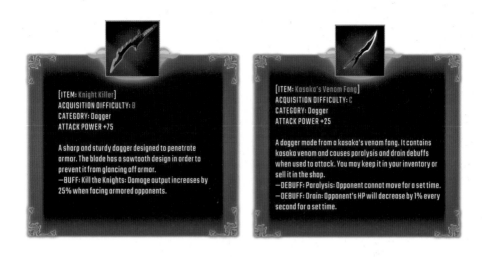

[ITEM: Knight Killer]
ACQUISITION DIFFICULTY: B
CATEGORY: Dagger
ATTACK POWER +75

A sharp and sturdy dagger designed to penetrate armor. The blade has a sawtooth design in order to prevent it from glancing off armor.
—BUFF: Kill the Knights: Damage output increases by 25% when facing armored opponents.

[ITEM: Kasaka's Venom Fang]
ACQUISITION DIFFICULTY: C
CATEGORY: Dagger
ATTACK POWER +25

A dagger made from a kasaka's venom fang. It contains kasaka venom and causes paralysis and drain debuffs when used to attack. You may keep it in your inventory or sell it in the shop.
—DEBUFF: Paralysis: Opponent cannot move for a set time.
—DEBUFF: Drain: Opponent's HP will decrease by 1% every second for a set time.

[SKILL: Ruler's Hand Lv. 1]
Active skill.
No mana required.

The user can physically manipulate objects without touching them.

[SKILL: Dagger Throw Lv. 1]
Active skill.
30 mana required.
Dagger-only skill.

Cause damage by throwing a dagger. The higher the level of the skill, the greater the accuracy rate and damage will become.

TO BE CONTINUED IN VOLUME 4...

VOLUME 4 PREVIEW

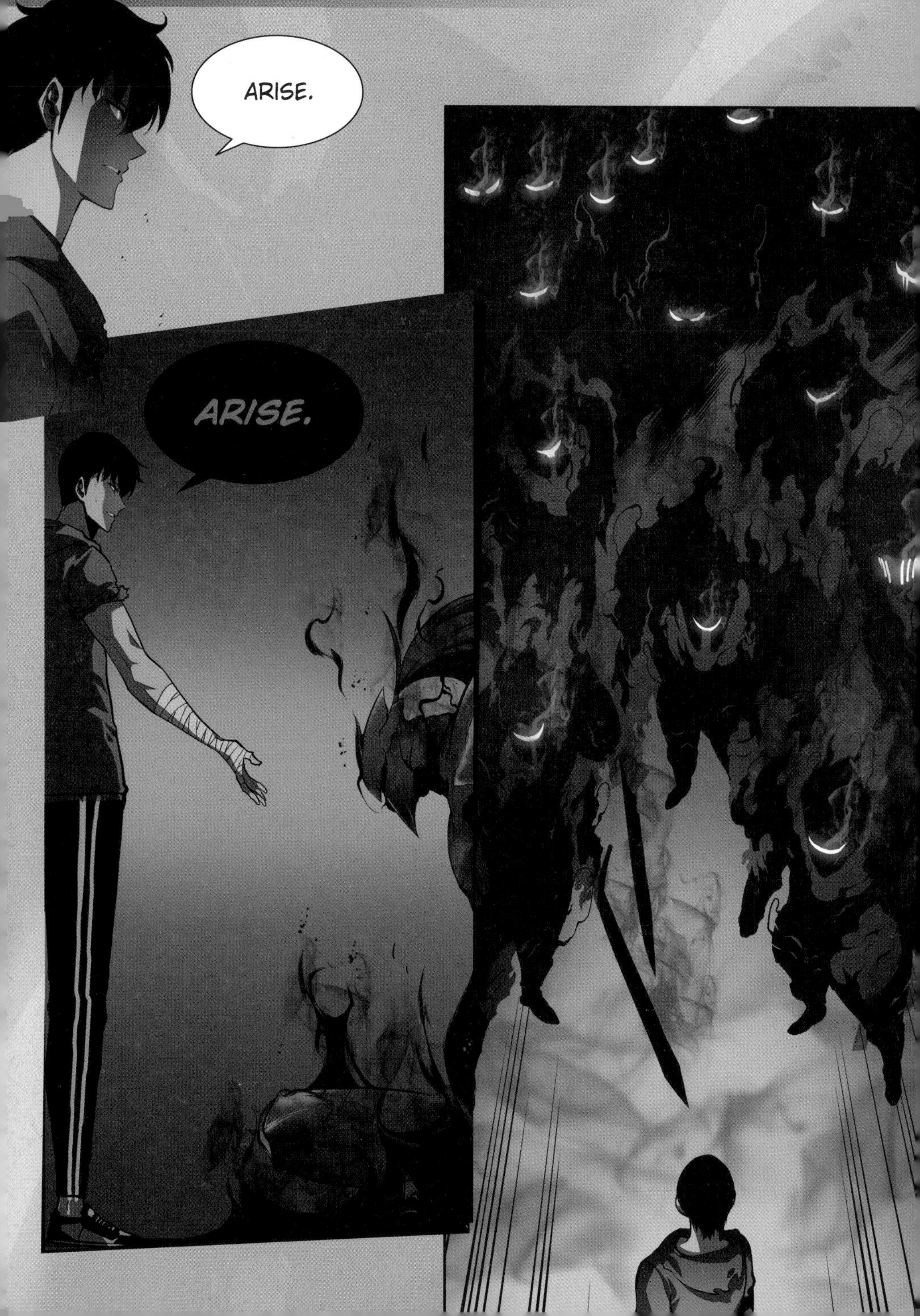
ARISE.
ARISE.

IT'S IMPOSSIBLE TO ESCAPE FROM THE RED GATE!

Those who leave or those who are left behind—
Who will survive?!

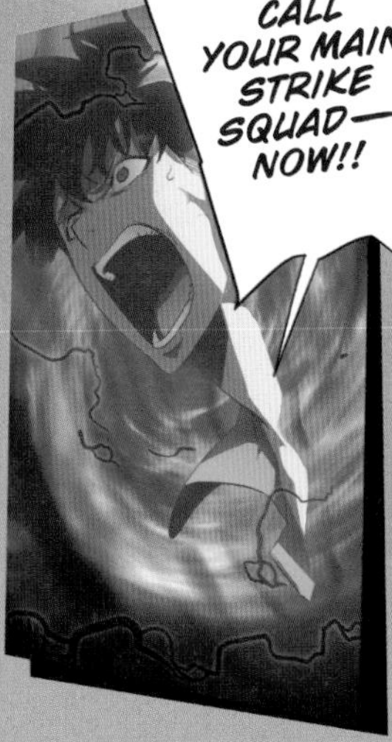
CALL YOUR MAIN STRIKE SQUAD—NOW!!

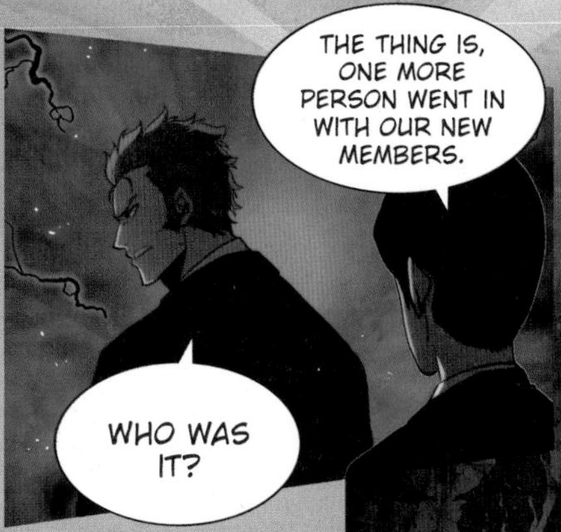
THE THING IS, ONE MORE PERSON WENT IN WITH OUR NEW MEMBERS.
WHO WAS IT?

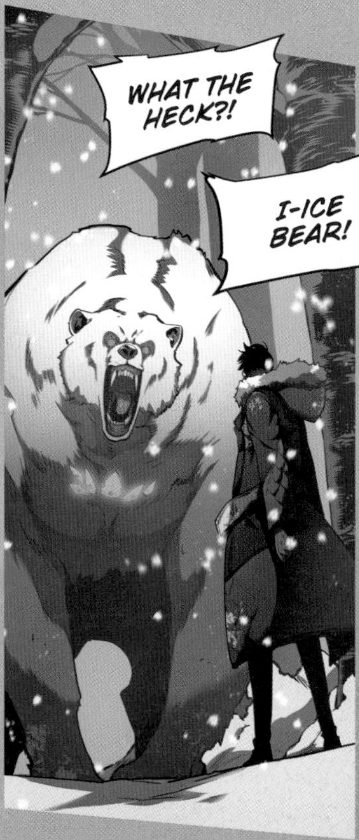
WHAT THE HECK?!
I-ICE BEAR!

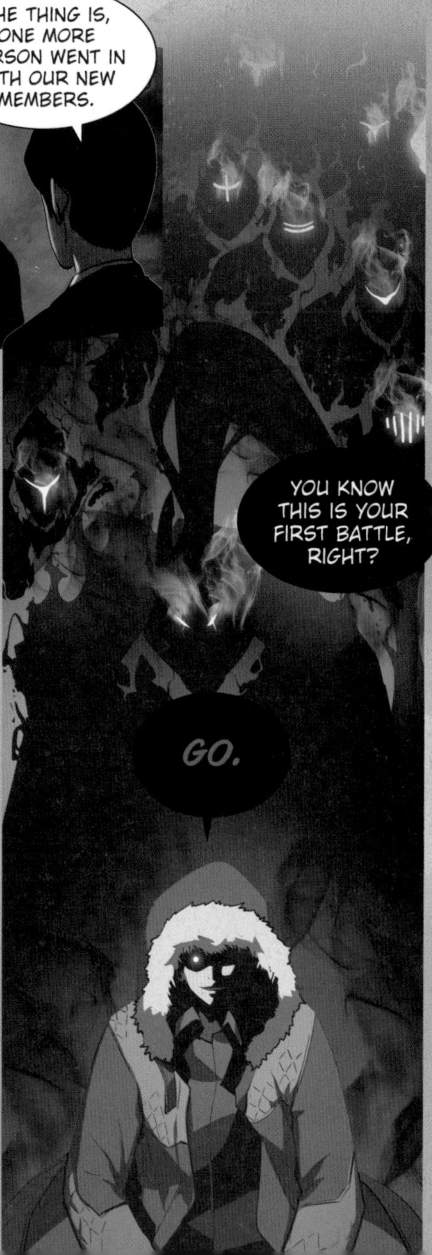
YOU KNOW THIS IS YOUR FIRST BATTLE, RIGHT?
GO.

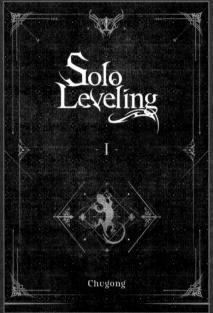

Solo Leveling

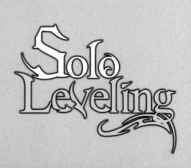

SOLO LEVELING

DUBU
[REDICE STUDIO]

3

ORIGINAL STORY
CHUGONG

Translation· Hye Young Im ◆ Rewrite· J. Torres ◆ Lettering· Abigail Blackman

SOLO LEVELING Volume 3
© DUBU(REDICE STUDIO), Chugong 2018 / D&C WEBTOON Biz
All rights reserved.
First published in Korea in 2018 by D&C WEBTOON Biz Co., Ltd.

English translation © 2021 by Yen Press, LLC

Yen Press
150 West 30th Street, 19th Floor
New York, NY 10001

Visit us at yenpress.com
facebook.com/yenpress
twitter.com/yenpress
yenpress.tumblr.com
instagram.com/yenpress

First Yen Press Edition: September 2021

Yen Press is an imprint of Yen Press, LLC.
The Yen Press name and logo are trademarks of Yen Press, LLC.

The publisher is not responsible for websites (or their content) that are not owned by the publisher.

Library of Congress Control Number: 2020950228

ISBNs: 978-1-9753-3651-6 (paperback)
978-1-9753-3652-3 (ebook)

10 9 8 7 6 5 4 3 2

TPA

Printed in South Korea